ISBN 978-1-331-10264-9
PIBN 10145138

THE

# JOURNAL

OF THE

# ROYAL ASIATIC SOCIETY

OF

## GREAT BRITAIN AND IRELAND.

NEW SERIES.

VOLUME THE SECOND.

LONDON:
TRÜBNER AND CO., 60, PATERNOSTER ROW.
H. LOESCHER, TURIN AND FLORENCE.
F. A. BROCKHAUS, LEIPZIG.

MDCCCLXVI.

STEPHEN AUSTIN,

PRINTER, HERTFORD.

# CONTENTS OF VOL. II.

[NEW SERIES.]

---

## ORIGINAL COMMUNICATIONS.

# JOURNAL

OF

# THE ROYAL ASIATIC SOCIETY.

---

## ART. I.—*Contributions to a Knowledge of the Vedic Theogony and Mythology.* No. II.—BY J. MUIR, ESQ.

### THE AṢVINS.

THE Aṣvins seem to have been a puzzle even to the oldest Indian Commentators. Yâska thus refers to them in the Nirukta, xii. 1: "Next in order are the deities whose sphere is the heaven; of these the Aṣvins are the first to arrive. They are called Aṣvins, because they pervade (*vyaṣnuvāte*) everything, the one with moisture, the other with light. Aurṇabhâva says they are called Aṣvins, from the horses (*aṣvaiḥ*, on which they ride). Who, then, are these Aṣvins? 'Heaven and Earth,' say some; 'Day and Night,' say others; 'The Sun and Moon,' say others; 'Two kings, performers of holy acts,' say the legendary writers. Their time is subsequent to midnight, whilst the manifestation of light is delayed; [and ends with the rising of the sun, *ibid.* xii. 5]. The dark portion [of this time] denotes the intermediate (god, = Indra), the light portion Aditya (the Sun)." [1] Professor Roth, on the strength of this passage considers that Yâska identifies the two Aṣvins with Indra and the Sun (Illustrations of Nirukta, p. 159).[2]

[1] See the different interpretation given by Professor Goldstücker, below.

[2] R. V. i. 181, 4, is quoted by Yâska in illustration of his view:—"Born here and there, these two have striven forward (?) with spotless bodies according to their respective characters. One of you, a conqueror and a sage [is the son of] the strong one (?); the other is born onward, the son of the sky." Comp. Roth's transl. in illustration of Nirukta, p. 159.

In the Journal of the German Oriental Society, iv. 425, the same author thus speaks of these gods: "The two Aṣvins, though, like the ancient interpreters of the Veda, we are by no means agreed as to the conception of their character, hold, nevertheless, a perfectly distinct position in the entire body of the Vedic deities of light. They are the earliest bringers of light in the morning sky, who in their chariot hasten onward before the dawn, and prepare the way for her." [1]

In a passage of the R. V., x. 17, 2 (quoted in my paper on Yama, p. 288), the Aṣvins are represented as the twin sons of Vivasvat and Saraṇyû. They are also called the sons of the sky (*divo napâtā*) in R. V., i. 182, 1; i. 184, 1;[2] x. 61, 4; and in i. 46, 2 *sindhumâtarâ*, the offspring of the Ocean[3] (whether aerial or terrestrial). In viii. 75, 1, they are said to have sprung (?) from the word of Daksha.

In i. 180, 2, the sister of the Aṣvins is mentioned, by whom the Commentator naturally understands Ushas. In vii. 71. 1, Ushas appears to be called the Sister of Night, whilst in i. 123, 5, she is said to be the sister of Bhaga and Varuṇa.

The Aṣvins are in many parts of the R. V. connected with Sûryâ, the youthful daughter of the sun (called also in one place, i. 119, 2, Urjânî (?) ), who is represented as having chosen them for her husbands (i. 119, 5; iv. 43, 6; vii. 69, 3; comp. x. 39, 11); and as having eagerly ascended their chariot (i. 34, 5; i. 116, 17; i. 117, 13; i. 118, 5; iv. 43, 2, 6; v. 73, 5; vi. 63, 5 f.; vii. 68, 3; vii. 69, 4; viii. 8, 10; viii. 22, 1; comp. viii. 29, 8).[4]

The commentator (on i. 116, 17) following the Brâhmaṇas, explains these allusions by saying that Savitri had destined his daughter Sûryâ to be the wife of Soma. But all the gods were anxious to obtain her hand, and resolved that the victor

[1] For some speculations of Professors Müller and Weber, on the Aṣvins, see the lectures of the former, 2nd series, p. 489, f, and the Indische Studien of the latter, vol. v., p. 234.

[2] In i. 181. 4, only one of them is said to be the son of the sky.

[3] On this the commentator remarks that although it is the Sun and Moon that are sprung from the sea, yet the same epithet applies equally to the Aṣvins who in the opinion of some are identical with the former.

[4] See also A. V. vi. 82, 2.

in a race which they agreed to run, should get her. She was accordingly won by the Aṣvins, and ascended their chariot.

Allusion is also made to Sûryâ in connection with the Aṣvins in x. 85, 9, where, however, they no longer appear as her husbands: "Soma was the wooer, the Aṣvins were the two friends of the bridegroom,[1] when Savitri gave to her husband Sûryâ consenting in her mind . . . . 14. When ye came, Aṣvins, to the marriage procession of Sûryâ, to make enquiries, all the gods approved, and Pûshan[2] as a son chose you for his parents."

The daughter of the Sun is connected with the Soma plant in ix. 1, 6: "The Daughter of the Sun purifies thy distilled Soma," etc.; and in ix. 113, 3, she is said to have brought it after it had been expanded by the rain.

If we look on Soma as the plant of that name, the connection between it and Sûryâ is not very clear; but if Soma be taken for the moon, as he appears to be in x. 85, 3 ("When they crush the plant, he who drinks fancies that he has drunk Soma; but no one tastes of him whom the priests know to be Soma,")[3] it is not unnatural, from the relation of the two luminaries, that he should have been regarded as son-in-law of the sun.

The Aṣvins are described as coming from afar, from the sky or from the lower air (i. 22, 2; iv. 44, 5; viii. 5, 30; viii. 8, 3, 4, 7); or as arriving from different unknown quarters, whether above or below, far or near (v. 73, 1; v. 74, 10; vii. 70, 3; vii. 72, 5; viii. 9, 2; viii. 10, 1, 5; viii. 26, 17; viii. 62, 5). Sometimes the worshipper enquires after their locality (i. 184, 1; v. 74, 2, 3; vi. 63, 1; viii. 62, 4). In one place (viii. 8, 23,) they are said to have three stations. The time of their appearance is properly the early dawn, when they yoke their horses to their car and descend to earth to receive the adorations and offerings of their votaries (i. 22, 1;

[1] Comp. A.V. xi. 8, 1, "when Manyu brought his bride from the house of Sankalpa, who were the bridegroom's friends?" etc.

[2] Weber asks (Ind. S. v. 183, 187,) whether Pûshan here is not meant to designate Soma the bridegroom. In vi. 58, 4, the gods are said to have given Pûshan to Sûryâ.

[3] See the part of my former paper referring to Soma, p. 140; and Weber's Ind. Stud. v. 179.

i. 184, 1; iv. 45, 2; vii. 67, 2;[1] vii. 69, 5; vii. 71, 1-3; vii. 72, 4; vii. 73, 1; viii. 5, 1, 2;[2] viii. 9, 17;[3] x. 39, 12;[4] x. 40, 1, 3; x. 41, 1, 2; x. 61, 4).[5] In i. 34, 10, Savitri is said to put their car in motion before the dawn. In other passages their time is not so well defined. Thus, in i. 157, 1, it is said: "Agni has awoke; the sun rises from the earth; the great and bright Ushas has dawned with her light; the Aṣvins have yoked their car to go; the divine Savitri has enlivened every part of the world:" where both the break of dawn and the appearance of the Aṣvins appear to be made simultaneous with the rising of the sun. The same is the case in vii. 71, 4. In v. 76, 3, the Aṣvins are invited to come at different times of the day, and in viii. 22, 14, it is said that they are invoked in the evening and during the day, as well as at dawn. It need not, however, surprise us that they should be invited to attend the different ceremonies of the worshippers, and therefore conceived to appear at hours distinct from the natural periods of their manifestation.

It may seem unaccountable that two deities of a character so little defined, and so difficult to identify, as the Aṣvins, should have been the object of so enthusiastic a worship as appears from the numerous hymns dedicated to them in the R. V. to have been paid to them in ancient times. The reason may have been that they were hailed as the precursors of returning day, after the darkness and dangers of the night. In one passage (viii. 35, 16 ff.) they are represented as being, like Agni, the chasers away of evil spirits.

The Aṣvins are said to be young (vii. 67, 10), ancient (vi. 62, 5), beautiful (vi. 62, 5; vi. 63, 1), honey-hued (viii. 26, 6), lords of lustre (viii. 22, 14; x. 93, 6), bright (vii. 68, 1),

[1] vii. 67, 2, "Agni, being kindled, has shone upon us; even the remotest ends of the darkness have been seen; the light preceding the dawn has been perceived, springing up for the glory of the daughter of heaven (Ushas). 3. Now, Aṣvins, the priest invokes you with his hymns," etc.

[2] viii. 5, 1, 2; "When the rosy-hued dawn, though far away, gleams as if she were near at hand, she spreads the light in all directions. 2. Ye, Aṣvins, like men, follow after Ushas in your car which is yoked by thought, and shines afar."

[3] viii. 9, 17, "Wake, o great and divine Ushas, the Aṣvins," etc.

[4] x. 39, 12, "The daughter of the sky (the dawn) is born when your car is yoked; as are also day and night."

[5] x. 61, 4, when the dark [night] stands among the tawny cows (rays of dawn), I invoke you, Aṣvins, sons of the sky."

of a golden brilliancy and sun-like radiance (viii. 8, 2), agile (vi. 63, 5), fleet as thought (viii. 22, 16), swift as falcons (v. 78, 4), possessed of many forms (i. 117, 9), wearing lotus garlands (x. 184, 2, and A. V. iii. 22, 4, Ṣ. P. Br. iv. 1, 5, 16); strong (x. 24, 4), mighty (vi. 62, 5), terrible, (*rudrâ*, v. 75, 3; x. 93, 7), skilful (*mâyinâ* or *mâyâvinâ*, vi. 63, 5; x. 24, 4), and profound in wisdom (viii. 8. 2). They are overthrowers of pride (viii. 22, 16); and traverse a golden (v. 75, 3,) or terrible (viii. 5, 11; viii. 8, 1; viii. 22, 1, 14; x. 39, 11), path.[1]

The car, golden in all its various parts (i. 180, 1; iv. 44, 4, 5; v. 77, 3; viii. 5, 28, 29, 35; viii. 22, 9), on which they ride, flying as on bird's wings (i. 183, 1), was formed by the Ribhus (x. 39, 12), and is singular in its formation, being three-wheeled, and triple in some other parts of its construction (*trivṛt, trivandkura*)[2] (i. 34, 2, 9; i. 47, 2; i. 118, 1, 2; i. 157, 3; vii. 71, 4; viii. 74, 8; x. 41, 1; comp. iv. 36, 1).

This car moves lightly (viii. 9, 8) and is swifter than thought (i. 117, 2; i. 118, 1; v. 77, 3; vi. 63, 7; x. 39, 12), or than the twinkling of an eye (viii. 62, 2). It is decked with a thousand ornaments and banners (*sahasra-nirṇij, sahasra-ketu* (i. 119, 1; viii. 8, 11, 14, 15) and has golden reins (viii. 22, 5). It is sometimes said to be drawn by a single ass, as the word *râsabha*[3] is, in two places at least,

[1] Two epithets very commonly applied to them are *dasrâ*, and *nâsatyâ*. The former term is explained by Sâyaṇa to signify destroyers of enemies, or of diseases (note on i. 3, 3), or beautiful (on viii. 75, 1). Professor Roth *s.v.* understands it to signify wonder-workers. The second word *nâsatyâ* is regarded by Sâyaṇa, following one of the etymologies given by Yâska (vi. 13) as equivalent to *satyâ*, truthful. If this is the sense, *satyâ* itself might as well have been used. In the later literature Dasra and Nâsatya were regarded as the separate names of the two Aṣvins. See Müller's Lectures, 2nd Series, p. 491.

[2] The word *vandhura* is variously explained by Sâyana as *nîḍabandhanâdhâra-bhûtam* (on i. 34, 9), *unnatânatarûpa-bandhana-kâshṭham* (on i. 47, 2), *veshṭhitam sâratheḥ sthânam* (on i. 118, 1), *sârathyâṣraya-sthânam* (on i. 157, 3), *sârathy-adhishṭhâna-sthânam* (on vii. 71, 4), and *trivandhura* as *triphalakâsanghaṭitena* (on viii. 74, 8). The epithet would thus mean either (1) having three perpendicular pieces of wood, or (2) having a triple standing place or seat for the charioteer. In i. 34, 2, the chariot is said to have three props fixed in it to lay hold of (*trayaḥ skambhâsaḥ skabhitâsa ârabhe*) which the commentator says were meant to secure the rider against the fear of falling when the chariot was moving rapidly. This explanation would coincide with one of the senses assigned to *vandhura*. In i. 181, 3, their chariot is called *sṛpra-vandhuraḥ*, which according to the commentator is = *vistîrṇa-purobhâgah*, "having a wide fore-part."

[3] See the legend in the Aitareya Brahmana, p. 270-273 of Dr. Haug's translation.

explained by the commentator (i. 34, 9; i. 116, 2; viii. 74, 7); but more frequently by fleet-winged, golden-winged, falcon-like, swàn-like horses, (i. 46, 3; i. 117, 2; i. 118, 4, 5; i. 180, 1; i. 181, 2; iv. 45, 4; v. 75, 5; vi. 63, 7; vii. 69, 7; viii. 5, 7, 22, 33, 35; viii. 10, 2; x. 143, 5). They carry a honied whip (*kaṣâ madhumatî*, i. 22, 3; i. 157, 4),[1] and traverse the regions (*tiro rajâmsi*, vii. 68, 3).

The Aṣvins are fancifully represented as doing, or as being requested to do, a variety of acts thrice over, viz., to move thrice by night and thrice by day, to bestow food thrice at even and at dawn, to bestow wealth thrice, come to the worship of the gods thrice, to bestow celestial medicaments thrice, and earthly thrice, etc. (i. 34, 1 ff; viii. 35, 7-9).

They are elsewhere compared to different twin objects, to two vultures on a tree, to two priests reciting hymns, to two goats, to two beautiful women, to husband and wife, to two ducks (*chakravâkâ*), to two ships, to two dogs, two eyes, two hands, two feet, two lips, two breasts, two noses, two ears, two swans, two falcons, two deer, two buffaloes, two wings of one bird, etc., etc. (ii. 39, 1 ff.; v. 78, 1-3; viii. 35, 7-9; x. 106, 2 ff.).

They are physicians[2] and restore the blind, the lame, the emaciated, and the sick, to sight, power of locomotion, health, and strength (i. 34, 6; i. 116, 16; i. 157, 6; viii. 9, 6, 15; viii. 22, 10; viii. 75, 1; x. 39, 3, 5; x. 40, 8). See also A.V. vii. 53, 1, where it is said that the Aṣvins are the physicians of the gods, and warded off death.

They place the productive germ in all creatures, and generate fire, water, and trees (i. 157, 5). They are connected with procreation and with love (x. 184, 2; x. 85, 26; A. V. ii. 30, 2; v. 25, 3; vi. 102, 1; xiv. 1, 36; xiv. 2, 5). See Weber's Ind. Stud. v. 219, 234.

The following are a few of the modes in which the divine

[1] See my paper on the "Progress of Vedic Religion, etc.," p. 363. Indra has a golden whip, viii. 33, 11.

[2] In Taitt. Br. iii. 1, 2, 11, the Aṣvins are called the physicians of the gods, the bearers of oblations, the messengers of the universe, the guardians of immortality; and in that and the preceding paragraph (10) they are connected with their own asterism (*nakshatra*), the Aṣvayuj.

power of the Aṣvins is declared in different hymns to have been manifested for the deliverance of their votaries.

When the sage Chyavâna had grown old, and had been forsaken, they divested him of his decrepit body, prolonged his life, and restored him to youth, making him acceptable to his wife, and the husband of maidens (i. 116, 10; i. 117, 13; i. 118, 6: v. 74, 5; v. 75, 5; vii. 68, 6; vii. 71, 5; x. 39, 4). This legend is related at length in the S. P. Br. in a passage which will be cited further on.

In the same way they renewed the youth of Kali[1] after he had grown old (x. 39, 8), and had married a wife (i. 112, 15).

They brought on a car to the youthful Vimada[2] a bride (i. 112, 19; i. 116, 1) named Kamadyû (x. 65, 12), who seems to have been the chaste wife of Purumitra (i. 117, 20; x. 39, 7).

They restored Vishṇâpû, like a lost animal, to the sight of Viṣvaka, son of Krishna, their worshipper, who, according to the commentator, was his father (i. 116, 23; i. 117, 7; x. 65, 12). The names both of Viṣvaka and Vishṇâpû occur in R. V. viii. 75, a hymn addressed to the Aṣvins; and the commentator connects the reference there made to them with the legend before us (on which, however, the hymn itself throws no light).

Another act recorded of the Aṣvins is their intervention in favour of Bhujyu, the son of Tugra, which is obscurely described in the following verses in R. V. i. 116, 3–5: "Tugra abandoned Bhujyu in the water-cloud, as any dead man leaves his property. Ye, Aṣvins, bore him in animated (*âtmanvatîbhiḥ*) water-tight ships, which traversed the air. 4. Three nights and three days did ye convey him in three flying cars, with a hundred feet, and six horses, which crossed over to the dry land beyond the liquid ocean. 5. Ye put forth your vigour in the ocean, which offers no stay, or standing-place, or support, when ye bore Bhujyu to his home, standing on a ship propelled by a hundred oars." R. V. i. 117, 14, 15: "Ye conveyed Bhujyu out of the liquid ocean with your

[1] The family of the Kalis is mentioned viii. 55, 15.

[2] A rishi of this name is mentioned R.V. viii. 9, 15; x. 20, 10; x. 23, 7; and a family of Vimadas in x. 23, 6.

headlong flying horses. 15. The son of Tugra invoked you, Aṣvins. Borne forward, he moved without distress over the sea. Ye brought him out with your well-yoked chariot swift as thought." Again in i. 182, 5 ff. it is said: "Ye (Aṣvins) made this animated (*âtmanvantam*) winged boat for the son of Tugra among the waters . . . 6. Four ships, in eager haste (?) impelled by the Aṣvins, convey to the shore Tugra, who had been plunged in the waters, and sunk in bottomless darkness. 7. What was that log, placed in the midst of the waves, which the suppliant son of Tugra embraced, as the wings of a bird, for support?" In vii. 68, 7, Bhujyu is said to have been abandoned by his malevolent companions in the middle of the sea. The story is also alluded to in i. 112, 6, 20; i. 118, 6; i. 119, 4; vi. 62, 6; vii. 69, 7; viii. 5, 22; x. 39, 4; x. 40, 7; x. 65, 12; x. 143, 5.

Again, when Viṣpalâ's leg had been cut off in battle, like the wing of a bird, the Aṣvins are said, when lauded by Agastya, to have given her an iron one instead (R. V. i. 112, 10; 1, 116, 15; i. 117, 11; i. 118, 8; x, 39, 8).[1]

They restored sight to Rijrâṣva, who had been made blind by his father for giving a hundred and one sheep to a she wolf to eat (i. 116, 16; i. 117, 17, 18). Rijrâṣva is mentioned in i. 100, 17, as praising Indra.

They restored Parâvṛj (or an outcast), who was blind and lame, to sight and the power of walking (i. 112, 8). Parâvṛj is connected with Indra in ii. 13, 12, and ii. 15, 7.

The Rishi Rebha has been hidden by the malignant, bound, overwhelmed in the waters (a well, according to the commentator), for ten nights and nine days, and abandoned till he was nearly, if not entirely, dead. The Aṣvins drew him up as soma-juice is raised with a ladle, or as a pot full of gold is dug out of the earth (i. 112, 5; i. 116, 24; i. 117, 4, 12; i. 118, 6; i. 119, 6; x. 39, 9).

Vandana seems to have been delivered from a somewhat similar calamity according to i. 112, 5; i. 118, 6; x. 39, 8. According to i. 119, 6, 7, however, he would appear to have been restored from decrepitude. From i. 116, 11, and i. 117,

[1] Compare the word *viṣpalâvasû* in R. V. i. 182, 1.

5, it would seem as if some person or thing had been restored to him.

So, too, the Aṣvins bestowed wisdom on their worshipper Kakshîvat, of the family of Pajra; and performed the notable miracle of causing a hundred jars of wine and honied liquor to flow forth from the hoof of their horse as from a sieve (i. 116, 7; i. 117, 6).

When invoked by the popular sage Atri Saptavadhri, who had been plunged by the malice and arts of evil spirits into a gloomy and burning abyss,[1] they speedily came to his assistance, mitigated the heat with cold, and supplied him with nutriment, so that his situation became tolerable, if not agreeable, till they eventually extricated him from his perilous position (i. 112, 7; i. 116, 8; i. 117, 3; i. 118, 7; i. 119, 6; v. 78, 4–6; vii. 71, 5; viii. 62, 3, 7-9; x. 39, 9). In x. 80, 3, the deliverance of Atri is ascribed to Agni.

They listened to the invocation of the wise Vadhrimatî, and gave her a son called Hiraṇyahasta (i. 116, 13; i. 117, 24; vi. 62, 7; x. 39, 7).

They gave a husband to Ghoshâ when she was growing old in her father's house (i. 117, 7; x. 39, 3, 6; x. 40); and, according to the commentator, cured her of the leprosy with which she had been afflicted (comp. i. 122, 5).

They caused the cow of the suppliant Ṣayu, which had left off bearing, to yield milk (i. 116, 22; i. 117, 20; i. 118, 8; i. 119, 6; x. 39, 13).

They gave to Pedu a strong, swift, white horse, of incomparable Indra-like prowess, which overcame all his enemies, and conquered for him unbounded spoils (i. 116, 6; i. 117, 9; i. 118, 9; i. 119, 10; vii. 71, 5; x. 39, 10).

Finally, to say nothing of the succours rendered to numerous other persons (i. 112, 116, 117, 118, 119,) the Aṣvins did not confine their benevolence to human beings, but are also celebrated as having rescued from the jaws of a wolf a quail by which they were invoked (i. 116, 14; i. 117, 16; i. 118, 8; x. 39, 13).

1 See Roth's explanation of the words *ṛbisa* and *gharma*, and his Illustrations of Nirukta, vi. 36.

The deliverances of Rebha, Vandana, Parâvṛj, Bhujyu, Chyavâna, and others are explained by Professor Benfey, (following Dr. Kuhn and Professor Müller) in the notes to his translations of the hymns in which they are mentioned, as referring to certain physical phenomena with which the Aṣvins are supposed by these scholars to be connected. But this allegorical method of interpretation seems unlikely to be correct, as it is difficult to suppose that the phenomena in question should have been alluded to under such a variety of names and circumstances. It appears therefore to be more probable that the Rishis merely refer to certain legends which were popularly current of interventions of the Aṣvins in behalf of the persons whose names are mentioned. The word Parâvṛj (in i. 112, 8), which is taken by the commentator for a proper name, and is explained by Professors Müller[1] and Benfey as the returning, or the setting, sun, is interpreted by Professor Roth in his Lexicon, *s.v.*, as an outcast.

In viii. 26, 8, the Aṣvins are invoked along with Indra, with whom they are also connected in x. 73, 4, and on whose car they sometimes ride, while at other times they accompany Vâyu, or the Âdityas, or the Ribhus, or participate in the strides of Vishṇu (viii. 9. 12). In i. 182, 2, they are said to possess strongly the qualities of Indra and of the Maruts. In x. 131, 4, 5, they are described as assisting Indra in his conflict with the Asura Namuchi (see my paper "Contributions," etc., p. 94, note), and as vigorous slayers of Vṛttra or of enemies (viii. 8, 22). They are greeted with affection (?) by the other gods when they arrive, x. 24, 5. In A. V. xii. 1, 10, they are represented as having meted out the earth.

The Aṣvins are supplicated with uplifted hands (vi. 63, 3,) for a variety of blessings, for long life, and forgiveness of sin (i. 157, 4); for offspring, wealth, victory, destruction of enemies, protection of friends, preservation of the worshippers themselves, of their houses and cattle (vii. 67, 6; viii. 8, 13, 15, 17; viii. 9, 11, 13; viii. 26, 7). They are exhorted to

[1] Lectures on language, second series, p. 512.

pass by and to destroy the man who offers no oblations, and to create light for the wise man who praises them (i. 182, 3).

No calamity or alarm from any quarter can touch the man whose chariot they place in the van (x. 39, 11).[1] The Rishi addresses them as a son his parents (vii. 67. 1). In x. 39, 6, a female suppliant, who represents herself as friendless and destitute, calls on them to treat her as parents do their children, and rescue her from her misfortunes. In another place (viii. 62, 11) they are reproached with being as tardy as two old men to respond to the summons of their worshipper. In vii. 72, 2, the Rishi represents himself as having hereditary claims on their consideration, and a common bond of union.[2]

The Aṣvins are described as being, like the other gods, fond of the soma juice (iii. 58, 7, 9; iv. 45, 1, 3; viii. 8, 5; viii. 35, 7-9).

The following version of the legend relating to the cure of Chyavana by the Aṣvins (to which allusion is made in the passages of the R. V. quoted above) is found in the Satapatha Brâhmaṇa, iv. 1, 5, 1 ff.:—

"Chyavana of the race of Bhṛgu, or Chyavana of the race of Angiras, having magically assumed a shrivelled form, was abandoned. Ṣaryâta, the descendant of Manu, wandered over this [world] with his tribe. He sat down in the neighbourhood [of Chyavana]. His youths, while playing, fancied this shrivelled magical body to be worthless, and pounded it with clods. Chyavana was incensed at the sons of Ṣaryâta. He created discord among them, so that father fought with son, and brother with brother. Ṣaryâta bethought him, 'what have I done? in consequence of which this calamity has befallen us.' He ordered the cowherds and shepherds to be called, and said, 'which of you has seen anything here to-day?' They replied, 'this shrivelled magical body which lies there is a man. Fancying it was something worthless,

[1] Compare the request preferred to Indra to bring forward the chariot of his worshipper from the rear to the front (viii. 69, 4. f.)

[2] The commentator explains this of a common ancestry by saying, in accordance with later tradition, that Vivasvat and Varuṇa were both sons of Kaṣyapa and Aditi, and that Vivasvat was the father of the Aṣvins, while Varuṇa was father of Vasistha the Rishi of the hymn. See Sanskrit Texts, i. 75, f.

the youths pounded it with clods.' Ṣaryâta knew then that it was Chyavana. He yoked his chariot, and taking his daughter Sukanyâ, drove off, and arrived at the place where the Rishi was. He said, 'Reverence to thee, Rishi; I injured thee because I did not know. This is Sukanyâ, with her I appease thee. Let my tribe be reconciled.' His tribe was in consequence reconciled; and Ṣaryâta of the race of Manu strove that he might never again do injury to any one. Now the Aṣvins used to wander over this world, performing cures. They approached Sukanyâ and wished to seduce her; but she would not consent. They said to her 'Sukanyâ, what shrivelled magical body is this by which thou liest? follow us.' She replied, 'I will not abandon, while he lives, the man to whom my father gave me.' The Rishi became aware of this. He said, 'Sukanyâ, what was this that they said to thee?' She told it to him. When informed, he said, 'If they address thee thus again, say to them, 'ye are neither complete nor perfect, and yet ye speak contemptuously of my husband;' and if they ask 'in what respect are we incomplete and imperfect?' then reply, 'make my husband young again, and I will tell you.' Accordingly they came again to her, and said the same thing. She answered, 'Ye are neither complete nor perfect, and yet ye talk contemptuously of my husband.' They enquired, 'In what respect are we incomplete and imperfect?' She rejoined, 'make my husband young again, and I will tell you.' They replied, 'take him to this pond, and he shall come forth with any age which he shall desire.' She took him to the pond, and he came forth with the age that he desired. The Aṣvins then asked, 'Sukanyâ, in what respect are we incomplete and imperfect?' To this the Rishi replied, 'The other gods celebrate a sacrifice in Kurukshetra, and exclude you two from it. That is the respect in which ye are incomplete and imperfect.' The Aṣvins then departed and came to the gods who were celebrating a sacrifice, when the Bahishpavamâna[1] text had been recited. They said, 'Invite us to join you.' The gods replied, 'We will not invite you, for ye have wandered about very

[1] See Haug's Ait. Br. ii. p. 120, note 13.

familiarly among men,[1] performing cures.' The Aṣvins rejoined, 'Ye worship with a headless sacrifice.' They asked, 'How [do we worship] with a headless [sacrifice]?' The Aṣvins answered, 'Invite us to join you, and we will tell you.' The gods consented, and invited them. They offered this Âṣvina draught (*graha*) to the Aṣvins, who became the two adhvaryu priests[2] of the sacrifice, and restored the head of the sacrifice. It is related in the Brâhmaṇa of the Divâkîrttyas, in what manner they restored the head of the sacrifice," etc., etc.

A story, varying in some particulars, is narrated in the Mahâbhârata, Vanaparva, 10316 ff. We are there told that the body of Chyavana, when performing austerity in a certain place, became encrusted with an ant-hill; that king Ṣaryâti came then to the spot with his wives and his daughter Sukanyâ; that the Rishi seeing her, became enamoured of her and endeavoured to gain her affections, but without eliciting from her any reply. Seeing, however, the sage's eyes gleaming out from the ant-hill, and not knowing what they were, the princess pierced them with a sharp instrument, whereupon Chyavana became incensed, and afflicted the king's army with a stoppage of urine and of the other necessary function. When the king found out the cause of the infliction, and supplicated the Rishi for its removal, the latter insisted on receiving the king's daughter to wife, as the sole condition of his forgiveness. Sukanyâ accordingly lived with the Rishi as his spouse. One day, however, she was seen by the Aṣvins, who endeavoured, but without effect, to persuade her to desert her decrepit husband, and choose one of them in his place. They then told her they were the physicians of the gods, and would restore her husband to youth and beauty, when she could make her choice between him and one of them. Chyavana and his wife consented to this; and

[1] In the Mahâbhârata, Sântip. v. 7589 f. it is said that the Aṣvins are the Sûdras of the gods, the Angirases being the Brahmans, the Âdityas the Kshatriyas, and the Maruts the Vaiṣyas. With the objection made against the Aṣvins of too great familiarity with mortals, compare the numerous instances of help rendered to their worshippers, which have been quoted above from the R. V., and which may have given rise to this idea.

[2] Comp. S. P. Br. viii. 2, 1, 3.

at the suggestion of the Aṣvins he entered with them into the neighbouring pond; when the three came forth of like celestial beauty, and each asked her to be his bride. She however recognized and chose her own husband. Chyavana in gratitude for his restoration to youth, then offered to compel Indra to admit the Aṣvins to a participation in the Soma ceremonial, and fulfilled his promise in the course of a sacrifice which he performed for king Ṣaryâti. On that occasion Indra objected to such an honour being extended to the Aṣvins, on the ground that they wandered about among men as physicians, changing their forms at will; but Chyavana refused to listen to the objection and carried out his intention, staying the arm of Indra when he was about to launch a thunderbolt, and creating a terrific demon who was on the point of devouring the king of the gods, and was only prevented by the timely submission of the latter.[1]

---

I have been favoured by Professor Goldstücker with the following note on the Aṣvins :—

The myth of the Aṣvins is, in my opinion, one of that class of myths in which two distinct elements, the cosmical and the human or historical, have gradually become blended into one. It seems necessary, therefore, to separate these two elements in order to arrive at an understanding of the myth. The historical or human element in it, I believe, is represented by those legends which refer to the wonderful cures effected by the Aṣvins, and to their performances of a kindred sort; the cosmical element is that relating to their luminous nature. The link which connects both seems to be the mysteriousness of the nature and effects of the phenomena of light, and of the healing art at a remote antiquity. That there might have been some horsemen or warriors of great renown who inspired their contemporaries with awe by their wonderful deeds, and more especially by their medical skill, appears to have been also the opinion of some old commentators mentioned by Yâska, for some "legendary writer," he says, took

[1] See the similar account of Chyavana's power in the passage from the Anuṣâsana parva quoted in Sanskrit Texts, i. 167 f.

them for "two kings, performers of holy acts;" and this view seems likewise borne out by the legend in which it is narrated that the gods refused the Aṣvins admittance to a sacrifice on the ground that they had been on too familiar terms with men. It would appear then that these Aṣvins, like the Ṛbhus, were originally renowned mortals, who in the course of time were translated into the companionship of the gods; and it may be a matter of importance to investigate whether, besides this *a priori* view, there are further grounds of a linguistic or grammatical character, for assuming that the hymns containing the legends relating to these human Aṣvins are posterior or otherwise to those descriptive of the cosmical gods of the same name.

The luminous character of the latter can scarcely be matter of doubt, for the view of some commentators—recorded by Yâska,—according to which they were identified with "heaven and earth," appears not to be countenanced by any of the passages known to us. Their very name, it would seem, settles this point, since *aṣva,* the horse, lit. "the pervader," is always the symbol of the luminous deities, especially of the sun. The difficulty, however, is to determine their position amongst these deities and to harmonise with it the other myths connected with them. I may here, however, first observe that though Yâska records opinions which identify the Aṣvins with "day and night," and "sun and moon," the passage relied upon by Professor Roth to prove that Yâska himself identified them with Indra and Âditya (the sun), does not bear out any such conclusion. For the passage in question, as I understand it, means: "their time is after the (latter) half of the night when the (space's) becoming light is resisted (by darkness); for the middlemost Aṣwin (between darkness and light) shares in darkness, whilst (the other), who is of a solar nature (âditya), shares in light." There is this verse relating to them: "In nights,"[1] etc. Nor does Durga, the commentator on Yâska, attribute to the latter

[1] *Nir.* xii. 1. tayoḥ kâlaḥ ûrdhvam ardharâtrât prâkâṣîbhâvasyânuvishtambham anu (the last word is omitted in Durga MS. I. O. L., No. 206) tamobhâgo hi madhyamo jyotirbhâga âdityaḥ; tayor eshâ bhavati Vasâtishu sma, etc.

the view which Professor Roth ascribes to him. His words, as I interpret them, are: "'their time is after the (latter) half of the night when the (space's) becoming light is resisted,' (means) when, after the (latter) half of the night darkness intersected by light makes an effort against light, that is the time of the Aṣvins. . . . . Then the nature of the middlemost (between them) is a share in that darkness which penetrates into light; and the solar one (âditya) assumes that nature which is a share in the light penetrating into darkness. These two are the middlemost and the uppermost: this is the teacher's (*i.e.* Yâska's) own opinion, for in order to substantiate it he gives as an instance the verse '*Vasâtishu sma,*'"[1] etc.

To judge, therefore, from these words, it is the opinion of Yâska that the Aṣvins represent the transition from darkness to light when the intermingling of both produces that inseparable duality expressed by the twin nature of these deities. And this interpretation, I hold, is the best that can be given of the character of the *cosmical* Aṣvins. It agrees with the epithets by which they are invoked and with the relationship in which they are placed. They are young, yet also ancient, beautiful, bright, swift, etc.; and their negative character—the result of the alliance of light with darkness—is, I believe, expressed by *dasra*, the destroyer, and also by the two negatives in the compound *nâsatya* (*na* + *a-satya*), though their positive character is again redeemed by the ellipsis of "enemies, or diseases," to *dasra*, and by the sense of *nâsatya*, not-untrue, *i.e.* truthful. They are the parents of Pûshan, the

[1] Durga I. O. L., No. 206; Tayoḥ kâla ûrdhvam ardharâtrât prakâṣîbhâvasyânu vishṭambham; jyotishâ vyatibhidyamânam ûrdhvam ardharâtrât tamo yadâ jyotir anu vishṭabhnâti so 'ṣvinoḥ kâlaḥ; [tataḥ prabhṛti sandhistotraṃ purodayâd âṣvinam, udite sauryâṇi]; tatra yat tamo 'nuvishtaṃ (The MS. of Prof. Müller, Lect. 2nd series, p. 490, reads, 'nupravishṭam) jyotishi tadbhâgo madhyamasya rûpaṃ (the MS. of Prof. M., ibid: tadbhâgo madhyamaḥ, tan madhyamasya rûpam); yaj jyotis tamasy anuvishṭaṃ (the same, ibid. anupravishṭam) tadbhâgam tadrûpam âdityaḥ. Tâv etau madhyamottamâv iti svamatam âchâryasya, yataḥ samarthanâyodâharati tayor eshâ bhavati Vasâtishu smeti. Professor Roth, in his illustrations of Nir. xii. 1, very correctly observes that the verse quoted by Yâska (vâsatishu sma, etc.) does not bear out the view that the Aṣvins are Indra and Âditya; but the proper inference to be drawn from this circumstance would seem to be, not that Yâska quoted a verse irrelevant to his view, but that Prof. Roth attributed to him a view which he had not entertained, and that it may be preferable to render âditya as proposed above: "the solar (Aṣvin)" or the Aṣvin of a solar nature.

sun; for they precede the rise of the sun; they are the sons of the sky, and again the sons of Vivasvat and Saraṇyû. Vivasvat, I believe, here implies the firmament "expanding" to the sight through the approaching light; and though Saraṇyû is to Professor Müller one of the deities which are forced by him to support his dawn-theory, it seems to me that the etymology of the word, and the character of the myths relating to it, rather point to the moving air, or the dark and cool air, heated and therefore set in motion by the approach of the rising sun. The Aṣvins are also the husbands or the friends of Sûryâ, whom I take for the representative of the weakest manifestation of the sun; and I believe that Sâyaṇa is right when by the sister of the Aṣvins he understands Ushas, the dawn. The mysterious phenomenon of the intermingling of darkness—which is no longer complete night—and of light—which is not yet dawn—seems to agree with all these conceptions, and with the further details of a cosmical nature, which are so fully given in the preceding paper.

---

## Notice of some of the Goddesses in the Vedic Hymns.

Of the goddesses mentioned in the Rig Veda some have been noticed already in this or preceding papers, viz., Aditi, the mother of the Âdityas, and representative of the universe; Diti, her counterpart; Nishṭigrî, the mother, and Indrâṇî, the wife of Indra;[1] Pṛiṣni, the mother of the Maruts; and Sûryâ, the daughter of the Sun, and spouse of the Aṣvins, or of Soma. Various other goddesses are also celebrated in the hymns of the Rig Veda, such as Agnâyî, Varuṇânî, Rodasî, Râkâ, Sinîvâlî, Ṣraddhā (Faith), and the Apsarases, whose names, however, occur but rarely; and Ushas, and Sarasvatî,

[1] Indrâṇî says in R.V. x. 86, 9: "This mischievous creature treats me with disdain as if I had no husband or sons, and yet I am the wife of Indra, and the mother of a hero," etc.; and in v. 11, it is said: "I have heard of Indrâṇî as the most fortunate of all these females, for never at any future time shall her husband die from decay." Indrâṇi is mentioned in the Taitt. Br. ii. 4, 2, 7, from which it appears that different goddesses had been competitors for the hand of Indra, and that Indrâṇî has been chosen because she surpassed them all in voluptuous attractions. In the same work, ii. 8, 8, 4, Vâch is said to be the wife of Indra.

with her cognates, who receive considerably greater prominence.

### Sarasvatî.

Sarasvati is a goddess of some, though not of very great, importance in the Rig Veda. As observed by Yâska (Nirukta ii. 23) she is celebrated both as a river and as a deity.[1] As an instance of the former character, he refers to R. V. vi. 61, 2, which I shall quote further on. She was no doubt primarily a river deity, as her name, "the watery,"[2] clearly denotes, and in this capacity she is celebrated in a few separate passages. Allusion is made in the hymns, as well as in the Brâhmaṇas (Ait. Br. ii. 19; Haug, vol. ii. p. 112) to sacrifices being performed on the banks of this river and of the adjoining Dṛishadvatî;[3] and the Sarasvati in particular seems to have been associated with the reputation for sanctity, which, according to the well-known passage in the Institutes of Manu (ii. 17 f.) was ascribed to the whole region, called Brahmâvartta, lying between these two small streams, and situated immediately to the westward of the Jumna. The Sarasvati thus appears to have been to the early Indians what the Ganges (which is only twice named in the Rig Veda) became to their descendants.[4] Already in R.V. i. 3, 10 (where, however, she is perhaps regarded as the goddess of sacrifice) she is described as "the purifier;" and in R. V. x. 17, 10 (=Vâj. San. 4, 2; A. V. vi. 51, 2), (after Sarasvati has been mentioned, vv. 7-9), the waters are thus celebrated: "May the Waters, the mothers, cleanse us, may they (the waters) who purify with butter,

[1] See also Sâyaṇa on R. V. i. 3, 12: *Dvividhâ hi Sarasvatî vigrahavad-devatâ nadî-rûpâ cha.*

[2] *Sarasvatî sara ity udaka-nâma sartes tad-vatî* (Nir. ix. 26). The Brahma-vaivartta-purana, ii. 5, as referred to in Prof. Aufrecht's Cat. p. 23, col. 2, has a legend that the Sarasvati was changed into a river by an imprecation of the Gangâ. In the A. V. vi. 100, 1, three Sarasvatis are spoken of, but no explanation is given of their difference.

[3] R. V. iii. 23, 4: "I place thee, Agni, on the abode of Iḷâ (comp. iii. 29, 4), on the most excellent spot of the earth, on the most auspicious of days. Shine, so as to enrich us, in a place of human resort, on the banks of the Dṛishadvatí, the Âpayâ, the Sarasvati."

[4] It is clear from the passages quoted in Sanskrit Texts, ii. 415 ff. that the Sarasvati continued in later times also to be regarded as a sacred river, but this character was shared by other Indian streams, if not by them all.

purify us with butter; for these goddesses bear away sin; I come up out of them pure and cleansed." When once the river had acquired a divine character, it was quite natural that she should be regarded as the patroness of the ceremonies which were celebrated on the margin of her holy waters, and that her direction and blessing should be invoked as essential to their proper performance and success. The connection into which she was thus brought with sacred rites seems to have led to the further step of imagining her to have an influence on the composition of the hymns which formed so important a part of the proceedings, and of identifying her with Vâch, the goddess of speech. At least, I have no other explanation to offer of this identification.

Sarasvati is frequently invited to the sacrifices along with several other goddesses, Iḷâ, Bhârati, Mahî, Hotrâ, Varûtrî, Dhishaṇâ (i. 13, 9; i. 142, 9; i. 188, 8; iii. 4, 8; v. 5, 8; v. 42, 12; ix. 5, 8; x. 110, 8), who, however, were never, like her, river nymphs, but personifications of some department of religious worship, or sacred science. She is also frequently invoked along with other deities (ii. 30, 8; iii. 54, 13; vii. 35, 11; viii. 38, 10; ix. 81, 4; x. 65, 1, 13; x. 141, 5).

In many of the passages[1] where Sarasvati is celebrated, her original character is, as I have intimated, distinctly preserved. Thus in vi. 52, 6; x. 30, 12, she is mentioned along with rivers, or fertilizing waters; and in x. 64, 9; x. 75, 5, she is specified along with the other well-known streams which are there named. In vii. 96, 2, and viii. 21, 18, reference is made to the kings and people living along her banks. In vi. 61, 10, and vii. 36, 6, she is spoken of as having seven sisters, as one of seven rivers, and as the mother of streams. In vii. 95, 1 and 2, she is said to pour on her fertilizing

[1] Sâyaṇa understands i. 3, 12, of the river, and explains it thus: "The Sarasvati by her act (of flowing) displays a copious flood." Roth in his Illustrations of the Nirukta (xi. 26) p. 152, translates, "A mighty stream is Sarasvatî; with her light she lightens, illuminates all pious minds." He, however, regards the commencing words as figurative, and not as referring to the river. Benfey renders: "Sarasvati by her light causes the great sea to be known: she shines through all thoughts." He understands the "great sea" as the universe, or as life, which he says is often designated in common Sanskrit also by the word *sâgara*. Benfey's explanation seems to me to be unsuitable. The conceptions of Sarasvatî as a river and as the directress of ceremonies may be blended in the passage.

waters, and to surpass all other rivers, to flow pure from the mountains to the sea, to be the swiftest of floods (*apasâm apastamâ* (vi. 61, 13); and in vi. 61, 2 and 8, to tear away the bases of the mountains on her banks with her impetuous and resounding current. In ii. 41, 16, she is called the best of mothers, of rivers, and of goddesses (*ambîtame, nadîtame, devîtame*).

In vii. 96, 4-6, a river god called Sarasvat is assigned as a consort to Sarasvati, who rolls along his fertilizing waters, and is invoked by the worshippers as the bestower of wives and offspring, as well as of plenty and protection.

In v. 43, 11, Sarasvatî is called upon to descend from the sky, from the great mountain,[1] to the sacrifice; and in vi. 49, 7, where she is called the daughter of the lightning (*pâvîravî kanyâ*)[2] and the wife of a hero (*vîra-patnî*),[3] she is supplicated to combine with the spouses of the gods to afford secure protection to the worshipper. In the first of these two passages the poet may perhaps be considered as assigning a celestial origin to the river as the offspring of thunder and rain.

In vi. 61, 11 f. she is said to fill the terrestrial regions and the air, and to occupy three abodes (*trisadashthâ*), and to have seven parts or elements (*sapta-dhâtuḥ*).

When regarded as a river nymph, Sarasvati is further described as an iron barrier or fortress, and a support (vii. 95, 1), as bestowing wealth, fatness, and fertility (vii. 95, 2), and is besought to listen to the prayer of her worshippers at their sacrifices (*ibid.* 4), to receive their praises, to shelter and protect them like a tree (*ibid.* 5), and to grant reputation to the unrenowned (ii. 41, 16). In vi. 61, 14, the rishi prays that he may not be removed to regions which are strange to her.

In vi. 61, 1, she is represented as having given to Vadhryaṣva a son Divodâsa, a canceller of his debts.

Viewed as the patroness of holy rites, (though it is

[1] Sâyaṇa says that *Mâdhyamikî Vâch*, or the goddess Vâch, who resides in the region intermediate between heaven and earth, is here intended.

[2] See Roth *s. v.* and compare x. 65, 13. Prof. Müller, in Kuhn and Schleicher's Beiträge, etc., iii. 448, assigns to *pâvîravî* the sense of "thundering."

[3] Sâyaṇa says her husband is Prajâpati. Would it not rather be Sarasvat?

not always easy to separate the one from the other of her characters), Sarasvatî is described as coming to the place of sacrifice in the same chariot with the oblations and the forefathers (x. 17, 8), as unctuous with butter, and as stimulating, directing, and prospering the devotions of the worshippers (i. 3, 10, 11; ii. 3, 8; vi. 61, 4). She affords secure protection, conquers enemies (ii. 30, 8; vi. 49, 7), and destroys the revilers of the gods (vi. 61, 3). She is dreadful, moves along a golden path,[1] and is a destroyer of Vrittra (vi. 61, 7). She yields prosperity and riches of all description from her prolific breasts[2] (i. 89, 3; i. 164, 49; viii. 21, 17; x. 17, 8, 9; ix. 67, 32), is the receptacle of all the powers of life (*viṣvâ âyûnshi*), and bestows offspring (ii. 41, 17). In x. 184, 2, she is associated with the deities who assist procreation. In ii. 1, 11, Agni is identified with her, and several other goddesses.

In R. V. x. 131, 5 (= Vâj. S. x. 34) where the Aṣvins are said to have defended Indra, Sarasvatî also is declared to have waited upon him. And in Vâj. S. xix. 12, it is said, "The gods celebrated a healing sacrifice, the Aṣvins physicians, and Sarasvatî too a physician through speech, communicated vigour to Indra." The Aṣvins and Sarasvati are also connected with each other in Vâj. S. xix. 12, 15, 18, 34, 80-83, 88-90, 93-95; xx. 56-69, 73-76, 90. In xix. 94, it is said that "Sarasvati, wife of the Aṣvins, holds a well-formed embryo in her womb. Varuṇa, king in the waters, produced Indra for glory, by the aqueous fluid as if by a *sâma* verse."

It does not appear that in the R.V. Sarasvati is identified with Vâch. For the passages of that collection in which the latter goddess is celebrated, I refer to Sanskrit texts, iii. 151-156; and to my former paper on "The progress of the Vedic Religion, etc.," pp. 354 f. (note) and p. 377.

[1] *Hiraṇyavarttiniḥ.* Sâyaṇa explains *varttini* as chariot, and the compound as meaning "having a golden chariot." The same word occurs again, applied to a river, in viii. 26, 18, where Sâyaṇa makes it mean "having a golden path," *i.e.* golden banks. The words *rudra-varttani*, "whose path is dreadful," and *ghṛta-varttani*, "whose path is unctuous," are also applied to different deities in the Rig Veda. *Kṛshṇa-varttani*, "he whose path is marked by blackness," is an epithet of Agni in viii. 23, 19, and the sense of that term is fixed by the use of the synonym *kṛshṇâdhvan*. The substantive *varttani* occurs in vii. 18, 16.

[2] Compare Ait. Br. iv. 1, at the end, where her two breasts are said to be truth and falsehood.

In the later mythology, as is well known, Sarasvati was identified with Vâch, and became under different names the spouse of Brahmâ, and the goddess of wisdom and eloquence, and is invoked as a Muse. In the Mahâbhârata she is called the mother of the Vedas (Ṣântiparva v. 12920), and the same is said of Vâch in the Taittirîya Br. ii. 8, 8, 5,[1] where (and in the preceding par. 4,) she is also said to be the wife of Indra, to contain within herself all worlds, and to have been sought after by the rishis who composed the Vedic hymns (*ṛishayo mantra-kṛitah*), as well as by the gods, through austerity.

In the Ṣântiparva v. 6811, it is related that when the Brahmarshis were performing austerities prior to the creation of the universe, "a voice derived from Brahmâ entered into the ears of them all; the celestial Sarasvati was then produced from the heavens."[2]

Excepting Aditi and Ushas the other goddesses mentioned in the Rig Veda are, as I have already intimated, of very little importance. Agnâyî, Varuṇânî, Aṣvinî, and Rodasî, the wives of Agni, Varuṇa, the Aṣvins, and Rudra respectively (Nirukta ix. 33 f.; xi. 50; xii. 46) are only alluded to in a few passages, i. 22, 12; ii. 32, 8; v. 46, 8; vi. 50, 5; vi. 66, 6; vii. 34, 22. No distinct functions are assigned to them, and they do not occupy positions at all corresponding to the rank of their husbands, with whom in fact they are never associated. The insignificance of these goddesses forms a striking contrast to the prominent position assumed by the spouses of Ṣiva and Vishnu, especially the former, in the later mythology.

### ARAṆYÂNÎ.

Araṇyânî (Nir. ix. 29, 30), is the goddess of forest solitude.

[1] In the S. P. Br. vii. 5, 2, 52, it is said, "Mind is the ocean. From mind, the ocean, the gods, with Vâch for a shovel, dug out the triple science (*i. e.* the three Vedas). Wherefore this verse (ṣloka) has been uttered," etc. In the Bhîshma-p. of the M. Bh. v. 3019, Achyuta (Krishna) is said to have created Sarasvati and the Vedas from his mind. In the Vana-p. *v.* 13432, the Gâyatrî is called the mother of the Vedas.

[2] Compare the verse quoted by Ṣankara on the Brahma sûtras (see Sanskrit Texts, iii. 68), from a Smṛti: "In the beginning a celestial voice, formed of the Vedas, eternal, without beginning or end, was uttered by Svayambhû, from which all activities have proceeded."

She is celebrated in R. V. x. 146, which I have translated in a preceding paper.

### Râkâ, Sinîvâlî, and Gungû.

Râkâ, Sinîvâlî, and Gungû (whom Sâyaṇa on ii. 32, 8, identifies with Kuhû) are three other goddesses mentioned in the R. V. (the first in ii. 32, 4, 5, 8; v. 42, 12; the second in ii. 32, 6 ff; x. 184, 2; and the third in ii. 32, 8). Sâyaṇa (on ii. 32, 4) says that Râkâ is the full moon.[1] She is, however, closely connected with parturition, as she is asked to "sew the work (apparently the formation of the embryo) with an unfailing needle), and to bestow a son with abundant wealth" (ii. 34, 4). Sinîvâlî and Kuhû are (as we are told by Yâska, xi. 31), wives of the gods according to the mythologists (*nairuktâḥ*), and the two new moons (*amâvâsye*) according to the ritualists (*yâjnikâḥ*), Sinîvâlî being the earlier and Kuhû the later. Sinîvâlî is, however, also connected with parturition, being called the broad-loined (or bushy-haired), the prolific, the handsome-armed, the handsome-fingered, supplicated for progeny (ii. 32, 6, 7), and asked to bestow pregnancy (x. 184, 2; A. V. v. 25, 3; vi. 11, 3). Yâska quotes from the Taitt. Br. iii. 3, 11, a verse regarding Kuhû, whose name does not occur in the Rig Veda.

### Ṣraddhâ.

Personifications of abstract ideas are not unknown in the Rig Veda, one hymn of which (x. 151) is addressed to Ṣraddhâ, or religious faith. By her, it is said, *v.* 1 (= Nir. ix. 31), "the (sacrificial) fire is kiṇdled, and by her the oblation is offered up." She is asked to prosper the liberal worshippers of the gods (*v.v.* 2, 3), and to impart faith; and is said to be an object of adoration in the morning, at noon, and at sunset (*v.* 5).[2]

[1] On these goddesses see Weber's Ind. Stud. v. 228 ff. and 237.

[2] In the Vâj. Sanhitâ, xix. 30, it is said that faith (*ṣraddhá*) is obtained by gifts (*dakshiṇá*) and truth (*satya*) by faith. In xix. 77 of the same work it is declared that "Prajâpati beholding, made a distinction between the forms of truth and falsehood (*satyánṛte*), connecting disbelief (*aṣraddhá*) with the latter, and faith or belief (*ṣraddhá*) with the former." This declaration, that truth is the only proper object of faith, has a far deeper signification than this ancient writer could possibly have assigned to it, viz., that it is the ultimate truth, and not the so-called orthodoxy of any proposition, which can alone entitle it to reception.

Ṣraddhâ is also celebrated in the Taitt. Br. ii. 8, 8, 6 f., where the above hymn of the R. V. is repeated; and she is there further said to dwell among the gods, to be the universe, and the mother of Kâma. (See my paper on the "Progress of the Vedic Religion," p. 377, note). In the same Taitt. Br. iii. 12, 3, 1, we are told that through Ṣraddhâ a god obtains his divine character, that the divine Ṣraddhâ is the support of the world, that she has Kâma (or the fulfilment of desire) for her calf, and yields immortality as her milk; that she is the first-born of the religious ceremonial, and the sustainer of the whole world: and she, who is the supreme mistress of the world, is besought to bestow immortality on her worshippers. In the S. P. Br. (xii. 7, 3, 11) she is called the daughter of Sûrya;[1] an appellation which is repeated in the M. Bh. Ṣântiparva, *v.* 9449,[2] where she is styled Ṣraddhâ Vaivasvatî, as well as Sûryasya duhitâ and Sâvitri.

## Lakshmî and Ṣrî.

Lakshmi is not found in the R. V. in the sense whieh the word bears in the later mythology, of a goddess personifying good fortune, though the word itself occurs in x. 71, 2,[3] in another signification. In the A. V., however, we have the following hymn which speaks of a plurality of Lakshmîs, some good and some bad: vii. 115, 1: "Fly away hence, o unlucky (or miserable) Lakshmi (*pāpi lakshmi*), perish hence, fly away from thence: with an iron hook we fasten thee to our enemy. 2. Savitri, do thou who art golden-handed, be-

[1] See what is said of the daughter of Sûrya above, in connection with the Aṣvins.

[2] In this passage a great deal is said in praise of Ṣraddhâ. She smites the man who smites her. The gods, it appears, had decided that the offerings of a niggardly student of the Veda (*ṣrotriya*) and a liberal usurer were of equal value. But Prajâpati determined that they were wrong (see the same sentiment in nearly the same words in Manu, iv. 224 ff.), and that the liberal man's oblation, being purified by his faith (*ṣraddhâ*), was to be accepted, whilst the other man's, being vitiated by his unbelief, was to be rejected. Unbelief, it is added, is the greatest of sins, but faith takes away sin.

A similar sentiment is expressed in the Vana-parva, 13461 ff.: "The doubter enjoys neither this world nor the next, nor any gratification. Those ancient sages who possess true knowledge have said that faith (*pratyaya*) is a sign of final liberation. . . . Abandoning fruitless (*lit.* dry) argumentations (*ṣushka-tarkam*), adhere to the *ṣruti* and the *smṛti*" (the Vedas and other books dependent on them).

[3] In the words *bhadrâ eshâm lakshmî nihitâ adhi vâchi*, "an auspicious fortune is attached to their words."

stowing on us wealth, send away from us to some other quarter the flying and inauspicious Lakshmî who mounts up on me, as a creeper[1] upon a tree. 3. A hundred Lakshmis are born together with the body of a mortal at his birth. Of these we chase away hence the most unlucky. Do thou, Jâtavedas, retain for us those which are fortunate. 4. Thus I divide them like the cows standing upon barren ground. May those Lakshmis which are auspicious (*puṇyâh*) rest here. Those which are unlucky (*pâpîh*) I destroy." (The expression *puṇyâ Lakshmî* occurs also in A. V. xii. 5, 6).

In the Vâj. S. xxxi. 22, Ṣrî and Lakshmi are said to be the two wives (of Âditya, according to the commentator). In the Ṣ. P. Br. xi. 4, 3, 1, Ṣrî is described as issuing forth from Prajâpati when he was performing intense austerity. Beholding her then standing resplendent and trembling,[2] the gods were covetous of her and proposed to Prajâpati that they should be allowed to kill her, and appropriate her gifts. He replied that she was a female, and that males did not generally kill females. They should therefore take from her her gifts without depriving her of life. In consequence, Agni, took from her food; Soma, kingly authority; Varuṇa, imperial authority; Mitra, martial energy (*kshattra*); Indra, force; Brihaspati, priestly glory (*brahma-varchasa*); Savitri, dominion; Pûshan, splendour; Sarasvati, nourishment, and Tvashtri, forms. Ṣrî then complained to Prajâpati that they had taken all these things from her. He told her to demand them back from them by sacrifice. This she accordingly did, and succeeded.

[1] *Vandanâ.* This word does not occur in Wilson's Dictionary, but I find there *vandâ* in the sense of a creeping plant.

[2] *Lelâyantî.* As fixing the sense of this word Prof. Aufrecht refers me to S. P. Br. p. 136; Bṛhad âraṇyaka p. 737; Muṇdaka Up. pp. 274, 276; and Ṣvetâṣvatara Up. p. 332.

## Art. II.—*Miscellaneous hymns from the Rig and Atharva Vedas.*[1] By J. Muir, Esq., D.C.L., LL.D.

The hymns of the Rig Veda are, as is well known, almost entirely of a religious character, designed, or at least, adapted, for recitation at the worship of the various popular deities, or at some of the ceremonials connected with various important events in the domestic or public life of the ancient Indians. Among these, however, are interspersed a few of a different description, which, from the wide celebrity they had acquired, were carefully preserved by the descendants of their authors, or by other interested persons, and have been incorporated in the great collection of sacred songs. Some of these productions, like the colloquy of Yama and Yami (translated in a former paper), the very obscure conversation between the hero Purûravas and the Apsaras Urvaṣî (R. V. x. 95),[2] and the Vrishâkapi hymn (R. V. x. 86), derived their importance from the interlocutors being personages regarded as divine, or ranked among the ancestors of the human race. Others, like the 72nd, the 90th, and the 129th hymns of the 10th Book (also quoted in previous articles) were venerated from the nature of the topics which they handled, or the depth or gravity of the speculations which they contain. Others, again, such as the hymns referred to by Professor Roth in his dissertation "on the historical matter contained in the Rig Veda,"[3] would possess an interest for the descendants of

[1] I have again to acknowledge the valuable aid which I have received from Professor Aufrecht in rendering some of the more difficult parts of the hymns translated in this paper.

[2] Professor Max Müller's Essay on Comparative Mythology, in the Oxford Essays for 1856, contains a translation of this myth as narrated in the Ṣatapatha Brâhmaṇa. The Brâhmaṇa, however, only quotes and illustrates the easiest verses of the hymn (R. V. x. 95), making no reference to its most obscure and difficult portions. Some of the verses not cited in the Brâhmaṇa are explained by Professor Müller. See also Roth's Illustrations of Nirukta, pp. 153 ff. and 230.

[3] Sur Litteratur and Geschichte des Weda, pp. 87.

the contending priestly races to whose rivalries they made allusion, and might even be valued for the purposes of imprecation to which they could be applied.[1] And those compositions which celebrate the liberality of different princes to their domestic priests would naturally be handed down with care by the successors of those favoured individuals.

In the following paper I shall adduce some other hymns, both from the Rig and the Atharva Vedas, which are only in part of a religious character, and possess a greater general interest than the bulk of those with which they are associated, from the references which they make to human character, dispositions, feelings, passions, and circumstances; from the light which they throw on the progress of sacerdotal pretensions, or from some other feature of their contents. In some of these hymns it will be seen that a considerable amount of shrewdness and worldly wisdom is expressed in a sentencious form.

### Hymn to Aranyâṇî, R. V. x. 146.

The first hymn which I shall adduce, addressed to the goddess of forest solitude, is distinguished by the poetical feeling which pervades it, and the natural manner in which the emotions arising from the situation there described are depicted, though some of the allusions which it contains are difficult to explain or comprehend. It is repeated in the Taittirîya Brâhmana, and explained by the Commentator on that work. (See also Roth's Illustrations of the Nirukta, p. 132).

1. "Araṇyânî, Araṇyânî, thou who seemest to lose thyself there, why dost thou not ask [the way to] the village? Does not terror seize thee (at thy solitude)? 2. When the chichchika (a bird) answers to the roar of bulls when it is uttered, flying about as if with cymbals, then [by their voices] Araṇyâni is lauded [as if by hymns]. 3. And the cows seem to eat, and the house appears to be seen, and at evening Araṇyânî seems to discharge the carts.[2] 4. One man calls to his cow,

[1] See Sanskrit Texts, i. 127 ff.

[2] Professor Aufrecht thinks this clause (*ṣakatîr iva sarjati*) should be rendered, ' In the evening the forest moves like a cart," with reference to the agitation of the branches by the evening air.

another fells a tree; a man lingering in the forest (in Araṇyâni) fancies that she [or some one] has screamed. 5. Araṇyânî is not [herself] murderous, if no one else (a tiger, etc.) assails; but after eating of sweet fruit, a man rests there at his pleasure. 6. I laud Araṇyânî, the mother of wild beasts, the unctuous-scented, the fragrant, who yields abundance of food, though she has no hinds to till her."

The next hymn which I shall quote refers to the great variety by which the aims and pursuits of different men are characterized. It is distinguished by a vein of naive observation, not unmingled with satire; and is curious as revealing to us the occupations pursued by the poet's father and mother, though it makes no reference to the class to which they belonged.

RIG VEDA, ix. 112.

1. "We different men have all our various imaginations and designs. The carpenter seeks something that is broken, the doctor a patient, the priest some one who will offer libations. O Indu (Soma), flow forth for Indra.[1] 2. With dried-up sticks, with birds' feathers, with metals, the artizan continually seeks after a man with plenty of gold. O Indu, etc., etc. 3. (= Nirukta, vi. 6) I am a poet, my father is a doctor, and my mother is a grinder of corn. With our different views, seeking to get gain, we run after [our respective objects] as after cattle.[2] O Indu, etc. 4. The draught horse desires an easy-going carriage; merry companions a laugh; the female sex the male; and frogs a pond. O Indu," etc.

RIG VEDA, x. 34.

The next hymn, which may possibly be the production of one who lays before us the sad results of his own bitter experience, describes with great vividness, graphic power, and truth of observation the seductions and miseries of gambling,

[1] This last clause, which is repeated at the end of each of the verses, and transforms the hymn into an address to Soma, is perhaps a later addition to an older song; as it seems to have no connection with the other parts of the verses to which it is attached.

[2] The three preceding verses are translated by Roth in his Illustrations of the Nirukta, p. 74.

which, we see, were as acutely felt in those early ages as they are in these later times.

1. (= Nirukta ix. 8). "The tumbling, air-born [products] of the great Vibhîdaka tree (*i.e.* the dice) delight me as they continue to roll on the dice-board. The exciting dice enchant me like a draught of the soma-plant growing on mount Mûjavat. 2. She (the gamester's own wife) never wronged or despised me. She was kind to me, and to my friends. But I for the sake of the partial dice, have spurned my devoted spouse. 3. My mother-in-law detests me; my wife rejects me. In his need [the gamester] finds no comforter. I cannot discover what is the enjoyment of the gambler any more than I can perceive what is the happiness of a worn-out hack horse. 4. Others pay court to the wife of the man whose wealth is coveted by the impetuous dice. His father, mother, brothers, say of him, "We know nothing of him; take him away bound." 5. When I resolve not to be tormented by them, because I am abandoned by my friends who withdraw from me,—yet as soon as the brown dice, when they are thrown, make a rattling sound, I hasten to their rendezvous, like a woman to her paramour.[1] 6. The gamester comes to the assembly, glowing in body, and inquiring, "shall I win?" The dice inflame his desire, making over his winnings to his opponent. 7. Hooking, piercing, deceitful, vexatious, delighting to torment, the dice dispense transient gifts, and again ruin the winner; they are covered with honey, but destroy the gambler. 8. Their troop of fifty-three disports itself [disposing men's destinies] like the god Savitri whose ordinances never fail. They bow not before the wrath even of the fiercest. The king himself makes obeisance to them. 9. They roll downward; they bound upward. Having no hands, they overcome him who has. These celestial coals, when thrown on the diceboard, scorch the heart, though cold themselves. 10. The destitute wife of the gamester is distressed, and so too is the mother of a son who goes she knows not whither. In debt and seeking after money, the gambler approaches with trepidation the

[1] These words are quoted in Nirukta xii. 7.

houses of other people at night. 11. It vexes the gamester to see his own wife, and then to observe the wives and happy homes of others. In the morning he yokes the brown horses (the dice); by the time when the fire goes out he has sunk into a degraded wretch. 12. He who is the general of your band, the first king of your troop,—to him I stretch forth [my] ten [fingers] toward the east [in reverence]:[1] I spare no expense [in my offering]. That I declare with perfect truth. 13. Never play with dice; practice husbandry; rejoice in thy property, esteeming it sufficient. 'There, o gamester, are thy cows; [this is] thy wife;'—so the adorable Savitri addresses me. 14. Be friendly [o dice]; be auspicious to us; do not bewitch us powerfully with your enchantment. Let your hostile wrath abate. Let others be subject to the fetters of the brown ones (the dice)."

That the passion for gambling prevailed very extensively at the time when the hymns of the Rig- and Atharva-vedas were composed is clear, from various other allusions to the practice which we find there. Thus in R. V. vii. 86, dice are mentioned along with wine, anger, thoughtlessness, etc., as causes of sin. The following verses from the A. V. prove the same point:

A. V. vii. 50-1. "As the lightning every day strikes the tree irresistibly, so may I to-day irresistibly smite the gamester with the dice. 2. May the wealth of the rich and of the poor unresisting be collected from every side into my hand as winnings."

vii. 109. 1. "This reverence be paid to the brown [die], who is ruler among the dice. With butter I worship Kali; may he thus be auspicious to us. 2. Bring, o Agni, butter to the Apsarases, but dust, sand, and water to the dice. Seeking oblations according to their several shares, the gods delight in both offerings. 3. The Apsarases hold a festival between the oblation and the sun. May they anoint my hands with butter, and overwhelm the gamester who is my opponent. 4. Dispense bad luck to our adversary, but moisten

[1] Compare A. V. v. 28, 11, and Vâjasaneyi Sanhitâ, xvi. 64.

us with butter. Strike, as lightning does a tree, the man who plays against us."

vi. 118, 1. "Whatever sins we have committed with our hands, seeking to obtain the host of dice,—remit to us to-day that debt, ye Apsarases Ugrampaṣyâ and Ugrajit."

A. V. iv. 38. 1. "I invoke hither the skilfully-playing Apsaras who cuts up and conquers, and gets gains in the game of dice. 2. I invoke hither the skilfully-playing Apsaras, who collects and scatters, and receives gains in the game of dice. 3. May she who dances about with the dice when she wins by gaming, grant gain to us, and obtain superiority, through her skill. May she come to us with abundance of riches. Let them not conquer our money. 4. I invoke hither the joyful and exulting Apsarases—those [goddesses] who delight in dice, and bring with them grief and anger."

It will be seen from these verses that the Apsarases are intimately connected with gambling. In A. V. ii. 2, 4, they are said to be "fond of dice," and "soul bewitching."

The next two hymns which I proceed to quote are in praise of generosity. The first of them celebrates liberality to the destitute in general; the second eulogizes the same virtue when exhibited in giving presents to priests.

## Rig Veda, x. 117.

1. "The gods have not ordained hunger to be our destruction. Even those who are full-fed are overtaken by various forms of death (*lit.* deaths). The prosperity of the liberal man never decays; while the illiberal finds no comforter. 2. He who, himself well provided with sustenance, hardens his heart against the poor man who approaches him, starving, and who has long courted him, desirous of food,—such a man meets with none to cheer him. 3. He is the bountiful man who gives to the lean beggar who comes to him craving food. Success attends that man in the sacrifice, and he secures for himself a friend in the future. 4. He is no friend who bestows nothing on his friend who waits upon him, seeking

for sustenance. Let every one depart from such a man;—his house is no home,—and look out for some one else who is liberal, even though he be a stranger. 5. Let the powerful man be generous to the suppliant; let him look along the path [of futurity]. For, oh, riches revolve like the wheels of a chariot: they come, now to one, now to another.[1] 6. In vain the fool obtains food: I tell the truth; it becomes his destruction (comp. v. 1). He nourishes neither his friend nor his companion. He who keeps his food to himself, has his sin to himself. 7. The ploughshare furrowing the ground, brings men plenty. A man moving onward with his feet, accomplishes his journey. A priest who speaks is more acceptable than one who is silent. A kinsman who is beneficent excels one who is stingy. 8. A one-footed being advances faster than a two-footed. The two-footed comes after the three-footed.[2] The four-footed follows in the rear of the two-footed, and moves on observing his steps. 9. The two hands, though alike, do not perform an equal amount of work. Two cows with the same mother do not yield the same quantity of milk. Two men, though twins, have not the same strength. And two others, though kinsmen, are not equally liberal."

## Rig Veda, x. 107.

1. "The great [lustre] of these opulent ones has been manifested. The whole living [world] has been liberated from darkness. The great light given by the Fathers[3] has arrived. The broad path of Largess has been beheld. 2. The givers of gifts abide aloft in the sky; the bestowers of horses live with the Sun; the givers of gold attain immor-

[1] It is curious to find in so ancient a composition this now trite comparison of the changes of fortune to the revolutions of a wheel. The same idea occurs in the Mahâbhârata, iii. 15489: "After happiness, suffering, and after suffering, happiness, visit a man in succession, as the spokes of a wheel [revolve round] the nave." According to Herodotus i. 207, Crœsus said to Cyrus: "If thou knowest that even thou art human, and rulest over mortals, learn first this lesson, that in the affairs of men there is a wheel which, by its revolution, renders it impossible for the same persons always to enjoy prosperity."

[2] Professor Aufrecht suggests that the one-footed may mean a cripple, and the three-footed, an old man with his staff.

[3] Compare R. V. x. 68, 11. "The Fathers have adorned the sky with stars .... and placed darkness in the night, and light in the day."

tality; the bestowers of raiment prolong their lives. 3. A gift which is a satisfaction of the gods, an offering to the deities, [proceeds] not from the illiberal; they bestow nothing; and many men of extensive liberality are bountiful merely through fear of reproach. . . . . 5. The giver of gifts, invited, advances first; he walks in the front as leader.[1] I regard as the king of men him who first presented a gift. 5. They call him a rishi, a priest, a reverend chanter of hymns and reciter of verses,—he knows the three forms of the resplendent (Agni),—the man who was the first to crown [his religious service] with a gift. 7. Largess bestows a cow, a horse, silver (?) and gold. Largess bestows (?) food, which is our life. The wise man makes largess-giving his breastplate. 8. Bountiful men neither die nor fall into calamity; they suffer neither wrong nor pain. Their liberality confers on them this whole world as well as heaven. 9. The bountiful conquer for themselves first, a pleasant abode, a well-dressed wife, and a draught of wine; they conquer those who walk in the front (?), uninvited. 10. A fleet horse is trained for the generous man; he obtains a brilliant damsel for his portion; this house of his resembles a lotus-pond, beautiful, embellished like a palace of the gods. 11. The liberal man is borne along by rapid horses. The car of largess rolls forward on easy wheels. Preserve, ye gods, the bountiful man in battle. He overcomes his enemies in the fight."

The next hymn, from the Atharva Veda, sets forth with great liveliness and vigour the advantages accruing to princes from the employment of a domestic priest.

### ATHARVA VEDA, iii. 19.

1. "May this prayer of mine be successful; may the vigour and strength be complete, may the power be perfect and undecaying, of those of whom I am the victorious priest (*purohita*). 2. I fortify their kingdom, and augment their

[1] Compare R. V. iv. 50, 8 f, where the prosperity and honor which attend a prince who retains and cherishes a domestic priest are described. See Professor Wilson's translation, and note on *v.* 9, in p. 214; and Roth's Art. on Brahma and the Brâhmans, Journ. Germ. Or. Society, i. 77 ff. See also the hymn from the A. V. iii. 19, next quoted in the text.

energy, valour, and force. I break the arms of their enemies with this oblation. 3. May all those who fight against our wise and prosperous [prince] sink downward, and be prostrated. With my prayer I destroy his enemies, and raise up his friends. 4. May those of whom I am the priest be sharper than an axe, sharper than fire, sharper than Indra's thunderbolt. 5. I strengthen their weapons; I prosper their kingdom rich in heroes. May their power be undecaying and victorious. May all the gods foster their designs. 6. May their valorous deeds, o Maghavat, burst forth; may the noise of the conquering heroes arise; may their distinct shouts, their clear yells, go up; may the gods, the Maruts with Indra as their chief, march forward with their host. 7. Go, conquer, ye warriors: may your arms be strong. Ye with the sharp arrows, smite those whose bows are powerless; ye whose weapons and arms are terrible (smite) the feeble. 8. When discharged, fly forth, o arrow, sped by prayer. Vanquish the foes, assail, slay all the choicest of them; let not one escape."

The two following hymns from the Atharva Veda declare the guilt, the peril, and disastrous consequences of oppressing Brâhmans, and robbing them of their property. The threats and imprecations of haughty sacerdotal insolence could scarcely be expressed more energetically.

### Atharva Veda, v. 18.

1. "King, the gods have not given thee [this cow] to eat. Do not, O Râjanya (man of royal descent), seek to devour the Brâhman's cow, which is not to be eaten. 2. The wicked Râjanya, unlucky in play, and self-destroyed, will eat the Brâhmin's cow, saying, 'Let me live to-day, [if I can] not [live] to-morrow.' 3. This cow, clothed with a skin, contains deadly poison, like a snake. Beware, Râjanya, she is ill-flavoured, and must not be eaten. 4. He [who eats her] forfeits his strength, destroys his own splendour, consumes everything like a fire which has been kindled. The man who looks upon the Brâhman as mere food to be eaten up, drinks serpent's poison. 5. Indra kindles a fire

in the heart of that contemner of the gods who slays the Brâhman, esteeming him to be inoffensive, and foolishly covets his property. Heaven and earth abhor the man who [so] acts. 6. A Brâhman is not to be wronged, as fire [must not be touched] by a man who cherishes his own body. Soma is his (the Brâhman's) kinsman, and Indra shields him from imprecations. 7. The wicked (?) man who thinks the priests' food is sweet while he is eating it, swallows [the cow] bristling with a hundred sharp points, but cannot digest her. 8. The priest's tongue is a bow-string, his voice is a barb, and his windpipe is arrow-points smeared with fire. With these god-directed, and heart-subduing bows, the priest pierces the scorners of the gods. Brâhmans bearing sharp arrows, armed with missiles, never miss their mark when they discharge a shaft. Shooting with fervour [austerity ?] and with anger, they pierce [the enemy] from afar. 10. The descendants of Vîtahavya who ruled over a thousand men, and were ten hundred in number, were overcome after they had eaten a Brahman's cow. 11. The cow herself, when she was slaughtered, destroyed them,—those men who cooked the last she-goat of Kesaraprâbandhâ. 12. Those hundred persons whom the earth shook off, after they had wronged the priestly race, were overwhelmed in an inconceivable manner. 13. He lives among mortals a scorner of the gods; infected with poison he becomes reduced to a skeleton; he who wrongs a Brâhman the kinsman of the deities, fails to attain to the heaven of the Forefathers. 14. Agni is called our leader; Soma our kinsman. Indra neutralizes imprecations [directed against us]; this the wise understand. 15. Like a poisoned arrow, o king, like a serpent, o lord of cows,—such is the dreadful shaft of the Brâhman, with which he pierces his despisers."

### Atharva Veda, v. 19.

1. "The Srinjayas, descendants of Vîtahavya, waxed exceedingly; they almost touched the sky; but after they had injured Bhrigu, they were overwhelmed. 2. When men pierced Brihatsâman, a Brâhman descended from Angiras, a

ram with two rows of teeth swallowed their children. 3. Those who spit, or throw filth (?) upon a Brâhman, sit eating hair in the midst of a stream of blood. 4. So long as this Brâhman's cow writhes (?) when being cooked, she destroys the glory of the kingdom; no vigorous hero is born there. 5. It is cruel to slaughter her; her ill-flavoured flesh is thrown away. When her milk is drunk, that is esteemed a sin among the Forefathers. 6. Whenever a king, fancying himself mighty, seeks to devour a Brâhman, that kingdom is broken up, in which a Brâhman suffers. Becoming eight-footed, four-eyed, four-eared, four-jawed, two-faced, two-tongued, she (the cow) shatters the kingdom of the oppressor of Brâhmans. 8. (Ruin) overflows that kingdom, as water swamps a leaky boat: calamity smites that country in which a priest is wronged. 9. Even trees, o Nârada, repel, and refuse their shade to, the man who claims a right to the property of a Brâhman. This [property], as king Varuṇa hath said, has been turned into a poison by the gods. No one who has eaten a Brâhman's cow continues to watch (*i.e.* to rule) over a country. 11. Those nine nineties [of persons] whom the earth shook off, when they had wronged the priestly race, were overwhelmed in an inconceivable manner (see v. 12 of the preceding hymn). 12. The gods have declared that the cloth wherewith a dead man's feet are bound shall be thy pall, thou oppressor of priests. 13. The tears which flow from a vanquished man as he laments,—such is the portion of water which the gods have assigned to thee, thou oppressor of priests. 14. The gods have allotted to thee that portion of water wherewith men wash the dead, and moisten their beards. 15. The rain of Mitra and Varuṇa does not descend on the oppressor of priests. For him the battle has never a successful issue; nor does he bring his friend into subjection." The attention of the reader is directed to the intensity of contempt and abhorrence which is sought to be conveyed by the coarse imagery contained in *vv.* 3, and 12-14, of the last preceding hymn.

In another hymn of the Atharva Veda, v. 17, the two following verses occur regarding the prerogative of Brâhmans;

8. "And if a woman have had ten former husbands, not Brâhmans, and a Brâhmana take her hand (*i.e.* marry her), he is the only husband. 9. It is a Brahman only who is a husband, and not a Râjanya, or a Vaiṣya. The Sun marches on declaring that to the five tribes of men."

The four hymns of the A. V. which follow contain incantations designed to save persons suffering under dangerous diseases, and on the point of death, from death, or rather perhaps to recall their spirits after their separation from the body. They supply various illustrations of the ideas entertained by the Indians of the period when they were composed regarding the vital principle, the relations of the different senses to the several elements, the deities by whom men's tenure of life was regulated, the power of incantations to arrest the approach of doom, and other kindred particulars.

### Atharva Veda, v. 30.

"1. From thy vicinity, from thy vicinity, from a distance, from thy vicinity [I call] to thee: remain here; do not follow, do not follow, the early Fathers. I firmly hold back thy breath. 2. Whatever incantations any kinsman or stranger has uttered against thee,—with my voice I declare thy release and deliverance from them all. 3. Whatever hurt thou hast done, or curse thou hast spoken, in thy folly, against woman or man, with my voice, etc. 4. If thou liest there in consequence of any sin committed by thy mother, or thy father,[1] with my voice, etc. 5. Receive the medicine which thy father, mother, sister and brother offer to thee. I make thee long-lived. 6. Come (?) hither, o man, with thy entire soul; do not follow the two messengers of Yama;[2] come to the abodes of the living. 7. Return when called, knowing the outlet of the path, the ascent, the advance, the

[1] Compare a curious passage from the Taittirîya Brâhmana iii. 7, 12, 3f. "May Agni deliver me from any sin which my mother may have committed when I was in her womb, or which my father may have committed. May my parents have received no injury from me, when I, a son, in sucking, squeezed my mother and father in my delight." Compare also R. V. vii. 86, 5, referred to in my paper, "Contributions to a knowledge of Vedic Theogony," etc., p. 82, line 19.

[2] See my former paper on Yama, pp. 292 and 297.

road of every living man. 8. Fear not; thou shalt not die; I make thee long-lived. I have charmed out of thy members the consumption by which they are wasted. 9. The consumption which racks and wastes thy limbs, and sickens thy heart, has flown away to a distance like a hawk, overcome by my word. 10. The two sages, Alert and Watchful, the sleepless, and the vigilant, these the guardians of thy life, are awake both day and night. 11. May this adorable Agni rise here to thee as a sun. Rise up from deep death,[1] yea even from black darkness.[2] 12. Reverence to Yama, reverence to Death, reverence to the Fathers, and to those who guide us. I place in front of this [sick] man, for his security, Agni who knows how to carry him across. 13. Let his breath, let his soul, let his sight come, and then his strength; let his body acquire sensation, and stand firm upon its feet. 14. Provide him, Agni, with breath, and with sight; restore him, furnished with a body, and with strength.[3] Thou hast the knowledge of immortality; let him not depart, or become a dweller in a house of clay. 15. Let not thy inhaled breath cease; let not thy exhaled breath vanish. Let the sun, the lord, raise thee up from death by his rays. 16. This tongue speaks within, bound, convulsive. By thee, I have charmed away the consumption, and the hundred torments of the fever. 17. This world is the dearest, unconquered by the gods. To whatever death thou wast destined when thou wast born—we call after thee, do not die before thou art worn out by old age."

ATHARVA VEDA, vii. 53.

1. "Brihaspati, thou hast delivered us from dwelling in the realm of Yama, from the curse. Aṣvins,—ye who, o Agni, are the two physicians of the Gods,—ye have repelled death from us by your powers. 2. Continue associated, ye two breaths, inspired and expired; forsake not his body: may they, united, remain with thee here. Live prosperously a hundred autumns. Agni is thy splendid protector

[1] Compare the *ἀιπυς ὀλεθρος* of Homer.
[2] Compare the passage quoted in my paper on Yama, p. 304.
[3] Compare the article just referred to, p. 8.

and lord. 3. May thy life which has been dissipated afar, may thy breaths, come back to thee again. Agni has snatched it from the lap of Nirriti (Destruction): and I introduce it again into thyself. 4. Let not his inspiration abandon him, nor his expiration quit him and depart. I commit him to the seven Rishis; may they carry him on in health to old age. 5. Enter into him, ye two breaths, like two steers forcing their way into a cow-pen. May this man flourish here, an unmolested depositary of old age. 6. We invigorate thy life. I drive away consumption from thee. May this excellent Agni sustain our life on every side. Ascending from the darkness to the uppermost heaven, we have reached, among the gods, the god Sûrya, the highest luminary."

### Atharva Veda, viii. 1.

1. "Reverence to Death the Ender! May thy inhaled and exhaled breaths rejoice here. May this man remain here united with his spirit in the domain of the sun, in the world of deathlessness. 2. Bhaga and Soma with his filaments, the divine Maruts, Indra, and Agni, have raised him up to health. Here is thy spirit, here thy breath, here thy life, here thy soul. We rescue thee from the bonds of Nirriti by a divine utterance. 4. Rise up hence, o man. Casting off the fetters of death, do not sink downward. Do not depart from this world, from the sight of Agni and the Sun. 5. May the Wind, Mâtariṣvan, blow for thee; may the waters shower immortality (or ambrosia) on thee; may the Sun shine healingly upon thy body; may Death pity thee; do not die. 6. Thou must ascend, o man, and not descend; I give thee life and vital power. Mount this pleasant and imperishable car; then, when aged, thou shalt declare a festival.[1] 7. Let not thy soul go away thither, let it not disappear; do not wander away from the living; do not follow the Fathers. May all the gods preserve thee. 8. Do not long after the departed, who conduct men afar. Ascend from the darkness; come into the light. We lay hold of thy hands. 9. Let not the two dogs sent by Yama,[2] the

[1] Compare R. V. x. 85, 17. [2] See A. V. v. 30, 6, above.

black and the brindled [seize thee]. Come hither; do not hesitate; do not remain here with averted mind. 10. Do not follow this path; it is terrible; I speak of that by which thou hast not hitherto gone. This, o man, is darkness; do not enter it. Beyond, thou hast fear; on this side, thou hast security. 11. May the fires which are in the waters preserve thee; may the fire which men kindle preserve thee; may Jâtavedas Vaiṣvânara (the fire which is common to all men) preserve thee; let not the celestial fire together with the lightning, consume thee. 12. Let not the flesh-devouring fire[1] be hostile to thee; go far from that wicked one. May the sky, the earth, the sun, and moon, preserve thee; may the air protect thee from the bolt of the gods. 13. May Wakeful and Watchful, may the sleepless and the waking preserve thee. May the guardian and the vigilant protect thee. 14. May they protect and guard you. To them be reverence. 15. May Vâyu, Indra, Dhâtri, and Savitri the deliverer, restore thee to converse with the living. Let not breath and strength abandon thee; we call back thy spirit. 16. Let not any violent devourer, let not darkness find thee. May the Âdityas and Vasus, with Indra and Agni, raise thee up to health. 17. The sky, the earth, Prajâpati have rescued thee. The plants with Soma their king, have delivered thee from death. 18. Let this man remain here, o gods; let him not depart hence to the other world. We rescue him from death with a charm of boundless efficacy (*sahasra-vîryyeṇa*). 19. I have delivered thee from death; may the vigorous breathe upon thee.[2] Let not the she-devils with dishevelled hair, or those that howl dreadfully, yell at thee. 20. I have snatched thee; I have caught thee; thou hast returned renewed. I have got, o man perfect in thy members, thy entire eye, and thy entire life. 21. [Life] has breathed upon thee. Light has come to thee. Darkness has departed from thee. We remove from thee death, Nirriti and consumption."

[1] There are three kinds of fire, the *kravyâd*, or funeral (here referred to), which devours dead bodies, the culinary (*âmâd*), and the sacrificial. See the Vâj. S. i. 17, and the commentary there.

[2] See the 4th verse of the next hymn.

## Atharva Veda, viii. 2.

1. "Seize this boon of immortality; may long life, which cannot be cut off, be thine. I restore to thee breath and life; do not depart to the mist (*rajas*) or to darkness (*tamas*); do not die. 2. Come hither to the light of the living; I rescue thee that thou mayest survive a hundred autumns. Loosing the bands of death and imprecation, I lengthen out thy existence. 3. I have recovered thy breath from the wind, thine eye from the sun.[1] I place in thee thy soul. Receive sensation in thy limbs. Speak, articulating with thy tongue. 4. I blow upon thee with the breath of bipeds, and of quadrupeds, as on Agni when he is born (*i.e.* on fire when kindled). I have paid reverence, o Death, to thine eye, and to thy breath. 5. Let this man live and not die. We restore him. I make for him a remedy. Death, do not kill the mau. I invoke for his safety a vivifying . . . . , living, delivering, strong, and powerful plant. 7. Befriend him; do not seize him; let him go; though he is thine only, let him abide here with all his strength; o Bhava and Ṣarva, be gracious; grant deliverance; remove evil, and confer life. 8. Befriend him, Death, pity him; let him arise. Unharmed, with all his limbs, hearing perfectly, let him obtain enjoyment during a life of a hundred years. 9. May the shaft of the gods pass thee by; I bring thee across from the mist (see v. 1); I have rescued thee from death. Removing far away the flesh-devouring Agni, I draw round thee a circle (see R. V. x. 18, 4) that thou mayest live. 10. Preserving him from that misty egress of thine, o Death, which no one may escape by menaces, we make prayer a protection for him. 11. I give thee thy breaths, death at thy full age,[2] long life and health. I drive away all the messengers of Yama, who roam about, sent by the son of Vivasvat. 12. We remove afar evil, Nirriti, Grâhi, and flesh-devouring Piṣâchas, and hurl all wicked Rakshases, as

[1] See my paper on Yama, p. 294, note 7. [2] Compare A. V. xix. 24, 4, 5, 8.

it were into darkness. 13. I seek thy life from the immortal, living, Agni Jâtavedas. I procure that thou mayest suffer no injury, that thou mayest also be immortal. May this be the fortunate result. 14. May heaven and earth in unison be auspicious and innocuous to thee. May the sun shine and the wind blow pleasantly to thy heart. May the celestial streaming waters drop down upon thee favourably. 15. May the plants be auspicious to thee. I have raised thee from the lower to the upper earth. There may both the sons of Aditi, the Sun and the Moon,[1] preserve thee. 16. Whatever garment for clothing, or whatever girdle thou makest for thyself, we cause it to be agreeable to thy body; may it be soft to thy touch. 17. When, as a barber, thou shavest our hair and beard with a sharp and cleansing razor, while cleansing our face, do not rob us of our life. 18. Let the rice and barley be auspicious to thee, innocuous, undisturbing. These destroy consumption, and deliver from suffering. 19. Whatever thou eatest or drinkest, the grain derived from husbandry, or liquid, whatever is or is not to be eaten—all that food I render for thee free from poison. 20. We commit thee to both the Day and the Night: preserve him for me from the goblins who seek to devour him. 21. We allot to thee a hundred, ten thousand, years, two, three, four, ages (yugas).[2] May Indra and Agni, may all the gods regard thee favourably, without anger. 22. We commit thee to autumn, winter, spring, summer. May the rains be pleasant to thee, in which the plants grow up. 23. Death rules over bipeds; death rules over quadrupeds. From that Death the ruler I rescue thee; do not fear. 24. Thou who art uninjured shalt not die; thou shalt not die; do not fear. They do not die there; they do not go to the nethermost darkness, (25) every thing lives there, cow, horse, man, beast, in the place where this prayer is used, the bulwark of life. May it preserve thee from curse from thy equals and friends. Be

[1] The Moon is not in the Vedas generally reckoned among the Âdityas. See my "Contributions to a knowledge of Vedic Mythology," etc., pp. 75-77.

[2] It would be difficult to say how great a duration is here denoted by this word; but it must be one of great length, if the long periods of years which are mentioned just before, may be taken as any indication.

undying, immortal, long-lived; let not thy breaths abandon thy body. 27. May the gods deliver thee from those hundred deaths, from those dangers which are surpassable, and from that Agni Vaiṣvânara (fire of the funeral pile?). 28. Thou art the body of Agni, the deliverer, the slayer of Rakshases, and of rivals; and thou, the medicament named *Pûtudru* (Butea frondosa), art the chaser away of diseases."

## ART. III.—*Five Hundred Questions on the Social Condition of the Natives of Bengal.*[1] By the Rev. J. LONG, of Calcutta.

(Read before the Royal Asiatic Society, 19th June, 1865).

DESIDERATA and Inquiries connected with the Presidency of Madras and Bombay were issued by the Secretary of the Royal Asiatic Society in 1827, on points relating to the language, literature, ancient history of families, antiquities, coins, people, architecture, landed tenures, arts and manufactures, of India.

The British Admiralty has published a Manual of Scientific Enquiry, so have the Statistical and other Societies.

Haxthausen, in his work on the Caucasus, remarks: "My travels and observations during more than twenty years, have convinced me that an acquaintance with the manners of a people, their moral and material interests, domestic relations, corporate associations, and specially the commercial relations of the lower classes, is indispensable to a real knowledge of the history and constitution of peoples and states."

The present time seems favourable in India to prosecute enquiries on this subject; with the rapid spread of education literary tastes are springing up among natives.

The following five hundred questions and desiderata—suggestive of a wide range of subjects, on "the proper study of mankind is man"—shew that a wide field is opened out for enquiry into the social life of the natives of India and their *folk-lore*, a species of knowledge not to be found exclusively in *books*, but mainly in the memories and traditions of the people. These questions were framed by the Rev. J. Long, in Calcutta, for an Association of educated native

[1] The majority of these questions are applicable to natives in other parts of India.

gentlemen of which he was the President; they were designed to map out the field of action on subjects relating to native social life in India.

Now is the time to "note the passing manners as they fly." Hindu society in various parts of India is in a *transition* state, and it is desirable to treasure up in writing the records of the past and the passing; an educated class of natives is rapidly rising, qualified not only to investigate but also to write in English the results of their investigations; literary societies, and periodical literature, are increasing among them. Natives alone can penetrate into native society. Europeans must remain on the surface; but the two classes can work in harmony. The natives are able and willing to supply the data and facts,—while the European can classify and arrange them on the plan laid down by Statistical and Sociological Societies, and publish them hereafter for the information of persons both in Europe and the East.

There is a wide field opened out, as the five hundred questions and desiderata in this paper shew, and the co-operation of the following classes of Europeans in India is earnestly solicited:—

1. *Collectors, Magistrates, and Commissioners in Districts*, who, associating much among the people, might through their native employés secure a large amount of valuable information on various points, and would find the inquiry profitable to themselves in promoting good feeling between them and the natives, deepening their interest in the country and occasionally relieving the tedium of a solitary hour.

2. *European Settlers* would find these questions of use in gaining a better acquaintance with the social condition of the natives with whom they are thrown so much in contact; it would shew them that natives can talk and think of other subjects besides rupees, while on the other hand the natives would see that the Sahibs are not mere indigo, tea and coffee producing machines, but take an interest in the welfare and condition of their dependents,—thus the asperities arising from antagonism of race would be softened.

3. *Principals and Teachers in Schools and Colleges*, would

find many of these questions suitable as subjects for essays to be given to native students, testing and calling out not only their powers of composition, but also their faculties of observation and knowledge of common things,—checking the tendency of education to make mere book-worms, separated from and having few sympathies with the masses.

4. *Missionaries* in their itinerancies and in mixing with the natives have excellent opportunities of filling up these gaps in our ignorance of social life, and by conversation on social questions of smoothing down any rancour that may arise from theological discussion.

5. *Students of the Vernacular, and Travellers,* would find an ample supply of materials for conversation with natives and teachers, which would in an agreeable manner facilitate the study of the vernacular.

## I.

## Aborigines.

The *Dhangars* and other hill tribes who do such important though dirty work in the drainage of Calcutta, are deserving notice as to their habitations, religion, customs, language. Sir J. Malcom's Essay on the Bhils—Hodgson's valuable papers on the Aboriginal tribes, etc., suggest various subjects of enquiry. Dr. Pritchard, Hodgson, etc., etc., devoted much labour to it; and Sir G. Grey, when Governor of New Zealand, learned the language of the Aborigines, and has since published a most interesting work on "the Poetry of the New Zealanders." He lived among them for a time, and has recorded all their legends, traditions, etc. The Maoris living in the *ultima Thule* of civilization speak a language in which there are many words derived from Sanskrit. The Santals, met with one hundred miles from Calcutta, use a language having strong affinities with that of the Tartars of Central Asia, who are Russian subjects. The Hindu poetical legends describe those aborigines as monkeys; Megasthenes writes of them as one-eyed, without noses, wrapped up in their ears (*hastikarnas*).

1. The mode of living, habits, morals, and food of the *Dhangars*,

and other aborigines in foreign places, contrasted with their native place?

2. Ditto of the hill men who go as *coolies* to the Mauritius, Ceylon, and the West Indies.

3. The social position and relation of the coolies to Zemindars on their return, how far do they acquire habits of thought and independence, a knowledge of improved means of cultivation, a taste for a higher order of amusements, and a greater pride of personal appearance?

4. Do the wives and families of the Aboriginal emigrants accompany them in their emigrations? What connexion do they keep up with their native villages?

5. The ceremonies observed by the Aborigines, etc., at births, marriages, funerals? What mode have they of settling their disputes? How far do they believe in witchcraft, omens?

6. Any traces of the Aborigines ever having lived in the plains of India?

## II.

### Agricultural Classes.

How desirable it would be in India to see the native landlord, like the English country gentleman, attending agricultural shows—joining with his tenants in the sports of the field—administering justice on the bench—sympathising with the peasants in their difficulties—deriving, from an agricultural education, that scientific knowledge of rural husbandry which would interest him in the country, and thus enable him to be independent of the false information of the agent (*gomasta*).

1. How far is the charge true that the *ryot* is *lazy*—if so, is it owing to his not having a proper incentive to industry, or to his natural disposition?

2. In what cases have *ryots* risen to be *peasant proprietors?*—what effect would a class of peasant proprietors have on cultivation as compared with large capitalists? Would the results be similar to those in France, where peasant proprietorship fosters economy, a respect for property, forethought and industry?

3. How far are *zemindars, absentees?*—the causes, remedies?

4. To what extent is a taste for *gardening* spreading among zemindars, and educated natives—how could it be more extensively promoted as a morning amusement for natives in offices? instances of any natives who have devoted much time and money to gardening.

5. How far could *public gardens*[1] be established in native towns?

6. In what respect would the introduction of the study of *agricultural chemistry* and *of the elements of Botany* in a popular form in Anglo-Vernacular schools tend to lessen that gulph which now exists between the educated classes and the rural population?

7. The practicability of *evening classes* for teaching the ryots to read.[2]

8. How far are the ryots becoming more aware of "the great world beyond their *market town?*"

9. *Poverty* among the ryots, how pre-disposing to disease? to cheating?

10. Would an *encumbered estate commission*, which has worked so well in Ireland, be suited for India?

11. Is there a strong desire among *ryots* for the possession of land, so as to lead to habits of prudence and economy?

12. Are there many remains of old *Jaghires* in Bengal?

13. Is the minute *sub-division of land* according to Hindu law carried out much? what are its effects?

14. The proportion of *landholders* to the rest of the population?

15. To what extent do the ryots purchase things not *produced in* their own district?

16. Any cases of poor *ryots* who have risen to be zemindars or to a good social position?

17. Many *sub-tenures* amounting to ten?

18. Do many of the rural population *emigrate to towns?* the effects on their morals and on wages?

19. To what extent are the *zemindars* "rotting in idleness?" its causes and remedies?

20. Are the ryots as attached to their *native villages* as formerly?

21. Has the *naib* (agent) as much influence as formerly over the zemindar?

22. Are *zemindars* as *litigious* as formerly?

23. Are the peasantry, though *unlettered*, not ignorant? Give examples, illustrations.

24. Signs of *agricultural improvement* within the last twenty years as contrasted with manufacturing improvement?

[1] In the North West Provinces of India in 1852, 10,000 Rupees were spent by Government in the establishment of public gardens. The author of *Seir Mutakherim* remarked last century "a garden, an orchard—being time out of mind as free to all the world all over India as is a well or a tank, nothing amazes and disgusts the Hindustanees more when they come to Calcutta than to find so many seats and gardens all shut up."

[2] I have met with cases of evening schools attended solely by ryots. In England one per cent. of the rural population attend such schools. In France 12 per cent. In Russia they are rapidly on the increase.

25. How far is there a growth of a feeling of *independence* among ryots? its causes and probable results?

26. Are *Middlemen* on the increase? the evils inflicted by them in rack-renting, etc., etc.

27. The condition of the *ryots* before the Permament Settlement, and their relation at that period to the landlords?

28. The different *abwabs* (fees) levied by zemindars?

29. *Torture*, how far practised now and formerly? the different modes?

## III.

### Astrology and Witchcraft.

Human nature in India, as in Europe, wishes to pry into the future, whether the fingers, the chattering of crows, or the stars are to be guides; in India the feeling against witches even lately was as strong as in England two centuries ago, thus in Mhow between 1800 and 1823, 2,500 witches were put to death.[1]

1. *Charmers for snake bites*, their numbers, pay, and how far really successful? the influence of music over snakes?

2. Are reputed *Expellers of Bhuts* or *Devils* many, their influence?

3. Various kinds of *mantras*, such as the *panch mantra*, etc., etc.?

4. *Witches*, their localities, emoluments, number, how detected, any put to death last century in Bengal, the various kinds of witchcraft?

5. *Divination* by the hand; its various kinds,—books on,—is the practice general?

6. *Auguries*, by what birds? how taken? what is the reliance placed on them now?

7. *Mesmerism* (*Jhárán Mantra*), to what extent known to the *old* Hindus—how practised now and by whom?

8. *Sleight-of-hand* tricks, the number and emoluments of its professors—instances of common tricks practised in Bengal?

9. Belief in *Fairies*, *Apparitions*, illustrations of its extent and influence? much on the decline?

10. *Gypsies* or *Naths*, their numbers, morals, means of support? influence among the people, language, religion, ceremonies at marriages, births, funerals?

11. Are casting the *evil eye* and other *incantations* common?

[1] See the Asiatic Annual Register, 1801; the Asiatic Journal 1823, on trials for witchcraft among Hindus.

12. *Treasure-finders,—thief detectors, fortune-tellers, astrologers,* their numbers, profits?

13. *Dreams*, various kinds of? who interpret them? their profits? analysis of vernacular books that treat of them?

14. *Omens, Charms*, and signs of futurity, various kinds in use?

## IV.

### Beggars and Vagrants.

The beggar class are not unworthy of consideration in India—in England they are the subjects of various books: who does not remember Burns's poem on the Jolly Beggars, or some of the exquisite traits about them in Goldsmith's and Crabbe's Poems?

1. The proportion of beggars from *choice* or from *necessity*, or on *religious* grounds?

2. The extent of beggars' beats?—more beggars in town or country? their profits, their amusements?

3. Are beggars much addicted to *thieving* or other crimes? Do many beggars feign *blindness, dumbness, lameness*, or practise other impositions?

4. *Fakirs* or *Sanyasis*—their habits, beat, profits, impositions, —which are worse, Hindu or Musulman fakirs? why do they call themselves Padris?

5. Mendicant *musicians*—their number, profits, skill, social position? Vagrant tradesmen, ditto.

6. Is not the present indiscriminate *charity* to *beggars* the mother of idleness and crime?

7. Where do beggars find shelter in the *rains*, in *illness*?

8. Are *Hindus* or Musulmans kinder to beggars?

9. Why do most of the mendicant orders choose *Ram* for their patron?

10. Do many beggars flock to towns? the causes? how far is the want of peasant proprietorship a cause of beggary?

## V.

### Calcutta.

Calcutta, the "city of palaces and pigsties," requires a separate Sociological niche for itself,—yet how little is really known of this *colluvies* of nations! Purnea furnishes to it syces,—Orissa, bearers,—Behar, Durwans,—Central India, opium merchants,—Kabul, horses and fruit-sellers,—Chittagong, boatmen;—while those semi-Asiatics, the Greeks, supply leading merchants.

In prosecuting enquiries on the various classes of population, the trades and handicrafts in Calcutta and the large cities of India, there is a model paper on that subject, published in the Royal Asiatic Society's Transactions, in relation to Bareilly, 1826, vol. i. pp. 467-484, treating of the progress in civilization, dress, amusements, food, houses, peculiar usages, habits and wants of the people of Bareilly. Many of the questions there propounded are applicable ceteris paribus to Benares, Bombay, Madras, etc.

1. The proportion of the *adult population* born in the city.[1]

2. The grouping of the population into classes inhabiting different localities according to *occupation, social grade,* and *birth place*?

3. *Afghans,* their numbers, occupation, moral condition—do they assert their Jewish descent?

4. *Armenians,*[2] ditto, their decrease; any connection kept up with Armenia or Russia; their colloquial language?

5. *Chinese,*[3] how far do they retain their country's mode of living? their morals, localities, numbers, language used, employments?

6. *East Indians.*[4] Not a welding of the European and Asiatic as the English were of the Norman and Saxon—effect of intermarriage among themselves; are they dying out?

7. *Feringhees,* who so called—origin of the word?

8. *Greeks* ditto, how far do they adopt English habits and customs—their habits as contrasted with those of English merchants; any connection kept up with Russia or Greece?

9. *Jains,* their numbers and social position?

10. *Jews,*[5] their numbers, wealth, and social position? what impression do they make on Hindus? their language, how far Indianised?[6]

11. *Merchant princes,* is the name still applicable in Calcutta and Bombay?

12. *Mixed Classes,* many such, as *Piralis,* etc., etc.

[1] Half the adult population of London is born in the Provinces.
[2] 636 Armenians in Calcutta in 1837.
[3] There were 362 in 1837.
[4] 4,746 in 1837.
[5] There were in Calcutta 307 Jews in 1837.
[6] The Alexandrian Jews were hellenised.

13. *Moguls*, their numbers, morals, social position,—many directly of Persian or Tartar origin?

14. *Musulmans*; are they very stationary? are they rising in social importance? their social morality as contrasted with that of the Hindus? are coffee shops common among them? ditto gambling? the number of Arabic and Persian schools among them? their feelings towards Hindus? many Hajis or Saids among them? Do they read the *Kulma* on Friday, in the mosques?

15. *Parsees*, their number, social status—are their prejudices decaying? their *Panchayats?* observance of New Year's day, and of the birth day of Zoroaster,—ceremonies in honor of the dead.—Commercial enterprise, charities, language, literature, caste disputes; when did they first come? the condition of their females,—their liturgies,—how far do they adopt Hindu customs; ditto English?

16. *Portuguese*, their number,[1] are they increasing? their influence; the language used; are any of pure origin? are their priests improving? the effect of their example on Hindus?

17. *Sanskrit Colleges.* Are there more than 100? the highest emoluments in them as contrasted with former days? state of learning among pupils and teachers?

18. *Seiks;* their numbers,—are many able to read the *Granth?* their occupations?

19. *Young Bengal;* how far does he really differ from his countrymen, and how far is it mere varnish? are his peculiarities on the increase or decrease? are there many out of Calcutta? The period when young Bengalism arose?

20. Account of the following *classes*, their numbers, profits, and social position,—bird sellers, glass-blowers, firework-makers, dyers, shell-workers, smiths, cattle doctors, yogis, weavers, divers, butchers, fowlers, bookbinders, druggists, bakers, gardeners, washermen, confectioners, barbers, sweepers, shoemakers, carpenters, masons?

21. The origin of the names of the *streets* with notices of the individuals, or of the circumstances or particular trades, that gave them those names?

22. The various cries made in the streets by hawkers or sellers?

23. Describe the numbers, profits, and social condition of the following classes—street sellers, street buyers, street finders, street performers, artists, showmen, street artizans or working pedlars, street laborers.

[1] 3,181 in 1837.

## VI.

### Ceremonies, Rites.

1. *Shraddhas*, the ceremonies and expenses connected with them now, as contrasted with former times, and in the various castes?

2. The chief *gram devatas* (village gods); the origin of their worship, the mode of conducting it. Are there more than 100?

3. Do *Hindus* or *Musulmans* expend more on their rites and ceremonies?

4. The profits and numbers of those who *burn* the *dead?*[1]

5. Is the practice of *shaking hands* and of other English customs increasing much?

6. On *investiture of the Poita*, is it usual to keep a piece of iron as a charm against *bhuts* (ghosts)? is the party confined for eleven days?

7. Are *compulsory pujas* much practised, such as throwing an image at night at a rich man's door that he may be compelled to perform a puja?

8. Describe the worship of *Sitola, Nag Manasa, Ulauta Devi;* the Shasti, Dheki, Govardan, and Ganesh Pujas,—their origin, extent, expenses, by what classes conducted, the temples, festivals connected with them?

9. *Agni Puja* and *Surjea Puja*, to what extent—with what pomp and expense, celebrated in former times? by what classes?

10. The various prayers and gesticulations connected with the *ahnik*, how far observed, and by what classes now?

11. Parrots, how trained to repeat *Radha Krishna?*

12. How far are the following practices now generally observed and by what classes? First morning prayer to the Guru? the *Gangástak; 24 Mudrás; prandyam? Gumukhi, Gaytrijap, Artipancha pradip, Panchagni, Das sanskar?*—marks of caste or sects in the forehead?—women worshipping the *dheki* to cure the scurvy and itch?

13. *Fasting*, how far observed now, compared with former days; the *Ekadasi* how kept, and by whom?

14. *Funerals*, their expense; ceremonies; period of mourning, in different castes; do women accompany the corpse? four modes of disposing of a corpse.—How far observed now, compared with former days?

15. Are *lamps* often sent floating down a stream as an omen?

[1] *Rama Murda Farish* died at Calcutta about 1835, worth five or six lacs, which he gained by burning the dead at Nimtollah.

16. Are thorns often put under the feet of a woman who dies pregnant?

17. Is there much observance now of *Das Snán, Das Dán?*

18. Describe the ceremonies, and among what classes practised, in the worship of books, birds, stones, fish?

19. Jogi's suspension of breath, postures, etc., etc., how far kept up now, and by what training?

20. In the *Holi festival*, are there less obscene words and figures than formerly? is the castor oil tree planted as a kind of maypole?

21. Is the *Navami* generally practised?[1]

22. *Chagdá*, near Calcutta, the reason for its being a city of refuge for outcasts, the numbers that resort to it? other similar places in Bengal.

23. Was the burying lepers alive much practised formerly? ditto burning alive?

24. *Human sacrifices* were formerly offered up at Kshir near Burdwan, at Yogadyea, at Kerilatta near Moorshedabad, to Kali at Brahmanitola near Nadaya, to Manasa, at Chitpore, Kalighat,—instances handed down by tradition?

25. How was the *charak* celebrated formerly? instances in its practice of the tongue being pierced with a bayonet? of a snake's tail put through the tongue?

26. *Birth ceremonies;* such as Jal karan or giving honey at first seeing a son; naming a child twelve days after birth; bringing him out at three months' old; feeding him at six months old; shaving the head at three years old—how far practised and by what castes?

27. In *marriages*, are the *laganpatrika*, tying the garments of parties together, much used? how do marriage ceremonies differ according to caste, rank, etc.

## VII.

### Classes.

1. In the *upper classes*, do many families die out? the causes?

2. Causes tending to create a *middle class* in Bengal?

3. Any probability of *approximating* the Hindus and *East Indians* in closer mutual sympathy—was the aversion less in former days than now?

4. The *Portuguese*—how many of European origin, their peculiar customs and mode of life? their influence over natives? their morals and energy as contrasted with those of natives?

[1] That is, placing the first fruits of grain in harvest time at the door.

5. The use of a native *landed aristocracy* as a shield against the despotism of a ruler or of a multitude?

6. Are there many *black Brahmans*? is their colour the effect of climate? are they of Hindu origin?

7. The *duration of life* among the upper and lower classes of Hindus, and the professional classes particularly, as showing the effect of temperance, mental occupation and bodily exercise?

8. Are *old men* very garrulous? are there many old men? to what age have some lived?

9. *Caste*, how far on the decline, and the causes of the decline? are the *varna sankara* or mixed castes on the increase? illustrations of the lower castes rising in the social scale, the causes? are the rules for expulsion from caste strictly observed?

10. *Families* that existed before the Muhammadan invasion.

## VIII.

### Commerce.

The commercial classes in India have always occupied a conspicuous place; even in Menu's time they held the purse strings, and have been less than other classes subject to priestly influence; hence the great sects of Jains in Rajputana and Central India, the Oswals of Behar, and Vaishnabs of Bengal have the greatest number of converts among the traders; the Marwari merchants are Jains, and the Ghosains are Vaishnabs. Religious reform found its votaries most in France among the Huguenot merchants; in the middle ages among the Belgian and Italian traders; and in Russia among the mercantile classes; the municipalities in the middle ages, mainly composed of the trading classes, were buffers against feudal and priestly oppression.

1. Why do *Buniyas* (shop keepers) in Behar rank with Vaisyas? their education and social position in Bengal—are many of them sureties—many foreigners among them—their profits?

2. *Mahajans* (money lenders) how far do their exactions extend—are they less now than formerly—their numbers—do many rise to a high position in native society?

3. The *native merchant princes*—their rise and social influence—do their sons follow their father's pursuits?

4. To what extent has the *decay* in ancient Indian articles of

production and trade been compensated by new sources of production and trade?

5. Indigo,[1] the accounts of it in Hindu books—also of tobacco, sugar, cotton?

6. The influences of *foreign trade* on the dress, food, habits, opinions, of natives?

7. How far are native merchants likely to form a quasi *aristocracy*, or an upper middle class?

8. *Native merchants*, how far liable to the charge of ostentation, avarice, vulgarity? how far do they rise into a higher grade, and their conduct in it?

9. The effect of *commercial legislature* on commercial morality, as shown in the Small Cause and Insolvent Courts?

10. *Shroffs* (bankers), their number, emoluments, social position?

11. Causes of the decreasing social intercourse between Europeans and natives—remedies?

## IX.

### Conversation and Social Intercourse.

Conversation, or the "feast of reason and the flow of soul," is as popular with the Bengali as with the European.

1. The subjects of conversation 20 *years ago* as contrasted with the present.

2. The subjects of conversation common to the *educated* and *uneducated* classes.

3. The favourite *times* for conversation; how different from the English?

4. Do any classes converse on subjects not relating to their *daily life and occupations*?

5. Are *Riddles* much used?—a collection of them a desideratum.

6. *Jesters* how far employed, their numbers and emoluments—is jesting much used? illustrations of it?

7. *Vaishnabs' or Saktas'* conversation—how do they differ in subject and moral tone?

8. Is there much *discussion* in Hindoo society—on what topics? is it angry at times?

9. The effect on conversation of the absence of *female society?*

10. Topics in the *zenana*, among educated, uneducated? among country or town people?

11. Among what classes are *Ghost stories* most common? mention twelve specimens of different kinds.

[1] In the *Pancha Tantra*, a work twelve centuries old at least, we have an account of a jackal who tumbled into an indigo vat.

## X.

### Criminal, or Dangerous, Classes.

1. How can a system of *education* be extended adapted to the circumstances of those who form the raw materials of the dangerous and criminal classes?

2. How far is *poverty* the parent of crime in Bengal? Do. *oppression?* Do. the *Guru Mahashay system?*

3. *Jails*, how far objects of terror and shame to natives? in what districts is the name "our father-in-law's house" given to the jail? are re-committals frequent? Are *Reformatories* for juvenile criminals desirable? the effect of teaching prisoners agriculture?

4. Is the *thannah* looked upon as a school where old offenders teach young ones crime?

5. Receivers of *stolen goods;* any approximate estimate of their number and profits?

6. Has the *punishment of death* much effect in lessening capital offences?

7. The proportion that can *read and write* intelligibly in the different jails?[1]

8. Is *infanticide* common among the poor?[2] Do. *incest?*

9. Is perjury or forgery on the increase? the causes?

10. River *Thagi* common? Ditto professional *poisoners?*

11. The influence of *age* and sex on crime?

12. Crime in different districts, and in various castes, particularly among Hindus and Muhammadans, how it differs in number, variety, heinousness?

13. Is there more crime in *town* or in the country?

14. Juvenile delinquents; their number, offences?

15. Has the autobiography of a thief ever been written?

16. Is Professor Wilson's remark correct, "in the great towns of India the profligacy bears no comparison to that of London or Paris?"

## XI.

### Debating Societies.

Debating Societies or Literary Clubs have sprung up in shoals both in Calcutta and the Mofussil within the last twelve

[1] In Liverpool it was ascertained lately that out of 19,336 persons apprehended in nine months, only 3 per cent. could read or write well enough for any available purpose.

[2] It is so in the manufacturing districts of England, and among the Rajputs.

years; they are nuclei for educated young men, and are congenial to the oriental habit which loves *dals:* we need a kind, however, like the Young Men's Associations of England, in which not only lectures might be delivered or essays read, but night classes might be formed for improvement in literature and science.

1. The number and duration of *Debating Societies* in cities during the last twenty years, the subjects discussed and social status of the members?
2. Ditto in the country?
3. In what respects are they improving as to the *choice of subjects* and the mode of conducting the meetings?
4. What *social influence* do they exercise in the family or on others?
5. A history of the *Dharma Sabha,* its leaders, quarrels, influenee?
6. Of the *Brahma Sabha,* ditto, ditto?
7. Account of any other meetings or reunions among Hindus with their social influence?

## XII.

### Diseases.

1. The social and moral causes of *insanity* among natives? Among what castes is it more prevalent, and why?
2. Are *Albinos* numerous, the causes?
3. What nervous diseases are regarded as being from a *bhut* (demon), requiring mantras?
4. *Nakra—Inoculation* for small pox—*Leprosy,*—their respective modes of treatment in ancient and modern times? how they differ? are lepers now treated kindly?
5. *Hindu Physicians,* their various remedies for *eye diseases?*
6. Are diseases from *dissipation* among Young Bengal on the increase?
7. What diseases indicate the *social condition* of the people, such as those of the eye, brain?
8. *Hospitals,* by what castes most attended, particularly Brahmans, Khaistas, Musulmans—and from what localities?
9. The relative *mortality and vitality* of each sex, and of the leading castes in Bengal.
10. Is the *duration of life* in inverse ratio to fecundity?
11. The influence of *employments* on health in Bengal, how shewn?

12. Various remedies for *snake bites?* any of real efficacy?
13. *Native medicines*, in what estimation held by educated natives?
14. Is mortality in *parturition* on the increase?
15. Was *Cholera* an epidemic among natives a century ago?

## XIII.

### Doctors.

The *kabiraj* (indigenous doctor) is a great favourite in native society and has been the cause of an enormous number of deaths. The Bengali class of the Medical College is, as it gradually developes, lessening this evil; Dr. Wise has written ably on this class and on Hindu medicine.

1. *Kabirajis*, whether are Hindu or Musulman ones more numerous or more skilful—their castes—their pay now and in former days?
2. *Inoculators*, are there more Hindus or Musulmans—the incantations used—their invocations of Sitola—their fees—caste—mode of treatment?
3. *Vaidyas* (native doctors), their chief localities in Bengal, the proportion that can read Ṣanskṛit, their pay and social position—an account of the *Atai Vaidyas*, *Dehatu Vaidyas*, *Chasi Vaidyas*, *Haturya Vaidyas?*
4. *Midwives*, *Cuppers*, *Leech sellers*, their skill, pay, numbers?
5. English educated native doctors, are their social position and pay increasing?
6. Ditto Bengali educated?

## XIV.

### Domestic.

Home has well been styled the "seed vessel of society, where the next generation must germinate."

1. Is *hospitality* as much practised now as formerly? and with as rigid a regard to caste?
2. The *home* influences of wives and daughters on educated natives?
3. Is the family tie very strong among Hindus? illustrate by examples.

## XV.

### Dramas, Jatras.

The Sanskrit Drama, so well translated by Dr. Wilson, presents a rich harvest of information on the social condition of the Indian aristocracy, females and Pandits, eighteen centuries ago. In the *Sárada tilaka* of the twelfth century, we have sketches of the various classes of females, of the Jogis, Buddhists, snake catchers, Pandits; the *Mriganlekhá* treats of the kings of Kalinga and Assam—as the Ramayan does of society 2,500 years ago. Nor have the last ten years been barren in the department of dramatic vernacular literature—as the many Bengali dramas on the subjects of "Kulinism," "Widow re-marriage," etc. show.

1. Account of the *bhaurs* or professional jesters.
2. A list of the various *játras*, their authors, subjects, influence.
3. Ditto *Rásas*.
4. An analysis of the vernacular dramas written during the last twenty years.

## XVI.

### Dress.[1]

1. Is the *Musulman* dress superior in any points to the Hindu?
2. Was the *needle* totally unknown to the Hindu? is there any Hindu word to express sewing with the needle?[2]
3. Do any Hindus now object to garments made by a *Moslem needle?*
4. Were there any *tailors* in ancient times among the Hindus?
5. Do Hindu *females* wash their linen often—is *soap* coming into use among them?

[1] A suitable dress for females, decent, yet national, is a desideratum. Some Hindu females have adopted the English dress, but they look exactly like Portuguese Ayahs, or the black dolls that hang in London over pawn-brokers' shops. Why should this be? The *sári*, it is true, is not sufficient, but in Bahar we find the petticoat (*lohanga*) and boddice (*kurta*) have been introduced from the west of India, and more than one-fourth of the Bahar women have adopted it. Some of the Rajput women in Bahar use long-drawers like the Musulman ladies. The males are better off as to dress, but in their disuse of the turban, substituting for it a cap, they benefit only the eye doctors and spectacle makers, furnishing them with more patients,—as the eyes having no shade like what the turban gives, become weak;—such has been the case in Egypt, since the Turkish Fez has been introduced.

[2] *Sui* properly means passing the shuttle in the act of weaving.

6. What Hindus will not drink water out of a girl's hands unless she is first *tattooed* on the arms and breast?

7. Would the wearing of *beards* be useful for Hindus?

8. Should Hindus take off their *shoes* in an European house, or their turbans on entering a place of worship?

## XVII.

### Drinking Habits.

In Menu's days liquors were allowed, and ancient Hindu history gives many a curious revelation on this point.

1. Are drinking habits more prevalent among the *Hindus or among Musulmans?* how was it 30 years ago compared with the present time?

2. Are Hindus quarrelsome in their cups?

3. Is smoking *Ganja, Charus, or Opium* more destructive;—which is more common? Do Hindu females *smoke* much? When was *smoking* introduced? Ditto *snuffing*?

4. How far is the increase of drinking owing to *domestic discomfort?*

5. How far do crimes attended with violence, arise from *intoxication?* how far is insanity the result of intemperance?

6. The effect of *intemperance* in producing pauperism?

7. The connection between *abkari shops*, public-houses, and crime?

8. Is *drinking brandy* a frequent practice with Young Bengal?

## XVIII.

### Education, in its Social Bearing.

The consideration of the School system in its *social* influences is a very important subject, as well as the enquiry, how far the competitive system is injurious so far as it treats boys as race horses,—trains them not for general use but to run for particular prizes,—promotes cramming, and mere book-knowledge;—leads to the neglect of the mass of the boys in a school, tempting the Masters, by attending to a few "fugle boys," to gain more praise for their school.

There is a tendency among Hindus like the man in the fable, to cry out nothing like leather, and to regard education as the panacea for *all* evils. Lord Brougham describes such persons as being like those who would trust to the effects of diet and regimen when the plague is raging, and Dr. Arnold remarked, "Education is wanted to improve the physical condition of the people: and yet *their physical condition must be improved, before they can be susceptible of education.*" You may educate the upper classes highly, but the masses are the basis of the social pyramid; without this being secure, the apex has no stability; brute force and the black cap are at best but temporary expedients.

1. How far are improved *habits* of cleanliness, order, punctuality, truthfulness, an improved standard of dress and living, and a development of character promoted by Anglo-Vernacular Schools?

2. Ditto by *Guru Mahashay* or village Schools?

3. The action of Anglo-Vernacular and Guru Mahashay Schools on the *family circle* in raising the moral and intellectual tone?

4. Any social evils arising from the training adopted for native girls in some Mission *female schools?* The remedy?

5. How far are the following remarks, made in England, applicable to India?

"There is a practical standard in the minds of the people, beyond which the education of the masses cannot be carried. If Government raise the standard, people diminish the time of children's attendance."

6. The social importance of teaching in all schools, the doctrines of *political economy* on labour, capital, wages, interchange, money, —as also the elements of agricultural chemistry.

7. Mental ignorance, how far productive of *moral depravity?*[1]

8. How far do *social discomforts* fret and enfeeble the masses, and render them unfit for higher thoughts?

9. Is *intemperance* greater in proportion among the educated or uneducated classes?

10. How far is the following statement, made by an educated native, correct?

"Natives educated in the *Government Colleges*, do not often fulfil the hope inspired by their academic career; they do not follow up their studies; they unlearn what they have learnt, sink in the mass with all the enervating environments of Indian life—the hookah and the zenana do their sure work."

11. Does not the social condition of the masses render a *grant-in-aid system* as inapplicable, as would be a voluntary system at the time of plague and pestilence?

[1] Dr. Mouat, Inspector of Jails in Bengal, shows in his Returns for 1860, that out of 73,000 criminals in the Bengal and Behar jails that year, 93 per cent. were utterly ignorant of reading and writing.

12. How far does school education mould the social institutions of the country and how far is it moulded by them?

13. The social importance of schools of *Industrial art*?

14. Ditto ditto of Agricultural schools?

15. The *tolas* (or Sanskrit Colleges)—the social causes leading to their decline. Any improvement in the subjects taught, or the mode of teaching? What great teachers are there now?

16. The probable reflex influence of requiring a knowledge of *reading and writing* from all classes, as a qualification for office?

17. The probable influence of the *university examination* in giving a preponderance to cramming and memory work, to the neglect of cultivating the faculty of observation?

18. Is it desirable that up to 6 years of age *girls* should be taught with boys?[1]

19. How far are the *Guru Mahashays*, as a class, guilty of the charges of teaching their pupils theft and lying, and of inflicting severe punishments? What has been the occupation of the fathers of those teachers generally?

20. A list of Vernacular authors and able teachers produced by the Sanskrit Colleges?

## XIX.

### FEMALES.

1. How far are the following remarks on Hindu females correct in different localities: "Ministers to the capricious sensuality of their arrogant lords.—The feeling of *natural affection* is comparatively weak—held under the jealousy of restraint, they become callous to all finer sensibilities?" Cases of *crim. con.* very seldom occur in respectable Hindu families. The life of a Hindu *widow* is wretched in the highest degree.

2. To what extent can *natch* (dancing) *girls* read? their influences and emolument now as compared with former days?

3. Do Hindu females often hear religious or other *books read* to them?[2]

4. What is the knowledge females acquire *independent of books*?

5. Mention female *authors* of past and present times.

6. Is the practice of females blackening their teeth and eyes, of Moslem origin?

7. Are the *angia, kurti, pyjamahs* much in use?

[1] In Kabul the custom is for boys and girls from 5 to 12 years of age to attend the same school.

[2] In Kabul many of the females are better acquainted with religious books than the males.

8. At what age are females considered old *women?* Do females become really *old* at thirty? what is their influence and conduct then?

9. Are Musulman females less luxurious and *extravagant* than Hindu ones?

10. What are the *recreations* of females? is kite flying such?

11. Are Hindu and Musulman females fond of *embroidering* and of *flowers?*

12. Are *quarrels* numerous among females? are they very jealous?

13. How far do females win and retain their *husband's affections?*

14. What is the average time men remain *widowers?*

15. How far practically is a system of austerity carried out with regard to *widows?* what means of support have they generally?

16. If a woman washes off *paint* from her forehead, is it considered a sign of her wishing her husband's death?

17. What has been the success of the working of the act for the remarriage of Hindu widows as to numbers and respectability?

18. How far do women rule their husbands at home? Many Hindu gentlemen "henpecked?"

## XX.

### Festivals.

Festivals for religious or commemorative purposes have always exercised great influence on social life, whether we look to the national games and assemblages of ancient Greeks, to those of the middle ages in Europe, or to those of recent times in England and France. Who can forget Washington Irving's vivid picture of Christmas and merry England in the olden time? But among the Hindus they have been pre-eminently influential as being interwoven so closely into the religion of the country. All the mighty minds of India in former days saw what a great effect they produced on all classes: hence Vaishnabs and Saktas alike, though differing in other points widely, have agreed in patronising them.

1. The *classes of society* that do not attend festivals now, but did once—why have they discontinued?

2. The influence of festivals on the *family relation,* particularly on women and children?

3. Any change and improvements in the mode of *conducting* festivals?

4. How far are festivals become more occasions of *trade* or *amusement* than formerly?

5. What festivals have become more *popular* than others—the causes?

6. How far is the observance of festivals on the *decline?*

7. Is there much *sale* of native books or of European articles at festivals?

8. Are festivals good times for holding *religious discussions*, such as are practised by missionaries?

9. The moral and social influence of festivals in bringing the male and female *sexes* more together?

10. The various customs, ceremonies, connected with the first day of *new year?*

11. How far festivals, such as the *Holi*, contribute to *idleness* and dissipation?

12. Any observance like April fool or the Maypole in the *Holi*?

13. Mention *Obsolete festivals*, and new ones, such as the *Jagadatri?*

14. *Barwari puja*, how far observed now, and by whom; its origin? Ditto the *Nag panchami* in Bengal.

15. An accurate description of the Hindu fasts and the festivals in the district? of their origin, the significance of their peculiar ceremonies, how observed by different castes?

16. Ditto of the Musulman.

17. *Sunday*, how spent by different classes of natives? Is it a day of pleasure?

18. On *Makar Sankranti*, *til* seeds are eaten after dinner, and the sun is the only deity worshipped—why?

19. Is the *Holi* a kind of All Fool's day?

20. Describe the following practices—On *Gadi padva*, *nim* leaves are chewed, and *puja* paid to an Almanac; on the *Ram Nabami* a recitation of Ramayun. *Narujal Purnima*, cocoa nuts are thrown into the sea. On the *Dewáli* worship is paid to books.

21. What festivals are observed by particular castes or by women only?

## XXI.

### Fishermen and Boatmen.

1. What *boats* are not in build of indigenous origin?

2. The *castes* that almost exclusively furnish boatmen,—why chiefly from Chittagong or Furridpore?

3. The *morals* of boatmen when separated from their families?

4. In what respects are *boatmen* equal in skill to sailors?

5. The peculiarities of the boatmen's *language;* is it the same as the Musulman-Bengali; a collection of the songs they sing when rowing?

6. Why few *Hindus* are boatmen?

7. The number of *boatmen* in Calcutta, are they on the increase or decrease? the causes?

8. *Sailors*, how victimised on landing, in punch-houses, and by crimps?

9. The various classes of *fishermen*, their profits now and formerly?

## XXII.

### Food.

The nature of food has much to do with bodily and mental vigour, although different nations in this point have their respective tastes; a Frenchman will eat a rat or a frog or horseflesh with a *gout,* that will make an Englishman almost vomit. The Englishman in like manner dislikes the oceans of ghi and quantities of high seasoning that enter into a Bengali's cuisine, while on the other hand the Bengali shudders at a calf being an object of mastication.

1. The different kinds of *curries*, their use, expense of preparation, and how far their high seasoning is conducive to health?

2. How far does the *diet of Hindus* preserve from certain diseases, but promote others?

3. The effect of a *vegetable diet* on certain mental qualities, such as courage?

4. *Tea* drinking, how far is it becoming popular?

5. Why was a *fish diet* allowed to Bengal, but prohibited to up-country Brahmans?

6. Is *adulteration* of food common? illustrations of it with its evils.

7. Illustrate the following statement: "the fare on which a Sonthal, a Cole, and a Garrow, will thrive, is utterly unsuited to the Bengali, the Assamese, and the Mugh."

## XXIII.

### Houses.

The dwellings of the poor and of the working classes have occupied much of the attention of philanthropists in England,

and ought to do so in India, where floors, walls, windows, are closely connected with questions of health and decency.

1. How far are the present *native houses* so built as to conduce to indecency, vice, quarrels, drunkenness, filth, bad ventilation?[1]

2. Is the *boitakhana* of Hindu origin?[2]

3. How far is the use of *chairs* preferable to the *Asan* or seat?

4. How can the following defects in tiled houses be remedied: exposure to wind and rain, cold in winter, hot in summer?

5. *Mud huts*, means to secure them against snake holes?

6. Is not the building of *suburban houses* for workmen in large towns desirable?

7. Is the northern side of a house invariably the *Thakur khana?*

## XXIV.

### KERANIS OR NATIVE CLERKS.

The Kerani system is so much the child of English trade and government as to demand special attention. One thing is clear, that as certain as English education has been limited almost exclusively in Bengal to the caste of Brahmans and Khaistas, so have the chief occupations of its alumni been those of keranis or copyists—an effectual way in many cases to turn an educated youth into a mere machine, and to render him simply an imitator or *copyer*—as he is a *copyist*. It is true in Northern India, from Katamandu to Mhow, the Bengali is the Englishman's right hand—in what?—is it not too often as a machine for copying, as a sort of looking glass to reflect his views without having any views of his own. A writer on Indian history remarks on the kerani in his work: "The eye seemed to communicate directly with the hand: there was no intervention of the brain. The intelligence of

[1] I allude here to an evil felt in England and Russia as highly demoralising, viz., a single sleeping-room for parties of different sexes. The Santals, semi-civilized though they be, are in this respect ahead of Bengalis; boys and girls arrived at the age of puberty, have to sleep separately away from their parents in a particular part of the village.

[2] Hamilton Buchanan's Bengal and Baher, vol. ii. p. 697, states, "Its name is moslem and that a place of receiving company was introduced, when the example or command of these haughty conquerors rendered it necessary to secrete the women; this practice is not common in the South of India, where the manners of the Hindus are less altered; the sofa made of wood, the carpets, and quilts seem to have been introduced by the Muhammadans."—See *Kirát Arjunya*.

the well tutored boy was seldom carried into the practicalities of actual life." I trust this taint on the Bengali may soon cease. Happily the introduction of iron copying machines will reduce in many cases the demand for machines of flesh.

1. The total number of *keranis* employed in the different offices in Calcutta; the average amount of their salaries?

2. The occupation of *keranis' leisure hours;* how far does the business of their offices afford material for conversation in their leisure hours?

3. Do *keranis* keep up *reading* habits—if not, why?

4. How far does their knowledge of *English* acquired at School decline in office?

5. How far do *keranis* read the new class of books in *Vernacular literature*?

6. Are *keranis* chiefly of the *khaista* caste or of the Brahman?

7. *Banians* (native) their past and present influence over Europeans, their profits?

## XXV.

### Language.

1. What is the source of that part of the *Vernacular language* which is not of Sanskrit or Persian origin? Has it, like the languages of South India, an affinity with the Tartarian dialects spoken in Central Asia.[1]

2. The *dialectical varieties in the vernacular*, how far are they divergencies of pronunciation and spelling, similar to those in the English and Italian dialects—their extent and causes? Are they on the increase or decrease?

3. How far is *Urdu* declining in certain parts of India, as a colloquial and written language? the causes?

4. What influence is likely to be produced on the *Bengali* language by increased intercourse with Central India and the North West?

5. What language is likely to supplant the *Santal*, is it the Bengali, Hindi, or Urdu? Ditto as regards the Asamese?

6. What effect on the structure of the vernaculars is likely to be produced by *English* educated natives?

7. What *idioms* in the vernacular language are most striking in contrast with those of the English and Urdu languages?

8. The language used at *Gour*, had it a closer affinity to Hindí than to Bengali.

[1] Caldwell's Dravidian grammar affords many valuable hints on this subject.

9. What old *Vernacular MSS.* exist among private families?[1]

10. Is the *Musulman-Bengali*, used chiefly by persons who cannot read or write the Bengali, increasing as a dialect?

11. The past and present influence of *Persian* in Bengal?

12. The *boundaries* of the Bengali language in the Midnapur district bordering on Orissa and in Birbhum on the Hindi-speaking districts?

13. The vernacular language, how far in its progress does it illustrate the varying features of *national character*, habits, pursuits, social and mental development?[2]

14. Are the educated Bengalis so different from Italians, Poles, or Hungarians, as to have little *patriotic feeling* in favour of their native language?

15. Words in the vernacular having affinities with any Tartar or *aboriginal* language?

16. Illustrations of the language of *Flowers* as used by Musulmans and Hindus?

17. A list of those *vernacular words* not derived from Sanskrit or Persian—their probable origin?

18. Names of places, persons, or things in the vernacular throwing any light on the origin and affinities of the *native race?*

19. *Cant* language used by particular classes?[3]

## XXVI.

### Law and Social State.

The laws of a people have a very important bearing on their social development; hence jurisprudence has well been defined, "the law of humanity in society," and the subject from this point of view has been taken up by the Social Science Association.

1. How far is the new *Penal Code*, as contrasted with the Regulations, likely to affect the social condition of the people and mould their character; and how far is the social condition of the people likely to modify the working of this Code?

[1] Research in other quarters ought to encourage it here: thus we find that the Pushtu, until lately considered a colloquial dialect, had, as Captain Raverty shows, MS. as early as 1417 A.D.

[2] Language has well been called a map of the manners and science of the people who speak it. Thus the term for a widow, *Vidhava*, showed that all widows were not burnt; so *pati*, a lord, the term for husband, indicated that he ruled.

[3] Colonel Sleeman in his Ramasceana gives the language of Thugs. We have in Bengal the language of boatmen.

2. How far has the *Punchayat* or native jury system tended to raise the character of the people? how far is it popular? would the English Jury system be more efficient in this respect?

3. The *Income Tax*, its probable bearings on the physical, social, and moral condition of the people?

4. Menu's laws, how far did they influence the masses?

5. The probable effects of making *English* the language of the Courts in its increasing the gulph between the English Judge and the masses? and in leaving the judge and the people at the mercy of the interpreter?

6. The effect on society of the Hindu law of *intestate property*.

7. Which is more favorable to the creation of a middle class and the elevation of the masses, a zemindary, a village, or a ryotwary system?

8 How would a law of *primogeniture* be likely to work in India?

9. Ditto a law like the French law of equal *sub-division?*

10. In what respects is the social condition of the people different now from what it was in the *Vedic* age—in Menu's—in Ram's—in Kalidasa's—in the Musulman ditto?

11. How far has law in India been the offspring, how far the parent of *public opinion?*

12. The working of the *Small Cause Courts* in checking or increasing a love for litigation and in promoting a regard to truth in dealings?

13. How far have native Educational *endowments* made the Pandits indolent by making them independent of their Scholars?

14. The value of village *Municipal Institutions* in preparing a people for self-government? the remains of the old system in different parts of India?

15. The importance to India of *English lawyers in India* having a training not only in law books, but also in a knowledge of the social condition of the people?

## XXVII.

### Marriages.

1. Illustrations of the effects of *early marriage* physically, mentally, socially?

2. The causes and consequences of the *expense* of marriage ceremonies?

3. How far do *marriage ceremonies* vary according to caste, social position, etc.?

4. What practices in the *marriage ceremonies* as to length, expense, rites, ought to be discountenanced, what to be continued?

5. Does *early marriage* in India tend to check vice?

6. Is there a marriage in practice among the Hindus corresponding to the *Muhammadan nikka?*

7. How far do marriages take place at a later period among *educated natives*—the effects?

8. Are *Ghataks* (Go betweens) many, their fees,—any ghatak registries extant from Bullal Sen's time, or three centuries ago?

9. The *expense* of marriage among the various castes or classes; are they on the increase or the decrease?

## XXVIII.

### Miscellaneous.

1. The different modes of *calculating time*, such as by sand, water, the sun, the stars?

2. Is the *Punchayat* much practised now? was it ever in Bengal as much a part of the village system as in Central India?

3. The practicability and advantage of *Mofussil Savings and Loan Banks* for the middle classes in the Mofussil, to promote provident habits and to rescue the Rayats from the Mahajans?[1]

4. Is the *cycle theory* for nations, of weakness, vigour, maturity, decay, inapplicable to India?

5. The *emigration* to the Mauritius and W. Indies in its effects on the social condition of the emigrants and their families; on the parties themselves on their return—are many remittances from emigrants made to their families?

6. To what type of the *European character* are the Bengalis likely to approximate—to the English or German, French or Italian?

7. Are not mere *English institutions* as little adapted for India as they would be for France?

8. *Oriental Epistles*, their various ornaments, superscriptions and envelopes?

9. Have cases been known in modern times of the following punishments being enforced—cutting off a Hindu's *tika* (top knot), putting lime on one side of his face and ink on the other side, and leading him about on an ass?

[1] In Birmingham in 1856, 84,000 accounts were opened for one penny and upwards; £4,500 being paid in. Through Dr. Chalmers' influence penny banks were established, fifty years ago in Scotland. Dr. Duncan established in Scotland Savings Banks for deposits of a shilling and upwards, and thirty-two-millions sterling have been deposited by 1,340,000 contributors.

10. *Names*, any change desirable in *Hindu names;* the various modes of giving them? are all expressive? are they ever *changed?* how many different *names* are there of men and of women?

11. *Salutations*, different modes of, any change in the form of in operation?

12. Are *large towns* in Bengal less favourable to morals than the country?

13. *Bazars*, their profits to the proprietors, changes in them within the last 20 years?

14. Are many new *Hindu temples* being built, where and at what cost?

15. *Spitting*, why practised so much by Hindus?

16. The history of the rise of the *old families* in Calcutta?[1]

17. What are the subjects of *national pride* with Bengalis?

18. Various forms of *oaths* among different castes; which are considered specially binding?

19. Are dwarfs numerous?

20. *Bankrupts* were formerly compelled to sit bare-headed before a blazing lamp, how long since that was practised?

21. Why do Hindus *count and divide* by 4? does it relate to time, such as 4 weeks, 12 hours?

22. To what extent is the *rise of prices* leading, among ryots and the working classes, to independence of feeling and action, to a desire for education and to increased domestic comfort?

23. Is *dusturi*, or servants' perquisites, in vogue in the same proportion among natives as among Europeans? was it practised in the Mogul time and at different rates according to occupation?

24. Does a *fixed price* for articles exist in any branch of Hindu trade?

25. Is there much *competition* among Hindus? Is the "cheap and nasty" system much practised?

26. Does population increase more in *town* or in the country?

27. *Longevity*, how does it vary in different districts—in *various employments?*

28. Has a variety of *soils* any influence on the character of the people, as low and marshy coasts are said to furnish a sordid, degraded race?

29. How far is there *real* tenderness to *animals* in India? Any places of refuge for lost or starving ones, or old ones?

30. Is *suicide* common in India? among what classes? the kinds? causes? on the increase?

[1] When I was in England 18 years ago, the late Professor Wilson directed my attention to this subject as one of great interest; only a native can write on it.

31. Different kinds of *ordeal* now among the Hindus, the balance, fire, water, poison, chewing rice, boiling oil, red hot iron?[1]

32. Twelve instances of English misunderstanding of native practices, ditto of natives mistaking English.

33. When were the natives first called *niggers?*

34. Refute the statement that natives have neither a word for gratitude in their language, nor a sense of it towards Europeans.

35. The advisability of introducing *fountains* and Turkish baths?

36. Any *Mahratta* females settled in Bengal?

37. The causes of the rise in *prices* in the district?

## XXIX.

### Musulmans.

The Musulmans live *among* the Hindus, but are not *of* them; they even now are in Europe objects of much interest to various nations, and in the middle ages they left in Europe undying memorials of their knowledge and progress in the arts and social life. The Musulmans in *Bengal* read Bengali, but speak a mixed dialect.

1. In what localities are there Musulmans of *Patan* or *Mogul* descent?

2. In what districts have Hindus become proselytes to Muhammadanism—how far by conviction? how far by compulsion? or from other causes?

3. To what extent do the Musulmans differ in their social life, hospitality, kindness to the poor, amusements, *manners and customs*, from the Hindus? do they practise polygamy or sensuality to a greater extent than the Hindus?

4. The number, education, emoluments and influence of *Kajis* and *Mullas* in various localities?

5. To what extent have the *Musulmans* and *Hindus* mutually adopted each other's religious and social practices?[2]

6. How far have the residence and influence of Musulmans diminished Hindu *superstitions*, as well as indecent and cruel practices?

7. Is not the following Hindu practice of Musulman origin—

[1] The trial by ordeal has been handed down in India from ancient times; it was prevalent in Europe in the middle ages.—*See Asiatic Researches, Vol. I.*

[2] In Purnea, Hindus contribute to the expense of the Mohurrum; while caste has throughout Bengal obtained a complete ascendancy over the Moslems.

writing with the *reed* instead of the style or iron pen? other instances?

8. How far have the strictness of Hindu caste and the easy terms on which Musulmans received converts, contributed to *Moslem proselytism?*

9. Is Muhammadanism on the increase? how has it gained so many converts from the *ryot* class?

10. Are the following *sects of Fakirs* in lower Bengal, Benawas, Takyahdars, Jalalis, Madari?

11. Murids—many? their conduct?

12. Many Hajis or *pilgrims;* do many go to *Mecca* from Bengal? by what route? do women often proceed? the effect on them when they return?

13. What line of *trade,* profession or art, are Musulmans taking to?

14. What are the descendants of the Moslem *gentry* doing; are they beginning to apply to trade? do they seek Government employ? their influence?

15. The number and endowments of *Pirsthans; Durgahs?* are many offerings made?

16. How far is *Sufeyism* spreading, and among what classes? any secret meetings among them? much asceticism?—their text books?—has the *Vedantic* system influenced Sufeyism in India? how far has Christianity?

17. How far are the *Ferazis* an offshoot of the Wahabees? are they spreading beyond Furridepore? are their influence and numbers on the increase?

18. Are the *Ramzan* and other feasts observed as strictly now as formerly; if not, in what particulars?

19. Do the *Ferazis* practise widow remarriage? what Musulman ceremonies do they reject—is any connection kept up by them with Arabia?

20. The difference between Hindu and Musulman *funerals,* birthdays, marriages, as to the number of ceremonies, expense, popularity?

21. How did *Musulmans* in former days persecute the Hindus—by conferring office and landed property on converts only—by rejecting Hindu evidence in Courts—by bringing Hindu children up as proselytes?

22. Are *Saids* numerous in Bengal? what estimation are they held in?

23. In Musulman *burial grounds,* describe the various monuments erected, the state in which they are kept?

24. In the *marriage ceremonies* are sitting in state—carrying and applying tumeric—measuring for wedding garments, kept up?

25. Describe *Kodali marna* at the Mohurrum; *Kadami rasal; Mui Moborak.*

26. Is the singing by *Dervishes* much practised?

27. Any practical checks to frequent *divorce?*

28. *Circumcision,* the ceremonies and expense attending it in different classes?

29. Is a musket fired at the *birth* of a male child?

30. Hindus or Musulmans, which are stronger believers in witches, ghosts?

31. The numbers, profits, and social position of the Arab seamen and Moguls who come to Calcutta and other ports for trade?

32. Anecdotes or MSS. illustrating the past and present social condition of the Musulmans in Calcutta, Dacca, Hugly, Murshidabad, Pandua?

33. Are drinking habits on the increase? the causes?

34. Are women more secluded among Musulmans or Hindus?

35. Is the attachment of the Musulmans to their religion declining in proportion to the political decay of the Moslems?

36. Is the hatred between Shiahs and Sunis lessening? ditto between other Musulman sects?

37. Describe the Musulman ceremonies at birth, circumcision, puberty, betrothal, marriages, funerals, exorcism, as practised now by different classes, and how different formerly?

38. Is there as strict a regard to omens in travelling now as formerly?

39. The effects still remaining of former Moslem rule in Bengali.

## XXX.

### The Native Press.

This power, though young at present, is gradually rising to a giant's strength; and even Young Bengal is coming round to acknowledge it to be a power, if not for himself, at least for his wife and daughters, who, not requiring to be copyists, do not need to work up a certain amount of China Bazar English; the publication of half a million copies of Bengali works in Calcutta annually for sale cannot be without its effects. It is very desirable to procure manuscript literature, such as ballads, proverbs, songs, family traditions. Of what great value, in an historical point of view to the Rajputs, are the ballads of Chand?

1. The circulation and profits of the following works: *Almanacs*, *Panchalis* or popular songs, tales.

2. Past and present *patrons* of native literature?

3. The use of *Vernacular Libraries* in making known new publications and creating a taste for reading?

4. A list of the various *libraries* for natives established in the Mofussil, their origin, success or failure, and the causes? the classes using them, the kind of books most popular?

5. A sketch of the history of native *editors*, past and present, of the former editors of the Bhaskar, Chandrika, Purna Chandraday, and Prabhakar *newspapers* in Calcutta?

6. The native press, how far an index of the *social*, moral, and intellectual condition of the people?

7. The recent *copyright* law, in its action on native authorship?

8. *Ballads*, are there many? any very old? how far illustrative of customs, history, morals?[1]

9. The *book trade*, its profits, mode of selling, canvassing, advertising?

10. *Pictures* of the gods and goddesses, where sold, in what numbers, by whom executed?[2]

11. *Female book hawkers*, the number, what class of books do they sell?

12. The working of the Act against *obscene publications?*

13. The practicability of procuring a volume of *Anecdotes of native social life* as drawn from their literature?

14. It has been affirmed that last century the Bengalis had no *moral books*, how far was that true?

## XXXI.

### PANDITS.

Pandits once occupied more important positions in social life than they do now. Many anecdotes are still afloat of the wonderful acquisition in Sanskrit lore made by the Tarkalankars and others of former days, of the lengthened period

[1] Ballad literature is not to be despised as an index of a popular mind, as Sir W. Scott has shown with regard to the Scotch, and Bp. Percy with respect to the English ballads. A queen of Denmark, ten centuries ago, had the Danish ballads published: they have lately been translated into English; they are chiefly written by women, and treat of history, and legends. The Guzerat Vernacular Society in its report for 1849 states that one of its great objects was the collecting and copying ancient MS. ballads and tales.

[2] It is calculated there may be two hundred shops for the sale of these; now Brahmanas and Khaistas come into the field as book agents.

of their grammatical studies, their profound acquaintance with the shastras, and their wonderful feats of memory. Their influence and emoluments are on the decay; the endowments they formerly had, which enabled them to maintain pupils according to the Hindu rule, that the master is to support the scholar, have been in many cases alienated. English education also has called for a more practical and paying knowledge than Sanskrit, though the latter is of the utmost value for philological and antiquarian purposes.

Raja Krishna Chundra Roy of Nuddea was the Mecenas of Pandits last century, and bestowed on them an immense amount of land. Adams, in his reports on education, has given us much information on the position of Pandits in 1835, so has Buchanan Hamilton on those of Behar at the beginning of this century. Though pandit learning is on the wane, still it is to be wished that Sanskrit studies were placed in this country on a proper basis—as a key to the chief Indian vernaculars—as a capital training in Philology—and as a means of throwing a flood of light on the origin of nations: how striking the fact, brought to light by Sanskrit, that the Highlanders of Scotland, the priests of Russia, and the Brahmans of Benares, use radically the same language!

1. *Pandits*—illustrations of their abstruse studies, deep knowledge as well as extensive reading on subjects now little studied?
2. The emoluments, fees, and endowments of *tols* (colleges), and their influence over the pupils in various localities?
3. The various causes that have led to the *decline* of the emoluments, influence, and studies of Pandits?
4. Were *Mithila brahmans* numerous and influential in Bengal?
5. Do *Pandits, Purohits,* or *Gurus* gain more emoluments, or have greater influence?

## XXXII.

### Proverbs.

Proverbs present a rich field in illustrating the social condition of the people, as is pointed out in Trench's admirable work on the Proverbs.

1. The *origin* of Vernacular Proverbs, how many are modern, how many from the Sanskrit?

2. The *extent* to which they are used, which are local?
3. Their contrast and similarity with Hindi, Urdu, Mahratta, Telugu?
4. Their resemblance to European Proverbs?
5. Proverbs illustrating the moral and social condition of the people.
6. Proverbs throwing any light on the history of the country?

## XXXIII.

### Readers.

In oriental countries where the masses cannot read, it is very common for the people to assemble to hear one read a book to them, and explain its more difficult passages; illustrations can be seen in the Arabian Nights. Among the Bengali this class of Readers or Reciters is called a *Kathak.*

1. The *Kathaks;* their number, mode of being trained, emoluments and chief localities; are they on the increase or decrease?
2. How far could the system be adopted of employing men like *Kathaks* to read interesting works?
3. Vernacular *lectures* on popular subjects illustrated with diagrams, pictures, the desirableness and practicability of having them?

## XXXIV.

### Recreations—Music.

Music, since the days of Orpheus, as well as before, has exercised a mighty spell on the popular mind: we know the famous saying "Give me the making the ballads of a nation, and I will give you the making its laws." Sir W. Jones has written well on Hindu music and has vindicated its claims, though Europeons and Asiatics will never agree on this point.

There is a Bengali work on this, but I have met very few pandits that could explain it.

1. The *popular songs* in use, their description, number and influence?
2. An account of the most popular *ballad writers?*
3. Any *English music* likely to be popular in this country?

4. Any men corresponding with the *Bhats* of Rajputana or the wandering minstrels of Europe in the middle ages?[1]

5. The numbers, profits of *musicians* who play for hire, their different classes?

6. Are *athletic exercises* as much practised now as formerly?

7. How far do Bengalis *sleep* more than Englishmen?[2]

8. What *English games* or athletic exercises might be naturalised in India?

9. The advantage of having a *half holiday* on Saturday?

10. *Field sports*, as fowling, fishing, riding, pigeon fancying, kite flying, how far practised?

11. *Gambling*, various kinds of—numbers of gamblers—gains—gambling houses?

12. The mode of spending the *evenings* among educated natives? much *discussion* on politics or religion?

13. Are *feats of skill*, such as balancing a row of water-pots on the head, dancing on poles, balancing, tumbling, rope-dancing, sleight of hand, common?

14. Native *musical instruments*, the various ones, by what classes used? the ones most popular?

15. *Analysis of Vernacular books* on music?

16. *Cock fighting*, bulbul fighting, ram fighting, how far practised?

17. The Hindu notation of music? any music on *European notation;* any counterpoint, describe the various *ragas;* any harp?

18. *Listening to tales*, and riddles of an evening, how far practised?

19. Various modes of *swimming* practised, can any women swim?

## XXXV.

### Sects.

Without trenching on theological controversy, there is a wide field in considering the social influence of the various sects of Hindus and Musulmans. Professor Wilson has almost exhausted the theological part of the question in his elaborate work on the "Sects of the Hindus," but there is much to fill up in the social part.

[1] In Behar zillah those *Bhats* rank next to the military tribes, amount to 380 families, most of which have endowments in land. "They are very impudent fellows, and when any one offends them, they make an image of cloth, and call it by their enemy's prototype."

[2] I mention this as the Bengalis sit up late.

1. How far are the *Vaishnabs* ahead of other sects in elevating the people or women, or in proselyting? have they made any proselytes among Muhammadans? their ceremonies for the initiation of converts?

2. The extent of the *Guru's* power and emoluments now? do they travel far? the greatest number of disciples any have? their visits, instruction, morals? the various kinds of Upadesh they whisper into the ear?

3. The duties, influence and punishment of the *Dalpati?*

4. Is this remark of Wilson correct: "In Bengal the *Lingum* worship has no hold on the people's affections, it is not interwoven with their amusements, nor must it be imagined that it offers any stimulus to impure passions." Lecture I. 22.

5. The *Saktas*, their mystical diagrams, rites, and gesticulations?

6. *Lingamites*, are their priests Jangams? are any Sudras?

7. Was *Sati* practised more among Saktas or Vaishnabs?

8. Who worship Ola Bibi (the goddess of cholera), when did it begin, and in what districts is it observed? ditto of Shitola, of the Karta Bhojas, of Dakin Ray, of Gazi?

9. What sects originating in the Upper Provinces have followers in Bengal, and what Bengali sects have adherents in the Upper Provinces?

10. Is the Tantric system spreading? its social influence?

11. The three leading divisions of Hindu *monks?* how far do they observe caste?

12. Among what sects is *Pantheism* spreading—is it spiritual or material pantheism?

13. The resemblances and differences between *Pantheism* and *Sufyism?*

14. The number of sects among the *Musulmans?* their respective social influences?

## XXXVI.

### Servants.

1. Do natives keep the same *number of servants* as Europeans in a corresponding rank of life? how do their pay, treatment, work, differ in the service of Europeans, East Indians, Hindus, and Musulmans?

2. The state of *slaves* in former days—their price and treatment?[1]

[1] Slavery was once very prevalent in Bengal, and especially in Behar; the Musulmans in the latter place, forbidden by their religion to purchase a freeman, in order to give a sop to their conscience, call it taking a lease of a man for ninety years.

3. The causes that *servants in Calcutta* and other parts in India are said to be inferior to what they used to be—is it that those who govern ill are served ill?

4. How far is the practice of exchanging *certificates* of character carried?

5. *Chubdars* (macemen) their numbers and pay in former days? when did their numbers become less?

6. Anecdotes, illustrative of the number, treatment, and cost of *slaves* in Bengal in former times.

7. How far are the rules of *caste* among servants really such? how far are they an invention for their own ease and profit? (In Madras, the land of real caste, one servant does the work of many).

8. *Ayahs*, their castes, emoluments, morals?

9. The moral and social effect of so many servants being separated from their wives and families? is it like the Scotch boothy system?

## XXXVII.

### Travelling.

Though pilgrimages may have conduced to encourage the Hindus to a love of adventure and to season them to hardship, still there is among Bengalis a strong clinging to their native place and their *bháilok*, and yet Bengalis are found like Jews everywhere in India, but with better effect now than what Hamilton records "of the Calcutta Babus sent to Dinagepore, which is invaded by strangers from Calcutta, most of them rapacious as kites, and eager to accumulate fortunes in order to be able to retire to their native country." We trust that one of the effects of the railroad will be to lead a different kind of Bengalis to visit Behar, viz., the educated native who wishes to see the remains of the former greatness of his country, as seen in the Buddhist ruins of Behar, the Hindu monuments of Benares, the Moslem grandeur of Agra and Delhi, the beauteous scenery in the valley of the Soane and the Jain·buildings of Rajputana, with the wide Champaign of Rewa—we hope this Indian *grand tour* may be considered necessary to crown a book education.[1]

[1] From Katamandu to Indore, the Bengali Babu is the copying machine in offices; in Benares alone there are about 7000 Bengalis settled.

1. Do the Bengalis travel more than the *Behar* men? is their love to it on the increase?

2. Do *pilgrimages in Bengal* contribute more to a travelling spirit than in the Agra Presidency?

3. Is much *correspondence* kept up between Bengalis located in the Agra Presidency and their friends in Bengal?

4. How far is *cheap postage* leading the lower classes to a desire to learn to write and read.

5. Different kinds of *lodging houses* for travellers, their various prices—accommodation—are they over crowded—do scenes of vice or robbery often occur?

6. *Railways*, their effects on third class travellers, in lessening caste prejudices—enlarging the powers of observation—promoting social comfort—how far are women availing themselves of them?

7. *News*, the various modes of procuring and publishing?

8. *Planting trees* by the road sides, how far practised in ancient and modern times?

9. The causes leading to natives *emigrating* to the Mauritius and other parts?

## XXXVIII.

### Vehicles.

1. The various changes in shape the *palankeen* has undergone.[1]

2. How far is it feasible to introduce into lower Bengal the use of the *ekka*, which is both cheap and expeditious?

3. *Palki bearers*, in Calcutta—their numbers, mode of life, localities, character, profit—their native country—many from Behar? *Ghari wallas* ditto ditto.[2]

4. *Syces* in Calcutta ditto ditto—were not syces formerly more swift of foot?[3]

5. The origin of the shape of the present *kiranchis* Is it taken from old English coaches?

## XXXIX.

### Working Classes.

In England, much interest has been taken in the working classes, as the great pillars of the social system.

In India in the *present* state of things, the working classes

[1] Last century they were arched.

[2] In Berlin, the cab drivers, while waiting for a fare, are to be often seen reading.

[3] The author of *Seri Mutakherim* writes that they make nothing of following and preceding Englishmen on a full gallop, and that common servants have been seen who would run down a hare.

afford a fine field for education and social improvement, as their improved social condition, the rise of wages, and their wants lead them to feel a stronger desire for education and its accompaniments; to them a knowledge of reading, writing, and arithmetic, is rendered by their daily occupations a matter of necessity, while a little colloquial English would in some cases be of use to them. What they especially need is not a smattering of book English, but a sound vernacular education, embracing the elements of mathematics and manufacturing skill, on the plan of the commercial schools in England, from which, a smattering of Latin has been excluded. How many eminent men have risen from this class, such as Stephenson and Hugh Miller, an encouragement to others; like as in the French army, every soldier is said to carry the baton of field marshall in his knapsack, or in Russia where several millionaires were originally serfs. In Jehanabad a century ago a Musulman tailor founded a sect composed of Musulmans and Hindus, who respect the Koran and Shastras; this tailor composed 18 sacred books in Hindi, and his followers now amount to 20,000. *Kabir*, sprung from a weaver family, was the founder of one of the greatest sects in north India, while among the village gods worshipped in Behar are those who were boatmen, domes, oilmen. Chandra Gupta's maternal grandfather was a barber.

The London Working Men's College, established in 1854, has 270 students in Mathematics, Drawing, French, Natural History; there are other Colleges in Manchester, Halifax, having among their alumni, carpenters, shoe-makers, weavers, tailors, porters. When will Bengal have hers—the working men now can scarcely read. When is India to have the literature of labour—like that of Burns the bard and ploughman—Clare the peasant poet—Hogg the shepherd poet—Cooper the shoemaker poet—Miller the stonemason geologist. Hood's literature of labour and the achievements of mind among the cottage, or "mind among the spindles" suggest many reflections on this.

1. *Weavers*, their numbers, profits, social position, localities; do many read; have many risen in the world?

2. *Tailors*, are all Musulmans?

3. *Shoemakers*, do any become rich? is the prejudice against them declining?

4. *Potters*, why inferior to those of former days?

5. *Dyers*, different kinds and nature of dyes?

6. *Masons and Stone cutters*, are they chiefly immigrants?

7. *Smiths*, the profits and social position of various classes as coppersmith, tinsmith, blacksmith, goldsmith.

8. *Confectioners*, any poisonous matter used in their colouring confectionery?

9. *Bookbinders*, any Hindus, if not, why?

10. *Shopkeepers*, why so many readers among them? what *class in society* do they come from?

11. *Idol makers*, their localities, profits, numbers?

12. *Firework makers*, ditto.

13. *Pansaries*, or *Grocers*, ditto.

14. Instances of *Revolutions in trade* in this country from change of employment, like that in Europe among weavers, manuscript copyers, coach proprietors?

15. Instances among the working classes of men who have *risen to wealth* or social distinction, or who have educated their sons well?

16. Is the *Shilpa Shastra* in use among any priests?[1]

17. Any strikes among the *working classes?*

18. The *middleman system*, its evils?

Among the most thriving trades is that of keepers of tatties, who profit as much by this dirty work as English undertakers do by their other division of it. I have heard of some of those men near Dharamtola bazar, Calcutta, who earn between two and three hundred rupis monthly. In the Congress General of Hygiene in France, 1852, one resolution passed was, "That the instruction of the young in the labouring classes ought to comprise all which relates to the cleanliness of their person and of their dwellings, to the benefits resulting from good ventilation and the evils arising from humidity." There is on the Continent the Association International de Bienfaisance, whose main objects are to bring into relationship all interested in the condition of the working classes, reformatory institutions and popular education.

[1] It is so among certain stonemasons in Behar zillah.

## CORRECTIONS TO ART. IV.

Page 88, note, line 1, instead of *bhisuwang* read *bhisuweng*.
„ 94, l. 6 and 7, instead of جمجما read جمجما
„ 98, note 4, instead of *Hĕnu* read *Ibĕnu*.
„ 112, note 1, instead of فنج read فنج. In the same note read *Tamil* instead of *Hindi*, and *Panchatantra* instead of *Hitopadeṣa*.
„ 120, line 8, instead of *shamsu-lbarrin* read *shamsu-lbarri*.
„ „ 16, instead of *Qamru-lbaḥrin* read *Qamru-lbaḥri*.
„ 133, note 2, instead of لربوبيه read الربوبيه

Page 87, line 25, add: It may not, perhaps, be devoid of interest to quote a remarkable passage from the Panja Tandăran (lithographed edition, p. 30), in which also mention is made of the human sacrifice performed by Yudhishṭhira before commencing the war. It occurs in the first book, in the story of the jackal, crow, and tiger persuading the lion, their master, to devour a camel:

مك سمبه ݢاݢق تونك ادله فد زمان درماراج تتكل مريكيئت
هندق فرݢي ميرڠ سبوه نݢري مك كات اهل النجومڽ يڠ برنام
كسنا جكلو تونك بونه انق تونك اين بوتكن قربان نسچاي دافتله
نݢري ايت مك سبب ضرورة دالم ايت مك دبونهپله انقڽ
تيادله بردوس كارن كيت مملهراكن پاو اورڠ باپق

"The Crow said to the King Lion: Lord! in the time of King *Dărmaraja*, when they intended to go to attack a certain state, that King's astrologer, called *Kăsna*, said: 'If your Majesty kills this your Majesty's child, making a sacrifice of it, that town (or state) is sure to be conquered.' Then, on account of the urgency of the case, the King killed his own child. Such an act is sinless, as we preserve by it the lives of the many."

## Art. IV.—*Short Account of the Malay Manuscripts belonging to the Royal Asiatic Society.* By H. N. van der Tuuk.

[Presented July 3, 1865].

### *A.*—Raffles Collection.

No 1 (large folio of 460 pages) contains the حكاية هڠ توه. About the hero see Malayan Annals, translated by Leyden, chapters xiv. and xvi. A small extract is found in Crawfurd's "History of the Indian Archipelago," ii. p. 51. Manuscripts of this work, the text of which might be available, are in the possession of Mr. J. Pijnappel, at Leyden; and of Mr. E. Netscher, at Riyow.[1] The last chapters of this tale are found in No. 2607 of the manuscripts of the India Office, commencing with that part where the king of Mălaka intends to make one of his sons king on Mount *Siguntang*.[2]

This composition is very interesting, as it exhibits a faithful picture of Malay life, and is written in genuine Malay.

No. 2 (large folio of 288 pages; the last four pages are filled up with doggrel rhymes by some transcriber). This manuscript appears to be a transcript made by a native of Java, for a great many words belonging to the Malay dialect of Java occur in it; as, for instance, *uribang*, flower of the

[1] I shall make mention of other copies, as it is my opinion that no Malay composition ought to be published without a supply of manuscripts bearing on the same subject. Texts from one manuscript, such as those published by Mr. J. J. de Hollander, in Holland, are not to be depended upon. Even quotations, found somewhere, I shall take notice of, as it may be useful to the editor of a Malay text to consult them.

[2] See No. 66 of my Kort Verslag der Maleische Handschriften in het East India House, London, where the reader will find a full account of those closing chapters. As the numbers in that account have been since changed, I shall give here the present numbers.

hibiscus rosa Sinensis; *bòpèng*, pock-marked; *kulòn*, west,[1] etc. It also abounds with Javanese titles, as *dĕmang*, *ngabéhi*, *kandurúwan*, etc. The manuscript is in many passages too corrupt to be of use in editing the text. The transcriber has often changed words he did not understand into such as resembled them in sound, or nearly so.[2] But what is very strange, it has now and then a form less corrupted than the Javanese; v.g. *nantabóga* (p. 188) instead of the Javanese *antaboga* (a corruption of the Kawi *anantabhoga*). As to the contents, it follows the Javanese poem only to a certain extent, whilst it often contains passages which are not explicable otherwise than by supposing that a Javanese original has been translated or imitated, which did not deviate so much from the original Kawi poem, as the one published by Mr. A. B. Cohen Stuart. Although it is evidently taken from the Javanese, its first and last pages contain matter not found either in the Kawi or Javanese work, whilst no trace is found of the introduction, wherein the king *Jáya Báya*, in whose reign *Mpu Sĕḍah*, the Javanese author, lived, is spoken of in laudatory terms; moreover, the title *Bărata yuda* (*Bhārata-yuddha*) which is given to the Javanese version, is not known in Malay; and the great war between the *Korawas* and *Pāṇḍawas*, wherever it is alluded to in Malay compositions, is always called *părang Pandáwa Jáya*, "the war of the victorious Pāṇḍawa." Not until p. 134 do the contents of this manuscript resemble the Kawi and Javanese composition. The Malay author says in the opening that his work, although containing the story of the *Pandawa Pancha Kalima*,[3] gives a great many beautiful tales in the beginning, and afterwards the tale named *Hikayat Pandawa Jaya*. These beautiful tales are, he says, a collection of Javanese dramatic compositions (*lălakon*), to which he gives no particular names. I shall, on another occasion, make an analysis of the whole

[1] Even Dutch words, as, for instance, بلاو (*blaauw*, blue), occur in it. (See p. 115).

[2] So, for instance, we find passim درهم (Ar.) instead of درما (alms, largesses of a king to priests and religious mendicants).

[3] Translation of *pancha*.

and divide it into three parts. The first will give a rapid view of the contents from page 1–134, being what is not found either in the Kawi or Javanese work. The second will be more circumstantial, as it may illustrate the difficult passages of the Kawi original, and will comprise what is found from p. 134–208, being the record of the great war. The third will give only a brief account of the contents from p. 208 to the end, as it deviates in this part almost in every respect from the Javanese version,[1] which closes with a eulogy of king *Jáya Báya*, of which no trace is found in this manuscript. The library of the India Office is possessed of two manuscripts bearing on the same subject, but only containing the description of the war. They are numbered 2384 (small 4to. 234 pages), and 2605 (8vo. 176 pages). Both commence with introducing to the reader the chief heroes who figure in it, and then speak of *Kăsna's*[2] mission to demand the half of the kingdom in behalf of the five sons of *Pandu.*[3] To enable the reader to form a judgment of the difference of the texts of the three manuscripts, some specimens are here given.

The names of the four holy men (*rĕṣi*) that join *Kăsna* when setting out for *Hastinapura* as mediator are in No. 2603 : رم فرسو , نراد , چنتيك , and چكرس ; in No. 2384, رما فرسو , اديكاون , چتيك , and جتركتر ; and in this manuscript, كوار , كنفي , بروسي , and رام فرسو .[4]

The passage where the Javanese version speaks of a human sacrifice being performed by either of the contending parties runs in No. 2384 as follows:

ستله هار سيڠ درفاڠ٢ هار مكث ماسڠ٢ مملنتس كوت كروا ايت
برهمان سكترا نماڽ دان ممفالسن كوت فندوا ايت انق سڠ رنجون

[1] Of the Kawi version only twelve copies (!) have been lithographed by order of the Dutch government. It is not complete, ending with the combat of *Arjuna* and *Aśwatthāmā*.

[2] *Krĕṣṇa.*

[3] Leyden (As. Res. x. 178) mentions the following separate tales about the *Pāndawas*: 1st. *The tale about their gambling*; 2nd, *that about their borrowing a hall*; 3rd, *that about their selling lime.*

[4] In the Kawi poem they are *Paraśurāma*, *Kaṇwa*, *Janaka*, and *Nārada* (the Javanese has the same, only differently spelt, according to the Javanese pronunciation).

دان سڠ رون نماڽ تله سده ممفالسن كوت ايت مك فندوا
فون كلورله در دالم كوتاڽ مڠادف متهار مات دان سرت ممبلاكڠكن
سوڠي فنچاك ايتَ etc.

No. 2603 has:

تله هارسيڠ مك ماسڠ٢ ممفلس كوتاڽ ادفون اكن ممفلس كوت
كروا ايت برهمان سكنتر نماڽ دان اكن ممفلس كوت فندو ايت
سڠ ايراوان تله سده مك فندو فون كلورله در دالم كوتاڽ مڠادف
متهار مات دان ممبلاكڠكن سوڠي فنچاك etc.

This manuscript has (p. 147):

ستله هارسيڠ مك ماسڠ٢ اكن ممااليس كوتاڽ ادفون فمااليس
كوت كوراو برنسكترا نماڽ مك فمااليس كوت فنداو ايت انق
سڠ ارجون روفاڽ ترلال ايلق اروان نماڽ ستله سده ممالس مك
ايفون كلورله در دالم كوتاڽ مڠادف كمتهار مات ممبلكاڠي سوڠي
فنچاك etc.

The Kawi (x. 6) has: *tuwin pada tlas makaryya bhisuweng*[1] *tgal paprangan | rawan ngaran i kang tawur nrĕpati pandawā murwwani | kunang tawur i sang nrĕpeng kuru ya kārilud brahmaṇa | rikan sira 'sināpa sang dwija sagotra mātyālaga.* "Then they all performed a sacrifice on the field of battle, *Rawan* was the name of the victim of the Pāndawa king, commencing; as to the victim of the Kuru king, a brahmaṇa was . . . . . , thence he was cursed by the twice born, to die with his [whole] family in fighting." This remarkable passage will perhaps attract the attention of some

[1] Instead of *bhisuwa* (*bhisuwang* is *bhisuwa* + *ing*) a manuscript on palm leaves in my possession has *bhisu-eng* (*bhisua* + *ing*). I should like to read here *bhiṣawa* (*abhiṣawa*). The Malay text gives no explanation, as it is evidently influenced by the Javanese version, where *sagotra* has become the name of a person. Moreover it identifies *Rawan* with a son of Arjuna (of the name of *Irawan*), who is afterwards killed by a demon (xii. 17). The word فمااليس in the Malay version is probably a substantive made from ممالس, which occurs in the *Hikayat Kumala bahrin* with the sense of *to turn off the evil influence of a ghost* from a person who is supposed to have been visited by a ghost, and in consequence of it has got some disease (compare the Ngaju-Dayak *palis*). فمالس must then have the meaning of what is used to turn off the evil influence of ghosts.

Sanskrit scholar, who may succeed in explaining it. In No. 21 (see below) I have not been able to find it.

No. 3 (large folio of 244 pages, imperfect at the end) contains the حکاية رڠڬ اري کود نستاف. It is one of the *Panji* tales, containing the adventures of *Inu Kărtapati*, prince of Kurípan. This manuscript commences with the king of Kurípan's getting a son, called on his birth *Asmára ning rat Ondákan Jáya*. Then the birth is related of *Lăsmining puri Chandra-kirana*, the princess of Daha, who was also named *Puspaning rat*,[1] and betrothed to the above-named prince of Kurípan. This princess, when yet a girl, was carried off by *Batára Kála*, and placed with her attendants in a forest, where she changed her name and that of her waiting women. The prince of Kurípan goes, attended by his followers, in quest of his intended bride, and in his rambles for that purpose takes the name of *Rangga Ariya Kuda Năstapa*, his followers too changing each his name.

No. 4 (folio of 246 pages and ending abruptly) and No. 73 (small 4to. of 420 pages) both contain the حکاية باين بديمن, an imitation of the Persian طوطي نامه. On comparing the introduction, where the owner of the parrot (خواجه ميمون) is spoken of, I found the readings to be nearly the same. In my possession is a copy (folio of 90 pages) wherein the parrot tells thirteen tales. In the library of the India Office there are two manuscripts of this composition (Nos. 2604 and 2606). The former contains twenty-two tales, but the latter only ten, whilst the introduction about *Khojah Meymún* is wanting in it.[2] According to Abdu-llah[3] the Moonshee this composition also goes by the name of حکاية خوجه ميمون after the parrot's owner. The two manuscripts of the India Office seem to belong to one and the same version, and only differ in the proper names, which have been changed to Malay ones in No. 2606. The versions in both differ from my manuscript.

No. 5 (folio of 315 pages) contains the حکاية دامربولن.

[1] Compare under No. 14.

[2] See further Kort Verslag der Maleische Handschriften van het E. I. House.

[3] See his Journal, p. 95 of the Singapore edition. Of this Journal there is also a reprint in the fourth volume of Meursinge's Maleisch Leesboek; and a French translation by Dulaurier.

It is an imitation in prose of the Javanese poem, the commencement of which has been published by Mr. J. J. de Hollander in the Reader, p. 158 sqq. at the end of his Handleiding bij de Beoefening der Javaansche Taal- en Letterkunde (Breda, 1848). A translation, as it would seem, of the Javanese poem is to be found in Roorda van Eysinga's Indië (Breda, 1843), p. 502 (3de boek, eerste deel.). No. 11 (folio of 151 pages, only written half way down, the open spaces being perhaps intended for a translation) contains the same tale, but considerably abridged.

No. 6. See No. 31.

No. 7 (folio) contains:

I. (71 pages) شعر بيدسار . This poem has been edited with a Dutch translation and annotations by Mr. R. van Hoëvell, in vol. xix. of the Transactions of the Batavian Society of Arts and Sciences, but may be had separately. A review of this edition is to be found in the Indisch Magazijn & Gids (1847), and quotations from another manuscript in Roorda van Eysinga's Maleisch-Nederduitsch Woordenboek, under بوكن , جمجم , دافت , دڠر , راون , سندر , سندير and سنڤم . Another copy is contained in No. 36 (folio of 130 pages, and ending abruptly). Both manuscripts may serve to correct the edited text. I subjoin here a specimen of the various readings:

The printed edition, page 3, line 9 from below, has:

*Satălah (baginda sampey)*[1] *kapantey* | *di lihatña părahu (di atas lantey)*[2] || *langkap (lah sakaliyan)*[3] *kajang dan lantey* | *(báik)*[4] *lah putări duduk bărjuntey* ||

Page 5, line 5 from above:

*Tidurlah anakku bulang hulu* | *biyarlah ayahnda bărjalan dăhulu* || *(anaḳku pandang)*[5] *hatiku pilu* | *bagey di hiris dăngan sămbilu* ||

Page 6, line 4:

*Sămbilan bulan sămbilan hari* | *(ku kandung)*[6] *di dulum (hutan duri)*[7] ||

[1] No. 7 has *sampey baginda*, and No. 36, *sampey tuwan turun*.
[2] No. 36, *tărlalu băsey*. [3] No. 36, *dan*. [4] Nos. 7 and 36, *ndıḳ*.
[5] No. 7, *anak kupandang*. [6] No. 7, *kukandung*. [7] No. 7, *diri*.

Page 6, line 2 from below:

*Bărjalan lah baginda (laju manulih)*[1] | *rasaña hăndak (băr-balik)*[2] *kămbali* ||

II. (69 pages) شعر كن تمبوهن . This poem has been twice edited by J. J. de Hollander, once in the Reader of the first edition of his Handleiding bij de beoefening der Maleische Taal- en Letterkunde, and once separately (Leyden, 1856), from a transcript evidently made in Java, and badly mutilated. The version of this manuscript has hardly anything in common with that of the one edited, but corresponds in many respects with that recension of the poem, from which Marsden has given extracts in the Reader at the end of his Grammar. The king mentioned in the opening is called here *Sări nara indăra di Chămpaka Jajar*, but in the one edited *Ratu Socha windu pura nagara*. As proper names of females, *Kin Tă-dahan* and *Kin Pangalipur* occur here; whilst the name of the heroine is sometimes shortened into *Kin Tăbuh* for the sake of rhyme and metre. *Wira Dandani, Wira Păndapa* and *Wira Kărta* are found as proper names of males. The hero, the prince who fell in love with the heroine, goes here by the names of *Puspa Kănchana, Raden Inu,*[3] *Anak Man-tări, Inu Bangsawan, Raden Inu Kărtapati,*[4] and *Anak Inu*. The beauty of the heroine is compared to that of *Januwati,*[5] the goddess of love (*yangyang kăsuma*), and the celestial nymph *Nila-utama*. Instead of *taman* (garden), this manuscript makes often use of the Kawi *lălangun.*[6] *Paduka Mahádewi, Paduka Matur* (?), and *Paduka Liku* are mentioned as inferior wives of the old king. The pages of the king employed on errands are called here *pangălasan*, instead of *băduwanda*. This version, moreover, does not end so tragically; Indra bringing the two lovers back to life, accost-

[1] A correction by the editor instead of the words of the manuscript, *sayang tărjalan*. No. 7 has the true reading (*sayang tărjali*).

[2] No. 7, *balik*.

[3] Rhyming on *tărmangu*. See also the extracts in the Reader of Marsden's Malay Grammar.

[4] A name of *Panji*.

[5] The name of *Samba's* sweetheart (see under No. 15).

[6] e.g. *mari-lah ămas ariningsun, kita mandi kalălangun*, and *tăngah hari baginda bangun, părgi mandi kalălangun*. The native tales speak always of delightful gardens, where a bathing-place is one of the first requisites.

ing the heroine with *anak galuh.*[1] One of the characters represented is *Si-Tuguk,*[2] who is described as a kind of Falstaff, big-bellied and fond of fun. There is also a version in prose which goes by the name of حكاية انداكن فنورت . In this version, the heroine is the daughter of a king of *Wanggar*, and the waiting-maid, who dies with her, is called here, as in the printed edition, *Kin Bayan.* One of her most beloved nurses has the name of *Antarăsmi*, and is addressed by her with *kakak* or the Javanese *ĕmbòk* (elder sister). The principal attendants of the hero are *Panta Wira Jaya* and *Jaran Angsoka.* The place where the heroine is killed is here the wood (Jav. *alas*) *Puchangan.* The lovers are brought to life by *Bătara Kala,* who changes them into lotus flowers, and then veils them in a cloud of incense. The residence is called in the end *Sochawindu,* but elsewhere only *Pura nagara.* Mr. H. C. Millies, at Utrecht, has a manuscript of this version. It is not worth publishing, but may be available for a new edition of the poem, of which there is a manuscript also in the library of King's College, if I recollect right. It is beyond all doubt, that the poem as well as the tale belong to the widely-spread cycle of the tales in which the adventures of *Panji* are related.[3]

III. (26 pages) شعر سلندغ داليم This poem is known on the west coast of Sumatra by the name of شعر سري بِنِين.[4] I possess two manuscripts of it (8vo. of 36 pages, and small 4to. of 68 pages). A prose version of it is contained in No. 2715 of the manuscripts of the India Office, and has been described in my Kort Verslag der Mal. Handschriften van het E. I. House.

IV. (10 pages) شعر ايكن تمبرا . This is a collection of erotic

[1] In the *Panji* tales the princess of Daha, the intended wife of *Chekel,* is commonly called *Raden-galuh.*

[2] One of the personating characters in the *Panji* tales.

[3] See Raffles' History of Java, ii., p. 88 sqq., i. 335 and 392; Cohen Stuart's *Djaja Lengkara,* and Roorda's Lotgevallen van *Raden Pandji,* in the Bijdragen tot de taal-land-en Volkenkunde van Nederlandsch Indië, vol. ii., p. 167 sqq., and vol. vii. nieuwe volgreeks, p. 1 sqq.

[4] In the end of this manuscript this proper name of the mother of the heroine is spelt سري بانين .

verses put into the mouths of two fishes (a *tambăra* and a *kakap*) who seem to be desperately in love.

No. 8. See under No. 17.

No. 9 (folio of 160 pages) contains, as do No. 37 (151 pages, and ending abruptly) and No. 55[1] (small 4to. of 262 pages) حكاية اندرا فترا. This tale contains the adventures of *Indăra Putăra*, son of *Bakărma Puspa*,[2] king of *Samanta-pura*, and is replete with wonderful narratives. The hero is carried off by a golden peacock; is sent by the king *Shahsiyān* to *Bărma Săqti;* kills a giant or demon on Mount *Indăra Kila;*[3] finds the wonderful sea in the midst of the world (*tasik samudăra*); meets with the princess *Kumála Rătna Sări;* contends with the prince *Lela Mangărna* in exhibiting supernatural feats; is carried off by a genie (of the name of تمربوك), whose son (called تمرجلس) he kills; meets consecutively with mountains of gold and other precious metals, the seas of wonder and love; journeys in a cavern during a month; kills a serpent (of the name of منندود), and a demon (called غورقسا); meets with *Dărma Gangga*, who instructs him in supernatural means of conquering his enemies, and with *Bărma Săqti*, etc. At last our hero comes home, and is made king of *Samanta-pura* with the title of Sultan *Indăra Mangindăra*. No. 55 terminates with a great many erotic verses not found in the other copies. Many quotations from this work are to be found in Werndly's Maleische Spraakkunst (pp. 133, 157, 162, 170 (twice), 171, 174 (three times), 176, 185, 186, 191, 193, 194 and 195), in Roorda van Eysinga's Maleisch-Nederduitsch Woordenboek (under *pantas*, *pandey*, *puji* and *gărak*), and in the annotations of Mr. van Hoëvell on the Sair Bidasari (pp. 289, 305, 333, 335, 348, 352, 375 and 399). Specimens of the reading of the three manuscripts:—

No. 9:

اد سؤرغ راج دنڬري سمنت فوري برنام راج بكرم بسف ترلال بسر

[1] Another copy is in the possession of Dr. Reinhold Rost (small 4to. 148 pages).

[2] Of course most proper names occurring in this account are transliterated guessingly, such as they would be pronounced by a Malay at first sight.

[3] Where *Arjuna* performed penance to get supernatural arms. Such proper names deserve being taken up in a Dictionary, as they occur very often.

كرجاءنڽ براف راج٢ يڠ تعلق كفد راج دان ممبري افتي كفد
سڬنف تاهن شهدان امفت فوله راج٢ يڠ مماكي ماكت كاءماسن
دباوهڽ دان ببراف هلبالڠ حاضر دڠن سنجتاڽ ددالم استان
دمكينله كبسارن راج ايت حتي ستله براف لماڽ مهاراج بكرم
بسف دالم كرجاءن مك استريڽ راج ايتفون حامله برنام استري
راج فتري جنجما رتن ديوي ادفون ستله براف لماڽ مك تون
فتري جنجما رتن ديوي ايت حامل

No. 27:

مك اد سوڠ راج دنڬري سمنت فوري برنام مهاراج بكرم فسف
اكن راج ايت ترلال بسر كرجاءن شهدان ببراف راج٢ يڠ تعلق
كفد بڬند ايت مڠنتر افتي كفد ستاهن سكال شهدان امفت فوله
راج٢ مماكي كله يڠ كاءماسن ننتياس اد حاضر دڠن سنجتاڽ دباوه
مهاراج فسف دمكينله كبسارن بڬند دياتس تخت كرجاءنڽ ايت
مك اد ببراف لماڽ مك استري مهاراج بكرم فسف يڠ برنام
تون فتري جمجم رتن ديوي ايتفون برانق سوڠ لاك٢

No. 55:

اد سوڠ راج دنڬري سمنت فور برنام راج بكرم بسف دان اكن
راج ايت ترلال بسر كرجاءنڽ شهدان ببراف راج٢ يڠ تعلق كفداڽ
ممبري افتي كفداڽ ڬنف تاهن شهدان امفت فوله راج٢ يڠ
مماكي كله كاءماسن دباوهڽ دمكينله كبسارن مهاراج بكرم بسف
سبرمول مك استري مهاراج بكرم بسف يڠ برنام تون فتري جنجم
رتن فون حامله

No. 10 (folio) contains a collection of transcripts of treaties between the Dutch E. I. Company and several native states in the Indian Archipelago. The first treaty is that between Admiral Speelman and the king of *Gowa* (Mangkasar), and the last that between the E. I. Company and the king of Jobor and Pahang.

No. 11. See under No. 5.

No. 12 (folio of 444 pages) contains the حكايت برما شهدان . It is very seldom that tales are divided into chapters (فصل), of which there are here sixteen. In the commencement of the tale there is a kind of summary, wherein the hero is said to be a great king, who visited Mount *Qāf*, China, and the land of the inferior gods (*dewa*), subjecting men and ghosts to his sovereignty. On p. 2 a state *Samanda-puri* is mentioned. Its king was called *Săriyawan*, and was sprung from *Indăra Dewa Maharáma Rupa*, whilst his queen was of mere mortal extraction. He had two sons called Raja *Ardān* and Raja *Marsádan*. The two princes went with a large retinue to the forest *Samanta Baranta*, where a dewa of the name *Saráma Dewa* was in the habit of enjoying himself. This god hated the king, their father, who had caused his residence to be destroyed in former times. He changed himself into an old man and visited the princes, saying that he wished to serve them. Contriving to separate them from their followers when engaged in hunting, the god transformed himself into an elephant, whom *Ardān* so hotly pursued, that he got the start of his brother, and at last found himself entirely alone. The god then flew away with the prince to the sky, but was killed by the young hero. *Ardān*, having arrived again on this sublunary orb, made the acquaintance of a *rĕṣi* called *Báyu Ráma*, who told him that he was not to revisit his country for many years. The prince remained in the dwelling of the holy man, who instructed him in all sorts of supernatural sciences. *Marsádan* goes in quest of his brother, and in his rambles arrives at *Indărapura*, where he marries the king's only daughter, and succeeds his father-in-law.[1] *Ardān* has a great many adventures of the same kind, delivering a princess with her waiting women, etc. *Bărma Shahdān*, the hero of the tale, is a son of *Marsádan Shāh*, king of *Kalingga dewa*,[2] and his eldest brother is

[1] Called *Bakărma Dáli raja*. The proper name *Bakărma* is very frequent in Malay tales, and is a corruption of the Sanskrit *wikrama;* it is often confounded with *Pakărma*.

[2] The manuscript has كالغك ديو (p. 32).

called here *Rájadirája*. This work is replete with *pantuns*, some of which are worthy of notice. The late Mr. P. P. Roorda van Eysinga possessed a manuscript (two volumes in folio), which he would have published, but for want of a sufficient number of subscribers: what has become of it I cannot say. J. J de Hollander (Handleiding bij de Beoefening der Mal. Taal-en Letterkunde, 3d edition, p. 332) says, I know not on what authority, that the author was *Sheikh Ibn Abu Omar*.

No 13 is a number I could not find. Dulaurier has also omitted it in the list he gives (Journal Asiatique, 3rd series, x. 69) of titles of the manuscripts of this collection.

No. 14 (folio of 456 pages: on the back of the cover, *Charang Kurina*) contains the حكاية چارڠ كلين. It is a tale belonging to the *Panji* cyclus. The commencement is about the king of Kuripan having two sons, the eldest being *Kărta Buwána*, and the youngest Raden *Asmára Jaya*, surnamed *Ondakan Rawisărăngga*, who was betrothed to the princess of Daha, called Raden *Puspita-ning Rat.*[1] The name by which this tale goes is the assumed name of the princess when she had fled from her father's residence in order to follow the prince, in the garb of a man.

No. 15 (small folio of 180 pages) contains the حكاية مهاراج بوم. The plot of this tale is nearly the same as that of the *Bhaumakawya*,[2] relating the adventures of *Boma* (the Sanskrit *Bhauma*, son of the earth). He was the son of *Bisnu* (*Wiṣṇu*) by the goddess *Părtiwi* (Sans. *prĕthiwī*, earth), and became a powerful king, whom even the gods stood in dread of. As he, demon-fashion, annoyed the penitents, *Kăsna* (*Kṛĕṣṇa*) sends his son *Samba* against him. *Boma* is at last killed by *Hanoman*, after having himself killed *Samba* and *Arjuna*, who were, however, called into life again by *Naráda* (*Nārada*) sent by *Batara Guru* for the purpose. The celebrated episode[3] of *Dărmadewa* and *Dărmadewi* is here inserted in the same way as in the Kawi poem, *Dărmadewa* following *Bisnu* when

[1] Compare under No. 3.
[2] Edited by Friederich in the Transactions of the Batavian Society.
[3] This episode is often alluded to in Malay tales and poems (comp. under No. 7, II.)

incarnating himself into *Kăsna* and becoming *Samba*, whilst *Dărmadewi*, after having burnt herself, becomes *Januwáti*,[1] and so is reunited to her former love. This tale is also named حكاية سڠ سمب . The R.A.S.'s MS. (see also under No. 21) slightly differs from the one in the India Office (No. 2905, 4to. 120 pages). Raffles (History of Java, i. p. 388, first edition) mentions the Javanese version under the titles *Buma Kalantaka* and *Embatali*. The first name is no doubt *Bhaumakalāntaka* (the death of the demon Bhaumà, *kala* being used in Javanese to denote demons and Titans), as may be inferred from the Kawi poem p. 233, where it is *Bhaumāntaka* (Bhauma's end, the hero dying by the hand of *Wiṣṇu*[2]). The Kawi version bears ap. Raffles l. l. the name *Anrakasura*, which is to be corrected into *Narakāsura* (the demon *Naraka*, another name of Bhauma). I shall give on another occasion an analysis of this Malay composition.

No. 16 (folio of 206 pages). A duplicate is No. 62, I. (158 pages). The two manuscripts differ but slightly. They contain the حكاية اسما يتيم. The work has been edited by Mr. P. Roorda van Eysinga (Batavia, 1821), who has also given an analysis of it in the tenth volume of the Transactions of the Batavian Society. The episode of the singing peacocks has been published from another version by Meursinge in the third volume of his Maleisch Leesboek. In the library of the India Office there are two manuscripts, Nos. 2429 and 2430 (?). Mr. J. Pijnappel has also a manuscript. A new edition of this work is desirable, as that by Roorda van Eysinga has long been out of print. Quotations from it are found in Werndly's Maleische Spraakkunst, pp. 142, 157, 170, 171, 172, 180, 182, and in the preface xl., xli.

[1] *Yajnawatī* is her constant name in the Kawi poem, where she is never called *Dărmadewi*.

[2] The Sanskrit words I transliterate according to the ancient Javanese pronunciation. The labial semi-vowel is represented by *w*, as it is very improbable that it was sounded *v*, the Sanskrit not having an *f*, of which the *v* is the corresponding sonant. The vowels *ṛ* and *ḷ* are represented by *rĕ* and *lĕ*, the *anuswara* by *ng*, the *wisarga* by *h*, and the lingual sibilant by *ṣ*, in accordance with the other linguals. The palatial sibilant is here represented by *ś*, and might be transliterated by *sh*, as it was probably pronounced as the French *ch*, which in the same way originated in a *k*, were it not that *sh* is in use with the English to represent the lingual *ṣ*.

No. 17 contains:

I. the 7th book of the بستان السلاطين (*ārtiña kăbon săgala raja raja*). No. 42 (folio of 440 pages: on the back, *Makota sagală raja raja*) contains but five books of this work, and No. 8 (folio of 367 pages) only four books and a few pages of the fifth; this copy is written with vowel-signs. This excellent work, complete copies of which are very rare, is divided into seven books, each book containing a certain number of chapters. The author calls himself *Nuru-ddīn ibn 'Alī ibn Hasanjī*, son of Muhammad of the Hamid tribe, and a native of Rānīr (see No. 78, IV.), and composed it at *Achih* (*Acheen*) in the year of the Muhammadan æra 1040, by order of Sultan *Iskander II. Aliyu-ddīn Mur̈ayat*[1] *Shāh Johan băr dawlat lillu-llahi fi'l'ālam.*[2] The first book (many chapters) treats of the creation of heaven and earth; the second (many chapters) is about prophets and kings; the third (six chapters) on just kings and clever ministers; the fourth (two chapters) on pious kings and holy men[3]; the fifth (two chapters) on unjust kings and foolish ministers; the sixth (two chapters) on honoured liberal men and heroes; the seventh (five chapters) on intelligence, and on all sorts of sciences, medical, physionomical, historical, etc. Everywhere a great many tales are given, which might be used for a new Malay Reader. This work gives more than it promises, which in Malay literature may be called a miracle. The twelfth chapter of the second book contains a summary of the history of Malay states; the thirteenth the history of *Achih* up to the time of the author. In the first chapter of the fourth book there are several tales about the celebrated *Ibrahīm Ibn Adham*, corresponding to some extent with the tale, published by Mr. P. Roorda van Eysinga (Batavia, 1822) and D. Lenting (Breda, 1846) under the title *Geschiedenis van Sultan Ibrahim vorst van Irak.*[4] I have in my possession a manuscript (4to. 194 pages) containing only the first four chapters of the seventh book.

[1] مغاية.  [2] The shadow of God on the world (ظل الله في العالم).

[3] اوليآء.  [4] The Sundanesse version has the title *Hikayat Surtan Oliya Henu Ibrahim waliyullah*, a copy of which is in my possession (small 4to. 90 pp.)

II. An incomplete copy of تاج السلاطين (see under No. 42).

No. 18 (folio of 202 pages) شجره ملايم. This collection of historical tales has been published for the greatest part by Dulaurier in his Chroniques Malayes, and translated by Leyden (Malay Annals, edited by Sir Stamford Raffles). This MS., however, contains chapters not found in other copies, and not translated by Leyden. The last chapter but one, for instance, is about *Sang Naya's* conspiracy against the Portuguese at Malaka. There are several versions of these chronicles, as the reader will see from the various readings in Dulaurier's edition. No. 35 (folio of 117 pages), No. 89 (folio 120 pages), and No. 68 (small 4to.) end with the death of *Hang Kăsturi*, the last-named number having besides an entirely different introduction, and being properly but an abridgement. In No. 76 (small 4to.) only a part is found commencing with the chapter on the depredations of a Mangkasar prince (كرايڠ مجوكو), and ending with the conquest of Malaka by the Portuguese. No. 80 (4to. of 312 pages), and No. 5 of the Farquhar collection (small 4to. 259 pages) both end also with the conquest of Malaka by the Portuguese. There are a great many copies of this work[1] in Holland as well as in the Indian archipelago, in the government offices, and in the possession of individuals.

No. 19 (folio of 331 pages) and No. 20 (folio of 365 pages) contain the حكاية دالڠ فڠود اسمار. This is again one of the *Panji* tales. The title is after a name by which the prince of *Kuripan* was known when he was changed by *Bătara Indăra* into a woman. The beginning of the second volume is not connected with the last words of the first, being—القصه مك ترسبتله فركتاان ستله ايت مك فڠيرن كسوم اڠكڠ فون اڠنديك اده كاكڠ امفو كدو بڠمان بجار كاكڠ كدو. No. 43 (small folio of 142 pages; on the back of the cover, *Hikayat Pangeran Ke-*

[1] That it contains for the greater part but fabulous history is beyond all doubt, as even the history of Malaka is tainted with the *Panji* tales; see, for instance, the chapter about the king of Malaka going to the court of Majapahit, and marrying a princess of the name of *Chandărakirana* (compare under No. 3).

*suma Agung*) contains the same, but only its last part,[1] the beginning words being—القصه مكئ ترسبتله فركتائن فغيرن كسوم اكغ دوالم نكري فكمباغن سهار٢ دغن ممال بون٢ئن دغن سكل كديثن etc. The name of the hero is in this volume دالغ فودق اسمار. No. 51 (small 4to. of 149 pages; on the back of the cover, *Hikayat Dalang pudak Asmara*) is the same, but the usual commencement is wanting, its first words being— القصه مكئ ترسبتله فركتائن سري بفات اغ كريفن سلام اي برفترا اكن انقد بگند رادن اينو كرتافات etc.

No. 20. See under No. 19.

No. 21 (small folio of 669 pages) contains the حكاية فنداو ليم. This is a collection of loosely connected tales, the greater part of which relate to the persons involved in the contest between the *Kaurawas* and *Pāndawas*. To distinguish this composition from that which only relates to the war, I propose to call the last حكاية فرغ فنداو جاي, on account of its being so popular (see under No. 2), and the first حكاية فنداو فنج كليم.[2] As to the contents of this number, it is evident that it is an entirely different work, and by no means to be identified either with No. 2, or the two MSS. at the India Office (see under No. 2). The commencement narrates the birth of *Parásu Rama* and *Dewa Bărata*, sons of بسنو روفن by the celestial nymph *Manik*. Then *Santánu* is mentioned, and the birth of his children, who had a peculiar fishy smell about them, as they had been cut out of the belly of a fish, who had swallowed the seed of *Santánu*. On p. 2, *Parasára* cures the stinking princess *Durgandini*, and calls her afterwards *Sayojana Suganda* (sweet-scented at the distance of a yojana), taking her as his wife. She becomes the mother of *Biyása*. Another part of the narrative is about *Băsmaka*, king of *Mandira-săpta*, who had three daughters, called

[1] This part is often found separately, as may be inferred from Bahru-ddīn's list (containing an account of Malay compositions found at *Surabaya*), wherein we find a حكايت فغيرن كسوم اكغ.

[2] This title I derive from the first pages of No. 2, where the author calls the part of his work not bearing directly on the war by this name (see under No. 2.)

*Amba, Ambi,* and *Ambalika. Amba* becomes the wife of *Dewabrata,* who kills her by inadvertence. He therefore vows to surrender his life to a woman, burns his wife's body, and then goes to his brother, *Parasurama,* who consoles him and changes his name into *Bisma.* On p. 34 we find mention made of the birth of *Dăstaráta,*[1] *Pandu Dewa Nata,*[2] and *Widura Săqma.*[3] *Dăstaráta* was born blind, because his mother, when visited by *Biyasa,* from fear closed her eyes; *Pandu's* body was white as crystal, because his mother had covered herself with a white veil when she conceived him; *Widura Săqma* was born with one lame leg, as his mother had pulled his leg (?). On p. 38 the birth of *Karna* is related: he was the son of *Sangyang Rawi,*[4] by *Dewi Păta.*[5] After this, the meeting is related of *Bisnu* and the goddess *Părtiwi* (see under No. 15), and then the birth of *Dărmadewa* and *Dărmadewi* (see under No. 15). On p. 91 we have the birth of *Kăsna* (*Krĕṣṇa*) and *Kakărsana* (a surname of *Baladewa*). The last chapters relate the contest of *Boma* against *Samba* (see under No. 15). Although this composition is but a collection of narratives with no plot whatever to deserve the name of *hikayat,* it is very interesting, as it introduces nearly all the persons acting in the *hikayat părang Pandáwa Jaya,* and the *hikáyat Mahárája Boma.*

No. 22 (folio of 720 pages; the commencement is wanting) contains the حكاية سري رام. It is a very elaborate recension of the Malay Ramayana, from which Marsden has given extracts in the Reader at the end of his Grammar. A far shorter version has been published by Mr. P. P. Roorda van Eysinga (Amsterdam, 1843). A MS. in the Dutch India Office contains also a version of it as elaborate as this; it is in two small 4to. volumes (marked Ned. Kolonien. Handschriften C. No. 1), the first volume being of 475, and the second of 654 pages.

No. 23 (folio of 698 pages) and No. 45 (4to. of 278 pages). Two copies of the چيكل وانيڠ فات. The first number corresponds in version with a manuscript belonging to the

[1] *Dhrĕtarāṣṭra.* [2] In Malay the name of *Pāṇḍu.* [3] *Widura.*
[4] The god Sun. [5] Instead of *Părta,* Sansc. *Prĕthā,* i.e. *Kuntī.*

Dutch India Office (folio of 185 pages, and marked Ned. Kolonien. Handschriften C. No. 21; it is not finished), but is more elaborate. No. 45 seems to belong to the same recension as the two copies of the India Office (No. 2875 small folio, and No. 2691 large 4to.[1]). Another version is contained in No. 27 (folio of 347 pages), and No. 28 (folio of 348 pages: on the back of their cover, *Hikayat Dalang Indra Kesŭma*). Both these volumes are divided into chapters, each of which contains a tale, connected with the chief story; the first volume contains fifty-four tales and the beginning of the fifty-fifth, whilst the second commences with the fifty-sixth tale. The title, جيكل etc., of this *Panji* tale is after a name which the hero takes on his rambles in search of the princess of Daha, disguising himself as a man of the lowest class. This is one of the most interesting Malay compositions, and has influenced almost every literary production of the Malays; on another occasion I shall give an analysis of it. This cycle of stories has received by mistake also the name of حكاية ناي كسوم from its commencement, where a *Bătara Naya Kăsuma*, an inhabitant of *Indra's* heaven, is spoken of as the grandfather of *Kărtapati*.

No. 24 (two folio volumes of 446 and 450 pages) contain the سلسله راج٢ دتانه جاو. The first volume commences of course with Adam, whose son was *Shīth* (شيث), whose son was *Nūrchaya*, whose son was *Sangyang Wĕnang*, whose son was *Sangyang Tunggal*, whose son was *Guru*, who had four sons and one daughter, being *Sangyang Sambu*, *Bărahma*, *Mahádewa*, *Bisnu*, and *Dewi Sări*. *Bisnu* became king of Java with the title Prabu Seta (? سيت). Then a chapter treats of the Ratu *Sela Părwata* of *Giling Băsi*. It ends with *Pangeran Dipati* taking the title of *Susunan Mangku Rat Senapati*, etc. The second volume commences with *Susunan Mangku Rat* being at *Bañu Mas*, and ordering the *Dipati* of *Tĕgal* to be fetched, and terminates with *Susunan Pakubuwana's* reign in *Kărtasura*. Two quotations from this work have been given by Dulaurier in the Journal Asiatique for 1846.

[1] See my "Kort Verslag der Mal. Handschriften van het East India House te Londen."

No. 25 (folio of 304 pages). This *Panji* tale goes by the name of حكاية اندغ[1] مالت رسمي from a name the heroine assumes when leading the life of a penitent. The commencement treats of the prince of *Kuripan*, called *Kuda Jaya Asmara*, surnamed *Kărtapati*, who was betrothed to the princess of Daha, *Raden Galuh Chandărakirana puspaning rat*. A god falling in love with the said princess asked her of *Batara Guru*, but meeting with a refusal, as she was to be the wife of *Kărtapati*, dropped her with her two waiting women into a forest, where she led the life of a penitent, and changed her name and that of her companions. She is afterwards married to the prince, here passim called *Raden Inu*, who succeeds his father with the title of *Părabu Anom ing Kuripan*, the old king retiring to the woods to do penance.

No. 26 (folio of 239 pages). This *Panji* tale goes by the name حكاية فنج ويل كسوم. The commencement is almost the same as that of No. 23, relating the birth of *Inu Kărtapati*, and that of the *Raden Galuh Puspaning rat*, surnamed *Chandărakirana*. Going in quest of his love, who is carried off by *Batara Kala* into a forest, the hero takes the name *Mesa*[2] *Taman Panji Jayeng Kăsuma*. Afterwards in the course of the narrative he is called *Sira Panji Wila Kăsuma* (p. 73 of MS.), but often merely *Sira Panji*. After a great many adventures he becomes king of all Jawa.[3] Werndly in his Maleische Boekzaal mentions a *Hikayat Mesa Taman Wila Kăsuma*, and van Hoëvell in his annotations on the Sair Bidasari has given quotations from a *Hikayat Panji Wila Kăsuma*, pp. 301, 326, 334, 339, 362, 363, and 374.

Nos. 27 and 28. See under No. 23.

No. 29 (folio, 645 pages; ends abruptly). This *Panji* tale has the lettering *Hikayat Naga Bersru* (on the fly-leaf within). I dare not decide whether this is right, as I did not succeed in finding the reason for this title. Leyden, in his Dissertation on the Indo-Chinese Nations (As. Res. x.) speaks of a

[1] From the Javanese *ẹṇḍang* (a female penitent or nun).
[2] Jav. *Maèsa* (*Mahiṣa*, buffalo) is frequent in proper names of Javanese personages, and is sometimes rendered by the equivalent Javanese *kĕbo*.
[3] *Amutĕr jagad jawa* (Jav.).

*Hikayat Naga Bisaru,*[1] or story of a princess of *Daha,* who was changed into a serpent, and banished to a lake. It is a pity he gave no explanation of the name. At all events this manuscript belongs to the *Panji* tales. It opens with the king of *Kuripan* asking for his son, the Raden *Inu Kărtapati,* the hand of the princess of *Daha, Chandărakirana.* The hero is here passim called *Sira Panji* and *Sări Panji.*

No. 30 (small folio of 74 pages; the wrong lettering on the back of the cover, *Salasilah nabi Muhammad,* is owing to the first words, which make *Nuru-ddīn* a descendant of the prophet's) contains the دفتر شجره چربون. It is a genealogical account of the kings of Cheribon (properly, *Chi-rĕbon*), commencing with a confused tale about Sheykh *Nūru-ddīn,* surnamed the *Suhunan Gunung Jati,* one of the apostles of the Islām in Java. It is probably translated from a peculiar dialect of the Javanese, its language being anything but Malay, and mixed up with Javanese and occasionally with Sundanese words too. Besides the said *Suhunan* ("*Reverend*"), other celebrated apostles, as the Suhunan's *Kali Jaga, Ampel Danta,* and *Bonang* are personated here as people endowed with miraculous gifts, and the conquest of *Majapahit, Bantĕn* (Bantam), and *Pajajáran* (called here too by its ancient name *Pakúwan*) is briefly narrated. The Panĕmbahan *Sura Sohan,* called also *Mowlānā Hasanu-ddīn,* introduces, according to this chronicle, the Islām in *Pajajaran,* the *Lampong* country, *Indărapura, Bangka-ulu* (Bencoolen), and *Balo.* His elder brother, the Panĕmbahan *Pakung Wati* rules the country from *Krawang* to Cheribon, he himself that from Bantam to *Krawang.* This manuscript makes use occasionally of the linguals ڊ and ط.[2] From it some valuable materials might be gleaned for a work on Javanese history, the last pages containing an account of the kings of Cheribon down to Sultan *Anom.*

No. 31 (folio of 411 pages) contains the حكاية شاه قباد.

[1] This *bisaru* and *bersru* of the lettering, I should like to explain by برسرو in the sense of *to cry invoking the gods.*

[2] e.g. منوڊعكن and بطار (*bhatára*).

The hero is the son of *Shāh Partsād*[1] *Indăra Lăqsana*, king of *Thăraf*,[2] situated in the neighbourhood of Mount *Qāf*. This king, although powerful, was forced to pay tribute to the monkey-king *Baliya Indăra*,[3] whose residence was *Kurdari* (كورداري). The king's eldest son, called in the commencement *Qubād Lela Indăra*,[4] and afterward *Shāh Qubād Johan 'Arifīn*, could not put up with his father's disgrace, and resolved to deliver his parent from the allegiance to the monkey-king. He is in several ways assisted by genii, who prove to be his relatives, and wages war against the powerful enemy. This manuscript ends abruptly, the last words being

مك بڠند شاه قباد فون ممبري تيته اكن انق راج ٢ توجه فوله دان كفد سري فادك كائندراٴن دان كفد راج مغرن چندرا دان كفد سڠل راج يڠ سلقسا توجه ريب انم راتس ايت كفد بچار همب بائيكله سڠل سودار همب

Another copy, in which some of the proper names are different, goes by the name of حكاية شهر القمر (No. 6, large folio of 414 pages). The father of the hero is called here *Shāh Părmat Indăra Lăqsana*, and the residence of the monkey-king *Kărdar* (كردر). An entirely different version is I. (85 pages, and ending abruptly) of No. 58; it goes by the name of حكاية راج شاه جوهن اندرا مغندرا. The hero is in this recension the son of *Bakărma*[5] *Chandăra*, king of *Baranta Indăra*. A specimen of the readings of No. 31 and No. 6 deserves being inserted:

[1] فرصاد [2] طرف

[3] According to the Malay history of *Ráma* the same as *Báli*, and brother of *Sugriwa*. Malay compositions borrow from each other proper names; so, for instance, we find *Indăra Kila* (mountain, where Arjuna lived as penitent), *Mintaraga* (name of a cave, where Arjuna did penance, Sanscr. and Kawi *wītarāga*, passionless), and other proper names from the Kawi poem *Wiwāha* (in Malay حكاية داتي نبل كواچ from a Titan conquered by Arjuna) occurring in other compositions. Such proper names ought to be received into the Dictionaries.

[4] Werndly in his Maleische Boekzaal mentions a tale about a person of this very name, and Bahru-ddīn (list of Malay works to be had at Surabaya) has a حكاية راج قبات ليلا.

[5] See under No. 12.

No. 6:

اد سبوه نڬري اتوق نماڽ همفر بوکت قاف نڬريڽ ايت ترلال
بسر کوتاڽ درفد بات فوته فنجڠڽ کوت ايت تيڬ بولن فد
فرجلانن دان نام رجاڽ شاه فرمت اندرا لقسان ادفون اکن بڬند
ايت اصلڽ درفد جن برمول اکن بڬند ايت ترلال بسر کرجاءنڽ
باڽق منتريڽ توجه راتس دان باڽق هلبالڠڽ تيڬ کتي دان
رعيتڽ تياد ترکير٢ لاڬ باڽقڽ ادفون اکن نڬري ايت ترلال جاوه
درفد نڬري يڠ لاين٢ جاڠنکن نڬري مانسي يڠ اد اکن همفر کفد
نڬري بڬند ايت ادفون بڬند ايت سننتياس اي مڠنترکن افتي
کفد راج کرا درفد ساعت جاوه درفد نڬري يڠ لاين شهدان دمکينله
ملاڽ مک سبب راج ايت مڠنتر افتي کفد راج کرا کارن اد
سوات راج کرا کردر نام نڬريڽ دان رجاڽ برنام مهاراج بليا ليلا
اندرا etc.

No. 31:

اد راج سبوه نڬري طرف نماڽ همفر بوکت قاف دان نام بڬند
ايت راج شاه فرصاد اندرا لقسان برمول اکن بڬند ايت ترلال امت
بسر کرجاءنڽ دان کوتاڽ درفد بات هيتم تيڬ بولن فرجلانن
جاوهڽ برمول اکن بڬند ايت اصلڽ درفد جن دان باڽق منتريڽ
توجه راتس دان هلبالڠڽ سفوله کتي رعيتڽ تياد ترکير٢ لاڬ باڽقڽ
ادفون اکن نڬري ايت ترلال امت مشهور کفد سکل مانسي دان
جن فري ممبڠ ديو٢ اندرا چندرا سکلين فون تياد دافت همفر
کفد نڬري بڬند تتاف اکن بڬند ايت سنتياس موسم مڠنترکن
افتي کفد راج کرا دمکينله اصلڽ يڠ جاد بڬند ايت مڠنترکن
افتي کفد کرا ايت الفصه اد سبوه نڬري کورداري نماڽ نڬري ايت
دان نام رجاڽ مهاراج بليا اندرا etc.

No. 32[1] (? folio) contains:

I. (11 pages). An account of various ceremonials, customs, and laws, *e.g.* of the chief ministers a king should have, the flags they wear, etc.

II. (5 pages). A short story about *Indărapura* being attacked by *todak*-fishes,[2] and the stratagem by which they were defeated.

III. (5 pages). The first arrival of the Portuguese, and their stratagem to get possession of Malaka.[3] A translation of it by Sir Stamford Raffles is to be found in the Asiatic Researches, xii, p. 115.

IV. Coloured figures representing the flags used by the sovereign and his chief ministers (belonging to I).

V. (63 pages). A tale the commencing words of which look more like a chapter than like a real commencement. They are:

القصه ترسبتله فركتائن اد سبوه نڬري برنام طوغان فوري رجاث برنام
سلطان امـمس ديو مكث راج ايت ترلال امت بسر كرجائن
استرين برنام فتري انتن چهيريم مكث تون فتري ايتفون ساڠت
هندق برانق etc.

The last words are:

حتي راج طاهر فري فون برفلق برچيم كفد راج ديو بسنو برتاڠس
تڠيسن لال بڠند فون تورن برجالن حتي بڠند راج سلطان امـمس
ديو فون دودقله يڠ بڠمان سلماث

It relates the adventures of *Dewa Bisnu*, son of the king spoken of in the commencement; from which it is probable that the title should be حكاية ديو بسنو.

No. 33 (folio) contains:

[1] Dulaurier in his list speaks of two folio volumes, both containing اندڠم, but I have only found one, on the back of which the number was obliterated. That number is consequently all but certain.

[2] The same is told of Singapura (see *Malayan Annals*, p. 83) and of *Barus* according to the *Sair Raja Tuktung* (شعر راج تقتڠ).

[3] The same narrative is found in one of the last chapters of No. 1.

I. (11 pages). A collection of laws, commencing with the finding of goods, and what is to be done with them.

II. (44 pages). Laws, some of which are maritime.

III. (8 pages). Fragments of a law book, beginning with the fencing of cultivated fields.

IV. (6 pages). باب فد مپتاکن کتیک رجغ. About the ominous qualities of the days of the months, having mystical names, mostly those of animals. The same is found in II. of No. 74.

V. (3 pages). باب فد مپتاکن کتیک توجه On the seven ominous times. The same is XVI. and XXXVII. of No. 34, and IV. of No. 74.

VI. (6 pages). فصل فد مپتاکن کتیک ليم On the five ominous times. Compare the Bataksch Woordenboek, p. 419. The same in No. 34 (x. and xxxv.) and No. 74 (v.)

No. 34 (folio; the number obliterated, and on the back of the cover, *undang undang*) contains:

I. (1 page). A fragment from a law book.

II. (1 page). باب فد مپتاکن ناک مغيدر درين. On the serpent turning itself round in the sky, the position of which is to be known, especially when going to war.

III. (3 pages). Charms and antidotes.

IV. (15 pages). Malay laws, commencing with the fencing of cultivated fields. The maritime part has been published by Dulaurier in the sixth volume of Pardessus's Collection de Lois Maritimes.

V. (7 pages). Treaty between the Admiral Speelman and Hasanu-ddīn, king of Gowa, and other Mangkasar chiefs (compare No. 10).

VI. (1 page). Chronicle of Mangkasar, commencing with اينله اصل يغ فرتام مول٢ يغ کرجائن دتلق ايت برنام کرايغ لوي د سيرو etc. (continued in VIII.)

VII. (1 page). Contract of *Aliyu-ddīn* of Gowa with the Malay merchants.

VIII. (3 pages). Continuation of VI. (continued in XII. and XVIII.)

IX. (9 pages). A chapter on the law of inheritance (فرائيصل).

X. (2 pages). See vi. of No. 33.

XI. (6 pages). Customs and laws commencing with the duties of the Băndhara, Tumănggung, and other functionaries of the Malays.

XII. (2 pages). Continuation of vi.

XIII. (1 page). A fragment about the discontinuance of praying according to the words of the prophet.

XIV. (1 page, 54th page). Formulas used as charms.

XV. (1 page). On ominous days (نحس).

XVI. (3 pages). The same as v. of No. 33.

XVII. (1 page). فصل مپتاكن [1] رجال الغيب

XVIII. (4 pages). Continuation of vi. (continued in xix.)

XIX. (3 pages). A fragment of a work on superstitions and continuation of vi. (continued in xxvi.) on charms, commencing with the means of seducing a woman, etc.

XX. (11 pages). Receipts against diseases, commencing with a precept about the regular course of a woman's sperm (ترتيب مني فرمفون).

XXI. (p. 78). Table of ominous events, which have to be expected on each day of the month.

XXII. (p. 79). Receipts, commencing with a prescription against stomach-ache.

XXIII. (p. 81). The letters of the alphabet with their mystical meaning under each of them.

XXIV. Regulations for the chief of the Malays settled at Mangkásar, his power, etc.

XXV. Prescription to conquer a woman's obduracy.

XXVI. (p. 82). Fragment of a chronicle (vi.) and continued in xxviii.

XXVII. Continuation of xxiv.

XXVIII. Continuation of vi.

XXIX. Combination of letters attributed to prophets, angels, and holy men.

XXX. (p. 98). A precept of the wise *Loqmān* about the future of a just-born child.

XXXI. (p. 99). On the ominous signification of earth-

[1] See Herklots' Customs, etc. p. 395.

quakes, lightning and eclipses, according to the time of their appearance. A fragment of a similar work is to be found in de Hollander's Reader, p. ٢٦٨.

XXXII. (p. 103). About the choice of the ground to erect a house upon, to make a field of, etc.

XXXIII. (p. 106). Means to know how a man and woman live together.

XXXIV. (p. 110). Means to know whether stolen goods may be recovered.

XXXV. (4 pages). See VI. of No. 33.

XXXVI. Astrological tables of the planets according to the days of the week.

XXXVII. See V. of No. 33. On p. 120, an illustrative table.

XXXVIII. (p. 121). A figure illustrative of the serpent's position (see II.).

No. 35. See under No. 18.

No. 36. See under No. 7.

No. 37. See under No. 9.

No. 38 (small folio of 87 pages), No. 59 (small 4to. of 138 pages), and No. 71 (small 4to. of 196 pages) contains the حكاية كليله و دمنه [1]. In the last-named number the introduction is wanting. Some fables from this book have been published by J. J. de Hollander in his Malay Reader, p. 18 sqq. I possess a manuscript of it (4to. of 205 pages). A specimen of the various readings of these four manuscripts may not be out of place. The reader may compare with it the fable published on p. 18 of the above-cited work.

No. 38:

اد سيکر دندڠ برسارڠ دياتس سفوهن برقس مها بسرادفون برقس
ايت برلوبڠ مک د لوبڠ فوهن برقس ايت اد سيکر اولر بسر
ددالم کايو ايت ديم دسان مک افبيل دندڠ ايت برانق دماکن
اولر ايت دمکين جو سلمان مک دندڠ ايت فرکي کفد صحابتن

[1] On the west coast of Sumatra it goes by the name of حكاية ستروبه (*si-tàrubuh*) after the name of the bull who became the lion's friend.

سيكر سريڬال مك كات سريڬال ايت افاته كهندقم داتڠ كفداك
مك كات دندڠ ايت هي تولنك ادفون اك داتڠ اين تله
ببراف كال اك برانق دماكنن جو اوله اولر بسر ايتله مك اك اين
داتڠ كفدام مڠدوكن حالك

No. 59:

اد سئكر دندڠ برسارڠ دياتس فوهن برقس مهابسر ادفون فوهن برقس
ايت اد برلوبڠ فوهن فرقس ايت اد سئكر اولر بسر ديم دسان مك
تيف٢ دندڠ ايت برانق دماكن اولر ايت دمكين جو سلمان مك
دندڠ ايتفون فرڬي كفد سئكر سريڬال مك كات سريڬال هي دندڠ
اف كهندق اڠكو داتڠ كفداك مك كات دندڠ ايت هي تولنك
ادفون اك داتڠ اين كارن تله براف كال اك برانق دماكن جو
اوله اولر بسر ابتفون مك اك داتڠ كفدام مڠدوكن حالك

No. 71:

مك ادله سئكر دندڠ برسارڠ دياتس فوهن كايو بسر مك ادله
فوهن ايت برلوبڠ٢ مك اولريڠ بسر سئكر دالم لوبڠ كايو ايت افبيل
برانقله دندڠ ايت داتڠله اولر دماكنن هابس سننتياس له يڠ دمكين
ايت مك دندڠ فون امت حيرانله اكندرين لال اي مڠادف كفد
سريڬال كتان هي هنديك افله داي افاياك سننتياس دالم
فرچنتاءنك افبيل اك برانق دماكنن اوله اولر ددالم كايو ايت

My manuscript:

اد سئكر دندڠ برسارڠ دياتس كايو برقس مهاتڠڬ مك اد سئكر
اولر ديم فد رڠك كايو برقس ايت تتكل دندڠ ايت برانق مك
دماكنن اوله اولر ايت اكن انق دندڠ ايت دمكينله سديكال مك
دندڠ ايتفون ترلال دكچت مك دندڠ فون فرڬيله كفد سريڬال
مڠدوكن حالن دمكين كتان سننتياس همب برانق دماكنن اوله اولر
ايت تولڠله بچاراكن اولهم اكنداك مكؤجر سريڬال هي هنديك

Hence it appears that the manuscript from which de Hollander published some fables must belong to another recension than these four manuscripts. All these versions are from the Persian.[1]

No. 39. See under No. 18.

No. 40 (folio of 320 pages) contains the حكاية ميس لاركسوم. The hero is the son of a king of كوناتن in West Java. This king had two wives, the youngest being *Ămas Ajĕng*, who bore him a son called جناكر نيت. She slanders the eldest, making the king believe she had tried to poison him. The elder queen is defended by her son, who in consequence falls into disgrace, and is incarcerated. The queen herself is conducted into a forest to be killed, but the executioner, pitying her condition, leaves her in a grotto, where بتار بناو supplies her wants. She is there delivered of a son, who receives the name of رادن ميس اريا مغكوستر. The story ends in a strange and abrupt way, as if not finished. I do not think it probable that this composition is the same as that mentioned by *Bahru-ddīn* under the title حكاية سير فنج لاركسوم, which is decidedly a *Panji* tale.

No. 41 contains a Malay translation of a Javanese *Wukon.*[2] It is a miserable composition, not readable without the Javanese original.

No. 42[3] and No. 64. Two copies of the تاج السلاطين. This work has been published with a Dutch translation by P. P. Roorda van Eysinga (*De Kroon der Koningen*, Batavia, 1827). A great many quotations in Werndly's Maleische Spraakkunst are from a better manuscript than that used by Roorda van Eysinga.

No. 43. See under No. 19.

No. 44 (4to. of 303 pages) contains the حكاية چابت تغكل a *Panji* tale; the title is derived from a banner (*tunggul*), the

[1] The Hindí version has been translated by *Abdu-llah* the Moonshee and published at Malaka. It is divided in the same way as the *Hitopadeśa*, and bears the title of فنج تندران.

[2] See Raffles' History of Java, i., p. 475 sqq. Tijdschrift voor Indische Taal-Land-en Volkenkunde (Batavia, vol. vi. and vii.)

[3] See also Nos. 17 and 47 II.

baneful influence of which occasioned a great mortality in the land,[1] being extracted (*chabut*) by the hero. It opens with the god *Naya Kăsuma* (see under No. 23) descending into the world, and taking the name of *Mesa Părta Jaya Kălana Banjáran.* He becomes king of *Majapahit,* with the title *Părabu Wira Kărta,* after having married the only daughter of the old king, who retired to do penance. His sons became kings of *Kurípan, Daha, Gagălang,* and *Singasári.* In the course of the narrative *Kărtapati* and *Chandărakiràna* are again the most conspicuous characters. In his perambulations the said prince calls himself *Kī-ramang Panji Wauhan*[2] (?), and the princess of *Daha,* when leading the life of a penitent, assumes the name of اندڠ اسماي دفوري (compare under No. 25). The language of this tale is crowded with Javanese words and expressions. As humble pronoun of the first person *pun titiyang*[3] (the man) is here used as in the Balinese.

No. 45. See under No. 23.

No. 46 (large 4to. of 306 pages) contains the حكاية ديو مندو. The hero's father is *Kărma Indăra,* king of *Kangsa Indăra.* This king has heard of a certain white elephant, and orders *Părba Indăra* to catch it. *Părba Indăra,* failing in executing the orders of his master, is discarded the court, and leaves with his family. He arrives at a hamlet, where a *Sheykh Jădīd* was living in religious solitude, and settles there. He afterwards begot there a daughter called *Siti*[4] *Mangărna Lela Chahya,* with whom the new king, *Pakărma*[5] *Raja,* falls in love when coming accidentally to her father's hermitage. *Siti Mangărna* is after due time delivered of a son, who is the hero of this tale. This prince leaves the residence, and rambles about to increase his knowledge of the world. In the course of his rambles he meets with the white elephant,

[1] Compare Cohen Stuart, l.l. p. 153.

[2] The manuscript: واوهن. A *Hikayat Mesa Kiramang* is mentioned in the Journal Asiatique, 1833, by Jaquet.

[3] Compare the use of *ulun* as pron. of 1st person, being the same as *ulun* (Lampong) and *úlună* (Malagasy spelling *olona*) which signify *man*, and *ngwang* (pron. 1st person) and *wwang* (*man*) in Kawi.

[4] The Arabic ستي.

[5] See under No. 12.

who was a princess of the name of *Lela Rătna Kumála*, and had been transformed by a demon, of the name of *Dewa Răqsa Malik*, out of spite, as he wanted her for his wife, but met with a refusal at her father's hands. Another copy of this tale is in the library of the India Office (No. 2871, folio volume), where the introduction is entirely different. According to the last words of that manuscript this tale goes also by the name of حكاية راج كڠس اندرا فكرم راج .

No. 47 (4to.) contains:

I. The حكاية ميس اندرا ديو كسوم . The hero is a son of a king of *Kuripan* by *Sakărba*,[1] a daughter of *Indăra*, a king of *Kăling*, who had made himself universal sovereign of the world (چكرا بوان وات) ; having subjected the kings of *Gujărat, Mogol, Abyssinia, Machulipatam, Bengal,* etc., he sends a fleet to conquer Java, going himself thither with his sons through the air. *Mesa Indăra Dewa Kăsuma* opposes the conqueror. Amongst the places the Indian king besieged is *Pajajáran*, the king of which had a son called *Ămas Tanduran*, and two daughters, called Raden galuh *Kumúda Răsmi*, and Raden galuh *Dewi Rina* (?). The opening of this tale is anything but clear. It is besides crowded with Javanese expressions, as for instance, *măngambah jumantára*[2] (to tread the air).

II. (64 pages). Fragments of the تاج السلاطين (see No. 42).

III. (18 pages). معزجة رسول الله ممڠكل بولن . Another copy in No. 62. This short tale about Muhammad's miracle of making the moon pass by halves through his sleeves, has been published by Robinson at the end of his "*Principles to elucidate the Malay Orthography*."[3] There are a great many manuscripts of this legend.[4]

IV. (5 pages) حكاية فرتن اسلام. On the duties of a married woman, about which the heroine of this tale consults the

[1] Corruption of the Sansk. *Suprabhā*.

[2] The Sansk. *dyumāntara*.

[3] P. 222 sqq. of the Dutch translation by E. Netscher.

[4] One in the possession of Mr. H. C. Millies at Utrecht, and another in mine (small 8vo. of 28 pages).

prophet.[1] A copy is in the possession of Mr. H. C. Millies, where the proper name is spelt فرتنا.

No. 48 (small 4to. of 210 pages) contains the شرح يغ لطيف اتس مختصر جوهرة التوحيد [2]. It is translated from the Arabic of *Ibrāhīm Laqānī*, by the Sheykh *Shihābu-ddīn*, surnamed the pilgrim, and son of *'Abdu-llah Muhammad*, surnamed the Malay (الجاوي).

No. 49 (4to. of 56 pages).[3] A poem the title of which is uncertain. It contains the celebration of a king of *Bintan*, and the splendour of his palace, garden, etc. The first verses are :

الحمد لله فوج يغ سدي     بك الله توهن يغ كاي
بركة محمد سيد الانبيا     برتمبه دولة راج يغ ملي
دولة مكت تله سجهترا     د فرنتهكن فادك ادند سودار
عارف باالله تاجم بچار     امفام شمس منراغي نگار
كامل فرنته سلطان مود     ممرنتهكن كرجأن فادك ككند

The last verses are :

برغكتله كدو ماكت عالم     مغارق فترا ماسق كدالم
دايرغكن نصب وزير الاعظم     مغنتركن فترا دار السلام
سجهتراله فكرجاءن دلي ماكت     دولة استعادة ددالم كوت
دڠن انگرا توهن سمست     سوات فون جاڠن مار سغكيت
سلسيله فترا دلي سمفاين     كلورله هداڠن برللاين
برفوله سمبرف برددااين     ممبري ايافن هلبالڠ سكلين
تمتله قصه دلي يغ غنا     دكارڠ فقير همب يغ هين

[1] It goes also by the name of حكاية بردان سلامة according to de Hollander, l. l p. 315.

[2] Another commentary on the same work is called, اتحاف المريد شرح علي جوهرة التوحيد .

[3] The lettering on the back of the cover (*Karangan Bantan*) is wrong. Dulaurier infers from it, that it is about the foundation of Bantam.

دمتري ددالم قرطاس چين سجقن[1] لارت باپق تأ كنا
تمتله رنچان دلي ماكت دكارغ ضعيف همب كنست
جكك اد سجق[1] يغ لت برباپق امفن دلي ماكت

No. 50 (small 4to. of 96 pages) contains the حكاية تميم الداري *i.e.* the adventures of *Tămīmu-ddāri*, an inhabitant of *Madīnah*, and originally a Christian. It is taken from the تاريخ الحجرات . He was carried off when bathing during the night, which the prophet had prohibited, by a spirit (*jīn*) to the country of the genii, that were yet infidels, and stayed there seven years and four months. He meets in the course of his rambles with the Antichrist (دجّال), appearing in the form of a bitch big with barking puppies, and becoming large when hearing bad reports about the Muslims, and small when they are favourable; with female cannibals on a certain island, with the angels *Jabarāil* and *Mikāil*, and the prophet *Hilir* (حضر), who gives an explanation of the wonderful things Tamīm sees and cannot account for. He meets a bird, too, which gives him a delicious beverage out of its bill, and is no other than the bird of *Ishāk*, and leads the erring faithful upon the right way. He sees a man filling out of a pond a pierced tub, being an usurer. On his return to this sub-lunary orb, he finds his wife re-married, and squabbles with her husband. '*Umar* (عمر) could not settle the quarrel, as *Tămīm*, not having shaved and pared his nails during his absence, looked quite another man, and was not recognised. '*Alī* (علی) then recollects a communication from the prophet about a sign by which *Tămīm* could be identified, being a whitish spot as large as a *dărham* behind the knee.

No. 51. See under No. 19.

No. 52 (4to. of 140 pages) contains the حكاية راج باب . In the opening a king of *Gunung bărapi Rantow panjang tăbing bărukir* is introduced, called طاهير شاه ڤري . He had forty wives, one of whom only, called *Indăra Sori*, became pregnant. Sending away the other thirty-nine on account of

[1] The Arabic سجع .

their sterility, he was cursed by them to have a hog as a son. After a pregnancy of seven years the queen was delivered of a boar of a terrifying appearance, with tusks as yellow as a ripe plantain fruit.[1] The king ordered his minister to throw his son into the woods, where the young hog conquered the king of the hogs, being assisted by a princess who was doing penance on the field of their contest. Having been victorious, he was bathed by that princess, and treated in her residence as her son After taking leave of her, he is carried away by a *jïn*, etc. This composition is replete with *pantuns*, and the text is not much corrupted. The language is genuine Malay as far as I have read it. After a great many adventures, the hero returns in a human shape to his father's residence, and is then called *Indăra Bărma Kala.*

No. 53 (small 4to.) contains:

I. (98 pages)[2] the حكاية سمسكين[3]. It has been published at Singapore (lithographed). There are a great many manuscripts of this tale. The one in my possession is badly mutilated by a Batavian transcriber, who has, for instance, changed سمايم into سمبهبغ!

II. (26 pages) شعرايكن. It commences with exhortations to children, and is a miserable jingling of rhymes about a great many fishes, introduced in it as would-be poets. The composition may be serviceable in correcting the existing Malay Dictionaries in the wrong pronunciation of fish-names. I possess a manuscript of it.

No. 54 (small 4to. of 293 pages) contains the حكاية احمد بسنو. In the commencement there is a kind of summary, relating that the hero was harmed by a genius called طبرسقتي, that on his rambles he came upon Mount *Langkări Rătna*, where he saw two princes of the genii, that he encountered the princesses *Săkanda Kumála Indăra* and *Bumáya Indăra*, fought the king *Makuta Indăra* on account of the first-named princess, and was thrown by order of that prince into

[1] باب تغڠل ترلال هيبة رفاڽ تارڠڽ كونڠ سفرت فيسڠ ماسق

[2] The lettering *Angkasa Dewa* is a mistake owing to the tale commencing with these words.

[3] *Si-miskin* ("the poor one").

the lake *Indăra Sătunang,* where he was swallowed up by a serpent, in whose belly he met the princess *Băranta Maya*; and a great many other adventures of the same kind are told. The hero was the son of *Sahfar Tsaf Indăra,*[1] king of *Burangga Dewa.* In one of the chapters طبرسقتي is said to be king of a state situated in the cavern of Mount *Dewa Rangga Indăra.*

No. 55. See under No. 9.

No. 56 (4to. of 412 pages; on the cover, *Badiulzaman Anak Hamzah*). In the commencement are contained the adventures of بديع الزمان, said to be the son of *Hamzah*;[2] then follow those of his father, and of *'Umar Maya,* with whose death it closes. Perhaps it is but a part of the حكاية حمزه .

No. 57 (4to. of 332 pages) contains the حكاية اندرا كياغن . *Mangindăra Chuwácha,* king of *Indăra Părchangga,* had two sons called *Raja Sháh Johan Mangindăra Rupa* and *Raja Thahir*[3] *Johan Shah.* The king having dreamt of a wonderful musical instrument, which sounded one hundred and ninety times when but once struck, and longing to have it, the two young princes go in quest of it. They are adopted by a ghost, of the name of راج سلم, who tells them where to find the wonderful instrument. He changes their names, calling the eldest prince *Indăra Mahádewa Săqti,* and the youngest *Bisnu Dewa Kaindàra-an,* surnamed *Indăra Lăqsana.* The brothers are separated afterwards, each of them achieving a great many stirring feats by the assistance of the *jin,* their adoptive father. Extracts from this composition are to be found in Marsden's Malay Reader at the end of his Grammar, according to a manuscript but slightly differing from this one, of which the lettering on the back of its cover, *Indra layang-*

[1] سحفر صف اندرا.

[2] Of the حكاية حمزه de Hollander in his Reader (p. 82 sqq.) has published extracts; and another extract is to be found in Roorda van Eysinga's Beknopte Maleische Spraakkunst (Breda, 1839), p. 102 sqq.

[3] طاهر

*an*, is a mistake for *Indăra Kiyángan*, as the extracts published by Marsden have it.

No. 58 (small 4to.) contains :

I. See under No. 31.

II. (34 pages). حكاية فتري جوهر مانكم, which is a more elaborate version of this tale than that published by de Hollander (Breda, 1845), and corresponds more with that of the manuscript from which quotations are found in Roorda van Eysinga's Maleisch-Nederduitsch Woordenboek (s. vv. *harām, hajī, chiyum, churi, khiyanat, khemah, durah, dapat, d'akap, dandam, diri, ridlā, rambut, zadah, salăsey, sălam, sanăschaya, surat, sayid, sisi, shetan, tsahib, pandey*, and *sahâya*). In this manuscript the heroine's brother is called منب شاهد. There was; and perhaps still is, also a MS. copy of this tale in the possession of Mr. Frederick Muller, at Amsterdam. On the west coast of Sumatra the heroine goes by the name of *Johor Malègan*, which name occurs in Bahruuddīn's list too. Of the Sumatra version[1] I possess an incomplete copy.

No. 59. See under No. 38.

No. 60 (small 4to. of 106 pages) contains the حكاية شاه مردان.[2] Another copy is No. 66 (small 4to. of 223 pages). The hero assuming in the course of his rambles the name of *Indăra Jaya*, this very popular tale goes also by the name of حكايه اندرا جاي. Part of it has been published by de Hollander in the first edition of his Handleiding bij de beoefening der Maleische Taal-en Letterkunde, p. ١٦٧-١٩٦. It is also called after the hero's father, حكاية[3] بكرم دتي راج. It is mentioned by Leyden (Asiatic Res. x.) under the title *Hikayat*

[1] About a Javanese version, see Raffles' History of Java, i., p. 394 sqq.

[2] The Persian pronunciation, *shâ-i mărdân* has occasioned the name شيخ مردان cited by van Hoëvell in the annotations to the Sair Bidasari. On the west coast of Sumatra شاه عالم is pronounced *sa-i alam;* hence confusion in the title of the dwarf deer between *shā-i 'ālam di rimba* and *shaykh 'ālam di rimba.*

[3] *Wikramāditya.* No. 60 and the extracts in de Hollander's Handleiding, Ll., have بكرم دنت جاي.

*Bikermadi(tya)*. A translated extract about the creation of the world is to be found in No. 60 of the Indo-Chinese Gleaner. A copy, too, is found in a volume, containing the *Hikayat Pălanduk Jănaka*, belonging to the library of the India Office (No 2673?). I possess a manuscript copy of it of 38 pages folio.

No. 61 (small 4to. of 150 pages) contains the حكاية شمس البر (*shamsu-lbarrin*). The hero, called "the sun of the earth,"[1] is the son of *Dărma Dikára*, king of *Paruwa Chakăra Nagara* in Hindustan. His name he owes to his being predestined to be a powerful king, ruling over the earth and sea, whence he was surnamed "the moon of the sea."[2] When twelve years old he was carried off by an infidel *jin*, in consequence of which he had a great many adventures before he returned home. On his return he succeeds his father with the title of Sultan *Qamru-lbahrin*.

No. 62 (quarto) contains:

I. See under No. 16

II. See under No. 49 III.

III. (about 60 pages) سريب مسايل. It contains one thousand questions put to Muhammad by a learned Jew of the Khaybar tribe. Having been answered by the prophet satisfactorily, a great many Jews of the said tribe embrace the Islām. It is translated from the Persian. A manuscript of this composition (small 4to. of 156 pages) I saw at Barus in the possession of the Tuwanku of *Sigambo-gambo*. A copy is also in the possession of Prof. H. C. Millies at Utrecht. It is a very interesting work, and reproduces the popular belief of the Malays about a great many questions of the Muhammadan faith. The orthodox priests condemn it as well as the حكاية محمد حنفية.

IV. (8 pages) جرترا نبي الله موسي مناجة د بوكت طورسين. Moses' ascent on Mount Sinai.

V. (5 pages) حكاية فاطمه كاون is a tract about the duties of a married woman, expounded by the prophet to his daughter.

[1] The manuscript explains the Arabic name by *artiña matahari di darat.*

[2] قمر البحر explained by *bulan yang dităpi láut.*

A copy of it is in the possession of Prof. H. C. Millies at Utrecht.

VI. (6 pages) حكاية رسول الله برچوكر. The prophet is shaved by Gabriel, and his hair gathered by the celestial nymphs for the purpose of making amulets of them. Published at Batavia (1853, in 12mo. Lange and Co.)

No. 63 (4to. of 349 pages; on the cover, *Raja 'adil*). It contains the حكاية بختيار.[1] The wrong lettering is owing to the commencement, where a just king (*Raja 'ādil*) whose name is not mentioned, is forced to flee from his dominions, and is afterwards made captive by an unjust king. This MS. however, contains another version than that from which de Hollander has given extracts in his Reader (p. 131 sqq.) and transliterated in his Handleiding tot de Kennis der Maleische Taal (Breda, 1845). The name of the person who found the child of which the queen was delivered during her flight with her consort, and which she was forced to leave, is here رسدس. The last tale in this manuscript is the story of Salomon and the queen of Sabā.[2] The text is pretty good, but occasionally corrupted. The introduction especially differs widely from that of other versions I know. I possess a copy (folio of 50 pages), wherein the number of tales told by *Bakhtiyār* amounts to nine. Its version differs from that of de Hollander's text. This tale goes also by the name of حكاية زاده بخت, حكاية ازباخ (from the name of the hero's father), and according to de Hollander, also حكاية غلام, which last name is by far not so popular, and does not convey an idea about its contents.

No. 64. See under No. 42.

No. 65 (small 4to. of 152 pages) contains the شعراغريني, a poem the plot of which is taken from the Javanese. It belongs to the *Panji* tales[3] relating the adventures of

[1] The Persian original was translated by Lescalier (*Bakhtiyar*, ou le Favori de la Fortune, Paris, 1805).

[2] Of this story there is an elaborate novel on the west coast of Sumatra, where it is called حكاية فتري بلقس. I possess three manuscripts of it, all written in the Menangkabow dialect.

[3] Other tales belonging to this cyclus, and not existing in this collection are—1.

*Panji* and *Angăreni*, daughter of the *patih*, with whom he fell in love after having been betrothed to *Sĕkar Taji*, the princess of *Kădiri*. His father ordered *Angăreni* to be killed when *Panji* was absent, having gone in quest of game.[1] This composition proves to be the story which has suggested the plot of the شعركن تمبوهن (see under No. 7). This manuscript breaks off abruptly, and is to such an extent replete with Javanese words, that a Malay would not understand it.

No. 66. See under No. 60.

No. 67. حكايه راج٢ فاسي. Published by Dulaurier in his Chroniques Malayes. A list of countries dependent on Majapahit, found in this manuscript, is published by the same in the Journal Asiatique for 1846.

No. 68. See under No. 18.

No. 69 (small 4to. of 128 pages). According to the lettering on the back of the cover, the title would be باب العقل كفد سگل اورغ بسر٢. It is an ethic work, laying down rules for ministers and great functionaries as to their conduct when officiating. It is illustrated by tales. In the commencement the manuscript says, that the tale came from Sultan *Aliyu-ddīn Shāh*, son of *Mantsūr Shāh*, king of *Pătani*. On page 10 there is a story about the sagacity of the dwarf-deer

حكاية فنج جاييغ كسوم (*jayeng kăsuma* is Javanese and means "victorious on the battle field," and is often changed in Malay into *Jaya Kăsuma*), from which quotations are to be found in van Hoëvell's annotations (p. 301, 326, 334, 362, 363, and 374). II. حكاية فنج سميرغ سمرنتاك (after an assumed name of *Chandărakirana*, when dressing as a male, and roving about to subject the states she came upon). III. حكاية ميس تندرامن (No. 2602, India Office). IV. حكاية سير فنج چترا (?) IV. حكاية چارغ ميس گمبرسار يغ برگلر رات انوم اغ ملاي. V. حكاية سبر فنج لاركسوم (see under No. 40. VI. (see II. under No 7). VII. حكاية جاي لغكار (a translation of which into Mangkasar is to be found in Mathes's *Makassaarsche Chresthomathie*). There are more tales belonging to this cyclus, as may be inferred from some manuscripts in the British Museum.

[1] The plot does not differ materially from that of the tale of which Mr. Taco Roorda has given an elaborate analysis (see *Lotgevallen van Raden Pandji* in the Bijdragen tot de Taal-Land en Volkenkunde van N.I. Vol. vii. Nieuwe Volgreeks). Compare also Raffles, History of Java, ii., 88.

(*pălanduk*[1]) settling a contest between an alligator and a young man about the propriety of the alligator eating the young man, who had delivered it when about to die on the dry. The last tale is about a Sultan *Al-'ālam Shāh.*

No. 70 (small 4to.) contains:

I. (186 pages). The seventh book of the بستان العارفين, an ethic work illustrated by a great many tales. According to the last words of this manuscript, the whole work is divided into seven books. On p. 163 the narrative about *Siti 'Abasah* (see No. 76) is found.

II. (8 pages). A small collection of tales,[2] belonging most probably to a larger composition (to I. ?). The first tale is about Moses and *Qārūn,* who bribed a pregnant woman to say, that Moses had committed adultery with her. The second is about a certain بلهم trying to outstrip Moses by the force of his penance. The third is about Moses' death. The fourth is about a woman called ربيعة العدوية getting ten-fold back what she had given to the poor. The fifth is about a man of the name of دانن مسر seeing the mercy of God to the just.

No. 71. See under No. 38.

No. 72 (small 4to. of 44 pages; on the back of the cover, *Kitab rasul*). It contains the حكاية مهاراج علي, another version of the *Story of King Skull*[3] (حكاية راج جمجمة), the plot being the same as that of the حكاية بسف وراج.[4] There are a great many copies of this tale. Prof. H. C. Millies at

[1] The حكاية فلندق جناك, two copies of which are in the Library of the India Office (Nos. 3049 and 2603), has a great similarity with the European tale about Reinard the fox. (See Kort Verslag der Maleische Handschriften van het E. I. House te London). The *pălanduk* acts in the Indian Archipelago the part that the fox acts with us.

[2] Such small collections of tales, the title of which is either arbitrary, or not to be fixed from the contents, are often found in the possession of the poor, who cannot afford to buy manuscripts of the extent of the *Bustānu-ssalāthīn, Taju-ssalāthīn,* and the like. A collection of the same kind is the حكاية ليم فصل in No. 2603 (Library of the India Office).

[3] Translated Asiatic Journal, 1823.

[4] Edited by Fraissinet under the title of *Geschiedenis van Vorst Bispoe Radja* (Breda, 1849).

Utrecht, possesses a copy (small 8vo.) bearing the title حكاية علي پادشاه (the Persian *p* is here strange). Of the story of King Skull there is a copy in the India Office, being the third tale in the حكاية ليم فصل (No. 2603). I myself possess two copies of it (one evidently mutilated by a Batavian transcriber).

No. 73. See No. 4.

No. 74 (small 4to.) contains:

I. Laws of Malaka, Johor, and Salangor.

II. (11 pages). See IV. of No. 33.

III. (1 page). Receipts, commencing with that against a kind of leprosy.

IV. (10 pages). See V. of No. 33.

V. (8 pages). See VI. of No. 33.

VI. Fragments of a religious work. On the last pages are found coloured tables representing the *five ominous times* (belonging to V.)

No. 75 (small 4to.; on the cover, *undang undang*) contains:

I. (6 pages). A fragment from a law book. The first chapter is about people having plantations and neglecting to fence them.

II. A fragment from some work on Muhammadan law, commencing with the rules about selling and buying (بيع), and ending with the law of inheritance (فرائض).

III. (2 pages). A fragment from an Arabic work on law with Malay interlinear translation.

IV. (15 pages). An Arabic-Malay Dictionary. Under each Arabic word the corresponding Malay is written. The last seven pages are not filled up with the Malay. I possess a complete copy, and a fragment of another work of the same kind.

No. 76 (small 4to.) contains:

I. See under No. 18.

II. (9 pages). حكاية ستي عباسه. It is properly but a tale taken from the بستان العارفين (I. No. 70), but often found separately. Two copies are in my possession (small 4to. of 20 pages, and small 8vo. of 24 pages).

III. (23 pages). A fragment from a work on religious observances, commencing with the sacrifices (قربان).

IV. (small 8vo. of 13 pages). Fragments of a work containing Malay laws, and commencing with goods found on the road.

No. 77 (small 4to.) contains:

I. (4 pages). شعر فيفت دان اڠڬڠ .

II. (61 pages). Maritime laws.

III. (20 pages). Orders issued by Sultan *Ahmad Tāju-ddīn Halīm Shāh* of *Kădah* (قدح), some of which refer to the suppression of piracy (Muh. year 1133).

No. 78 (small 4to.) contains:

I. (62 pages) شعر فرڠ اڠڬرس د بتاوي . A poem, celebrating the conquest of Java by the English forces under Lord Minto. The first words are:

دڠرکن تون سوات القصه  جندرل مسکالق[1] امفوڽ ماس
تتکل بڬند بربوت جاس  د مستير كورنيلس[2] ساڠت فرقس
بربوت بنتڠ د مستير كرنيلس  برهمفنله كونن سكلين فرنچس

It closes with the description of a market, and teems with Batavian Malay words.

II. (2 pages) شعر چنت براه . A short love-letter[3] in verses, of which the following lines may serve as a specimen:

ككند ملايڠكن قرطاس سچارق  دتربڠكن اڠن ريحان العاشق
ڬنت فرتمون يڠ امت باٸك  كفد ادند وجه يڠ تحقيق

[1] The Dutch *Maarschalk* (Marshal).

[2] *Meester Cornelis* is the name of a district of Batavia, where there are barracks.

[3] In No. 2609 (India Office) there is a love-letter, the title of which is yet to be ascertained. Its commencing verses are:

سلام دعا در فد ككند  يڠ دفلهراكن الله تعالي
داتڠ كفد تون ادند  بدن يڠ سوچ سدي ترعالي
ايو هي امس مانس شهدا  تمباهن فولق ادند يڠ ملي
تله ترمذكور ددالم داد  اورڠ يڠ عارف مندافتكن دي

It contains 18 pages.

No. 79 (small 4to.) contains:

I. (46 pages) the laudatory terms Malay letters commence with, varying according to the rank of the person addressed. Thc specimens given here are nearly all in Arabic (continued in III.)

II. (7 pages). Fragments of a Muhammadan law work containing the fines to be paid for wounds inflicted. The مثقال is here explained by انم كوفغ امس فوته نكري قده يائت تيك سوك ريل. Each of the Arabic law terms is explained by a Malay phrase written under it, and containing the amount of the fine; an example will suffice:

سمحاق (wound touching the pericranium) is explained by:

لوك فوتس داڠغ لال سمفي فد سلافت تولغ امفت مثقال هركان
امفت ايكر انت

III. (49 pages) continuation of I. It closes with the model of a letter to the Dutch Governor-General and the Dutch India counsellors (Raden van Indie). I. and III. are consequently fragments from the *kitāb tarāsul,* a book in which precepts are laid down how to write letters.

IV. (7 pages) رسالة شفاء القلوب (a figurative title, "the physic of hearts"). The author calls himself *Nūru-ddīn Ibn 'Alī Ibn Hasanjī Ibn Muhammad Hamīdi.*[2] This is a treatise about the sense to be attached to the word شهادة. He composed it, he says, in order to combat those that entertain wrong opinions about the nature of God.

V. (8 pages). A tract, the title of which I could not ascertain without reading it through. It begins with stating the best time for building a house, and contracting a marriage, and closes with a recommendation of forbearance towards a slave, even when guilty. It is addressed to 'Ali (علي), each article ending with يا علي.

VI. (2 pages). Questions and answers about the sense of سقشي (testimony), perhaps belonging to IV.

[1] حسنجي. [2] حميدي (See about this author Note 1, p. 47.)

VII. (9 pages). رسالة فد ميتاكن صفة دو فوله. A tract on the qualities of God.

VIII. (34 pages). محمدة الاعتقاد.[1] This treatise is divided into two introductory chapters (مقدم), four books (باب), and one concluding chapter (خاتم).

The first introductory chapter: فد ميتاكن اعتقاد اكن عالم دان الله سبحانه و تعالي.

The second introductory chapter: فد ميتاكن اكم.

The first book: فد ميتاكن ايمان دان سكلين ركنن.

The second book: فد ميتاكن اسلام دان سكل ركنن.

The third book: فد ميتاكن توحيد.

The fourth book: فد ميتاكن معرفة.

IX. (15 pages). Arabic fragment from a commentary on the Qur'an, with Malay translation.

No. 80. See under No. 18.

## *B.*—Farquhar Collection.[2]

No. 1 (small 4to. of 51 pages; within, *Cherita Sultan Iskander*). It contains a pretty good copy of the انڠدڠ٢ راج ملاك commencing with what is reserved for the sovereign. The seventeenth chapter is about people going to hunt.

No. 2 (small 4to. of 202 pages; imperfect at the end). It contains the حكاية راج اسكندر ذو القرنين. The last pages give the history of the defeat by Alexander of a king who was a worshipper of the sun. A small extract from this tale is to be found in Roorda van Eysinga's Malay Reader at the end of his Beknopte Maleische Spraakkunst (Breda, 1839), p. 120-123; and innumerable quotations from it are to be found in Werndly's Maleische Spraakkunst, and in Roorda van

[1] It is translated by ارتمن فوهن اعتقاد. A note by a transcriber calls the author شيخ نور الدين (the same as the author of IV. ?).

[2] The manuscripts of this collection were not numbered. I have put numbers on them in accordance with the list Dulaurier gave of them, with the exception of two volumes he did not examine.

Eysinga's Mal. Nederduitsch Woordenboek; some also in van Hoëvell's aant. op de Sair Bidasari.

No. 3 (small 4to. of 175 pages) شعر كمفني ولند برفرڠ دڠن چين, relating the war of the Dutch Company with the Chinese, and the well-known murder of the Chinamen of Batavia under Valkenier. It is translated from the Javanese.

No. 4 (small 4to. of 80 pages) عادة سڬل راج٢ ملايو. This interesting work was composed at the request of the Señor Gornador دبرين at Malaka in the Muhammadan year 1193. It is an account of Malay observances during the pregnancy of the wives of chiefs, the birth of their children, etc. After the introduction it continues thus: القصه فري مپتاكن عادة سڬل راج٢ ملايو يڠ فرب كال راج يڠ بسر٢ تتكال استري بڬند ايت حامل سمفي توجه بولن لماڽ مك دفڠڬل بيدن اوله بڬند. On p. 71 there is an elaborate description of the bier of a king.

No. 5. See No. 18 of the Raffles Collection.

No. 6 (small 8vo.) contains:

I. (17 pages). An erotic poem, the title of which I could not ascertain. The first verses are:

دڠركن تون سوات رنچان    فقير مڠارڠ سوات بين
اوصل يڠ مانس مود ترون    لاڠ جوهري بجقسان

And the last:

دڠ ساجي دودق مپوج    منكت اون تيڠ لافس
افاته داي دڠن بود    قلمن فاته قرطاسن هابس

II. (14 pages). A love-letter in verses. The last verses are literally the same as those on the two last pages of II. of No. 9, commencing with

تون سولت سيا لراڠن    سامله سام ممبله دير
فاته فارڠ لاوت تموُدان    اورڠ مموكت بتورس باتڠ
سمفي سكارڠ دراسق دندم    كاسه ترايكت بنچان داتڠ
تتف بوله فاڬركن دليم    دڠ جوده ددالم فون
متهار توجه بولن ليم    باروله سده دڠن مو تون

The last verses are

اغڠرس لاوت ملاك      كناله ريبت دتنجڠ تون

تاجمله كرس هلت سنجات      هندق مربت ڤاو تون

III. (11 pages). The same as I. of No. 9.

IV. (27 pages). According to the end the title is شعر فنتن. The beginning verses are literally the same as those of II. of No. 9.

V. (23 pages). A poem without title, commencing:

كود د اون بردنديڠن      باڠي كن فوتس راس تلين

مود بڠساون برتنتاڠن      باڠيكن فوتس راس هتين

The last words are:

انچئ علي فرڠي كبڠك      سارت برموت لاد سبيج

هاره سكال تيدق كسڠك      ݢاجه دتلن سِنُولر ليد

No. 6* (small 4to.) contains:

I. (14 pages). The same as I. of No. 6.

II. (19 pages). A love-letter in verses. The last verses are:

مرفات برتلر ليم      برتكرُ دياتس تنجڠ بالي

منجاد بسي افاله كيت      هندق د تمف توكڠ يڠ فندي

توكڠ برنام نخود براهيم      فافن فنتو لب برڬنتڠ

چيت تيدق فد يڠ لائن      كفد تون تمفت برڬنتڠ

بهاۑت كتاڠن در فساڠن      لنتڠكن باتڠ تيڠك دفا

فسن فتري در كياڠن      اين سكارڠ هندق برجمفا

No. 7 (small 8vo. of 55 pages). According to the end the title should be شعر جوهن انق راج فيرق. It is a tragic love-story, as the hero dies.[1]

[1] On page 45 we find:

ملك الموت داتڠ در حضرة      منجنجڠكن فرمان ترلال برت

جوهن سڠرا لال له معرت      كمبال فولڠ كنڠري اخرة

معرت (frequent spelling of the Ar. معراج) *merat*, is in poetry used for *to die.*

No. 7* (small 8vo. of 55 pages). Another copy of No. 7.

No. 8 (small 4to. of 175 pages, imperfect at the end; within: Presented by Colonel W. M. G. Colebrooke, 6th July, 1832), contains the بداية الهداية.[1] The Malay author calls himself *Muhammad sayn*,[2] son of *Jalālu-ddīn*, an Achinese of the Shafi-'i sect. A quotation from this composition is to be found in van Hoëvell's annotations on the Sair Bidasari, p. 378, where he cites p. 983 of the manuscript. The author of this work says, that he took the subject from the ام البراهين of *Abu 'Abdillah Muhammad ben Yusuf Assanūsī Alhasanī.*

No. 9 (small 4to.) contains:

I. (17 pages) شعر بوڠ . A poem where flowers are introduced singing *pantuns*, in this way:

مول برمدح كنتم دليم    وجهڽ سفرت بولن فرنام
لقسان ديوي نيلا اوتام[3]    سكلين عالم تياد اكن سام
دليم د سورباي    بغان جاته كدالم كولم
تياد كسيهن ممندڠ سهيا    دودق برچنت سبڠ دان مالم
مپهوتي مدح بوڠ فندن    منتڠ درجا ترلال حبران

II. (7 pages). A collection of *pantuns*, commencing with:

نخود راكم رقنا سولي    بوڠ تنجڠ دياتس كوت
راج مأنكم انتن بدوري    د جنجڠ بائك جاد مأكت

(See No. 6, II.)

No. 10 (small 4to. of 53 pages). اندڠ٢ راج ملاك وقتو اي كرجاءن ددالم نڬري ملاك هڠڬ سمفي كنڬري جوهر . This work deserves being published; its language is pure, and the text, as far as I have examined it, not mutilated.

[1] Also mentioned in Bahru-ddīn's list.

[2] He is the author also of a Malay work called كشف الكرام في بيان النية عند تكبيرة الاحرام (a copy of which I saw at Batavia, small 4to. of about 30 pages).

[3] *Nila-utáma*, name of a celestial nymph (Tobasche Spraakkunst, § 30, VII. *b*).

## Note 1.

### *About the Author of* IV. *of No.* 79 (*Raffles Collection*).

The author, who calls himself also الرانيري, from *Ranīr* the place where he lived (مسكنا), composed, besides the بستان السلاطين (No. 17), also the following works:

I. (No. 39, large 4to. India Office at Batavia) درة الفرائد بشرح العقائد يائت منيار يڠ تركارڠ فد مپتاكن سڬل اعتقاد .

II. (No. 3, small 4to. India Office at Batavia) هدية الحبيب في ترغيب والترهيب يائيت هلون اكن نبي محمد صلي الله عليه وسلم فد مپتاكن سڬل عمل كبجيكن دان منجاؤهي درفد سڬل عمل كجهاتن .

III. (No. 24, Library of the India Office at Batavia) اسرار الانسان في معرفة الروح والرحمن, commenced under *Iskandar II. ʻAlā uddīn,* and finished under the queen *Tāju-l'ʻālam T'safiyatu-ddīn.*

IV. (No. 14, Library of the India Office at Batavia) جواهر العلوم في كشف المعلوم .

V. فتح المبين علي الملحدين ارتين كمفاڠن يڠ امت پات اتس سڬل ملحد, composed by order of Sultan *Muqul Mar̉āyat Shāh,*[1] against the tenets of the Pantheistical sect, the followers of which were put to death by the said king of Achih, their books being burnt before the mosque *Beytu-rrahman.* I saw a copy of this work at Barus (small 4to. of 40 pages), from which I took this notice.

VI. نبذة في دعوي الظل مع صاحبه ارتين رسالة فد مپتاكن دعوي بايڠ٢ دڠن يڠ امفون دي, a refutation of *Shamsu-ddīn's* heretical tenets. (cf. VII.)

VII. تبيان في معرفة الاديان فكانه ماء الزلال علي قلب الضمان الي

[1] مقل مغاية شاه .

الطريق الرحمن ارتبن ميتاكن سيڬل اكم مك ادله سؤله٢ اير يڠ امت سجق مموسكن هات يڠ دهاڬ كفد جالن توهن يڠ برنام رحمن, composed under queen *Tāju-l-'ālam Tsafiyatu-ddīn Shāh*,[1] daughter of Sultan *Iskandar Muda Johan bàrdowlat*, son of Sultan *'Alā u-ddīn 'Alī Ri-'āyat Shāh*, son of Sultan *Farmān Shāh*, son of Sultan *Mutlafar*[2] *Shāh*, son of Sultan *'Ināyat Shāh*. It is divided into two books, the first giving an account of the religions from Adam till Muhammad, and the second summing up the heterodox tenets of several Muhammadan sects. The purpose of the author was to combat the opinions of *Shamsuddīn* of *Pasey*[3] and his followers. A copy in small 4to. (of 72 pages) is in my possession.

VIII. ماء الحياة لاهل الممات. A fragment of this work is found in a manuscript belonging to the Batavian Society (No. 55 ?).

IX. حُجّة الصديق لدفع الزنديق. A copy of this work exists in the Library of the Batavian Society (No. ?).

Most of these works are directed against the popular writings of *Hamzah* of *Barus*,[4] and the above-named *Shamsu-ddīn* of *Pasey*. The works of *Hamzah* are, as far as I know:

I. اسرار العارفين. I saw a copy of this at Barus (small 8vo. of 24 pages). I read only the preface, which says, that it is an abridgement of a greater work of the same name and by the same author; and that there are three works of this name, the two already mentioned, the large and the abridged one, and one treating on عشق, عاشق and معشوق. This is all I could read, as the owner would not lend it me even for a day.

[1] تاج العالم صفية الدين شاه. [2] مظفر.

[3] الشمطرائي as the Arabic introduction has. *Shamaṭarā* is an Arabic corruption of *Samudăra*, the ancient name of *Pasey*, which occasioned the whole island to be called by the Portuguese, who sailed with Arabic pilots, *Sumatra*, a name with which natives, not used to mix with Europeans, are not acquainted.

[4] الفنصوري *Fantsur* being the ancient name of Barus; hence the Barus camphor (كافر بارس) is called in Arabic كافور الفنصوري.

II. شعر سبورغ فيغي , an allegorical poem,[1] wherein the soul of man is spoken of as that of a bird (*kalow tărbang siburung pingey, 'alāmat badan di makan ulat*, if the pingey flies away, it is a sign that the body will be eaten by the worms).

III. شعر فراه. An allegorical poem, wherein mankind is spoken of as a vessel tossing about on the waves. A small fragment is in my possession.

IV. شعر سيدغ فقير . A copy is in my possession (small 4to. of 14 pages). It is also an allegorical poem, speaking of mankind as forlorn and indigent.

V. كشف السر التجلي السبحاني, a short exposition of God's nature, qualities, and works. Werndly knew it (see his Boekzaal, p. 354). It is quoted in the second book of the *Tabyān* (see above, p. 47, VII.) as a book deserving to be burnt.[2]

VI. كتاب منتهي فد مراجناكن سبد نبي . It is mentioned in the *Tabyān*, and seems to be an exposition of the sayings of the prophet.

VII. شعر داكغ. A fragment is in my possession. It has the same tendency as No. III.

The works of *Shamsu-ddīn*[3] of *Pasey* are:

I. مرأة المحققين كتاب فري نسبة ارتين بغس مخلوق دغن حق تعالي. It is cited in the second book of the *Tabyān*. A badly mutilated copy is in the Leyden University Library (No. 1332). The Sultan in whose reign it was composed is there only called مرحوم ماكت .

[1] The poems of Hamzah were yet much read in Valentyn's time, but that he was a native of Barus that author did not know (see Beschrijving van Sumatra, p. 21).

[2] The other books, the author of the *Tabyān* speaks of in this way are the مرأة المحقق, the حرقة, the حق اليقين, the ديرة الوجود, the سر لربوبيه and the سر الانوار.

[3] He calls himself sometimes ابن عبدالله . He seems to have lived at *Achih* (Ar. اشية). A namesake of his is شمس الدين الحاذق محمد ابن فضل الله and is cited as the author of a تحفة المرسلة.

II. شرح رباعي حمزة الفنصوري . I saw at Padang a copy (8vo. of 16 pages), but the owner would not part with it. It is a commentary on the anything but transparent poems of *Hamzah* of *Barus*.

III. مرآة المؤمن. Werndly (Maleische Boekzaal) knew it, and says of it, that it is divided into 211 questions and answers, explaining the principal religious terms. In the preface to his Grammar a small quotation from this work is given.

### Note 2.

*The Manuscripts of the India Office Not Mentioned in my "Kort Verslag der Maleische Handschriften van het E. I. House te Londen."*

1. حكاية مهاراج بوم . (See No. 15 of the Raffles Collection.)

2. Another copy of the حكاية فرغ فنداو جاي. (See No. 2 of the Raffles Collection.)

3. سمرقندي (17 pages in No. 2906,[1] 4to.). Arabic with an interlinear Malay translation. It contains the first precepts of the Islām in questions and answers. The commencement is: "If people enquire of you: what is the *imān*? the answer is: I believe in God, etc." The author is ابو الليث محمد ابن ابي نصر ابن ابراهيم, surnamed of *Samarqand* (السمرقندي). This little book goes universally by the name of *Samarqandī*. Copies with an interlinear Javanese translation[2] are numerous in the west of Java. A commentary on it (شرح على السمرقندي) is in the Library of the Batavian Society (No. 29); it has an interlinear Javanese translation. Two

[1] The other 51 pages of this volume contain, 1. the several positions of the body when praying; 2. the application of the five letters of الحمد to the five obligatory prayers; 3. the formulas of prayers for the dead; and 4. on marriage (حكم نكاح).

[2] A copy is in the Library of the Batavian Society (No. 26).

copies in Sundanese are in my possession, one of which is in the Arabic character.

4. (No. 2672, folio) contains:

I. (133 pages). Another copy of the شعرجارن تماس. It is of the same version as the other manuscript (No. 2610).

II. (127 pages). Another copy of the حكاية بودق مسكين (or حكاية فارغ فوتغ so called after a miraculous chopping-knife, the hero was possessed of). It seems to belong to the same recension as No. 2877.[1]

AMSTERDAM, *November* 25, 1865.

[1] There may be other Malay manuscripts in the Library of the India Office which I have overlooked, the Persian, Arabic, and Malay manuscripts being mingled together. I am in hopes the deficiencies in this notice may be filled up by other scholars, who will also call attention to the many valuable Malay manuscripts in the Libraries of London. A new Malay Chrestomathy is urgently needed at the present time, as those published by Marsden, Meursinge, and de Hollander, are anything but trustworthy, each of the texts they contain having been taken from a single manuscript only. It is only by a careful comparison of many that a text can be furnished which may be depended upon by persons desirous of obtaining an adequate idea of the grammatical structure of the Malay language, and reluctant to trust the assertions of those who pretend that Malay is devoid of grammar.

ART. V.—*Brief Prefatory Remarks to the Translation of the Amitâbha Sûtra from Chinese.* By the Rev. S. BEAL, Chaplain R. N.

[Read 6th February, 1865.]

The following translation of the Amitâbha Sûtra is made from the Chinese edition of that work, prepared by Kumârajîva, and bound up in a volume known as the "Daily Prayers of the Buddhist Priests belonging to the Contemplative School" (Shan-mun).

No doubt the Chinese version is much abbreviated. We are told that Kumârajîva omitted repetitions and superfluities in making his translations. We have reason to be thankful that he did so.

The Amitâbha Sûtra contains a description of the Western Heavens, the Sukhavatî, or Happy Land, to which so many millions of Buddhists look as their reward in another life. It is a question of some importance at what time this belief in a Western Paradise incorporated itself with Buddhism.

In fixing the period we may be certain that it was before the date of Kumârajîva, *i.e.* 400 A.D.; and if it be correct that the Chinese translation of the "Wou-liang-sheu-king," *i.e.* the Sûtra of Amitâbha, under the name of the "Eternal," dates from the Han dynasty (Edkins), we may go back to the first century A.D. as the latest admissible date for the origin of this belief.

Wassiljew hazards the remark that the idea of a Western Paradise was borrowed from foreigners, with whom the Buddhists of Southern India were brought into contact (Wassiljew, Der Buddhismus, § 121). We know that merchants from Alexandria frequented the Western shores of the peninsula at an early date. There was a Christian mission established in the same direction as early as the days of Pantænus (Fabricius, Lux Evang., c. 36, p. 637; Hough's

Christianity in India, I. 51). We know also that two of the principal writers in the developed schools of Buddhism, viz., Nâgârjuna and Âryadeva, were born and lived in South India (Wassiljew, § 212). Taking the date of Âryadeva to be about 100 A.D., for he was the fourth patriarch after Aṣvaghosha, who was contemporary with Kanishka, we may again regard this as an approximate date for the origin of the belief in a Western Paradise, and of the writings bearing on that belief. The connection of this worship with South India is still further illustrated by the reverence paid to Avalokiteṣvara, the reputed son of Amitâbha, in that quarter. Hiouen Thsang relates that "in the country of the Mo-lo-ye (Malayas), in South-western India, there is a celebrated peak called Potalaka, on which Kwan-tseu-tsai, *i.e.* Avalokiteṣvara, frequently locates himself in coming and going, and appears under various shapes to pilgrims visiting the neighbourhood" (Julien). Now this peak Potalaka may be either the celebrated Pedura-talla-galla, one of the highest mountain crags in Ceylon, and belonging to the Malaya-giri of Burnouf, or the Maleæ Montes of Pliny and Ptolemy; or it may be one of the eminences of the southern ghâts of Malabar. In either case it is certain that with this mountain is connected the extensive worship paid to Avalokiteṣvara; and he again is spoken of as the Bodhisattva, or active power of Amitâbha, whose worship may therefore be presumed to have arisen in the same locality, *i.e.* South India. Avalokiteṣvara, being spoken of as the son of Amitâbha, seems to confirm the idea of the presence of a foreign, and perhaps a Christian, element in this singular cultus. Whether the term "Western Paradise," and its description found in the Sûtra which follows, bears out this idea we leave others to judge.

In popular Buddhist language, Amitâbha is spoken of as the fourth Dhyâni Buddha, corresponding to Ṣâkya Muni amongst the Mânushi Buddhas. Respecting the land over which he rules, we find the following description in a popular work on the subject:—"Amitâbha reigns over the land Sukhavatî, which, compared with our world, bears due west exactly 100,000 billions of Sakwalas. In respect to the tiers of Sakwalas, which rise one above the other, springing from the mystic Lotus, this land Sukhavatî belongs to the thirteenth tier. In about the middle of this tier is our own world, and at the extreme western border of it the land of Amitâbha" (Fah-kai-lih-to).

The hold which the worship of Amitâbha has taken upon the popular mind, in China and Japan, can hardly be exaggerated—in every direction his name is engraved or inscribed, to call the attention of the passer-by to the efficacy of repeating it, and the great majority of popular Buddhist writings have relation to the same subject. Amongst many thousand tracts, which came under my own notice, in the Temples of Canton, after its capture in 1857, the larger number related either to Kwan-yin (Avalokiteṣvara) or to the Western Paradise of Amitâbha. One particularly attracted my attention,—this was a sheet representing a boat, full of people, passing over the sea to the opposite shore, guided by Amitâbha himself, and steered by Kwan-yin; upon this sheet there was an exhortation within, in which the power of Amitâbha is set forth, by way of comparison with other modes of salvation, much to the advantage of the former—for it asserts "other methods of deliverance are like the progress of an insect up a high mountain, but this method (*i.e.* of Amitâbha) is like the advance of a boat sailing with a fair wind and propitious tide; on once entering the Western Paradise (continues the exhortation) there is no return—the highest rank there, is that of Buddha, the lowest, that of the most exalted Deva. Again, whilst the happiness of this condition is so great, the mode of attaining it is equally simple. In this mode of salvation, there are no distinctions of rich and poor, of male and female, of people and priests: all are equally able to arrive at this condition. Let every virtuous person therefore nourish in himself a principle of faith—let him with constant and undivided attention, invoke the name of Amitâbha Buddha, and thus he shall eventually be saved in the Paradise of the Western Heavens."

On the sail of the boat (which bears a flag, inscribed with the word Sukhavatî, and which is represented as being full of happy disciples, male and female,) is written this scroll. "The one name of O-mi-to (Amitâbha) is a precious sword for destroying the whole concourse of evils. This one name, O-mi-to, is the brave champion that defies the power of hell —this one name, O-mi-to, is the bright lamp that dissipates darkness—this one name, O-mi-to, is the boat of mercy, on which we may cross the sea of trouble—this one name, O-mi-to, is the direct path for escaping the entanglement of frequent transmigration—this one name, O-mi-to, is the perfect mode by which to avoid life and death—this one name, O-mi-to, is the mysterious power which endows us with superhuman faculties—this one name, O-mi-to, is the best mode for divining secrets. These six letters, *i.e.* Na-mo, O-mi-to, Fuh, include all the 84,000 methods of salvation; they are able, with one stroke, as it were, to divide the bonds that hold us captive; there is no such invocation as that of O-mi-to, which, in the twinkling of an eye, is able to transport us to the Western Heavens."

This is a fair sample of the popular mode of Buddhist teaching among the lower orders in China, and as a natural result, the highest aim of the convert to this doctrine is to repeat, with little intermission, the name of O-mi-to, Fuh, O-mi-to, Fuh, till the desired result be attained—*i.e.*, emancipation from all earthly troubles, and a certain admission after death to Paradise.

The southern schools of Buddhism, viz., in Ceylon, Siam, and Annam, know nothing of Amitâbha or his Western Paradise. This fact seems to point to the late development of the doctrine in India. Probably, however, intercourse between the island and the mainland was prevented at an early date by the warlike character of the Malabar population. Fah Hian, we know, arrived at the island by sea, and Hiouen Thsang, for some reason or other, avoided all the southern portion of the peninsula, and did not visit Ceylon. In fact, there appears to be an early break between the Buddhist current of teaching followed by the Indian teachers and those in Ceylon, the result of which is the vastly different aspect under which that religion presents itself in those countries. It was, however, from Southern India that the great teacher of the doctrine of a Western Paradise arrived in China. Bodhidharma, the twenty-eighth patriarch, and the founder of the contemplative school, reached that country by sea A.D. 526. He seems to have brought with him the very name which is now used in China to denote the school of which he was the first patriarch. The word "Shan," according to Edkins, was formerly written "jan," and this contracted from jan-na, pointing evidently to the Indian word Jaina. This confirms the opinion that the Jaina religion is but an off-shoot of later Buddhism. With respect to Bodhidharma, there is a legend still existing in China which exemplifies his belief in the doctrine of a Western Heaven, "for as he lay in his coffin (we are told) he held one shoe in his hand. Whilst thus situated, his remains were visited by a celebrated priest called Sung-yun, who asked him where he was going; to which he replied, 'To the Western Heavens.' Sung-yun then returned home; but afterwards the coffin of Bodhidharma was opened and found empty, except one of his shoes, which still remained. By imperial command this shoe was preserved as a sacred relic. Afterwards, in the Tang dynasty, it was stolen, and no one now knows where it is" (Edkins).

I now pass at once to the translation.

## THE AMITÂBHA SÛTRA.

*Extracted from the work called "Shan Mun Yih Tung," or Daily Prayers of the Contemplative School of Priests.*

Thus have I heard. On a certain occasion Buddha was residing at Ṣrâvastî, in the garden of Kita, with the great Bhikshus, 1,250 in all, being great Rahats, possessed of perfect knowledge, to wit, the venerable Ṣâriputra, the great Maudgalyâyana, the great Kâṣyapa, the great Kâtyâyana, the great Gochira, Revata, Ṣrutaviṃṣatikoṭi, Nanda, Ânanda, Rahula, Gavâmpati, Piṇḍola, Bharadvâja, Kâlâditya, the great Kapphiṇa, Vakula, Aniruddha, and so forth, all great disciples. And in addition to these were all the great Bodhisattvas; to wit, Manjuṣrî, king of the law, Ajita, Maitreya, and so forth, all great Bodhisattvas; and, moreover, there were present Ṣakra râjâ and others, with innumerable Devas. At this time Buddha addressed the venerable Ṣâriputra as follows:—"In the western regions more than one hundred thousand myriads of systems of worlds beyond this, there is a Sakwala named Sukhavatî. Why is this region so named? Because all those born in it have no griefs or sorrows: they experience only unmixed joys; therefore it is named the infinitely happy land. Again, Ṣâriputra, this happy region is surrounded by seven rows of ornamental railings, seven rows of exquisite curtains, seven rows of waving trees—hence, again, it is called the infinitely happy region. Again, Ṣâriputra, this happy land possesses seven gemmous lakes, in the midst of which flow waters possessed of the eight distinctive qualities (viz., limpidity and purity, refreshing coolness, sweetness, softness, fertilizing qualities, calmness, power of preventing famine, productiveness of abundance). Spreading over the bottom of these lakes are golden sands, whilst the four sides have pleasant walks enriched with gold, silver, crystal, lapis lazuli, beryl, ruby, and cornelian. In the middle of the lakes are lotus flowers, large as a chariot wheel, blue, yellow, red, and white, each reflecting brilliant hues of its own colour, and possessed of the most perfect and delightful fragrance. Thus, O Ṣâriputra, this blessed region is perfected and thoroughly adorned.

"Again, Ṣâriputra, the land of that Buddha ever shares in heavenly delights (or, music), the ground is resplendent gold, at morning and evening showers of the Divine Udumbara flower descend upon all those born there, at early dawn the most exquisite blossoms burst out at their side: thousand myriads of Buddhas instantly resort here for refreshment, and then return to their own regions, and for this reason, Ṣâriputra, that land is called most happy. Again, Ṣâriputra, that region is possessed of every species of pleasure delightful to the senses, birds of every hue, the white stork, the peacock, the macaw, garudas, birds of every kind, all these, at morning and evening, unite to sing the praises of the Law, so that all born in that land, hearing these notes, are led to invoke

Buddha, the Law and the Assembly. But, Ṣâriputra, you must not suppose that these birds are born in this state in the way of retribution for sins in a superior condition, and why not? Because, in that region there exists not either of the three evil ways of birth (*i.e.*, as a beast, demon, or asura). Ṣâriputra! that land being emphatically free from these evil ways of birth, is thereby more fully possessed of the superior ways of birth, and these different kinds of birds are all of them the different apparitional forms of superior beings, whom Amitâbha Buddha causes thus to chaunt the various sounds of the land. Ṣâriputra! in that land of Buddha, whenever a gentle breeze moves softly, then the various precious waving trees, and the gemmous curtain that surrounds the land, emit a gentle and mysterious sound, like a thousand different kinds of music, all at the same time; on hearing which, the dwellers in that land conceive, spontaneously, a heart full of adoration for Buddha, the Law, and the Assembly.

"Ṣâriputra, this land is thus perfectly adorned, and complete in pleasure.

"But now, Ṣâriputra, you would perhaps enquire, why the Buddha of that region is called Amitâbha. Ṣâriputra! it is because he is unmeasurably bright and glorious, so that his splendour fills the lands of the ten regions, and no obstacle can oppose the diffusion of the rays of his glory,[1] for this reason, he is called Amitâbha. Again, Ṣâriputra, the years of the life of that Buddha, as men compute them, are endless, and without bound, in asankhyas of years—for this reason, also, he is called Amitâbha. For ten kalpas of years, that Buddha has enjoyed his present condition, and has for his disciples an endless and incalculable number of Ṣrâvakas, all of them Rahats, innumerable, and not to be expressed for multitude, and Bodhisattvas equally vast in number. So it is, Ṣâriputra, that land of Buddha is perfected. Again, Ṣâriputra, in that land of perfect joy all who are born, are born as Avaivartyas (never to return),[2] whilst among these there are numbers who make *this* their resting place, before

[1] Burn. Introd., p. 100. [2] Lalita Vistara, 267.

that one birth more (which shall end in their arriving at Buddhaship); infinite are these in number, not to be expressed for multitude, simply innumerable.

"Ṣâriputra! all mortals who hear this account, ought to offer up this one vow—that they may be born in that country—and why? because, if once born there, they obtain the felicity of only one more appearance as superior sages (and then obtain the condition of Buddha.) Ṣâriputra, it is not possible to be born in that country possessing an inferior Karma; Ṣâriputra! if there be a virtuous man or woman, who hears this account of Amitâbha Buddha, and who assiduously invokes his name for one day or two, up to seven, and during this time maintains a heart unaffected by worldly thoughts, or confused ideas—that man or woman, when about to die, shall be blessed with a clear vision of Amitâbha and all his saints, and at the last moment, if his heart be not turned back, he shall depart, and forthwith be born in that most blessed land of Amitâbha Buddha. Ṣâriputra! I perceive that such will be the happy consequence (of so doing) and therefore I repeat these words; whatever men they be who hear them, they ought at once to utter this vow, that they may be born in that land.

"Ṣâriputra! thus it is I would recite in stanzas of commendation, the excellences of that infinitely glorious land of Amitâbha Buddha.

[The Sûtra then proceeds to speak of the various Buddhas towards each of the four points, and also in the zenith and nadir. This being a mere recital of names, is omitted here.]

"Ṣâriputra! what say you as to the meaning of this expression, the saving power which resides in the repetition of the names of all the Buddhas? Ṣâriputra! if there be a virtuous man or woman who hears and receives this Sûtra, and who hears the names of all the Buddhas, these virtuous men or women, in consequence of the saving power which resides in the repetition of these names, shall all obtain the privilege of not passing through and revolving in the condition of Anuttara Samyak Sambodhi, *i.e.* the unsurpassably just and enlightened heart. (This is the condition usually assigned to the Bodhisattva, before arriving at the state of Buddha). Wherefore, Ṣâriputra, ye all ought to receive and believe these my words, and the words of all the Buddhas.

"Ṣâriputra! if there be a man who has vowed, or now vows, or shall vow and desire, to be born in that region, all these men shall be privileged not to remain or revolve in the condition of Anuttara Samyak Sambodhi, but to be born at once in their various conditions in the land of that Buddha, whether in time past, now, or henceforth. Wherefore, Ṣâriputra, whatever faithful man or woman there be, they ought all to put up this prayer, that they may be born in that land. Ṣâriputra, as I have now thus recounted the praises of all these Buddhas, their indescribable excellences, so those Buddhas likewise recount my praises and infinite excellences, and speak thus:—'Ṣâkya Muni Buddha is he that is able (शक्) to accomplish most difficult results (prompted by) his exceeding love—he it is who is "able" in the So-ho world (Sahâlokadhâtu), the evil world of five impurities (viz., violence, perception, calamities, birth, death); he it is who is "able," in the midst of these, to arrive at the condition Anuttara Samyak Sambodhi, and on account of all sentient creatures to repeat his Law, difficult to be embraced by those for whom it is said.'

"Ṣâriputra! know, then, that I, in the midst of this evil and calamitous world, preaching these difficult doctrines, have arrived at the condition of Anuttara Samyak Sambodhi, and now, on account of all creatures, have declared this Law difficult to be believed, and this is that which is most difficult."

Buddha having repeated this Sûtra, Ṣâriputra and all the Bhikshus, and all the assembly, the Devas, Asuras, and so on, having heard what Buddha said, joyfully received and believed it, and having prostrated themselves in adoration, departed.

## Art. VI.—*The Initial Coinage of Bengal.* By Edward Thomas, Esq.

Towards the end of August, 1863, an unusually large hoard of coins, numbering in all no less than 13,500 pieces of silver, was found in the Protected State of Kooch Bahár, in Northern Bengal, the contents of which were consigned, in the ordinary payment of revenue, to the Imperial Treasury in Calcutta. Advantage was wisely sought to be taken of the possible archæological interest of such a discovery, in selections directed to be made from the general bulk to enrich the medal cabinets of the local Mint and the Museum of the Asiatic Society of Bengal. The task of selection, and with it of inevitably final rejection, was entrusted to Bábu Rajendra-lál-Mitra,—an experienced scholar in many branches of Sanskrit literature, and who, in the absence of more practised Numismatists, courageously encountered the novel study and impromptu exposition of Semitic Palæography as practically developed in his own native land six centuries ago. The Bábu, after having assiduously completed his selections for the Government,[1] was considerate enough to devote himself to renewed and more critical examinations of this mass of coined metal, with a view to secure for Colonel C. S. Guthrie (late of the Bengal Engineers), any examples of importance that might have escaped his earlier investigations. The result has been that more than a thousand additional specimens have been rescued from the Presidency Mint crucibles, and now contribute the leading materials for the subjoined monograph.

An autumnal fall of a river bank, not far removed from the traditional capital of *Kunteswar Rája,* a king of mark in provincial annals,[2] disclosed to modern eyes the hidden trea-

[1] J. A. S. Bengal, 1864, p. 480.

[2] Col. J. C. Haughton, to whom we are mainly indebted for the knowledge of this *trouvaille*, has been so obliging as to furnish me with some interesting

sure of some credulous mortal who, in olden time, entrusted his wealth to the keeping of an alluvial soil, carefully stored and secured in brass vessels specially constructed for the purpose, but destined to contribute undesignedly to an alien inheritance, and a disentombment at a period much posterior to that contemplated by its depositor. This accumulation, so singular in its numerical amount, is not the less remarkable in the details of its component elements—whether as regards the, so to say, newness and sharpness of outline of the majority of the pieces themselves, the peculiarly local character of the whole collection, or its extremely limited range in point of time. It may be said to embrace compactly the records of ten kings, ten mint cities, and to represent 107 years of the annals of the country. The date of its inhumation may be fixed, almost with precision, towards the end of the eighth century A.H., or the fourteenth century A.D. A very limited proportion of the entire aggregation was contributed by external currencies, and the imperial metropolis of Dehli alone intervenes to disturb the purely indigenous issues, and that merely to the extent of *less* than 150 out of the 13,500 otherwise unmixed produce of Bengal Mints.[1]

details of the site of discovery and illustrations of the neighbouring localities. Col. Haughton writes:—"The place where the coin was found is about three miles S.W. of Deenhatta, not far from the Temple of Kunteswaree (or Komit-Eswaree) on the banks of the river Dhurla. Near to this temple is a place called Gosain Moraee, a short distance from which are the ruins of Kuntesur Raja's capital called Kunteswaree-Pat, consisting of a mound of considerable extent, which has been surrounded with several ditches and walls, which are again protected at the distance of a mile or two by enormous mounds of nearly 100 feet high. The brass vessels, in which the treasure was deposited, were ordinary brass *lotahs*, to which the top or lip had not been fixed, but in lieu thereof the vessels were covered by canister tops, secured by an iron spike passing from side to side."

[1] I wish to explain the reservations I make in thus stating this total below that given in Rajendra lál's list of 150 coins of *seven* Dehli kings (J.A.S.B., September, 1864, p. 481). In the first place, I greatly mistrust the reading of the sixth king's title. Muhammad bin Tughlak was called *Fakhr-ud-din* Júnah in his youth only; on his first mission to the Dakhin in 721 A.H. the higher title of *Ulugh Khán* was conferred upon him by his father, but from the date of his accession to the throne of Hindustan, he contented himself with the use of his simple name and patronymic; no longer the "glory of the faith," he was the far more humble الوثق بتائيد الرحمن, or the conventional المجاهد في سبيل الله (Ziá-i-Barni, Calcutta edit., p. 196), both of which were so persistently copied by the independent Bengal Sultan. Certainly no such title as فخرالدين occurs on *any* of the specimens of the *Kooch*

The exclusively home characteristics of the great majority of the collection are enlivened by the occasional intrusion of mementos of imperial re-assertions, and numismatic contributions from other independent sources aid in the casual illustration of the varying political conditions of the province, and of the relations maintained from time to time between the too-independent governors of a distant principality and their liege suzerains at Dehli.

Muhammadan writers have incidentally preserved a record of the fact, that on the first entry of their armies into Bengal, they found an exclusive *cowrie* or shell currency, assisted possibly by bullion in the larger payments, but associated with no coined money of any description;[1] a heritage of primitive

*Bahár* collection, that the Bábu has selected for Col. Guthrie, with the exception of those bearing the names of Fakhr-ud-dín *Mubárak Sháh*.

The second question, of the altogether improbable intrusion of coins of Muhammad 'Ádil Sháh ("new type"), I must meet in a more direct way, by assigning the supposed examples of his money to the potentate from whose mints they really came, that is, *Ikhtiár-ud-dín* GHÁZÍ SHÁH (No. vii. infra), giving a difference in the age of the two kings, as far as their epochs affect the probable date of the concealment of this *trouvaille*, of more than two centuries (753 A.H. against 960 A.H.). The Bábu has himself discovered his early error of making Shams-ud-dín Pírúz, *one of the Dehlí Pathâns* (as reported in the local newspapers), and transferred him, in the printed proceedings of the Asiatic Society of Bengal, to an anomalous position at the end of the Bengal Patháns (p. 483), while omitting to deduct him from the total number of "*eight* Dehlí Pathâns," which reckoning has been allowed to stand at p. 480. In the matter of date, we are not informed why this king should be assigned to A.D. 1491, instead of to the true 1320 A.D. which history claims for him.

[1] Minháj-ul-Siráj, who was resident in Lakhnauti in A.H. 641, writes چنان تقریر کردند که دران بلاد کوده بعوض چیتل روان است Tabakát-i-Násiri, p. 149, Calcutta printed edition (1864). Ibn Batutah gives an account of the collection of the cowrie shells in the Maldive Islands, from whence they were exported to Bengal in exchange for rice; the gradational quantities and values are detailed as follows: سیاه = 100 cowries. فال = 700. کتّي = 12000. بُستو = 100,000, four *bustús* were estimated as worth one gold *dinár*; but the rate of exchange varied considerably, so that occasionally a *dinár* would purchase as many as twelve *bustús*, or twelve laks of cowries! (French edit., iv., p. 121. Lee's Translation, p. 178.) Sir Henry Elliot mentions that "in India, in 1740, a rupee exchanged for 2,400 cowries; in 1756, for 2,560 cowries; and (in 1845) as many as 6,500 could be obtained for a rupee." —Glossary of Indian Terms, p. 373. They were estimated in the currency scheme of 1833 at 6,400 per rupee.—Prinsep's U.T., p. 2. Major Rennell, who was in Silhet in 1767-8, speaking of the cowrie money, remarks: "I found no other currency of any kind in the country; and upon an occasion when an increase in the revenue of the province was enforced, several boat loads (not less than 50 tons each) were collected and sent down the Burrampooter to Dacca." As late as 1801 the revenues of the British district of Silhet "were

barter, indeed, which survived undisturbed in many of the outlying districts up to the early part of the present century. The consistent adherence of the people to this simple medium of exchange, goes far to explain an enigma, recently adverted to,[1] as to the general absence of all specimens of money of high antiquity within certain limits northward of the seaboard, and may serve to reconcile the anomaly of conterminous nationalities appearing in such different degrees of advancement when tried by similar isolated tests of local habitudes. For the rest, the arms of Islám clearly brought with them into Bengal what modern civilization deems a fiscal necessity—a scheme of national coinage; and the present enquiry is concerned to determine when and in what form the conquerors applied the theory and practice they themselves had as yet but imperfectly realized.

When Muhammad bin Sám had so far consolidated his early successes in India into a design of permanent occupancy, leaving a viceroy and generalissimo in Dehli, in the person of Kutb-ud-dín Aibek, while his own court was still held at Ghazní, the scattered subordinate commanders each sought to extend the frontiers of *the* faith beyond the limits already acquired. In pursuance of this accepted mission, Muhammad Bakhtiár Khiljí, *Sipahsálár* in Oude, in A.H. 599, pushed his forces southward, and expelled, with but little effort, the ancient Hindu dynasty of Nuddeah, superseding that city as the capital, and transferring the future metropolis of Bengal to the proximate site of Lakhnautí, where he ruled undisturbed by higher authority till his own career was prematurely cut short in A.H. 602.

Considering the then existing time-honoured system of valuation by shells—which would certainly not invite a hasty issue of coin—and Muhammad Bakhtiár's acknowledged subordination to Kutb-ud-dín, who, so far as can be seen, uttered no money in his own name, it may fairly be inferred that if a single piece was produced, it formed a part only of an occasional, or special,

collected in cowries, which was also the general medium of all pecuniary transactions, and a considerable expense was then incurred by Government in effecting their conversion into bullion."—Hamilton's Hindostan, London, 1820., i. p. 195.

[1] J.R.A.S., vol. i., N.S., p. 473-4.

medallic mintage—a numismatic Fatah-námah, or assertion and declaration of conquest and supremacy alone, designedly avoiding any needless interference with the fixed trade by adventitious monetary complications, which so unprogressive a race as the Hindus would naturally be slow to appreciate.

Similar motives may be taken to have prevailed in the north, where the least possible change was made in the established currency of the country, extending, indeed, to a mere substitution of names in the vernacular character on the coin, which was allowed to retain the typical "Bull and Horseman" device of Prithvi Rája and his predecessors. The pieces themselves, designated from their place of mintage *Dehli-wálas*,[1] were composed of a mixture of silver and copper in intentionally graduated proportions, but of the one fixed weight of thirty-two ratis, or the measure of the old *Purána* of silver of Manu's day. Progressive modifications were effected in the types and legends of these coins, but no systematic reconstruction of the circulating media took place until the reign of Altamsh; who, however, left the existing currencies undisturbed, as the basis for the introduction of the larger and more valuable and exclusively silver الفضة popularly known in after times as the *Tankah*,[2] a standard which may also be supposed to have followed traditional weights in the contents assigned to it, as the 96 rati-piece modern ideas would identify with the *Tolah:* or it may possibly have been originated as a new 100 rati coin, a decimal innovation on the primitive

[1] The name is written دلی ال in Kutb-ud-dín Aibek's inscription on the mosque at Dehli. (Prinsep's Essays, i. 327). The Táj-ul-Maásir and other native authorities give the word as دهليوال. Hasan Nizámi, the author of the former work, mentions that Kubáchah, ruler of Sind, sent his son with an offering of 100 láks of Dehli-wáls to Altamsh, and no less than 500 láks of the same description of coin were eventually found in Kubáchah's treasury, many of which were probably struck in his own mints. (See Ariana Antiqua, pl. xx., fig. 19; J.A.S.B., iv., pl. 37, figs. 28, 29, 47; and Prinsep's Essays, i., pl. xxvi., figs. 28, 29, 47.)

[2] Erskine derives this name from the Chagatai Túrki word, *tang*, "white." (History of India under Báber. London, 1854, vol. i. p. 546). Vullers gives a different and clearly preferable derivation in تنگه (fort. ex. تَنُک s. تَنگ tenuis, suff. ه). Ibn Batutah carefully preserves the orthography as تَنگَه, s. टंक and टङ्क.

Hindu reckoning by fours, a point which remains to be determined by the correct ascertainment of the normal weight of the rati, which is still a debated question. My own results, obtained from comparative numismatic data of various ages, point to 1·75 grains,[1] while General

[1] In attempting to ascertain the relation of the weights of ancient and modern days, and to follow the changes that time and local custom may have introduced into the static laws of India, the capital point to be determined is the true weight of the *rati*, as it was understood and accepted when the initiatory metric system was in course of formation. Two different elements have hitherto obstructed any satisfactory settlement of the intrinsic measure of this primary unit—the one, the irregularity of the weight of the *gunja* seeds themselves, which vary with localities and other incidental circumstances of growth;* the other, the importance of which has been rather overlooked, that the modifications in the higher standards, introduced from time to time by despotic authority, were never accompanied by any rise or fall in the nominal total of *ratis* which went to form the altered integer. From these and other causes the rate of the *rati* has been variously estimated as† 1·3125 grains, 1·875 grains, 1·953 grains, and even as high as 2·25 grains.

We have Manu's authority for the fact that 32 *ratis* went to the old silver *dharana* or *puráṇa*, and we are instructed by his commentator, in a needlessly complicated sum, that the *kárshu* was composed of 80 *ratis* of copper. We have likewise seen that this *kársha* constituted a commercial static measure, its double character as a coin and as a weight being well calculated to ensure its fixity and uniformity in either capacity within the range of its circulation. I shall be able to show that this exact weight retained so distinct a place in the fiscal history of the metropolis of Hindustán, that in the revision and re-adjustment of the coinage which took place under Muhammad bin Tughlak, in A.D. 1325, this integer was revived in the form of silver coin, and was further retained as a mint standard by his successors, till Shír Sháh re-modelled the currency about the middle of the sixteenth century. In the same way I have already demonstrated elsewhere,‡ in illustration of an independent question, that a coin retaining with singular fidelity the ponderable ratio of the ancient *puráṇa*, was concurrent with the restored *kársha* under Fírúz Sháh (A.D. 1351–1388) and other kings. And to complete the intermediate link, I may cite the fact that when the effects of Greek and Scythian interference had passed away, the 32-*rati puráṇa* re-appeared in the Punjáb and Northern India, as the silver currency of the local dynasty of SYÁLA and SAMANTA DEVA,§ and furnished in its style and devices the prototype of the Dehli CHOHÁN series of "Bull and Horseman" coins, *the Dehliwálas*, which were retained, unaltered in weight, by the Muhammadans, in joint circulation with the silver double *Dirhams* of 174 grains of their own system.||

Extant specimens of Syála's coins in the British Museum weigh 54·4 grains and upwards.

If this double series of weights, extending over an interval of time represented by 24 or 25 centuries, and narrowed to an almost identical locality, are found not only to accord with exactitude in themselves, but to approach the only rational solution of the given quantities, the case may be taken as proved.

The ancient *puráṇa* hall-marked silver pieces range as high as 55 grains; copper coins of *Rámadata*¶ are extant of 137·5 grains; and other early coins of

* Colebrooke, As. Res. v. 93.

† Sir W. Jones, As. Res., ii. 154, "*Rati* = 1 $\frac{5}{16}$ of a grain." Prinsep, U. T. (180÷96); Jervis, Weights of Konkan, p. 40; Wilson, Glossary, sub voce *Rati*.

‡ Num Chron., xv., notes, pp. 138, 153, etc.

§ J. A. S. Bengal, iv. 674; J. R. A. S., ix. 177; Ariana Antiqua, p. 428; Prinsep's Essays, i. 313.

|| N. C., xv. 136; Prinsep's Essays, U. T., p. 70.

¶ Prinsep's Essays, i. p. 216, pl. xx., figs. 47, 48.

Cunningham adheres to the higher figures of 1.8229 grains.[1]

about 70 grains; while, in parallel exemplification, the latter standard weights, under the Muhammadans at Dehli, are found to be 56 and 140 grains. Hence—

$$140 \div 80 \text{ ratis} = 1{\cdot}75 \text{ grains}$$
$$56 \div 32 \;\; ,, \;\; = 1.75 \;\; ,,$$

and this is the weight I propose to assign to the original *rati;* there may be some doubt about the second decimal, as we are not bound to demand an exact sum of *even* grains, but the 1.7 may be accepted with full confidence, leaving the hundred at discretion, though from preference, as well as for simplicity of conversion of figures, I adhere to the $1\frac{3}{4}$. Under this system, then, the definition of each ancient weight by modern grains will stand as follows:—

| | | | | |
|---|---|---|---|---|
| SILVER...... | 1 Mâsha | = | 2 Ratis or | 3·5 grains. |
| | 1 Dharaṇa or Purâṇa | = | 32 ,, | 56·0 ,, |
| | 1 Satamâna | = | 320 ,, | 560· ,, |
| GOLD ...... | 1 Mâsha | = | 5 ,, | 8·75 ,, |
| | 1 Suvarṇa | = | 80 ,, | 140· ,, |
| | 1 Pala or Nishka | = | 320 ,, | 560· ,, |
| | 1 Dharaṇa | = | 3200 ,, | 5600· ,, |
| COPPER .... | 1 Kârsha | = | 80 ,, | 140· ,, |
| Subdivisions of Kârsha ...... | $\frac{1}{2}$ | = | 40 ,, | 70· ,, |
| | $\frac{1}{4}$ | = | 20 ,, | 35· ,, |
| | $\frac{1}{8}$ | = | 10 ,, | 17·5 ,, |

—*Numismatic Chronicle*, vol. iv., N.S. p. 131, March, 1864.

[1] General Cunningham's deductions are founded on the following estimates:—"I have been collecting materials for the same subject [Indian Weights] for nearly twenty years, and I have made many curious discoveries. I see that Mr. Thomas quotes Sir William Jones as fixing the weight of the *Krisĥnala*, or *Rati* seed, at $1\frac{5}{16}$ grain; but I am satisfied that this is a simple misprint of Jones's manuscript for $1\frac{5}{6}$ or 1·833 grain, which is as nearly as possible the average weight of thousands of seeds which I have tested. The great unit of mediæval and modern times is the *táka* of not less than 145 grains, of which six make the *chha-táka*, or *chhatak*, equal to 870 grains, or nearly two ounces; and 100 make the *sataka*, or *ser*, the derivation being *sat-táka*, or 100 *tákas.* For convenience I have taken, in all my calculations, the *rati* seed at 1·8229 grain. Then 80 *ratis* or 145·832 was the weight of the *tanyka* of copper, and also of the golden *suvarna*, which multiplied by six gives 874·99 grains, or exactly two ounces for the *chhatáka* or chhatak."—J.A.S. Bengal, 1865, page 46.

Mr. N. S. Maskelyne, of the Mineral Department, British Museum, who, some time ago, entered into an elaborate series of comparisons of Oriental weights, with a view to determine the identity of one of our most celebrated Indian diamonds, has been so obliging as to draw up for me the following memorandum, exhibiting the bearing of an entirely independent set of data upon the question under review, the true weight of the Indian *Rati.* The value of this contribution in itself, and the difficulty of doing justice to it in an abstract, must plead my excuse for printing it *in extenso* in this place:—

I shall confine my answer to your question about the rati to the estimate of it as derived from the Mishkâl. The other channel of enquiry, that namely of Hindoo metrology and numismatics, is too complicated, and so far as I have been able to follow it, too unsatisfactory in its results, to justify my urging any arguments derived from it. Indeed, the oscillations in the currencies, and our knowing so few very fine coins of reigns before Shír Sháh, of critical value, make this branch of the subject almost unapproachable to one who is not an Oriental scholar. I would premise, however, that I do not believe very accurate results are to be obtained solely from the weights of coins, except in the few cases where, as in the coins of Akbar, or of Abd-el-Malek ben Merwân, we have some literary

However, these silver coins of Altamsh—let their primary static ideal have been based upon a duplication of the dirhams

statements about them. Nor can you get any result from weighing carob beans to determine the carat, or abrus seeds to determine the *rati*. I weighed, long ago, hundreds of ratis, that Dr. Daubeny lent me, with an average of 1.694 troy grains. Sir William Jones found, I believe, one of 1.318, and Professor Wilson, I think, another value again. They vary according to the soil and climate they are grown in, and the time and atmosphere they have been kept in.

My investigation of the rati originated in a desire to determine whether the diamond, now the Queen's, was the same that Baber records as having been given to Humáyún at the taking of Agra, after the battle of Paniput, and which had once belonged to Alá-ed-dín (Khilji). I also was led to suppose that the diamond Tavernier saw at the Court of Aurungzebe was the same, and that he had confounded it with one that Meer Jumla gave to Shâh Jehân, and that had been recently found at Golconda. I would here observe that Tavernier's weights can be very little trusted; I can give you my reasons for this assertion, if you wish for them.

Bâber, in his memoirs, says the weight of Humâyún's diamond, was about 8 mishkâls. In his description of India, he gives the following ratios of the weights in use there:—

| | | | | | | | |
|---|---|---|---|---|---|---|---|
| 8 ratis | = | 1 máshah. | | | | | |
| 32 ,, | = | 4 ,, | = | 1 tang (tank). | | | |
| 40 ,, | = | 5 ,, | | | = | 1 mishkâl. | |
| 96 ,, | = | 12 ,, | | | = | 1 tola. | |

Jewels and precious stones being estimated by the tang. Furthermore he states 14 tolas = 1 sír, 40 sírs = 1 man, etc. Thus, then, the 8 mishkâls would be 320 ratis.

Tavernier says the diamond he saw weighed 319½ ratis. The Koh-i-Nûr, in 1851 (and, I believe, in Baber's day also), weighed 589.5 grains troy. The theory that it was Alá-ed-dín's diamond, would demand—

| | | | | |
|---|---|---|---|---|
| a mishkâl | (8) | weight of | 73.7 | grains. |
| a tola | ($3\frac{1}{3}$) | ,, | 176.85 | ,, |
| a tank | (10) | ,, | 58.95 | ,, |
| a mâsha | (40) | ,, | 14.745 | ,, |
| a rati | (320 of 8 to the mâsha) | | 1 8425 | ,, |
| —— | (240 of 6 ,, ) | | 2.533 | ,, |

Now, as to the mishkâl—the Mahommadan writers speak of it as not having altered from the days of the Prophet. Doubtless, it has been a pretty permament weight, and very likely, in Makrizi's time, was but slightly various in different places. At present, the following table represents the different mishkâls, so far as I have been able to ascertain them.

| | | |
|---|---|---|
| The gold and silver mishkâl of *Bassorah* = 1½dirham ........ | =72 | grains. |
| The ,, ,, mussal or mishkâl of *Gamroon* (71.75 miscals = 100 mahmoudias = 5136 grains).................... | =71.6. | ,, |
| The gold and silver miscal of *Mocha* = 24 carats = $24\frac{1}{160}$ vakya (of 480 grains, nearly) .............................. | =72 | ,, |
| That of *Bushire* = $\frac{1}{720}$ of a maund of 53784 grains .......... | =74.7 | ,, |
| The metical of *Aleppo* and *Algiers* ........................ | =73 | ,, |
| The ,, of *Tripoli* ........................................ | =73.6 | ,, |
| In *Persian*, the demi mishkâl = $\frac{1}{1200}$ of the batman of Chessay (of 8871 grains)................................ The taurid batman and mishkâl = half the above | =73.96 | ,, |
| The mishkâl corresponding to the (½) dirham used for gold and silver, in Persia .................................... | =74.5 | ,, |
| The abbasi corresponding to 1 mishkal, Marsden says ........ | =72 | ,, |
| The modern debased mishkâl of *Bokhara* .................. | =71 | ,, |

Bâber, in speaking of the mishkâl, may either mean his own Bokharan mishkâl, or, as seems more probable, the current mishkâl as existing at that time in India;

of Ghazní, or, as is more probable, elaborated out of the elements of ancient Indian Metrology—may be quoted in their

in short, the "Indian or Syrian mishkâl" of the Mahommadan writers—which was the Greek mishkâl + 2 kirats. The modern debased mishkâl of Bokhara we may leave out of our comparisons. It is surely a degraded weight in a country that has undergone an eclipse.

The old "Greek Dinar" is of course the Byzant, or solidus aureus—the denarius of Byzantium. It was nominally coined 72 to the Roman lb. The Byzantian Roman lb. in the British Museum weighs 4995 grains, so the solidus was *nominally* coined at 69.4 grains. It *really* issued from the mint at a maximum weight of 68 (a very few of the most finely preserved coins reaching this amount). Now taking Makrizi's statement that the mishkâl was 24 kirats, and that of the Ayin-i-Akberi that the Greek mishkâl was 2 kirats less than this; we find the weight of the mishkâl $= 68 + \frac{68}{11} = 74.18$ grains troy. Again, Makrizi mentions that Abd-el-malek ben Merwan coined dinars and dirhams in the ratios of $21\frac{3}{4}$ kirats: 15 kirats. Now this Caliph's gold coins in the British Museum (in a very fine state of preservation), weigh 66.5 grains, and his silver, also well preserved, 44.5. Taking the former as coined at 67, we have the ratio:

$$\text{Dinar} : \text{Dirham} = 21\tfrac{3}{4} : 15 = 67 : 46.2,$$

which latter gives a probable weight for the dirham as originally coined. (In Makrizi's time the ratio was dinar : dirham $= 10 : 7 = 21.75 : 15.22$; or supposing the gold coin unchanged at 67, the silver dirham would become 46.88). Then, as the ratio of the dinar (or gold mishkâl) to the mishkâl weight $= 21\frac{3}{4} : 24$ we have for the mishkâl weight a value of 73.93 grains.

These two values, thus severally adduced from different data—viz., 74.18 and 73.93—sufficiently nearly accord to justify, I think, our striking the balance between them, and declaring the ancient mishkâl—("the Syrian or Indian mishkâl") to have been very nearly 74 grains. Hence the kirat would be 3.133 grains, troy. The modern carat varies from 3.15, the modern Indian carat, to 3.28, the old French carat (made thus probably to be an aliquot part of the old French ounce). The English carat = 3.168; the Hamburgh = 3.176, and the Portuguese = 3.171.

The above value of the mishkâl accords extremely well with my theory about the diamond.

That the "Greek Dinar" of Makrizi was the Sassanian gold is not at all likely, although the silver dirham was, no doubt, originally derived from the Sassanian drachma. Of the few gold pieces of Sassanian coinage, the one in the Museum, of Ardashir I., weighs now 65.5, and could not have been coined at less than 66.5 grains—which would give a mishkâl of 72.04. But under the Sassanidæ, the gold coinage was quite exceptional, and was not large enough to have formed the basis of the monetary system of the Caliphs, which was professedly founded on Greek coins, *current*.

As to the Bokhâran mishkâl of Bâber's time, how are we to arrive at it? You—and if you can't, who can?—are able to make little firm ground out of the weights of Sassanian, or Ghasnavid coins—nor will the coins of the Ayubite, Mamluke, and Mamluke Bahrite, Caliphs (of which I have weighed scores), give any much more reliable units on which to base the history of the progress of change in the mishkâl. The limits of its variation in modern times seem to have lain between 74.5 and 72 troy grains; I believe 74 as near as possible its true original weight, the weight of the Syrian and of the Indian mishkâl. This would give the rati on the goldsmith's standard of 8 to the mâsha, and 40 to the mishkâl, as 1.85 grains, and the limits of this rati would be 1.862 and 1.80. The value of the jeweller's rati (6 to the mâsha) would be for the 74 grain mishkâl 2.47 grains, and its limits would be 2.483 and 2.40.

That Bâber's and Humâyún's now worn and dilapidated coins of 71 and 71.5 grains were mishkâls is not improbable; but they certainly were not coined at less than 74 grains.

Without entering into the Indian numismatical question, I may remind you of surviving integrity of weight and design, as having furnished the prototypes of a long line of sequent Dehli mintages, and thus contributing the manifest introductory model of all Bengal coinages.[1]

The artistic merits of the produce of the southern mints,

Tuglak's coin of 174 grains (one in the British Museum = 172.25), probably coined at 175 or 176; a fair weight of issue for a coin nominally of some 177 or 178 grains. These coins, I believe, you consider to represent the tola. A tola of 177.6 would accord on the ratios of Báber's table with a mishkál of 74 grains. I am strongly tempted to enter further into this question of the ponderary systems of India, but I am warned by your own able papers of the difficulties in the path of one who deals only in translations and in the weight of coins.

24th Nov., 1865.

[1] There are three varieties of Altamsh's silver coinage, all showing more or less the imperfection of the training of the Indian artists in the reproduction of the official alphabet of their conquerors. The designs of these pieces were clearly taken from the old Ghazní model of Muhammad bin Sám's Dirhams and Dínárs, and the indeterminate form of the device itself would seem to indicate that they mark the initial effort of the new Muhammadan silver currency which so soon fixed itself into one unvarying type, and retained its crude and unimproved lettering for upwards of a century, till Muhammad bin Tughlak inaugurated his reign by the issue of those choice specimens of the Moneyer's art, which stand without compeers in the Dehli series.

No. 1, Silver. Size, vii.; weight, 162·5. Supposed to have been struck on the receipt of the recognition of the Khalif of Baghdád in 626 A.H.

Obverse: Square area, with double lines, within a circle.

Legend, لا اله الا الله محمد رسول الله

Reverse: Square area, with double lines, within a circle.

Legend, في عهد الامام المستنصر امير المومنين

No. 2, Silver. Size, viii.; weight, 163·5. Date, 630 A.H.

Obverse: Square area, with double lines,

Legend, السلطان الاعظم شمس الدنيا والدين
ابو المظفر اليتمس السلطان ناصر امير المومنين

Reverse: Circular area.

Legend, لا اله الا الله محمد رسول الله المستنصر
امير المومنين

Margin, ضرب هذا الـ

Mr. Bayley notices the occasional change of the name of the piece to the generic السكة as well as the ignorant substitution of المستنصر بامر الله for the Khalif's true title. J.A.S.B., 1862, p. 207. Col. Guthrie's coin (Type No. 2) discloses a similar error.

Legend, في عهد الامام المستنصر امير المومنين

Margin, ضرب هذة الفضة

No. 3, Silver. Size, viii.; weight, 163·5 gr.

Obverse, as No. 2, but the square area is enclosed in a circle.

Reverse: Square area enclosed within a circle, identical with the obverse design.

though superior in the early copies to the crude introductory issues of Altamsh, seldom compete with the contemporary design or execution of the Dehli die-cutters, and soon merge into their own provincialisms, which are progressively exaggerated in the repetition, until, at last, what with the imperfection of the model, the progressive conventionalism of the designers, and the ignorance and crude mechanical imitation of the engravers, their legends become mere semblances of intelligible writing, and, as the plates will show, like Persian *shikastah*, easy to read when one can divine what is intended, but for anything like precision in obscure and nearly obliterated margins, a very untrustworthy basis for the search after exact results.

The different mints each followed its own traditions, and the school of art stood generally at a higher level in the eastern section of the kingdom, especially when Sonárgaon was held by its own independent rulers. The lowest scale of die execution, exemplified in the present series, was reserved for the capital of the united provinces under the kingship of Sikandar (No. 22 infrà). The numismatic innovations of Muhammad bin Tughlak were felt and copied in the south, especially in the reproduction of the titular legends; but his own coins struck at the "city"—he would not call it capital—of Lakhnautí, evince the haste and carelessness of a temporary sojourn, and still worse, the hand of a local artist, all of which short-comings may be forgiven to a monarch who, in his own imperial metropolis, had raised the standard of the beauties of Arabic writing, as applied to coin legends, to a position it had never before attained, and which later improved appliances have seldom succeeded in equalling.

The Bengal Sultáns, mere imitators at first, were original in their later developments of coin illumination, and the issues of the fully independent kings exhibit a commendable variety of patterns in the die devices, damaged and restricted, however, in the general effect by the pervading coarseness and imperfection of the forms of the letters. Then, again, the tenor of the inscriptions is usually of independent conception, especially in the refusal to adopt the ever recurring *kalimah*, and in the suggestive mutations of titles assigned to the lieutenants of the prophet on earth, whose names they did not care to learn. So also was their elaboration of the titular adjuncts of the four Imáms uninfluenced by northern formulæ; many of which conventionalisms survived for centuries, till Shír Sháh, in the chances of conquest, incorporated them into the coinage of Hindustán, during the exile of the temporarily vanquished Humáyún.

The standard of the Bengal coinage was necessarily, like the pieces themselves, a mere imitation of imperial mint quantities, and the early issues will be seen to follow closely upon the proper amount in weight contemplated in the Dehli prototypes; but one of the curious results the Kooch Behár collective find determines is, that, though the first kings on the list clearly put forth money of full measure, their pieces were, in most cases, subjected to a well understood Indian process of boring-out, or reduction to the exact weight to which we must suppose subsequent kings lowered the legal standard of their money, so that, although some of the silver pieces of Kai Káús and Fírúz have escaped the debaser's eye, and preserve the completeness of their original issue denomination, the great majority of the older coins have been brought down to the subsequent local standard of 166 grains, at which figure, in troy grains, the bulk of the hoard ranges, or, in more marked terms, 166 grains is the precise weight of the majority of the very latest and best preserved specimens, which must have been consigned to their recent place of concealment when very fresh from mints but little removed from the residence of the accumulator of the treasure, and be held to represent coin which could scarcely have changed hands.

The intrinsic value of the money of these sovereigns follows next in the order of the enquiry. This department of fiscal administration might naturally have been expected to have been subject to but limited check or control, when regulated by the uncertain processes of Oriental metallurgy; but, in practice, it will be seen that some of the native Mint-masters were able to secure a very high standard of purity, and, what is more remarkable, to maintain a singularly uniform scale in the rate of alloy. In the case of the imperial coins subjected to assay in Calcutta, specimens spreading over, and in so far, representing a sequent eighty years of the issues of the northern metropolis, vary only to the extent of six grains in the thousand, or 0.6 per cent. As the Dehli coinage proves superior, in point of weight, to the southern standard, so also does it retain a higher degree of purity; the 990 and 996 of silver to the test total of 1,000 grains, sinks, in the earliest examples of the Bengal mintages, to 989, from which figures it experiences a temporary rise, in possibly exceptional cases, under Bahádur Sháh, who may be supposed to have brought down, with his reinstituted honors and the coined treasure so lavishly bestowed upon him by Muhammad bin Tughlak on his restoration to the government of Sonárgaon, certain implied responsibilities for the equity and fulness of his currencies; while in the subsequent irregularly descending scale, Aâzam Sháh's officials arrived at the most unblushing effort of debasement, in the reduction of silver to 962 grains. Among other unexpected items for which the aid of modern science may be credited, is the support which the intrinsic contents of the erroneously-classed coins of 'Ádil Sháh under native interpretation, lend to the correctness of the revised attribution of the pieces themselves suggested by the critical terms of their own legends, in the manifest identity of their assay touch with the associate coins of the lower empire of India.

Colonel Guthrie has furnished me with the following data, concerning the âssay of the various coins composing the Kooch Bahár hoard:—"When the Bengal Asiatic Society made their selection of coins from the trove, they set apart four of each description for the Mint, two being for special assay, two for the Mint collection. The result of the assay was as follows (1,000 represents absolute purity):"

DEHLI COINS.

1. Balban (A.H. 664) ... 990 and 996
2. Kai Kobád (A.H. 685) 990 and 996
3. Ghiás-ud-dín Tughlak (A.H. 720) 990.
4. 'Ádil Sháh [i.e. Ghází Sháh of Bengal, A.H. 751] 989.

BENGAL COINS.

1. Shams-ud-dín Fírúz........... 989
2. Bahádur Sháh ...... 988 and 993
3. Mubárak Sháh...... .......... 987
4. Iliás Sháh (1st type) 939; (2nd) 982; (3rd) 988.
5. Sikandar Sháh (return lost).
6. Aâzam Sháh (1st type) 981; (2nd) 989; (3rd) 962; (4th) 977; (5th) 985.

A question that has frequently puzzled both Oriental and European commentators on the history of India, has been the intrinsic value of the current coin at the various epochs referred to, so that the most exact numerical specifications conveyed but a vague notion of the sterling sum contemplated in the recital of any given author. Numismatists have been for long past in a position to assert that the Dehli Tankah contained absolutely 173 grains, which would presuppose a theoretical issue weight of 174 or 175 grains, and a touch of nearly pure silver; but assuming this specific coin to have been a *white* or *real* "Tankah of Silver (تنكه نقره), a doubt necessarily remained as to what was to be understood by the alternative black Tankah (تنكه سياه). Nizám-ud-dín Ahmad, in his Tabakát-i-Akbari, seems to assign the introduction of these black Tankahs to Muhammad bin Tughlak, who notoriously depreciated the currency to a large extent, before he resorted to the extreme measure of a forced currency, though it may be doubted whether any such depreciation would have been thought of, even if there had been time to effect the conversion, at the very commencement of his reign, to which period Nizám-ud-dín attributes the issue of these pieces, in the apparent desire of explaining the bare possibility of the possession of such numerical amounts as are stated to have been squandered in largesses by the newly-enthroned monarch. However, the real debasement of the coin need not have extended much beyond the point indicated by the superficial aspect of his own Bengal mintages, and Aâzam Sháh's coins of the same locality probably exceed that accusatory measure of debasement; while, on the other hand, Muhammad bin Tughlak, on reverting to specie currencies, after his futile trial of copper tokens, seems to have aimed at a restoration of the ancient purity of metal in his metropolitan issues, as I can quote a coin of his produced by the Dehli Mint in A.H. 734, which has every outward appearance of a sole component element of unalloyed silver, and equally retains the fair average weight of 168 grains.[1] All

[1] This coin is similar, but not identical in its legends with the gold piece,

these evidences would seem to imply that the Bengal ratio of purity was intentionally lower, and that a very slight addition to the recognised alloy would bring the local issues fairly within the category of "black Tankahs." Such a supposition of the inferiority of the coinages of the southern kingdom appears to be curiously illustrated by Báber's mentioning that, in A.H. 932, a portion of the revenues of the district of Tirhút, a sort of border-land of his kingdom, which did not extend over Bengal, was payable in *Tankah Nukrah*, and the larger remainder in *Tànkah Siáh*,[1] an exceptional association of currencies in a given locality, which can scarcely be explained in a more simple and reasonable manner than by assuming the lower description of the conventional estimate piece to have been concurrent with a better description of the same coin, constituting the prevailing and authorized revenue standard of the northern portions of the conquering Moghul's Indian dominions.

Another important element of all currency questions is the relative rate of exchange of the precious metals *inter se.* And this is a division of the enquiry of peculiar significance at the present moment, when Her Majesty's Government are under pressure by the European interest to introduce gold as a legal tender at a fixed and permanent rate, or, in effect, to supersede the existing silver standard, the single and incontestable measure of value, in which all modern obligations have been contracted, and a metal, whose present market price is, in all human probability, less liable to be affected by

No. 84, of 736 A.H., p. 50, Pathân Sultâns. The following are the inscriptions:

*Obverse*— والله الغني وانتم الفقرا

*Reverse*— في عهد محمد بن تغلق

Margin— بدار الاسلام سنة اربع وثلثين وسبعماية

[1] Báber has left an interesting account of the revenues of his newly-acquired kingdom in India, as estimated after the battle of Panipat, in A.H. 932, to the effect that "the countries from Bhíra to Bahâr which are now under my dominion yield a revenue of 52 krores" of Tankas. In the detail of the returns from different provinces, Tirhút is noticed as Tribute (Khidmatâna) of the Tirhúti Raja 250,000 *tankah nukrah*, and 2,750,000 *tankah siáh*. William Erskine, History of India under Báber and Humáyun, London, 1854, vol. i., p. 540. See also Leyden's Memoirs of Baber, London, 1826, p. 334.

over production than that of gold: the bullion value of which latter had already begun to decline in the Bazárs of India, simultaneously with the arrival of the first-fruits of Australian mining.

If the contemplated authoritative revolution in the established currency had to be applied to a fully civilized people, there might be less objection to this premature experiment; but to disturb the dealings of an empire, peopled by races of extreme fixity of ideas, to give advantages to the crafty few, to the detriment of the mass of the unlettered population, is scarcely justified by the exigencies of British trade; and India's well-wishers may fairly advance a mild protest against hasty legislation, and claim for a subject and but little understood nationality, some consideration, before the ruling power forces on their unprepared minds the advanced commercial tenets of the cities of London and Liverpool.

The ordinary rate of exchange of silver against gold in Marco Polo's time (1271-91 A.D.),[1] may be inferred to have been eight to one; though exceptional cases are mentioned in localities within the reach of Indian traders, where the ratios of six to one and five to one severally obtained.

Ibn Batutah, in the middle of the fourteenth century,

[1] The Province of KARAIAN. "For money they employ the white porcelain shell found in the sea, and these they also wear as ornaments about their necks. Eighty of the shells are equal in value to a saggio of silver, or two Venetian groats, and eight saggi of good silver to one of pure gold." Chap. xxxix.

The Province of KARAZAN. "Gold is found in the rivers, both in small particles and in lumps; and there are also veins of it in the mountains. In consequence of the large quantity obtained, they give a saggio of gold for six saggi of silver. They likewise use the before-mentioned porcelain shells in currency, which, however, are not found in this part of the world, but are brought from India."—Chap. xl; also Pinkerton (London, 1811), vol. vii., 143.

The Province of KARDANDAN. "The currency of this country is gold by weight, and also the porcelain shells. An ounce of gold is exchanged for five ounces of silver, and a saggio of gold for five saggi of silver, there being no silver mines in this country, but much gold; and consequently the merchants who import silver obtain a large profit." Chap. xli.

The Kingdom of MIEN (*Ava*). "You then reach a spacious plain [at the foot of the Yunnan range], whereon, three days in every week, a number of people assemble, many of whom come down from the neighbouring mountains, bringing their gold to be exchanged for silver, which the merchants who repair thither from distant countries carry with them for this purpose; and one saggio of gold is given for five of silver." Chap. xliii. Travels of Marco Polo, by W. Marsden, London, 1818; and Bohn's Edition, 1854.

when he was, so to say, resident and domesticated in India, reports the relative values of the metals as eight to one.[1]

[1] رايت الارزيُباع في اسواقها خمسة وعشرين رطلًا دهلية بدينار فضي
والدينار الفضي هو ثمانية دراهم ودرهمهم كالدرهم النقرة سوآءً iv. 10,

"J'ai vu vendre le riz, dans les marchés de ce pays [Bengale], sur le pied de vingt-cinq ritbl de Dihly pour un dínár d'argent: celui-ci vaut huit drachmes, et leur drachme équivaut absolument à la drachme d'argent" (iv. 210).

The difficulty of arriving at any thoroughly satisfactory interpretation of the obscure Arabic text, as it now stands, may be frankly admitted, nor do I seek to alter or amend the French translation, further than to offer a very simple explanation of what probably the author really designed to convey in the general tenor of the passage in question. It was a crude but established custom among the early Muhammadan occupying conquerors of India, to issue gold and silver coins of equal weights, identical fabric, and analogous central legends; hence, whenever, as in the present instance, the word *Dínár* is used in apposition with and contrast to the secondary term *Dirham*, the one *primâ facie* implies gold, the other silver; and there can be little doubt but that the original design of the text was to specify that one gold piece of a given weight passed *in situ* for eight silver pieces of similar form and of slightly greater bulk. It is possible that the term *Dínár* may in process of time have come to stand for a conventional measure of value, like the "pound sterling," susceptible by common consent of being liquidated in the due equivalent of silver; but this concession need not affect the direct contrast between the Dínârs and Dirhams so obviously marked in the case in point.

Ibn Batutah in an earlier part of his work (iii. 426) [Lee's edition is imperfect at this portion, p. 149] gives us the comparative Dehli rate of exchange—of which he had unpleasant personal experiences: he relates that he was directed to be paid (55,000 + 12,000 =) 67,000 pieces of some well understood currency neither the name or the metal of which is defined, but which may legitimately be taken to have been "Silver Tankahs," and in satisfaction of this amount, deducting the established one-tenth for *Dastúrí*, which left a reduced total of 60,300, he received 6,233 gold tankahs. Under this scale of payment the gold must have borne a rate of exchange of one to 9·67 of silver, or very nearly one to 10, a proportion which might be supposed to clash with the one to eight of the more southern kingdom, but the existing state of the currencies of the two localities afford a striking illustration of the consistency of the African observer's appreciation of money values in either case. His special patron, Muhammad bin Tughlak, Emperor of Dehli, had, from his first elevation to the throne, evinced a tendency to tamper with the currency, departing very early in his reign from the traditional equality of weights of gold and silver coins; he re-modelled both forms and relative proportions, introducing pieces of 200 grains of gold, styled on their surfaces *dínárs*, and silver coins of 140 grains, designated as *adalis*, in supersession of the ancient equable tankahs, both of gold and silver, extant examples of which in either metal come up to about 174 grains. More important for the present issue is the practical result, that, from the very commencement, Muhammad Tughlak's silver money is invariably of a lower standard than that of his predecessors, whether this refers to the early continuation of the full silver tankah, or to his own newly devised 140 grain piece, a mere reproduction of the time-honoured local weight, which the Aryan races found current in the land some twenty-five centuries before this Moslem revival, but in either case, this payment to Ibn Batutah seems to have been made after the Sultan had organised and abandoned that imaginary phase of perfection in the royal art of depreciating the circulating media, by the entire supercession of the precious metals, and following the ideal of a paper currency, the substitution of a copper simulacrum of each and every piece in the

The Emperor Akbar's minister, Abúl Fazl, has left an official record of the value of gold in the second half of the sixteenth century, at which period the price was on the rise, so that the mints were issuing gold coin in the relation of one to 9·4 of silvre. But a remarkable advance must have taken place about this time, as in the second moiety of the seventeenth century, Tavernier[1] found gold exchanging against fourteen times its weight of silver, from which point it gradually advanced to one to fifteen, a rate it maintained when the East India Company re-modelled the coinage in 1833.[2] Afterwards, with prospering times, the metal ran up occasionally to fabulous premiums, to fall again ignominiously, when Californian and Australian discoveries made it common in the land.

I revert for the moment to a more formal recapitulation of the computations, which serve to establish the ratios of gold and silver in Akbar's time.

Abúl Fazl's figured returns give the following results:—

First.—Chugal, weight in gold Tolah 3, Másha 0, Rati $5\frac{1}{4} = 30$ Rs. of $11\frac{1}{2}$ Máshas each : 549·84 :: 172·5 × 30 (5175·0) : 1::9·4118.

Second.—Áftábí, gold, weight T. 1, M. 2, R. $4\frac{3}{4}$=12 Rs. : 218·90 ::172·5×12 (2070·0):1::9·4563.

order of its degree from the *Dinár* to the lowest coin in the realm, the values being authoritatively designated on the surface of each. This forced currency held its own, more or less successfully from 730 to 733, when it came to a simple and self-developed end. Taking the probable date of this payment as 742-3 A.H. (Ibn, B. vi., p. 4, and vol. iii., p. xxii.), it may be assumed that the 174 (or 175) grain old gold tankah, which had heretofore stood at the equitable exchange of one to eight tunkas of good silver, came necessarily, in the depreciation of the new silver coins, to be worth ten or more of the later issues. Pathán Sultáns, p. 53).

[1] "All the gold and silver which is brought into the territories of the Great Mogul is refined to the highest perfection before it be coined into money."—Tavernier, London Edition, 1677, p. 2. "The roupie of gold weighs two drams and a half, and eleven grains, and is valued in the country at 14 roupies of silver."—Page 2. "But to return to our roupies of gold, you must take notice that they are not so current among the merchants. For one of them is not worth above fourteen roupies." The traveller then goes on to relate his doleful personal experiences, of how, when he elected to be paid for his goods in gold, "the king's uncle" forced him to receive the gold rupee at the rate of fourteen and a half silver rupees, whereby he lost no less than 3428 rupees, on the transaction. Sir James Stewart, writing in 1772, also estimates the conventional proportionate value of silver to gold, as fourteen to one—"The Principles of Money applied to the present state of the Coin of Bengal." Calcutta, 1772.

[2] Prinsep's Useful Tables, pp. 5, 72, 79.

Third.—Ilahí, or Lál Jalálí, also Muíanni, gold, weight M. 12, R. $1\frac{3}{4}$ = 10 Rs. : 183·28 :: 172·5 × 10 (1725·0) : 1::9·4118.

3 A.—The larger piece, the Sihansah, in value 100 Lál Jalális, gives an identical return. Weight in gold, T. 101, M. 9, R. 7 = 1000 Rs. : 18328· :: 172,500 (172·5 × 100 × 10):1::9·4118.

Fourth.—Adl.-Guṭkah, or Muhar, also called Mihrábí, gold, weight 11 Máshas = 9 Rs. : 165 :: 172·5 × 9 (1552·5) : 1 ::9·40909.

4 A.—The higher proportions specified under the piece of 100 round Muhars, produce a similar result. Weight in gold, T. 91, M. 8 = 900 Rs. : 16500 :: 155250· (172·5 × 100 × 9) ·:1::9·40.

These sums are based upon the ordinary Tolah of 180 gr., Másha of 15, and Rati of 1·875 grs. The question of corresponding values in the English scale need not affect the accuracy of comparisons founded upon the conventional measure by which both metals were estimated.

I have given more prominence to the above calculations, and even tested anew my earlier returns by the independent totals afforded by the larger sums now inserted, because the obvious result of gold being to silver as one to 9·4, has been called in question by an official of the Calcutta Mint (a Dr. Shekleton), who, however, while unable either to correct my data, or to produce any possible evidence against my conclusions, ventures to affirm, that "9·4 to one is a relative value of gold to silver, which never could really have existed."[1] Nevertheless, here is a series of comparative weights and values, furnished by the highest authority of the day, and each and all produce returns absolutely identical up to the first place of decimals. My original estimates were sketched and published at Dehli, in 1851, where I had access to the best MSS., to the most comprehensive range of antiquarian relics, and at command the most intelligent oral testimony in the land. When reprinting Prinsep's "Useful Tables" (London, 1858), I had occasion to quote these calculations, and was able to fortify them, had it been needed, by the precisely analogous

[1] Jour. As. Soc. Bengal, 1864, p. 517.

results obtained by Colonel W. Anderson, who had tried Abúl Fazl's figures, from a different point of view, and for altogether independent purposes.[1] But if there were the faintest reason for doubting so moderate a rate as one to 9·4, the whole discussion might be set at rest by Abúl Fazl's own statement as translated into English in 1783 when, in concluding a very elaborate review of the profit and loss of refining gold, for the purpose of coinage, he concludes, and the process "leaves a remainder of about *one-half a tolah* of gold, the value of which is four rupees."[2] It may be as well that I should add, that some of my totals differ from those to be found in Gladwin's translation of the original Persian text.[3] I do not recapitulate the several divergencies, but it is necessary to prove the justice of one, at least, of my emendations. Gladwin's MSS. gave the rupee at 11¼ *máshas* (i. p. 34). The more carefully collated Dehli texts showed the real weight to be 11·5 *máshas*, a static fact of some importance, which is curiously susceptible of proof from Gladwin's own data: at page 46 of his Calcutta edition, a sum is given of the refining charges and profits, as understood by the mints of those days, wherein 989 tolas, 9 máshas of impure silver is stated to be reduced by 14 T. 9 M. 1 R. in refining, and a further 4 T. 10 M. 3 R. in manipulation, leaving 11641 *máshas* of silver (989. 9. 0. — 14. 9. 1. — 4. 10. 3. = 11641) which is officially announced as ordinarily coined into 1012 rupees, (1012 × 115 = 11638) giving, as nearly as may be, the essential 11½ máshas, which the translated text *should* have preserved in its earlier passages.

Richard Hawkins, who was at Agra, in A.D. 1609-11, during the reign of Jahángír, has left a notice of certain accumulated treasures of that prince which he was permitted to behold, and amongst the rest he specifies "In primis of Seraffins Ecberi, which be ten rupias apiece;" to this passage is added in a marginal note, that, "a tole is a rupia challany [current] of silver, and ten of these toles are of the value of one of gold."[4] This evidence might at first sight seem to militate against the conclusion arrived at from the official

[1] U.T., vol. ii., p. 32. [2] Gladwin, i. 44. [3] 4to., Calcutta, 1783.
[4] Purchas' Travels, folio, 1625-26, i. 217.

returns above summarized, but the value of gold was clearly on the rise, and one of the aims of Akbar's legislation on metallic exchanges, which had necessarily been disturbed by progressive modifications in the relative values of the precious metals, was manifestly to secure an authoritative *even* reckoning by tens and hundreds. The old round *muhar*, (No. 4 of the above list) represented the inconvenient sum of nine rupees, or 360 *dáms;* by raising the weight of the piece to the higher total given under No. 3, the gold *ilahi* was made equivalent to ten rupees, or in fiscal reckoning to 400 *dáms.* Similarly, in the case of the silver coin, the old rupee passed for 39 *dáms;* in the new currency a value of 40 *dáms* was secured, not by an increase of weight, but by the declared and doubtlessly achieved higher standard of the metal employed, aided by the advantage that contemporary mintages so readily secured in India.

The subdivisions of the standard silver Tankah, as well as the relative exchange ratios of silver and copper in their subordinate denominations, claim a passing notice. Though Bengal proper probably remained satisfied with its lower currency of cowries, supplemented by the occasional intervention of copper, for some time after the introduction of gold and silver money, yet as the earliest copper coins of that kingdom must have been based upon and, in the first instance, supplied by Dehli mintages, the Imperial practice comes properly within the range of the local division of the general enquiry.

It has been seen that Minháj-ul-Siráj, in comparing the circulating media of Hindustán and Bengal, speaks of the currency of the former as composed of *Chitals*, a name which is seemingly used by himself and succeeding authors in the generic sense for money, as if these pieces continued to constitute the popular standard both in theory and practice, notwithstanding the introduction of the more imposing *tankahs* of gold and silver. Up to this time it has not been possible satisfactorily to demonstrate the actual value of the coin in question; in some cases indirect evidence would seem to bring its intrinsic worth down to a very low point; while, at times, the money calculations for large sums, in which its name alone is used, appear to invest it with a metrical position far beyond the subordinate exchanges of mere bazár traffic.

In the details of the "prices-current" in the reign of Alá-ud-dín Muhammad, as well as in the relation of certain monetary re-adjustments made by Fírúz Sháh III., the name of the *Chital* is constantly associated in the definition of comparative values with another subdivision entitled the Káṇi, which may now be pronounced with some certainty to have been the $\frac{1}{64}$ of the original *Tankah*, of 175 grains, and $\frac{1}{50}$ of the new silver coin of 140 grains, introduced by Muhammad bin Tughlak. The temporary forced currency of this Sultán necessitated in itself the positive announcement of the names, and authoritative equivalents of each representative piece, and in this abnormal practice contributes many items towards the elucidation of the quantitative constitution of the real currency of the day, which these copper tokens were designed to replace. In illustration of this point, I insert a woodcut and description of a brass coin, which was put forth to pass for the value of the silver piece of 140 grains, to whose official weight it is seemingly suggestively approximated.

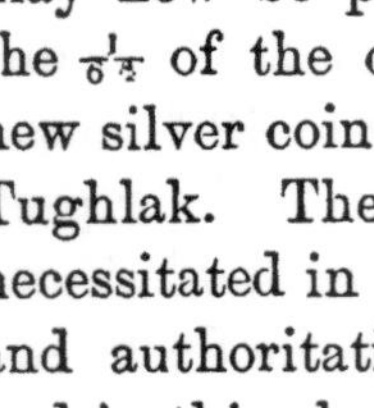

Brass; weight, 132 grs.; A.H. 731; *Common.*

*Obverse.*—مهرشد تنكه پنجاه كاني در روزكار بنده اميدوار محمد تغلق. Struck (lit. *sealed*), a tankah of fifty kánis in the reign of the servant, hopeful (of mercy), Muhammad Tughlak.

*Reverse.*—Area, من اطاع السلطان فقد اطاع الرحمن. "He who obeys the king, truly he obeys God."[1]

Margin, در تخت كاه دولت اباد سال بر هفصد سي يك. At the capital Daulat-ábád, year ? 731.

In addition to the 50 *káni*-piece may be quoted extant specimens of this Sultán's forced issues, bearing the definitive names of "*hast-káni*" (8 káṇis). "*Shash-káni*" (6 káṇis) and *Do-káni* (2 káṇis.) An obverse of the latter is given in the margin.

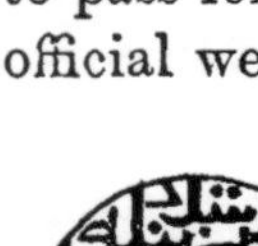

The reverse has the unadorned name of محمد تغلق.

[1] In other examples of the forced currency, he exhorts his subjects in more urgent terms to submit to the Almighty, as represented in the person of the

Next in order, may be quoted historical evidence of Fírúz Sháh's fiscal re-organizations, in the course of which mention is made of pre-existing pieces of 48, 25, 24, 12, 10, 8, and 6 káṇis, the lowest denomination called by that name; afterwards the narrative goes on to explain that, in addition to the ordinary *Chital* piece already in use, Fírúz Sháh originated, for the benefit of the poorer classes of his subjects, subdivisional ½ Chital and ¼ Chital pieces.

As the spoken languages of the Peninsula enable us to restore the true meaning to the misinterpreted Sanskrit *karsha*,[1] so the Dravidian tongues readily explain the term *káṇi*, which finds no place in Aryan vocabularies, but which was incorporated into the vernaculars of Hindustán, during the southward migrations of the Scythic tribes. In Telugu, *káṇi* means $\frac{1}{64}$, or one quarter of a sixteenth" (Brown). In Canarese $\frac{1}{64}$ (Reeve), and in Tamil $\frac{1}{80}$ (Winslow). Wilson's Glossary gives "*Káṇi*, corruptly, *Cawney*. Tel. Tam. Karn. $\frac{1}{80}$, or sometimes $\frac{1}{64}$."[2]

The term *káṇi*, in addition to its preferable meaning of $\frac{1}{64}$, was, as we see, also used for the fraction $\frac{1}{80}$, but its application in the former sense to the ruling integer in the present instance, seems to be conclusively settled by the relative proportions assigned to the modified *tankah* of Muhammad bin Tughlak, when compared with the normal weight of the earlier coin (: 64 : : 175 : 50 : : 136·718).

The method in which the subdivisional currency was arranged, consisted, as has already been stated, of an admixture of the two metals, silver and copper, in intentionally varying proportions in pieces of identical weight, shape and device; so that the traders in each case had to judge by the eye and hand of the intrinsic value of the coin presented to them. To European notions this system would imply endless doubt and uncertainty, but under the practiced vision and delicate perceptive powers of touch, with which the natives of India are endowed, but little difficulty seems to have been experi-

ruling monarch, and to adopt, in effect, the bad money he covers with texts from the Kurán—the "Obey God and obey the Prophet and those in authority among you," and "Sovereignty is not conferred upon every man," but "some" are placed over "others"—were unneeded on his coinage of pure metal.

[1] Num. Chron. iv. 58; J. A. S. B. xxxiii. 266.

[2] There is a coin called a "Do-gáni or Doodee," still quoted in the Madras Almanacks.

enced; and I myself can testify to the accuracy of the verdicts pronounced by the experienced men of Dehli, whose instinctive estimates were tested repeatedly by absolute assay. I published many of these results, some years ago, in the Numismatic Chronicle,[1] where the curious in these matters may trace many of the gradational pieces of the *káṇis* above enumerated. As some further experiments in reference to the intrinsic values of these coins were made, at my instance, in the Calcutta Mint, I subjoin a table of the authoritative results, which sufficiently confirms the previous less exhaustive assays by the native process.

LIST OF DEHLI COINS,

*Composed of Silver and Copper in varying proportions forwarded for examination by Edward Thomas, Esq., C.S.*, 10 *June*, 1853.

| No. of Packet. | A. H. | Reference to Numbers of Coins in "Pathán Sultáns." | No. of Coins in Parcel. | Weight in Grains. | Dwts. Fine Silver per lb. in each. |
|---|---|---|---|---|---|
| 1 | 716 | Mubárak Sháh. No. 66. | 1 | 53·22 | 5·375 |
| 2 | 726 | Muhammad bin Tughlak. No. 91. | 1 | 55·15 | 13·300 |
| 3 | 895 | Sikandar Bahlol. No. 163. | 1 | 143·438 | 1·900 |
| 4 | 896 | ,, ,, | 4–1 | 142·163 | 2·025 |
| ,, | ,, | ,, ,, | 1 | 142·936 | 1·925 |
| ,, | ,, | ,, ,, | 1 | 138·913 | 1·615 |
| ,, | ,, | ,, ,, | 1 | 140·088 | 2·200 |
| 5 | 898 | ,, ,, | 1 | 141·500 | 1·5625 |
| 6 | 900 | ,, ,, | 2–1 | 140 800 | 2·6000 |
| ,, | ,, | ,, ,, | 1 | 127·600 | 3·0125 |
| 7 | 903 | ,, ,, | 1 | 143·100 | 4·650 |
| 8 | 904 | ,, ,, | 3–1 | 142·500 | 5·624 |
| ,, | 907 | ,, ,, | 3–1 | 143·250 | 15·5 |
| ,, | ,, | ,, ,, | 1 | 141·150 | 16·0 |
| ,, | ,, | ,, ,, | 1 | 139·900 | 16·0 |
| 9 | 905 | ,, ,, | 1 | 144·500 | 17·5 |
| 10 | 909 | ,, ,, | 1 | 141·500 | 15·0 |
| 11 | 910 | ,, ,, | 1 | 140·200 | 15·0 |
| 12 | 912 | ,, ,, | 2–1 | 142·500 | 12·0 |
| ,, | ,, | ,, ,, | 1 | 135·500 | 15·0 |
| 13 | 913 | ,, ,, | 2–1 | 132·250 | 15·0 |
| ,, | ,, | ,, ,, | 1 | 140·750 | 15.0 |
| 14 | 914 | ,, ,, | 4–1 | 140·000 | 15·0 |
| ,, | ,, | ,, ,, | 1 | 138·500 | 15·5 |
| ,, | ,, | ,, ,, | 1 | 141·000 | 16·5 |
| ,, | ,, | ,, ,, | 1 | 140·500 | 16·0 |
| 15 | 918 | ,, ,, | 4–1 | 138·250 | 10·0 |
| ,, | ,, | ,, ,, | 1 | 133·250 | 10·0 |
| ,, | ,, | ,, ,, | 1 | 139·750 | 9·0 |
| ,, | ,, | ,, ,, | 1 | 125·000 | 8·0 |
| 16 | 919 | ,, ,, | 3–1 | 135·250 | 32·0 |
| ,, | ,, | ,, ,, | 1 | 137·250 | 8·0 |
| ,, | ,, | ,, ,, | 1 | 137·500 | 8.0 |

[1] Vol. xv. 1852, p. 121, *et seq.*

The Institutes of Manu have preserved a record, reproduced in the subjoined table, of the various weights in use, some centuries before Christ,[1] and among other things explain, that the values of gold and copper, were calculated by a different metric scheme, to that applied to silver. A larger number of Ratis went to the Másha in the former, and the progression of numbers commenced with a five (5 × 16), while the silver estimates were founded on the simple arithmetic of *fours* (2 × 16), which constituted so special a characteristic of India's home civilization. Still, the two sets of tables starting from independent bases, were very early assimilated and adapted to each other in the advancing totals, so that the 320 ratis constituting the *ṣatamána* of the quaternary multiplication, is created in the third line by the use of a *ten*, and the quasi exotic scheme corrects its independent elements by multiplying by *four*, and produces a similar total in the contents of the *Pala* or *Nishka*. The second lines of the tables are severally filled in with the aggregate numbers, 32 and 80, and as the duplication of the former, or 64, has

[1] Manu, viii. 131.—"Those names of copper, silver, and gold (weights) which are commonly used among men for the purpose of worldly business, I will now comprehensively explain. 132.—The very small mote which may be discerned in a sunbeam passing through a lattice is the first of quantities, and men call it a *trasareṇu*. 133.—Eight of those *trasareṇus* are supposed equal in weight to one minute poppy-seed (*likshá*), three of those seeds are equal to one black mustard-seed (*rájasarshapa*), and three of these last to a white mustard-seed (*gaura-sarshapa*). 134.—Six white mustard seeds are equal to a middle-sized barley-corn (*yavá*), three such barley-corns to one *kṛshṇala* [raktika], five *kṛshṇalas* of gold are one *másha*, and sixteen such *máshas* one *suvarṇa*. 135.—Four *suvarṇas* make a *pala*, ten *palas* a *dharaṇa*, but two kṛshṇalas weighed together are considered as one silver máshaka. 136.—Sixteen of those máshakas are a silver *dharaṇa* or *puráṇa*, but a copper *kársha* is known to be a *paṇa* or *kárshápana*. 137.—Ten *dharaṇas* of silver are known by the name of a *ṣatamána*, and the weight of four suvarṇas has also the appellation of a *nishka*." These statements may be tabulated thus as the

ANCIENT INDIAN SYSTEM OF WEIGHTS.

| | | | | |
|---|---|---|---|---|
| SILVER. | | | | |
| 2 ratis | = 1 másha | | | |
| 32 ,, | = 16 ,, | = 1 dharaṇa, or puráṇa. | | |
| 320 ,, | = 160 ,, | = 10 ,, | | 1 ṣatamána. |
| GOLD. | | | | |
| 5 ratis | = 1 másha. | | | |
| 80 ,, | = 16 ,, | = 1 suvarṇa. | | |
| 320 ,, | = 64 ,, | = 4 ,, | = 1 pala, or nishka. | |
| 3200 ,, | = 640 ,, | = 40 ,, | = 10 ,, | 1 dharaṇa. |
| COPPER. | | | | |
| 80 ratis | = 1 kárshápaṇa. | | | |

been seen to do duty in the one case, the probability of the use of the 160 naturally suggests itself in connexion with the theoretical organization of the copper coinage.

In proceeding to test the relations of the minor and subordinate currencies, the cardinal point to be determined is, the exchangeable value of copper as against silver. It has been affirmed by Colebrooke,[1] that the ratio stood in Manu's time at 64 to 1: accepting the correctness of this estimate, which has, I believe, remained unchallenged, and supposing the rate to have remained practically but little affected up to the Muhammadan conquest, the 175 grains of *silver* of Altamsh's new coinage, would be equivalent in metallic value to 11,200 grains of *copper*. The ancient copper *kárshápaṇa* is recognised and defined as 80 ratis in weight, so that under the above conditions, and calculating the rati at 1·75 grains, each kárshápaṇa was equal to 140 grains, and eighty of these, under the same calculations, give a return of 11,200 grains. Without at present advancing any more definite proposition, or quoting dubious coincidencies, it may be as well to test these preliminary results by the Numismatic data Fírúz Sháh's Mints have left as an heritage behind him. Among the incidents quoted regarding that monarch's monetary innovations, he is stated to have introduced, for the first time, *half* and *quarter* Chitals. On the occasion of a very elaborate revision of my monograph on the Patháu Sultáns of Dehli, while residing under the very shadow of so many of their memorial edifices, I acquired and described, among others, two specimens of the money of this king, which seemed to be closely identifiable with his Utopian productions of new and infinitesimal subdivisions of the leading copper coinage, in his expressed desire of securing for the poorest of the poor, the fractional change they might be entitled to in the most limited purchases.[2] These coins responded singularly in their mutual proportions, and contributed in the form of once

[1] As. Res. v. 95.

[2] Shams-i-Siráj, in his work entitled the Táríkh-i-Fírúz Sháhi, gives the following incidents regarding Fírúz Sháh's coinages :—

شرح بیان احوال سکهٔ مہر شش کانے نقلست سلطان فیروزشاه در

current money, definitive weights in copper amounting severally to 34·5 and 17·8 grains, from which a very low estimate was deduced of 34·8 and 17·4, as a normal official standard. If the 34·8 grain of the first of these be multiplied by 160, it will give a return of 5568·0 grains, and accepting this trial piece, conditionally, as Fírúz's novel *half-Chital*,[1] it will be seen to furnish a general total of 11,136 grains for the copper equivalent of the 175 grains of silver contained in the old Tankah, and confirms the range of the Chital at 69·6 grains, or only ·4 short of the full contents tradition would assign it, as the unchanged *half kárshápaṇa* of primitive ages.[2] To pass to the opposite extreme for a test of the copper exchange rate, it is found that when Shír Sháh reorganised the northern coinage of Hindustán, by the lights of

¼ Chital of Fírúz.

طور عظمت و دور مکنت خویش چون سلاطین اهل گیتي سکهاء
بچندین نوع پدید اورد چنانچه زر تنکه و نقره و سکه چهل وهشت
کانی و مهر بیست و پنجکانی و بیست وچهار کانی ودوازده کانی وده کانی و
هشتکانی و ششکانی و مهر یک جیتل چون فیروزشاه بچندین اجناس
بي قیاس مهر وضع کردانید بعده در دل مبارك بالهام حضرت حق
تبارك تعالی گذرانید اگر بیچاره فقیران از اهل بازار چیزي
خرید کنند واز جمله مال نیم جیتل و یا دانکي باقي ماند آن
دوکاندار دانکه خود ندارد اگر این راهگذري ان باقي بر او بگذارد
ضایع رود اگر ازان دوکاندار طلب کند چون این مهر نیست از
کجا بچه دهد باقی او دهد برین وجوه میان بایع و مشتري مقالت
این حالت بتطویل کشید سلطان فیروزشاه فرمان فرمود که مهر
نیم جیتل که انرا اده گویند و مهر دانک جیتل که انرا پنکه گویند
وضع کنند تاغرض فقرا و مساکین حاصل شود

The original and unique MS., from which the above passage is extracted, is in the possession of the Nawáb Zíá-ud-dín of Lohárú, in the Dehli territory.

[1] I once supposed these two coins to be whole and half Chitals, instead of the half and quarter pieces now adopted.

[2] It may be as well to state distinctly that the most complete affirmation of the numismatic existence of a *Chital* of a given weight and value, supported even by all anterior written testimony, in no wise detracts from the subsequent and independent use of the name for the purposes of account, a confusion which perchance may have arisen from the traditional permanency of the term itself, which

his southern experience, and swept away all dubious combinations of metals, reducing the copper standard to its severe chemical element; his Mint statistics show that the 178 grains of silver, constituting his revised Tankah, exchanged against 40 *dáms*, or quadrupled chitals of copper, of an ascertained weight of 323·5 grains each, producing in all a total of 12,940 grains of the latter metal, as the equivalent of 178 grains of silver, or in the ratio of 72·69 to 1; though, even in the altered weights and modified proportions, still retaining inherent traces of the old scheme of *fours*, in the half *dám* of 80, and the quarter *dám* of 160 to the new "Rupee."

in either case might eventually have been used to represent higher or lower values than that which originally belonged to it. Ziá-i-Barni at one moment seems to employ the term as a fractional fiftieth of the *Tankah*, while in other parts of the same or similar documents he quotes a total of "sixty Chitals," and in his statement of progressive advances of price, mentions the rise from twenty Chitals to *half a Tankah*. Ferishtah following, with but vague knowledge, declares that fifty Chitals constituted the *Tankah;* while Abúl Fazl, who had real information on these matters as understood in his own day, asserts that the *dám* was divided "in account" into twenty-five Chitals. (See Suppt. Pathán Sultáns, p. 31; N. C. xv. 156; Ferishtah, p. 299; Gladwin A. A., I., p. 36.) Then again there seems to have been some direct association between *Chitals* and *Káṇis*, as General Cunningham has published a coin which he as yet has only partially deciphered, bearing the word جتله on the one side, and بكاني [? يكاني ] on the other. J. A. S. B., 1862, p. 425.

I have received from Mr. C. P. Brown the following note in reply to my queries as to the probable derivation of the word Chital:—

"I have been considering the inquiry you make regarding *chital* چيتل. You probably are aware that it is mentioned in the Ayín-i-Akbari, in the chapter on coins. There it evidently is an ideal money, like the farthing. You believe it may be connected with *chhe tol* چھے تول, but I rather judge it to be merely the Sanskrit *chitra* चित्र meaning 'odd' as a species; or as an odd sum, a fraction; the smallest coins in copper, which in Marata and Dakhni are called *khurda* خورده (see Wilson's Glossary, p. 288), and in America *bits;* or a fraction even of these, which in the bazar are often represented or paid in a few pinches of grain. As the Sanskrit month *Chaitra* is in Bengali *Chait*, and the *Chitra-durgam*, or 'odd coloured hill,' is in Dakhni called چيتل درگ *Chittle droog*, I think this may be the true derivation. The *cauri*, kowry, is not mentioned in the Ayín-i-Akbari, and probably was not yet introduced into India. We still call the smallest fractions 'grains;' and that which is indefinite would be *chitra*, or, according to the Musulmâni pronunciation, *cheetul*. There is also a form of it, *chillara* चिल्लर or *chilra* چلرا used in the Madras countries. Wilson notices it in his Glossary, p. 112, but fails to perceive its origin. It is precisely the same in sense. In Sanskrit scientific treatises, after a general rule, *chitram* is given as being a species, or sub class: *chillara* may often be rendered miscellaneous; and this is the same in idea."

It remains to discover upon what principles the new silver coinage of Altamsh was based. That copper was the ruling standard by which the relative values of the more precious metals were determined, there can scarcely be a doubt. The estimate by Paṇas of the ancient Law-giver, the constant reckoning by Chitals of the early Muhammadan intruders, down to the revenue assessments of Akbar, all of which were calculated in copper coin, sufficiently establish the permanency of the local custom, and the intrinsic contents of Altamsh's *Sikkah* or الفضّة of 174 or 175 grains, must primarily have been regulated by the silver equivalent of a given number of Chitals. Had the old silver *Puráṇas* been still in vogue, the new coin might have been supposed to have been based upon their weights and values; three of which Puráṇas would have answered to an approximate total of 96 ratis; but although the weight of the old coin had been preserved in the more modern *Dehli-wálas*, the metallic value of the current pieces had been so reduced, that from 16 to 24 would probably have been required to meet the exchange against the original silver *Tankah*; on the other hand, although the number of 96 ratis does not occur in the ancient tables, the combination of the inconvenient number of *three* Puráṇas into one piece, is by no means opposed to Vedic ideas; and there can be no question but that the traditional 96 ratis, of whatever origination, is constant in the modern *tolah;* but, as I have said before, the question whether the new coin was designed to constitute an even *one hundred* rati-piece, which, in process of time, by wear or intentional lowering of standard weights, came to settle down to the 96 rati *tolah,* remains to be proved by the determination of the decimals in troy-grains, which ought to be assigned to the normal *rati.*

I now proceed to notice the historical bearings of the coins of the Bengal series.

Any general revision of a special subject, coincident with the discovery of an unusually large amount of new illustrative materials, owes a first tribute to previous commentators—whose range of identification may chance to have been circumscribed by more limited archæological data, the application of which may equally have been narrowed by the inaccessibility of written history, heretofore confined, as in the present instance, to original Oriental MSS., or the partial transcripts and translations incidentally made known to the European world. At the head of the list of modern contributors must be placed, in point of time, M. Reinaud, who, so long ago as 1823, deciphered and described several types of the Bengal Mintages, commencing with those of Iliás Sháh (No. viii. of this series).[1] Closely following appeared Marsden's elaborate work, which, among other novelties, displayed a well-sustained sequence of Bengal coins, with corresponding engravings *still unequalled*, though in point of antiquity, producing nothing earlier than the issues of the same Iliás Sháh, who had inaugurated the newly-asserted independence of the southern monarchy, with such a wealth of coinages.[2] Next in order, must be cited a paper, in the Journal of the Asiatic Society of Bengal, by Mr. Laidlay, which added materially to the numismatic records of the local sovereigns, though still remaining deficient in the development of memorials of the more purely introductory history of the kingdom.[3] I myself, in the course of the publication of the Imperial Coins of the Pathán Sultáns of Dehli,[4] had occasion to notice two pieces of Bahádur Sháh, one of which proved of considerable interest, and likewise coins of both Shams-ud-dín Fírúz, and Mubárak Sháh, whose defective marginal legends, however, defeated any conclusive assignment to their original producers.

The chronicles of a subordinate and, in those days, but little accessible country were too often neglected by the national historians at the Court of Dehli, even if their means of information as to the course of local events had not necessarily been more or less imperfect. Two striking exceptions to the ordinary rule fortuitously occur, at conjunctions specially bearing upon the present enquiry, in the narrative of

[1] Journal Asiatique, Paris, vol. iii., p. 272.
[2] Numismata Orientalia, London, 1825, pp. 561–585.
[3] Vol. xv. (1846), p. 323.
[4] Wertheimer, London, 1847, pp. 37, 42, 82, and Supplement printed at Dehli in 1851, p. 15. See also Numismatic Chronicle, vol. ix., pp. 176, 181; vol. x., p. 153; and vol. xv. p. 124.

Minháj-ul-Siráj, Juzjáni, and the "Travels of Ibn Batutah," the former of whom accompanied Tughán Khán to Lakhnauti, in A.H. 640,[1] where he resided for about two years. The Arab from Tangiers,[2] on his way round to China, as ambassador on the part of Muhammad bin Tughlak, found himself in Eastern Bengal at the inconvenient moment when Fakhr-ud-dín Mubárak was in a state of undisguised revolt against the emperor, to whom they jointly owed allegiance; but this did not interfere with his practical spirit of enquiry, or his placing on record a most graphic description of the existing civilization and politics of the kingdom, and further compiling a singularly fresh and independent account (derived clearly from *vivâ voce* statements) of the immediately preceding dynastic changes to which the province had been subjected. So that, in effect, Ibn Batutah, with his merely incidental observations, has done more for the elucidation of the obscurities of the indigenous history of the period represented by the earlier coins of the Kooch Bahár hoard than all the native authors combined, to whose writings we at present have access.

The merits of these authors may or may not appear upon

[1] The Tabakát-i-Násiri of Abú Umar Minháj-ud-dín bin Siráj-ud-dín, *Juzjáni*, has been printed and published in the Persian series of the Bibliotheca Indica. under the auspices of the Asiatic Society of Bengal (Calcutta, 1864, pp. 453). The chapters on Indian and Central Asian affairs, with which the author was more or less personally conversant, have alone been reproduced. The usual Oriental commencement with the history of the world, the rise of Muhammadanism, etc , being mere compilations from secondary sources, have been very properly excluded from this edition. A full notice of the original work will be found in Mr. Morley's Catalogue of the MSS. of the R. A. S., p. 17 (London, 1854). Several other works of native historians, bearing upon the subject of this paper, have also been made accessible to the public in a printed form in the same collection, among which may be noted the Táríkh-i-Fíráz Sháhí (the third king of the name in the Dehli list), by Ziá-i-Barni (Calcutta, 1862, pp. 602), and the Muntakhab-ul-Tawáríkh of Abd ul Kádir, *Badáúni* (Calcutta, 1865, pp. 407). The editors have unadvisedly, I think, omitted the early portions of the original relating to India, and commence the publication with the accession of Akbar. An outline of the entire contents of the work will be found in Sir H. Elliot's Historians of India (Calcutta, 1849, p. 305).

[2] An English version of Ibn Batutah's Travels (taken from an abridged text), by Dr. S. Lee, was published in the series of the Oriental Translation Fund in 1829 (1 vol., 4to., London). A new and very complete edition of his entire Arabic Text, with a French Translation, chiefly the work of the late M. C. Defrémery, has been issued within the last few years by the Société Asiatique of Paris (4 vols. 8vo., Paris, 1853-1858).

the surface in the subsequent pages, as it is only in doubtful or difficult cases that their aid may chance to be invoked, but for the obscure series of the first Governors of Bengal, the one stands alone, and for the space of time intervening between the provincial obscuration of Násir-ud-dín Mahmúd, the unambitious son of Balban, to the revival of public interest in Bengal, consequent upon the subjection and capture of a rebel vassal by Ghiás-ud-dín Tughlak Sháh, the chance traveller describes more effectively the political mutations and varying monarchical successions than the professed historiographers treating exclusively of the annals of their own land.

The following list of Local Governors has been compiled, the early portion from the precise statements of Minháj-ul-Siráj, the latter part from the casual notices of Bengal, to be found in Ziá-i-Barni, who professed to continue the history of India from the latest date reached by the former author, or from A.H. 658 to 753, being a period of 95 years, covering the reigns of eleven kings. The last-named work was finally completed in A.H. 758.

The arrangement of the names and the dates of accession of the chiefs will be found to depart occasionally from the details given by Stewart,[1] in his excellent History of Bengal, but I have designedly sought to draw my materials independently from the original authorities, whom he was perhaps in a less favourable position for consulting than the student of the present day.

## GOVERNORS OF BENGAL.

| ACCESSION. A.H. | NAMES OF GOVERNORS. | REMARKS. |
| --- | --- | --- |
| 600 | 1. محمد بختيار خلجي | First Muhammadan conqueror of Bengal, under Kutb-ud-dín of Dehli. |
| 602 | 2. عزالدين محمد شبران خلجي | Succeeds to the local government after the death of Muhammad Bakhtiár. |

1 The History of Bengal, by Charles Stewart. London, 1813. 4to.

## GOVERNORS OF BENGAL—*continued.*

| ACCESSION, A.H. | NAMES OF GOVERNORS. | REMARKS. |
|---|---|---|
| 605 | 3. علاء الدين علي مردان خلجي | Nominated to the government by Kutb-ud-dín, on whose decease in A.H. 607, he assumes independence.[1] |
| 608 | 4. حسام الدين عوض خلجي (سلطان غياث الدين) | Commandant at Deokót, establishes his power and assumes royal honors. He submits to Altamsh in A.H. 622, but almost immediately commences an active revolt, which is put an end to in his capture by Násir-ud-dín Mahmúd, the eldest son of Altamsh, in A.H. 624. |
| 624 | 5. ناصر الدين محمود بن سلطان التمس | Násir-ud-dín had been appointed by his father Governor of Oudh, in A.H. 623, from whence he advanced against Hisám-ud-dín in 624, and recovered the kingdom of Bengal, where he remained as sub-king till his death early in 626. |
| 627 | 6. علاء الدين جاني | After temporary disturbances in the province, Altamsh, having restored order in A.H. 627, designated Alá-ud-dín Jání to the charge of Bengal. |
| | 7. سيف الدين ايبك يغان تت | Nominated to Bengal on the dismissal of Alá-ud-dín Jání (date not given). Dies in 631 A.H. |

[1] Minháj-ul-Siráj, who treats of the history of his own and immediately preceding times, introduces the reigns of the more powerful sovereigns with a full list of the Court notabilities, forming a sort of *Almanach de Gotha* of Muhammadan India. These lists embrace the various branches of the Royal Family, Ministers, Judges, and Governors of Provinces. The following names of the ضابط's or military administrators of Bengal, which appear in the official returns, may serve to check or confirm the imperfect data obtained from the casual notices of local history to be met with in the general narrative of the events of the Empire at large. There is this discrimination, however, to be made that these imperial nominations were often merely titular, while the effective executive was in other and independent hands:

Under Altamsh, A.H. 607–633.

ملك لكهنوتي ملك اختيار الدين محمد برادر زاده

Under Násir-ud-dín Mahmúd, A.H. 644–664.

الملك الكبير عزالدين طغرل طغانخان ملك لكهنوتي

الملك الكبير تمرخان قيران ملك اوده و لكهنوتي

الملك الكبير جلال الدين خلج خان ملك جاني ملك لكهنوتي وكره

## GOVERNORS OF BENGAL—*continued.*

| ACCESSION. A.H. | NAMES OF GOVERNORS. | REMARKS. |
| --- | --- | --- |
| 631 | 8. عزالدين طغرل طغان خان | Pledges his allegiance to Rizíah on her elevation in A.H. 634; continues in the government till 642 A.H., when he surrenders the kingdom to No. 9. (Minháj-ul-Siráj, the historian, was at his court at this latter period. |
| 642 | 9. قمرالدين تمرخان قيران | Obtains possession of Lakhnauti on the 5th Zul Káad, A.H. 642—dies in 644. |
| | 10. اختيار الدين يوزبك طغرل خان | Dates uncertain. First appointed during the reign of Násir-ud-dín Mahmúd of Dehlí. He seems to have been a powerful ruler and a daring commander, and finally met his death in his retreat from an over-venturesome expedition into Kámrúp. He had previously assumed independence under the title of سلطان مغيث الدين. |
| 656 | 11. جلال الدين مسعود ملك جاني | Appointed in A.H. 656. (قتلغ خان subsequently in temporary possession). |
| 657 | 12. عزالدين بلبن اوزبكي | Recognised, on receipt of his tributary presents at head-quarters, in the early part of A.H. 657. |
| 657 | 13. تاج الدين ارسلان خان سنجر خوارزمي | Obtains a momentary advantage over No. 12 in his absence from his capital; eventually taken prisoner and superseded by No. 12. |
| 659 | 14. (محمد ارسلان خان) تتر خان | Son of No. 12.[1] On the accession of Balban in A.H. 664, he forwards elephants and tribute to Dehli. |
| 676? | 15. مغيث الدين طغرل | Appointed by Balban.[2] He afterwards asserts his independence, and assumes the title of سلطان مغيث الدين. Balban sends armies against him without success, and at last proceeds in person to Bengal. Finally, Toghral is surprised and killed. |
| 681 | 16. بغراخان ناصرالدين محمود | Second son of Balban, installed with royal honors. |

[1] Zíá-i-Barni in one place, page 53, calls him تترخان پسر ارسلان خان, and again, at page 66, محمد ارسلان خان كه اورا تتر خان گفتندي.

[2] Zíá-i-Barni, pp. 82–92.

As I have such frequent occasion to quote the names of the Kings of the Imperial Dynasty of Dehli, I annex for facility of reference a full list of these Sovereigns.

LIST OF THE PATHA'N SULTA'NS OF HINDUSTAN. (DEHLI).

| DATE OF ACCESSION. A.H. | NO. | NAMES OF SULTANS. |
|---|---|---|
| 589 | 1 | Mũiz-ud-dín Muhammad bin Sâm (1st Dynasty). |
| 602 | 2 | Kutb-ud-dín Aibek. |
| 607 | 3 | Arâm Sháh. |
| 607 | 4 | Shams-ud-dín Altamsh. |
| 633 | 5 | Rukn-ud-dín Fírúz Sháh I. |
| 634 | 6 | Sultán Rizíah. |
| 637 | 7 | Mũiz-ud-dín Bahrâm Sháh. |
| 639 | 8 | Alá-ud-dín Masãúd Sháh. |
| 644 | 9 | Násir-ud-dín Mahmúd. |
| 664 | 10 | Ghíás-ud-dín Balban. |
| 685 | 11 | Mũiz-ud-dín Kaikubâd. |
| 688 | 12 | Jalál-ud-dín Fírúz Sháh II., *Khiljí* (2nd Dynasty). |
| 695 | 13 | Rukn-ud-dín Ibráhím. |
| 695 | 14 | Alá-ud-dín Muhammad Sháh. |
| 715 | 15 | Shaháb-ud-dín Umar. |
| 716 | 16 | Kutb-ud-dín Mubârak Sháh I. |
| 720 | 17 | Násir-ud-dín Khusrú. |
| 720 | 18 | Ghíás-ud-dín Tughlak Sháh (3rd Dynasty). |
| 725 | 19 | Muhammad bin Tughlak. |
| 752 | 20 | Fírúz Sháh III., *bin Salur Rajab.* |
| 790 | 21 | Tughlak Sháh II. |
| 791 | 22 | Abúbakr Sháh. |
| 793 | 23 | Muhammad Sháh bin Fírúz Sháh. |
| 795 | 24 | Sikandar Sháh. |
| 795 | 25 | Mahmúd Sháh bin Muhammad Sháh (Timúr, 800). |
| 797 | 26 | Nusrat Sháh, *Interregnum*, Mahmúd restored, 802. |
| 815 | 27 | Daulat Khân Lodí. |
| 817 | 28 | Khizr Khân *Syud* (4th Dynasty). |
| 824 | 29 | Mũiz-ud-dín Mubárak Sháh II. |
| 839 | 30 | Muhammad Sháh bin Faríd Sháh. |
| 849 | 31 | 'Aálam Sháh. |
| 854 | 32 | Bahlól Lódí (5th Dynasty). |
| 894 | 33 | Sikandar bin Bahlól. |
| 923 | 34 | Ibráhím bin Sikandar (Bâber, 930 A.H.) |
| 937 | 35 | Muhammad Humâyún, *Moghul.* |
| 946 | 36 | Faríd-ud-dín Shír Sháh, *Afghán.* |
| 952 | 37 | Islâm Sháh. |
| 960 | 38 | Muhammad 'Aádil Sháh. |
| 961 | 39 | Ibrâhím Súr. |
| 962 | 40 | Sikandar Sháh (Humâyún, 962 A.H.) |

The unenlivened Chronicles of the Local Governors of Bengal enter upon a more interesting phase, in the nomination of Násir-ud-dín Mahmúd, the son of the Emperor Balban, who subsequently came to prefer the easy dignity of Viceroy, in the more even climate of the south, in derogation of his birth-right's higher honours, and the attendant dangers of Imperialism at Dehli. One of the most touching chapters of Indian history is contributed by the incidents of this monarch's meeting with his own arrogant son, Muiz-ud-dín Kaikubád, who had succeeded to the superior dignities abjured by the father.[1] They then met as nominal Vassal and Suzerain, but little unequal in power, and each occupying independent and preparedly hostile camps, on the ordinary route between their respective capitals. Oriental etiquette, and more reasonable distrust, for a time, delayed the interview, in which, at last, nature was destined to re-assert its laws, and to reconcile even conflicting royal interests, by subduing, for the moment, the coarse vices of the son in the presence of the tempered virtues of the father. Repeated amicable conferences, however, merely resulted in each returning on his way, with but little change in the relative political position of either; and the comparatively obscure repose of Násir-ud-dín Mahmúd remained undisturbed, while other successors filled his son's throne at Dehli. The more immediate question bearing upon the attribution of the earliest coins in the Kooch Bahár treasure, is exactly how long did Násir-ud-dín continue to live and reign. Ziá-i-Barni,[2] and those who follow his ill-digested history, affirm that he retained his provincial kingship till 699 A.H., when he divested himself of all symbols of royalty in the mere dread of the confessedly overwhelming power of Alá-ud-dín Muhammad Sháh, to be, however, reinstated by that Sultán; and, finally, it is asserted that Násir-ud-dín was still in existence, and once again reinvested with the full insignia of a king, by Tughlak Sháh, in A.H. 724.

Ziá-i-Barni, p. 142; Ibn Batutah, iii., p. 178; Lee's Translation, p. 117; and قران السعدين of Amír Khusrú, *Dehlivi*.

[2] Printed edition, p. 451; Budauni MS.; Ferishtah (Briggs, i. p. 406).

Ibn Batutah, a higher authority in proximity of time, and obviously more intimate with the purely indigenous history, states that Násir-ud-dín, on his return from his interview with his son, reigned some years (سنين),[1] an expression which is scarcely compatible with the idea of a nearly continuous rule of "forty-three solar years," and a decease in A.H. 725, as adopted by Stewart:[2] a prolongation of administrative functions indeed altogether inconsistent with the direct evidence of the dates on the money of Kai Káús, or the parallel proof of Shams-ud-dín's exercise of the functions of sovereignty in 702 A.H., associated as they are with the uncontested historical and numismatic demonstration of the succession of one grandson, Shaháb-ud-dín, whose ejection from his inherited section of the kingdom by his more powerful brother, Bahádur, formed so prominent a ground for imperial interference in the affairs of Bengal, are each and all too well ascertained to leave any doubt that the authors who make Násir-ud-dín's reign extend to 725 must be in error; the source of the mistake seems as simple as it is obvious, the mere omission of the son's name as preceding that of the father, in Persian MS. writing, or simple ignorance of the order of local successions, would account for the whole difficulty. And, as is obvious, Ibn Batutah's own personal knowledge, and possibly correct autograph version, reproduced independently in other lands, have not saved later transcripts of his work from analogous imperfections.[3]

But there are other and more direct internal evidences in the texts of the Indian authors, of confusion and imperfect knowledge in the relation of the incidents attendant upon the re-settlement of Bengal by Alá-ud-dín in A.H. 699, where it is stated that "a chief, named Bahádur Khân," was at this time appointed to "the eastern districts of Bengal,"[4] with the object of dividing the province, and thus rendering its rulers

[1] French edition, iii., p. 179, and xiii. Dr. Lee's سنتين "two years," p. 118, is an error.
[2] Stewart's Bengal, p. 80.
[3] Ex.gr., Bahádur is made the *son* of Násir-ud-dín, at p. 179, vol. iii., instead of the grandson, which the text at p. 210, vol. iii., and p. 213, vol. iv., affirms him to have been. Lee's MS. authorities again, in omitting the intermediate name of Násir-ud-dín, skip a generation, and ante-date Shams-ud-dín (Fírúz) in constituting him a son of Ghiás-ud-dín Balban (p. 128).
[4] Ferishtah, Briggs, i., p. 406; Stewart, p. 79.

"more subservient to the Court of Dehli." It is highly improbable, had Násir-ud-dín been living at the epoch in question, that a grandson of his should have been selected for such a charge to the supercession of his own father, Shams-ud-dín, or in priority to the son of that father, Shaháb-ud-dín, who was the elder or perhaps better-born brother of Bahádur, each of whom, Ibn Batutah certifies, in turn succeeded to royal honours in the old capital of Bengal.

Having completed this simple outline of the historical data, I now proceed to describe the coins in their due order; first on the list in priority of time is a piece which I can only doubtfully assign to Bengal, and whose individual appropriation, moreover, must remain to a certain extent inconclusive. The coin itself will be seen to bear the hereditary name of the first Moslem Conqueror of India, *Mahmúd* of Ghazní, and the oft-revived title of the founder of the dynasty, *Násir-ud-dín* Subuktagín, a conjunction of royal designations already seen to have been applied to a succession of Pathán princes, whose intitulation followed antecedent conventionalisms.

*Násir-ud-dín.* Mahmúd Sháh.

No. 1.

Silver. Size, viii. Weight, 163.1 grs. Unique, *British Museum.*

| Obv. | Rev. |
| --- | --- |
| السلطان الاعظم | فى عهد الامام |
| ناصر الدنيا والدين | المستنصر بالله امير |
| ابو المظفر محمود | المومنين لله |
| شاه بن سلطان | |

Margin, illegible.

The incidental details of the legends restrict the assignment of this piece to one of *two* individuals, the eldest or the youngest son of Altamsh, the latter of whom was authoritatively designated by the like name and title on the decease of his brother, in 626 A.H.[1] The citation of the formula, "during the reign of (the Khalif) Al Mostansir billah," on the reverse, limits the final period of the issue of the coin, not exactly to the 5th month of the year A.H. 640, when that Pontiff died, but with clear precision to A.H. 641, when the knowledge of his death was officially declared by the substitution of a new name in the Mintages of the capital of Hindustán.[2]

This younger son was destined eventually to succeed to the throne of his father at Dehli, in 644 A.H., after the intervening reigns of Rukn-ud-dín Fírúz Sháh, Rizíah, Muiz-ud-dín Bahrám Sháh, and Alá-ud-dín Masâúd Sháh, in all, however, extending only over a space of eleven years, posterior to the death of Altamsh. The second Mahmúd, must, under these conditions, have been but of tender years, and though, at this conjuncture, promoted to the titular honours of an elder brother, not in any position to exercise authority in his own person, and less likely to have had medallic tribute paid to him by his father, should such have been the origin of the exceptional specimen under review. To the first-born Násir-ud-dín Mahmúd, no such objections apply; he was very early invested by his sire, with the administration of the important government of Hánsi, and in 623 A.H., advanced to the higher charge of the dependencies of Oudh, from which *quasi* frontier, he was called upon to proceed against Hisám-ud-dín Avaz, (No. 4 in the list of Governors, *suprà*), who had already achieved a very complete independence in the province of Bengal. Here, his arms were fortuitously, but not the less effectually, successful, so that he had honours thrust upon him even to the Red Umbrella, and its attendant dignities,[3] what-

[1] سلطان اسلام ناصر الدين محمود چنانچه وارث اسم ولقب او است Tabakát Násirí, p. 181; بلقب و نام پسر مهتر مخصوص گردانيده p. 201.

[2] Pathán Sultáns of Dehli, coin No. 33, p. 22.

[3] His title is usually limited by Minháj-ul-Siráj to ملک pp. 177, 181, 201;

ever the exact measure of these may have been. Under such triumphant coincidences, it is possible that the universal favourite, the still loyal heir-apparent, may have placed his own name on the coinage, without designed offence, especially as at this time Moslem Mints were only beginning to adapt themselves to their early naturalization on Indian soil, and when the conqueror's camps carried with them the simple machinery, and equally ready adepts, for converting bullion plunder on the instant into the official money of a general, or his liege sovereign. Altamsh's own circulating media were only in process of crude development at this period, and had scarcely risen superior to the purely Hindu currencies it had served the purpose of his predecessors to leave virtually intact: his own strange *Túrki* name,[1] and that of many of his successors, continued to figure in the *Nágarí* letters of the subject races on the surfaces of the mixed silver and copper coins of indigenous origin, at times commemorative of imperfectly achieved conquests, and the limited ascendancy implied in the retention of the joint names of the conqueror and the momentarily subject monarch;[2] while the Sultán's own trial-

but on one occasion سلطان crops out incidentally in the Court list where, in his place among the sons of the Emperor Altamsh, he is so designated, p. 178.

[1] This name I have, as a general rule, retained in the form accepted as the conventional English orthography—*Altamsh*. The correct rendering of the original is still an open question, but the more trustworthy authors reproduce the designation as التتمس, a transcription supported in a measure by the repetition of the third letter in the Kufic dies, and made authoritative, in as far as local pronunciation is concerned, by the Hindí correlative version of लितितिमिसि (Pathán Sultáns, Coin No. 14). The inscription on the Kutb Minár, at Dehli, has ايلتتمش, which accords with the Arabic numismatic rendering on the reverses of the Hindí Coins now cited.

See also Táj-ul-Maásir, *Alitimish:* Wasâf, *Alitmish*, and at times اَتَلْمِش Badauni, *Ailtitimish.*

Elliot's Historians of India, p. 111.

[2] See coins of *Chahir deva.*

*Obverse.* Bull. Legend: असावरी श्री समसोरलदिवि

*Reverse.* Horseman. Legend: श्री चाहड देव

—Pathán Sultáns, No. 15; Ariana Antiqua, pl. xix. 16. 31, 34; Prinsep's Essays, i. 333, pl. xxvi. 31; Minháj-ul-Siráj, pp. 215, 240; Tod's Rajasthan, ii. 451; and J.A.S. Bengal, 1865, p. 126.

pieces, in silver, were indeterminate in their design and legends, as well as utterly barbarous in their graphic execution.

Had the coin under review followed the usual phraseology and palæography of the Imperial Násir-ud-dín Mahmúd's Mint legends, it might have been imagined that an ancient and obsolete reverse had been by hazard associated with a new obverse. But the obverse inscription in the present instance differs from the later Dehli nomenclature in the addition of the word *Sháh* after the name of *Mahmúd*,[1] and contrasts as singularly in the forms of the letters, and the insertion of the short vowels with the more deferred issues, as it, on the other hand, closely identifies itself in these marked peculiarities with the initial dies of Altamsh and the closely sequent coinages of Rizíah, two of which latter are now known to be the produce of the Lakhnauti Mint.

## RIZÍAH.

The earliest coins that can be definitely attributed to a Bengal mint, are those of the celebrated Queen Regnant of Muhammadan India—Rizíah, the daughter of Altamsh. The ministers at her father's court were scandalized at the preference it was proposed to extend to a daughter, in supercession of the claims of adult male heirs to the throne; but the Sultán justified his selection, alike on account of the demerits of his sons, and the gifts and acquirements of his daughter, who had been brought up under the unusual advantages of freedom from the seclusion enjoined for females by the more severe custom of ordinary Moslem households, aided by the advantages incident to the exalted position occupied by her mother as the leading and independently-domiciled wife. After the brief reign of Rukn-ud-dín Fírúz, extending over

[1] So, in written history, Násir-ud-dín Mahmúd, the Emperor, is called by his own special biographer, سلطان المعظم ناصر الدنيا والدين محمود بن السلطان (pp. 9, 177, 178, 201, etc.) which is in contrast to the nominal adjunct so constant with his predecessors, Fírúz Sháh, Bahrám Sháh, Masáúd Sháh. On one occasion only does the additional Sháh appear in a substituted list of Altamsh's Court (p. 178), where the text gives—1. Sultán Násir-ud-dín * * 2. Sultán Násir-ud-dín Mahmúd; and at the end, after the name of Rukn-ud-dín Fírúz Sháh, comes "Násir-ud-dín Mahmúd *Sháh*."

less than seven months—who freely exemplified by his misconduct his father's prophetic reproach—Rizíah succeeded in establishing her supremacy in the city of Dehli (A.H. 734), and Eastern eyes witnessed the singular spectacle of an unveiled and diademed Queen—the first in India—directing the hosts of Islám, under the canopy of the immemorial regal seat on an elephant. Rizíah's early inauguration was attended with no inconsiderable danger and difficulty, arising from the organised military resources of the various governors of provinces, who hesitated in conceding their allegiance. Eventually, however, to use the expression of Minháj-ul-Siráj, quiet was established throughout the empire, and Rizíah's sway was acknowledged from "Daibal to Lakhnautí." In A.H. 737, the Empress proceeded in person to quell an outbreak on the part of Ikhtíár-ud-dín Altúníah, Governor of Tiberhind; but was taken captive in the engagement that ensued, and, possibly with scant ceremony, introduced into the harem of the conqueror, who shortly afterwards advanced upon Dehli in the hope of recovering the sovereignty, to which he had thus acquired an adventitious claim; but his army was in turn defeated, and himself and Rizíah met their deaths near Kaithal in the month of Rabi-al-Awal, A.H. 738.[1]

The contemporary biographer in his official lists styles this queen السلطان رضية الدين, a title which she affects on the ordinary copper coins,[2] but on the silver money she adopts the designation of جلالة الدين.

*Jalálat-ud-dín.* Rizíah.

COIN No. 2.

Laknautí, A.H. ?

Silver. Size, vii. Weight, 168 grs. Plate I., figure 1.

Type, *Obverse*, the whole surface is occupied by the legend.

*Reverse*, circular area, enclosing a double-lined square. Narrow margin.

[1] Tabakát Násiri, pp. 183, 185, 251. See also Ibn Batutah, iii. pp. 167, 168.
[2] Patháu Sultáns, Nos. 28, 29.

PL. I.

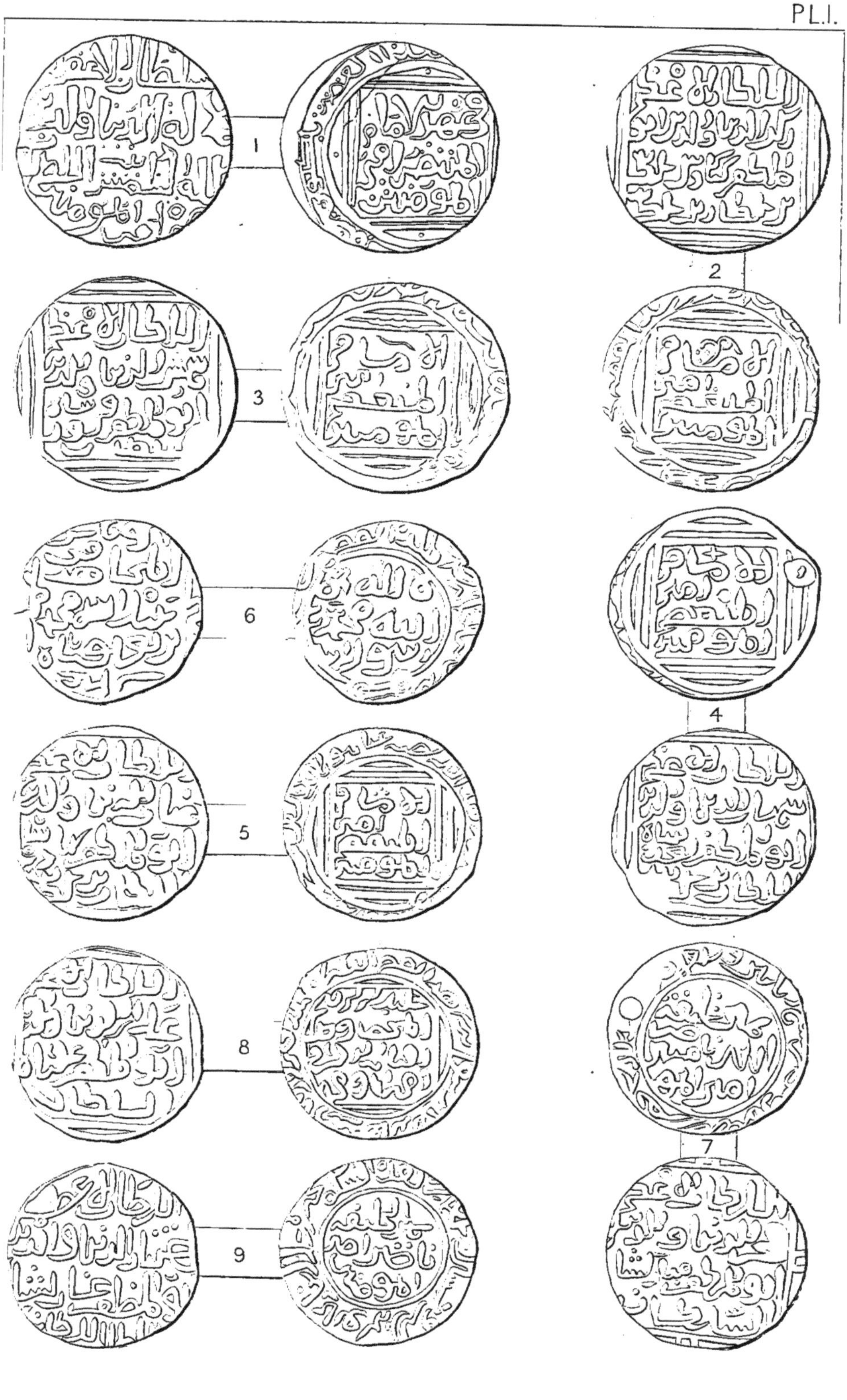

| Obv. | Rev. |
|---|---|
| السلطان الاعظم | في عهد الامام |
| جلالة الدنيا والدين | المستنصر امير |
| ملكه ابنت التمش السلطان | المومنين |
| مهرة اميرالمومنين | |

*Reverse* Margin, * * هذا الفضة بلكنوتي سنة * *

(See also a similar coin from the Laknautí Mint, Plate i., fig. 27, page 19. Coins of the Pathán Sultáns of Hindústán.[1]

[1] It would seem from the orthography adopted in this earliest record of the name of *Lakhnauti* (لكنوتي) that the original Semitic transcription was designed to follow the classical derivation of *Lakshmaṇavatí* (लक्ष्मणावती), which was soon, however, adapted to the more colloquial *Luchhman* (لچهمن) by the addition of an *h* after the *k*, as لكهنوتي; in which form it appears under the first local Sultáns (coin No. 3, etc.), Minháj-ul-Siráj relates its elevation to the rank of the capital in supercession of Nuddeah by Muhammad Bakhtiár in the following terms: چون محمد بختيار آن مملكت را ضابط كرد شهر نوديه را خراب بگذاشت و بر موضعي كه لكهنوتي است دارالملك ساخت Printed edit. p. 151. The same author at p. 162 gives a full account of the remarkable size, progress, and general topography of the city as existing in 641 A.H. on the occasion of his own visit.

It is difficult to say when the name of the city was changed to *Gaur*, a denomination which is never made use of by the older authorities. Abul Fazl says, "Formerly it was called Lucknouty, and sometimes Gour" (A. A. ii. p. 11); while Budáuni gives a ridiculous version of the origin of the designation as being derived from غوري. He writes و محمد بختيار معابد و بتخانهاي كفاررا ويران ساخته مساجد و خوانق و مدارس كرد و دارالملك بنام خويش تعمير فرمود كه كور نام دارد. The obvious imperfection of the critical philology of the derivation, however, debars it reception, as does the caustic alternative of گور = "grave," which the often deserted site, under the speedy action of water and a semi-tropical vegetation, may have deservedly earned for it. But it is quite legitimate to infer that as गौड was the ancient name for central Bengal (Wilson, Glossary, *sub voce*; Albírúní, quoted J.R.A.S. i., N.S., p. 471), and so intimately associated with the tribal divisions of the indigenous Brahmans, that the designation originated in the popular application of the name of the country to its own metropolis, and that the town continued to be called *Gaur* in vernacular speech in spite of the new names so frequently bestowed upon it by its alien lords.

### I.—RUKN-UD-DÍN KAI KÁÚS.

The full and satisfactory identification of the king who ruled under the designation of Kai Káús has yet to be accomplished. Rajendra lál Mitra has suggested a notion that Násir-ud-dín Mahmúd, the son of Balban, so often mentioned in this article, sought, as local ruler of Bengal, "to continue his allegiance to his grandson Kaimurs [momentarily king of Dehli], even after his deposition, and possibly after his death,"[1] by retaining his name on the public money. I should be disposed to seek a less complicated explanation of the numismatic evidences. Kai Káús' date, tested by the examples of his mintages in the Kooch Bahár hoard, is limited, in range of time, to five years (691–695 A.H.);[2] a latitude might be taken beyond the ascertained units, which are somewhat indeterminate in their tracings, and have equally suffered from abrasion, on the exposed margins of the coins, but the *ninety* and the *six hundred* can scarcely be contested. If we examine the political state of India at this period, we find that Hindustán was abnormally quiet under the feeble rule of Jalál-ud-dín Fírúz (687–695 A.H.): Alá-ud-dín's conquests in the Dakhin could have but little affected Bengal, so that any changes that may have taken place in the latter kingdom were probably due to successional or revolutionary causes arising within its own limits. We can scarcely build up a theory of an access of vigour and assumption of independence by Násir-ud-dín himself; nor is it probable that, in such a case, he would have changed both his title and his name. Besides, the array of titles on the coins in the triple succession of *Sultáns* is altogether inconsistent with his actual origin. Though he was the son of one emperor of Dehli, and the father of another, he could scarcely ignore the rise of the former from a state of slavery, or conceal the fact that Balban himself never pretended to have been the offspring of a king. The two alternatives remain of either supposing

[1] Jour. As. Soc. Beng., 1864, p. 508.

[2] Rajendra lál says, "the units *one* and *three* are perfectly clear." Col. Guthrie's three coins are imperfect in the word for the unit. I observe traces of a *four* on two specimens; and I read, with some certainty, 695 on another.

that Násir-ud-dín died before 691 A.H., a question discussed elsewhere, or to conclude that his son Rukn-ud-dín Kai Káús temporarily assumed kingship during the lifetime of his father,[1] and that his limited reign and local obscurity saved his memory from the comments of history. I fully endorse Rajendra lál's suggestion that Kai Káús would have been likely to be selected as a name for one of a family who took so many of their designations from Persian heroic ages, and the elaborate intitulation adopted by that prince, on his coins, of the "Son and grandson of a Sultán," favours such an identification.[2] It will be seen that although the opening terms of his obverse legends follow the conventional and unvarying mint phraseology in the use of السلطان, *the* (reigning) Sultán, yet after his own proper name he styles himself merely سلطان, and seemingly desired to strengthen his position by the insertion of the regal titles of his father and grandfather, though there is so far room for questioning this supposition in the fact that the father had fallen short of supreme power, and was only doubtfully authorized to call himself Sultán, while in strictness the Imperial *Balban* should have been designated *the Sultán* (past *regnant*); but, on the other

[1] The following is the genealogical tree, according to Ibn Batutah. See vol. iii., pp. 174-5, 179, 210, 462; vol. iv., p. 212.

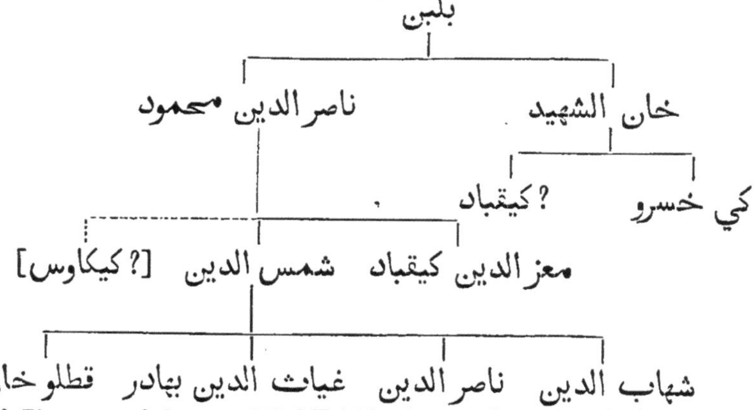


[2] The name of the son of Kai Kobád, who was elevated to the throne of Dehli on the death of his father, is variously given by Oriental writers as Shams-ud-dín كيومرث and كيكاوس. Budáuní and the Mirát-ul-Alam (MS.) give *Kai Káús*, but the majority of authors prefer the *Kaiomurs*. Ziá-i-Barni does not state the name of the boy, but mentions a son of Altamsh, in the previous generation, as having been called *Kaiomurs* (printed ed. p. 126).

hand, Násir-ud-dín had been so long virtually a king in the south, that the complimentary use of the term was quite within heraldic licence; and it is to be remarked, that a similar omission of the supreme prefix occurs in *Násir-ud-dín Mahmúd Sháh's* coin (No. 1), which, if correctly attributed, would prove the legitimacy [1] of the optional use of one or the other form.

These are avowedly mere speculations; but when it is considered how much attention was paid in India, in those days, to every varying shade and degree of honorary rank, how much importance was attached to even the colours of official umbrellas,[2] and other, to us, minor observances, it cannot but be felt that these subordinate indications may chance to prove of material aid in illustrating doubtful interpretations.

Kai Káús.

No. 3.

Lakhnautí, A.H. "691, 693," [3] and 694-695.

Silver. Size, vii. Weight, 168 grs. Very rare. Plate I. fig. 2.

Type, as in the previous coins.

| Obv. | Rev. |
|---|---|
| السلطان الاعظم | الامام |
| ركن الدنيا والدين ابو | المستعصم |
| المظفر كيكاوس سلطان | امير المومنين |
| بن سلطان بن سلطان | |

Margin, ضرب هذا الفضة بحضرت لكهنوتي سنة خمس وتسعين وستماية

[1] The Bengal Mints, after the initial uncertainty, soon settle themselves down to follow the established Dehli models. In the latter, it will be seen, great care was taken by all those sovereigns who could boast of a Royal descent, to define the fact upon their coins. Bahrám Sháh, Masáûd Sháh, Násir-ud-dín Mahmúd bin Altamsh, and Ibrahim bin Fírúz all entitle themselves بن السلطان. Balban, Kai Kubád, Jalál-ud-dín Fírúz, and the great Alá-ud-dín Muhammad Sháh have to be content with their own self-achieved السلطان.

[2] وسه چتر برداست لعل وسياه و سپيد Minháj-ul-Siráj, p. 263; اقطاع بداون وچتر سبز يافت ditto, p. 181, A.H. 625.

[3] Babu Rajendra lál Mitra notices four coins of this king with the dates 691 and 693. Journ. As. Soc. Bengal, 1864, p. 579 He was disposed to read the mint as Sunárgaon. Of Col. Guthrie's three specimens, two bear distinct traces of the name of Lakhnautí.

## II.—SHAMS-UD-DÍN FÍRUZ.

Whatever may have been the actual date of Násir-ud-dín's decease or political obscuration, we tread upon more firm ground in the conjoint testimony of the coins and the historical reminiscences of Ibn Batutah, in the assurance that his son, Shams-ud-dín Fírúz, was in full possession of power in Western Bengal at the time of Muhammad bin Tughlak's abortive revolt against his own father, in 722–3 A.H.[1] The African traveller incidentally mentions that, to the court of this southern monarch fled the nobles who had engaged in the contemplated treason, which originated in the camp of the army of the Dakhin, of which the imperial heir was commander. Professedly written history is altogether at fault in establishing the existence or illustrating the reign of this sovereign; and even Ibn Batutah[2] does little more than place upon

[1] As this passage presents no particular difficulty, beyond the difference of the texts from which English and French translators have drawn their inspiration, I merely annex the rendering given in the amended Paris edition, vol. iii., p. 210. "Les autres émirs s'enfuirent près du Sultan Chems eddîn, fils du sultan Nâcir-eddîn, fils du sultan Ghiyâth eddîn Balaban, et se fixèrent à sa cour. . . Les émirs fugitifs séjournèrent près du sultan Chems eddîn. Dans la suite, celui-ci mourut, léguant le trône à son fils Chihâb eddîn. Ce prince succéda à son père; mais son frère cadet, Ghiyâth eddîn Behâdoûr Boûrah (ce dernier mot signifie, dans la langue indienne, *le noir*), le vainquit, s'empara du royaume, et tua son frère Kothloû Khân, ainsi que la plupart de ses autres frères. Deux de ceux-ci, le sultan Chihâb eddîn et Nâsir eddîn, s'enfuirent près de Toghlok, qui se mit en marche avec eux, afin de combattre le fratricide. Il laissa dans son royaume son fils Mohammed en qualité de vice-roi, et s'avança en hâte vers le pays de Lacnaouty. Il s'en rendit maître, fit prisonnier son sultan Ghiyâth eddîn Behadoûr et reprit avec ce captif le chemin de sa capitale." See also Lee's Translation, p. 128.

[2] Ibn Batutah in the following extract tells us so much about the real history of Bengal at, and previous to his own visit, that I quote the Arabic text *in extenso*; I feel it is the more necessary to reproduce the original version on this occasion, as Dr. Lee's translation is altogether deficient in any reference to the passage, which was clearly wanting in the MSS. at his disposal.

ذكر سلطان بنجالة وهو السلطان فخر الدين الملقب بفخرة * *
سلطان فاضل محبّ فى الغربآء وخصوصًا الفقرآء والمتصوفة وكانت
مملكة هذه البلاد للسلطان ناصر الدين بن السلطان غياث الدين
بلبن وهو الذى ولى ولدُه معز الدين الملك بدهلى فتوجه لقتاله والتقيا
بالنهر وسمى لقاؤهما لقاء السعدين وقد ذكرنا ذلك وانه ترك الملك
لولده وعاد الى بنجالة فاقام بها الى انّ توفى وولى ابنه شمس الدين

record the affiliation, elevation, and decease of Shams-ud-dín, whose own coins alone furnish the additional item of his regal name of Fírúz; and in their marginal records establish the fact of his possession of Lakhnautí during the period embraced between the years 702–722, and at some moment of

الى ان توفى فولى ابنه شهاب الدين الى انْ غلب عليه اخوه غياث الدين بهادور بور فاستنصر شهاب الدين بالسلطان غياث الدين تغلق فنصره وأخذ بهادور بور اسيرًا ثمّ اطلقه ابنه محمد لمّا ملك على ان يقاسمه ملك فنكث عليه فقاتله حتّى قتله وولى علي هذه البلاد صهرًا له فقتله العسكر واستولى على ملكها على شاه وهو إذذاك ببلاد اللكنوتى فلما راى فخر الدّين انّ الملك قد خرج عن اولاد السلطان ناصر الدين وهو مولى لهم خالف بسُدكاوان وبلاد بنجالة واَستقلّ بالملك واشتدّت الفتنة بينه وبين على شاه فاذا كانت ايام الشتاء والوحل اغار فخر الدين على بلاد اللكنوتى فى البحر لقوته فيه واذا عادت الايام التى لامطر فيها اغار على شاه على بنجالة فى البرّ لقوته فيه

Vol. iv. p. 212, Paris edition.

TRANSLATION.

C'est le Sultan Fakhr eddîn, surnommé Fakreh, qui est un souverain distingué, aimant les étrangers, surtout les fakîrs et les soufis. La royauté de ce pays a appartenu au Sultan Nâssir eddîn, fils du Sultan Ghiyâth ed dîn Balaban, et dont le fils, Mo'izz eddîn, fut investi de la souveraineté à Dihly. Nâssir eddîn se mit en marche pour combattre ce fils; ils se rencontrèrent sur les bords du fleuve, et leur entrevue fut appelée la rencontre des deux astres heureux. Nous avons déjà raconté celá, et comment Nâssir eddîn abandonna l'empire à son fils et retourna dans le Bengale. Il y séjourna jusqu'à sa mort, et eut pour successeur son (autre) fils, Chams eddîn, qui, après son trépas, fut lui-même remplacé par son fils, Chihâb eddîn, lequel fut vaincu par son frère, Ghiyâth eddîn Béhâdour Boûr. Chihâb eddîn demanda du secours au Sultan Ghiyâth eddîn Toghlok, qui lui en accorda, et fit prisonnier Béhâdour Boûr. Celui-ci fut ensuite relâché par le fils de Toghlok, Mohammed, après son avénement, à condition de partager avec lui le royauté du Bengale; mais il se révolta contre lui, et Mohammed lui fit la guerre jusqu'à ce qu'il le tuât. Il nomma alors gouverneur de ce pays un de ses beaux-frères, que les troupes massacrèrent. 'Aly Châh, qui se trouvait alors dans le pays de de Lacnaouty, s'empara de la royauté du Bengale. Quand Fakhr eddîn vit que la puissance royale était sortie de la famille du Sultan Nâssir eddîn, dont il était un des affranchis (ou clients), il se révolta à Sodcâwân et dans le Bengale, et se déclara indépendant. Une violente inimitié survint entre lui et 'Aly Châh. Lorsqu'arrivaient le temps de l'hiver et la saison des pluies, Fakbr eddîn faisait une incursion sur le pays de Lacnaouty, au moyen du fleuve, sur lequel il était puissant. Mais quand revenaient les jours où il ne tombe pas de pluie, 'Aly Châh fondait sur le Bengale par la voie de terre, à cause de la puissance qu'il avait sur celle-ci.

his ownership the Eastern Province of Bengal represented by the mint of Sonárgaon. A subordinate incident is developed in the legends of the coins, that he felt himself sufficiently firm in his own power to discard the superogatory adjuncts of descent or relationship, and relied upon the simple affirmation of his own position as السلطان.

*Shams-ud-dín.* Fírúz Sháh.

No. 4.

Lakhnautí, A.H. 702,[1] 715 (Col. Bush) 720, 722.

Silver. Size, vii. Weight, 168.4 grs. Very rare. Plate I., fig. 3. Type as above.

| Obv. | Rev. |
| --- | --- |
| السلطان الاعظم | الامام |
| شمس الدنيا والدين | المستعصم |
| ابو المظفر فيروز شاه | امير المومنين |
| السلطان | |

Margin, ضرب هذاالفضة بحضرت لكهنوتي سنة عشرين و [سبعماية]

No. 5.

Sonárgaon, A.H. ?

Silver. Size, vii. Weight, 168 grs. Unique. Type as above.

### III.—SHAHA'B-UD-DI'N. *BUGHRAH* SHA'H.

Neither history, incidental biography, nor numismatic remains avail to do more than prove the elevation, as they seem to indicate the brief and uneventful rule, of Shaháb-ud-dín, the son of Shams-ud-dín Fírúz, and grandson of the once recognised heir-apparent of Balban.

[1] See also Pathán Sultáns of Hindústán, p. 37, coin dated 702 A.H. This coin was published by me in 1848. I then read the date as 702 A.H. I was not at the time unversed in the decipherment of Arabic numbers, and probably from the very difficulty of placing the piece itself, I may the more rely upon the accuracy of my original interpretation. I mention this fact as I am at present unable to refer to the coin itself.

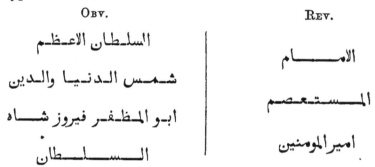

The singularly limited number of the coins of this prince, confined—if Calcutta selections be not at fault[1]—to three examples amid the 13,500 accumulated specimens of the currencies of other kings of the land over which he temporarily held sway, sufficiently mark his status in the general list of the potentates of the century in which he lived. No date or place of mintage is preserved on his extant money, and the single additional item supplied by their aid is his personal or proper name, which appears on their surfaces as نعده ; a crude outline which might suggest a doubt as to the conclusiveness of the transcription of بغره, now confidently adopted as expressing an optional rendering of the grandfather's title of بغراخان,[2] a name which was even further distorted from the Túrki original by the conversion of the medial ر *r* into the vernacular *cerebral* ड or ڈ = *ḍ*. For the rest, the pieces themselves, under the mechanical test, in their make, the forms of their letters, and the tenor of their legends, evidently follow closely upon Shams-ud-dín's mintages, and as clearly precede the money of the same locality, issued by Ghiás-ud-dín *Bahádur Sháh*, who in 724 A.H. drove this, his own brother, Shaháb-ud-dín to take refuge with Ghiás-ud-dín Tughlak Sháh. Bahádur's career has yet to be told in connexion with his own coins; but to dispose of Shaháb-ud-dín,[3]

[1] The name of this king does not appear in any of Rajendra lál's lists.

[2] The ancient name of طنغاج بغراخان of Bokhára notoriety in 350 A.H. (Fræhn Recensio Numorum Muhammadanorum, pp. 139, 593, 578), was subjected to strange mutations on Indian soil. My authority for the substitution of the final ة in place of the vowel ا is derived from Ibn Batutah, who uniformly writes the word with an ة (iii. 231, 5, 293). Ferishtah (*text*, p. 131) has بقرا, whence Stewart's *Bagora* (p. 74). Dow gave the name as *Kera*, and Briggs as *Kurra* (i. pp. 265, 270, etc.).

[3] Those who delight in interesting coincidences might see, in this name of Shaháb-ud-dín, a most tempting opportunity for associating him with a really important record by the Indigènes themselves, inscribed on a stone slab in the fort of Chunár, setting forth their victory over a "*Malik*" Shaháb-ud-dín, quoted as acting under Muhammad bin Tughlak, in Samvat 1390 (A.H. 734); but I confess I do not myself encourage the identification. Chunár is certainly not out of the range of access from Bengal; but other men of mark may have filled this command, and the name of the fortress itself is never heard of in reference to the affairs of the kingdom of Lakhnauti, in those early days, though the main road of communication between the two capitals of the north and the south took its course through Budáun or Kanauj and Jaunpore. The inscription

as far as the exercise of his Mint prerogatives are concerned, he seems to have been lost to fame, from the date when he was absorbed with an associate fugitive brother (Násir-ud-dín) under the ægis of the Emperor of Dehli.

is otherwise well worthy of further examination, in as far as it concerns the history of imperial influence upon proximate localities; and as such I transcribe both the text and Dr. Mills' translation of the brief passages which may chance to illustrate the general subject.

Verse 5:

सहाब्द्दीनादिदुष्टात्मयवनेन्द्रमहम्मदा ।
सैराजो मि[लितोऽम]त्यो वैरिणापि कृपानिधिः ॥

"By MUHAMMAD, lord of the hostile Yavanas SHAHÁB-UD-DÍN and the rest, though an enemy, was SAIRÁJA, the treasure of benignity, employed as prime minister."

Verse 11:

संवत् १३९० भाद्रपदि ५ गुरौ सैराजदेवनश्वर
णागतमलिकसहाबद्दीनरक्षितं ॥

"Samvat 1390, in the month of Bhadra, fifth day of the waning moon, on Thursday, was the kingdom set free from MALIK SHAHÁB-UD-DÍN, acting under the protecting favour of SAIRÁJA DEVA aforesaid."
—(See Journal As. Soc. Bengal, vol. v., 1836, p. 341).

A subordinate but still more open inquiry also suggests itself in connexion with the mention of Shaháb-ud-dín in 734 A.H., as to whether, amid the strange confusion of names and titles, *the* "Kadr Khán," who is noticed by Ferishtah under the original designation of Malik Bídar Khilji, may not, perchance, have been the identical Shaháb-ud-dín *Bughrah* reinstated as simple governor in Lakhnauti as his brother Bahádur was restored to power in Sonárgaon. I am aware that this is treacherous ground to venture upon; but such a supposition is not without other incidental support, especially in Ibn Batutah's passage (original, iii. 214, quoted at p. 192), where Kadr Khán is spoken of as if he had been in effect the last scion of the family of Násir-ud-dín Mahmúd Bughrah.

The original passages in Ferishtah are as follows (i. p. 237):—

و ملك بيدار خلجي را قدر خان خطاب كرده چون شاه ناصر
الدين فوت شده بود اقطاع لكهنوتي باو داد (i. p. 244). درين وقت
يكي از نوكران قدر خان كه اورا ملك فخر الدين گفتندي بعد از
فوت بهرام خان در بنكاله بغي ورزيد و قدر خان را كشته خزاين
لكهنوتي متصرف شد

See also Briggs' Translation, i. pp. 412, 423.

The Táríkh Mubárak Sháhi has the name in manifest mistranscription as *Bandár*.

و ملك بندار خلجي قدر خان شد و اقطاع لكهنوتي يافت

A difficulty necessarily suggests itself in regard to the tribe of *Khilji*, but the use of the name in its non-ethnic sense might readily be explained by the old subordination of the Bengal family to the Khilji dynasty of Fírúz, or the specially *Khilji* serial succession of the earlier governors of Bengal.

*Shaháb-ud-dín.* Bughrah Sháh.

No. 6.

Mint, ?

Silver. Size, vii. Weight, 168.5 grs. Two coins only, *Col. Guthrie.* Plate I., fig. 4.

Type as usual.

| OBV. | REV. |
|---|---|
| السلطان الاعظم | الامام |
| شهاب الدنياو الدين | المستعصم |
| ابو المظفر بغده شاه | امير المومنين |
| السلطان بن سلطان | |
| Margin, (remainder illegible) | ضرب هذا الـ |

### IV.—BAHÁDUR SHÁH.

The single point in the biography of Bahádur Sháh, which remains at all obscure, is the date of his first attaining power. Ibn Batutah records with sufficient distinctness, that he conquered and set aside his regnant brother *Shaháb-ud-dín*, sometime prior to Ghiás-ud-dín Tughlak's reassertion of the ancient suzerainty of Dehli over the lightly-held allegiance of Bengal, and his eventual carrying away captive the offending Bahádur, who was, however, soon to be released, and restored with added honours,[1] by Muhammad bin Tughlak, almost immediately on his own accesssion. Indian home-authors, who so rarely refer to the affairs of the Gangetic delta, give vague intimations of the first appointment of Bahádur to Eastern Bengal by 'Alá-ud-dín Muhammad in A.H. 799,[2] assigning to him an inconceivable interval of

[1] چون سلطان بهادر سنارکامی را بملک اوده رخصت کرد انچه زر نقد در خزانه بود بیکبار در انعام اوداد. Tabakát-i-Akbari.

See also Ziá-i-Barni, printed edit. p. 461.

[2] Stewart, p. 75. Ferishtah (Briggs) i. 406.

placid repose until A.H. 717, when he is stated to have broken out into the turbulent self-assertion for which he was afterwards so celebrated.

The two statements are certainly at variance, but Ibn Batutah's is the most readily reconcilable with probabilities, and the demands of the up to this time legible dates on the coins which Bahádur put into circulation in Bengal. I might have some doubt as to the conclusiveness of the reading of the date 710 on his money in the Kooch Bahár *trouvaille*, but I have none as to the clear expression of A.H. 711 and 712, though the singular break occurring between 712 (or 714) and 720 suggests a suspicion of an originally imperfect die-rendering of the عشر = 10 for عشرين = 20;[1] which would bring the corrected range of Bahádur's dates to 720–724; but even these figures leave something to be reconciled in reference to their associate place of mintage, for in 720–722, his father, Shams-ud-dín Fírúz, was clearly in possession of the already commemorated "*Lakhnauti;*" but such an anomaly might be explained by the supposition that Bahádur, in the earlier days, used the name of *Lakhnauti* as a geographical expression for a portion of the dominions ordinarily administered from that capital. Undoubtedly the first appearance of the contrasted designation of the Eastern capital "Sonárgaon," occurs on a coin of his father; but even this sign of discrimination of Urban issues would not be altogether opposed to a continuance by Bahádur of the loose usage of Camp Mints, of naming the metropolis as the general term for the division at large, or inconsistent with the subsidiary legitimate employment of the designation of the province on a coinage effected anywhere within its own boundaries,—either of which simple causes may have prevailed, and been utilized with a new motive, if any covert ulterior meaning might be designed, as implying that Bahádur himself had special successional or other claims to the metropolitan districts.

[1] Among more critical Arabic scholars than the Bengal Mint Masters ever affected to be, this point would have been easily determined by the insertion or omission of the conjunction و *wau*, which, as a rule, is required to couple the *units* and the *twenties*, but is not used with the *units* and *tens*.

Tughlak Sháh's intervention in the affairs of Bengal seems to have originated in an appeal on the part of the ejected Shaháb-ud-dín against the usurpation of his brother Bahádur. The result of the Imperial expedition to the South was the defeat, capture, and transport to Dehli of Bahádur Sháh; but among the first acts of the new Sultán, Muhammad bin Tughlak, was the release and re-installation of the offender, showing clearly that he was something more than an ordinary local governor, transferable at will, and that possibly the interests of the father and son, in their newly-established dynastic rank, and the confessed insubordination of the latter, were independently advocated by the opposing members of the royal line of Bengal, whose family tree could show so much more ancient a series of regal successions than their parvenu Suzerains, whose elevation dated scarce five years back. One of the most interesting illustrations of the present series is contributed by coin No. 9, in the legends of which Bahádur acknowledges the supremacy of Muhammad bin Tughlak over Eastern Bengal during A.H. 628.[1] The subjection seems, however, to have been of brief duration, as sometime in or after the year A.H. 730 Bahádur appears to have reverted to an independent coinage, in a new capital called after his own title *Ghiáspúr* (coin No. 8), and in A.H. 733 Muhammad bin Tughlak is found issuing his own coin in Bengal, and Bahádur, defeated and put to death, contributed an example to insurgent governors in his own skin, which was stuffed and paraded through the provinces of the empire.

[1] Ibn Batutah gives the following additional particulars of Bahádur's reinstallation:—"Il [Muhammad bin Tughlak] lui fit de nombreux cadeaux en argent, chevaux, éléphants, et le renvoya dans son royaume. Il expédia avec lui le fils de son frère, Ibráhím Khân; il couvint avec Behâdour Boûrah qu'ils posséderaient ledit royaume par égales moitiés; que leurs noms figureraient ensemble sur les monnaies; que la prière serait faite en leur nom commun, et que Ghiyâth eddîn enverrait son fils Mohammed dit Berbath (برباط), come ôtage près du souverain de l'Inde. Ghiyâth eddîn partit, et observa toutes les promesses qu'il avait faites; seulement, il n'envoya pas son fils, comme il avait été stipulé. Il prétendit que ce dernier s'y était refusé, et, dans son discours, il blessa les convenances. Le souverain de l'Inde fit marcher au secours du fils de son frère, Ibrâhîm Khân, des troupes dont le commandant était Doldji altatiry (دُلجي التتري). Elles combattirent Ghiyâth eddîn et le tuèrent; elles le dépouillèrent de sa peau, qu'on rembourra de paille, et qu'on promena ensuite dans les provinces."—Vol. iii. p. 316.

IV. Bahádur Sháh.

No. 7.

Lakhnautí, A.H. 710?, 711, 712, 7-3, 7-4,[1] *break*, 720, 721, 722.

Silver. Size, vii. to viii. Weight, ordinarily, 166 grs.; one example is as high as 167.5 grs. Rare.

| Obv. | Rev. |
|---|---|
| السلطان الاعظم | الامام |
| غياث الدنيا والدين | المستعصم |
| ابو المظفر بهادر شاه | امير المومنين |
| السلطان بن سلطان | |

Margin, ضرب هذالفضة بحضرت لكهنوتي سنة احد عشر وسبعماية

No. 8.

Second Mint, Ghiáspúr. Date, 730.

Silver. Size, vii. Weight, 166 and 164.5 grs. Very rare. Two coins. *Col. Guthrie.* Plate I., fig. 5.

Margin, * هذ السكة قصبه غياثپور سنة ثلاثين *

IV. Bahádur Sháh,
as Vassal *under* Muhammad bin Tughlak.

No. 9.

Sonárgaon, A.H. 728.

Silver. Weight, 140 grs. Unique. *Dehli Archæological Society.*

*Obverse,* السلطان المعظم غياث الدنيا والدين ابوالمظفر بهادر شاه
السلطان ابن السلطان

*Reverse,* Area, ضرب بامرالواثق بالله محمد بن تغلق شاه

Margin, هذه السكه بحضرة سناركانو سنه ثمان وعشرين و سبعمايه

[1] The dates 7-3, 7-4, may perchance be obliterated records of 723 and 724. I have placed them among the lower figures, but I have no sanction for retaining them in that position.

Muhammad *bin Tughlak Sháh,* Emperor of Hindustán, (in his own name) after the re-conquest of Bengal.

No. 10.

Lakhnauti, A.H. 733.

Silver. Small coins. Size, v. to v¼. Weight of well-preserved coins, 168.5 grs. Five specimens, *Col. Guthrie.* Plate I., fig. 6.

| Obv. | Rev. |
|---|---|
| ابوبکر | |
| المجاهد فی | لا اله الا |
| سبیل الله | الله محمد |
| محمد بن تغلق شاه | رسول الله |
| ٧٣٣ | |

*Reverse,* Margin,

ضرب هذه الفضه بشهر لکهنوتي سنه ثلاث وثلثين وسبعمايه

If the place of mintage of these imperial coins had been illegible, I should almost have been prepared, on the strength of the peculiarity of the forms of the letters, to have assigned their execution to a Bengal artist. The original model for the type of coinage may be seen in fig. 90, page 54, Pathán Sultáns. The late Mr. G. Freeling, of the Bengal C.S., has left on record his acquisition of a gold piece of the same design (from the Dehli Mint) dated A.H. 725.

### V.—FAKHR-UD-DÍN. MUBÁRAK SHÁH.

On the departure of Muhammad bin Tughlak from Bengal, Tátár Khán, honorarily entitled Bahrám Khán, an adopted son of Ghíás-ud-dín Tughlak, seems to have been left in charge of the provinces included in the government of Sonárgaon, while the Lakhnauti division of the kingdom of Bengal was entrusted to Ḳadr Khán. On the death of Bahrám Khán,[1] which is stated to have taken place in 739—but may probably have to be antedated to 737—Fakhr-ud-dín Mubárak, his *Siláhdár,* took possession of the government, and proclaimed his independence. He was in the first instance defeated by

[1] Nizám-ud-dín Ahmad says, Mubárak killed Bahrám Khán; while Abul Fazl affirms that Mubárak put Ḳadr Khán to death.—Ayín-i-Akbari, ii. 21.

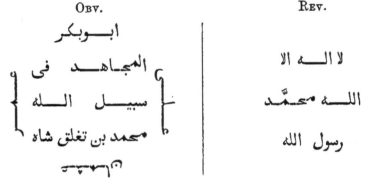

the troops sent against him from Lakhnauti, but finally succeeded in maintaining his authority, and, as the coins prove, in retaining his hold on Sonárgaon and its dependencies throughout the nine years, from 741 to 750 A.H., comparatively undisturbed. The history of the period is confused, and the dates given by the native authors prove of little value;[1] but the coins establish the fact that in 751 another ruler, designated *Ikhtiár-ud-dín* Ghází Sháh, presided over the Mints of Eastern Bengal.

v. *Fakhr-ud-dín.* Mubárak Sháh.

No. 11.

Sonárgaon, A.H. 737, — 741, 742, 743, 744, 745, 746, 747, 748, 749, 750.

Silver. Size, vi. to vi½. Weight, 166.0 grs. Unique.

Plate I., fig. 7.

| Obv. | Rev. |
|---|---|
| السلطان الاعظم | يمين خليفه الله |
| فخر الدنيا والدين | ناصر امير |
| ابو المظفر مباركشاه | المومنين |
| السلطان | |

Margin,

ضرب هذة السكة بحضرة جلال سنارکانو سنه سبع وثلثين وسبعماية

The above specimen is unique in date, and varies in the opening legend of the reverse from the less rare coins of later years, which commence with يمين الخليفة[2]

VI.—'ALÁ-UD-DÍN. 'ALÍ SHÁH.

'Alí Sháh, whom Muhammadan writers, by a strange jumble, have endowed with the surname of his adversary Mubárak, and ordinarily refer to as "'Ali Mubárak,"[3] assumed kingship on the death of Ḳadr Khán, Muhammad Tughlak's representative at Lakhnauti, entitling himself 'Alá-ud-dín. The

[1] Ferishtah, Briggs, i. pp. 412–423; iv. 328. Stewart, pp. 80–83.
[2] See also an engraving of his coin (dated 750) Pathán Sultáns, fig. 151 and page 82.
[3] Budauni MS. Ferishtah, iv. 329. Stewart, p. 82. Ayín-i-Akbari, ii. 21.

more important incidents of his reign are confined to his hostilities with his rival, Fakhr-ud-dín Mubárak of Sonárgaon, who possessed advantages in his maritime resources, while the rivers remained navigable for large vessels during the rainy season, but which were more than counterbalanced by Alí Sháh's power on land, which availed him for the greater part of the year, and which finally enabled him to establish his undisputed rule in the Western provinces.

His coins exhibit dates ranging from 742 to 746 A.H., and bear the impress of the new mint of the metropolis, Fírúzábád, an evidence of a change in the royal residence, which clearly implies something more than a mere removal to a new site proximate to the old Lakhnauti, whose name is henceforth lost sight of, and may be taken to indicate a strategetic transfer of the court to the safer and less exposed locality of the future capital, Pandua.[1] 'Alí Sháh is stated to have been assassinated by his foster brother, Hájí Ilíás.[2]

*'Alá-ud-dín.* 'Alí Sháh.
No. 12.
Fírúzábád, 742, 744, 745, 746

Silver. Size, vi½. Weight, 166.7 grs. Rare. Plate I. fig. 8.
Type as usual.

| Obv. | Rev. |
|---|---|
| السلطان الاعظم | سكندر الزمان |
| علاء الدنيا والدين | المخصوص |
| ابو المظفر عليشاه | بعنايت الرحمن ناصر |
| السلطان | امير المومنين |

Margin,

ضرب هذالفضة السكة في البادة فيروزاباد سنة اثني اربعين وسبعماية

[1] Stewart, speaking of Fírúz's advance against Ilíás, says, "the Emperor advanced to a place now called Feroseporeábad, where he pitched his camp and commenced the operations of the siege of Pundua," p. 84. There is a *Mahal* Fírúzpúr in *Sircar* Tandah, noticed in the Ayín-i-Akbari, ii. p. 2. See also the note from Shams-i-Siráj, quoted below (p. 205), under the notice of Ilíás Sháh's reign.

[2] Stewart, p. 83.

## VII.—IKHTÍAR-UD-DÍN. GHÁZÍ SHÁH.

At the period of this king's accession to the sovereignty of Sonárgaon in A.H. 750 or 751, we lose the aid of our most trustworthy recorder of the annals of Bengal during his own time. The conclusion of Ibn Batutah's narrative leaves Fakhr-ud-dín Mubárak still in power, while the native authorities are clearly at fault in their arrangement of dates and events, and altogether silent as to any change in the succession in Eastern Bengal except in their allusions to the more than problematical capture of Fakhr-ud-dín and his execution by 'Alí Mubárak in 743 A.H., with the final accession of Ilíás "one year and five months afterwards." [1]

The numismatic testimony would seem to show that Mubárak was succeeded by his own *son*, as the *Ul Sultán bin Ul Sultán* may be taken to imply. The immediately consecutive dates, and the absolute identity of the fabric of the coins, as well as the retention of the style of Right-hand of the Khalifat on the reverse, alike connect the two princes; while the cessation of the issues of Ghází Sháh simultaneously with the acquisition of Sonárgaon by Ilíás, in A.H. 753, would seem to point to the gradual spread of the power of the latter, which is stated to have been at its zenith just before Fírúz III. assailed him in his newly consolidated monarchy in 754.[2]

---

[1] Stewart, p. 83.

[2] Shams-i-Siráj, speaking on hearsay, affirms that Shams-ud-dín Ilíás captured and slew Fakhr-ud-dín after Fírúz III.'s first expedition into Bengal; and that the main object of the latter's second invasion of that province was for the purpose of reasserting the rights of Zəfar Khán, the son-in-law of Fakhr-ud-dín (who had fled for protection to Dehli), to the kingdom of Eastern Bengal. It is asserted that although Fírúz succeeded in obtaining this concession from Sikandar, who, in the interval, had succeeded to his father's throne, Zafar Khán himself was wise enough to decline the dangerous proximity to so powerful a rival monarch, and to return in the suite of the Sultán. The Bengálí troops, under Zafar Khán, subsequently distinguished themselves in an opposite quarter of India, near Tattah, and their commander was eventually left in charge of Guzrát. —Shams-i-Siráj, book ii. cap. 9, etc.—See also Journal Archæological Society of Dehli (Major Lewis' abstract translation), 1849, p. 15.

The Tárikh-i-Mubárak Sháhi (dedicated to Mubárak II.), the concluding date of which is 838 A.H., also declares that Hájí Ilíás killed Fakhr-ud-dín in 741 A.H. This last date is a manifest error; as is also, probably, the omission, by both authors, of the words *son of* before the name of Fakhr-ud-dín.

*Ikhtiár-ud-dín.* Ghází Sháh.
No. 13.
Sonárgaon, A.H. 751–753.

Silver. Size, vi. Weight, 166 grs. Very rare indeed. Three coins, *Col. Guthrie.* Plate I. fig. 9.

| OBV. | REV. |
| --- | --- |
| السلطان الاعظم | يمين الخليفة |
| اختيار الدنيا والدين | ناصر امير |
| ابو المظفر غازيشاه | المومنين |
| السلطان بن السلطان | |

Margin,

ضرب هذه السكه بحضرة جلال سناركانو سنه احدي وخمسين وسبعماية

VIII.—SHAMS-UD-DÍN. ILÍÁS SHÁH.

The modern application of old coins divides itself into two branches—the suggestive development of obscure tradition and the enlargement and critical revision of accepted history. The transition point between these archæological functions, in the present series, declares itself in the accession of Ilíás Sháh, the first recognised and effectively independent Moslem Sultán of Bengal, the annals of whose reign have been so often imperfectly reproduced in prefatory introduction to the relation of the magnificent future his successors were destined to achieve as holders of the interests and the commercial prosperity of the Delta of the Ganges, to whose heritage, indeed, England owes its effective ownership of the continent of India at the present day.

The compiler of the English version of the early history of Bengal[1] adopts the conclusion that Hájí Ilíás first obtained power on the assassination of "'Ali Mubárak" in 745-6, but the previous rectification of the independent personality and status of the two individuals thus singularly absorbed into one, will prepare the reader for the corrections involved, though not,

[1] Stewart, p. 83.

perhaps, for the apparent anomalies the coins disclose. Medallic testimony would seem to indicate a long waging of hostile interests between the real 'Alí Sháh and Hájí Iliás, before the latter attained his final local triumph; for although Iliás is seen to have coined money in Fírúzábád in 740 A.H., the chance seems to have been denied him in 741; and in 742 his adversary, 'Alí Sháh, is found in full possession of the mint in question. The Kooch Bahár hoard reveals no coin of either party dated 743, but in 744 the two again compete for ownership, which 'Alí Sháh for the time being continues through 745 into 746, when the annual series is taken up and carried on successively for an uninterrupted twelve years by his more favoured opponent. It is needless to speculate on the varying course of these individual triumphs; suffice it to say, that the increasing power of the ruler of Pandua, in 754, excited the Emperor Fírúz III. to proceed against him in all the pomp and following of an Oriental suzerain—resulting only in the confession of weakness, conveniently attributed to the periodical flooding of the country[1]—which effectively laid

[1] Stewart felt a difficulty about the right position of *Akdálah*, the real point of attack, and a place of considerable importance in the local history of Bengal. The following is Zíá-i-Barni's description of the place, taken from the concluding chapters of his history on the occasion of Fírúz Sháh's (III.) invasion of Bengal in 754 A.H.:—

واکداله نام موضعي است نزدیک پنڈوه که یک طرف ان آب
است وطرف دوم جنگل است دران اکداله تحصین کرد واز پنڈوه
مردم کارامدهرا با زن وبچه در اکداله برد P. 588, printed edit.

Rennell gives another Akdallah north of Dacca. "Map of Hindoostan."

In the following passage Shams-i-Siráj desires to make it appear that Fírúz III. gave his *own* name to the city of Pandua; but, as we have seen that the designation was applied to the new capital either in 740 or 742—that is, long before Fírúz became king of Dehli, it will be preferable to conclude that the name was originally bestowed in honour of the Shams-ud-dín Fírúz of Bengal, of the present series. The quotation is otherwise of value, as it establishes, beyond a doubt, the true position of the new metropolis:—

(فیروز شاه) در پندوه رسید درآن مقام خطبه بنام حضرت فیروز
شاه خواندند و نام شهر فیروزآباد نهادند چون سلطان فیروز شاه
اکدالهرا آزادپور نام کرد و شهر پندوهرا فیروزآباد * * * * (hence)
آزادپور عرف اکداله و فیروزآباد عرف پندوه

From the original MS. in the possession of Zíá-ud-dín Khán of Lohárú.

the foundation of the ultimate independence of Bengal. A monarchy which was destined so to grow in power and material wealth as to be competent, indirectly, in the person of Shír Sháh, to recover for the old Muhammadan interest the cherished capitals of the north, and to eject from Hindustán the Moghuls who too hastily boasted of an easily-achieved conquest of the country "from Bhíra to Bahár."

*Shams-ud-dín.* Ilíás Sháh.

No. 14.

Fírúzábád, A.H. 740, 744, 746, 747, 748, 749, 750, 751, 754, 755, 756, 757, 758.

Silver. Size, vii. Weight, selected specimens, 168.0 grs.; ordinary weights, 166.0 grs.

Type No. 1. The old Dehli pattern.

*Obverse,* Square area.

*Reverse,* Square area, within a circle.

| Obv. | Rev. |
| --- | --- |
| السلطان الغازي | |
| شمس الدنيا والدين | سكندر الثاني |
| ابو المظفر الياس | يمين الخلافة ناصر |
| شاه السلطان | امير المومنين |

Margin,

ضرب هذالفضة السكة في البلد فيروزاباد سنة اربع وخمسين وسبعماية

Type No. 1. Variety A. Silver. Size, vii. Weight, 166 grs.

*Obverse,* Lettered surface.

*Reverse,* Small circle, area.

No. 15.

Fírúzábád, A.H. 758.

Type No. 2. Broad coin. Size, ix. Weight of the best and selected specimens, 166.0 grs. only.

*Obverse,* Plain lettered surface.

*Reverse,* Circular area, with narrow margin.

Legends, both obverse and reverse as in No. 1 type.

Marginal legend,

ضرب هذه السكه بحضرة فيروزاباد سنه ثمان وخمسين وسبعماية

PL. II.

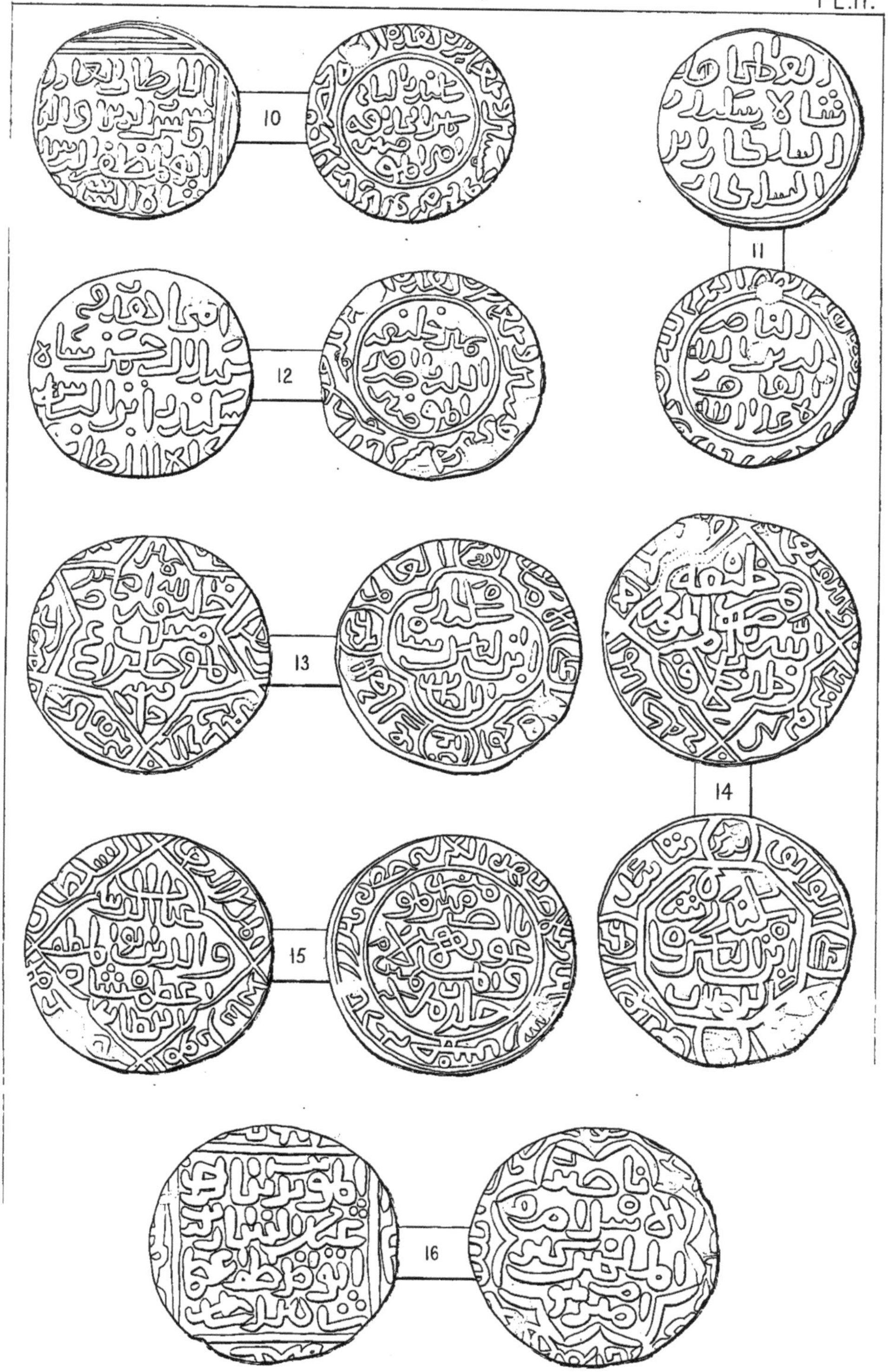

The Kooch Bahár trove must have been rich in this type of coin, and of the particular year A.H. 758, as out of 109 specimens in Col. Guthrie's collection, there is no single example of any other date.

No. 16.

Sonárgaon, A.H. 753, 754, 755, 756, 757, 758.

Type No. 3. Size, vii. Present weight, 166 grs. after the obvious reduction by boring out. Plate II., fig. 10.

*Obverse*, Square area.

*Reverse*, Circular area, with broad margin.

| Obv. | Rev. |
|---|---|
| السلطان العادل | سكندر الثاني |
| شمس الدنيا والدين | يمين الخلافة |
| ابو المظفر الياس | امير المومنين |
| شاه السلطان | |

Margin,

ضرب هذه السكه بحضرة جلال سناركانو سنة خمس وخمسين وسبعماية

IX.—SIKANDAR BIN ILIÁS.

This king—the second only in the still-incomplete assertion of local independence of allegiance to the throne of Dehli—exhibits in the material wealth of his national coinage the striking progress incident to comparative freedom and identity of home interests, which may be achieved, almost on the instant, by the denizens of a commercial centre so favoured by nature as the Delta of the Ganges.

Tried by such a test, few statistical returns could present more effectively the contrast disclosed in the Kooch Bahár treasure between the accumulated produce of the Bengal Mints, representing a century and a quarter's limited activity, attended with all the advantages of a diffused circulation, but under a subordinate government, as compared with the overwhelming array of coins bearing the impress of a single unfettered monarch, whose money was, in effect, new from the dies. To numismatists the enhanced proportion will be more significantly shown by a reference to the additional number of Mint-cities, the singular variety of new types produced, and above all, by the sustained series and corroborating repetitions of annual dates. It is under the latter aspect alone that I have now to comment on the history of a reign already sufficiently told in other pages. Sikandar Sháh placidly succeeded his father towards the end of 759 A.H., and the coins of the period sufficiently support the date of such a transfer of power, in the final 758 recorded on the issues of the father, though proof of the accession of the son is less marked, as the seeming anomaly obtained—under the conjoint efforts of father and son to achieve release from thraldom to a distant suzerain—of a concession to the son of much independent power, and, coincidently, the right to coin money in his own name, whether in his own camps or in his father's royal cities. Though some of the earlier designed coins give evidence of due humility in titular phraseology, the same simplicity is adhered to, in continuous mintages, long after the removal of any possible impediments or restrictions to the adoption of comparatively exalted titles; though in the more independent governmental mintages of 758 A.H. (No. 21) the السلطان المعظم is affected even during the life-time of the father, and, after his own accession, higher assumptions, and a more definite approach towards personal hierarchical honors, are discovered in the metropolitan issues of 766-780 (No. 22), while special service against the infidels seems to be implied in the novel intitulation of القاهر الاعدا الله, "The conqueror of the enemies of God," on the Fírúzábád money of 769 A.H. (No. 23).

But the most interesting details furnished by Sikandar's coins are those which illustrate the geographical distribution of the chief seats of government. Unlike the Northern Moslems, who, in the difficulty of moving the Eastern hosts—conventionally deemed essential to an Imperial progress—over the imperfect highways of Hindustán, confined themselves ordinarily to one fixed metropolis, the kings of Bengal enjoyed facilities of river communication almost unprecedented: their various capitals, situated within easy distance of one another, were at all times accessible by water,—a differently constructed State barge secured at any season free approach to the seaboard cities of the Great Ganges or the towns on the narrow channels of the western streams. These frequent regal visitations are incidentally recorded on the coinage of the day, by the insertion of the prefix of حضرت to the name of the selected residence, which term colloquially marked the presence of royalty within the limits of the favoured fiscal division.

Sikandar's mint cities were five in number—No. 2, *Fírúzábád;* 3, *Satgaon;* and 4, *Shahr Nau,* in Western Bengal; with 5, *Sonárgaon;* and 6, *Muâzamábád,* in the Eastern division of the province.

2. The first-named mint, in addition to the preferential *Hazrat,*[1] is styled variously *Baldat* and بلدة المحروسة "fortified city," a specification which probably refers to the separate though closely proximate citadel of *Akdálah,* so celebrated in the military annals of the time (coin No. 26).

3. Satgaon is distinguished by the prefix of عَرْصَة (Atrium) a term which, in India, came to be conventionally used for a tract or geographical division of country,[2] a sense which would well accord with its application to Satgaon, as the third circle of government of Bengal proper.[3] In the subsequent reign of Aâzam the mint specification is more directly brought into

[1] حَضْرَة "Præsentia, Majestas; urbs, in qua est regis sedes."

[2] عرصهٔ زمين in Persian, means "surface of the earth." Sir Henry Elliot remarks, "The words used before Akbar's time to represent tracts of country larger than a *Pergunnah* were شق, خطه, عرصه, ديار, ولايت, and اقطاع —Glossary of Indian Terms, *sub voce,* "Circár."

[3] Ziá-i-Barni, in introducing his narrative of Tughlak Shâh's expedition to Bengal (A.H. 724), speaks of that province as consisting of the three divisions of "Lakhnauti, Sunárgaon, and Satgaon" (p. 450, printed edit.).

The Ayín-i-Akbari, in the xvi. cent. A.D., thus refers to Satgaon, "There are two emporiums a mile distant from each other; one called Satgaon, and the other Hoogly with its dependencies; both of which are in the possession of the Europeans."—Gladwin, ii. p. 15. See also Rennell, p. 57. Stewart's Bengal, pp. 186, 240, 243, 330.

association with the town itself in the seemingly more definite localization involved in the word قَصَبَة[1]

4. *Shahr Nau,* I suppose to have been the intitulation of the new city founded near the site of the old Lakhnauti:[2] it is variously denominated as the simple *'Arsat* or عَرْصَة المعمورة (populous, richly cultivated).[3] This progressively less appropriate name may be supposed to have merged into the official Jannatábád, which follows in Mint sequence.

4. *Sonárgaon,* as a rule, retains its ancient discriminative designation of حضرة جلال, a title which it eventually had to cede to its rival Muâzamábád.

6. *Muâzamábád.* There is no definite authority for the determination of the site of this city, which, however, seems to have been founded by Sikandar about 758-759 A.H.,

[1] From قَصَبَ "amputavit:" hence قصبة "oppidum, *vel* potior, præcipua pars oppidorum."

[2] The decipherment of the name of this mint (as Col. Yule reminds me) determines for mediæval geography the contested site of Nicolò Conti's *Cernove.* The Venetian traveller in the East in the early part of the fifteenth century is recorded to have said that "he entered the mouth of the river Ganges, and, sailing up it, at the end of fifteen days he came to a large and wealthy city called Cernove. . . . On both banks of the stream there are most charming villas and plantations and gardens. . . . . Having departed hence he sailed up the river Ganges for the space of three months, leaving behind him four very famous cities, and landed at an extremely powerful city called Maarazia . . . . having spent thirteen days 'on an expedition to some mountains to the eastward, in search of carbuncles' . . . he returned to the city of Cernove, and thence proceeded to Buffetania."—The travels of Nicolò Conti, Hakluyt Society, London, pp. 10, 11. See also Purchas, vol. v. p. 508; and Murray's Travels in Asia, ii. 11.

There are also many interesting details regarding the geography of Bengal, and a very full and lucid summary of the history of the period, to be found in "Da Asia de João de Barros" (Lisboa, 1777, vol. iv. [viii.], p. 465 *et seq.*). At the period of the treaty of Alfonso de Mello with, "El Rey Mamud de Bengala" (the king whom Shír Sháh eventually overcame) the name of Shahr Nau had merged into the old provincial designation of *Gaur,* which is described as "a principal Cidade deste Reino he chamada *Gouro,* situada nas correntes do Gange, e dizem ter de comprido tres leguas das nossas, e duzentos mil vizinhos" (p. 458). Satigam makes a prominent figure on the map, and Sornagam is located on a large island within the Delta, the main stream dividing it from Daca, which is placed on the opposite or left bank of the estuary.

More modern accounts of the old city may be found in Purchas, i. 579; Churchill, viii. 54; also Rennell, Memoir of a Map of Hindoostan, London, 1788, p. 55; Stewart, p. 44, and in a special work entitled "The Ruins of Gour," illustrated with maps, plans, and engravings of the numerous Muhammadan edifices extant in 1817, by H. Creighton, 4to., London, Black, Parbury and Allen. See also Elliot's Glossary of Indian Terms, *sub voce,* Gour Brahmin.

[3] The adjective (derived from عَمَرَ, Coluit) will admit of other meanings, and, if understood as applying to a town, might signify "well-built," locally *Pakká.*

when his own coins record that he himself assumed the title of المعظم, without trenching upon the superlative الاعظم usually reserved for the reigning monarch. I conclude that there was a gradual migration from the ancient Sonárgaon to the new city, which grew in importance from the governmental centre implied in the اقليم معظماباد (No. 19) of 760 A.H., to the بلدة المعظم معظماباد, "the great city of Muâzamábád" (No. 28) of about 780 A.H., till, on the disappearance of the name of Sonárgaon from the marginal records of the general currency, the new metropolis appropriates to itself the immemorial حضرة جلال of Eastern Bengal (No. 32 A.)

With a view to keep these brief geographical notices under one heading, I advert for the moment to No. 7, *Ghiáspúr*, of which locality I have been able to discover no trace; and likewise anticipate the due order of the examination of Aâzam Sháh's mint cities in referring to the sole remaining name of *Jannatábád*, an epithet which is erroneously stated to have been given by Humáyún to the re-edified Lakhnauti,[1] but which is here seen to have been in use a century and a half before the Moghuls made their way into Bengal.

The single item remaining to be mentioned in regard to Aâzam's mints is the substitution of the word قصبة in lieu of بلدة[2] as the prefix to Fírúzábád (No. 35), in parallel progress towards centralization with the Mint phraseology adopted in the case of Satgaon.

Sikandar Sháh *bin Ilíás Sháh.*

No. 17.

Fírúzábád, A.H. 750, 751, 752, 753, 754, 758, 759, 760.

Type No. 1. Ordinary simple obverse, with reverse circular area and margin.

[1] Ayín-i-Akbari, ii. p. 11; Stewart's Bengal, 124. Bengal itself was called جنة البلاد, "The Paradise of Regions." Ibn Batutah, iv. p. 210, says the Persians called Bengal دوزخ بور نعمة, "ce qui signifie," en arabe, "un enfer rempli de biens." Marsden, Num. Orient. p. 578, gives a coin of 'Alá-ud-dín Husain Sháh, of A.H. 917, purporting to have been struck at "*Jannatabad.*"

[2] بلد "regio;" also "oppidum." The plurals are said to vary, in correspondence with the independent meanings, as بلاد and بُلْدَان.

| Obv. | Rev. |
|---|---|
| سکنـــــدر شاه | المجـاهـــد |
| ابن الـيـاس شـاه | في ســـبيـل |
| الســـلـطـان | الـــرحمـن |

Margin,

ضرب هذ الفضه السکه في البلده فیروزاباد سنه ثلاث وخمسین وسبعمایه

No. 18.

Sonárgaon, A.H. 756, 757, 759, 760, 763.

Type No. 2. The usual lettered obverse with circular area and margin reverse.

| Obv. | Rev. |
|---|---|
| المجـاهــــد في | یمین خلیفـه |
| ســبیـــل الـــرحمـن | اللـه ناصر امیر |
| سکـنـدر شاه ابن الیاس | المـــومـنـین |
| شاه الســـلطان | |

Margin,

ضرب هذه السکه بحضرة جلال سنارگانو سنه ستین وسبعمایه

No. 19.

Muâzamábád, A.H. 760, 761, 763, 764. Plate II. fig. 12.

Variety A.

Margin,

ضرب هذه السکه اقلیم معظماباد سنه احدي وستین وسبعمایه

No. 20.

Fírúzábád, A.H. 764.

Variety B.

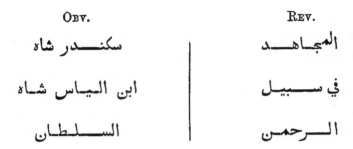

### No. 21.

Sonárgaon, A.H. 758, 759.

Type No. 3. As usual.

| Obv. | Rev. |
| --- | --- |
| السلطان المعظم | يمين خليفه |
| سكندر شاه | الله ناصر امير |
| ابن الياس شاه | المومنين |
| السلطان | |

Margin as usual.

### No. 22.

Fírúzábád, A.H. 765, 766, 770, 771, 772, 773, 776, 779, 780.

Type No. 4. Coarse coins, badly formed letters. *Obverse,* simple ettered surface. *Reverse,* circular area.

| Obv. | Rev. |
| --- | --- |
| الامام | يمين خليفه |
| الاعظم ابو | الله ناصر امير |
| المجاهد سكندر | المومنين |
| شاه ابن الياس | خلد الله خلافة |
| شاه السلطان | |

Margin, هذه السكه بحضرت فيروزاباد سنه سبعين وسبعمايه

### No. 23.

Fírúzábád, A.H. 769.

Silver. Size, vii. Weight, 166 grs. Very rare. Plate II. fig. 11.

Type No. 5. Similar design to type 1.

| Obv. | Rev. |
| --- | --- |
| ابو المجاهد | الناصر |
| سكندر شاه | لدين الله |
| السّلطان ابن | القاهر |
| السّلطان | لاعدا الله[1] |

Margin,

ضرب هذ الفضه السكه في البلده فيروزاباد سنه تسع وستين و * *

No. 24.

Satgaon, A.H. 780, 781, 782, 783, 784, 788. Plate II. fig. 13.

Type No. 6. *Obverse*, a quadrated scalloped shield, with open bosses on the margin containing the names of the "four friends," the intermediate spaces being filled in partially with the king's titles.

*Reverse*, hexagonal star-shaped lozenge, with exterior marginal legend.

| Obv. | Rev. |
| --- | --- |
| | يمين |
| سكندر شاه | خليفه الله ناصر امير |
| ابن الياس شاه | المومنين خلد الله |
| السلطان | خلافة |

*Obverse* Margin,

الامام العالم العادل ابو المجاهد — ابوبكر عمر عثمان علي

*Reverse* Margin,

ضرب هذه السكه المباركه في عرصه ستكانو سنه احد وثمانين وسبعمايه

[1] The pattern legend of this mint-die seems to have been taken from oral data, as it is engraved as القاهرُلاعد الله instead of the more critical القاهر أل اعدا الله The increased facilities of intercourse by sea probably aided the colloquial knowledge of Arabic in the estuaries of Bengal; while the learned of Dehli had to rely more upon books and occasional teachers. Ibn Batutah tells us, that Muhammad bin Tughlak, though pretending to speak Arabic, did not distinguish himself in the act, while *Háji* Ilíás must himself have performed the pilgrimage to Mecca.

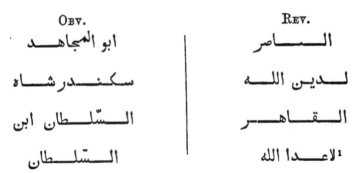

### No. 25.

Shahr Nau, A.H. 781, 782, 783, 784, 785, 786. Plate II. fig. 14.

Type No. 7. *Obverse*, a simple octagon, with four circlets in the margin containing the names of the four friends of the Prophet, the rest of the exergue being filled in with the king's own titles.

*Reverse*, a diamond-shaped area with the crossed lines prolonged to the edge of the piece; the lines are slightly scalloped outwards to form an ornamental field.

| OBV. | REV. |
|---|---|
| سكندر شـــاه | يمين خلـــيفه |
| ابن الـياس شـــاه | الله ناصر امير المـــومنين |
| السـلــطان | خلـد خلافـــة |

*Obverse* Margin,

ابوبكر عمر عثمان علي      الوثق بتايئد الرحمن ابو المجاهد

*Reverse* Margin,

ضرب هذه السكه المباركه في عرصه شهرنو سنه اثني وثمانين وسبعمايه

The name of the mint is imperfectly expressed on even the best specimens, and great latitude has been permitted in the omission or insertion of entire words in the reverse marginal legend.

Variety A. differs merely in the pattern of the reverse area, which is ornamented with double instead of single scallops.

### No. 26.

Fírúzábád, A.H. 780, 781, 782, 783, 784, 785, 786, 787, 788, 789, 790, 791, 792.

Type No. 8. *Obverse*, circular area, with a broad margin divided by circlets enclosing the names of the four friends of the Prophet, the intermediate spaces being filled in with their titles.

*Reverse*, octagonal rose scalloped lozenge, with narrow margin.

*Obverse*,

الواثق بتائيد الرحمن ابو المجاهد سكندر شاه ابن الياس شاه السلطان

Margin,

ابوبكر الاعظم عمر ابوالخليفه عثمان المعظم علي الامام.

*Reverse,*

بمين الخليفة ناصر امير المومنين[1] عون الاسلام والمسلمين خلد خلافته

Margin,

ضرب هذة السكة المباركة فى بلدة المحروسة فيروزاباد سنة ثمانين وسبعماية

No. 27.

Satgaon, A.H. 780.

Variety A. *Reverse* Margin,

ضرب هذه السكه المباركه فى عرصه المعموره ستكانو etc.

No. 28.

Muâzamábád (the great city), A.H. ?

Variety B. Mint, بلدة المعظم معظماباد

No. 29.

Shahr Nau, A.H. 781.

Variety C. Mint, عرصة المعمورة شهرنو سنه احدو ثمانين

No. 30.

Col. Guthrie has a gold piece of type No. 8, size vii. and a half, weighing 158 grains. The coin is inferior in execution to the ordinary silver money. The letters are badly formed, and the marginal legend is altogether obliterated.[2]

No. 31.

Fírúzábád, A.H. 781, 782, 783, 784, 785, 786, 787.

Type No. 9. *Obverse*, circular area, with a broad margin, broken by small shields containing the names of the four companions of the

[1] M. Reinaud interpreted the word as عون, *Defensor* (Journal Asiatique, 1823, p. 272), in which he is followed by Marsden (ii. p. 567). Sayud Ahmad again, in his transcript of 'Alá-ud-dín's Inscription of 710 A.H., reproduces the title as غوث الاسلام و المسلمين, which, in effect, carries a nearly identical meaning (Asár-ul-sunnádíd, p. 53).

[2] The only other Bengal gold coins I am at present able to refer to are a well-preserved piece of *Jálál-ud-dín* Fatah Sháh bin Mahmúd (dated A.H. 890), now in the possession of Colonel Guthrie, weighing 161.4 grains, and a coin in the B. M. assigned to 'Alá-ud-dín Husain (A.H. 905–927) which weighs 159.5 grains.

Prophet; the intermediate spaces are filled in with titles which occasionally pertain to the king, but at times exclusively belong to the Imáms.[1]

*Reverse*, hexagonal field; narrow margin.

| Obv. | Rev. |
|---|---|
| ابو المجاهد | يمين خليفه |
| سكندر شاه ابن الياس | الله ناصر امير المومنين |
| شاه السلطان | عون الاسلام والمسلم |
| | خلد ملك |

*Obverse* Margin,

الامام (ابوبكر) الاعظم (عمر) الواثق (عثمان) بتائيد الرحمن (علي)

*Reverse* Margin,

ضرب هذه السكه المباركه في بلده فيروزاباد سنه ست وثمانين وسبعمايه

## X.—A'AZAM SHÁH.

The accession of Ghiás-ud-dín Aåzam Sháh was disgraced by rebellion against his own father and coincident open war, in the course of which Sikandar fell in a general action between his own and his son's troops. Native historians are more than ordinarily obscure in the narration of these incidents, and the dates relied upon are singularly untrustworthy when brought to the test of numismatic facts. Aåzam's initial revolt is admitted to have gained force chiefly in Eastern Bengal, where his coinage substantially proves his administrative supremacy, whether as nominally subordinate or covertly resistant to paternal authority, dating from 772 A.H.,—an increase of power seems to be associated with the mint record of a hold over Satgaon in 790 A.H., and a real or pretended occupancy of a portion of the territory of Pandua in

[1] الواثق in many instances is replaced by ابوالخليفه while المعظم follows the name of عثمان.

791, though the final eclipse of the royal titles of the father is delayed till 792 A.H.[1]

Ghíás-ud-dín Aåzam Sháh, *bin Sikandar Sháh.*

No. 32.

Muåzamábád, A.H. 772, 775, 776.

Silver.   Size, viii½.   Weight, 166 grs.   Plate II. fig. 16.

Type No. 1.   *Obverse,* square area occupying nearly the whole surface of the coin, as in the old Dehli pattern.

*Reverse,* scalloped lozenge, forming an eight-pointed but contracted star.

| Obv. | Rev. |
|---|---|
| المويد بتائيد الرحمن | ناصر الاسلام و |
| غياث الدنيا والدين | المسلمين كين |
| ابو المظفر اعظم شاه | امير المـومنين |
| السلطان | |

*Obverse* Margin : On the upper edge, ابوبكر ; on the left, عمر ; in consecutive reading at the foot, عثمان ; and on the right, على

*Reverse* Margin,

هذه السكه المباركه في بلدة معظمابــاد سنه ثمان وسبعين وسبعمــاية

Variety A.   In one instance بحضرت جلال supplies the place of في بلدة .

There is a doubt about the reading of the word كين "being humble;" the عين "Oculus" of Marsden would certainly be preferable in point of sense, but the forms of the letters of the word scarcely justify such a rendering, unless we admit of an unusual degree of even Bengálí imperfection in the fashioning these dies.

On two examples of this mintage *in silver,* the marginal legend bears the words هذه الدينار in clearly cut letters; but I imagine this seeming anomaly to have arisen from a fortuitous use of the dies for gold coins, which, in device, were identical with those employed for the silver money.

---

[1] Stewart supposes that Sikandar met his death in 769 A.H. (p. 89); and an even more patent error places the decease of Aåzam in 775 A.H. (p. 93). The Tabakát-i-Ákbari, which devotes a special section to the history of Bengal, implies an amiable and undisturbed succession in this instance.

No. 33.

Jannatábád, A.H. 790.

Variety A. Similar obverse with circular reverse.

Mint, جنتاباد سنه تسعين و

Rev. Obv.

No. 34.

Type No. 2. There is a subordinate class of coins, following the devices of Type No. 1 (in size vii. and upwards), struck from less expanded dies, and generally of very inferior execution in the outlining of the letters. These are also from the mint of Muȁzamábád, and are dated in bungled and almost illegible words— احدوثماثما, ثماثما, ثمانوسعو, سبعوسبعمايه, which may be designed to stand for 770 odd, 778, 780, and 781 respectively.

No. 35.

Fírúzábád, A.H. 791, 792, 793, 794, 795, 796, 797, 798, 799.

Type No. 3. Size, viii. to viii¼. Weight, 166 grs. Plate II. fig. 15.

*Obverse*, scalloped diamond field; broad margin.

*Reverse*, circular area.

| Obv. | Rev. |
|---|---|
| غياث الدنيا | ناصر امير |
| والدين ابو المظفر | المومنين عون الاسلام |
| اعظم شاه | و المسلمين |
| السلطان | خلد ملكه |

*Obverse* Margin, السلطان الاعظم المويدبتائيد الملك الرحمن

*Reverse* Margin,

هذة السكة بقصبة فيروزاباد سنة ثلاث وتسعين وسبعماية

The Reverse marginal records vary in the prefix to the name of the mint from the Kasbah above given, في حضرة and في حضرة المباركه being occasionally used.

No. 36.

Satgaon, A.H. 795, 798.

Variety A.

No. 37.

Satgaon, A.H. 790, 795, 796.

Type No. 4. '*Obverse*, area, a square, with a looped semicircle at each of the sides, forming a kind of amalgamation of the margin with the central device.

*Reverse*, area, a four-pointed star-shaped lozenge; the outside spaces being filled in with the marginal legend.

| Obv. | Rev. |
| --- | --- |
| ابــــوبكر | |
| المويد بتائيد الرحمن | ناصــرالاســلام و |
| غياث الدنيا والدين | المسلمين كين |
| ابو المـظفراعـــظـم | امير المـومنين |
| شـــاه الســـلطان | |

*Reverse* Margin,

ضرب هذ السكه * * في عرصه ستكانو سنه تسعين وسبعمايه

No. 38.

Type No. 5. Size, v. Weight, 166 grains.

*Obverse*, lettered surface.

*Reverse*, circular area; narrow margin.

| Obv. | Rev. |
| --- | --- |
| غياثّ الدنيا | ابـــد اللـــه |
| و الدين ابو المظفر | خلد اللهُ دولته |
| اعـــظـمـشـــاه | مـــلـــكـــه |
| السـلـطـان | |

Margin? * معظماباد سنه احد

The singular orthography adopted in the rendering of the term *Abdallah*, and the substitution of an initial ا *alif* in lieu of the grammatical ع *ain*, affords another instance of the ignorance of the local mint officials, and their tendency to reproduce the approximate *sounds* of words, without regard to the true powers of the letters employed.

---

A vacant space in the final setting up of this article invites me to extend it so far as to notice a limited series of coins which have hitherto been erroneously associated with the mintages of Bengal proper,—I allude to the money of Táj-ud-dín Fírúz, whose date has, in like manner, been misapprehended by Marsden (p. 575), and by Mr. Laidlay, who follows his interpretation (J.A.S.B. xv. p. 330). The subjoined examples will show that the supposed date of 897 A.H. should be 807; and the consecutive numbers on the different coins now cited establish the fact that the potentate whose name they bear reigned at least from 804 to 823, having a capital entitled *Hájíábád*, which may, with sufficient reason, be identified with the *Hájípúr* of modern nomenclature. The introductory piece A. seems to have been issued by Táj-ud-dín's predecessor, and their several mintages alike depart from the ordinary style of Bengal coinages in the phraseology and finished execution of the Arabic legends, as well as in the weights of their currencies, which approximate closely to the full Dehli standard, in contrast to the reduced southern range of 166 grains.

A. Silver. Size, vii½. Weight, 165 grs. Unique. A.H. 797.

| Obv. | Rev. |
| --- | --- |
| الناصرلدين | الواثق بتايد |
| لدنان العامى | الرحمن ابو المظفر |
| الاهل الايمان | محمد شاه السلطان |
| | ٧٩٧ |

B. Silver. Size from vi½ to viii½. Weight, 168 grs., the full and *sustained* weight of several specimens.

| Obv. | Rev. |
|---|---|
| سُلَطان | تـاج الـدنـيا |
| العَهد و الزمان | وَالدين فيروز |
| الوَاثق بتائيد الرحمن | شاه السلطان |
| ابو المظفر | ٨٠٤ |

*Obverse*, lettered surface.

*Reverse*, square area, with imperfect marginal records, usually consisting of ضرب بحضرت حاجياباد with the figured dates *at the foot*, ranging onwards from 804 to 807 [Marsden], 810, 813, 814, 818, 819, 820, 822, and 823 A.H.

These coins are chiefly from the collection of the late Sir R. Jenkins, but have now passed into Colonel Guthrie's possession.

Among other rare and unpublished coins, having more or less connexion with the progress of events in Bengal, I may call attention to the subjoined piece of Shír Sháh (C.), which seems to mark his final triumph over Humáyún in 946 A.H. and his own assumption of imperial honours in Hindustán. The gold coin (D.) is of interest, as exhibiting the model from whence Akbar derived one of his types of money, which Oriental authors would have us believe were altogether of his special origination, even as they attribute so many of Shír Sháh's other admirable fiscal and revenue organizations to his Moghul successor. In coin E. we follow the spread of Shír Sháh's power northwards to the ancient capital of the Patháns, and the piece F. illustrates the retention of the family sway over the other extreme of the old dominion.

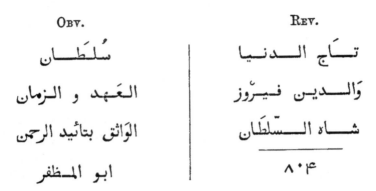

C. Silver. Size, vi¼. Weight, 163 grs. A.H. 946. Well executed Western characters.

*Obverse*, السلطان العادل المويد بتائيد الرحمن فريد الدنيا و الدين

*Reverse*, ابو المظفر شير شاه سلطان خلد الله ملكه و سلطانهٔ ٩٤٦

D. Gold. Square coin. Weight, 168½ grs. Unique. (R. J. Brassey, Esq.).

*Obverse*, the Kalimah.

*Reverse*, شير شاه سلطان خلد الله ملكه

At the foot, श्री सेर सहि.

E. Silver. Size, vii. Weight, 168 grs. Dehli. A.H. 948.

*Obverse*, Square area. لااله الاالله محمد رسول الله

Margin, the names and titles of the four Imáms.

*Reverse*, Square area. ٩٤٨ السلطان شير شاه خلد الله ملكهٔ

At the foot, स्री सीरी साह.

Margin, ضرب بحضرت دهلي * * *

F. Silver. Size, viii. Weight, ? Satgaon, A.H. 951 (from the collection of the late G. H. Freeling, Bengal C.S.)

Circular area, اسلام شاه ابن شير شاه سلطان خلد الله ملكه و سلطانه و اعلي امره و شانه

Margin,

جلال الدنيا و الدين ابو المظفر स्री इसलाम साह ضرب ستكانو ٩٥١

## BENGAL MINTS.

| | 1 Lakhnautí. | 2 Fírúzábád. | 3 Satgaon. | 4 Shahr Nau. | 5 Sonárgaon. | 6 Muãzamábád. |
|---|---|---|---|---|---|---|
| I. Kai Káús ............ ..... | A.H. 691.........695 | ... ... ... | ... ... | ... ... | ... ... ... | ... ... |
| II. Shams-ud-dín ............ | 702.........722 | ... ... ... | ... ... | ... ... | *in possession.* | ... ... |
| III. Shaháb-ud-dín............ | ... ... ... | ... ... ... | ... ... | ... ... | ... ... ... | ... ... |
| IV. Bahádur Sháh ............ | 710, 712.........720-722 | ... ... ... | ... ... | ... ... | IV. *Under Muhammad bin Tughlak*, 728 | ... ... |
| *Muhammad bin Tughlak (himself)* | .........733 | ... ... ... | ... ... | ... ... | ... ... ... | ... ... |
| V. Mubárak Sháh............ | ... ... ... | ... ... ... | ... ... | ... ... | 737.........741 to 750 | ... ... |
| VI. 'Alí Sháh .................. | ... ... ... | 742.........746 | ... ... | ... ... | ... ... ... | ... ... |
| VII. Ghází Sháh ............... | ... ... ... | ... ... ... | ... ... | ... ... | 751.........753 | ... ... |
| VIII. Iliás Sháh ............... | ... ... ... | 740.........758 | ... ... | ... ... | 753.........758 | ... ... |
| IX. Sikandar Sháh............ | ... ... ... | 750.........792 | 780......784 | 781......786 | 756.........764 | 760......764 |
| X. Aãzam Sháh............... | ... ... ... | 791.........799 | 790......798 | ... ... | ... ... ... | 772......781 |

Mint No. 7. Ghiáspúr............IV. Bahádur Sháh, 730 A.H. Mint No. 8. Jannatábád...........X. Aãzam Sháh, 790 A.H.

## Art. VIII.—*Specimen of an Assyrian Dictionary.* By Edwin Norris, Esq., Hon. Sec.

The following paper is a Specimen of what pretends to be no more than a Skeleton Dictionary of the Assyrian Language, which the few who know anything of the matter will assuredly expect to find incomplete, and often erroneous. The compiler, though well aware that such expectation will not be disappointed, believes that no apology is required; for many years must necessarily elapse before an approach can be made to completeness in such a work, and the best Assyrian decipherers are the most assured of the vague character of their interpretations, whenever the subject goes much beyond plain narration, or whenever words of infrequent occurrence are made use of. He ought rather, with Semitic knowledge limited to a superficial acquaintance with Hebrew, and with but little leisure, to apologize for venturing at all upon such an attempt; but having got together a very large number of words while assisting Sir Henry Rawlinson in the preparation of inscriptions for publication, and being, moreover, of opinion that a work like the present, which requires little more than persevering industry, will never be compiled by men of greater powers who are better employed, he was unwilling that his labour should be thrown away, and hopeful that it might be of some use. He believes that his compilation may serve as a repository in which Assyrian students may jot down their difficulties, and where they may occasionally look for help, by collating passages containing the words they are investigating. He only asks credit, in the words of an early critic lately reprinted, for "his diligence in breaking "the yce, and givinge lighte to others, who may moore "easely perfecte then begyne."*

If the Specimen given should be thought satisfactory, the compiler would propose to commence at once the printing of the whole Dictionary; and he hopes that our Rawlinsons and Hinckses will gradually fill up deficiencies, and correct the errors which they will certainly find in most pages; he scarcely ever looks over the sheets himself without making additions, and, he trusts, improvements.

He has to acknowledge, with thanks, much valuable help from Dr. Hincks in a considerable part of this Specimen, and he feels bound to declare that he is indebted for almost everything he knows of Assyrian to the direct communications or to the writings of Sir Henry Rawlinson.

* Francis Thynne's Animadversions, &c., page 9; reprinted in 1865.

---

THE arrangement of words written with a syllabary must always be more difficult than with an alphabet; but with the Assyrian syllabary, encumbered as it is by monograms, determinatives, polyphones, unpronounceable proto-Babylonian symbols, and varying orthography, the difficulty is greatly increased. We must work by compromise, and sometimes elude a difficulty we cannot conquer. After trying and giving up several schemes, the compiler has adopted the following:—

Words are arranged according to the order of the Hebrew alphabet, and no notice is taken of inherent unwritten vowels, or of the complementary vowels following them, which serve at most only to lengthen the syllable. Thus,  [*bu ur*] is entered as BR, [*e mu uk*] as EMK, [*as ti*] as ST, or [*a ga, a ga a*] as AG, [*su a tu*] as SAT. is entered as H.

, which appears to be etymologically equivalent to ע, is often used as a complementary vowel to a syllable with inherent *i*, and is transliterated as *e*.* As Assyrian writing made no distinction between the hard and soft sounds [surds and sonants] of final consonants, using only one form for *ab* and *ap*, one for *ug*, *uk*, and *uq*, &c., such consonants are always arranged as soft [sonants], mainly because *b*, *g*, *d*, come before *p*, *k*, *t*, in the alphabet. Polyphones will also be entered under their earliest initial; for example, which may be read *dan*, *kal*, or *lib*, will come under D. This rule, limiting each character to one place, is in accordance with our own usage: we place Caius and Cicero under C, although the initial sound of one is *k*, of the other *s*; and the words *physic*, *psalm*, *ptisan*, and *paper*, appear in our dictionaries under P, although pronounced with initial *f*, *s*, *t*, and *p*. An exception to the rule of taking the earliest letter of the alphabet is made when the polyphone is a character of the ordinary syllabary, and likewise when the polyphone has usually one sound only, any other being rarely found.

In this way the student will generally know where to look for any given word; the few which remain doubtful will be placed, if the initial be known, at the end of the class of words having that initial; other doubtful words will be put at the end of the Dictionary.

In all this the notation for purposes of arrangement must be distinguished from the transliteration, which will be mentioned presently.

---

* It is curious that when the Jews write German in Hebrew letters, they have for centuries represented the vowel *e* by ע, making der Mensch דער מענש, &c.

In the body of the work the compiler, of course, begins each paragraph with the word to be explained—he will give it first in the cuneiform character, in all the forms he has noted, and then in Roman letters; the English equivalent will follow, and any cognate word known to him in another Semitic language. He will quote one or more phrases containing the word in question, with a literal translation, word for word; when he is unable to read or translate a passage, he must leave it for more advanced students. The cuneiform character may be occasionally omitted in these phrases, to save room and avoid repetition, when the original is published in some work easily procurable. He apprehends that this plan will exhibit pretty clearly the limits of his knowledge, but he disclaims any pretence of knowing all, or even a very large proportion of all that is known; he has not read carefully, with the idea of preparing a dictionary, even all that is in print, and not a twentieth part of what remains on the clay slabs, which may be fairly termed "in manuscript."

The verbs will follow separately, with classified examples of all the forms which the compiler has recorded, together with any obvious nominal derivatives, which may be referred to the earlier part of the Dictionary.

He has included in his plan the names of persons and places, which may be useful historically and geographically; also extracts from syllabaries and bilingual lists, sometimes fragmentary, mostly without any attempt at explanation. Some groups of characters may also be found which are no words at all, but only parts of one or more words from sentences of which he could make nothing.

The transliteration will be, so far as practicable, the most usual representation of the Hebrew letters, with the phonology of which language that of the Assyrian appears to have a greater analogy than with that of any other Semitic idiom. The ח, ט, ס, and צ, will be distinguished from ה, ת, ש, and ז, by a dot below—ḥ, ṭ, ṣ, and ẓ; the ambiguous characters representing both *m* and *v* will be made *m* or *v*, as accordant with etymology; in doubtful cases *m* will be preferred. What is called *mimmation* will be made by a line over the vowel so affected, *e.g.*,  will be made *tā*,  *lī*, &c.

Accad or proto-Babylonian words will be generally rendered as if they were Assyrian, and left to take their chance in that form; with the exception of a few of frequent occurrence, whose Assyrian equivalents are well known from vocabularies and variant readings, and which could not be conveniently transliterated, such as  , which will be written *nahr* (river), *same* (heaven), *yom* (day), *eni* (eyes), *uzni* (ears), *kappi* (hands), *naru* (tablet), *ḥuraz* (gold), *kaspu* (silver), and perhaps a few more. No positive rule can be laid down, but in any uncertainty both forms will be given; there is no doubt whatever, strange as it may appear, that the Assyrians in such cases wrote a word in one language and pronounced it in another.* Determinatives before

* This we ourselves do when we write "viz." and pronounce it "namely." It appears from the following French translation of a passage in the "Fihrist" by Mons. de Quatremère, that this was also done by another eastern nation, many centuries ago:—"Les Perses ont aussi un alphabet appelé *zewaresh*, dont les lettres "sont tantôt liées, tantôt isolées. Le vocabulaire se compose d'environ mille mots, "et ils s'en servent pour distinguer les expressions qui ont une forme semblable. "Par exemple, quiconque veut écrire le mot *gouscht*, qui, en arabe, signifie *lahm* "(chair), écrit *bisra*, qu'il prononce *gouscht;* si l'on veut écrire *nan* qui signifie *pain*, "on trace le mot *lahm*, que l'on pronouce *nan*. Il en est ainsi des autres mots, "à l'exception de ceux qui n'ont point besoin d'être déguisés, et que l'on écrit comme "ils se prononcent."—Journ. Asiat. Paris, March, 1835. p. 256. This refers, of course, to the so-called Pahlavi language.

proper names will be generally omitted in transliteration, and the name printed with a capital letter. Throughout the work a normal character will be used, as near to the older Assyrian forms as the disposable typographical arrangements will admit; consequently all the hieratic and the more recent Babylonian and Persian words will be written in the same ancient alphabet.

---

*List of Abbreviations used in Referring to Inscriptions.*

| | |
|---|---|
| Beh. .. .. | Behistun Inscription, in Journ. R.A.S., 1851. |
| 1 Beltis .. | R. I., Vol. II, Sh. 66. To Beltis as Goddess of War. |
| 2 „ .. | „ „ „ Execution of Susian Chiefs. |
| Birs .. .. | „ Vol. I, Sh. 51. No. 1. Nebuchadnezzar, from Birs Nimrud. |
| Bl. St. .. .. | „ „ Sh. 49, 50. Lord Aberdeen's Black Stone; Esar Haddon. |
| B.M. .. .. | Layard's Inscriptions, published by the British Museum in 1850; the figure preceding denotes the number of the sheet, the following figure shows the line. |
| Botta .. .. | From Botta's Monument de Ninive. 1849–1850, Paris. When a double reference is given, the second denotes Oppert's Inscription, printed in the Journal Asiatique, Paris, 1863. |
| Br. Cyl. .. | R. I., Vol. I, Sh. 69. Nabonidus. Fragments. |
| Br. Obel. .. | „ „ Sh. 28. Sardanapalus. |
| E. I. H. .. | „ „ Sh. 53–64. Nebuchadnezzar. First published by the Hon. East India Company, in 1807. |
| Esar .. .. | „ „ Sh. 45–47. Annals of Esar Haddon. |
| Gyges .. .. | Notice of Gyges, King of Lydia, from a fragment of Assurbanipal. Not published. |
| 1 Mich. .. | R. I., Vol. I, Sh. 70. A block of basalt, usually called Michaux' Stone. First published in Millin's Monuments Antiques Inédits; Paris, 1802. |
| 2 „ .. / 3 „ .. | Two similar stones, in the British Museum, in Hieratic. Not published. |
| Monolith .. | R. I., Vol. I, Sh. 27. Sardanapalus, in British Museum. |
| Nabonid. .. | „ „ Sh. 68. Cylinder of Nabonidus, from Mugheir. |
| Neb. Bab. .. | „ „ Sh. 52, No. 3. Nebuchadnezzar, from Babylon. |
| Neb. Gr. .. | „ „ Sh. 65, 66. Ditto. First published by Grotefend, Göttingen, 1848. |

| | |
|---|---|
| Neb. Senk. .. | R. I., Vol. I, Sh. 51, No. 2. Ditto, from Senkereh. |
| Nebi Yun. .. | „ „ Sh. 43, 44. Sennacherib, from Nebi Yunus. |
| Nerig. .. | „ „ Sh. 67. Cylinder of Neriglissar, from Babylon. |
| Obel. .. .. | L. I., Sh. 87–98. Nimrud Obelisk, Shalmaneser. |
| New Div. .. | Monolith of the same King. Not published. |
| 1 Pul. .. .. | All in R. Ins., Vol. I, Sh. 35. No. 3 was first printed in L. Ins., No. 70, with some slight differences. |
| 2 „ .. .. | |
| 3 „ .. .. | |
| 4 „ .. .. | |
| Rich .. .. | R. I., Vol. I, Sh. 52, No. 4. Nebuchadnezzar. First published in Rich's Babylon and Persepolis, 1839; Pl. 9. |
| Sarg. .. .. | „ „ Sh. 36. Sargina, from Khorsabad. |
| Sard. .. .. | „ „ Sh. 17–26. Annals of Sardanapalus. |
| Sen. B. .. | Sennacherib, on four large slabs, in British Museum. Not published. |
| Sen. Gr. .. | Sennacherib. Published by Grotefend, Göttingen, 1850. |
| Sen. T. .. | R. I., Vol. I, Sh. 37–42. Sennacherib, from Koyunjik. Taylor's Cylinder. |
| Sh. Ph. .. | „ „ Sh. 29-34. Shamas-Phul or Shamas Vul. From Nimrud, Hieratic. |
| St. .. .. | L. I., Sh. 1–11. The Standard Inscription of Sardanapalus. |
| Tig. .. .. | R. I., Vol. I, Sh. 9-16. Annals of Tiglath Pileser I. |
| Tig. jun. .. | „ Vol. II, Sh. 67. „ „ „ II. |

*** In the above List L.I. refers to Layard's Inscriptions, printed in 1850; and R.I. to Rawlinson's Inscriptions, in 2 vols., 1861 and 1866.

The smaller Inscriptions of the Persian empire will be designated by capital letters, as is done in the publications of Westergaard, and by the numbers in Rawlinson's Memoir, Journ. R.A.S., 1845.

---

Many additions and corrections were communicated by Sir H. Rawlinson while this specimen was preparing for the press; they are denoted by the letter R.

*Conventional Alphabet for the Arrangement of Words in the Dictionary.*

A 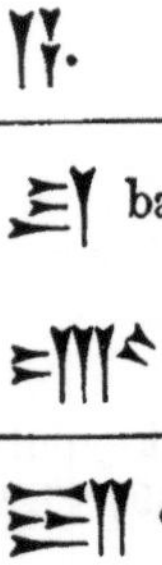

B ba,  bi, 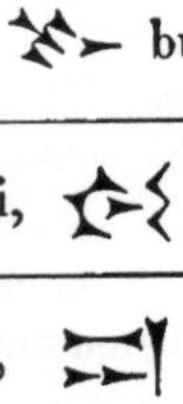 bu, 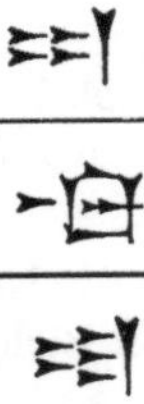 ab, 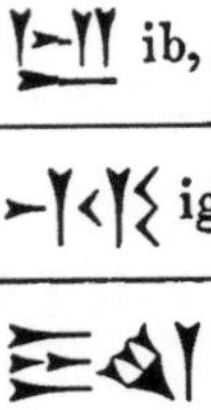 ib, 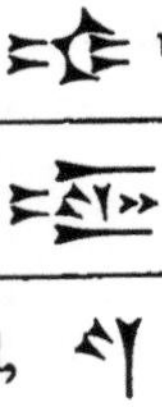 ub.

G ga, gi, gu, ag, ig, ug.

D da, di, du, ad, id, ud.

*or* y, *or* hiatus.—V  hu,  u.

 la,  li,  lu,  al,  il,  ul,  lī.

 ma,  me,  mi,  mu,  am,  im,  um.

 sa,  si,  su.—E  e.

 pa,  pi,  pu.—Z  ẓi,  zu.

,  ar,  ir, , 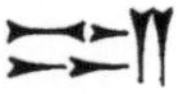 ur.

si, ,  su,  as,  is,  us.

A [cuneiform], in Scythic [cuneiform], equivalent to *a* or *ha*.

Dr. Hincks, in the Report of the British Association, 1857, page 136. derives the character from *drops of water;* sounded in Accadian a or hwa, the meaning would be *water;* soūnded pur, *river;* as in Purrat, *Euphrates.*

[cuneiform], giltanú.—Syl. 562.

¶ [cuneiform], A SON, much used in filiation, and pronounced *pal*, or *bal*. The full pronunciation was *ablu*, in const. *abil.*

[cuneiform], *Merodach-bal-adan.*—Esar. ii. 32.

[cuneiform]. sa Arame, bal Aguṣi, *of Aramu, son of Aguṣu.**—Obel. 130.

[cuneiform] would be *son's son*, as [cuneiform], pal pal sa Mutaggil Nebo, *grandson of Mutaggil Nebo.*—Tig. vii. 45.

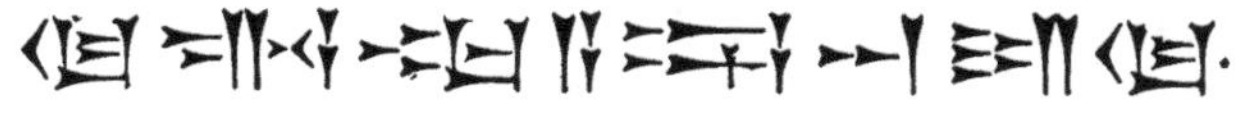

[cuneiform]. *Thy tents(?) son of Babel*, or perhaps, *O Babel.*—Sen. T. v. 23, 24.

I do not know the phonetic power of [cuneiform], but it probably had a final dental, being followed by [cuneiform] in Sen.T. i. 22, and v. 29.

¶ [cuneiform], abu, FATHER.—Vol. II, pl. 31, ii. 28.

Cf. also [cuneiform].—Vol. II, pl. 32, ii. 59.

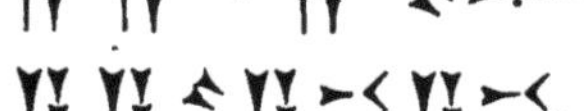

And [cuneiform]. „ „ 61.

---

* I usually put a name in the nominative case in the translation, when I think I am sure of it, but the distinction of cases is not always clear to me.

¶ WATER, written phonetically, *mie*, Heb. מֵי, is generally in the plural, but when followed by was perhaps sounded *miat;* it is, however, more commonly followed by.

ana mie inadú, *into waters shall cast* (moisten R.).—Tig. viii. 65.

asar muzú sa mie, *place of exit of waters.*—Obel. 69.

mie nahri-su, *waters of his rivers.*—Botta 151, 22 (10)=130.

mie nakbi, *water-courses.*—Botta 151, 20 (8)=128.

miat-su nádi kazuti ana zumme-ya lu asti; *of its flowing nauseous waters for my thirst I drank.*—Sen. T. iii. 80.

Doubtful; see קוץ Gen. xxvii. 46. Hincks reads "Its clear waters were abundant for my thirst when I drank."—Polyph. p. 45. Rawlinson suggests "the muddy overflow of its waters for my thirst I drank."

rádu sa mie, *tempest of the waters.*—Nab. Brok. Cyl. ii. 57. Cf. Birs. ii. 1.

Esar. iii. 54. Sard. ii. 132; iii. 32, 136. Sh. Ph. iv. 25, 29.

*water of gods = rain.* mie ili sa mie ili [zunnu sa zunni] salgu, *much rain and snow.*—Sen. T. iv. 77. Given repeatedly as in the meteorological tables.—R.

*waters of the Turnat.*—Obel. 76; 15 BM 24. Name of a town in Kardunias, written in Sh. Ph. iv. 4. The river Turnat is mentioned in l. 9. Torna of the Arabs, and Tornadatus of Pliny.—R.

.—1 Mich. i. 3. Oppert reads Mi Kaldas (Gyndas, Diala). Tal., Ami kalkal (Tigris); but see Vol. II, pl. 51, l. 31.

¶ ........ , suffixed, *my;* more commonly .

, bili-a, *my lords.*—Sh. Ph. iv. 6.

, niri-a, *my yoke* (my feet).—Ibid.

, ummanati-a, *my soldiers.*—Sh. Ph. iv. 25.

, gatú-a, *my hand.*—Birs. i. 14.

AA , ai, *the female power of the sun.*

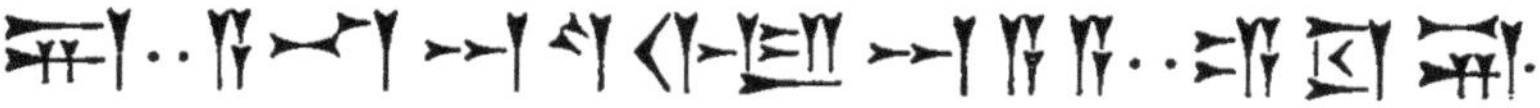

Bit .. ana Shams va Ai .. epus, *a house .. for the sun and for ...... I made.*—Neb. Gr. ii. 40, 42.

See Rawlinson's Herodotus, Vol. I, p. 612. See also R. Insc., Vol. II, pl. 57. i. 11–32, for the twenty names of this goddess.

¶ , negative particle, usually of deprecation, *let it not, be it not,* perhaps the Hebrew אִי; Job. xxii. 30; 1 Sam. iv. 21.

, ai isi nakiri, *may I not have enemies.*—E.I.H. x. 15; Neb. Bab. ii. 31.

, mugallitu ai arsi [arli].—Neb. Bab. ii. 31.

, mugalliti ai arsi.—E. I. H. x. 16.

These readings are doubtful. A comparison of the concluding lines of E.I.H. of Neb. Gr. and of Neriglissar, may, perhaps, suggest a translation to a good Semitic scholar. Dr. Hincks's copy of Neb. Bab. ii. 31, has 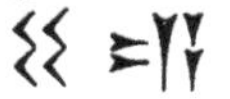 at the end, instead of .

 ai irsá ḥiditi.—Nabon. ii. 29; Brok. Cyl. ii. 27. In Br. Cyl. i. 23, we have the same sentence, with the word printed , irsán.

Dr. Hincks would translate "may he not give way to sinners;" perhaps agree or consort with sinners.

, ai ipparkú idá-sa, *may its walls (?) not be broken.*—Sen. B. iv. 43=42 BM 53.

, followed by umma, which is like the Latin cunque, or Sanscrit chiya, means *any one whatever* (cf. מְאוּמָה Heb.), as 

, aiumma ina libbi-sunu asar-su ul umassí ma susub-su ul idi ma ḥire nahr-su ul izkur; *any one among them its site not touched, and its restoration not undertook, and the digging of its water not laboured at.*—Sarg. 36.

;

aiumma ina libbi-sunu ana bit rab garbi-su ṭamu ribat biluti-sa nin aḥḥar, subat ṣuleṣu ul idá, libbús ul iḥṣuṣ; *any one among them to the palace therein in the height of its power (?) stayed not, the seat of its buildings knew not, into it ventured not.*—Sen. Gr. 40—Some words doubtful.

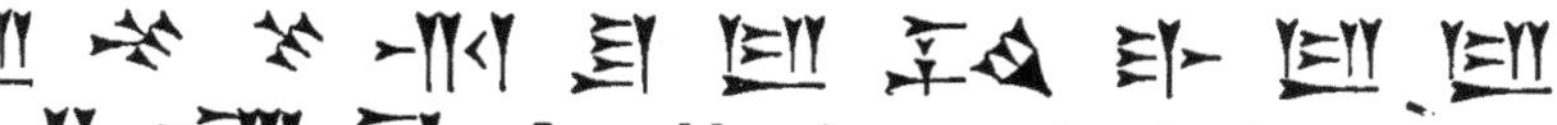
 Lu aklu, lu nuturda, lu ḥazannu, lu muserisu, lu tiggallu, lu aiumma; *whether aklu, or nuturda, or ḥazannu, or muserisu, or tiggallu, or any one whatever.*—2 Mich. i. 33.

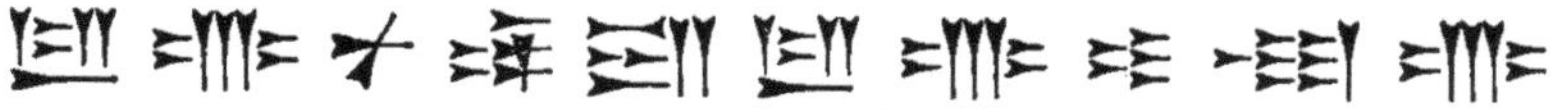
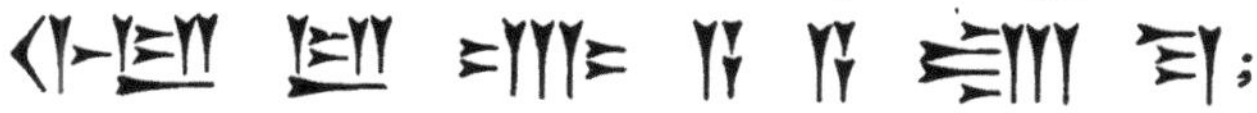 lú nuturda, lú itú, va lú aiumma; *whether naturda, or itú, or any one whatever.*—1 Mich. ii. 6.

All these Accadian words appear to designate classes of men; some additional appellations occur in a like passage in 3 Mich. iii. 8—14.

¶ . .  as a termination, makes a gentile noun, signifying the *people*, or *country*, or *city*, as preceded by the respective determinative , , or 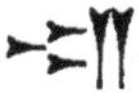.

, Parṣai tur Parṣai, *a Persian, son of a Persian.*—N. R. 6, 7. In the Persian, Pársa, Pársahyá putra.—l. 13, 14.

. Madai, *Media.*—N.R. 11; Beh. 14, 16, 23, 26, 43, 47, &c. In Persian, Mada.

1 Pul. 7; Botta 145, 5=17; 147, 5=65; Sen. T. ii. 30; Sarg. 14, 30; Esar. iv. 9, 22.

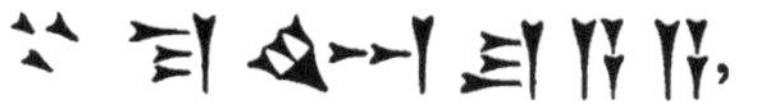, Mahbai, *Moab.*—Sen. T. ii. 53; Tig. jun. 60.

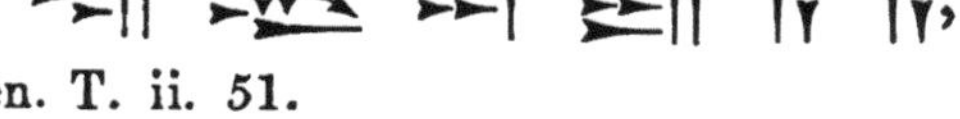, Azdudai, *Ashdod.*—Sen. T. ii. 51.

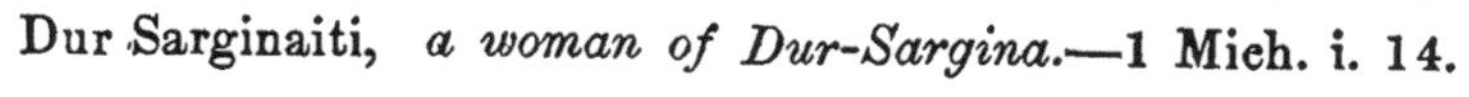, Sal Dur Sarginaiti, *a woman of Dur-Sargina.*—1 Mich. i. 14.

The final *ti* represents the oblique case, feminine.

AAB , , , ayab, st. const., aibi, aibut, pl. ENEMY. Heb. אֹיֵב.

, ayab Babel, *enemy of Babylon.*—Esar. ii. 43. , zalbat aibi, *smiter of enemies.*—Tig. i. 8.  var. , kasid aibi-su, *capturing his enemies.*—Sard. i. 40. , kasid aibut Assur, *capturing the enemies of Assur.*—Sard. i. 28.

Tig. i. 11; Sard. i. 15; E.I.H. vi. 39; Nerig. i. 27.

, Aibursabū.—E.I.H. v. 38.

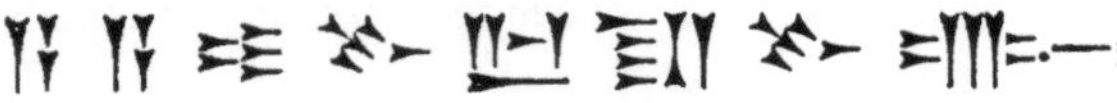.—Ibid. v. 45.

.—Ibid. v. 15.

.—Ibid. vii. 46.

,—Nerig. ii. 17; Rich. i. 22.

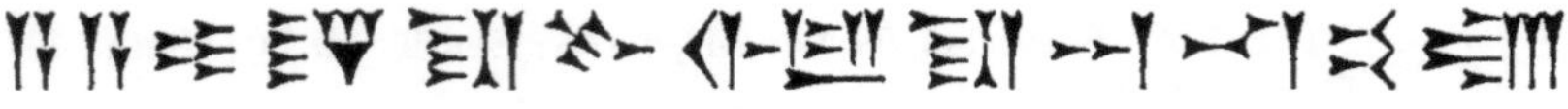
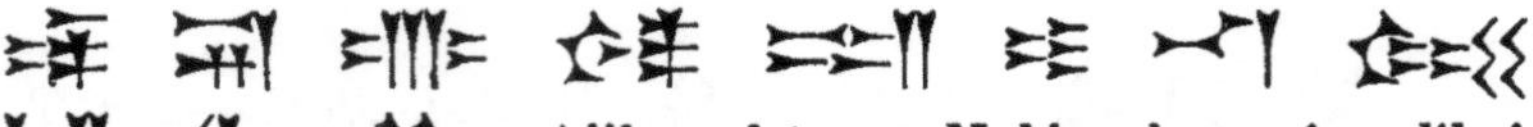
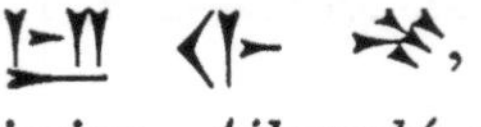, Aiibursabú sa Nabiupaluẓur ina libni ipsivu, *Aibursabú which Nabopolassar in brick had extended.*—E.I.H. vii. 46.

A piece of water near Babylon, often connected with *ṣule Babel*, the mound of Babylon. Probably an artificial pond, lined with brick. Dr. Hincks would read this name *Aya-ipur-sapú*, "let not the edge crumble," connecting *ipvr* with עפר, dust. May it not be rather from the verb פור, to break in pieces?—See Oppert's note in E. M. p. 290.

**AB** 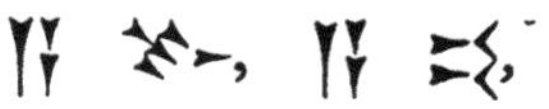 abu, nom., abi, gen., FATHER. Heb. אָב.

Nom.—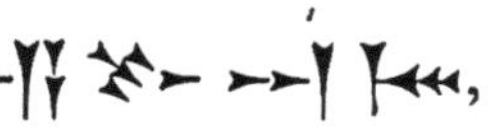, abu ili, *father of gods.*—42 BM 52; Botta 152, 23=167; Obel. 4.

Gen.—, abi alidi-ka, *of the father begetting thee.*—Birs. ii. 27.

, abi alidi-ya, *of the father begetting me.*—E. I. H. vii. 12.

*Di* is not on the printed copies, but it is clear on the slab.

, kima abi va ummi, *like a father and a mother.*—K. 66, quoted by Oppert, Journ. Asiat. Aug.-Sept. 1857, p. 172.

Abi appears to be irregularly *my father* in the nom. case in the following:

, itti sa abi ipusu, *with what my father did.*—E. I. H. v. 51.

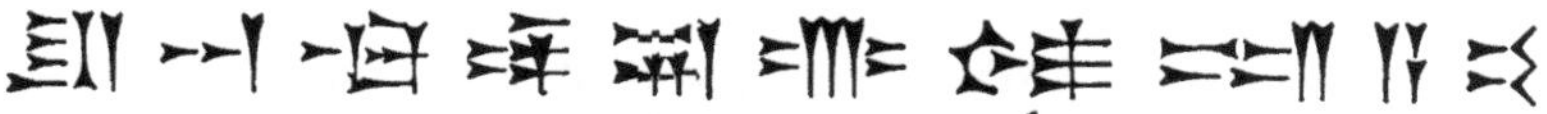
, sa Nabupalhuẓur abi banú-a ipusu; *which Nabopolassar, my father begetting me, made.*—E. I. H. iv. 71.

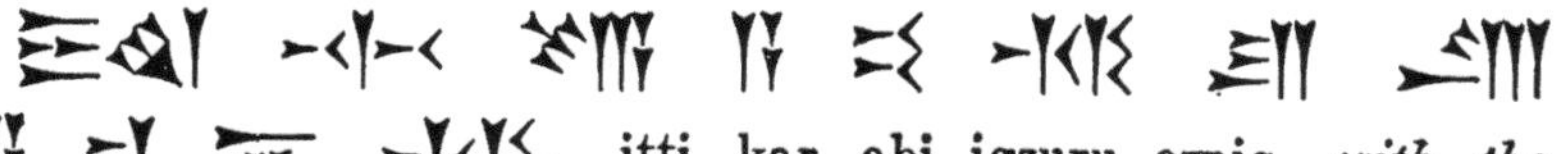
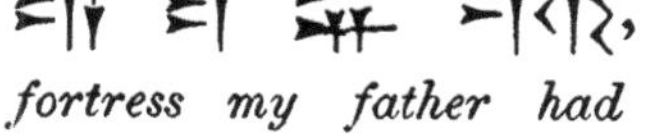, itti kar abi igzuru ezniq, *with the fortress my father had damaged I joined.*—E. I. H. v. 30.—Doubtful.

Aba. , &c. 
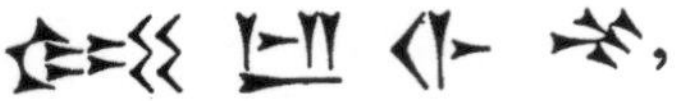, sa N. aba banú-a ina libni ipsivu, *which Nabopolassar, the father begetting me, in brick had extended.*—E.I.H. vii. 48.

Dr. Hincks suggests that *a* in aba, is *my*, in this passage.

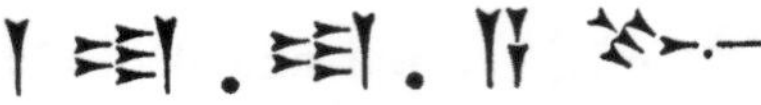.—Syl. 92.

 is very generally used for abu, *father*.

¶ , Abu, *the fifth month* (Heb אָב), on a slab containing all the months, written phonetically. Usually written .—See Neb. Yun. 42.

¶ 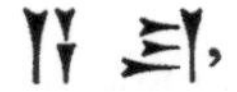, Aba, some *law officer*. Accadian.

, Aba of the Assyrians.—Vol. II, Sh. 31. l. 64.

, Aba of the Arameans.—l. 65.

The officer who signs the legal tablets, treated of by Sir Henry Rawlinson, in Journ. R.A.S. 1864, is so called.—See p. 246 of Journal, where it is rendered *judge*.

¶ , abba (habba), The SEA.—Any large river?

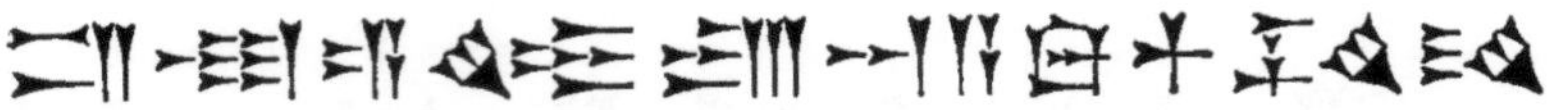
, istu ebirtan nahr Tiggar adi Libnana va habba rabte, *from the passage of the river Tigris to Lebanon and the great sea.*—Stand. 8. Nearly the same in Sard. ii. 127.

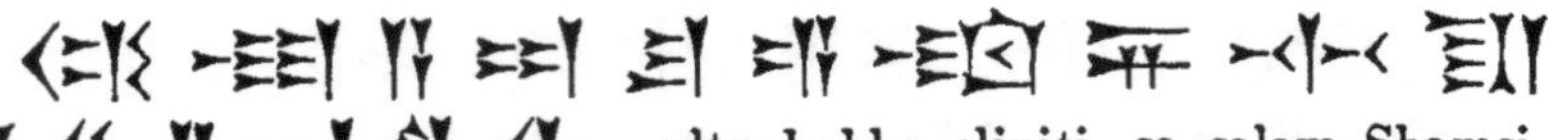
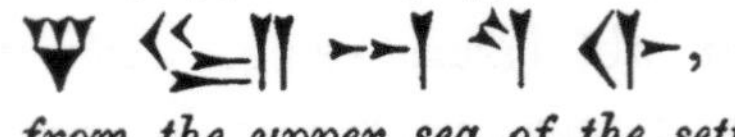, ultu habba eliniti sa salam Shamsi, *from the upper sea of the setting sun.*—Sen. T. i. 13.

Tig. iv. 4, 50, 99; vi. 43. Sard. iii. 85. Br. Ob. i. 3. Neb. Yun. 21.

, sa ina ebirtan habba, *which (is) in the crossing of the sea.*—Neb. Yun. 21.

, nahira in habba rabte iduk, *a porpoise in the great sea he killed.*—Brok. Ob. i. 3.

, istamdaḥu sate u habbai, *hath passed over mountains and seas.*—N. Div. i. 10. A parallel passage in 12BM9 has *tamáte.*

¶ , abba, f., CAMEL. Accadian.

 , habbai sa sunai ẓiri-sina, *camels which two (are) their backs.*—Obel. Epig. 1 and 3.

To judge from the Hebrew שֶׁנְהַבִּים, shen-habbim, *ivory,* habba should be *elephant,* but the obelisk with its figures is decisive; we have a similar confusion in the Gothic ulband, for *a camel;* also in the Slavonic dialects. It would appear, from several parallels cited by Sir Henry Rawlinson, that gammal and habba are used indiscriminately; the former word being Semitic, the latter Accadian.—See Vol. II, p. 44, iii, l. 6 and 7. But in pl. 31, i. 54, 55, we have the  and , apparently contrasted.

¶ , , abub, const. abubi, obl., CORN.—Heb. אָבִיב.

, abub uthari, *green corn of battle,* i.e., *warriors.*—Tig. i. 50; v. 43. *Sickle of war.*—R.

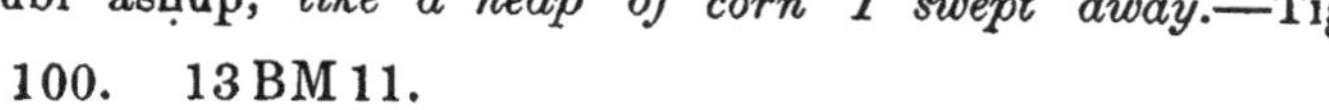, kima tel abubi asḥup, *like a heap of corn I swept away.*—Tig. iii. 75; v. 100. 13BM11.

, kip abubi, *giver of corn.*—Sh. Ph. i. 10.

.—Syl. 394.

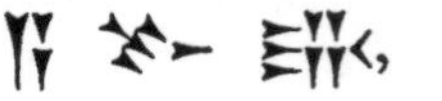

, abubis, adv., *like corn.*   , rizi-su abubis asbun, *his helpers like corn I swept.*—Neb. Yun. 7.

Abubis appears to be used in Tig. ii. 78, instead of abubi.

, abunanis, adv., *like a field of corn.*

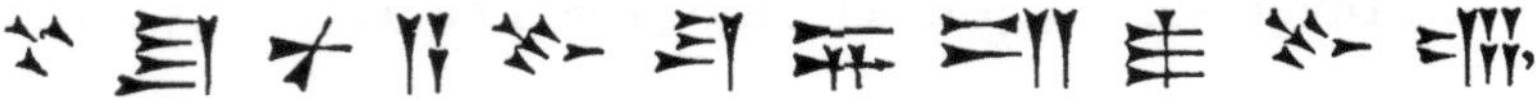

, mat-sunu abubanis asbun ; *their country like a field of corn I swept.*—Obel. 158. See Obel. 21 ; 12 BM 14.

, abbanú, *I was made (?). Niphal of Bana.*—E.I.H. i. 27. See Verbs.

ABG 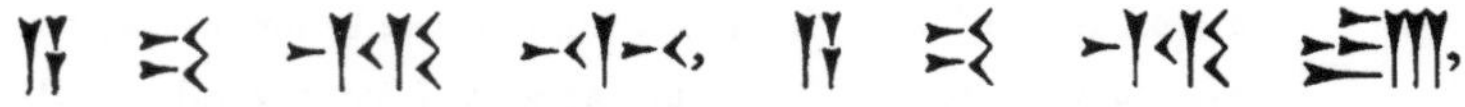 , abikti, obl., abikta, acc., DEFEAT ; a frequent variant is  , an Accadian word.

, abikta-sunu lu askun, *their defeat I effected.*—Tig. i. 76.

, abikti ummani-su liskunu, *the defeat of his troops may they effect.*—Tig. viii. 81.

I do not see why the oblique case is put here.

.—Sard. iii. 39.

.—N. Div. i. 38.

See also Tig. iii. 23; iv. 17; v. 76, 89; viii. 81.

**ABD** , abat, PETITION. abat tur-sal sarri, *petition of the daughter of the king.* A small unpublished slab, l. 1. Usually .—R.

.—Syl. 261.

Printed copy imperfect; a fresh fragment has been found recently.

**ABI** , abaya. Proto-Babylonian.

—Vol. II, pl. 37, i. 6.

—Vol. II, pl. 37, i. 56.

Umme mee, *mother of waters;* perhaps *pelican.*—R.

**ABL** , , ablu, n., abil, con., A SON.

, ablu, kenū, *eldest son,* var. .—Birs. ii. 16. See p. 6.

, abil-su kinū, *his eldest son.*—E.I.H. i. 33 ; vii. 28.

¶ , abal, *title of an Official.*—Vol. II, pl. 31, l. 80.

This title is Accadian.—R.

¶ , abullī.—Vol. II, pl. 37, ii. 63. Abullī is proto-Babylonian.

**ABM** , abime, *wood of some sort.* Hincks suggests doubtfully abies.

, iz abime kulab babi emad, *wood for posts of gates he placed.*—Esar. vi. 2.

**ABN** , abn, STONE ; Var. .—Sard. iii. 55, 63.

is phonetically *tag*, or *tak*.

, var. ,
iltakkanu, var. iltakanu.—Sard. i. 30.

, abni ẓipa ina eli-su azru, *stones firm upon it I laid down.*—Tig. vi. 14. A variant omits .

, lamaṣṣi sa abni, *sacred figures of stone.*—Esar. v. 41.—R.

.—Syl. 175.

See Esar. v. 41; vi. 53. Sen. T. vi. 52; and Rawlinson's note in J. R. As. Soc., 1864, p. 240.

, Tel Abnai, "*Mound of stones.*" *Name of a city near Orfa and Arbela.* See Rawlinson's Herodotus, Vol. I, p. 466.

Determ. ,
IV urmahi sa admas, *four lions of adamant (?)*—Br. Ob. ii. 17.

**ABṢ** , abuṣa, var. abubuṣa ; *stable, manger.* Heb. אֵבוּס ; *granary,* Heb. מַאֲבוּס.

.—Sard. i. 7.

Dr. Hincks has collated many copies, and has not seen one with the omission of the second . He has seen one copy with beginning a line, which would militate against the above meaning. I do not understand the passage.

,
Bit Abuṣate, sa bit rab biluti-ya ; *Bit Abuṣate, which is the palace of my lordship.*—Brok. Obel. ii. 1.

ABE , Abaeni, *a country of Nairi.*—Tig. iv. 79.

ABQ , Abuqu, *a city of Susiana,*  *with several other towns.*—Sard. i. 46.

ABR , var. , *strengthening.* אַבִּיר Heb.

, abir salimmate, la adiru tukmate, *strengthening the peaceful, not sparing opposition.*—R. Sard. i. 19; St. 13.

Dr. Hincks would read "not fearing opposition."

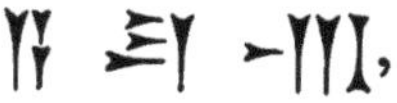, abari, *mighty deeds.*—Opp.

, Ninib bil abari, *Ninib, lord of mighty deeds.*—Oppert's Harem Inscription, l. 1; E. M. p. 333.

¶ , Syl. 726.

¶ , abars, *a metal classed with iron, tin, &c.*—Oppert makes it *antimony.*—Botta 152, 16 = 160.

The Gold Tablet in the Expédition en Mésopotamie, p. 343, has , which Dr. Oppert reads as one word, *i.e.*, puyâk, *antimony;* but we have in Botta , anna, anbar, abars; *lead, iron (?), antimony.* A Bilingual slab has anna=anaku; Heb. אֲנָךְ, *lead.*—R.

¶ , Abarṣihuni, *a country of Nairi.*—Tig. iv. 82. Amaṣṣihuni.—R.

¶ , abarti, *across, over, along,* from Heb. עֵבֶר.

makát agurri abarti Buratti urakkiṣu ; *buttresses of brick along the Euphrates he constructed.*—E.I.H. v. 8.—R.

ABT , Abitigna, *with other towns of the country of Kakmí.*—Sarg. 28.

Botta 146, 21=57 imperfect. Oppert refers to 139, 10, and 140, 1.

I do not remember seeing any of the following pronouns in documents older than those of the Persian period:

AG 

, agá, agah, agata, THIS.

, agá sa anku ebusu, *this which I have done.*—Beh. 11.

, bit agá, *this house.*—No. 17, C. 17.

, ziqqaru agah, *this earth.*—No. 15, D. 2.

, ziqqaru agá, *this earth.*—No. 5, O. 2 ; No. 13. E. 1.

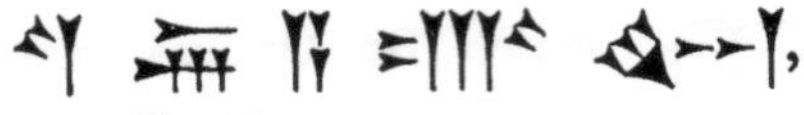, Parṣa agah, *this Persia.*—No. 15, D. 13.

, ana mati-ya agá, *to this my country.*—No. 6, N.R. 33.

adi eli sa sarrutu agata . . . . . . . *until that this kingdom (I obtained).*—Beh. 10.

 irẓitī agáta, *this earth.*—No. 17, C. 3.

 ziqqari agáta, *this land.*—No. 17, C. 11.

 ziqqaru agáta, *this land.*—No. 13, E. 6; No. 5, O. 17.

 must be plural in Beh. 4; but the substantive is lost.

 and  appear to have been used for both numbers and genders. We find the former with *ziqqaru* in O. 2 and E. 1, and the latter with the same noun in D. 2; and this same noun appears with the feminine *agáta* in O. 17, E. 6, and D. 7. *Agá* must, however, be rather considered the masculine, as it is found with the names of men on all the detached inscriptions at Behistun. All these words occur in a degenerate period of the language, and the inscriptions may have been written by Persians. *Aga*, in the opinion of Sir H. C. Rawlinson, was taken from the Accadian  or , "here," or "there."

¶ Aga, combined with the personal pronouns sú, *he*, sunu, *they:*

 biti sa ili sa Gumátū aga-sú Magusu ibbulu; *the houses of the gods which Gumata, he the Magian, had destroyed.*—Beh. 25; see also l. 12, 23, 28, 82.

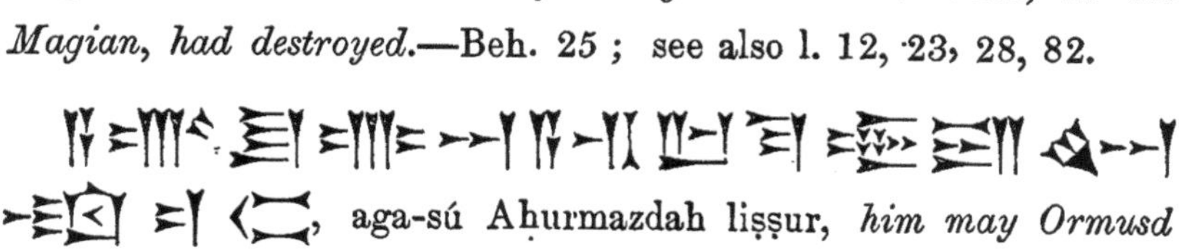 aga-sú Aḥurmazdah liṣṣur, *him may Ormusd protect.*—No. 17, C. 24.

 nikrutu aga-sunu, *those rebels.*—Beh. 46. In Beh. 65, with , nikrut.

The following are compounds of aga and the demonstrative annu:—

sú agannu ana sar ittur, *he here became king.*—Beh. 12.

, sa aganna ibnu, *which here he made.*—No. 3, H. 14.

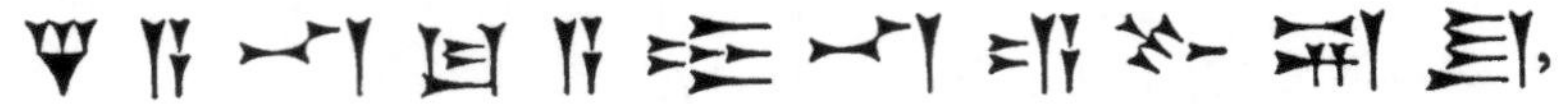

sa anaku aganna ebussu, *which I here made.*—No. 13, E. 8.

In the above passages the Persian inscription has *idá*, "here."—R.

Pl. mas., , zalmánu agannutu, *these images.*—Beh. 106.

Pl. fem., 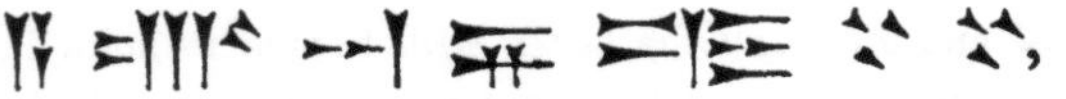, agannitā mati, *these provinces.*—No. 3, H. 13.

, mati aganetū, *these provinces.*—Beh. 8, 9.

, aganetū mati, *these provinces.*—Beh. 7.

, doubtful, seems to mean *we are.*—Beh. 3.

The declension appears to be as follows:—Sing. com., agá and agah; fem., agata; plural, agá. Compounded with annu:—Sing. nom., agannu; accus., aganna; plural mas., agannut; fem., agannet.

¶ 

agú, nom., agá, acc., age, pl., CROWN.

, agú rabá sa risdu, *a crown large for the head.*—Slab K. 162, i. 45.

The example is completed from ii. 16, a parallel passage.

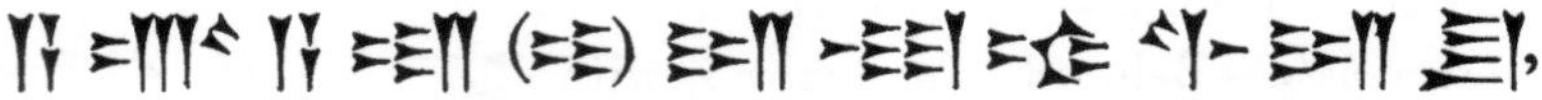

agá ẓira tuppira-su, *a crown lofty ye have granted him.*—Tig. i. 21.

[cuneiform], bil age, *lord of crowns.*—Tig. i. 5.

[cuneiform], sar age, *king of crowns.*—Obel. 6.

[cuneiform], nadin ḥaruṭ (izpa) va age, *giver of sceptre and crowns.*—Tig. i. 2.

Query.—Sen. Gr. 47; = 28 BM 13; = Sen. B. iii. 29.

¶ Aga: Sir H. Rawlinson considers this a genitive or possessive termination allied to the terminal nasal in Scythic, Turkish, &c.:—[cuneiform], rabaga, *greatness.* [cuneiform], Bil rabaga nu bilá, *Lord of greatness without end.*—1 Mich. iii. 13.—See [cuneiform].

AGB [cuneiform].—Brok. Cyl. ii. 29, 48. Mr. Talbot reads this Agaba, and renders it *Arbela;* it is more probably Agani.—See Rawlinson's Herodotus, Vol. I, p. 611.

Vol. II, pl. 50, i. 9, [cuneiform], Bit-andadia, *a tower* (ziggur) *in Agani.*

AGZ [cuneiform], Agazi, *a country in Media.*—Botta 147, 9=69. Oppert has Agagi.

AGL [cuneiform], agali, GOATS. اجل cervus rupicaper, bos sylvestris.

[cuneiform], pare, agali, *cows, goats.*—N. Div. ii. 65.

[cuneiform], pare, agali, va marsit; *cows, goats, and young.*—Tig. v. 6.

[cuneiform]; sumuli, agali, ibili; *mules (?), goats, rams.*—Sen. T. vi. 55.

The identification of these animals is somewhat doubtful.

AGM , agammu, agamme, אֲגַם, A POOL.

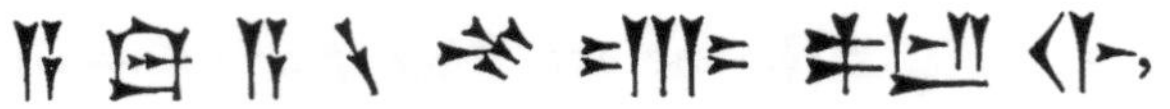, nahr agammu usapsi, *the water Agammu I expanded.*—42 BM 44.

, kirib nahr agamme va apparate, *near the pools and lakes.*—Sen. T. iii. 59.

An artificial lake, made by Sennacherib.—Hincks.

AGN , aganáte, BASONS, BOWLS.—אַגָּן Heb., pelvis.

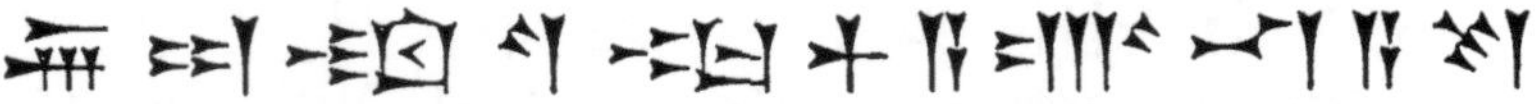
, ṣapli utkabar, aganáte utkabar; *bowls of copper and basins of copper.*—Sard. ii. 122.

AGṢ , Aguṣi, *the father of Aramu.*—Obel. 130; N. Div. ii. 27. Made Guṣi in N. Div. ii. 12, and I think in ii. 83.

AGR , agar, FIELD.—1 Mich. i. 2. אִכָּר, ager, *acre?* 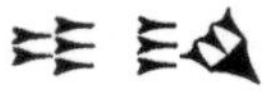 in E.I.H. iv. 64.

, agar-su l'irhiz, *his field may he inundate.*—1 Mich. iv. 11.

, eli agari-sun, *upon their fields.*—Sen. Gr. 30.

¶ , agarin, MOTHER.

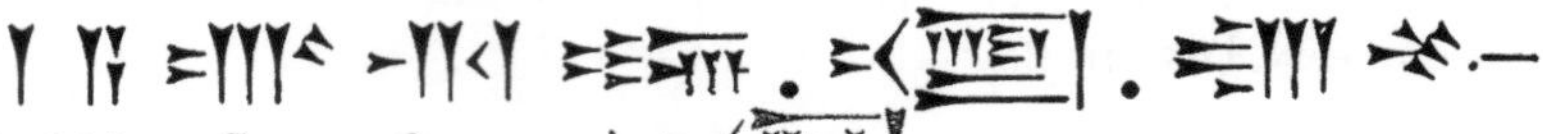—Syl. 192. In another copy 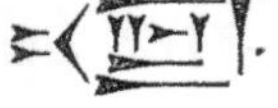.

This singular word is found in the following passage:

, ina lib ibba agarinni alatti-ya, *in the fair body of the mother who bore me.*—38 BM 3.

¶  aguri, agurri, obl. case, BURNT BRICK.

var.  , ina aguri arẓip, *in brick I built.*—Tig. viii. 6.

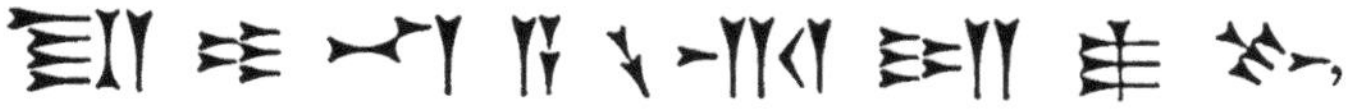

, sa ina aguri raspu, *which of brick (was) built.*—Tig. vi. 11 ; see also vi. 19, &c.

—E.I.H. iv. 12 ; vi. 51. Birs. ii. 3.

—Birs. i. 25 ; E.I.H. iii. 16, 69. Porter's transcript of vi. 51.

Agurri differs from liban, which is *sun-dried* only.

, aguris, *made of brick.* Porter's transcript is  , agurris.

. . . . .  , malak bit aguris mare . . . . . ubannū, *further (?), a house of brick conspicuous . . . I built.*—E.I.H. iii. 56.

¶  , agartu, VALUABLE. אֲגוֹרָה, *a piece of silver*, 1 Sam. ii. 36. Hunutu, ḥuraz, kaspu, agartu, nintaksu ; *wealth, gold, silver, valuables, furniture.*—Sen. T. i. 28.

, abn agartū, *precious stones.*—Sen. B. i. 6 ; Esar. i. 19.

, idem.—Botta 154,12=180.

Always accompanying *gold, silver,* &c.

, kima napsati agarti, *like precious work.*—E.I.H. vii. 30 ; ix. 52.

**AGS** [cuneiform], agis, *urgently, strongly.* أجّ *properare, instigare.*

[cuneiform], agis umahruni, *urgently they impelled me.*—43 BM 6.

See aggis [cuneiform] and [cuneiform] in passages very nearly parallel; Sard. i. 42, and N. Div. i. 14.

**AD** [cuneiform], adi, prep. *to ;* conj. *also, together with.*

[cuneiform], adi habba elinite lu ardi sunuti, *to the upper sea I pursued (?) them.*—Tig. iv. 99.

[cuneiform], adi maḥri-ya isbura, *to my presence he sent.*—Botta 153, 9 = 153.

With ultu, istu, ta, *from :—*

[cuneiform] v. [cuneiform] istu ebirtan nahr Zabi supalí . . . . .· adi ebirtan nahr Buratta, *from the crossing of the lower Zab . . . . . to the crossing of the Euphrates.*—Tig. vi. 42.

[cuneiform], istu ris sarruti-ya adi 5 pal-ya, *from the beginning of my reign to my fifth year.*—Tig. vi. 45.

[cuneiform], ultu zit shamsi adi erib shamsi, *from rising of sun to setting of sun.*—Esar. i. 7.

¶ *And, together with.* Interchanges with ; cf. Obel. 80 and 15 BM 26, parallel passages. , var. .—St. 8.

, sarrani mati Nairi, adi sa ana niraruti-sunu illikuni ; *Kings of the countries of Nairi, together with (those) who to their aid went.*—Tig. iv. 97.

, nisi adi marsiti-sunu, *people and their children(?)*—Botta 147, 11 = 71.

See also Tig. iii. 3. Sen. T. i. 20 ; ii. 13. Obel. 153, 169. New Div. ii. 52.

¶ , adi eli sa, *until that, whilst.*

, adi eli sa anku allaku an Madai, *until that I went to Media.*—Beh. 47.

. . . adi eli sa bit attunu in asri-su . . . *until that our house to its place* (imperfect).—Beh. 27.

, adi eli sa agá ebus, *(Ormuzd gave me help) whilst I was doing this.*—N. R. 32.

¶ , *over,* adverbially.

, adi eli mie lu'usabil, *over (it) the water I brought.*—Sard. ii. 132 ; iii. 136.

¶ , ade, *acknowledgment* [*religious*], עד.
*Dependence on, union with.*—Hincks. *Precepts.*—Oppert.

,
ade ili rabi ebuk, *the acknowledgment of the great gods he forsook.*—Botta 148, 7=79 ; 151, 14=122.

 . . . ,
sa Padí sar-sunu, bil-ade va mabad sa Assur . . . iddu, *who Padi their king, holding the belief and service of Assyria . . . had expelled.*—Sen. T. ii. 70.

Avaient trahi leur roi Padi, inspiré d'amitié et de zèle pour l'Assyrie.—Op.

In Sen. B. i. 23, parallel passage, we have  for . *Commander of troops (?).*

¶ 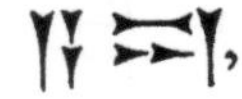, equ. .—Vol. II, pl. 31, ii. 24.

ADA , Adia, *one of 27 strong cities.*—Sh. Ph. i. 45.

ADL 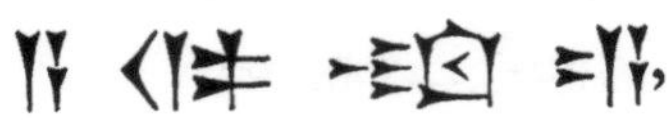, Adile, *one of several tribes.*—Tig. jun. 6.

ADM 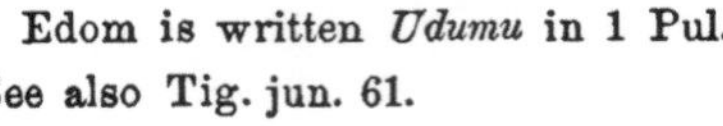, Adumú, *Edom.*—Esar. ii. 55.

Edom is written *Udumu* in 1 Pul. 12, and *Udummai* in Sen. T. ii. 54. See also Tig. jun. 61.

¶ .—Syl. 357.

¶ 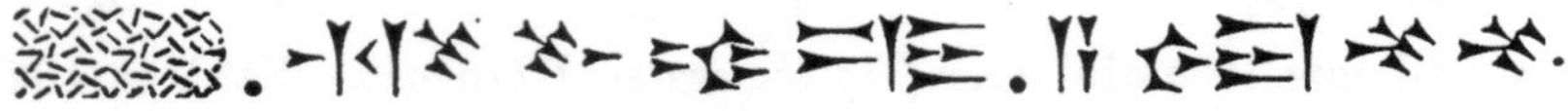.
Adammumu.—Vol. II, pl. 37, ii. 14 ; Trilingual list of Birds.

**ADN** , two Accad. words, *water great, i.e.,* FLOOD; in Assyrian, *mili.* See , Vol. II, pl. 39, iv. 7; and , in E.I.H. vii. 51.

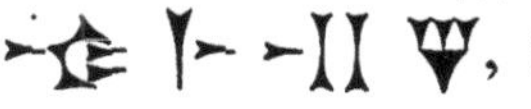, ina mili kissati (ina ussi-sa abbu usapsu va) uribbu timmen-sa; doubtfully rendered, *by the gathered floods (in its foundation hollows abounded, and) was dilated its platform.*—Sen. Gr. 48.

Same in Sen. B. iii. 30, and 38 BM 14, omitting the clause bracketed.

, ina mili kissati timmen-su la enise, *by the gathering floods its platform was not damaged.*—Sen. Gr. 53= 39 BM 18.

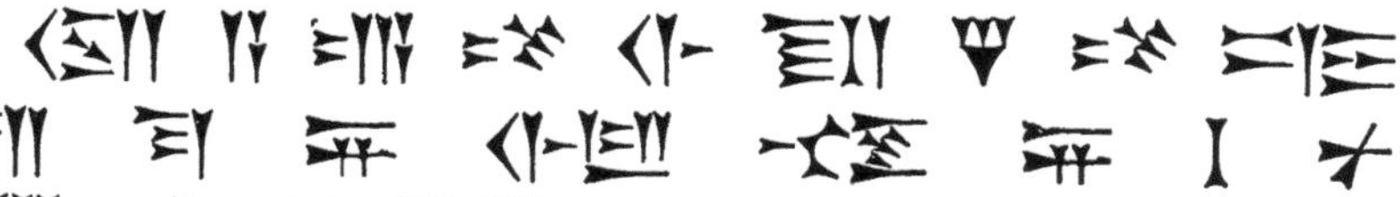
, kima mili kissati sagabtā ṣimani va munni-sunu usardá.—Sen. T. v. 78.

¶ , Adani.—Sard. iii. 98. See Adaeni, p. 32.

¶ , adanni. Opp. *old age;* Talbot renders it *foundation,* from אדן.

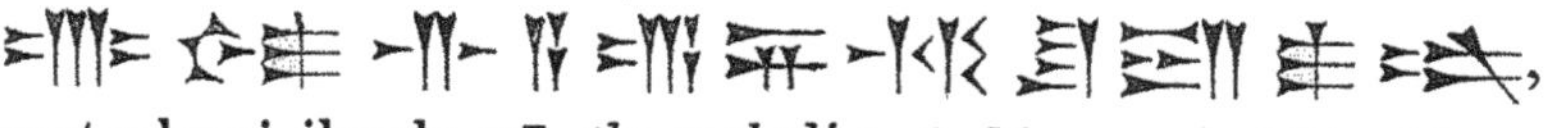,
huẓurat adanni iksuda-ssū, *the maladies of old age seized him (?).*—Botta 151, 9=117. Oppert.

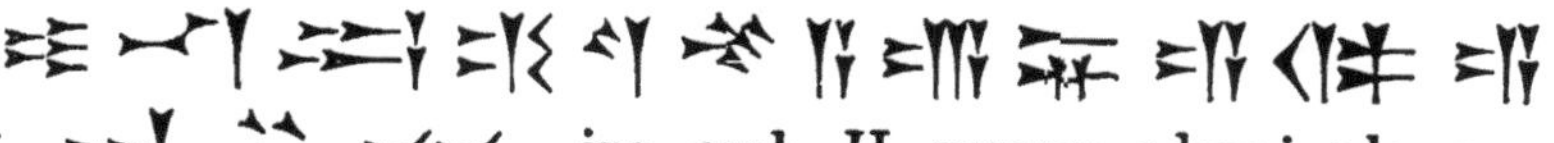
, ina aruḫ II yommu adanni ede pan matti.—38 BM 10.

¶ , Adini, *father of Aḫunu.*—Sard. iii. 61; Obel. 36, 46; frequent in Obelisk and New Div.

, Bit Adini, *country beyond the Tigris.*—Sard. iii. 64. Without  in l. 60 and 134.

¶ , Adinnu, *a city of Hamath.*—N. Div. ii. 88.

¶ , Adaeni, *a country of Nairi.*—Tig. iv. 79. See Adani, p. 31.

ADR , adir, *honouring.* Heb. הדר.

, 'la adir zikri ili, *not honouring the memory of the gods.*—Botta 151, 4=112.

¶ , adiru, *timid, cowardly; avoiding.*

, bulḫu adiru melam Asur bil-ya lu isḫup sunuti, *timid fear of the approach (?) of Assur my lord overwhelmed them.*—Tig. ii. 38.

, ri'u [sab] tabráte la adiru tukmate, *prince . . . . . not sparing opposition.*—Sard. i. 13=St. 3.

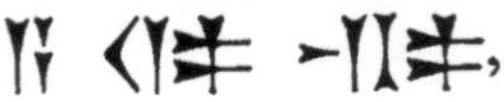, adiris, *like a coward, cowardly.*

, in buzrat sadí marẓi adiris usib, *in the fastnesses of rugged mountains cowering he remained.*—Botta 146, 5=41.

# JOURNAL

OF

# THE ROYAL ASIATIC SOCIETY.


## Art. VIII.—*On the Relations of the Priests to the other Classes of Indian Society in the Vedic Age.*[1] By J. Muir, Esq.

In a former paper on "Manu, the progenitor of the Aryan Indians," published in the Society's Journal,[2] I have attempted to shew that in general the authors of the hymns of the Rig-veda regarded the whole of the Aryan people, embracing not only the priests and the chiefs, but the middle classes also of the population, as descended from one common father, or ancestor, whom they designate by the name of Manu. This reference to a common progenitor excludes, of course, the supposition that the writers by whom it is made could have had any belief in the myth which became afterwards current among their countrymen, that their nation consisted of four castes, differing naturally in dignity, and separately created by Brahmâ.

That essay, however, leaves out of consideration any notices which the Rig-veda may contain regarding the different classes of which the society contemporary with its composition was made up. As this great collection of hymns embodies numerous references, both to the authors themselves and to the other agents in the celebration of divine worship, it may be expected to supply, incidentally or indirectly, at least, some

[1] This subject has been already treated in Professor Roth's book, Zur Litt. u. Geschichte des Weda; in his essay "Brahma und die Brahmanen," in the 1st vol. of the Journal of the Germ. Or. Society; in Dr. Haug's Tract on "the Origin of Brahmanism," and in the 1st vol. of my "Sanskrit Texts."

[2] Vol. xx. p. 406 ff.

information respecting the opinion which these ministers of religion entertained of themselves, and of the relation in which they stood to the other sections of the community. I shall now endeavour to shew how far this expectation is justified by an examination of the Rig-veda.

I have elsewhere[1] enquired into the views which the authors of the hymns appear to have held on the subject of their own authorship. The conclusion I arrived at was, that they did not in general look upon their compositions as divinely inspired, since they frequently speak of them as the productions of their own minds (*ibid.* pp. 128–140). But though this is most commonly the case (and especially, as we may conjecture, in regard to the older hymns), there is no doubt that they also attached a high value to these productions, which they describe as being acceptable to the gods (R.V. v. 45, 4; v. 85, 1; vii. 26, 1, 2; x. 23, 6; x. 54, 6; x. 105, 8), whose activity they stimulated (iii. 34, 1; vii. 19, 11), and whose blessing they drew down. In some of the hymns a supernatural character or insight is claimed for the Rishis (i. 179, 2; vii. 76, 4; iii. 53, 9; vii. 33, 11 ff.; vii. 87, 4; vii. 88, 3 ff.; x. 14, 15; x. 62, 4, 5), and a mysterious efficacy is ascribed to their compositions (Sanskrit Texts, vol. iii. pp. 173 f.) The Rishis called their hymns by various names, as *arka, uktha, ṛch, gir, dhî, nîtha, nivid, mantra, mati, sûkta, stoma, vâch, vachas*, etc. etc.; and they also frequently applied to them the appellation of *brahma*, as, for instance, in the whole, or most, of the following passages:—i. 31, 18; i. 37, 4; i. 61, 16; i. 62, 13; i. 80, 16; i. 117, 25; i. 152, 5, 7; i. 165, 14; ii. 18, 7; ii. 23, 1, 2; ii. 34, 6; ii. 39, 8; iii. 18, 3; iii. 29, 15; iii. 51, 6; iii. 53, 12; iv. 6, 11; iv. 16, 20, 21; iv. 22, 1; iv. 36, 7; v. 29, 15; v. 40, 6; v. 73, 10; v. 85, 1; vi. 17, 13; vi. 23, 1, 5; vi. 38, 3, 4; vi. 47, 14; vi. 50, 6; vi. 52, 2, 3; vi. 69, 4, 7; vi. 75, 19; vii. 22, 3, 9; vii. 28, 1, 2, 5; vii. 31, 11; vii. 33, 3, 4; vii. 35, 7, 14; vii. 37, 4; vii. 61, 2, 6; vii. 70, 6; vii. 72, 3, 4; vii. 83, 4; vii. 97, 3, 9; vii. 103, 8; viii. 4, 2; viii. 32, 27; viii. 51, 4; viii. 52, 2; viii. 55, 11; viii. 78, 3; viii. 87, 8; x. 13, 1; x. 54, 6;

[1] Sanskrit Texts, vol. iii. pp. 116—164.

x. 61, 1, 7; x. 80, 7; x. 89, 3; x. 114, 8. That in these passages *brahma* has generally the sense of hymn or prayer is clear from the context of some of them (as in i. 37, 4; viii. 32, 27, where *brahma* is joined with the verb *gâyata* "sing," and in vi. 69, 7, where the gods are supplicated to hear it), as well as from the fact that the poets are said (in i. 62, 13; v. 73, 10; vii. 22, 9; vii. 31, 11; x. 80, 7) to have fashioned or generated it, in the same way as they are said to have fashioned or generated hymns in other texts (as i. 109, 1; v. 2, 11; vii. 15, 4; viii. 77, 4; x. 23, 6; x. 39, 14), where the sense is indisputable; while in other places (iv. 16, 21; v. 29, 15; vi. 17, 13; vi. 50, 6; vii. 61, 6; x. 89, 3) new productions of the poets are spoken of under the appellation of *brahma*.

That *brahma* has the sense of hymn or prayer is also shown by the two following passages. In vii. 26, 1, it is said: "Soma not poured out does not exhilarate Indra; nor do libations without hymns (*abrahmâṇaḥ*=*stotra-hînâḥ*, Sâyaṇa). I generate for him a hymn (*uktha*) which he will love, so that like a man he may hear our new (production). 2. At each hymn (*uktha*) the soma exhilarates Indra, at each psalm (*nîtha*) the libations (exhilarate) Maghavat, when the worshippers united, with one effort invoke him for help, as sons do a father."[1] Again in x. 105, 8: "Drive away our calamities. With a hymn (*ṛchâ*) may we slay the men who are hymnless (*anṛchaḥ*). A sacrifice without prayer (*abrahmâ*) does not please thee well."

I have said that great virtue is occasionally attributed by the poets to their hymns and prayers; and this is true of those sacred texts when called by the name of *brahma*, as well as when they receive other appellations, such as *mantra*.

[1] It is clear from the context of this passage that *abrahmâṇaḥ* means "unattended by hymns," and not "without a priest." After saying that soma-libations without hymns are unacceptable to Indra, the poet does not add that he is himself a *priest*, or that he is attended by one, but that he generates a hymn; and the same sense is required by what follows in the second verse. Accordingly we find that Sâyaṇa explains *abrahmâṇaḥ* by *stotra-hînâḥ*, "destitute of hymns." The same sense is equally appropriate in the next passage cited, x. 105, 8. On iv. 16, 9, where *abrahmâ* is an epithet of *dasyu*, "demon," Sâyaṇa understands it to mean "without a priest," but it may mean equally well or better, "without devotion."

Thus it is said, iii. 53, 12, "This prayer (*brahma*) of Viṣvâmitra protects the tribe of Bharata;" v. 40, 6, "Atri with the fourth prayer (*brahmaṇâ*) discovered the sun concealed by unholy darkness;" vi. 75, 19, "Prayer (*brahma*) is my protecting armour;" vii. 33, 3, "Indra preserved Sudâs in the battle of the ten kings through your prayer, o Vasishṭhas." In ii. 23, 1, Brahmaṇaspati is said to be the "great king of prayers," and in v. 2 to be the "generator of prayers" (*janitâ brahmaṇâm*); whilst in x. 61, 7, prayer is declared to have been generated by the gods.

Brăhmăn in the masculine is no doubt derived from the same root as brăhmăn neuter, and though differing from it in accent as well as gender, must be presumed to be closely connected with it in signification, just as the English "prayer" in the sense of a petition would be with "prayer," a petitioner, if the word were used in the latter sense. As, then, *brăhmăn* neuter means a hymn or prayer, *brahman* in the masculine must naturally be taken to denote the person who composes or repeats a hymn or prayer. We do not, however, find that the composers of the hymns are in general designated by the word *brahman*, the name most commonly applied to them being *ṛshi*, though they are also called *vipra*, *vedhas*, *kavi*, etc. (see "Sanskrit Texts," vol. iii. pp. 116 ff.). There are, however, a few texts, such as i. 80, 1; i. 164, 35; ii. 12, 6; ii. 39, 1; v. 31, 4; v. 40, 8; ix. 113, 6, etc., in which the priest (*brahmâ*) may perhaps be understood as referred to in the capacity of author of the hymn he utters. So, too, in ii. 20, 4 and vi. 21, 8, a new composer (or, perhaps, merely a new reciter) of hymns is spoken of under the appellation of *nutânasya brahmaṇyataḥ*; in ii. 19, 8, the Gṛtsamadas are spoken of both as the fabricators of a new hymn (*manma navîyaḥ*) and as (*brahmaṇyantaḥ*) performing devotion; while in another place (x. 96, 5) Indra is said to have been lauded by former worshippers, *pûrvebhir yajvabhiḥ*, a term usually confined (as *brăhmăn* was frequently applied) in after times to the offerers of sacrifice. In three passages, vii. 28, 2; vii. 70, 5; and x. 89, 16, the *brahma* and *brahmâṇi* "prayer" and "prayers" of the *ṛshis* are spoken of; and in vii. 22, 9, *ṛshis* are said to have generated prayers (*brahmâṇi*). In i. 177, 5, we find *brahmâṇi kâroḥ*, "the prayers of the poet." The fact that in various hymns the authors speak of themselves as having received valuable gifts from the princes their patrons, and that they do not speak of any class of officiating priests as separate from themselves, would also seem to indicate an identity of the poet and priest at that early period. The term *brahman* must therefore, as we may conclude, have been originally applied (1) to the same persons who are spoken of elsewhere in the hymns as *ṛshi*, *kavi*, etc., and have denoted devout worshippers and contemplative sages who composed prayers and hymns which they themselves recited in praise of the gods. Afterwards, when the ceremonial gradually became more complicated, and a division of sacred functions took place, the word was more ordinarily employed (2) for a minister of public worship, and at length came to signify (3) one particular kind of priest with special duties. I subjoin a translation of the different passages in which the word occurs in the Rig-veda; and I have attempted to classify them according as it seems to bear, in each case, the first, second, or third of the senses just indicated. This, however, is not always an easy task, as in many of these texts there is nothing to fix the meaning of the term with precision, and one signification easily runs into another, as the same person may be at once the author and the reciter of the hymn.

I. Passages in which *brahman* may signify "contemplator, sage, or poet."

(In order to save the repetition of the word *brăhmăn* in parenthesis after *priest*, I have put the latter word in italics whenever it stands for *brahman*).

i. 80, 1.[1] "Thus in his exhilaration from soma juice the *priest* (*brahmâ*) has made (or uttered) a magnifying[2] (hymn)."

i. 164, 34. "I ask thee (what is) the remotest end of the

[1] I have to acknowledge my obligations to Professor Aufrecht for the assistance which he has freely rendered to me in the preparation of this paper, and especially in the translation of the more difficult texts which occur in the course of it.

[2] *Varddhanam* = *vṛddhi-karaṃ stotram* (Sâyaṇa).

earth; I ask where is the central point of the world; I ask thee (what is) the seed of the vigorous horse; I ask (what is) the highest heaven[1] of speech. 35. This altar is the remotest end of the earth; this sacrifice is the central point of the world; this soma is the seed of the vigorous horse; this *priest* is the highest heaven of speech."[2]

ii. 12, 6. "He (Indra) who is the quickener of the sluggish, of the emaciated, of the suppliant *priest* who praises him," etc.

vi. 45, 7. "With hymns I call Indra, the *priest*,—the carrier of prayers (*brahma-vâhasam*),[3] the friend who is worthy of praise,—as men do a cow which is to be milked."

viii. 16, 7. "Indra is a *priest*, Indra is a rishi,[4] Indra is much and often invoked, great through his mighty powers."

x. 71, 11. (See the translation of the entire hymn below. The sense of *brahmâ* in v. 11 will depend on the meaning assigned to *jâta-vidyâ*).

x. 77, 1. (In this passage, the sense of which is not very clear, the word *priest* appears to be an epithet of the host of Maruts).

x. 85, 3. "A man thinks he has drunk soma when the plant (so called) has been crushed. But no one tastes of that which the *priests* know to be soma (the moon). 16. The *priests* rightly know, Sûryâ, that thou hast two wheels; but it is sages (*addhâtayaḥ*) alone who know the one wheel which is hidden. 34. The *priest* who knows Sûrya deserves the bride's garment."[5]

x. 107, 6. "They call him a rishi, him a *priest*, reverend, a chanter of Sâma verses (*sâma-gâm*), and reciter of *ukthas*,—he knows the three forms of the brilliant (Agni)—the man who first worshipped with a largess."

x. 117, 7. "A *priest*[6] who speaks is more acceptable than one who does not speak."

[1] Compare R.V. iii. 32, 10; x. 109, 4, below, and the words, "the highest heaven of invention."

[2] Compare R.V. x. 71 and x. 125.

[3] Compare *v.* 19 and stoma-vâhasaḥ, iv. 32, 12.

[4] Different deities are called *ṛshi*, *kavi*, etc., in the following texts: v. 29, 1; vi. 14, 2; viii. 6, 41; ix. 96, 18; ix. 107, 7; x. 27, 22; x. 112, 9.

[5] See Dr. Haug's Ait. Br., vol. i., Introduction, p. 20.

[6] The word here seems to indicate an order or profession, as the *silent* priest is still a priest.

(See Dr. Haug's remark on this verse, Ait. Br. Introd. p. 20; also the contexts of the two last passages in my article "Miscellaneous Hymns from the R. and A. Vedas," pp. 32 f.)

x. 125, 5. "I (says Vâch) make him whom I love formidable (*ugram*), him a *priest*, him a rishi, him a sage (*sumedhâm*)."

II. In the passages which follow the word *brahman* does not seem to signify so much a "sage or poet," as a "worshipper or priest."

i. 10, 1. "The singers (*gâyatriṇaḥ*) sing thee, the hymners (*arkiṇaḥ*) recite a hymn, the *priests* (*brahmâṇaḥ*), O Ṣatakratu, have raised thee up like a pole."

(Compare i. 5, 8; i. 7, 1; viii. 16, 9. See Dr. Haug's remark on this verse, Ait. Br. Introd. p. 20).

i. 33, 9. "Thou, Indra, with the believers, didst blow against the unbelievers, with the *priests* thou didst blow away the Dasyu."

i. 101, 5. "Indra, who is lord of all that moves and breathes, who first found the cows for the *priest*, who hurled down the Dasyu."

i. 108, 7. "When, o adorable Indra and Agni, ye are exhilarated in your own abode, or with a *priest* or prince (*brahmaṇi râjaṇi vâ*),[1] come thence, ye vigorous (deities), and then drink of the poured out soma."

i. 158, 6. "Dîrghatamas, son of Mamatâ, being decrepit in his tenth lustre, (though) a *priest*, becomes the charioteer of (or is borne upon) the waters which are hastening to their goal."

(Prof. Aufrecht understands this to mean that Dîrghatamas is verging towards his end, and thinks there is a play on the word "charioteer" as an employment not befitting a priest).

ii. 39, 1. "Ye (Aṣvins) are like two vultures on a tree; like two *priests* singing a hymn at a sacrifice."

[1] A distinction of orders or professions appears to be here recognized. In the following verse (v. 54, 7) a *rishi* and a prince are distinguished much in the same way as a *priest* and king are in i. 108, 7: "That man, whether rishi or prince, whom ye, O Maruts, support, is neither conquered nor killed, he neither decays nor is distressed, nor is injured; his riches do not decline, nor his support." Compare v. 14, where it is said, "Ye, O Maruts, give riches with desirable men, ye protect a rishi who is skilled in hymns (*sâma-vipra*); ye give a horse and food to Bharata, ye make a king prosperous." In iii. 43, 5, reference is found to Viṣvâmitra, or the author, being made by Indra both a prince and a rishi.

iv. 50, 7 ff. "That king overcomes all hostile powers in force and valour who maintains Bṛihaspati in abundance, who praises and magnifies him as (a deity) enjoying the first distinction. 8. He dwells prosperous in his own palace, to him the earth always yields her increase,[1] to him the people bow down of themselves,—that king in whose house a *priest* walks first[2] (*yasmin brahmâ râjani pûrva eti*). 9. Unrivalled, he conquers the riches both of his enemies and his kinsmen—the gods preserve the king who bestows wealth on the *priest* who asks his assistance."[3]

(The benefits resulting from the employment of a domestic priest (*purohita*) are also set forth in A.V. iii. 19, translated in my former article, "Miscellaneous Hymns from the R. and A. Vedas," in the volume of this Journal, p. 33).

iv. 58, 2. "Let us proclaim the name of butter (*ghṛta*), let us at this sacrifice hold it (in mind) with prostrations. May the *priest* (Agni ?) hear the praise which is chanted. The four-horned bright-coloured (god) has sent this forth."

v. 29, 3. "And, ye Maruts. *priests*, may Indra drink of this my soma which has been poured out," etc

v. 31, 4. "The men[4] have fashioned a car for thy (Indra's) horse, and Tvashtṛ a gleaming thunderbolt, o god greatly-invoked. The *priests*, magnifying Indra, have strengthened him for the slaughter of Ahi."

v. 32, 12. "I hear of thee thus rightly prospering, and bestowing wealth on, the sages (*viprebhyaḥ*). What do the *priests*, thy friends, obtain who have reposed their wishes on thee, O Indra?"

v. 40, 8. "Applying the stones (for pressing soma), performing worship, honouring the gods with praise and obeisance, the *priest* Atri placed the eye of the sun in the sky, and swept away the magical arts of Svarbhânu."

[1] Compare R.V. v. 37, 4 f.

[2] Compare viii. 69, 4; x. 39, 11; x. 107, 5; and the word *purohita*, used of a ministering priest as one *placed in front*. Prof. Aufrecht, however, would translate the last words, "under whose rule the *priest* receives the first or principal portion."

[3] See on this passage Roth's Art. on Brahma and the Brâhmans, *Journ. Germ. Or. Soc.*, i. 77 ff. See also Aitareya Brâhmaṇa, viii. 26.

[4] Ṛbhus?

vii. 7, 5. "The chosen bearer (of oblations), Agni, the *priest,* having arrived, has sat down in a mortal's abode, the upholder."

vii. 33, 11. "And thou, o Vasishṭha, art a son of Mitra and Varuṇa (or a Maitravaruṇa-priest), born, o *priest,* from the soul of Urvaṣî. All the gods placed in the vessel thee, the drop which had fallen through divine contemplation."

vii. 42, 1. "The *priests,* the Angirases, have arrived," etc.

viii. 7, 20. "Where now, bountiful (Maruts), are ye exhilarated, with the sacrificial grass spread beneath you? What *priest* is serving you?"

viii. 17, 2 f. "Thy tawny steeds with flowing manes, yoked by prayer (*brahma-yujâ*),[1] bring thee hither, Indra; listen to our prayers. 3. We *priests,* offerers of soma, bringing oblations, continually invoke the drinker of soma."

viii. 31, 1. "That *priest* is beloved of Indra who worships, sacrifices, pours out libations, and cooks offerings."

viii. 32, 16. "There is not now any debt due by the active *priests* who pour out libations. Soma has not been drunk without an equivalent."

viii. 33, 10. "Look downward, not upward; keep thy feet close together; let them not see those parts which should be covered; thou, a *priest,* hast become a woman."

"viii. 45, 39. "I seize these thy tawny steeds, yoked by our hymn (*vacho-yujâ*) to a splendid chariot, since thou didst give (wealth) to the *priests.*"

viii. 53, 7. "Where is that vigorous, youthful, large-necked, unconquered (Indra)? What *priest* serves him?"

viii. 66, 5. "Indra clove the Gandharva in the bottomless mists, for the prosperity of the *priests.*"

viii. 81, 30. "Be not, o lord of riches (Indra), sluggish like a *priest.*[2] Be exhilarated by the libation mixed with milk."

viii. 85, 5. "When, Indra, thou seizest in thine arms the thunderbolt which brings down pride, in order to slay Ahi,

[1] Compare viii. 45, 39, below.

[2] Dr. Haug (Introd. to Ait, Br. p. 20) refers to Ait. Br. v. 34, as illustrating this reproach. See p. 376 of his translation. This verse clearly shows that the priests formed a professional body.

the (aerial) hills and the cows utter their voice, and the *priests* draw near to thee."

ix. 96, 6. "Soma, resounding, overflows the filter, he who is *priest* among the gods, leader among poets, rishi among the wise, buffalo among wild beasts, falcon among kites, an axe among the woods."

ix. 112, 1. "Various are the thoughts and endeavours of us different men. The carpenter seeks something broken, the doctor a patient, the *priest* some one to offer libations.[1]

ix. 113, 6. "O pure Soma, in the place where the priest, uttering a metrical hymn, is exalted at the soma sacrifice through (the sound of) the crushing-stone, producing pleasure with soma, o Indu (soma) flow for Indra."

x. 28, 11. (The word *brahmaṇaḥ* occurs in this verse, but the sense is not clear).

x. 71, 11. (See translation of this verse below, where the entire hymn is given).

x. 85, 29. "Put away that which requires expiation (?). Distribute money to the *priests*. 35. Behold the forms of Sûryâ. But the *priest* purifies them."

x. 141, 3. "With hymns we invoke to our aid king Soma, Agni, the Âdityas, Vishṇu, Sûrya, and Bṛhaspati, the *priest*.

III. In the following passages the word *brahman* appears to designate the special class of priest so called, in contradistinction to *hotri*, *udgâtri*, and *adhvaryu*.

ii. 1, 2 (=x. 91, 10). "Thine, Agni, is the office of *hotri*, thine the regulated office of *potri*, thine the office of *neshṭri*, though art the *agnidh* of the pious man, thine is the office of *praṣâstri*, thou actest as *adhvaryu*, thou art the *brahman*, and the lord of the house in our abode. 2. Thou, Agni, art Indra, the chief of the virtuous, thou art Vishṇu, the wide-stepping, the adorable, thou, o Brahmaṇaspati, art the *priest* (*brahmâ*), the possessor of wealth, thou, o sustainer, art associated with the ceremonial."

[1] This verse also distinctly proves that the priesthood already formed a profession. Verse 3 of the same hymn is as follows: "I am a poet, my father a physician, my mother a grinder of corn." Unfortunately there is nothing further said which could throw light on the relations in which the different professions and classes of society stood to each other.

iv. 9, 3. "He (Agni) is led round the house, a joyous *hotri* at the ceremonies, and sits a *potri.* 4. And Agni is a wife (*i.e.* a mistress of the house) at the sacrifice, and a master of the house in our abode, and he sits a *brăhmăn.*"

x. 52, 2. "I have sat down an adorable *hotri*; all the gods, the Maruts, stimulate me. Day by day, ye Aṣvins, I have acted as your *adhvaryu;* the *brahman* is he who kindles the fire: this is your invocation."

I shall now bring forward the whole of the texts in which the word Brâhmăṇa, meaning a son, or descendant, of a *brăhmăn,* occurs in the Rig-veda.[1] They are the following:

i. 164, 45. "Speech consists of four defined grades. These are known by those Brâhmans who are wise. They do not reveal the three which are esoteric. Men speak the fourth grade of speech."

This text is quoted and commented upon in Nirukta xiii. 9.

vi. 75, 10. "May the Brâhman fathers, drinkers of soma, may the auspicious, the sinless, heaven and earth, may Pûshan preserve us," etc. etc.

vii. 103, 1 (= Nirukta 9, 6). "After lying quiet for a year, those rite-fulfilling Brâhmans[2] the frogs have (now) uttered their voice, which has been inspired by Parjanya...7. Like Brâhmans at the Atirâtra soma rite, like (those Brâhmans) speaking round about the full pond (or soma-bowl[3]),

[1] There are two more texts in which the word *brâhmana* is found, viz., i. 15, 5, and ii. 36, 5, on which see the following note. The word *brahmaputra,* son of a brahman, is found in ii. 43, 2: "Thou, O bird, singest a sâma verse like an *udgâtri*; thou singest praises like the son of a *brahman* at the libations."

[2] In the Nighantus, iii. 13, these words *brâhmaṇâ vrata-chârinaḥ* are referred to as conveying the sense of a simile, though they are unaccompanied by a particle of similitude. In his Illustrations of the Nirukta, p. 126, Roth thus remarks on this passage: "This is the only place in the first nine mandalas of the R.V. in which the word Brâhmaṇa is found with its later sense, whilst the tenth mandala offers a number of instances. This is one of the proofs that many of the hymns in this book were composed considerably later (than the rest of the R.V.). The word *brâhmaṇa* has another signification in i. 15, 5; ii. 36, 5; and vi. 75, 10. (In the first of these texts, Roth assigns to the word the sense of the Brâhman's soma-vessel. See his Lexicon, *s.v.* It does not appear what meaning he would give to the word in vi. 75, 10. He has in this passage overlooked R.V. i. 164, 45, which, however, is duly adduced in his Lexicon). See Wilson's translation of the hymn; as also Müller's, in his Anc. Sansk. Lit. p. 494 f.

[3] *Saras.* See R.V. viii. 66, 4, quoted in Nirukta v. 11, where Yâska says, "The ritualists inform us that at the mid-day oblation there are thirty *uktha* platters destined for one deity, which are then drunk at one draught. These are here called *saras.*" (Compare Roth's Illustrations on the passage.) See also R.V. vi. 17, 11, and viii. 7, 10, with Sâyana's explanations of all three passages).

you frogs surround (the pond) on this day of the year, which is that of the autumnal rains. 8. These soma-offering Brâhmans (the frogs) have uttered their voice, performing their annual devotion (*brahma*); these adhvaryu priests sweating with their boiled oblations (or in the hot season) come forth from their retreats like persons who have been concealed."

x. 16, 6. "Whatever part of thee any black bird, or ant, or serpent, or wild beast has mutilated, may Agni cure thee of all that, and Soma who has entered into the Brâhmans."[1]

x. 71, 1.[2] "When, ó Bṛhaspati, men first sent forth the earliest utterance of speech, giving a name (to things), then all that was treasured within them, most excellent and pure, was disclosed through love.

2. = Nirukta iv. 10). "Wherever the wise,—as if cleansing meal with a sieve,—have uttered speech with intelligence, there friends recognize acts of friendliness; good fortune[3] dwells in their speech.[3]

3. "Through sacrifice they came upon the track of speech, and found her entered into the rishis. Taking, they divided her into many parts:[4] the seven poets celebrate her in concert."

4. (=Nir. i. 19.) "And one man, seeing, sees not speech, and another, hearing, hears her not;[5] while to a third she discloses her form, as a loving well-dressed wife does to her husband."

5. (=Nir. i. 20.) "They say that one man has a sure defence in (her[6]) friendship; he is not overcome even in the

[1] Compare A.V. vii. 115, 1 ff—xii. 5, 6.

[2] I cannot pretend that I am satisfied with the translation I have attempted of this very difficult hymn. Verses 4 and 5 are explained in Sâyaṇa's Introduction to the Rig-veda, pp. 30 f., of Müller's edition.

[3] I quote here as somewhat akin to this hymn another from the A.V. vi. 108, being a prayer for wisdom or intelligence. 1. "Come to us, wisdom, the first, with cows and horses; (come) thou with the rays of the sun; thou art to us an object of worship. 2. To (obtain) the succour of the gods, I invoke wisdom the first, full of prayer, inspired by prayer, praised by rishis, imbibed by Brahmachârins. 3. We introduce within me that wisdom which Ṛbhus know, that wisdom which divine beings (*asurâḥ*) know, that excellent wisdom which rishis know. 4. Make me, o Agni, wise to-day with that wisdom which the wise rishis—the makers of things existing—know. 5. We introduce wisdom in the evening, wisdom in the morning, wisdom at noon, wisdom with the rays of the sun, and with speech" (*vachasâ*).

[4] Compare x. 125, 3; i. 164, 45; (x. 90, 11); and A.V. xii. 1, 45.

[5] Compare Isaiah vi. 9, 10; and Matthew xiii. 14, 15.

[6] *Vâk-sakhye*, Yâska.

conflict (of discussion). But that person consorts with a vain delusion who has listened to speech without fruit or flower."

6. "He who abandons a friend who understands friendship, has no portion whatever in speech. All that he hears, he hears in vain, for he knows not the path of righteousness."

7. "Friends gifted both with eyes and ears have proved unequal in mental efforts. Some have been (as waters) reaching to the face or armpit, while others have been seen like ponds in which one might bathe."

8. (=Nir. xiii. 13.) "When Brâhmans who are friends strive (?) together in efforts of the mind produced by the heart,[1] they leave one man behind through their acquirements, whilst others walk about boasting to be priests." (This is the sense Prof. Aufrecht suggests for the word *ohabrăhmâṇaḥ*. Prof. Roth *s.v.* thinks it may mean "real *priests*." The author of Nirukta xiii. 13, explains it as meaning "reasoning *priests*," or "those of whom reasoning is the sacred science.")

9. "The men who range neither near nor far, who are neither (reflecting) Brâhmans nor yet pious worshippers at libations,—these, having acquired speech, weave their web imperfectly, (like) a female weaver,[2] being destitute of skill."

10. "All friends rejoice at the arrival of a renowned friend who rules the assembly; for such a one, repelling evil, and bestowing nourishment upon them, is thoroughly prepared for the conflict (of discussion)."

11. (Nir. i. 8.) "One man possesses a store of verses (*ṛchâm*); a second sings a hymn (*gâyatra*) during (the chanting of) the *ṣakvarîs;* one who is a *priest* (*brahman*) declares the science of being (*jâta-vidyâm*), whilst another prescribes the order of the ceremonial.[3]

R. V. x. 88, 19 (=Nir. vii. 31). "As long as the fair-

[1] Compare i. 171, 2; ii. 35, 2; vi. 16, 47.

[2] Such is the sense which Prof. Aufrecht thinks may, with probability, be assigned to *sirîs*, a word which occurs only here.

[3] According to Yâska (Nir. i. 8), these four persons are respectively the *hotri*, *udgâtri*, *brahman*, and *adhvaryu* priests. The brahman, he says, being possessed of all science, ought to know everything; and gives utterance to his knowledge as occasion arises for it (*jâte jâte*). See Dr. Haug's remarks on this verse. Ait. Br. Introd. p. 20.

winged Dawns do not array themselves in light, o Mâtariṣvan, so long the Brâhman coming to the sacrifice, keeps (the fire), sitting below the hotri-priest."

(See Prof. Roth's translation of this verse in his Illustrations of the Nirukta, p. 113).

x. 90, 11 (= A.V. xix. 5, 6; Vâj. S. xxxi.). "When they divided Purusha, into how many parts did they distribute him? What was his mouth? what were his arms? what were called his thighs and feet? 12. The Brâhman was his mouth, the Râjanya was made his arms, that which was the Vaiṣya was his thighs, the Ṣûdra sprang from his feet."

(See the translation of this entire hymn in Sanskrit Texts, i. 6 ff.; and in my paper on "The Progress of the Vedic Religion," in Journal Roy. As. Soc. vol. i. new series, pp. 353 ff.).

x. 97, 22. "The plants converse with king Soma,[1] (and say), "for whomsoever a Brâhman acts (*kṛṇoti*, officiates), him, o king, we deliver."

x. 109, 1. "These (deities), the boundless, liquid Mâtariṣvan (Air), the fiercely-flaming, ardently-burning, beneficent (Fire), and the divine primeval Waters, first exclaimed against the outrage on a *priest* (*brahma-kilbishe*). 2. King Soma,[2] unenvious, first gave back the priest's wife; Varuṇa and Mitra were the inviters; Agni, the invoker, brought her, taking her hand. 3. When restored, she had to be received back by the hand, and they then proclaimed aloud, 'This is the *priest's* wife;' she was not committed to a messenger to be sent:—in this way it is that the kingdom of a ruler (or Kshattriya) remains secured to him.[3] 4. Those ancient deities, the Rishis, who sat down to perform austerities, spoke thus of her, 'Terrible is the wife of the Brâhman; when approached, she plants confusion in the highest heaven.[4] 5. The Brahmachârin[5] (religious student) continues to perform observances.

[1] Compare *oshadhîḥ Soma-râjnîh*, "the plants whose king is Soma," in *vv.* 18 and 19 of this hymn.

[2] Compare R.V. x. 85, 8 f., 40 f.; and my contributions to Vedic Mythology, No. ii., p. 2 f.

[3] I am indebted to Prof. Aufrecht for this explanation of the verse.

[4] See R.V. i. 164, 34, 35, above.

[5] See my paper on the Progress of the Vedic religion, pp. 374 ff.

He becomes one member[1] of the gods. Through him Bṛhaspati obtained his wife, as the gods obtained the ladle which was brought by Soma. 6. The gods gave her back, and men gave her back; kings, performing righteousness, gave back the *priest's* wife. 7. Giving back the *priest's* wife, freeing themselves from sin against the gods, (these kings) enjoy the abundance of the earth, and possess a free range of movement."

This hymn is repeated in the Atharva-veda, with the addition of ten more verses, which I subjoin.

Atharva-veda, v. 17.

(*vv.* 1-3 = *vv.* 1-3 of R.V. x. 109).

4. "That calamity which falls upon the village, of which they say, 'this is a star with dishevelled hair,' is in truth the *priest's* wife, who ruins the kingdom which is visited by a hare attended with meteors."

(*vv.* 5-6 = *vv.* 5-4 of R.V. x. 109).

7. "Whenever any miscarriages take place, or any moving things are destroyed, whenever men slay each other, it is the *priest's* wife who kills them. 8. And when a woman has had ten former husbands not Brâhmans, if a *priest* (*brahmâ*) take her hand (*i.e.* marry her), it is he alone who is her husband 9. It is a Brâhman only that is a husband, and not a Râjanya, or a Vaiṣya. That (truth) the Sun goes forward proclaiming to the five classes of men (*panchabhyo mânanebhyaḥ.*"

(*vv.* 10-11 = *vv.* 6-7 of R.V. x. 109).

12. "His (the king's) wife does not repose opulent (*ṣatavâhî*) and handsome upon her bed, in that kingdom where a *priest's* wife is foolishly shut up. 13. A son with large ears (*vikarṇaḥ*) and broad head is not born in the house in that kingdom, etc. 14. A charioteer with golden neckchain does not march before the king's hosts (?)[2] in that kingdom, etc. 15. A white horse with black ears does not make a show, yoked to his (the king's) chariot in that kingdom, etc. 16. There is

[1] See A.V. x. 7, 1 ff., 9, 26.

[2] The word here in the original is *sûnânâm*, with which it is difficult to make any sense. Should we read *senânâm?*

no pond with blossoming lotuses in his (the king's) grounds in that kingdom where, etc. 17. His (the king's) brindled cow is not milked by his milkmen in that kingdom, etc. 18. His (the king's) milch cow does not thrive, nor does his ox endure the yoke, in that country where a Brâhman passes the night wretchedly without his wife."

I will now refer to a number of texts in which liberality to the authors of the hymns is mentioned with approbation.

Of these passages i. 125; i. 126; v. 27; v. 30, 12 ff.; v. 33, 8 ff.; v. 61, 10; vi. 27, 8; and vi. 47, 22 ff., may be consulted in Prof. Wilson's translation; and a version of R.V. x. 107 will be found in my article, "Miscellaneous Hymns from the Rig and Atharva Vedas," p. 32 f. The following are further instances:[1] —

vii. 18, 22 ff. "Earning two hundred cows and two cars with mares, the gift of Sudâs the grandson of Devavat and son of Pijavana, I walk about, as a priest does round a house, offering praises. 23. The four robust richly caparisoned brown[2] horses of Sudâs, the son of Pijavana, standing on the earth, carry me, son to son,[3] onward to renown in perpetuity." (See the translation of these verses in Roth's Litt. u. Geschichte des Weda, p. 100.) In i. 126, 3, and vi. 27, 8, also, the word *vadhûmantaḥ* is used as here, and is probably to be taken in the first of these passages of mares, and in the latter of cows, *vinṣatiṃ gâ vadhûmanto*, being "twenty bulls with their cows." The same sense of cows or mares is probably to be understood in viii. 19, 36. That the preced-

[1] The fourth volume of Professor Wilson's Rig-veda, edited by Mr. Cowell, having been published since this paper was written, the reader may compare his version of such of the following passages as are included in it with mine.

[2] The word here rendered is *smaddishṭayaḥ*. In his explanation of this passage Sâyaṇa considers it to mean *praṣastâtisarjanaṣraddhâdidânângayuktâḥ*, *i.e.* "possessing the approved constituents of a gift, viz., generosity, faith," etc. It occurs in three other texts, viz., in iii. 45, 5, as an epithet of Indra, where Sâyaṇa takes it to signify *bhadravâkya*, "speaking auspicious words;" in vi. 63, 9, where he takes it as = *praṣasta-darṣanân*, "of approved look;" and in x. 62, 9, Prof. Aufrecht considers the word to mean "strong," "robust," a sense which suits the context of iii. 45, 5 (where it cannot possibly bear the interpretation assigned by Sâyana on vii. 18, 23), and apparently also that of x. 62, 9. From the etymology (apparently *smat* for *sumat*, "good" or "well," and *dishṭi*, "pleasure" or "good luck,") one would suppose it ought to mean "blessed" or "fortunate," a sense which might also suit the context of iii. 45, 5.

[3] *Tokaṃ tokâya.* The sense is obscure.

ing passages refer to the females of bulls or horses is made likely by comparing viii. 57, 17, which will be quoted below. In viii. 46, 37, however, reference is distinctly made to the gift of a woman (*yoshaṇâ*).

viii. 3, 21. "(The horse?) which Indra, the Maruts, and Pâkasthâman, the son of Kurayâṇa, gave to me, the most brilliant of all, like (the sun) careering in the sky. 22. Pâkasthâman gave me a tawny (horse) well broken in, and filling his traces, an indication of riches. 23. Like to which other ten swift steeds also bear the yoke, like those which carried the son of Tugra to his home. 24. Soul, food, body, raiment, the giver of vigour, and ornament—(all this Pâkasthâman is). I celebrate him as the fourth liberal bestower of a tawny horse."

viii. 4, 19. "We have celebrated among the Turvaṣus the profuse riches, consisting of hundreds of horses (bestowed) at the festivals of Kuranga, at the distributions made by this powerful and fortunate king. 20. After sixty thousand pure cows,[1] I, a rishi, have driven away herds of cattle obtained by the Priyamedhas with faces upturned to heaven, through the prayers of the sacrificing son of Kaṇva. 21. Even the trees[2] rejoiced at my arrival, (exclaiming), 'they have obtained cows in abundance, they have obtained horses in abundance.'"[3]

viii. 5, 37. "May ye, Aṣvins, take notice of my new gifts, how Kaṣu, of the race of Chedi, has bestowed on me a hundred camels and ten thousand kine. 38. The people are prostrate beneath the feet of the descendant of Chedi, and the men about him are but leather-workers (before him), who presented to me ten kings brilliant as gold. 39. Let no one try to walk in the path which these Chedis tread. No sage is regarded as a more bountiful man (than this prince."[4]

viii. 6, 46. "I have received a hundred from Tirindara, a

[1] Sâyaṇa explains *nirmajâm* as *niḥṣcsheṇa ṣuddhânam gavam*. Roth leaves the word unexplained; and Prof. Aufrecht suggests *nirṇijâm*, "garments," as perhaps the true reading.

[2] Compare Psalm xcvi. 12.

[3] This verse is translated in Benfey's Glossary in the Sâma-veda, *s.v. meha*.

[4] Or, "No one, (as) the sage expects, will (prove to be) a more munificent person."

thousand from Parşu, the riches of the Yâdvas. 47. They gave three hundred horses, ten thousand cows, to Sâman the Pajra. 48. The exalted prince overpassed the sky, giving a yoke of four camels; he (overpassed) the Yâdva tribe by his renown."

viii. 19, 36. "Trasadasyu, son of Purukutsa, the bountiful lord, the patron of the virtuous, gave me fifty females (cows or mares).[1] 37. And while I was travelling . . . . at the ford of the Suvâstu, Şyâva, the wealthy lord of the Diyas (or of gifts) brought three seventies."

viii. 21, 17. "Was it Indra who gave to me, the worshipper, all this wealth? or was it the blessed Sarasvatî who gave this riches, or was it thou, Chitra? 18. King Chitra and other kings who (dwell) along the Sarasvatî, diffused himself (over us) like Parjanya, in a shower, bestowing a thousand and tens of thousands."

viii. 24, 29. "May the gift of Nârya reach the Vyaşnas, offerers of Soma-libations, together with abundant wealth, in hundreds and thousands. 30. If any one, sacrificing, enquire of thee (o Ushas), wheresoever thou art engaged, where (he is), reply, 'This Vala dwells remote on the banks of the Gomatî.'"[2]

viii. 46, 21. "Let the ungodly man come forward[3] who has received as large a present as this which Vasa, the son of Aşva, has received at the break of to-day's dawn from the Pṛthuşravas, the son of Kanîta. 22. I have received the sixty thousand and ten thousand (appropriated to) the son of Aşva, two thousand camels, ten hundreds of brown (mares), ten of (mares) with three ruddy spots, and ten thousand cows. 23, 24. Ten brown, impetuous, irresistible, swift, overbearing steeds of the bountiful Pṛthuşravas, son of Kanîta, cause the circumference of the chariot wheel to whirl round. Bestowing a golden chariot, he has shewn himself a most bountiful sage, and acquired the most extended renown . . . . . . 30. As oxen approach the herd, so they

[1] See in note above the remarks on vii. 18, 22.
[2] Compare the similar expressions in R.V. v. 61, 19.
[3] This challenge seems to mean that no ungodly man had received such gifts.

draw near to me. 31. Then when he had called for a hundred camels from amongst the grazing herd, and two thousand among the white cattle, 32. I, the sage, received a hundred from the Dâsa[1] Balbûtha, the deliverer. These men of thine, O Vâyu, protected by Indra, rejoice; protected by the gods, they rejoice. 33. Then that large woman is led away, covered with jewels, towards Vaṣa, son of Aṣva."

viii. 54, 10. "May the opulent prince, who bestows on me speckled cows with golden housings, never perish, o gods. 12. Over and above the thousand speckled cows, I received a bright, large, broad, shining piece of gold. 13. Men have exalted to the gods the renown of the grandson of Durgaha,[2] who was bountiful to me in (bestowing) a thousand (cows)."

viii. 57, 14. "Near me stand six men in pairs, in the exhilaration of the Soma juice, bestowing delightful gifts. 15. Of Indrota I received two brown horses, from the son of Ṛksha two tawny, and from the son of Aṣvamedha two ruddy horses. 16. From the son of Atithigva (I received) horses with a beautiful car, from the son of Ṛksha horses with beautiful reins, and from the son of Aṣvamedha horses of beautiful form. 17. Along with Pûtakratu, I obtained six horses with mares[3] from Indrota, the son of Atithigva. 18. Among these brown horses was perceived a bay mare with a stallion, and with beautiful reins and a whip. 19. May no mortal, however desirous of reviling, fasten any fault upon you, o ye possessors of food."

x. 33, 4. "I, a rishi, have solicited king Kuruṣravaṇa, descendant of Trasadusyu, the most bountiful of sages. 5. Let me celebrate, at the (sacrifice), attended with a thousand gifts, (that prince) whose three tawny mares convey me excellently in a car. 6. Of which father of Upamaṣravas, the agreeable words were like a pleasant field to him who uttered them. 7. Attend, o Upamaṣravas, son (of Kuruṣravaṇa), and grandson of Mitrâtithi—I am the encomiast of thy father.

[1] Roth, *s.v. dâsa*, conjectures that instead of *dâse*, the proper reading is here *dâsân*, which would alter the sense to, "I received a hundred slaves from Balbûtha."

[2] Langlois *in loco* refers for illustration of this to R.V. iv. 42, 8.

[3] Sâyaṇa here understands *vadhûmataḥ*, of mares, *vaḍavâbhis tadvataḥ*.

8. If I had power over the immortals, or over mortals, my magnificent (patron) should still be alive. 9. The man even of a hundred years lives not beyond the period ordained by the gods;[1] so hath (everything) continually revolved."

x. 62, 6. "The Virûpas, who sprang from Agni, from the sky, Navagva, and Daṣagva, who perfectly possesses the character of an Angiras, is elevated to the gods. 7. The sages (princes) in concert with Indra lavished a herd of cows and of horses. Men have exalted to the gods[2] the renown of me, Ashṭakarṇî, who bestowed a thousand. 8. Let this man[3] now multiply; may he shoot up like a sprout, he who at once lavishes a thousand hundred horses for a gift. 9. No one equals him, as no one succeeds in grasping the summit of the sky.[4] The largesses of the son of Savarṇa have been diffused as widely as the sea. 10. Yadu and Turva gave two robust bondmen to serve (me) with abundance of kine. 11. Let not this man, the leader of the people, who lavishes thousands, suffer calamity. Let his largesses go on vying with the sun. May the gods prolong the life of the son of Savarṇa, from whom we, without fatiguing labour [or without cessation], have received food."

x. 93, 14. "I have spoken this (in praise) of Duhsîma, Pṛthavâna, Vena, and Râma,—a god among the magnificent,—who, having yoked five hundred (horses) for our benefit,—their (liberality) became renowned by (this) course. 15. Over and above this, Tânva straightway assigned, Pârthya straightway assigned, Mâyava straightway assigned (to us) here seventy-seven."

If we consider that the various texts which have just been quoted are the productions of the class whose pretensions they represent and whose dignity they exalt, and further, if we take into account the indications, supplied by various

[1] Compare R.V. viii. 28, 4: "As the gods desire so it comes to pass; no one—no mortal, however hostile—can hinder that (will) of theirs."

[2] Compare viii. 54, 12, above.

[3] In my article on "Manu, the progenitor of the Aryan Indians," Jour. R. A. S., xx. p. 416, note, I translated this word *manu* as a proper name, perhaps wrongly.

[4] Comp. Ṣ. P. Br. xiii. 5, 4, 14: "Neither former nor later men of the five races have reached this great work of Bharata (performed) to-day, as no mortal has reached the sky with his arms."

other passages which I shall cite below, of indifference to the gods and to their ministers manifested by the other sections of the community, we may think it necessary to make some deduction from the impression which we had at first received of the estimation in which the priestly order was held at the time when the hymns of the Rigveda were composed. But after every such allowance has been made, it will remain certain that the *brahman*, whether we look upon him as a sage and poet, or as an officiating priest, or in both capacities, was regarded with respect and reverence, and even that his presence was considered an important condition of the efficacy of the ceremonial. Thus, in i. 164, 35, the priest is described as "the highest heaven of speech;" in x. 107, 6, a liberal patron is called a rishi and a priest, as epithets expressive of the greatest eulogy; in x. 125, 5, the goddess Vâch is said to make the man who is the object of her special affection a priest and a rishi; in vi. 45, 7; vii. 7, 5; viii. 16, 7; and ix. 96, 6, the term "priest" is applied honorifically to the gods Indra, Agni, and Soma; in iv. 50, 8, 9, great prosperity is declared to attend the prince by whom a priest is employed, honoured, and succoured; and in iii. 53, 9, 12; v. 2, 6; vii. 33, 2, 3, 5; and vii. 83, 4, the highest efficacy is ascribed to the intervention and intercession of priests.

Again, although the commendations which are passed in the hymns on liberality to priests have been composed by interested parties, and though the value of the presents bestowed has no doubt been enormously exaggerated, there is no reason to doubt that the ministers of public worship, who possessed the gift of expression and of poetry, who were the depositaries of all sacred science, and who were regarded as the channels of access to the gods, would be largely rewarded and honoured.[1]

[1] It is to be observed that, in these eulogies of liberality, mention is nowhere made of Brâhmans as the recipients of the gifts. In two places, viii. 4, 20, and x. 33, 4, a rishi is mentioned as the receiver. In later works, such as the Ṣatapatha Brâhmaṇa, on the contrary, the presents are distinctly connected with Brâhmans. Thus it is said in that work, ii. 2, 2, 6: "Two kinds of gods are gods, viz., the gods (proper), whilst those Brâhmans who have the Vedic tradition, and are learned, are the human gods. The worship (*yajna*) of these is divided into two kinds. Oblations constitute the worship offered to the gods, and presents

It is further clear, from some of the texts quoted above (ii. 1, 2; iv. 9, 3; x. 52, 2), as well as i. 162, 5, and from the contents of hymns ii. 36; ii. 37; ii. 43; and x. 124, 1,[1] that in the later part of the Vedic era, to which these productions are probably to be assigned, the ceremonial of worship had become highly developed and complicated, and that different classes of priests were required for its proper celebration.[2] It is manifest that considerable skill must have been required for the due performance of these several functions; and as such skill could only be acquired by early instruction and by practice, there can be little doubt that the priesthood must at that period have become a regular profession.[3] The distinction of king or noble and priest appears to be recognized in i. 108, 7, as well as in iv. 50, 8, 9; whilst in v. 47, 7, 14, a similar distinction is made between king and rishi; and it is noticeable that the verse, in other respects nearly identical, with which the 36th and 37th hymns of the eighth mandala respectively conclude, ends in the one hymn with the words, "Thou alone, Indra, didst deliver Trasadasyu in the conflict of men, magnifying prayers" (*brahmâṇi vardhayan*); whilst in the other the last words are, "magnifying (royal) powers" (*kshattrâṇi vardhayan*), as if the former contained a reference to the functions of the priest, and the latter to those of the prince.

While, however, there thus appears to be every reason for supposing that towards the close of the Vedic period the priesthood had become a profession, the texts which have been quoted, with the exception of one (x. 90, 12) which will

(*dakshiṇâ*) that offered to the human gods, the Brâhmans, who possess the Vedic tradition, and are learned. It is with oblations that a man gratifies the gods, and with presents that he gratifies the human gods, the Brâhmans, who possess the Vedic tradition, and are learned. Both these two kinds of gods, when gratified, place him in a state of happiness" (*sudhâyâm*); (or "convey him to the heavenly world," as the expression is varied in the parallel passage of the same work, iv. 3, 4, 4.)

[1] See also i. 94, 6, where it is said: "Thou (Agni) art an *adhvaryu*, and the earliest *hotri*, a *praśâstri*, a *potri*, and by nature a *purohita*. Knowing all the priestly functions (*ârtvijyâ*) wise, thou nourishest us," etc.

[2] See Prof. Müller's remarks on this subject, Anc. Sansk. Lit., pp. 485 ff.; and Dr. Haug's somewhat different view of the same matter in his Introd. to Ait. Br., pp. 11 ff.

[3] In regard to the great importance and influence of the priests, see Müller's Anc. Sansk. Lit., pp. 485 ff.

be further adverted to below, do not contain anything which necessarily implies that the priests formed an exclusive caste, or, at least, a caste separated from all other by insurmountable barriers, as in later times.[1] There is a wide difference between a profession, or even a hereditary order, and a caste in the fully developed Brahmanical sense. Even in countries where the dignity and exclusive prerogatives of the priesthood are most fully recognized (as in Roman Catholic Europe), the clergy form only a profession, and their ranks may be recruited from all sections of the community. So, too, is it in most countries, even with a hereditary nobility. Plebeians may be ennobled at the will of the sovereign. There is, therefore, no difficulty in supposing that in the Vedic era the Indian priesthood—even if we suppose its members to have been for the most part sprung from priestly families—may have often admitted aspirants to the sacerdotal character from other classes of their countrymen. Even the employment of the words *brâhmaṇa* and *râjanya* in the Rig-veda does not disprove this. The former word, derived from *brahman*, "priest," signifies, as already intimated, nothing further than the son or descendant of a priest (the word *brahmaputra*, "son of a priest," is, as we have seen, actually used in one text),—just as the latter (*râjanya*) means nothing more than the descendant of a king or chief (*râjan*).

The paucity of the texts (and those, too, probably of a date comparatively recent) in which the word *brâhmaṇa*

[1] Dr. Haug, in his tract on the "Origin of Brâhmanism," p. 5, thus states his views on this question: "It has been of late asserted that the original parts of the Vedas do not know the system of caste. But this conclusion was prematurely arrived at without sufficiently weighing the evidence. It is true the caste system is not to be found in such a developed state, the duties enjoined to the several castes are not so clearly defined as in the Law Books and Purâṇas. But nevertheless the system is already known in the earlier parts of the Vedas, or rather presupposed. The barriers only were not quite so insurmountable as in later times." This view he supports by a reference to the Zend Avesta, from which he deduces the conclusion that the people had been divided into three classes even before the separation of the Indian from the Iranian Aryans, and adds: "From all we know, the real origin of caste appears to go back to a time anterior to the composition of the Vedic hymns, though its development into a regular system with insurmountable barriers can be referred only to the latest period of the Vedic times." As thus stated, the difference between Dr. Haug and other European scholars is one of degree and age, not of principle, for none of them assert any distinction of race, or congenital difference, between the castes or classes.

occurs, when contrasted with the large number of those in which *brăhmăn* is found, seems to prove conclusively that the former word was but little used in the earlier part of the Vedic era, and only came into common use towards its close. In some of these passages (as in vii. 103, 1, 7, 8; x. 88, 19) the Brâhman is merely alluded to as a priest, and in vii. 103, the comparison of frogs to Brâhmans may seem even to imply a want of respect for the latter and their office.[1] In other places (i. 164, 45, and x. 71, 8, 9) a distinction appears to be drawn between intelligent and unintelligent Brâhmans, between such as were thoughtful and others who were mere mechanical instruments in carrying on the ceremonial of worship,[2] which, however, certainly points to the existence of a sacerdotal class. In another passage (x. 97, 22) the importance of a Brâhman to the proper performance of religious rites appears to be clearly expressed. In x. 109, where the words brăhmăn (*passim*) and brâhmaṇa (in *v.* 4) seem to be used interchangeably—the inviolability of Brâhmans' wives, the peril of interfering with them, and the blessing attendant on reparation for any outrage committed against them, are referred to in such a way as to shew at once the loftiness of the claims set up by the Brâhmans on their own behalf, and to prove that these pretensions were frequently disregarded by the nobles. In x. 16, 6, the Brâhmans are spoken of as inspired by Soma, and in vi. 75, 10, the manes of earlier Brâhmans are reckoned among those divine beings who have power to protect the suppliant. But in none of these texts is any reference made to the Brâhmans constituting an exclusive caste or race, descended from an ancestor distinct from those of the other classes of their countrymen. In fact, it is proved by one of the additions (cited above) which have been made in the Atharva-veda (v. 17, 8 f.) to one of the hymns just referred to (x. 10, 9), that, even at that later period when that addition was made, Brâhmans had but little regard to the purity of the sacerdotal blood, as they did not intermarry

[1] See Müller's remarks on this hymn in his Anc. Sansk. Lit., p. 494.

[2] In R.V. viii. 50, 9, it is said: "Whether an unwise or a wise man, O Indra, has offered to thee a hymn, he has gladdened (thee) through his devotion to thee."

with women of their own order only, or even with women who had previously lived single, but were in the habit of forming unions with the widows of Râjanyas or Vaiṣyas,[1] if they did not even take possession of the wives of such men while they were alive.[2] Even if we suppose these women to have belonged to priestly families, this would only show that it was no uncommon thing for females of that class to be married to Râjanyas or Vaiṣyas—a fact which would, of course, imply that the caste system was either quite unknown, or only beginning to be introduced among the Indians of the earlier Vedic age. That, agreeably to ancient tradition, Brâhmans intermarried with Râjanya women at the period in question, is also distinctly shewn by the story of the Rishi Chyavana and Sukanyâ, daughter of king Ṣaryâta, narrated in the Ṣatapatha Brâhmaṇa, and quoted in my former paper, "Contributions to a Knowledge of Vedic Mythology," No. ii., pp. 11 ff. See also the stories of the

[1] That the remarriage of women was customary among the Hindus of those days is also shewn by A.V., ix. 5, 27 f., quoted in my former paper on Yama, p. 299

[2] This latter supposition derives a certain support from the emphasis with which the two verses in question (A.V. v. 17, 8, 9) assert that the Brâhman was the only true husband. Whence, it may be asked, the necessity for this strong and repeated asseveration, if the Râjanya and Vaiṣya husbands were not still alive, and prepared to claim the restoration of their wives? The verses are, however, explicable without this supposition.

It is to be observed, however, that no mention is here made of Ṣûdras as a class with which Brâhmans intermarried. Ṣûdras were not Âryas, like the three upper classes. This distinction is not recognised in the following verse of the A.V. xix. 62, 1: Make me dear to gods, dear to princes, dear to every one who beholds me, both to Ṣûdra and to Ârya." (Unless we are to suppose that both here and in xix. 32, 8, *ărya* = a Vaiṣya, and not *ārya*, is the word.) In Ṣatapatha Brâhmaṇa, Kâṇva Ṣâkhâ (Adhvara Kâṇḍa, i. 6), the same thing is clearly stated in these words, for a copy of which I am indebted to Professor Müller:—*Tan na sarva eva prapadyeta na hi devâḥ sarveṇaiva sangachhante | ârya eva brâhmaṇo vâ kshattriyo vâ vaiṣyo vâ te hi yajniyâḥ | no eva sarveṇaiva samvadeta na hi devâḥ sarveṇaiva samvadante âryeṇaiva brâhmaṇena vâ kshattriyeṇa vâ vaiṣyena vâ te hi yajniyâḥ | yady enam ṣûdreṇa samvâdo vindet "itthum enam nichakshva" ity anyam brûyâd esha dîkshitasyopachârah.* "Every one cannot obtain this (for the gods do not associate with every man), but only an Ârya, a Brâhman, or a Kshattriya, or a Vaiṣya, for these can sacrifice. Nor should one talk with every body (for the gods do not talk with every body), but only with an Ârya, a Brâhman, or a Kshattriya, or a Vaiṣya, for these can sacrifice. If any one have occasion to speak to a Ṣûdra, let him say to another person, 'Tell this man so and so.' This is the rule for an initiated man."

In the corresponding passage of the Mâdhyandina Ṣâkhâ (p. 224 of Weber's Edition) this passage is differently recorded.

From Manu (ix. 149–157; x. 7ff.) it is clear that Brâhmans intermarried with Ṣûdra-women, though the offspring of these marriages were degraded.

Rishi Ṣyâvâṣva, who married the daughter of king Rathavîti, as told by the commentator on Rig-veda, v. 61, and given in Prof. Wilson's translation, vol. iii. p. 344.

We have, however, still to consider the single text of the Rig-veda, x. 90, 11, 12, which seems at first sight to prove the existence of a belief in the separate creation of the four castes at the time when it was composed. A careful examination of the context in which these verses are found,[1] or even of the verses themselves, will, however, I think, lead to the conclusion that the representation is allegorical, and implies no opinion regarding the literal origination of the four classes. It is not even said that the Brâhman was produced from the mouth, the Râjanya from the arms, or the Vaiṣya from the thighs of Purusha; but that these classes formed respectively those members of his body. It is the Ṣûdra alone who is asserted to have sprung from the part of the body with which he is associated—the feet.

It is further to be noticed that as this hymn probably belongs to the close of the Vedic age, no conclusion can, on any interpretation of its meaning, be drawn from it in regard to the opinion regarding the different classes which prevailed in the earlier portion of that era. Dr. Haug, it is true, denies that the hymn is comparatively modern. He thinks that there is no sufficient evidence to prove this, but that, "on the contrary, reasons might be alleged to shew that it is even old." He is of opinion that the hymn had been used at human sacrifices, which he considers to have been customary in the earliest Vedic period, though they were afterwards abandoned as revolting to human feelings ("Origin of Brâhmanism," p. 5). Notwithstanding what is here urged by Dr. Haug, I cannot help agreeing with the opinion stated by other scholars, such as Colebrooke (Essays, i. 309, note; or p. 197 of Williams and Norgate's edition) and Max Müller (Ancient Sansk. Lit., p. 570 f.), that this hymn is of a later date than the great bulk of the collection in which it is found. As compared

[1] The entire hymn is translated in my paper on the Progress of the Vedic Religion, pp. 353 ff., and also in "Sanskrit Texts," vol. i. pp. 6 ff., where some remarks are made on it.

with by far the larger part of the hymns, it has every character of modernness both in its diction and ideas.

It is not denied that the hymns which we find in the Rig-veda collection are of very different periods. They themselves speak of newer and older hymns. So many as a thousand compositions of this sort could scarcely have been produced within a very short space of time, and there is no reason to imagine that the literary activity of the ancient Hindus was confined to the age immediately preceding the collection of the hymns. But if we are to recognize any difference of age, what hymns can we more reasonably suppose to be the oldest than those which are at once archaic in language and style, and naive and simple in the character of their conceptions; and on the other hand, what compositions can more properly be set down as the most recent than those which manifest an advance in speculative ideas, while their language approaches to the modern Sanskrit? These latter conditions seem to be fulfilled in the Purusha Sûkta, as well as in hymns x. 71; x. 72; x. 81; x. 82; x. 121; and x. 129. The pantheistic character of the opening parts of the Purusha Sûkta alone would suffice to demonstrate its comparatively recent date.

That even the legendary genealogies of the Purâṇas frequently assign to members of the four so-called castes a common origin, has been shown in my Sanskrit Texts, vol. i. chap. ii.; and for the evidence discoverable, both in the Rig-veda itself and in the epic poems and Purânas, that hymns were composed, and sacerdotal functions exercised, by persons who in later ages were called Râjanyas or Kshattriyas, as well as by Brâhmans, I may refer to the same volume, pp. 86–151 where the stories of Viṣvâmitra and Devâpi are told.

In later times, when none but Brâhman priests were known, it seemed to be an unaccountable, and—as contradicting the exclusive sacerdotal pretensions of the Brâhmans—an inconvenient circumstance, that priestly functions should have been recorded as exercised by Râjanyas; and it therefore became necessary to explain away the historical facts, by inventing miraculous legends to make it appear that these men of the royal order had been in reality transformed into Brâhmans, as the reward of their superhuman merits and austerities (see Sanskrit Texts, vol. i., pp. 95 ff., 148 ff.). The very existence, however, of such a word as *râjarshi*, or "royal rishi," proves that Indian tradition recognized as rishis or authors of Vedic hymns persons who had belonged to Râjanya families. A number of such are named (though without the epithet of *râjarshi*) in the Anukramaṇikâ or index to the Rig-veda; but Sâyaṇa, who quotes that old document, gives them this title. Thus, in the introduction to hymn i. 100, he says: "Ṛjrâṣva and others, sons of Vṛshâgir, in all five râjarshis, saw this hymn in a bodily form (*sadehaṃ sûktaṃ dadṛṣuḥ*). Hence they are its rishis (or seers)." The 17th verse of this hymn is as follows: "This hymn the Vârshâgiras, Ṛjrâṣva, with his attendants Amvarîsha, Sahadeva, Bhayamâna, and Surâdhas, utter to thee, the vigorous, o Indra, as their homage;" on which Sâyaṇa repeats the remark that these persons were râjarshis. Ambarîsha is also said to be the rishi of ix. 98. Again, "Trasadasyu, son of Purukutsa, a Râjarshi," is said by Sâyaṇa on R.V. iv. 42, to be the rishi of that hymn. In the 9th verse Trasadasyu is thus mentioned: "Purukutsânî worshipped you, o Indra and Varuṇa, with salutations and obeisances; then ye gave her king Trasadasyu, a slayer of enemies, a demigod." Similarly Sâyaṇa says on v. 27: "Tryaruṇa son of Trivṛshṇa, Trasadasyu son of Purukutsa, and Aṣvamedha son of Bharata, these three kings conjoined, are the rishis of this hymn; or Atri is the rishi." As the hymn is spoken by a fourth person, in praise of the liberality of these kings, it is clear they cannot well be its authors. However, the Hindu tradition of their being so, is good proof that kings could, in conformity with ancient opinion, be rishis. Trasadasyu and Trayaruṇa are also mentioned as the rishis of ix. 110.[1] The rishis of iv. 43 and iv. 44 are declared by Sâyaṇa, and by the Anukramaṇikâ, to be Purumîlha, and Ajamîlha, sons or descendants of Suhotra. Though these persons

[1] In the Vishṇu Purâṇa, Trayyâruṇa, Pushkarin, and Kapi are said to have been sons of Urukshaya, and the last of them to have become a Brâhman. In the Matsya P., Trayyaruṇi, Pushkarâruṇi, and Kapi are said to have all become Brâhmans. (Wilson, V. P., p. 451, and note.)

are not said by either of these authorities to be kings, yet in the Vishṇu Purâṇa they are mentioned as being of royal race, and as grandsons of Suhotra, and according to the Bhâgavata P. a tribe of Brâhmans is said to have been descended from the son of Ajamîlha. In the sixth verse of iv. 44, the descendants of Ajamîlha are said to have come to the worship of the Aṣvins. The following hymns are said by tradition to have had the following kings for their rishis, viz.: x. 9, Sindhudwîpa, son of Ambarîsha (or Triṣiras, son of Tvashtṛ); x. 75, Sindhukshit, son of Priyamedha; x. 133, Sudâs, son of Pijavana; x. 134, Mândhâtṛ, son of Yuvanâṣva; x. 179, Sibi, son of Uṣînara, Pratardana, son of Divodâsa and king of Kâṣî, and Vasumanas, son of Rohidaṣva; and x. 148 is declared to have had Pṛthî Vainya as its rishi. In the fifth verse of that hymn it is said: "Hear, o heroic Indra, the invocation of Pṛthî; and thou art praised by the hymns of Venya." In viii. 9, 10, also, Pṛthî Vainya is mentioned among rishis "Whatever invocation Kakshîvat has made to you, or the rishi Vyaṣva, or Dîrghatamas, or Pṛthî, son of Vena, in the places of sacrifice, take notice of that, o Aṣvins." Here Sâyaṇa refers to Pṛthî as the "royal rishi of that name."[1]

I have observed above that the contents of R.V. x. 109 not only display the high pretensions of the priestly order, but also indicate clearly that those pretensions were often disregarded by the ruling class. In fact, the hymns of the Rigveda contain numerous references to persons, apparently of different descriptions, who were either hostile or indifferent to the system of religious worship which the rishis professed and inculcated. We find there a long list of condemnatory epithets applied to these persons, such as *adeva, adevayu, anindra, abrahman, ayajyu, ayajvan, anyavrata, apavrata, avrata, devanid, brahmadvish*, etc., etc.; *i.e.*, "godless," "destitute of Indra," "without devotion," "unsacrificing," "following other rites," "averse to religious rites, or to law," "without rites, or lawless," "revilers of the gods," "haters of

[1] Even females are said to be authors of hymns or parts of hymns, as Romaṣâ, "daughter of Bṛhaspati, an utterer of hymns" (i. 126), Lopamudrâ (i. 179, 1), and Viṣvavârâ, of the family of Atri (v. 28).

devotion," etc. (i. 33, 3, 4; i. 51, 8, 9; i. 101, 2, 4; i. 121, 13; i. 131, 4; i. 132, 4; i. 147, 2; i. 150, 2; i. 174, 8; i. 175, 3; ii. 12, 10; ii. 23, 4, 8, 12; ii. 26, 1; iii. 30, 17; iii. 31, 9; iii. 34, 9; iv. 16, 9; v. 2, 9, 10; v, 20, 2; v. 42, 9, 10; vi. 14, 3; vi. 49, 15; vi. 52, 2, 3; vi. 61, 3; vi. 67, 9; vii. 6, 3; vii. 61, 4; vii. 83, 7; vii. 93, 5; viii. 31, 15 ff.; viii. 45, 23; viii. 51, 12; viii. 53, 1; viii. 59, 7, 10, 11; ix. 41, 2; ix. 63, 24; ix. 73, 5, 8; x. 22, 7 f.; x. 27, 1 ff.; x. 36, 9; x. 38, 3; x. 42, 4; x. 49, 1; x. 160, 4; x. 182, 3.) In most of these passages, no doubt, the epithets in question are connected with the words *Dâsa* or *Dasyu,* which—whether we understand them of barbarous aboriginal races, then partially occupying the Punjab, or of the evil spirits with which the darkness was peopled by the lively imagination of the early Indians—certainly did not ordinarily designate tribes of Aryan descent. But there are other texts containing denunciations of religious hostility or indifference, where no express reference is made to Dasyus, which may with more or less probability be understood of members of the Aryan community. Such are the following:—

i. 84, 7. "Indra, who alone distributes riches to the sacrificing mortal, is lord and irresistible. 7. When will Indra crush the illiberal (*arâdhasam*) man like a bush with his foot? when will he hear our hymns?"

i. 101, 4. "Indra, who is the slayer of him, however strong, who offers no libations."

i. 122, 9. "The hostile man, the malicious enemy, who pours out no libations to you, o Mitra and Varuṇa, plants fever in his own heart, when the pious man has by his offerings obtained (your blessing)."

i. 124, 10. "Wake, o magnificent Dawn (Ushas), the men who present offerings; let the thoughtless niggards (*paṇayaḥ*)[1] sleep." (Comp. iv. 51, 3.)

1. 125, 7. "Let not the liberal suffer evil or calamity; let not devout sages decay; let them have some further term; let griefs befall the illiberal (*apṛṇantam*)."

[1] This sense of the word is confirmed by i. 33, 3, where the rishi says to Indra, "*mâ paṇir bhûr asmad adhi,*" "Be not niggardly towards us."

i. 147, 2. "One man contemns (*pîyati*), whilst another praises, thee. Reverent, I adore thy manifestation, o Agni."

i. 176, 4. "Slay every one who offers no oblations—though difficult to destroy[1]—who is displeasing to thee. Give us his wealth; the sage expects it."

i. 182, 3. "What do ye here, o powerful (Aṣvins)? Why do ye sit in the house of any man who offers no sacrifice, and yet is honoured? Assail, wear away the breath of the niggard (*paṇer asum*), and create light for the sage who desires to praise you."

i. 190, 5. "Those persons who, flourishing, but wicked, regarding thee, o god, as a feeble being, depend upon thee who art gracious—thou bestowest nothing desirable upon the malignant, thou, o Bṛhaspati, avengest thyself on the scorner (*piyârum*)."

ii. 23, 4. "By thy wise leadings thou guidest and protectest the man who worships thee: no calamity can assail him who hates devotion (*brahma-dvishaḥ*), and the queller of his wrath: this, o Bṛhaspati, is thy great glory."

ii. 26, 1. "The upright worshipper shall slay those who seek to slay (him); the godly shall overcome the ungodly; the religious shall slay in battle even him who is hard to conquer; the sacrificer shall divide the spoils of the unsacrificing."

iv. 24, 2. "In battle Indra bestows riches upon the man who offers prayers (*brahmaṇyate*) and libations. . . . . . 5. Then some men worship the mighty (Indra); then the cooker of oblations will present his offering of meal; then Soma will abandon those who offer no libations; then (the impious) will be fain to worship the vigorous (god)."

iv. 25, 5. "Dear is the righteous man, dear to Indra is the man who reveres him, dear is the worshipper, dear to him is the offer of soma. 6. This impetuous and heroic Indra regards as peculiarly his own the cooked oblation of the devout soma-offerer; he is not the relation, or friend, or kinsman, of the man who offers no libations; he destroys the prostrate irreligious man. 7. Indra, the soma-drinker, approves not

[1] Roth, *s.v.* understands *dûṇâṣam* to mean "continually."

friendship with the wealthy niggard (*revatâ paṇinâ*) who offers no libations. He deprives him of his riches, and destroys him when stripped bare, whilst he is the exclusive favourer of the man who offers libations and cooks offerings."

iv. 51, 3. "The magnificent dawns, appearing, have to-day aroused the liberal to the bestowal of wealth. Let the niggards (*paṇayaḥ*) sleep in gloom, and the regardless in the midst of darkness." (Compare i. 124, 10.)

v. 34, 3 (= Nirukta vi. 19). "Whoever offers soma-libations to Indra, either in sunshine or darkness, becomes glorious. The mighty god drives away the ostentatious; the opulent god (drives away) the man who decks out his person, and is the friend of the degraded. (Yâska adds to these epithets of the objects of Indra's enmity that of *ayajvânam*, 'one who does not worship.') 5. Indra desires no support from five or from ten (allies); he consorts not with the man who offers no libation, however flourishing; but overwhelms, and at once destroys such a person, whilst he gives the godly man a herd of kine as his portion. 6. . . .. The enemy of him who makes no libations, the promoter of him who offers libations, Indra, the terrible subduer of all, the lord, brings the Dâsa into subjection. 7. He gathers together the goods of the niggard (*paṇeḥ*) to be spoiled; he allots to the sacrificer wealth beneficial for men. Every one who provokes his fury is deeply involved in difficulty."

v. 42, 7. "Praise the first depositary of gems, Bṛhaspati, the bestower of riches, who is most propitious to the man that hymns and lauds him, who comes with abundant wealth to the man that invokes him. 8. Those who are attended by thy succours, Bṛhaspati, are unharmed, affluent, rich in men. The possessions of those who bestow horses, cows, and raiment, are blest. 9. Make unblest the wealth of those who enjoy themselves while they do not gratify (thee) with our hymns.[1] Drive away from the sunlight those haters of devotion (*brahma-dvishaḥ*) who are averse to religious rites, while they increase in progeny. 10. Hasten, o Maruts, with-

[1] Or, according to Sâyaṇa, "who do not satisfy us who are possessed of laudatory hymns."

out wheels[1] against the man who attends at the sacrifice of a Rakshas (or sinner).[2] He who reviles the man who celebrates your service secures but contemptible pleasures, however much he may sweat."

vi. 13, 3. "That lord of the virtuous by his power destroys Vrittra (or the enemy); o wise Agni, offspring of the ceremonial, that sage whom thou in concert with the son of the waters prosperest with wealth, divides the spoil of the niggard (*paṇeḥ*)."

vi. 44, 11. "Abandon us not, o vigorous god, to the destroyer; let us not suffer injury whilst we live in the friendship of thee who art opulent. Thy former bounties to men (are known); slay those who offer no libations; root out the illiberal (*apṛṇataḥ*)."

vi. 52, 1. "By heaven or by earth I approve not that, nor by (this) sacrifice, nor by these rites.[3] Let the strong mountains crush him; let the priest (*yashṭâ*) of Atiyâja fall. 2. Whoever, o Maruts, regards himself as superior to us, or reviles our worship when performed, may scorching calamities light upon him; may the sky consume that hater of devotion (*brahma-dvisham*).[4] 3. Why, o Soma, do they call thee the protector of devotion, or our preserver from imprecations? Why doest thou see us reviled? Hurl thy burning bolt against the hater of devotion (*brahma-dvishe*)." (These verses perhaps refer to the struggles of rival priests. Professor Aufrecht renders the words *atiyâjasya yashṭâ*, by "he who tries to outdo us in sacrifices." Sâyaṇa, who is followed by Professor Goldstücker, makes *atiyâja* the name of a rishi. Professor Roth takes it to mean "very pious.")

vi. 53, 3. "Impel to liberality, o burning Pûshan, even

[1] *Achakrebhiḥ*, easily, swiftly, noiselessly, suddenly. Compare the phrase *achakrayâ svadhayâ varttamânam* in x. 27, 19, and *nichakrayâ*, viii. 7, 29.

[2] This latter rendering of the words *ya ohate rakshaso devavîtau*, is suggested by Professor Aufrecht. Compare the words *mâ no martâya ripave rakshasvine*, etc., viii. 49, 8, and *yo naḥ kaşchid ririkshati rakshastvena martyaḥ*, etc., viii. 18, 13. Sâyaṇa renders the words under consideration by "who brings Rakshases to to the sacrifice,—by irregular observances, etc., makes it demoniacal (*âsura*)."

[3] The sense of this is not very clear, unless, as Professor Aufrecht proposes, we understand the words as an oath.

[4] This verse occurs in a modified form in the A.V. ii. 12, 6, but without any perceptible difference of sense.

the man who wishes to give nothing. Soften[1] the soul even of the niggard (*paṇeḥ*). 4. Open up paths by which we may obtain food; slay our enemies; let our ceremonies be successful, o terrible god. 5. O wise deity, pierce the hearts of the niggards (*paṇînâm*) with a probe; and then subject them to us. 6. Pierce them with a goad, o Pûshan; seek (for us) that which is dear to the heart of the niggard (*paṇeḥ*); and then subject them to us. 7. Penetrate and tear the hearts of the niggards (*paṇînâm*), o wise deity, and then subject them to us. 8. With that prayer-promoting probe (*brahmachodinîm ârâm*) which thou holdest, o burning Pûshan, penetrate and tear the heart of every (such man)."

vii. 83, 4. "O Indra and Varuṇa, unrivalled with your weapons, slaying Bheda, ye preserved Sudâs; ye listened to the prayers of these men in the battle; the priestly office of the Tritsus proved efficacious. . . . . 6. Both invoke you, Indra and Varuṇa, for the acquisition of spoil (as) in the conflicts where ye protected Sudâs with the Tritsus, when he was assailed by the ten kings. 7. Ten unsacrificing (*ayajyavaḥ*) kings did not, o Indra and Varuṇa, vanquish Sudâs. The praises of the men who partake in the sacrificial feast were effectual; the gods were present at their invocations. 8. O Indra and Varuṇa, ye gave succour to Sudâs when surrounded in the battle of the ten kings, where the devout white-robed Tritśus, with knotted hair, worshipped you with reverence and prayer."

[In the first verse of this hymn Indra and Varuṇa are said to have slain both the Dâsa and Ârya enemies of Sudâs. His enemies were therefore in part Âryas, and the ten kings alluded to in the verses I have quoted were no doubt of this race. And yet it is to be observed that in *v.* 7 they are described as *ayajyavaḥ*, "unsacrificing." If, therefore, this expression is to be taken literally, it would follow that these Aryan kings were not worshippers of Indra and Varuṇa. Perhaps, however, the epithet is only to be understood in a general way, as meaning "ungodly." If we are to take the indefinite word "both" (*ubhayâsah*) in verse 6, as meaning

[1] Or, "crush" (*vi mrada*).

"both the contending hosts," it would, indeed, result that not only Sudâs but also the ten kings who were fighting against him offered supplications to the same gods; but this would seem to be in contradiction to the literal sense of the word "unsacrificing" in the following verse; and Sâyaṇa understands "both" to refer to Sudâs and the Tritsus who were his helpers].

vii. 19, 1. "Who (Indra) bestows on the man who offers many libations the wealth of the family which does not worship (him)."

viii. 2, 18. The gods love a man who offers oblations; they do not approve sleep. The active obtain delight." (Compare viii. 86, 3).

viii. 14, 15. "Thou, o Indra, a drinker of soma, who art supreme, hast scattered and destroyed the hostile assembly which offers no oblations."

viii. 31, 15. "Impetuous is the chariot of the godly man, and he is a hero in every battle. The sacrificer who seeks to please the gods overcomes the man who does not sacrifice. 16. Thou dost not perish, o sacrificer, nor thou, o offerer of libations, nor thou, o godly man."

viii. 45, 15. "Bring to us the wealth of the man who, being rich, but no sacrificer, refuses to present offerings. . . . 23. Let not violent fools, let not deriders insult thee. Love not the haters of devotion (*brahmadvishaḥ*)."

viii. 51, 12. "Let us praise Indra truly, not falsely. Great destruction overtakes the man who offers no libations, whilst he who offers them has many lights."

viii. 53, 1. "Let our hymns exhilarate thee; give us wealth, o Thunderer. Slay the haters of devotion (*brahmadvishaḥ*). 2. Crush with thy foot the niggards (*paṇîn*), who bestow nothing;[1] thou art great; no one equals thee."

viii. 59, 7. "O long-lived god, the ungodly man shall not obtain food. . . . . 10. Thou, Indra, lovest our rites; thou satiatest (? ironically) those who revile thee. . . . . . . . ." Perhaps these expressions may refer to the Dâsas and Dasyu, who are mentioned in the context.

[1] In ix. 101, 13, we find *ṣvânam arâdhasam*, "the dog who bestows nothing."

viii. 86, 2. "Bestow, o Indra, upon the worshipper who offers libations and gives presents, and not upon the niggard (*paṇau*), the horse and cow which thou possessest, as an undecaying portion. 3. Let the godless man who performs no rites, and sleeps an incessant sleep, destroy by his own acts[1] the wealth which sustains him; sever him from it."

x. 27, 1. "The impulse comes upon me (says Indra) to bestow (blessings) on the sacrificer who offers libations. I slay the man who utters no praises, who is an enemy of truth, a sinner, and empty."[2]

x. 32. "May the (worshippers) who constantly bring thee to the sacrifices slay the boasters (or talkers) who give no presents" (*vagvanân arâdhasaḥ*).

x. 38, 3. "Whatever godless man (*adevaḥ*), whether Dâsa or Ârya, o much-lauded Indra, seeks after us to vanquish us, let these enemies be easy for us to overcome; through thee may we slay them in the conflict."

[This passage shows that Âryas as well as Dâsas were charged with being deniers of the Aryan gods (compare vii. 83, 7); unless we are to consider the term "godless" as employed, as in modern times,[3] to describe persons who were practically, though not theoretically, unbelievers. This latter view is confirmed by A.V. v. 8, 3, where an enemy plotting against the worshipper, and employing a *priest* (*v.* 5), is yet described as "godless."]

x. 42, 4. . . "Here the hero (Indra) takes for a friend the man who brings offerings; he desires no friendship with the man who pours out no libations."

x. 49, 1. . . "I (says Indra) bestow the earliest riches on the man who praises me: I have made for myself a hymn which magnifies me. I am the encourager of the man who sacrifices. I overwhelm in every conflict those who do not sacrifice."

x. 160, 4. "Whoever, loving the gods, offers libations of soma to Indra with an ardent soul, with his whole heart,—Indra does not give up his kine (to spoliation), but makes for

[1] Compare viii. 18, 13.
[2] "Empty-handed," *âbhum*, as explained by Böhtlingk and Roth *s.v.*
[3] *e.g.* in the case of the Government Colleges in Ireland.

him (the soma-libation) approved and pleasing.[1] 4. That man is observed by Indra who, though rich, offers to him no libations of soma. Maghavat grasps him in his fist,[2] and slays the haters of devotion (*brahmadvishaḥ*) though unsolicited."

That the wealthy man here referred to is an Âryan is rendered probable by the tenor of the following text, where the rich man there alluded to, after contemning Indra during a period of security, concludes by invoking the god when he has been terrified into devotion by the manifestations of his power and anger:

viii. 21, 14. "Thou takest not a rich man for thy friend. Drunkards contemn thee. When thou utterest a sound, and musterest (thy hosts), then thou art invoked as a father."[3]

1 Prof. Aufrecht suggested that the words "the soma libation," should be understood in this verse, and compares vii. 84, 3, and x. 39, 2. The blessings which attend a devout worshipper of Indra are also described in vi. 28, 2 ff.

2 See Prof. Goldstücker's Sanskrit Lexicon *s.v. aratni.* Sâyaṇa's interpretation of this verse, as there quoted and translated by Prof. G., is as follows: "Indra manifests himself (to the pious); (the sacrificer), who, though not wealthy, offers him the soma libation,—him, Indra, the wealthy, holds in his hand (lit. *fist*, *i.e.* he protects him), after having defeated (*niḥ* scil. *kṛshya*) his enemies; even unsolicited he slays the foes of the Brâhmans." I am, I confess, bold enough to consider the rendering I have given in the text as preferable to Sâyaṇa's in the parts where mine differs from his. His connection of the negative particle *na* which follows *revân* with that word (so as to make it = *arevân*), instead of with the verb *sunoti*, seems forced and unnatural, especially as rich men are often censured as non-sacrificers (as in iv. 25, 7; v. 34, 5, v. 42, 9; viii. 45, 15). Prof. Roth conjecturally interprets *aratnau nirdadhâti* as meaning "he finds him out in a corner." Prof. Aufrecht would render, "holds him at arm's length, despises him."

3 Compare the following additional passages.—i. 110, 7; i. 113, 18; i. 121, 13; i. 131, 4; i. 132, 4; i. 133, 7; i. 151, 7; i. 152, 2; i. 174, 6; vi. 22, 8; vi. 23, 2, 3, 9. We read in i. 51, 8: "Distinguish between the Âryas and those who are Dasyus; chastising the men who are destitute of rites (or lawless), subject them to the sacrificer. Be a strong supporter of thy worshipper," etc.; and in i. 130, 8: "Indra preserved the sacrificing Ârya in battle." But it does not follow from such texts that the Âryas are always identifiable with the worshippers of the gods, though the two classes would generally include the same persons.

As the people named in the following verse (iii. 53, 14), the Kîkaṭas, seem to have lived on the outskirts of Âryan civilization, no conclusion can be drawn from it in reference to the point before us. "What are thy cows, (o Indra) doing among the Kîkaṭas? (These people) neither draw (from these cows) milk to mix with the soma, nor do they heat the sacrificial kettle. Bring to us the wealth of Pramaganda (or the usurer); subject to us the degraded people." The Kîkaṭas, according to Yâska (Nir. vi. 32), are a non-Âryan race; though he and Sâyaṇa give *nâstikas* or atheists as an alternative sense. Prof. Weber (Indische Studien, i. 186) thinks that as Kîkaṭa is an old name for Magadha or Behar, we may understand the word *anâryya* used by Yâska as meaning an Âryan tribe which

(See "Contributions to Vedic Theogony," etc., p. 101, note 1.) In vi. 47, 16, Indra is said to be the enemy of the prosperous man (*edhamânadviṭ*), probably an Ârya who rendered him no service.[1]

In two other passages we are even told that doubts were entertained by some in regard to Indra's existence; ii. 12, 5: "Have faith in that terrible being of whom men ask 'where is he?' and declare that he is not. He destroys the possessions of the foe, etc. . . . . 15. Thou art true, who being irresistible, continually providest food for him who pours out libations and cooks oblations."

viii. 89, 3. "Seeking food, present a hymn to Indra, a true hymn, if he truly exists. 'Indra does not exist,' says some one; 'who has seen him? whom shall we praise?' 'This is I, o worshipper (exclaims Indra), behold me here, I surpass all beings in greatness.'"

It seems evident from the preceding texts that the *parcus deorum cultor et infrequens* was by no means a rare character among the Âryas of the Vedic age, and that the priests found no little difficulty in drawing forth the liberality of their lay contemporaries towards themselves, and in enforcing a due regard to the ceremonials of devotion. It would even appear that the ministers of religion had to encounter a considerable amount of contempt and hostility from the ungodly, for such words as *brahmadvish*,[2] "hater of devotion," and *piyâru*,

did not follow Âryan rites, but were in the same condition as the Vrâtyas described by him in p. 33, and by Prof. Aufrecht at pp. 138 f. of the same volume, who were admissible by a particular rite within the Brahmanical pale. From Atharva Veda, v. 22, 14, however, it would appear that the Magadhas were regarded by the writer with enmity, and the people designated in the verse before us as Kîkatas, are described as hostile or indifferent to Âryan rites. (See Sanskrit Texts ii. 362 ff. and Wilson's note *in loco*.)

[1] As however it is said in the same verse that Indra subdues the terrible, and brings forward others, it is possible that these expressions may be meant merely to declare Indra's absolute control over the destinies of men, and to describe the Nemesis that overtakes pride, with an indication of the Herodotean idea τὸ θεῖον φθονερόν. (Herod. iii. 40; vii. 10, and 46.)

[2] This word *brahma-dvish* might mean either "hater of *priests*," or "hater of devotion," but in the R.V. it seems to have the latter sense. Sâyaṇa, on ii. 23, renders it *mantrâṇâm brâhmaṇânâm vâ dveshṭuḥ*, "hater of *mantras* (hymns), or of Brâhmans;" and similarly, on v. 42, 9, *brâhmaṇa-dveshṭrîn mantra-dveshṭrîn vâ*, "hater of Brâhmans or of mantras;" whilst on iii. 30, 17, he explains it by *brâhmaṇa-dvesha-kâriṇe*, "hater of Brâhmans;" and the same on vi. 22, 8; vi.

"despiser," which seem to be sometimes applied to irreligious Âryas, express something more than passive opposition. It may perhaps be further gathered from a few passages, which I shall now cite, that the recognized Âryan worship of the national gods, Agni, Indra, Varuṇa, etc., was not kept free from a certain admixture of demonolatry borrowed most probably from the aboriginal tribes; and it is indeed easy to conceive, or even a thing to be assumed as natural and necessary, that the religion as well as the language, manners, and customs of the Âryans should, in process of time, have undergone some modification from the close contact into which they must have been brought with these barbarous neighbours.[1]

From the first text which I shall quote, and which is ascribed by tradition to the rishi Vasishṭha, it seems that that distinguished personage himself had been accused, whether truly or falsely, of worshipping false gods, of familiarity with evil spirits, and the practice of devilish arts. A charge of this kind could scarcely have been made with any chance of being credited, unless such demonolatry was commonly known to have been practised either by him, or by other members of the same community. The passage referred to (R.V. vii. 104, 12 ff.) is as follows: "The intelligent man can easily discern, (when) true and false words contend together, which of them is true, and which of them is correct. Soma protects the former, and destroys untruth. 13. Soma does not prosper the sinner, nor the man who wields royal power deceitfully.

52, 3; vii. 104, 2; viii. 45, 23; and viii. 53, 1. The context of ii. 23, 4; v. 42, 9; vi. 52, 2, 3; x. 160, 4, seems to be in favour of the sense "haters of devotion," and the other passages contain nothing inconsistent with this interpretation. No use can therefore be made of this word to prove the importance of priests in the Vedic age.

[1] The demons mentioned in the Rig-veda are called by various names, such as *Rakshas*, *Yâtu*, *Yâtudhâna*, of which the feminine Yâtudhânî is also found, and apparently also *Dasyu* and *Dâsa*. The word *piṣâchi* (masculine) also occurs in R.V. i. 133, 5, and *piṣâcha* frequently in the A.V. The *Yâtus* are conceived as of different kinds, *ṣva-yâtu*, *ulûka-yâtu*, *susulûka-yâtu*, *koka-yâtu*, *suparṇa-yâtu*, *gṛdhra-yâtu*, the dog-, owl-, vulture-, etc. etc. formed Yâtus (vii. 104, 22); and *ṣaphâruj yâtus*, perhaps, such as wound with their hoofs (x. 87, 12). Indra and Agni are the destroyers of the Yâtus who seek to disturb and vitiate the sacrifices and to slay these deities (vii. 104, 18, 20 f.; x. 87, 9 ff.). The Yâtus are described as devouring, insatiable, eaters of raw flesh, of the flesh of men and cattle, drinkers of milk, haters of devotion, maleficent, glaring-eyed, furious, the offspring of darkness (vii. 104 and x. 87 passim).

He slays the Rakshas, he slays the liar, they both sleep in the fetters of Indra. 14. If I am either one whose gods are false,[1] or if I have conceived of the gods untruly;—why art thou angry with us, o Jâtavedas; let slanderers fall into thy destruction. 15. May I die to-day if I am a Yâtudhâna, or if I have injured any man's life. Then let him be separated from his ten sons, who falsely addresses to me (the words) 'o Yâtudhâna.' 16. He who addresses to me who am no Yâtu[2] (the words), 'o Yâtudhâna,' or who (being) himself a Rakshas says, 'I am pure;'[3] let Indra slay him with his mighty bolt; let him sink down the lowest of all creatures." Sâyaṇa in his note on v. 12 refers to a legend according to which a Râkshasa had taken the form of Vasishṭha, and killed a hundred sons of that rishi, and that these verses were uttered by Vasishṭha to repel the charge of his having been possessed by the demon. This legend, however, which was no doubt manufactured to explain the verses, does not in reality answer this purpose. And it would seem, as I have above assumed, that Vasishṭha, or the speaker in these verses, whoever he may have been, had been charged with worshipping false gods, and with being under the influence of demons; and that while repelling the accusation, he here retorts upon his accuser by calling *him* a Rakshas.

Again in vii. 34, 8, the rishi says: "I who am no Yâtu (undemoniacal) invoke the gods; fulfilling (the ceremony) in due form, I offer a hymn." In another place[4] (vii. 21, 5) it is said: "Neither, o Indra, have Yâtus inspired[5]

[1] *Anṛta-devaḥ:* i.e. *asatya-bhûtâ devâ yasya,* "one whose gods are untrue, or unreal" (Sâyaṇa). Prof. Goldstücker *s.v.* interprets the word as meaning, "one to whom the gods are untrue." Prof. Max Müller renders the phrase, "If I had worshipped false gods." Prof. Roth who had originally *s.v.* taken the word to mean "a false prayer." withdraws this sense, and adheres to that given by Sâyaṇa, at the close of his article on *deva.*

[2] Roth *s.v.* explains the word *ayâtu* as meaning, "not demoniacal, free from demoniacal (magic)." Goldstücker *s.v.* defines the word, "a no-demon, a being different from, or the reverse of, a fiend."

[3] See Prof. Goldstücker's Dict. *s.v. ayâtu.*

[4] Quoted with its context in Sanskrit Texts, iv. 345.

[5] Or, "impelled," *jûjuvuḥ.* This is the sense given by Roth *s.v.* who explains the words thus: "Demons do not impel us:" *i.e.* "We are not in league with demons." Compare *deva-jûta,* "god-inspired," or "god-impelled," applied to

us . . . . .[1] Let the lord (Indra) triumph over the hostile race; let no priapic (or long-tailed) demons,[2] approach our ceremony."

In vi. 62, 8, a person characterized as *rakshoyuj* is devoted to the vengeance of the gods. The commentator explains the term as either "the lord, or the instigator, of demons, or a priest possessed of, or by, demons" (Rakshases).

In vii. 85, 1, the word *arakshas* is used in a sense perhaps akin to that of *ayâtu:* "I consecrate (or polish, *punîshe*) for you twain an undemoniacal (*arakshasam*) hymn, offering a libation of soma to Indra and Varuṇa." The same word is also employed in viii. 90, 8, where the Aṣvins are thus addressed: "Since we offer to you an undemoniacal gift (*râtim arakshasam*)," etc. Compare ii. 10, 5; v. 87, 9.

If we should assign to the words *Rakshaso devavîtau* in R.V. v. 42, 10 (a passage quoted above), the sense of "the sacrifice offered to a Rakshas," the preceding conclusions would be still further confirmed.

If such demonolatry really existed to any extent among the Âryas, it is quite conceivable (I throw this out as a mere conjecture), that the intense hatred of the evil spirits whom, under the appellations of Yâtudhânas, Rakshases, Asuras, etc., Agni, Indra, and other deities, are so frequently represented in the R. V. (i. 133; iii. 15, 1;

Viṣvâmitra in iii. 53, 9; and, on the other hand, *dasyujûtaya* in vi. 24, 8, where it is said: "Indra does not bow to the strong nor the firm, nor to the bold man *impelled by a Dasyu* (or evil spirit)."

[1] The sense of the following words *na vandanâ vedyâbhiḥ* is obscure.

[2] *Ṣiṣnadevâḥ.* The same word occurs in x. 99, 3: "When, irresistible, he conquered by his force the treasures of the (city) with a hundred gates, slaying the priapic (or long-tailed) demons." (See Sanskrit Texts, iv. 346). If this word *ṣiṣnadeva* is correctly rendered as above, the demons in question may have some affinity with the Gandharvas, who are represented as objects of apprehension in A.V. iv. 37, in consequence of their propensity for women, whom, though themselves hairy like dogs or monkeys, they attempted to seduce by assuming an agreeable form (vv. 11, 12). The author of the hymn accordingly wishes that they may be emasculated (v. 7). [Professor Aufrecht thinks that *ṣiṣnadevâh*, being a *bahuvrîhi* compound, must mean "lascivious" (*ṣiṣnam devo yeshâm*).] These Gandharvas are also described (vv. 8, 9) as *havir-adân*, "eaters of oblations." In A.V. xviii. 2, 28, the Dasyus (who must here be demons) are spoken of as mingling with the Pitris under the appearance of friends, though they had no right to partake in the oblations; and Agni is besought to drive them away from the sacrifice. Compare the disputes regarding the admission of Rudra to a share in sacrifices, Sanskrit Texts, iv. 203, 241, 312 ff.

vii. 13, 1; vii. 15, 10; vii. 104; viii. 23, 13; viii. 43, 26; x. 87; x. 187, 3, etc.) as destroying or chasing away from the sacrifices which they disturbed and polluted (vii. 104, 18; x. 87, 9, 11), may not have been inspired by the dread which the superstitious worshippers entertained of those goblins, so much as by the fact that they were rival objects of adoration for whom their votaries claimed a share in the oblations, whilst the adherents of the gods described their patrons as triumphing by their superior power over the hostile intruders, and their magical arts (vii. 104, 20, 21, 24; x. 87, 19).[1]

Is it possible to look upon Rudra as having been originally a demon worshipped by the aborigines as the lord of evil spirits, and subsequently introduced into the Aryan worship? And that he was then, as well as originally, supplicated to abstain from inflicting those evils of which he was regarded as the author, and flattered by being addressed as the great healer of those sufferings which had their origin in his malevolence? (See the reference made to the late Rev. Dr. Stevenson's paper on the "Ante-Brahmanical Religion of the Hindus," and to Lassen's Ind. Antiq. in Sanskrit Texts, iv. 344). His malignant, homicidal, and cattle-destroying character (R.V. iv. 3, 6; i. 114, 10, Sanskrit Texts iv. 339), assimilates him to the Rakshasas and Yâtudhânas (though it is true that they are not, as he is, specifically described as the inflicters of disease and death); and he is described in the Ṣatarudriya (Vâj. S. xvi. 8, 20), as having attendants (*satvânaḥ*), while in A.V. xiii. 4, 27, all the Yâtus are said to obey his commands, and in *v.* 25 of the same hymn he is declared to be death, and immortality, vastness (*abhvam*), and a Rakshas (*sa eva mṛtyuḥ so 'mṛtaṃ so 'bhvaṃ sa rakshaḥ*); and in xi. 2, 30 f., reverence is offered to his wide-mouthed howling dogs, and to his shouting, long-haired, devouring armies. It is true that in the 11th verse of the same hymn he is asked to drive away dogs and shrieking female (demons) with dis-

[1] Perhaps, however, it is unnecessary to resort to this supposition in order to account for the dread and hatred of Rakshases which prevailed in the Vedic age. Such horror and hatred of demons appear to be natural to men in a certain stage of civilization. See Lecky's History of the Rise and Progress of Rationalism, i. 17 f.

hevelled hair; that in A.V. iv. 28, 5, Bhava (a deity akin to, or identical with, Rudra) and Ṣarva are solicited to destroy the Yâtudhâna who uses incantations (compare x. 1, 23) and makes men mad; that in Vaj. 16, 5, Rudra is besought to drive away Yâtudhanîs; that in A.V. xi. 2, 28, Bhava is asked to be gracious to the sacrificer who has faith in the existence of the gods, and in *v.* 23 is said to destroy the contemners of the deities who offer them no sacrifice;—all of these latter traits being common to him with the other Vedic gods. If, however, Rudra really represents a god or demon borrowed by the Âryas from the aborigines, it was to be expected that when adopted by the former he would be invested with the general characteristics which they assigned to their other deities, and that his connection with the evil spirits, of whom he was originally the chief, should as far as possible be kept out of sight and ultimately forgotten.

It is true that this theory leaves unexplained the connection of Rudra with the Maruts, in conformity with which he ought to be the god of tempests. (See the extract from Weber's Ind. Stud. in Sansk. Texts, iv. 334 ff.). But Rudra may be a composite character, and modified by the addition of heterogeneous elements in the course of ages.

There is no proof in the Rig-veda that the introduction of the worship of Rudra, even if it was more recent than that of the other Vedic gods, was met with any opposition. But we find there are hints that the adoration of the Rudras or Maruts was regarded as an innovation. These deities are described in many places (see my paper, "Contributions to a Knowledge of Vedic Theogony," etc., p. 110), as the sons of Rudra and Pṛṣni, and might, therefore, be supposed to have had some connection with Rudra. In one passage, too, (R.V. vii. 56, 17), a cattle-destroying and homicidal character (*gohâ nṛhâ vadho vaḥ*), akin to his, is ascribed to them. On the other hand, they are frequently represented as in close relation with Indra; and in fact it is almost inevitable that these deities of the tempest should be associated with the Thunderer, who could scarcely fulfil his function as dispenser of rain without their co-operation. But there are some hymns, viz., the 165th, the 170th, and the 171st, of the first Maṇḍala, in which Indra is introduced as regarding them with jealousy, and as resenting the worship which was paid to them. Thus in i. 160, 6 ff., he boasts that he is quite independent of their aid, while they reply that their assistance had been of importance to his success in battle. (Compare viii. 7, 31, and viii. 85, 7; iv. 18, 11). Again, in i. 170, Indra, who complains (*v.* 3) that the rishi Agastya was despising him and neglecting his worship, is besought (*v.* 2) to come to terms with the Maruts, and to associate with them at the sacrifice (*v.* 5); and in i. 171, 4, the rishi asks forgiveness from the Maruts, because, through dread of Indra, he had discontinued the sacrifice which he had begun in their honour. From all this it would seem as if the worshippers of Indra had entertained some objection to the adoration of the Maruts, and ascribed to the god the aversion to it which they themselves entertained. If there is any truth in the hypothesis that Rudra may have originally been a deity or demon who was introduced from the worship of the aborigines into that of their Aryan conquerors, the same may have been the case with the Rudras or Maruts, the sons of Rudra. Only, if this be the fact, these gods have been transformed in character in the course of their reception into the Indian pantheon, and rehabilitated by the ascription to them of different functions and milder attributes than those which belonged to them as deities, or demons of the aborigines.

The supposition which I have here made of the gradual transformation of Râkshasas into deities, is illustrated by the story told in the Mahâbhârata of the Râkshasî Jarâ, who is called a household goddess, and is represented as seeking to requite by benefits the worship which was paid to her. (See Sanskrit Texts, iv. 247).

I have already quoted from the Atharva-veda (v. 17) some evidence of the greater development which the Brahmanical pretensions had received subsequently to the age when the greater part of the Rig-veda was composed. Farther illustration of the same point may be found in the two hymns which follow the one just referred to, viz., A.V. v. 18, and

v. 19, which have been already translated in my former paper, "Miscellaneous Hymns from the Rig and Atharva Vedas," pp. 34 ff.). There is another section of the same Veda, xii. 5, in which curses similar to those in the last two hymns are fulminated against the oppressors of Brâhmans. The following are specimens: "4. Prayer (*brăhmăn*) is the chief (thing); the Brâhman is the lord (*adhipati*). 5. From the Kshattriya who takes the priest's cow, and oppresses the Brâhman, (6) there depart piety (*sûnṛta*), valour, good fortune, (7) force, keenness, vigour, strength, speech, energy, prosperity, virtue, (8) prayer (*brahman*), royalty, kingdom, subjects, splendour, renown, lustre, wealth, (9) life, beauty, name, fame, inspiration and expiration, sight, hearing, (10) milk, juice, food, eating, righteousness, truth, oblation, sacrifice, offspring, and cattle;—(11) all these things depart from the Kshattriya who takes the priest's cow. 12. Terrible is the Brâhman's cow, filled with deadly poison. . . . 13. In her reside all dreadful things and all forms of death, (14) all cruel things, and all forms of homicide. 15. When taken, she binds in the fetters of death the oppressor of priests and despiser of the gods." A great deal more follows to the same effect, which it would be tiresome to quote.

I subjoin some further texts of the Atharva-veda in which reference is made to priests (*brăhmăn*) and Brâhmans, and as I suppose these two words had by this period become nearly synonymous, there will no longer be any sufficient reason for separating the passages in which they respectively occur.

iv. 6, 1. "The Brâhman was born the first, with ten heads and ten faces. He first drank the soma; he made poison powerless."[1]

In xix. 22, 21 (= xix. 23, 30) it is similarly said: "Powers are assembled, of which prayer (or sacred science, *brahman*) is the chief. Prayer in the beginning stretched out the sky.

[1] I may mention for the benefit of any Indian Student who may see this article that this hitherto undiscovered variety of Brâhman, who was never anything but a "sky-flower," created by the prolific imagination of the author of this verse, was not again heard of, as far as I am aware, till he was resuscitated as Râvaṇa by the author of the Râmâyaṇa and his followers, who describe the enemy of Râma and ravisher of Sîtâ as a monstrous Brâhman with ten heads.

The *priest* (*brăhmăn*) was born the first of beings. Who, then, ought to vie with the *priest?*"

A superhuman power appears to be ascribed to the priest in the following passages,—unless by *priest* we are to understand Bṛhaspati:—

xix. 9, 12. "May a prosperous journey be granted to me by prayer, Prajâpati, Dhâtri, the worlds, the Vedas, the seven rishis, the fires; may Indra grant me felicity, may the *priest* (*brahman*) grant me felicity."

xix. 43, 8. "May the *priest* conduct me to the place whither the knowers of prayer (or of sacred science) go by initiation and austerity. May the *priest* impart to me sacred science."

The wonderful powers of the Brahmachârin, or student of sacred science, are described in a hymn (A.V. xi. 5), parts of which are translated in my paper on the progress of the Vedic Religion, pp. 374 ff.

And yet with all this sacredness of his character the priest must be devoted to destruction, if, in the interest of an enemy, he was seeking by his ceremonies to effect the ruin of the worshipper.

v. 8, 5, "May the *priest* whom these men have placed at their head (as a *purohita*) for our injury, fall under thy feet, o Indra; I hurl him away to death" (compare A.V. vii. 70, 1 ff.).

## Art. IX.—*On the Interpretation of the Veda.* By J. Muir, Esq.

I am led to make some remarks on the subject of this paper by a passage in Mr. Cowell's preface to the fourth volume of the late Professor Wilson's translation of the Rig-veda, which appears to me unduly to depreciate the services which have already been rendered by those eminent scholars both in Germany and in England who have begun to apply the scientific processes of modern philology to the explanation of this ancient hymn-collection. Mr. Cowell admits (p. vi.),—

"As Vaidik studies progress, and more texts are published and studied, fresh light will be thrown on these records of the ancient world; and we may gradually attain a deeper insight into their meaning than the mediæval Hindus could possess, just as a modern scholar may understand Homer more thoroughly than the Byzantine scholiasts."

But he goes on to say:—

"It is easy to depreciate native commentators, but it is not so easy to supersede them; and while I would by no means uphold Sâyaṇa as infallible, I confess that, in the present early stage of Vaidik studies in Europe, it seems to me the safer course to follow native tradition rather than to accept too readily the arbitrary conjectures which continental scholars so often hazard."

Without considering it necessary to examine, or defend, all the explanations of particular words proposed by the foreign lexicographers alluded to by Mr. Cowell, I yet venture to think that those scholars have been perfectly justified in commencing at once the arduous task of expounding the Veda on the principles of interpretation which they have adopted and enunciated. This task is, no doubt—(as those who undertake it themselves confess)—one which will only be properly accomplished by the critical labours of many scholars, I may even say, of several successive generations. This is clear, if any proof were wanted, from the parallel case of the Old

Testament; on the interpretation of which Hebraists, after all the studies of many centuries, are yet far from having said their last word. But what are those texts, and additional materials and appliances which Mr. Cowell desires to have within reach before we are to suffer ourselves to distrust the authority of native commentators, and to make any efforts to attain that deeper insight into the meaning of the Vedas which he feels to be desirable? The Rig-veda, as every one admits, stands alone in its antiquity, and in the character of its contents, and must therefore, as regards its more peculiar and difficult portions, be interpreted mainly through itself. To apply in another sense the words of its commentator, it shines by its own light, and is self-demonstrating.[1] But the whole text of the Rig-veda Sanhitâ has been already published with the commentary on the first eight books. The texts of the Sâma-veda (which contains only a few verses which are not in the Rig-veda) and of the White Yajur-veda, have also been printed. It is true that only a part of the Black Yajur-veda has yet been given to the world, but there is no reason to suppose that it contains any very large amount of matter which will throw light on the real sense of the older hymns. Besides, we already possess in print the texts of the two most important Brâhmanas, and a portion of a third, so that any aid which can be derived from them is also at our command. But even if additional materials of greater value than are ever likely to be brought to light were still inaccessible, why should not competent scholars proceed at once, with the very considerable means which they already possess, to lay the foundation of a true interpretation of the Rig-veda, leaving the mistakes which they may now commit to be corrected by their own future rcsearches, or by those of their successors, when further helps shall have become available? *Ars longa vita brevis.*

I propose in the course of this paper to show, by a selec tion of instances from the Nirukta, and from Sâyaṇa's commentary, the unsatisfactory character of the assistance which those works afford for explaining many of the most difficult

[1] See Müller's Rig-veda, vol. i., p. 4, lines 21ff.

passages of the hymns, and the consequent necessity which exists that all the other available resources of philology should be called into requisition to supply their deficiencies. But before proceeding to this part of my task, I wish to allow the representatives of the different schools of Vedic interpretation to state their own opinions on the subject under consideration.

Professor Wilson professes to have based his translation of the hymns of the Rig-veda on the commentary of Sâyaṇa Acharya, who lived in the fourteenth century of the Christian era, and on whose work he remarks that—

"Although the interpretation of Sâyaṇa may be occasionally questioned, he undoubtedly had a knowledge of his text far beyond the pretensions of any European scholar, and must have been in possession, either through his own learning or that of his assistants, of all the interpretations which had been perpetuated by traditional teaching from the earliest times."—Introduction to Translation of Rig-veda Sanhitâ (published in 1850), vol. i., p. xlix.

And in a note to his translation of the 10th hymn of the 1st Book (vol. i., p. 25) he observes, on certain proposed renderings of Prof. Roth and M. Langlois, that "Sâyaṇa, no doubt, knew much better than either of the European interpreters what the expression intended." In the introduction to his second vol., p. xix. (published in 1854), Prof. Wilson returns to the subject, and remarks, among other things, as follows:—

"With respect to unusual words, there are no doubt a great number employed in the Veda, and it is possible that the lexicographic significations given by the commentators may be sometimes questionable, sometimes contradictory; but from what other authority can a satisfactory interpretation be derived? It has been supposed that a careful collation of all the passages in which such words occur might lead to a consistent and indisputable interpretation; but this assumes that they have always been employed with precision and uniformity by the original authors, a conclusion that would scarcely be tenable even if the author were one individual, and utterly untenable when, as is the case with the Sûktas, the authors are indefinitely numerous: it is very improbable, therefore, that even such collation would remove all perplexity on this account, although it might occasionally do so; at any rate such a concordance has still to be established, and until it is effected we may be satisfied with the interpretation given us by the most distinguished native scholars, availing themselves of all the Vaidik learning that had preceded them," etc. etc.

Again in p. xxii. he says:—

"The more unmanageable difficulties are those which are utterly insuperable except by guess: they are not the perplexities of commission, but of omission: not the words or phrases that are given, but those that are left out: the constant recurrence of the abuse of ellipsis and metonymy, requiring not only words, but sometimes sentences, to be supplied by comment or conjecture, before any definite meaning can be given to the expressions that occur. . . . . . It may not always require extraordinary ingenuity to hit upon what is intended by such elliptical expressions from correlative terms or context; but such a mode of interpretation by European scholars, whose ordinary train of thinking runs in a very different channel from that of Indian scholarship, can scarcely claim equal authority with the latter," etc.

In regard to one of these elliptical texts, Prof. Wilson expresses himself very unhesitatingly when he says (p. xxiii.):

"The original author alone could say with confidence that he meant '*rivers*,' which thenceforward became the traditional and admitted explanation, and is, accordingly, so supplied by the scholiast."

In the following passage (p. xxv.), however, Prof. Wilson admits that it is doubtful whether these explanations had always actually come down from the age of the authors of the hymns:—

"How far his" (*i.e.* the author's) "lecture and amplification may have been preserved uncorrupted through successive generations, until they reached Yâska, and eventually Sâyaṇa, may be reasonably liable to question; but that the explanations of these scholiasts were not arbitrary, but were such as had been established by the practice of preceding schools, and were generally current at their several eras, can admit of no doubt. Even if it were not so, their undeniable learning and their sympathy with the views and feelings of their countrymen, amongst whom were the original authors and expounders of the Sûktas, must give a weight to their authority which no European scholar, however profound his knowledge of Sanskrit or of the Vedas, can, in my opinion, be entitled to claim."

The following is Prof. Rudolph Roth's explanation of the system which he has pursued in the interpretation of Vedic words in the great Sanskrit and German Lexicon published by himself and Dr. Boehtlingk. I translate from the preface to the first vol. of the Lexicon published in 1855 :

"As the aids furnished to us by recent authors for the understanding of the Vedic texts are but scanty, we are the more dependent on the contributions made to their interpretation by Indian scholarship itself, *i.e.*, on the commentaries. And, in fact, so far as regards one of the branches of Vedic literature, the treatises on theology and worship, we can desire no better guides than these commentators, so exact in all respects, who follow their texts word by word, who, so long as even the semblance of a misconception might arise, are never weary of repeating what they have frequently said before, and who often appear as if they had been writing for us foreigners rather than for their own priestly alumni who had grown up in the midst of these conceptions and impressions. Here, where their task is to explain the widely-ramified, ingenious, and often far-fetched symbolism of their ceremonial, to elucidate the numberless minutiæ on the observance of which in religious worship, eternal salvation or perdition depends, they are on their proper ground. For in the Brâhmaṇas there breathes the same spirit which works downward through the whole course of orthodox Indian theology, and in particular has pervaded those Brahmanical schools which some centuries ago were so zealously engaged in investigating and explaining the most prominent treatises of their ancient theological literature.

"The case, however, is quite different when the same men assume the task of interpreting the ancient collections of hymns. These texts are not the creations of theological speculation, nor have they sprung out of the soil of that rigidly prescribed, minute, liturgical ceremonial to which we have alluded, but they are for the most part productions of the oldest religious-lyrical poetry, the artistic cultivation of which was as little confined to particular families or castes as was the offering of daily sacrifice and prayer: in them a world of deities lives, and a worship is mirrored, which are essentially distinct from the system taught in the Brâhmaṇas; they speak a language divided from that of the Brâhmanas (which scarcely differs from the so-called classical Sanskrit) by a chasm as wide as that which separates the Latin of the Salic hymns from that of M. Terentius Varro. Here, therefore, there were required not only quite different qualifications for interpretation, but also a freedom of judgment and a greater breadth of view and of historical intuitions. Freedom of judgment, however, was wanting to priestly learning among all the nations of heathen antiquity, whilst in India no one has ever had any conception of historical development.

"Thus the very qualities which have made those commentators excellent guides to an understanding of the theological treatises, render them unsuitable conductors on that far older and quite differently circumstanced domain. As the so-called classical Sanskrit was perfectly familiar to them, they sought its ordinary idiom in the Vedic hymns also. Since any difference in the ritual appeared to them inconceivable, and the present forms were believed to have existed from the beginning of the world, they fancied that the patriarchs of the Indian religion must have sacrificed in the very same manner. As the recognized mythological and cosmical systems of their own age appeared to them unassailable and revealed verities, they must necessarily (so the commentators thought) be discoverable in that centre-point of revelation, the hymns of the ancient Rishis, who had, indeed, lived in familiar intercourse with the gods, and possessed far higher wisdom than the succeeding generations.

"It is unnecessary to enlarge on this state of things, or to illustrate it by examples.[1] Nor will it be expected that we should here indicate at length the very considerable advantage which is derivable from the works of these interpreters, in spite of all their imperfections. The whole state of the case is neither difficult to recognise, nor singular in its kind. The sacred books of the ancient nations were, as a general rule, explained in the same manner by later generations according to the prevailing systems of theology and the higher or lower state of science; and in every case this interpretation was given out as being a tradition, that is, it claimed for itself an antiquity and a dignity of which it could not always boast with truth. Besides, to give an example, it has never occurred to any one to make our understanding of the Hebrew books of the Old Testament depend on the Talmud and the Rabbins, while there are

1 [Though Prof. Róth does not consider it necessary to give instances in proof of his assertions, I may allude to the way in which Sâyaṇa considers the dwarf-incarnation of Vishṇu to be referred to in R.V. i. 22 16 ff., and identifies the Rudra of the hymns with the husband of Pârvatî; see his note on R.V. i. 114, 6; and Sanskrit Texts, iv. 57 and 257. Yâska, however, and the older authors referred to by him, Nir. xii. 19, seem to know, or, at least, they say, nothing of the dwarf-incarnation.—J.M.]

not wanting scholars who hold it as the duty of a conscientious interpreter of the Veda to translate in conformity with Sâyaṇa, Mahîdhara, etc. Consequently, we do not believe, like H. H. Wilson, that Sâyaṇa, for instance, understood the expressions of the Veda better than any European interpreter; but we think that a conscientious European interpreter may understand the Veda far better and more correctly than Sâyaṇa. We do not esteem it our first task to arrive at that understanding of the Veda which was current in India some centuries ago, but to search out the sense which the poets themselves have put into their hymns and utterances. Hence we are of opinion that the writings of Sâyaṇa and the other commentators do not form a rule for the interpreter, but are merely one of those helps of which the latter will avail himself for the execution of his undoubtedly difficult task, a task which is not to be accomplished at the first onset, or by any single individual. . . . . .

"We have, therefore, endeavoured to follow the path prescribed by philology, to derive from the texts themselves the sense which they contain, by a juxtaposition of all the passages which are cognate in diction or contents;—a tedious and laborious path, in which neither the commentators nor the translators have preceded us. The double duty of exegete and lexicographer has thus devolved upon us. A simply etymological procedure, practised as it must be by those who seek to divine the sense of a word from the sole consideration of the passage before them, without regard to the ten or twenty other passages in which it recurs, cannot possibly lead to a correct result. Such a procedure, even if practised in conformity with philological principles, moves in far too wide logical circles to admit of its always hitting the right point, and gives rise to conceptions which are far too general and colourless, which, perhaps, indeed, include within them the firmly defined and sharply stamped meaning which the word contains, but fail to reproduce it in its peculiarity, and therefore in its power and beauty.

"Of this nature is the procedure which the commentators have adopted, and whereby they clearly demonstrate that they have not simultaneously mastered the entire vocabulary of these books, and at the same time that they have not handled the individual passages according to any fixed traditional interpretation. Hence it happens that they have assigned to a large number of nouns in the Veda the sense of *power*, *sacrifice*, *food*, *wisdom*, etc., and to many verbs, that of *going*,[1] *moving*, etc., when all these words are distinct from one

[1] [The Nighaṇṭu ii., 14, contains no less than 122 verbs, to which the sense of *going* is assigned.—J.M.]

another, have a definite value and a clear significance of their own, and in many cases have scarcely the most distant connection with those general conceptions. And it is only by the reinstatement of these misapprehended words in their lost rights that the Veda acquires a striking meaning, force, and richness of expression, and gives us an entirely different image of the world of thought in the earliest antiquity.

"No one who knows the difficulties of such an occupation will refuse us indulgence for our undoubtedly numerous mistakes, mistakes which, in the progress of the work, will become first and most distinctly manifest to ourselves."

I have considered it proper to give this long extract from the preface to the St. Petersburg Lexicon, as though Prof. Roth is by no means the sole representative of the school of interpretation which he here defends, he has, by the compilation of the large portion of his Dictionary which has already appeared, done far more than any other Sanskritist has yet accomplished to carry his principles into practice.

Before adverting to the criticism which this passage has received from Prof. Goldstücker, I shall make a short quotation from Prof. Max Müller's preface to the 3rd vol. of his Rig-veda, which must be understood as laying down principles of interpretation similar to those which are advocated by Roth. After remarking that "the conviction seems to be growing more and more general, that without this (Sâyaṇa's) Commentary an accurate and scholarlike knowledge of the Veda could never have been obtained;" Müller goes on to say:—

"It would have been equally wrong, however, to consider Sâyaṇa's commentary as an infallible authority with regard to the interpretation of the Veda. Sâyaṇa gives the traditional, but not the original, sense of the Vaidik hymns. . . . If, therefore, we wish to know how the Brahmans, from the time of the composition of the first Brâhmaṇa to the present day, understood and interpreted the hymns of their ancient Rishis, we ought to translate them in strict accordance with Sâyaṇa's gloss. . . . . Nor could it be said that the tradition of the Brahmans, which Sâyaṇa embodied in his work, after the lapse of at least three thousand years, had changed the whole character of the Rig-veda. By far the greater part of these hymns is so simple and straightforward, that there can be no doubt that their original meaning was exactly the same as their traditional interpretation. But no religion, no poetry, no law, no language can resist the tear and wear of thirty centuries; and in the Veda, as in other works, handed down to us from a very remote antiquity, the sharp edges of primitive thought, the delicate features of a young language, the fresh hue of unconscious poetry, have been washed away by the successive waves of what we call *tradition*, whether we look upon it as a principle of growth or decay. To restore the primitive outlines of the Vaidik period of thought will be a work of great difficulty." pp. vii., f. He then goes on to quote a passage from a previous essay of his own, in which, after laying it down as a rule that, "not a corner of the Brâhmaṇas, the Sûtras, Yâska, and Sâyaṇa should be left unexplored before we venture to propose a rendering of our own," he, a little further on, proceeds thus: "To make such misunderstandings" (as are found in the Brâhmaṇas) "possible, we must assume a considerable interval between the composition of the hymns and the Brâhmaṇas. As the authors of the Brâhmaṇas were blinded by theology, the authors of the still later Niruktas were deceived by etymological fictions, and both conspired to mislead by their authority later and more sensible commentators, such as Sâyaṇa. Where Sâyaṇa has no authority to mislead him, his Commentary is at all events rational; but still his scholastic notions would never allow him to accept the free interpretation which a comparative study of these venerable documents forces upon the unprejudiced scholar. We must therefore discover ourselves the real vestiges of these ancient poets," etc.

I now come to Prof. Goldstücker's strictures (Pâṇini, pp. 241 ff.) on the principles of Vedic interpretation laid down by Prof. Roth. He thus expresses his opinion of the value, and of the method, of the Indian commentators:—

"Without the vast information these commentators have disclosed to us,—without their method of explaining the obscurest texts,—in one word, without their scholarship, we should still stand at the outer doors of Hindu antiquity. . . . The whole religious life of ancient India is based on tradition. . . . Tradition tells us, through the voice of the commentators, who re-echo the voice of their ancestors, how the nation, from immemorial times, understood the sacred texts, what inferences they drew from them, what influence they allowed them to exercise on their religious, philosophical, ethical,—in a word, on their national, development. . . . But it would be utterly erroneous to assume that a scholar like Sâyaṇa, or even a copy of him, like Mahîdhara, contented himself with being the mouthpiece of his predecessors or ancestors. They not only record the sense of the Vaidik texts and the sense of the words of which these texts consist, but they endeavour to show that the interpretations which they give are *consistent with the grammatical requirements of the language itself.*"

Prof. Goldstücker then quotes (pp. 245 f.) a portion of the remarks of Prof. Roth which I have cited above, and proceeds to controvert a statement, which he ascribes to that scholar, that Sâyaṇa and the other commentators give us "only that sense of the Veda which was current in India some centuries ago:"—

"A bolder statement," writes Prof. Goldstücker (p. 248), "I defy any scholar to have met with in any book. Sâyana incessantly refers to Yâska. All his explanations show that he stands on the ground of the *oldest legends and traditions*,—of such traditions, moreover, as have no connection whatever with the creeds of those sects which represent the degenerated Hindu faith of his time."

Prof. Goldstücker then goes on (pp. 248 ff.) to argue that Prof. Roth, from imperfect acquaintance with the labours of the Indian commentators, is not entitled to depreciate their qualifications for the correct interpretation of the Veda, or to assert the superior fitness of European scholars for this task; rejects as absurd the idea of the former not being able, as well as the latter, to bring together and compare all the passages in which particular words occur; maintains that in the case of those words which occur but once in the Veda, and in regard to which, therefore, no comparison with other passages is possible, the guesses of Sâyaṇa are as good as those of his critic; reiterates his opinion that Sâyaṇa's method of procedure was not purely etymological, but involved a reference to tradition; and ridicules the assertion that a European scholar can understand the Veda more correctly than Sâyaṇa, or arrive more nearly at the meaning which the Rishis gave to their own hymns.

With reference to the strictures of Prof. Goldstücker on the assertion which he attributes to Prof. Roth, that Sâyaṇa and the other later commentators give "*only* that sense of the Veda which was current in India some centuries ago,"

I would remark that I find nothing in the passage quoted by Prof. Goldstücker, and by myself, from Roth, to show that the latter scholar, although he refuses to be bound by the interpretations of the mediæval scholiasts, and may regard these interpretations as having been in great part initiated by those scholiasts themselves, is therefore disposed to deny that they may in part have been founded on older materials handed down by former generations. Because a body of interpretation is spoken of as *existing* at a particular date, it does not follow that no part of it is admitted to have had an earlier origin. In fact, Prof. Roth cannot for a moment be imagined to have ignored the assistance which Sâyaṇa had derived from the older work of Yâska, the Nirukta, a book of which he himself had, only three years before the preface to his Dictionary was written, published an edition. From the concluding pages of that work (which appeared in 1852), I translate the following additional observations on the Indian commentators, which shew that in Roth's opinion Yâska, though much more ancient, and otherwise more advantageously situated, than Sâyaṇa, stood yet essentially on the same footing with the latter, being rather a learned exegete, working, in all cases of difficulty, by an etymological process, than the depositary of any certain interpretation of the hymns handed down by tradition from the period when they were intelligible to every one who recited them:—

"In regard to the point how much or how little the Indian commentators from Yâska downwards contribute to the understanding of the Veda, a more correct judgment than that hitherto current will be formed as soon as some of them shall have become completely known. The interpretation of the Veda can lay upon itself no heavier fetters than by believing in the infallibility of these guides, or in the existence of a valuable tradition supposed to have been enjoyed by them. A superficial observation has already shown that their mode of interpretation is simply the reverse of a traditional one, that it is in fact a grammatical and etymological one, which has only so much in common with the traditional method, that it explains each verse, each line, each word by itself, without enquiring how far the results so obtained agree with those derived from other quarters.

"If any person is disposed to find tradition in the fact that the commentators coincide in having in their minds one tolerably simple scheme of conception, *e.g.*, in regard to the functions of a particular god, or even in regard to the entire contents of the hymns, which they unceasingly force into the texts, he may indeed call that tradition, but he will at the same time admit that this poverty of intuition is nothing which we should very much covet. This scheme embraces the scholastic conceptions, which had become fixed at an early period, but yet not before the date when the Vedic hymns had already become the object of a purely learned study, and when the religious ideas and social circumstances on which they are based had for a long time lost their vitality. In spite of all the irregularities of their imaginative faculty, the Indians have at all times had a longing for arrangement, classification, systematizing, and have through these, in themselves praiseworthy, tendencies very frequently given rise to the greatest confusion. The Vedic literature, too, affords numerous proofs of this.

"The same remarks apply, in all essential points, to Yâska, as to Sâyaṇa, or any other of the later writers. Yâska, too, is a learned interpreter, who works with the materials which science had collected before his age; but he has a prodigious advantage in point of time before those compilers of detailed, continuous commentaries, and belongs to a quite different literary period, when Sanskrit still existed in a process of natural growth. And his work gains for us a greater importance from the fact that it is indeed the only one of its kind which has been preserved. Even those commentators who lived five centuries and more before us know of no other comparable to it in rank and antiquity, and are consequently unwearied in their appeals to Yâska's authority. The half of the Nirukta might be restored out of Sâyaṇa's Commentary on the Rig-veda."

Prof. Roth then goes on to give some account of the different schools of interpretation, as well as the names of individual teachers, anterior to Yâska (pp. 220 ff.).

I will add here the opinion of one other eminent scholar, Prof. Benfey, on the points at issue between Profs. Roth and Goldstücker. I quote at second hand from the Gött. Gel. Anz. 1858, p. 1608 f., as extracted by Prof. Weber at the end of his reply to Prof. Goldstücker's Pâṇini, in the Indische Studien, v. 174 f.:—

"Every one who has carefully studied the Indian interpretations is aware that absolutely no continuous tradition, extending from the composition of the Vedas to their explanation by Indian scholars, can be assumed; that, on the contrary, between the genuine poetic remains of Vedic antiquity and their interpretations a long-continued break in tradition must have intervened, out of which at most the comprehension of some particulars may have been rescued and handed down to later times by means of liturgical usages and words, formulæ, and perhaps, also, poems connected therewith. Besides these remains of tradition, which must be estimated as very scanty, the interpreters of the Veda had, in the main, scarcely any other helps than those which, for the most part, are still at our command, the usage of the classical speech, and the grammatical and etymological-lexicographical investigation of words. At the utmost, they found some aid in materials preserved in local dialects; but this advantage is almost entirely outweighed by the comparison which we are able to institute with the Zend, and that which we can make (though here we must of course proceed with caution and prudence) with the other languages cognate to the Sanskrit,—a comparison which has already supplied so many helps to a clearer understanding of the Vedas. But quite irrespectively of all particular aids, the Indian method of interpretation becomes in its whole essence an entirely false one, owing to the prejudice with which it chooses to conceive the ancient circumstances and ideas which have become quite strange to it, from its own religious stand-point, so many centuries more recent; whilst, on the other hand, an advantage for the comprehension of the whole is secured to us by the acquaintance (drawn from analogous relations) with the life, the conceptions, the wants, of ancient peoples and popular songs, which we possess,—an advantage which, even if the Indians owed more details than they actually do owe, to tradition, would not be eclipsed by their interpretation."

It appears, therefore, that the views of Prof. Roth, in regard to the proper principles of Vedic interpretation, are shared by Professors Müller, Weber, and Benfey; whilst even my learned friend, Prof. Goldstücker himself, cannot be altogether acquitted (as I shall hereafter show) of a certain heretical tendency to deviate in practice from the interpretations of Sâyaṇa,—a tendency which may, perhaps, as his Dictionary advances, become by and by developed into a more pronounced heterodoxy.

I now proceed to inquire, in some detail, whether any considerable traces exist in ancient Indian literature of a tradition of the sense of the Vedic hymns handed continuously down from the earliest period. If any such traces are extant, they must be found primarily in the Brâhmaṇas, or the Âraṇyakas, or in Yâska. Do these works then contain any interpretations, at once positive and satisfactory, of any considerable portion of the hymns? I begin with the oldest works,—the Brâhmaṇas. In a quotation which I have made above from Prof. Max Müller, he states his opinion that "we must assume a considerable interval between the composition of the hymns and the Brâhmaṇas." There is no doubt that this is true. The language and the contents of these two classes of works are alike widely different. Referring to the same author's "History of Ancient Indian Literature" for a complete account of the Brâhmaṇas, I will merely quote from it a few sentences, to show how little in his estimation these books are likely to aid us in understanding the hymns:—

"There is throughout the Brâhmaṇas," he writes, p. 432, "such a complete misunderstanding of the original intention of the Vedic hymns, that we can hardly understand how such an estrangement could have taken place, unless there had been at some time or other a sudden and violent break in the chain of tradition. The authors of the Brâhmaṇas evidently imagined that those ancient hymns were written simply for the sake of their sacrifices, and whatever interpretation they thought fit to assign to those acts, the same, they supposed, had to be borne out by the hymns. This idea has vitiated the whole system of Indian exegesis. . . . . . Not only was the true nature of the gods, as conceived by the early poets, completely lost sight of, but new gods were actually created out of words which were never intended to be names of divine beings."

Müller goes on, p. 433, to illustrate this by referring to the fact that a god, Ka (Who), was invented out of certain interrogative verses of the Rig-veda in which the worshipper asks to *whom* he shall address his worship. Thus, for example, the Ṣatapatha Brâhmaṇa, vii. 4, 1, 19, after quoting the first verse of R.V. x. 121, ending with "to what god shall we offer our oblation?" says, "Ka (Who) is Prajâpati; to him let us offer our oblation."[1] Müller then refers to the taste-

[1] Compare "Sanskrit Texts," iv. 13, note.

less explanation given in a Brâhmaṇa of the epithet "golden-handed" applied to the Sun in the hymns, that the Sun had lost his hand, and had got instead one of gold.[1] The Ṣatapatha Brâhmaṇa, xiii. 6, 1, 2, understands, very improbably, the Virâj alluded to in Rig-veda, x. 90, 5 ("From him (Purusha) was born Virâj, and from Virâj, Purusha"), to be the metre of that name, and declares that Purusha, the sacrifice, was begotten by Purusha on Virâj. Again, Rig-veda, x. 61, 7, which apparently refers in a figurative manner to some atmospheric phenomenon, is explained in Ṣatapatha Brâhmaṇa, i. 7, 4, 1, as referring to a legend about Prajâpati having literally had sexual intercourse with his own daughter, so as to occasion scandal and indignation among the gods. The same Brâhmaṇa contains (xi. 5, 1, 1 ff.) the legend of Purûravas and Urvaṣî, in the course of which five verses of the 95th hymn of the 10th book of the R.V. are introduced as part of the conversation which passed between the hero and the nymph, but it does not give any detailed explanation of these verses, and it does not quote at all the verses which make up the rest of the hymn, and which are generally far more difficult to interpret. Again, in the Aitareya Brâhmaṇa vii. 13-18, where the story of Ṣunaḥṣepa is told, a large number of verses, composing the 24th to the 30th hymns of the first book of the R.V., and a few from the fourth and fifth books, are referred to as having been uttered by the hero of the legend, but are not even quoted at length, much less explained. (See Dr. Haug's Ait. Br., vol. ii. pp. 466 ff.) There is indeed in Ait. Br. viii. 26 (see Haug, vol. ii. pp. 530 ff.) an interpretation given of three verses of R.V. iv. 50 (vv. 7-9), but this, whatever its value otherwise may be, is but an inconsiderable contribution to the exposition of the hymns. Ṣ. P. Br. x. 5, 3, 1, contains a paraphrase of R.V. x. 129, 1, which is not without value. (See my former article on the "Progress of the Vedic Religion," p. 346 f.) Some explanation of R.V. i. 25, 10, also is given in Ṣ. P. Br. v. 4, 4, 5. But as far as I have looked into the Brâhmaṇas,

[1] See "Contributions to a Knowledge of Vedic Theogony," etc. in this Journal, for 1864, p. 116, note.

I have seen but very little which can be of much service in throwing light on the original sense of the hymns.

I observe, indeed, that Professor Müller thus expresses himself (Anc. Sansk. Lit., p. 153) in regard to the use which he thinks may be made of the Brâhmaṇas, etc., for the purpose referred to:—

"For explanations of old Vedic words, for etymologies and synonymous expressions, the Brâhmaṇas contain very rich materials. . . . . Whole verses and hymns are shortly explained there; and the Âraṇyakas and Upanishads, if included, would furnish richer sources for Vedic etymologies than even the Nirukta itself. The beginning of the Aitareya Âraṇyaka is in fact a commentary on the beginning of the Rig-veda; and if all the passages of the Brâhmaṇas were collected where one word is explained by another with which it is joined merely by the particle *vai*,[1] they would even now give a rich harvest for a new Nirukta."

This passage, however, must be taken in connection with those which have been quoted above from the same writer. I am unable to refer to the Aitareya Âraṇyaka to which he alludes. But judging from the views which he has expressed elsewhere, I conclude that he does not expect, as the result of the researches which he recommends (even if pushed to the utmost extent) into all the existing remains of Indian literature exterior to the hymns themselves, any very extensive or material assistance towards the restoration of the original sense of the latter. But whatever might be the issue of the course of investigation thus suggested, it is at least presupposed in Prof. Müller's recommendation that this process of carefully searching the Brâhmaṇas and Âraṇyakas for interpretations of obsolete Vedic words and phrases has not yet been pursued to a sufficient extent by any of the Indian etymologists or commentators. But if this be true—if any considerable amount of important materials suitable to their purpose has been neglected by Yâska or Sâyaṇa—it is clear that we cannot look to either of those writers as our final or sufficient authority.

[1] [As, for instance, in the cases *viṣo vai pastyáḥ* (Ṣ. P. Br. v. 4, 4, 5) *Prajâpatir vai Kaḥ*, Ṣ. P. Br. vii. 4, 1, 19.—J.M].

I now come to the Nighaṇṭus, and the Nirukta of Yâska. The Nighaṇṭus[1] form a vocabulary of terms, many of which are obsolete. The first three sections are almost entirely made up of lists of so-called synonymes, varying in number from two to one hundred and twenty-two, of nouns or verbs of well-known signification, such as *pṛthivî*, "earth," *hiraṇya*, "gold," *antariksha*, "atmosphere," *jval*, "to burn," *gam*, "to go." The remaining two sections consist of mere lists of words of different significations, which are left unexplained. There does not seem to be any reason to doubt that in the first three sections of this work the general sense of many obsolete words has been preserved by tradition; though as the terms declared to be synonymous are often very numerous, it is clear from the nature of the case, as Prof. Roth observes (see above), that the specific sense, and particular shade of meaning, represented by each, must be often left in the dark. And an examination of the lists puts this beyond a doubt. Thus under the synonymes of *vâch*, "speech," we find such words as *ṣloka*, *nivid*, *ṛk*, *gâthâ*, *anushṭup*, words denoting different kinds of verses or compositions, which can never have been employed as simple equivalents of speech in the abstract. The value of these lists therefore for the purpose of defining the precise signification of words is very limited. And even if the first three sections were of more value than they are in this respect, they are far from embracing the whole of the difficult words in the Veda. The fourth section contains two hundred and seventy-eight words which are not explained at all, though there are, no doubt, a good many among them which do not require any explanation, as their sense is notorious. The Nirukta of Yâska is a sort of commentary on the Nighaṇṭus. It begins with these words: "A record has been composed, which we have to explain. It is called the Nighaṇṭus." The introduction to the work (i. 1—ii. 4) contains the outlines of a grammatical system, and an ex-

[1] Prof. Roth considers this vocabulary to be older than Yâska. (Introduction to Nirukta, p. xii. f.). Müller, too, (Anc. Ind. Lit. 154), says, "probably these lists existed in his family long before his time."

planation of the advantages, objects, principles and methods of exegesis. This is followed (ii. 5—iii. 22) by remarks suggested by the lists of explained synonymes composing the first three sections of the Nighaṇṭus. In the succeeding chapters (iv.—vi.) of the Nirukta, the unexplained terms in the fourth section of the Nighaṇṭus are interpreted; whilst in the last six books the list of words, chiefly names of deities, contained in the fifth section of the Nighaṇṭus, is elucidated.[1] The thirteenth and fourteenth chapters, styled Nirukta-pariṣishṭa, appear to be the work of a later writer.

The Nirukta makes frequent reference to the Brâhmaṇas, adduces various legends, such as those about Devâpi (xi. 10) and Viṣvâmitra (ii. 24), and also alludes to various schools of Vedic interpretation which existed anterior to the time of its author, such as the Nairuktas or etymologists, the Aitihâsikas or legendary writers, and the Yâjnikas or ritualists.[2] In the course of his work, Yâska supplies some specimens of the mode of explaining the hymns adopted by these different classes of expositors, from which it would appear that each school interpreted from its own special point of view, and according to its own literary, moral, or professional tendencies and prepossessions. Thus we are told (Nirukta, xi. 29 and 31) that the Nairuktas understood Anumati, Râkâ, Sinîvâlî, and Kuhû to be goddesses, while the Yâjnikas took them for the new and full moons. On one point the greatest diversity of opinion prevailed. The gods called Aṣvins were a great enigma. The Nirukta (xii. 1) gives the following answers to the question who they were: "'Heaven and Earth,' say some; 'Day and Night,' say others; 'the Sun and Moon,' say others; 'two kings, performers of the holy acts,' say the Aitihâsikas."[3] In his explanation of R.V. i. 164, 32, Yâska

[1] See all this more fully stated in Roth's Illustrations of the Nirukta, p. 3.

[2] See Roth's Illustrations of the Nirukta, pp. 220 ff.

[3] Sâyaṇa also mentions some of these different schools of interpreters in different parts of his commentary. Thus on R.V. i. 64, 8, he says: *Pṛshatyaḥ*, the Maruts' instruments of conveyance, are does marked with white spots according to the Aitihâsikas, and a line of variously coloured clouds according to the Nairuktas." Again, he tells us that writers of the former class understood R.V. i. 174, 2, of the cities belonging to Vṛttra's Asuras, whilst those of the latter class

(ii. 8) refers to the Parivrâjakas (ascetic mendicants) as attributing one sense to the close of that verse, while the Nairuktas assigned a different one.[1] It is thus clear that from the earliest period there were diversities of opinion in regard to the sense of the hymns. As we come down to later times, when speculation had been further devèloped, we find some new varieties of interpretation. Thus in the Nirukta-pariṣishṭa, i. 9, the "four defined grades or stages of speech" referred to in R.V. i. 164, 45, are said to be diversely explained, "by the Rishis as meaning the four mystic words *om, bhûḥ, bhuvaḥ, svar;* by the grammarians as denoting nouns, verbs, prepositions, and particles; by the ritualists as referring to the hymns, the liturgical precepts, the Brâhmaṇas, and the ordinary language; by the etymologists as designating the Ṛik, the Yajush, the Sâman texts, and the current language; whilst by others they are thought to signify the languages of serpents, birds, reptiles, and the vernacular; and the spiritualists (*âtmapravâdâḥ*) understand them of the modes of speech in beasts, musical instruments (?), wild animals, and soul."

Yâska gives also the names of no less than seventeen interpreters who had preceded him,[2] and whose explanations of the Veda are often conflicting. Thus we are informed (Nir. iii. 8) that some understood the "five peoples" (*panchajanâḥ*) mentioned in R.V. x. 53, 4, to be the Gandharvas, Pitris, gods, Asuras, and Rakshases; whilst Aupamanyana took them for the four castes and the Nishâdas.[3] From Nir. iv. 3, it appears that while Yâska himself understood the word *ṣitâma* which occurs

understood it of the clouds. In like manner, on viii. 66, 10, he gives us two separate interpretations of that verse, the first that of the Nairuktas, who expounded it of natural phenomena, of showers brought by the sun (represented by Vishṇu), and the second that of the Aitihâsikas, who explained it mythologically in conformity with a story drawn from the Brâhmaṇa of the Charakas.

[1] The ascetics, influenced, perhaps, by their own feelings of estrangement from family life, gave to the words in question the meaning "The father of many children suffers distress." The Etymologists understood the same clause of the fructifying effects of rain.

[2] Roth, Illustrations, pp. 221 f.

[3] In Nir. iii. 15, several different derivations of the word *vidhavâ*, "widow," are given. It is said to be either = *vidhâtṛkâ*, "without a supporter;" or, according to Charmaṣiras (one of Yâska's predecessors), to come from *vidhavana* or *vidhâvana;* or to be derived from *vi* + *dhava*, "without a man."

in the Vâjasaneyi Sanhitâ, xxi. 43, of the *shoulder* of the sacrificial victim, Ṣâkapûṇi took it for the *female organ*, Taiṭîki for the *liver*, and Gâlava for the *fat*. Again, Nir. vi. 13, tells us that Aurṇabhâva understood the word *Nâsatyau* (an epithet of the Aṣvins) to mean "true, not false" (*satyau, na asatyau*; Âgrâyaṇa took it to mean "leaders of truth" *satyasya praṇetârau*); whilst Yâska himself suggests that it may signify "nose-born" *nâsikâ-prabhavau*). From Nir. vii. 23, it appears that whilst the early ritualists held the deity lauded in R.V. i. 59, 6, to be the Sun, Ṣâkapûṇi on the contrary held that it was Agni Vaiṣvânara. Further, in Nir. viii. 2, we are informed that Kraushṭuki held Draviṇodas to mean Indra, but Ṣâkapûṇi considered the term to denote Agni. Kâtthakya was of opinion that the word *idhma* signified merely the wood employed in sacrifice, while Ṣâkapûṇi thought it stood for Agni (Nir. viii. 4, 5). So, again, Kâtthakya understood Narâṣansa to designate "sacrifice," but Ṣâkapûṇi took it for a name of Agni (*ibid.* 6); Kâtthakya explained the "divine doors" (R.V. x. 110, 5), of the house-doors at sacrifice, but Ṣâkapûṇi took them to stand for Agni (*ibid.* 10); the former interpreter held Vanaspati to be the sacrificial post, but Ṣâkapûṇi asserted that it was a name of Agni (*ibid.* 17). In like manner, Yâska's predecessors were not agreed as to what was meant by Vishṇu's three steps mentioned in R.V. i. 22, 17, Ṣâkapûṇi maintaining that they were planted on the earth, the atmosphere, and the sky respectively; and Aurṇabhâva that it was the hill over which the sun rises, the meridian, and the hill where he sets, that were the localities referred to. Finally, the etymologists declared that the word *Sâdhyas* in R.V. x. 90, 16, denoted the gods residing in the sky, whilst according to a legend (*âkhyâna*) it represented a former age of the gods (*pûrvaṃ deva-yugam*: comp. R.V. x. 72, 2, 3).

There was one of Yâska's predecessors who had actually the audacity to assert that the science of Vedic exposition was useless, as the Vedic hymns and formulæ were obscure, unmeaning, or mutually contradictory. As instances of obscurity, he cites the texts in which the words *amyak* (R.V.

i. 169, 3), *yâdṛṣmin* (R.V. v. 44, 8), *jârayâyi* (R.V. vi. 12, 4), and *kâṇukâ* (R.V. viii. 66, 4), occur. In regard to this charge of obscurity, Yâska replies that it is not the fault of the post that the blind man does not see it; it is the man's fault.[1] It would appear from the objections of this rationalist, that in his day many learned men had great difficulties in regard to the sense of different passages of the hymns. It is true indeed that Durgâchârya, the commentator on the Nirukta, seems to consider Kautsa a mere man of straw, into whose mouth these objections are dramatically put for the sake of their being refuted;[2] but I do not see why Kautsa should be regarded as a fictitious personage any more than any of the other predecessors of Yâska who are named in the Nirukta. And even if he were admitted to be so, it may be assumed as certain that Yâska, an orthodox believer, would never have alluded to sceptical doubts of this description unless they had been previously started by some of his predecessors, and had been commonly current in his time. We shall see further on how he succeeds in the attempt he makes to explain some of the texts which Kautsa charges with obscurity.

The question how far Yâska can be regarded as the depositary of a real and satisfactory Vedic tradition has been thus already, in part, answered, and in an unfavourable sense, by the account I have given of the differences of opinion existing among his predecessors. I now proceed to enquire further how far his own language and method of interpretation show him to have been walking in the clear light of day, or groping in the dark, and merely guessing at the sense of the hymns.

It is extremely unlikely that, with all the appliances which it appears he had at his command in the works of his predecessors, which he quotes, and probably others besides, Yâska should not have been able to determine the sense of many words which later scholars like Sâyaṇa had no means of dis-

[1] See Nirukta, i. 15 f.; Roth's Illustrations, pp. 11 f.; and "Sanskrit Texts," ii. 181 ff.
[2] "Sanskrit Texts," ii. 184.

covering. According to Prof. Max Müller,[1] Yâska lived in the fourth century before our era. Prof. Goldstücker holds that he was anterior to Pâṇini, whose date he considers to be involved in impenetrable obscurity, and yet, he thinks, must have been anterior to that of Buddha, whose death again he speaks of as the remotest date of Hindu antiquity which can be called a real date,[2] agreeing apparently with Lassen in placing it in 543 B.C.,[3] whilst Müller refers it to 477 B.C. Yâska was thus some two thousand years older than Sâyaṇa. We may therefore often assume, that when he affirms positively that a word unknown to later Sanskrit has such and such a meaning, even though he attaches to it an etymology, and when the sense suits the passage, he had grounds for his assertion. Thus, when he says (iv. 15) that *tugvan* means a "ford," or (v. 22) *ṣvaghnin*, a "gambler," or (vi. 26) that *bekanâṭa* signifies a "usurer," there is no reason to dispute his affirmation. But whenever he seems to draw the meaning from the etymology, and his interpretation does not yield a good sense, we must doubt whether his opinion rested on any trustworthy tradition. And again, when he gives two or more alternative or optional explanations of the same word, all apparently founded on mere etymology, we are justified in supposing that he had no earlier authority for his guide, and that his renderings are simply conjectural. Many instances, I believe, can be given where the phenomenon last described occurs; and I shall proceed to bring forward some specimens. There are also cases in which Yâska is positive as to the meaning he assigns, but in which the sense of the passage, or a collation of other texts, justifies us in departing from his rendering. In all these passages I shall at the same time give the interpretation proposed by Sâyaṇa, if it be within my reach. And as it will sometimes be found that Sâyaṇa departs from Yâska, we shall, in such instances, either have to conclude that the older interpreter is wrong—in which event ancient tradition must in that particular instance

[1] "Last Results of Sanskrit Researches" in "Bunsen's Christianity and Mankind," vol. iii. p. 137.

[2] Pâṇini, pp. 225, 227.

[3] *Ibid*, pp. 231, 233.

be of no value—or that Sâyaṇa does not there follow tradition at all. In such cases either the value of the supposed tradition, or its faithful reproduction by the later commentator, will be disproved.

The following are specimens of these different cases, together with some instances of words which do not occur in the Nirukta, but in which Sâyaṇa gives a variety of inconsistent explanations:—

1. *Atharyu* is an epithet of Agni. Yâska (v. 10) renders it by *atanavantam*, "going" or "moving." Sâyaṇa, in R.V. vii. 1, 1, explains it by *âgamyam atanavantaṃ vâ, i.e.*, either "to be gone to, approached," or "going," "moving."[1] It thus appears that he does not implicitly follow Yâska, and was not sure of the sense. Prof. Goldstücker, *s.v.*, renders it "moving constantly." Prof. Roth, *s.v.*, thinks it means "having sharp points like a lance."

2. *Anânuda* is an adjective not found in the Nirukta, but in different passages of the R.V. On i. 53, 8, Sâyaṇa explains it as *anuchara-rahitaḥ*, "without followers;" on ii. 21, 4, and ii. 23, 11, as "one after whom no other gives," *i.e.*, "unequalled in giving." On this Prof. Goldstücker remarks: "Both meanings of the word, as given according to the Comm., seem doubtful;" but he proposes no other. Roth, *s.v.*, translates it by "unyielding."

(1) *Anushvadham*, (2) *anu svadhâm*, (3) *svadhâm anu*, (4) *svadhayâ*, (5) *svadhâbhiḥ*, (6) *svadhâvat*. The first of these words occurs in various texts of the R.V., one of which, iii. 47, 1, is quoted in Nir. iv. 8, where the word is explained by *anv annam*, "after food." Prof. Goldstücker, *s.v.*, explains it thus: 1, "in consequence of (partaking of) food, through food, viz., soma, etc.; 2, food for food, to every food (as clarified butter); 3, after every oblation." The sixth word, *svadhâvat*, occurs in two places in the Nirukta, viz., in x. 6 (where R.V. vii. 46, 1, is quoted), when it is an epithet, in the dative, of Rudra; and in xii. 17 (where R.V. vi. 58, 1, is quoted), when it is an epithet, in the vocative, of Pûshan. In both places the

[1] Prof. Wilson has misunderstood the latter of the two words when he translates it, "not spreading or dispersing." See his note *in loco*.

word is rendered by *annavat*, "having food." *Anushvadham* is found in R.V. i. 81, 4; ii. 3, 11; iii. 47, 1.[1] In the first of these texts Sâyaṇa explains it to mean "during the drinking of food in the shape of soma;" in the second by "at every oblation" (*prati haviḥ*); and in the third by "followed by," or "following," the oblations (*savanîya-puroḍâśâdi-rûpeṇânnenânugatam* ...... *svadhâm anugamya varttamânam*). The words *anu svadhâm* are found separately in R.V. i. 33, 11; viii. 77, 5; and in the reverse order *svadhâm anu* in i. 6, 4, and viii. 20, 7.[2] In the first of these texts Sâyaṇa renders the words by "the waters flowed *with reference to* Indra's *food in the shape of rice*," etc. (*annaṃ vrîhy-âdi-rûpam anulakshya*); in the second (viii. 77, 5), by "*after* our *food* or *water*;" in the third (i. 6, 4), by "*with reference to the food or water* which was about to be produced;"[3] and in the fourth (viii. 20, 7), by, "with reference to food having the character of an oblation." *Svadhayâ* is found in R.V. i. 64, 4, applied to the Maruts, where it is correctly rendered by Sâyaṇa *svakîyena balena*, "by their own strength." In iv. 13, 5, too, *kayâ svadhayâ* is explained as = *kena balena*, "by what strength?" It also occurs in vii. 78, 4; ix. 71, 8; x. 27, 19; x. 88, 1; x. 129, 2. In the first of these passages the word is rendered by *annena*, "by food."[4] Surely there can be little doubt that here it means "by its own power," "spontaneously." To say, "she (Ushas) ascended her car yoked *by food*,[5] which her well-yoked horses

[1] It also occurs in ix. 72, 5; but I have no access to Sâyaṇa's Comm. on that passage.

[2] See also R.V. i. 165, 5; vii. 56, 13.

[3] Sâyaṇa here gives the following derivation of *svadhâ*, viz.: *svaṃ lokaṃ dadhâti pushṇâti iti svadhâ*. This word has three senses assigned to it in the Nighaṇṭus, viz. "water" (i. 12), "food" (ii. 7), and "heaven and earth" in the dual (iii. 30).

[4] The same general sense is assigned in i. 154, 4; v. 34, 1: vii. 47, 3. See also Sâyaṇa on i. 164. 38.

[5] I am not aware that in any passage the chariots or horses of the gods are said to be yoked by food, as denoted by any word which certainly bears that sense. The horses of Indra are, indeed, represented as being yoked by prayer (*brahma-yuj*) in R.V. i. 177, 2; iii. 35, 4; viii. 1, 24; viii. 2, 27; viii. 2, 17; and as being yoked by a hymn (*vacho-yuj*) in viii. 45, 39; but in these cases, generally, at least, the god is supposed to yoke his car in consequence of this invitation to come and partake of the oblation, or libation, and not after partaking of it. It is true that the word *brahman* (neuter) has sometimes the sense of "food" or "oblation" ascribed to it, and that in two of the above texts, viii. 1, 24, and viii. 2, 27, one of the optional senses assigned by Sâyaṇa to *brahma-yuj* is, "yoked by our oblation," two other senses, "yoked by the lord, Indra," and "yoked by our

bring hither," makes but an indifferent sense, whilst it would yield an appropriate poetical meaning to say that she ascended her car yoked "by its own inherent power." Compare R.V. iv. 26, 4, where the phrase *achakrayâ svadhayâ* is rendered by Sâyaṇa a "wheel-less car," the word *svadhâ* having here, he says, the sense of chariot (*atra svadhâ-ṣabdo ratha-vâchî*); and for proof he refers to R.V. x. 27, 19,[1] where we have the words *achakrayâ svadhayâ varttamânam*, etc., "I beheld the troop borne from afar, moving by a wheel-less *inherent power*," which is no doubt the proper rendering in iv. 26, 4, also. It is clear that *svadhâ* could not have the sense of chariot in vii. 78, 4, above cited, as it would be absurd to speak of the *car* (*ratha*) of Ushas being yoked by a *car* (*svadhâ*). Having no access to Sâyaṇa's comment on x. 27, 19, I am not aware how he translates it; but he probably adheres to the rendering given on iv. 26, 4, as it would make nonsense to say, "moving by wheel-less *food*."[2] As regards R.V. x. 129, 2, 5, I gather from Mr. Colebrooke's translation (Misc. Essays, i. 34), than even Sâyaṇa abandons the sense of food as appropriate in that hymn, since *svadhâ* is there rendered by "her who is sustained within him." It seems, however, better to render it in verse 2 by "through its inherent power," and in *v.* 5, by "a self-supporting principle." The sense, "by their own power" seems appropriate in x. 88, 1, though here too it is rendered by "food," Nir. vii. 25. *Svadhâbhiḥ* (*loc.* pl.) is explained in i. 95, 4, and i. 164, 30, by "sacrificial food;" in v. 60, 4. by "waters;" in vii. 104, 9, by "forces;" and in viii. 10, 4, by "praises which are the cause of strength." I come lastly to *svadhâvat*, which I find in R.V. v. 3, 2; vi. 58, 1; vii. 20, 1; vii. 37, 2; vii. 46, 1; vii. 86, 5, and elsewhere. In vi. 58, 1, and vii. 46, 1, as we have already seen, the word is rendered by Yâska, "having food;" and in

hymn," being proposed in the former case, and one alternative sense, "yoked by our hymn," being proposed in the latter. In i. 177, 2; iii. 35, 4; and viii. 17, 2, however, "yoked by our hymn" (*mantra*) is the only rendering given. *Vacho-yuj* in viii. 45, 39, is explained, "yoked by our hymn."

[1] This and some other instances show that Sâyaṇa did occasionally resort to parallel passages for the elucidation of the text under his consideration, but he did not carry the practice far enough.

[2] Compare *achakrebhiḥ* in R.V. v. 42, 10, and *nichakrayâ* in viii. 7, 29.

these passages (as well as in vii. 31, 7; vii. 88, 5), he is followed by Sâyaṇa, who, again, in i. 95, 4; v. 3, 2, translates it by "having sacrificial food." In vi. 21, 3; vii. 20, 1; vii. 37, 2; and vii. 86, 4, however, Sâyaṇa departs from Yàska, and from his own practice elsewhere, in rendering *svadhâvat* by *balavat* or *tejasvin*, "strong," or "vigorous." Prof. Roth has treated of *anushvadham*, etc., in his Illustrations of the Nirukta, pp. 40 f.; and in his Lexicon he translates the word in question by "willingly," "spontaneously," "gladly." In his new translation of the R.V., in the "Orient und Occident," Prof. Benfey renders *svadhâm anu*, *anu svadhâm*, and *anushvadham*, in i. 6, 4; i. 33, 11; and i. 81, 4, in a similar manner. This interpretation, in fact, will probably be found to suit nearly all, if not the whole, of the texts in which the phrase is found.

*Aprâyu* is explained in Nir. iv. 19, where R.V. i. 89, 1, is quoted, as meaning in that passage (where it is an epithet of the gods) *apramâdyantaḥ*, "not careless." Sâyaṇa, in his comment on the same text, declares it to be equivalent to *apragachhantaḥ svakîyaṃ rakshitavyam aparityajyantaḥ*, "not departing, not forsaking him whom they have to protect." (Mahîdhara, the commentator on the Vâj. S. (where this text is repeated, xxv. 14), explains the word by *anâlasâḥ*, "not sluggish.") The word occurs again in R.V. viii. 24, 18, as an epithet of sacrifices, where Sâyaṇa interprets it to mean *either* sacrifices which are conducted by men who are "not careless" (*apramâdyat*), *or* by "careful men who perform the rite remaining together, and do not go elsewhere after they have begun it." In the first passage, at least, he departs from Sâyaṇa. Prof. Goldstücker, *s.v.*, renders the word "attentive," "assiduous," adding, "according to Yâska . . .; but Sâyaṇa gives to this word in one verse the meaning, 'not going forth, not leaving' . . . .; while in another he admits also the former meaning, which seems more congenial to the context."

*Ambhriṇa* is given in Nigh. iii. 3, as one of the synonyms of *mahat*, "great." It occurs in R.V. i. 133, 5, as an epithet of *piṣâchi*, "a goblin," and is interpreted by Sâyaṇa as meaning *either* "shrieking very terribly" *or* "very huge." It is clear, therefore, that Sâyaṇa did not know by any certain tradition what the sense of the word was.

*Amyak.*—This word is found in one of the passages which Kautsa (see above) charges with obscurity, R.V. i. 169, 3; *amyak sâ te Indra ṛshṭir asme;* and I therefore think it as well to give some account of it, although it does not afford any very strong evidence in favour of any of the propositions I have undertaken to establish. Yâska, Nir. vi. 15, explains the term by *amâkteti vâ abhyakteti vâ,* meaning apparently either "arrived near," or "arrived towards." The fact of his giving an alternative etymology shows that he did not know for certain what the real derivation was, though his mind may have been made up as to the sense. Prof. Roth (Illustrations of Nir. p. 81) considers *amyak* to be the third per. aor. of *myaksh,* which, from a comparison of other passages, he believes to have the sense of "gleaming." The words would thus mean: "Thy bolt *gleamed* upon us, o Indra." Sâyaṇa, without offering any etymology, translates the clause thus: "Thy thunderbolt *comes* (*prâpnoti*) near the clouds for us, for rain to us." As both Yâska (in the passage above cited) and Sâyaṇa in his introduction to the R.V. (p. 5 of Müller's edition) had referred to and ridiculed the objection taken against the intelligibility of this verse, they were bound in honour to make it yield some sense or other; though from the obscurity of which it was cited as an instance—perhaps a proverbial instance—even so far back as the time of the former, it seems difficult to suppose that they had any certain tradition to go upon as to its meaning. Prof. Goldstücker translates the word *amyak* (see *s.v.*) "towards, near;" and adds: "This is apparently the meaning of the word in the following Rig-veda verse, where it seems to be used with the ellipsis of 'come.'" He then, after quoting the verse before us, goes on: "Yaska, who, in a discussion in his introduction, denies that this word can be called obscure, renders it in this verse *amâkteti vâbhyakteti vâ,* 'come here,' or 'come towards;' and Sâyaṇa explains it by *prâpnoti,* without, however, giving its etymology. This formation of the word corresponds with that of other compounds ending iu *ach.*" Prof. Goldstücker holds that it would be "against all grammatical analogy" to take *amyak* for an aorist, as Roth proposes. There is no proof, however, that either Yâska or Sâyaṇa concurred with Prof. Goldstücker in holding the word for a particle in *ach.*

*Alâtṛṇa* occurs in two passages of the Rig-veda. One of these, iii. 30, 10, is quoted in Nir. vi. 2, where it is explained as = *alam âtardanaḥ,* "greatly-splitting, or split." If this explanatory phrase be understood in the passive sense, it will coincide with Sâyaṇa's interpretation, "that which, from being full of water, is exceedingly broken." In i. 166, 7, the word is an epithet of the Maruts, and is explained by Sâyaṇa as susceptible of three different senses, viz., as standing either—1st, for *anâtṛṇâsaḥ* = *âtardana-rahitâḥ,* "free from splitting;" or, 2nd, as *alam âtardanâḥ ṣatrûṇâm,* "great cleavers of their enemies;" or, 3rd, as *alam dâtâraḥ phalânâm,* "great bestowers of rewards." Who will say that Sâyaṇa is here either a confident, or a satisfactory, guide?

*Askṛdhoyu* is explained by Yâska (in Nir. vi. 3, where he quotes R.V. vi. 22, 3) as = *akṛdhv-âyuḥ,* "not short-lived;" *kṛdhu,* being = *hrasva,* "short." Sâyaṇa renders it in two passages (vi. 22, 3; vi. 67, 11) by *avichhinna,* "not cut off," which would coincide with Yâska's interpretation; but on vii. 53, 3, he takes it for *ahrasvam analpam,* "not short," "not little," which seems to differ somewhat from the former sense, inasmuch as it refers not to duration but to quantity.

*Asridh* does not occur in the Nirukta. It is variously interpreted by Sâyaṇa either as "free from decay," or "desiccation" (i. 3, 9; i. 13, 9), or as "free from desiccation, always remaining in the same state (the Maruts," i. 89, 3), or as "innocuous" (iv. 32, 24; iv. 45, 4; v. 46, 4).

*Ahimanyu* does not occur in the Nirukta. It is applied to the Maruts in R.V. i. 64, 8, where Sâyaṇa offers a choice of interpretations, making it either = *âhanana-ṣîla-manyu-yuktâḥ,* "filled with wrath disposed to smite," or = *ahîna-jnânâḥ,* "of eminent wisdom." He was, therefore, only guessing at the sense.

*Ahimâya* is not found in the Nirukta. It is understood by

Sâyaṇa on i. 190, 4, as an epithet of Vṛttra and his class, and translated as either = "those whose enchantments come and destroy," or "those whose enchantments come in the atmosphere." On vi. 20, 7, he understands it as = "those who have destructive enchantments;" and on vi. 52, 15, as = "those who have destructive wisdom." I am not aware how he renders it in x. 63, 4. Another epithet of the gods, *ehimâya*, which Roth thinks may be a corruption of *ahimâya*, occurs in R.V. i. 3, 9, where Sâyaṇa assigns two possible senses—1st, "having all-pervading wisdom;" and, 2nd, that of a designation of the deities, derived from their having said to Agni when he had entered into the waters, *ehi mâ yâsîḥ*, "come, do not go."

*Âṣuṣukshaṇi*, which occurs R.V. ii. 1, 1, and Vâj. S. xi. 27, as an epithet of Agni, is explained in Nir. vi. 1 as meaning either "one who quickly slays, or gives, by his flame" (*âṣu ṣuchâ kshaṇoti iti vâ sanoti iti vâ*), or "desiring to consume." Sâyaṇa translates the word "flaming on all sides," or "one who quickly gives pain to his enemies by consuming," etc. Mahîdhara, on Vâj. S. xi. 27, translates *âṣuṣukshaṇi* as either = "quickly drying the wet ground," or as = "quickly destroying the darkness with his flame, or giving, distributing, by his flame." Roth (Illustrations of Nirukta, p. 72) compares *ṣuṣukvani* in R.V. viii. 23, 5, where Sâyaṇa renders "glowing."

*Âsâ* occurs frequently in the Rig-veda, and is diversely explained by Sâyaṇa. In his comments on ii. 1, 14; iv. 5, 10; vi. 3, 4; vi. 32, 1, he renders it by *âsyena*, "with the mouth;" on v. 17, 2, by *âsyena vâchâ*, "with the mouth, by speech;" on v. 17, 5; v. 23, 1, by *âsyena stotreṇa*, "with the mouth, with a hymn;" on i. 76, 4; vi. 16, 9, by *âsyena âsya-sthânîyayâ* (or *âsya-bhûtayâ*) *jvâlayâ*, "with the mouth, with the flame in the mouth;" on vii. 16, 9, as an epithet of *jihvayâ*, "the tongue," by *âsya-sthânîyayâ*, "situated in the mouth;" on i. 129, 5, by "near, in the place of sacrifice;" and on i. 168, 2, by "near." Similarly, he varies in the sense of *âsayâ*, making it stand in one place (i. 20, 1) for "with the mouth," and in another (i. 127, 8) for "near."

In the Nighaṇṭus, ii. 16, the word *âsât* is found as one of the synonyms of "near."

*Ishmin* is variously interpreted by Sâyaṇa in different places, viz., on i. 87, 6, and vii. 56, 11, as "going, moving;" on v. 52, 16; v. 87, 5, as "going," or "possessing food." Yâska gives the three derivations of *îshaṇinaḥ*, *eshaṇinaḥ*, and *arshaṇinaḥ* (Nir. iv. 16).

*Îvat.*—This word occurs in R.V. iv. 4, 6; iv. 15, 5; iv. 43, 3; v. 49, 5; vi. 73, 2; vii. 23, 1; vii. 56, 18; viii. 46, 21. In all these passages, without exception, Sâyaṇa renders it either simply by "going," "moving," or by some modification of that sense, as "coming," "approaching," "coming with prosperity," "occupied," "moving creatures." And yet there seems no reason to doubt that the word signifies "so much," "so great," as it is explained by Roth, *s.v.*, as being an old Vedic form for *iyat*, just as *kîvat* is for *kiyat*, as is (in the latter case) recognised both by Yâska (Nir. vi. 3) and by Sâyaṇa on R.V. iii. 30, 17, the only passage where it occurs. From this it appears that just as in ordinary Sanskrit *îdṛk* and *kîdṛk* are formed in the same way as *etâdṛk*, *tâdṛk*, *yâdṛk*, so, too, in ancient times the series of *etâvat*, *tâvat*, *yâvat*, was completed by *îvat* and *kîvat*, though at a subsequent period the two latter forms became obsolete, whilst *iyat* and *kiyat*, which are also found in the R.V., were regarded as alone correct. Their sense of "so much," "so great," etc. etc., appears, as far as I can judge, to suit all the passages of the R.V. where the word *îvat* occurs.

*Urugâya* (generally an epithet of Vishṇu) is interpreted by Yâska (Nir. ii. 7) in his comment on R.V. i. 154, 6, as = *mahâgati*, "making large strides." Sâyaṇa, however, wavers in his explanation, making it either "hymned by many" (on i. 154, 3; ii. 1, 3); "wide-going," or "much-praised" (on iii. 6, 4); "hymned by many," or "of great renown" (on iv. 3, 7); "great goers" (of the Aṣvins, iv. 14, 1); "celebrated by many" (on vii. 100, 1); "to be hymned by many," or "moving in many places," or "of great renown," or "one who, by his power, makes all his enemies howl" (on viii. 29, 7); "hymned by the great" (on i. 154, 1); "to be hymned by many great persons" (i. 154, 6). See also i. 155, 4; vi. 28, 4; vi. 65, 6; vii. 35, 15; x. 109, 7, where Prof. Roth considers the word to be a substantive. Looking to R.V. i. 22, 16 ff., about the striding of Vishṇu, there can be little doubt that the adjective *urugâya* means "wide-striding."

*Ṛdûdara* occurs in R.V. viii. 48, 10, as an epithet of Soma, and is interpreted by Yâska (vi. 4) in his explanation of part of that verse as = *mṛdûdara*, and as meaning "soft-bellied," or "soft in (men's) bellies." Sâyaṇa (on the same verse) renders it, "not hurting the belly" (*udarâbâdhakena*). On ii. 33, 5, where the word is applied to Rudra, he adopts the first of Yâska's two meanings; whilst on iii. 54, 10, where it is applied to the Âdityas, he repeats both of his predecessor's interpretations, modifying the second so as to signify, "those in whose bellies Soma is soft."[1]

*Ṛjîshin*, according to Yâska (v. 12, where he explains R.V. x. 89, 5), means Soma, but is also an epithet of Indra. "That which remains of soma when it is being purified is *ṛjîsha*, or rejected; therefore *ṛjîshin* is soma. There is also a text referring to Indra as *ṛjîshî vajrî*." Mahîdhara, on Vâj. S. xix. 72, says that *ṛjîsha* is the squeezed and juiceless refuse of the soma-plant. Sâyaṇa generally interprets the word *ṛjîshin* as an epithet of Indra by, "he who has the soma after it has been pressed and has lost its juice or taste" (on iii. 32, 1; iii. 36, 10; iv. 16, 1, 5; vi. 20, 2). On i. 64, 12, and i. 87, 1, where *ṛjîshin* is an epithet of the Maruts, he explains that at the third libation when those deities are worshipped this *ṛjîsha* is offered, and hence they are said to have it. On v. 40, 4 (where the word is applied to Indra) he says that after the soma has been offered at the first and second libations, and has become juiceless, that which is offered at the third libation is called *ṛjîsha* = *soma*. On iii. 46, 3, he makes *ṛjîshin* simply equivalent to *somavân*, "having soma." In two places, however, where the word is applied to the Maruts, Sâyaṇa gives alternative interpretations, viz., on ii.

[1] The Sanskrit scholar may also examine Yâska's desperate attempt (vi. 33) to explain the two words *ṛdûpâ* and *ṛdûvṛdh*, which occur in R.V. viii. 66, 11. Sâyaṇa merely repeats Yâska; but his text of the passage differs somewhat from Roth's.

34, 1, he says it means either "having water," or "having tasteless soma;" and on i. 87, 1, "either having such soma, or, being providers(?) of moisture" (*prârjayitâro rasânâm*). In i. 32, 6, where the word *ṛjîsha* (not *-shin*) is applied to Indra, Sâyaṇa makes it=*ṣatrûṇâm apârjakam*, "repeller of enemies." It thus appears that he wavers in his interpretation. The sense of "drinker of tasteless or spiritless soma" is not a very probable one. Indra is generally represented as greatly exhilarated by the beverage he quaffs, and it seems a poor compliment to him to call him the drinker of a vapid draught. Besides, in one of the texts of which *ṛjîshin* is the first word, *soma-pâvan*, a term which indubitably means soma-drinker, is found at the end of the same line, and it is unlikely that two epithets so closely resembling each other as "soma-drinker" and "spiritless-soma-drinker" should occur so near. In his glossary to the Sâma-veda, and in his translation of S.V. i. 248 and ii. 789, Prof. Benfey renders the word by "victorious;" and it appears from his note on the last of these two texts that the commentator there gives a choice of interpretations. Prof. Roth *s.v.* translates it by "forward-rushing;" and Benfey, in his translation of R.V. i. 87, 1, renders it similarly by "gradaus schreitenden" (Orient und Occident, ii. 249).

*Evayâvan*, which is not found in the Nirukta, is diversely interpreted by Sâyaṇa as="moving with horses" (applied by him to the Maruts, i. 90, 5); as="going to the hymn or sacrifice to which they should go" (ii. 34, 11, spoken of the same); as="moving with horses, or with the waters of the atmosphere,—coming with showers for the pleasure of others also" (vi. 48, 12, *evayâvarî*, spoken of the cow); or as="bringing to his worshippers the objects which they desire to obtain" (on vii. 100, 2, spoken of Vishṇu).

*Kâṇukâ* is one of the terms objected to by Kautsa as obscure (see above). It occurs only once, in R.V. viii. 66, 4; and Yâska does his utmost to explain it in Nir. v. 11. The whole verse runs thus: "Indra drank at one draught thirty lakes (or cups) of soma. . . . . ," the word *kâṇukâ* being the last of the verse. Yâska takes it either for a neuter plural, agreeing with *sarâṃsi* (cups) and meaning "desired" (*kântakâni*), or "entirely full" (*krântakâni*), or "properly formed" (*kṛtakâni*), or for an epithet of Indra, signifying "fond or beloved of soma" (*somasya kântaḥ*), or "overcome by love of soma" (*kaṇe ghâta iti vâ kaṇe hataḥ kântihataḥ*). "The ritualists" (*yâjnikâḥ*), (Yâska proceeds), "say that the thirty bowls which are destined for one deity at the mid-day libations, and are drunk off at once, are denoted in this verse by the word *sarâṃsi*, whilst the etymologists (*nairuktâḥ*), consider that they stand for the thirty nights and days constituting respectively the first and second halves of the month. In the second half the rays drink up the collected waters of the moon." According to the latter interpretation, Indra is (as Sâyaṇa remarks) the deity personifying time (*kâlâbhimânî*). In his explanation Sâyaṇa merely abridges Yâska's.

*Kârudhayaḥ* is in three places (vi. 21, 8: vi. 24, 2; vi. 44, 12) explained by Sâyaṇa as "upholder of poets or worshippers". (*kârûṇâṃ dhârakaḥ*, or *dhârayitâ*.) In another passage (iii. 32, 10) he gives a different sense, "maker of works" (*karmaṇâṃ vidhâtâ*). This latter sense would be appropriate enough here if it exists in the component elements of the word.

*Kiyedhâḥ* is explained by Yâska (vi. 20, where he quotes R.V. i. 61, 12), in two ways, as = either to *kiyaddhâḥ* "holding how much?" or to *kramamâṇa-dhâḥ*, "holding those who advance." Sâyaṇa, on i. 61, 6, renders it by *balavân*, "strong," and declares the two interpretations of the Nirukta to mean (1) "one who has strength of which no one knows the extent," and (2) "one who stops the advancing might of others. On verse 12 of the same hymn, he repeats the same explanations. It appears from Roth's Illustrations, *in loco*, that Durga, the commentator on the Nirukta, refers the epithet to Vṛttra, whilst others referred it to Indra. And Roth remarks, that by his double interpretation, "holding how much (water or power)?" and "holding the advancing (waters or hostile powers)," Yâska has left the application to one or other of these personages open.

*Kuchara* is explained by Yâska i. 20 (where R.V. i. 154, 2, is quoted), as meaning (if applied to a wild beast) "doing an evil deed," or if taken for a designation of the god (Vishṇu), as signifying "whither does he not go?" Sâyaṇa, on the same passage, gives it the sense either of "doer of evil deeds, such as killing," or "going to inaccessible places," or, if understood of the gods, as meaning either "doing evil deeds, such as the slaughter of enemies," or "one who ranges in all places throughout the three worlds." (*Kushu, sarvâsu bhûmishu, lokatraye, sanchârî.*) We have thus between Yâska and Sâyaṇa three derivations, according as we conceive the word to be compounded of *ku*, "bad," *ku*, "earth," or *kva*, "where," prefixed to *chara*, "going," or "acting." Such a play upon words in a double sense, though common enough in the modern rhetorical poetry of the Hindus, is scarcely to be looked for in the ancient hymns of the Veda.

*Kuṇâru* is explained by Yâska (Nir. vi. 1, where he quotes R. V. iii. 30, 8) as meaning a "cloud" (*parikvaṇanaṃ megham*). Sâyaṇa (on the same passage) gives two interpretations of the words *sahadânuṃ kshiyantaṃ saṃ piṇak kuṇârum*, viz., either (1) "crush the destroying (*kshiyantaṃ*) *kuṇâru* = a certain yelling Asura, associated with Dânu, Vṛttra's mother, or with the Dânavas," or (2) "Crush the thundering (*kuṇâru*) Vṛttra, having the gift of bestowing water (*sahadânum*), dwelling (*kshiyantam*) in the sky." Thus there are no less than three words in this single line (viz., *sahâdanum, kshiyantam,* and *kuṇârum*), of which Sâyaṇa offers alternative explanations.

*Kshayadvîra* does not occur in the Nirukta. It is variously explained by Sâyaṇa as "very strong, he in whom all heroes are destroyed" (on i. 106, 4); or, "he in whom heroes perish, or whose sons, the Maruts, rule" (on i. 114, 1, 2); or "he who has heroes, sons and servants, dwelling with him" (on i. 125, 3); or "possessed of heroes, sons and others, dwelling or moving" (*nivasadbhir itvarair vâ*, on R.V. viii. 19, 10). It will be seen, that as regards the root *kshi*, which forms the first member of this compound, Sâyaṇa wavers between the three senses of "perishing," "ruling," and "dwelling."

*Girikshit*, an epithet of Vishṇu (in i. 154, 3), is translated by Sâyaṇa as "residing in speech" (*giri* locative of *gir*), or "in a region high as a mountain." In this passage, however, it has, probably, one single sense.

*Jâtûbharman* is not in the Nirukta. Sâyaṇa explains it as meaning either "having the lightning for a weapon," or "supporter of creatures."

*Jârayâyi* is another of the words objected to by Kautsa as obscure. (See above.) It occurs only once in the R.V., vi. 12, 4, which is quoted by Yàska in vi. 15, where he explains it by *ajâyi*, to which his commentator Durga gives the meaning "is, or was, born." (See Roth's Illustrations, etc , p. 82.) Sâyaṇa, on the contrary, renders it by *stûyate* "is praised."

*Jîradânu* is not found in the Nirukta, though *jîra* is given in the Nighaṇṭus, ii. 15, as one of the synonymes of *kshipra*, "quick." In one passage (i. 165, 15) it is rendered by Sâyaṇa *jaya-ṣîla-dânam*, "having victorious gifts;" but in all the following texts he takes it for, "whose gifts are quick" (ii. 34, 4; v. 53, 5; v. 54, 9; v. 62, 3; v. 83, 1; vii. 64, 2; viii. 51, 3).

*Joshavâka* is found in R.V. vi. 59, 4, and is explained by Yâska (v. 21, 22, where he quotes this passage) as "that of which the name is unknown, that which is to be pondered (?)" *avijnâta-nâmadheyaṃ joshayitavyaṃ bhavati*). He renders the whole verse thus: "Ye, o Indra and Agni, eat the offering of the man who praises you when the soma libations are poured out. Ye do not eat (that) of the prater (?) who speaks *joshavâka*." Sâyaṇa renders: "Ye, o Indra and Agni, do not eat the (offering) of the man who, when the soma-libations are poured out, praises you badly, who, in the midst of them, speaks unpleasing words when he ought to speak pleasing ones." It is to be observed, however—and I perceive that Wilson also, in his note on the passage, has adverted to the fact—that in the quotation made from Yâska (v. 22) in Müller's edition of the R.V., the reading of the passage is different from what it is in Professor Roth's edition, as in Roth's text the first clause has no negative particle (*na*), whilst the negative particle is found there in Müller's. The meaning of that clause of the Nirukta is thus reversed. The sense given by Roth's reading appears to me to be the most conformable to the apparent meaning of Yâska, as two kinds of worshippers evidently appear to be contemplated in his explanation, one of whom the two gods approve and whose oblation they eat, and another whose oblation they do not eat. Sâyaṇa, in conformity with the reading of Yâska given by Müller, makes both clauses of the verse relate to one kind of worshipper, *i.e.*, to one whose offering the two gods disapprove. There would thus appear to be a difference between Yâska and Sâyaṇa as to the sense of the verse of the R.V. which they are expounding. What is its real sense, it is not necessary for me to decide. Roth considers that the future participle *joshayitavyam*, employed by Yâska, means "requiring consideration." Wilson renders the clause of which it forms a part, "that being of unknown name is to be propitiated." (Compare Roth's Lexicon, *s.v.*, and his remarks in his Illustr. of Nir. p. 68.)

*Daksha-pitaraḥ* is an epithet of the gods which is not found in the Nirukta. It occurs in three passages of the R.V. On the first (vi. 50, 2) Sâyaṇa takes the word for "those who have Daksha for their forefather," and refers to two other texts (R.V. x. 15, 3, and x. 72, 5)), the one to prove that the word *pitṛ* may stand for "forefather," and the second to show that the gods are elsewhere declared to have Daksha for their ancestor. On the second passage (vii. 66, 2) Sâyaṇa translates the word by "preservers, or lords, *i.e.* givers, of strength;" and on the third (viii. 52, 10) by "preservers, lords, of food." The word also occurs in the Taittirîya Sanhitâ, i. 2, 3, 1, where the commentator explains it much as Sâyaṇa on vi. 50, 2, does; and in Vâj. S. xiv. 3, where it is explained by "preserver of vigour."

*Danaḥ* is a word occurring in R.V. i. 174, 2, in regard to which Yâska (vi. 31) and Sâyaṇa contradict each other; the former taking it for an adjective meaning "liberally-minded" (*dâna-manasaḥ*), whilst the latter makes it a verb in the second person singular imperfect, meaning either "thou didst subdue," or "thou didst cause to cry."

*Dasrâ*, a frequent dual epithet of the Aṣvins, and sometimes of other gods (Indra and Vishṇu, vi. 69, 7), is explained by Yâska (vi. 26, where he quotes R.V. i. 117, 21), as=*darṣanîyau*, "to be seen, sightly." Sâyaṇa sometimes understands it in that sense (as on i. 47, 6; i. 117, 5, 20, 21; i. 118, 3; i. 120, 4; vi. 69, 7; viii. 22, 17); sometimes as "destroyers of enemies" (on i. 92, 16; i. 139, 3; i. 158, 1; i. 180, 5; i. 182, 2; i. 183, 4; iii. 58, 3; iv. 43, 4; v. 75, 2); once, at least, as either "destroyers of enemies," or "from their being the physicians of the gods, destroyers of diseases" (on i. 3, 3); sometimes as either "to be seen," or as "destroyers of enemies" (on viii. 5, 2; viii. 8, 1; viii. 26, 6; viii. 75, 1); sometimes as gods "having the name of Dasrâ," or as "to be seen" (on i. 116, 10). See my article on the Aṣvins, above, p. 5, note. It appears from Roth's Illustrations of Nirukta, p. 92, that Durga, the commentator on the Nirukta, explains Dasrâ by "destroyers of enemies," or "causers of works, agriculture," etc.

*Divishṭi* is explained by Yâska (vi. 22, where he quotes R.V. viii. 4, 19), as, in the loc. pl.=*divaḥ eshaṇeshu*, "longings after the sky." Sâyaṇa, on the same passage, makes it mean "sacrificial rites which are the causes of obtaining heaven." Similarly, on iv. 9, 2, he makes it = *yâgeshu*, "sacrifices." On iv. 46, 1, he takes it for "sacrifices which confer heaven," or "our longings after heaven being the causes."[1] And, again, on iv. 47, 1, he interprets it *divo dyulokasya eshaṇeshu satsu*, "there being longings after the sky;" on i. 139, 4, he translates, "longings after heaven, or longings, or goings, of sacrifice which enlightens, being causes;" on i. 86, 4, he renders it by "sacrificial days;" on viii. 65, 9, by "the arrivals of our days, or longings for heaven, being causes;" on vii. 74, 1, by "people who desire heaven, priests;" and on i. 141, 6, "longings after days being the cause."

*Dvibarhas* means, according to Yâska (vi. 17, where he quotes R.V. vi. 19, 1), "lord (*parivṛḍhaḥ*) in both regions, the middle and the upper" (*i.e.* atmosphere and sky). Sâyaṇa,

[1] Sâyaṇa's note on this verse (iv. 46, 1) affords another instance of his referring to a parallel text (R.V. vii. 92, 1) to prove that the first draught of soma was offered to Vâyu.

on the same passage, and also on iv. 5, 3; vii. 24, 2; viii. 15, 2, follows Yâska. On i. 71, 6, he has, "grown (*vṛṃhito varddhitaḥ*) in the middle and upper regions." On i. 114, 10, he makes it, "lord in the two regions, the earth and the sky, or in the two paths, the southern and the northern, or lord of knowledge and of works." On i. 176, 5, he renders it, *stotra-havî-rûpa-dvividha-parivṛḍha-karmavataḥ-yajamânasya*, "of the worshipper who is eminent in both kinds of worship, *i.e.* hymns and oblations."

*Nichumpuṇa* is explained by Yâska (v. 17, 18, where he quotes R.V. viii. 82, 22), as a designation of soma, "that which pleases by being swallowed" (*nichânta-pṛṇo nichamanena prîṇâti*). The ocean, too, he says, is called *nichumpuṇa;* as is also the *avabhṛtha* (or cleansing of vessels and worshippers after a sacrifice), as that "in which they sound lowly, or place lowly" (*nîchair asmin kvaṇanti nîchair dadhati iti vâ*). Sâyaṇa explains in conformity with Yâska. The word also occurs in the Vâjasaneyi Sanhitâ, iii. 48, and viii. 27, on the former of which passages Mahîdhara explains it as meaning either "slow-going" (*nitarâṃ chopati mandaṃ gachhati nichumpuṇaḥ*), or "that in which they sound lowly, perform the rite with a low voice." On viii. 27, he mentions only the first of these two explanations. The sense of the word is thus left doubtful.

*Naichâṣâkha* and *pramaganda* are two words occurring in R.V. iii. 53, 14, a text which is quoted and explained in Nir. vi. 32. Yâska there gives various senses to *pramaganda.* He first says *maganda* is "a usurer." The descendant of such a person is *pramaganda,* "a person sprung from a very usurious family." Or, secondly, the word is = *pramadakaḥ,* "one who desires that there should be no future state." Or, thirdly, it it is = *paṇḍakaḥ,* a "catamite," or "eunuch." He derives *naichâṣâkha* from *nîchâṣâkha,* apparently "of a low stock." Sâyaṇa understands it of the property of degraded people. He adopts the first of the three senses of *pramaganda* proposed by Yâska. It appears from an objection made to the eternity of the Veda which Sâyaṇa quotes in his Introduction, p. 7, and answers in p. 10 (as cited in Sanskrit Texts, iii. 62), that

*Pramaganda* was considered by the objectors to be the name of a king, and *Naichâṣâkha* that of a town.

*Nema* is given in Nir. iii. 20 as = *arddha*, "half," in which sense it is taken by Sâyaṇa on R.V. v. 61, 8. In other places (i. 54, 8; iv. 24, 4, 5; vi. 16, 18), he translates it by "these," "some," "others." But in viii. 89, 3, he holds it to be the proper name of a descendant of Bhrigu. In this he appears to be wrong. Compare R.V. ii. 12, 5.

*Nishshidh, nishshidhvan, puru-nishshidh, puru-nishshidhvan.* These words are not found in the Nighaṇṭus or Nirukta. The first of them, which occurs in the R.V. in different numbers and cases, is variously interpreted by Sâyaṇa in different places; as = "constantly discharging rain-clouds" (on R.V. i. 169, 2); or "commands, ordinances" (*anuṣâsanâni*, iii. 51, 5);[1] or "destructive light" (*hiṃsikâṃ dîptim*, iii. 55, 8); "hinderers, enemies" (iv. 24, 1), or "hindrances to enemies," or "cords to restrain enemies" (vi. 44, 11). *Nishshidhvarîḥ* (the feminine form of *nishshidhvan*) occurs in iii. 55, 22, where Sâyaṇa makes it = *nitarâṃ tvat-kartṛka-siddhimatyaḥ, i.e.*, "having eminently perfections created by thee" (Indra). *Puru-nishshidh* is found in i. 10, 5[2] as an epithet of Indra, and is there translated by Sâyaṇa as = "hinderer of many enemies; and *puru-nishshidhvan*, in iv. 38, 2, as a designation of Dadhikrâ, where it is understood by him in the same sense. It is, therefore, quite impossible to suppose that the commentator could have had any certain tradition of the sense of these words. Prof. Wilson, who translates *pûrvîr asya nishshidho martyeshu* in iii. 51, 5, by "many are his [Indra's] prohibitions (against evil enjoined) to men," has a note on this verse, in which he remarks that "a similar phrase in a former passage [i. 10, 5] *purunishshidhe* has been rendered 'repeller of many foes:' there is no material incompatibility, the latter being a compound epithet, and the substantive in both cases being derived from *shidh*, to succeed, to go, with the preposi-

[1] We have, in his comment on this verse, a further instance of Sâyaṇa quoting another passage for illustration, as he here cites i. 10, 5 as referring to Indra's function of command. See further on.

[2] This verse is repeated in Sâma-veda i. 363, where Benfey renders it "vielgebietend," "many ruling."

tion *nir*, out, *ex*, to exclude, to prohibit." Prof. Wilson, however, while taking notice of this one passage to which Sâyaṇa himself had drawn his attention, has not adverted to the other texts which I have adduced: and when words identical in tenor with those in iii. 51, 5, are repeated in vi. 44, 11, viz., *pûrvîsh ṭe Indra nishshidho janeshu*, he translates them differently, thns: "many are the hindrances (opposed) to thee amongst men." This does not, however, correctly reproduce Sâyaṇa's meaning.

*Paritakmyâ* is translated "night" in Nir. xi. 25, where R.V. x. 108, 1 is explained. This sense is adopted by Prof. Müller in translating the verse. (Lectures on Language, second series, p. 464, and note.) Prof. Aufrecht, on the other hand, renders the word by "necessity." (Journal of Ger. Or. Society, vol. xiii., pp. 496 and 498.) Prof. Roth, who in his Illustr. of the Nir. had taken the same view, assigns in his Lexicon, *s.v.*, another signification, that of "wandering," as the proper one for this passage. For most other texts of the R.V. he adopts the sense of "night," "darkness." In two passages he gives it the sense of "causing anxiety," "dangerous." Sâyaṇa renders the word by "night" in i. 116, 15; iv. 43, 3; vi. 24, 9; by "dark," apparently, in v. 30, 13; by "night," or "battle,' or " sacrifice," in vii. 69, 4; by "surrounding," (*paritakane nimittabhûte sati*) or "night" in iv. 41, 6; by "battle" in v. 31, 11; by "to be gone round, or surrounded," as an epithet of *dhane*, wealth, in i. 31, 6; and by "surrounding," as an epithet of *râtrî*, "night," which goes before, in v. 30, 14. It thus appears that in some places he is uncertain about the sense.

*Paryabhûshat* in R.V. ii. 12, 1, is explained by Yâska (x. 10) as = *paryabhavat paryagṛhṇât paryarakshad atyakrâmad iti vâ*, *i e.*, "overcame, or comprehended, or protected, or surpassed." He could not, therefore, it would appear, have been very sure of its meaning. Sâyaṇa renders simply *rakshakatvena paryagrahît*, "surrounded as a protector." The same word is found in the imperative (*pari bhûsha*) in R.V. i. 15, 4, where Sâyaṇa renders it, "adorn," and Benfey, "encircle;" and in i. 31, 2, where Sâyaṇa, followed by Benfey, translates the clause, *devâ-*

*nâṃ pari bhûshasi vratam*, "thou adornest the ceremonial (*karma*) of the gods." The same root, preceded by the particle *vi*, occurs in i. 112, 4, *vi bhûshati*, where Sâyaṇa offers two explanations, "is diffused," or "eminently adorns," and in vi. 15, 9, *vi bhûshan*, where he renders, "adorning." The word *âbhûsha*, in R.V. vii. 92, 1 (=Vâj. S. vii. 7) is understood by both commentators, Sâyaṇa and Mahîdhara, in the sense of "come."

*Pânta* is explained in Nir. vii. 25 (where R.V. x. 88, 1 is quoted) as = *pânîya*, "to be drunk." It occurs also in R.V. i. 122, 1, where Sâyaṇa renders it by "preserving, or to be drunk, sacrifice, or instrument of sacrifice." On i. 55, 1, also, he gives it the sense of either "protecting, or to be drunk."

*Purukshu* is not found in the Nirukta; but *kshu* is given in the Nighaṇṭus, ii. 7, as a synomyme of *anna*, "food." Sâyaṇa interprets it variously, for the most part as = *bahvanna*, "having much food" (on i. 68, 5; iii. 25, 2; iii. 54, 21; iv. 34, 10; vi. 19, 5); also as = "greatly renowned" (ii. 40, 4); as having one or other of the two preceding senses (iv. 29, 5; vi. 68, 6); and, again, as "having much food, or many cattle" (vi. 22, 3). The commentator on the Vaj. S., xxvii. 20, renders it "that which dwells in many" (*bahushu kshiyati nivasati*).

*Pṛthupâjas* does not occur in the Nirukta; but *pâjas* is given in the Nighaṇṭus, ii. 9, as one of the synonymes for *bala*, "strength." In Nir. vi. 12, it is said to derive its name from preserving. *Pṛthupâjas* is variously rendered by Sâyaṇa as "having great strength" (iii. 27, 5; iv. 46, 5); as "having great vigour (or lustre," *tejas*, iii. 5, 1; iii. 27, 5); as "having great strength or much food" (iii. 3, 1; viii. 5, 2); as "having great vigour (or lustre) or great velocity" (iii. 2, 11).

*Pṛthushṭuka* occurs as an epithet of Sinîvâlî in R.V. ii. 32, 6. This passage is quoted in Nir. xi. 32, and the word is there explained as either "broad-loined," or "having broadly plaited (or a broad mass of) hair" (*pṛthukeṣa-stuke*), or *pṛthu-stuke*. Sâyaṇa renders by *pṛthu-jaghane pṛthu-saṃhate vâ*, "having broad loins," or "broadly built" (?) The passage is repeated in Vaj. S. xxxiv. 10, where Mahîdhara makes the word = *he pṛthukeṣa-bhâre mahâstute vâ pṛthukâme vâ* "having a large mass of hair, or greatly praised, or having large desires." On the sense of the word *stukâ*, compare Weber, Ind. Stud., v. 233 and 237.

*Pvadivaḥ* is met with in the Nighaṇṭus, iii. 27, as one of the synonymes of *purâṇa*, "old." The same sense is assigned to it in the Nirukta, viii. 19, as well as in iv. 8, where it is rendered by *pûrveshu api ahassu* "even in former days." Sâyaṇa, in his note on the passage here illustrated by Yâska (R.V. iii. 47, 1), adheres to the interpretation of the latter. He also retains the sense "old" in i. 53, 2; ii. 3, 1; iii. 36, 2; iv. 6, 4; iv. 7, 8; v. 8, 7; vi. 5, 3; vi. 23, 5; but in iii. 38, 5 and iv. 34, 3 he assigns to the word the meaning of "extremely shining" (*prakarsheṇa dyotamâna*).

*Bakura* is found in R.V. i. 117, 21, a passage quoted by Yâska (vi. 25, 26), where (after saying that *bakura* is = *bhâskaro bhayankaro bhâsamâno dravati iti vâ*, "illuminator, terrible, or that which runs shining") he assigns to the word the sense of "light or water" (*jyotishâ udakena vâ*. Sâyaṇa gives it the meaning of the "shining lightning." Prof. Roth thinks it denotes a wind instrument. Whether he is right or not, it is clear that Yâska had no certain knowledge of its sense.

*Bîriṭa*, as we are told in Nir. v. 27, means, according to Taiṭîki, the "atmosphere," the first syllable being from *vî*, "to go," and the second being from *ir*, "to go," and the whole denoting that wherein the birds or the clouds move. Yâska then quotes the only passage in which it occurs, R.V. vii. 39, 2 (=Vâj. S. xxxiii. 44), giving it first the sense of atmosphere, and next suggesting the sense of "assemblage of men." Sâyaṇa repeats the two interpretations of Yâska. Mahîdhara adopts the second, but quotes Yâska.

*Madachyut* does not occur in the Nirukta. It is generally understood by Sâyaṇa as "humbler of the pride of enemies" (on R.V. i. 51, 2; i. 81. 3; viii. 1, 21; viii. 85, 5), or, "humblers of enemies," viii. 22' 16. But on i. 85, 7, he takes it for "that which sheds forth joy, the sacrifice."

*Mṛdhravâch* is explained by Yâska (vi. 31, where he quotes R.V. i. 174, 2) as = *mṛdu-vâchaḥ* "softly-speaking." This translation is quoted by Sâyaṇa at the end of his note on the passage without remark. His own rendering is different, as he either, according to the interpretation of the Aitihasikas (legendary writers), makes the word = *marshaṇa-vachanâḥ*, "uttering angry words," or, according to that of the Nairuktas, takes it as = *marshaṇa-dhvani-yuktâḥ*, "having a threatening sound." On v. 29, 10; v. 32, 8; and vii. 6, 3, he understands the term to stand for "with organs of speech destroyed," or "with speech destroyed;" and on vii. 18, 13, he assigns a sense similar to that given on i. 174, 2, viz., *bâdhavâcham*, "injuriously speaking." The meanings he assigns are thus mutually inconsistent, as well as at variance with that proposed by Yâska.

*Amṛdhra* occurs frequently in the R.V., as in v. 37, 1; v. 43, 2, 13; vi. 19, 7; vi. 22, 10; vi. 75, 9; vii. 67, 5, in all which places it is rendered by Sâyaṇa *ahiṃsita*, or *hiṃsâ-rahita*, "uninjured," or *hiṃsitum aṣakya*, "uninjurable." On iii. 58, 8, he translates "not despised by any one." On i. 37, 11, besides "uninjurable," he proposes an alternative sense, "not wetting," which Prof. Goldstücker regards as not very probable (see *s.v.*). On viii. 69, 2 (where, however, Müller puts the texts in brackets), he renders it in an active sense, *ahinsaka*, "not injuring." On Vaj. S. xxix. 46, Mahîdhara renders the word "hard-limbed, or giving stern commands."

*Mehanâ* (an undeclined word) is found in Nir. iv. 4 (where R.V. v. 39, 1 is quoted), and is explained as either = *maṃhanîyaṃ*[1] *dhanam*, "to be given, wealth," or *me iha na* "(that which) I have not here."[2] Sâyaṇa, following Yâska's first interpretation, understands *mehanâ* as = *maṃhanîya*, on v. 38, 3 and v. 39, 1. On viii. 4, 21, repeating both Yâska's explanations, he makes it either *maṃhanîyâṃ praṣasyâm*, "laudable,

[1] The verb *maṃh* is found in Nigh. iii. 20, as signifying "to give."

[2] See on this word Roth's Illust. of Nir. p. 39, where other passages in which it occurs are given. Roth mentions that Durga, the commentator on the Nirukta, says that, in the R.V., *mehanâ* is one word, whilst in the Sâmaveda it is considered to be made up of three. On the sense of the term see also Benfey's Gloss. to S.V., p. 151.

excellent," agreeing with both *gâm* (fem.) "cow," and *aşva* (masc.) "horse," or, *me iha na*; and the latter words he explains thus: "In this king (*iha*) there was not (*na*) to me (*me*) that gift of excellent wealth." On viii. 52, 12 (=V.S. 33, 50), he takes the word as = *udaka-sechana-yuktâḥ*, or *sechanena yuktâḥ*, "shedding water." Mahîdhara, on the same verse, explains, "shedders of wealth," etc., *dhanâdi-sektâraḥ*. In iii. 49, 3, the word *mehanâvân* is met with, which Sâyaṇa explains thus: *mihyate sichyate dîyate arthibhyaḥ iti mehanam dhanam tadvân*, "*mehana* is wealth, that which is shed forth, given, to suppliants; he who has it is *mehanâvat*."

*Reṇukakâṭa* is not mentioned in the Nirukta. It is found as an epithet of *arvan*, "horse," in R.V. vi. 28, 4, where Sâyaṇa takes it for "stirring up dust," spoken of a horse come for battle. The word is also found connected with *arvan* in Vâj. S. xxviii. 13, where it is differently understood by Mahîdhara as follows: *kâṭaḥ kûpaḥ, kutsitaḥ kâṭah kakâṭaḥ, reṇubhiḥ kṛtvâ kakâṭaḥ reṇukakâṭaḥ*, "*kâṭa* is a well; *kakâṭa* is a bad well; a bad well with dust is a *reṇukakâṭa*." Such a well, into which calves and youths fall, is to be removed. Wells, etc., which obstruct sacrifices and offspring are to be removed from the road. Such is this scholiast's explanation. It will be seen that the two Commentators are far from agreeing, and the word is so constructed that there is no reason to suppose it has both senses.

*Vavakshitha* and *vivakshase* are given in Nigh. iii. 3, among the synonymes of *mahat*, "great;" and in Nir. iii. 13, are said to be derived from the root *vach*, "to speak," or from *vah*, "to carry." Sâyaṇa seems (except in one case, vii. 100, 6), to regard the different forms of this word as coming from *vah*, "to bring," and interprets as follows: *vavakshuḥ*, "they wish to bring" (R.V. i. 64, 3); *ati vavakshitha*, "thou exceedingly wishest to carry, art a supporter of" (i. 81, 5); ditto, "thou exceedingly wishest to carry" (i. 102, 8; iii. 9, 3); *vavakshitha*, "thou wishest to carry all" (ii. 22, 3); *vavakshe* = *uvâha*, "he carried" (iv. 16, 5); *vavakshatuḥ* = *avahatâm*, "they two carried" (viii. 12, 25–27); *anuvavakshitha* =

*anuvoḍhum ichha*, "desire to carry" (viii. 77, 5). *Pravavakshe*, in vii. 100, 6, is rendered both by Yâska (v. 8) and by Sâyaṇa in loco, as=*prabrûshe*, "thou sayest." Setting aside the last passage, it appears to me that in most of the rest which I have quoted the sense of "carrying" is inappropriate. In i. 64, 3, Sâyaṇa has to supply the words, "what is desired by their worshippers," in order to make the word "bring" yield a tolerable sense; whilst, if we take the verb to signify "waxed, grew," the meaning will be "the Rudras waxed like mountains." So, too, in i. 81, 5, and i. 102, 8, it makes a better sense to say of Indra, "thou hast waxed greater than the whole universe," than to say, "thou exceedingly wishest to bear the universe." And in iii. 9, 3, where Sâyaṇa explains the words *ati tṛshṭam vavakshitha*, "thou (Agni) exceedingly wishest to bring, in order to fulfil the desire of thy worshipper, by bestowing an appropriate reward." Roth (*s. v. tṛshṭa*) proposes to render "thou (Agni) hast overcome that which bites, *i.e.* the smoke." Similarly, in ii. 22, 3; iv. 16, 5; viii. 77, 5, the sense of "waxing" seems by far the most appropriate (though not, apparently, in ii. 34, 4). Even in viii. 12, 25–27, where at first sight the meaning "carried" seems to suit the context,—"when, Indra, the gods placed thee in the front in the battle, then thy beautiful steeds *carried* (*thee*)",—the other sense, "grew great," would be admissible, especially as there is no noun in the line to be governed by *vavakshatuḥ*, and as in the next verse following the three where this verb occurs, another verb with that very signification (*vavṛdhâte*, "grew") is actually applied to the horses. Other forms of this verb, *vakshati* and *vakshataḥ*, occur in R.V. i. 2, 2; iv. 8, 2; viii. 6, 45; where they are treated by Sâyaṇa as futures, or precatives. Can *vakshati* be a third per. pres., "he brings?" *Âvakshat* and *vakshat* (R.V. x. 20, 10, and x. 176, 2) seem to have the sense of "bringing." *Vakshatha* occurs as a substantive in vii. 33, 8, where Sâyaṇa assigns the sense of *prakâṣa*, "brightness." Perhaps it may mean "full splendour." Roth (Illustr. of Nir. p. 30) thinks the root *vaksh* has the sense of "waxing;" so, too, Benfey (gloss to S.V.), who, however, gives it the sense of "carrying" in R.V. iv. 7, 11. In his translation of i. 64, 3; i. 81, 5; i. 102, 8, he translates "growing." Westergaard also *s.v.* adopts the sense of "growing," "being strong," etc.

*Ṣarman* has in the Nighaṇṭus, iii. 4, the sense of "house." In Nir. ix. 19, 32; xii. 45, it has the meaning of "refuge" (*ṣaraṇam*). In i. 174, 2, Sâyaṇa renders *ṣarma* by *sukhaṃ yathâ bhavati*, "easily," whilst in another verse, vi. 20, 10, where the context is the same, he translates it by "thunderbolt" (*ṣarma ṣarmaṇâ vajreṇa*).

*Ṣârada*, "autumnal," (which is not found in the Nirukta), is a word applied in several passages of the R.V. to the cities of the Dasyus. On i. 131, 4, Sâyaṇa explains it as = "fortified for a year;" on i. 174, 2, as "new," or "fortified for a year;" on vi. 20, 10, as "belonging to an Asura called Ṣarad."

*Ṣurudh*, in the plural, means, according to the Nirukta, vi. 16, "waters," which "prevent distress" (*ṣucham saṃrundhanti*). The word is mentioned in two other passages of the Nir. viz., x. 41 and xii. 18 (where R.V. iv. 23, 8, and vi. 49, 8, are cited), in the former of which no further explanation of it is given, whilst in the later (xii. 18) it is rendered by *dhanâni*, "riches." Sâyaṇa, on i. 72, 7, takes the word for "food which prevents suffering in the shape of hunger" (*kshud-rûpasya sokasya rodhayitrîr ishaḥ*); on iii. 38, 5, for "preventives of thirst, waters;" on iv. 23, 8, for "waters;" on vi. 3, 3, for "preventives of suffering, cows;" [1] on vi. 49, 8 (=Nir. xii. 18) the same (in opposition to Yâska, who here renders it "riches"); on vii. 23, 2, for "things which prevent suffering, herbs;" and on vii. 62, 3, for "preventers of suffering," but taken as nom. masc. and as an epithet of Varuṇa and other gods; or, optionally, in the accus., for "plants." In i. 169, 8, the word is interpreted of "distress-preventing desiccating lines of clouds," *ṣokasya rodhayitrîḥ ṣoshakâḥ . . . . megha-panktîḥ*. R.V. vi. 49, 8, is repeated in the Vâj. S. xxxiv. 42, where *ṣurudhaḥ* is explained as "a means of removing suffering."

[1] These cows belong to the Râkshasas, whom Sâyaṇa considers to be denoted by the word *aktu*, "night," in which such spirits move about.

*Salalûka* is explained in Nir. vi. 3 (where the only text in which it occurs, R.V. iii. 30, 17, is cited), as=" covetous (*saṃ-lubdha*), wicked, according to the Nairuktas, or etymologists; or it may be for *sararûka*, from *sṛ* (to go), reduplicated." Durga understands it to mean "confounded," or "fugitive," of the Râkshases. Sâyaṇa takes it for *saraṇa-ṣîla*, "moving."

*Santya* is found as an epithet of Agni in R.V. i. 18, 2; i. 36, 2; viii. 19, 26. In the first of these passages Sâyaṇa explains it as meaning "bestower of rewards," and in the second as "liberal," deriving it in both cases from the root *san*, "to give." In the third passage he makes it =*sam-bhajanîya*, "to be served, or possessed."

*Sarvatâti* is interpreted in Nir. xi. 24 (where R.V. i. 94, 15, is quoted) by *sarvâsu karma-tatishu*, "in all performances (*lit.* extensions) of works." Sâyaṇa on the same passage repeats these words of Yâska, and adds, "or to him who is present at all sacrifices." On iv. 26, 3, he translates it simply by "sacrifice." On vi. 12, 2, also, he renders it by "sacrifice" ("performed by all," *sarvais tâyamâne yajne*), or, (taking *tâti* for a suffix), the "totality" of worshippers (*sarvaḥ stotâ*). On i. 106, 2, he renders it by "that which is extended by all heroes, battle," which sense he also assigns to it in vii. 18, 19. On iii. 54, 11, he gives it the signification of "every desired good." In this last text, where Savitṛ is asked to give the worshippers *sarvatâti* (*âd asmabhyam âsuva sarvatâtim*), it could not well signify either battle, or sacrifice, or anything but blessing in some form or other. On vi. 56, 6, the scholiast assigns the sense of "sacrifice," or "the extension of all enjoyments," *sarveshâṃ bhogânâṃ vistârâya*. The word also occurs in ix. 96, 4; x. 36, 14; and x. 100, 1 ff., but Sâyaṇa's explanations of those passages are not within my reach. See Prof. Benfey's Excursus on the word *sarvatâti* in his "Orient und Occident," ii. 519 ff., referred to in my article on "Vedic Theogony," etc., p. 70, note.

*Sumajjâni* (not in the Nirukta), is an epithet of Vishṇu in R.V. i. 156, 2. Sâyaṇa thinks it may mean one of two things, either "self-born" (*sumat* being = *svayam* according to Nir. vi. 22, and *jâni* being taken for "birth"), or "having a wife (*jâni*) who gladdens" (*sumat* being here = *sutarâṃ mâdayati*). The epithet will in the latter case be equivalent to the "lord of the world-gladdening Ṣrî." Here we have an importation of later ideas into Vedic mythology. I am not aware of any other passage of the R.V. in which a wife is assigned to Vishṇu. In the Vâj. S. xxix. 60, Aditi is called his wife; as Sinîvâlî appears to be in A.V. vii. 46, 3.

*Spaṣ*, as a verb, is found in R.V. i. 10, 2. where Sâyaṇa translates it by "touched, began;" in i. 22, 19 (= Vâj. vi. 14; Sâma-veda, ii. 1021), where he renders it by "(every worshipper) touched, performed," the root *spaṣ* having the two senses of injuring and touching (*bâdhana-sparṣanayoḥ*). Mahîdhara on Vâj. S. vi. 4, explains the same word by "bound, fashioned," or "bound in himself," or "fixed," *spaṣ* having the sense of binding (*bandhane*). In i. 128, 4, Sâyaṇa translates by *atyarthaṃ spṛṣati svîkaroti*, "touches exceedingly, accepts," (the sense of "oblations, etc.," being given to *jâtâni*); in i. 176, 3, by *bâdhayasva*, "injure." The verb also occurs without a preposition in x. 102, 8, and with *anu* prefixed in x. 14, 1, and x. 160, 4. I am not aware what sense Sâyaṇa assigns in the first two passages, but in the third he translates *anuspashṭa* by *dṛshṭigochara*, "visible" (see Goldstücker's Dict. *s.v. aratni*). *Spaṣ*, as a noun, is found in R.V. i. 25, 13; i. 33. 8; iv. 4, 3; v. 59, 1; vi. 67, 5; vii. 61, 3; vii. 87, 3; viii. 50, 15; ix. 73, 4, 7; and A.V. iv. 16, 4. In the first passage Sâyaṇa renders it, *hiraṇya-sparṣino rasmîn*, "gold-touching, rays;" in the second (i. 33, 8), *bâdhakân Vṛttrânucharân*, "the injurious followers of Vṛttra;" in the third (iv. 4, 3) by *parabâdhakân raṣmîn chârân vâ*, "destroying others, rays, or spies;" in the fourth (vi. 67, 5) by "rays, or spies; in the fifth (vii. 61, 3)[1] by *rûpam*, "form;" in vii. 87, 3, by *charâḥ*, "spies," (though here, too, the root *spaṣ* is said to have the sense of *spṛṣ*, "touch.") In v. 59, 1, *spaṭ*, nom. sing., is said by the scholiast to be = *sprashṭâ hotâ*, "priest;" whilst in viii. 50, 15, where it is an epithet of Indra, he makes it mean *sarvasya jnâtâ*,

[1] In vii. 61, 3, there is another instance of Sâyaṇa's making a reference back to a preceding passage, i. 61, 9. See also his notes on i. 154, 1; ii. 2, 5; iii. 17, 1; vi. 26, 4, vii. 76, 4.

"knower of all things." The sense of the noun *spaṣ* is pretty well fixed by A.V. iv. 16, 4, to be generally that of spies or messengers. And I do not see why in some, at least, of the texts of the R.V. above quoted the verb too should not have the sense of "seeing," or "shewing." The root *spaṣ* has the significations of "making evident," "informing," given to it among others in Wilson's Dictionary. The participles *spashṭa* and *anuspashṭa*, "manifest," seem to come from a verb meaning "to see." *Spaṣ*, "a spy," also appears to be derived from a root having the same sense. And in the cognate languages the root has the same signification. See Roth's Illustrations of the Nirukta, p. 138 f.

*Smaddishṭi*, *smadishṭa*, are not to be found in the Nirukta.. The former word (divided into *smad* + *dishṭi* in the Pada text) occurs several times in the R.V., viz., in iii. 45, 5, as an epithet of Indra, where Sâyaṇa translates it by *bhadra-vâkya*, "auspiciously speaking;" in vi. 63, 9, where he takes it for an epithet of chariots or horses, and renders it "handsome-looking," *praṣasta-darṣanân* (where *dishṭi* must be taken to stand for *dṛshṭi*); in vii. 18, 23, where it is an epithet of *dânâḥ*, "horses," and is explained by him as "possessing all the approved attributes of a gift, liberality, faith," etc. (*praṣastâti-sarjana-ṣraddhâdi-dânânga-yuktâḥ*). These interpretations seem to be mutually discrepant. His commentary on x. 62, 10, where the word is also found, is not accessible to me. The second word, *smadishṭa*, differs from the first, in that it ends not in *ṭi* but in *ṭa*, and is compounded of *smat* + *ishṭa*, occurs in R.V. vii. 87, 3, where Sâyaṇa renders it, "either good goers, or, sent together," according as *smat* is taken in the sense of "good," or "with."

*Kuṇḍṛṇâchî* is explained by Sâyaṇa on R.V. i. 29, 6, as denoting the tortuous movement of the wind; whilst in Vâj. S. 24, 35, as interpreted by Mahîdhara, it signifies some kind of wild animal. The words *prâvo yudhyantam ṛshabhaṃ daṣadyum* occur both in R.V. i. 33, 14, and in vi. 26, 4, but are differently explained by Sâyaṇa in these two places. In the former he renders, "thou hast preserved the eminent (rishi) Daṣadyu when fighting;" whilst in the latter he makes Vṛshabha a proper name and Daṣadyu an epithet, translating, "thou hast preserved (the king) Vṛshabha fighting for ten days." This discrepancy is pointed out by Prof. Benfey in his note 294 to the former text (Orient und Occident, i. p. 51), and he then proceeds: "I am far from imputing this to Sâyaṇa as an offence. He was as little aware of it as we are now. I make the remark only for the sake of those who attach so great importance to him that, instead of the Veda, they translate his Commentary, and while doing so, pretend to be giving a translation of the hymns."

*Pṛshṭa* in R.V. i. 98, 2, is explained by Sâyaṇa as meaning either *saṃspṛshṭa*, "touched," or *nishikṭa, nihita*, "shed, placed."

*Prashṭi* is explained by Sâyaṇa on R.V. i. 39, 6, as "a particular kind of yoke between the three animals which draw the chariot," *etat-sanjnako vâhana-traya-madhya-vartti yuga-viṣeshaḥ*. On viii. 7, 28, he takes *prashṭi* to mean either "swift," or "a buck yoked in front." See Prof. Wilson's note on the former passage. The words *puruṇîthâ jarasva* in R.V. vii. 9, 6, are interpreted by Sâyaṇa to mean either "praise with much laudation," or "consume the Râkshasas who move by many paths."

*Gûrttaṣravas* is explained by Sâyaṇa on i. 61, 5, as *praṣasyânna*, "having approved food;" and on i. 122, 10, as *ud-gûrṇa-dîpti, prakhyâtânno vâ*, "having exalted light," or "having renowned food."

*Vîtahavya*, in R.V. vi. 15, 2, is said by Sâyaṇa either to mean a rishi so called, or, if Bharadvâja be the rishi of the hymn, then *vîtahavya* will be an epithet signifying "he by whom an oblation has been presented." The word occurs again in vii. 19, 3, where the scholiast takes it for an epithet of Sudâs, meaning, "he who has given, or generated, an oblation."

*Ṣvaitreya*, which in R.V. i. 33, 14, is taken by Sâyaṇa for a proper name, the son of *Ṣvitrâ*, is in v. 19, 3, understood of the "lightning-fire produced in the atmosphere," although the word has the appearance of being a proper name in that passage also.

*Akavâri* is not in the Nirukta. It is found in R.V. iii. 47, 5, as an epithet of Indra, and is there explained by Sâyaṇa as =*prabhûta-ṣatrukam,* "having many enemies," or *akutsitârim,* "having foes not contemptible." The last sense he illustrates by a reference to R.V. i. 61, 9, where the epithet *svari,* "having glorious enemies," is applied to Indra, as implying that the vanquisher of such enemies must be most heroic. In vii. 96, 3, *akavârî* is spoken of Sarasvatî, and is interpreted in quite a different manner by Sâyaṇa, as *akutsita-gamanâ,* "not badly going." The first of the preceding verses is repeated in Vâj. S. vii. 36, where *akavâri* is taken as either "he whose enemies even are not bad," or "he who obtains what is not bad," *i.e.* "has eminent dominion."

*Akshṇayâvan* is not in the Nirukta, but is found in R.V. viii. 7, 35, where Sâyaṇa gives two explanations, viz., either "going pervadingly" (*vyâptaṃ gachhantaḥ*), or "going quicker than even the eye."

*Adha-priya, kadha-priya, kadha-prî.* The first of these words occurs as an epithet of the Aṣvins in R.V. viii. 8, 4, where Sâyaṇa offers two interpretations, either (1) "fond of that which exists here *below,* viz., Soma," or (2) "fond of praise," *adha* standing for *kadha,* shorn of its initial *k.* Prof. Roth, *s.v.,* renders, "then pleased." Prof. Goldstücker does not give the word. *Kadha-priya* is found in R.V. i. 30, 20, as an epithet of Ushas, and *kadha-prî* in i. 38, 1, and viii. 7, 31, as an epithet of the Maruts, and both terms are uniformly rendered by Sâyaṇa "fond of praise," *kadha* being said to stand for *katha* or *kathâ,* "speaking." Prof. Roth, *s.vv.,* suggests, "friendly to whom?" And, certainly, when it is observed that all the three passages in which the two words are found are interrogative, this rendering seems more probable than Sâyaṇa's. Compare *kuhayâkṛte* in viii. 24, 30. Prof. Benfey translates in i. 30, 20, "where lovest thou?" and in i. 38, 1, "where do ye like to linger?"

*Anarviṣ.* On this word it will be sufficient to quote Prof. Goldstücker's explanation in his Dictionary: "(*ved.*) i. A car-man, one going with, or on a cart." . . . "(or, according to another explanation, which appears, however, to be an artificial one), ii. one who does not arrive where he is to go to, one not attaining the end or aim of his journey." The artificial explanation here alluded to is that of Sâyaṇa on i. 121, 7.

*Amavat* is explained by Prof. Roth, *s.v.*, as "violent," "strong," etc.; and by Prof. Goldstücker, *s.v.*, "powerful, mighty, strong." The latter scholar remarks that "this meaning of *amavat* seems to apply satisfactorily to all other instances in which the word occurs. . . . . . There are, however, other meanings . . . . mentioned by Yâska, and accordingly by Sâyaṇa and Mahîdhara, which deserve noticing, not only because the first of them is plausible, but also on account of their high antiquity." The words of Yâska (vi. 12) explanatory of the word before us are *amâtyavân abhyamanavân svavân vâ, i.e.*, either "with ministers, or with diseases, or with riches." See Goldstücker, *s.vv. amavat* and *abhyamanavat.* Yâska seems thus to have been undecided as to the sense. See also Sâyaṇa on R.V. iv. 4, 1, and Wilson's note on the same passage, as also Mahîdhara on Vâj. S. 13, 9.

*Amina* is explained by Sâyaṇa on R.V. vi. 19, as=*ahiṃsanîya*, "uninjurable;" and on this passage he gives no other sense. Prof. Goldstücker, *s.v.*, after assigning the two senses (1) "of an unlimited measure or quantity (of strength), or (2) uninjured," goes on to say: "According to Yâska (vi. 16) the word may have either of these meanings in the following verse of the R.V. (vi. 19, 1);" and quotes Durga, the commentator on Yâska, to show that the words of the latter are to be so understood. Durga also observes that from the form of the word, and the suitableness of both senses, either is admissible. But we are not yet arrived at an end of the optional meanings proposed for this adjective. I learn from Prof. Goldstücker's next article that in another text (R.V. x. 116, 4), where this same term occurs (applied, too, as in vi. 19, 1, along with *dvibarhas*, as an epithet of Indra), it has two other meanings assigned to it by Sâyaṇa, *both different from those assigned by Yâska* to the word in R.V. vi. 19, 1 (and one of which he (Sâyaṇa) himself adopts in his note on that passage). These two new meanings are "going everywhere" (*sarvayantâ*), and "all-beloved" (*sarvaiḥ kâmyamânaḥ*).

Could anything show more demonstratively the conjectural and etymological character of many of Sâyaṇa's interpretations?

*Amatra* is found as an epithet of Indra in R.V. i. 61, 9, where it is explained by Sâyaṇa as either = "expert in moving in battles, etc., or devoid of any limit." It is also found in iii. 36, 4, where the Commentator renders it, "a vanquisher of enemies." This latter text is quoted in Nir. vi. 23, where the senses of "measureless, great, or uninjured," are assigned to the word. See Goldstücker, *s.v. abhyamita.*

*Amîtavarṇa,* spoken of the Dawns in R.V. iv. 51, 9, is explained by Sâyaṇa as = *ahiṃsitavarṇâ aparimitavarṇâ vâ,* "either of uninjured colour, or of unlimited colour." He could not therefore have had any precise idea of the sense.

*Amanda,* applied to hymns in R.V. i. 126, 1, is by Yâska, (ix. 10) in his explanation of that passage, rendered as = *abâliṣân analpân vâ,* "either not foolish, or not few." Sâyaṇa contents himself with the second sense.

*Ayâsya* has more than one signification assigned to it by Sâyaṇa in i. 62, 7, and viii. 51, 2. See Prof. Goldstücker's Dictionary, *s.v.*

*Aptur,* said to be derived from *ap,* "water," and *tur,* "to hasten," an epithet of the gods in general (R.V. i. 3, 8), of Agni (iii. 27, 11), of Indra (iii. 51, 2, and according to the scholiast, in ii. 21, 5 also, though there it may be a nom. pl.), is declared by Sâyaṇa to have in all these passages the sense of "sender, or senders, of water." In i. 118, 4, where it is an epithet of the horses (according to Sâyaṇa), or the falcons, of the Aṣvins, he ascribes to it the signification of "quick like the waters" (*âpa iva tvaropetâḥ*). Prof. Goldstücker follows the Scholiast in assigning to it both these senses, viz.: "(1) sending water (*i.e.* rain), an epithet of Indra, Agni, etc.; (2) quick as water (*i.e.* as the falling rain), an epithet of the horses of the Aṣwins." I confess I do not think the commentator's opinion a sufficient reason for concluding that the word has two different meanings. It also occurs in R.V. ix. 61, 13 = S.V. i. 487, where Prof. Benfey renders it "flood-conquering" (while in his Glossary he makes it "water-shedding"). In his translation of R.V. i. 3, 8, in Orient und Occident, he gives it the sense of "active in works," and in i. 118, 4, of "hastening through the air." Prof. Roth, in his Lexicon, *s.v.*, renders it "active, zealous." The substantive *aptûryam* is rendered with some variation by Sâyaṇa in two passages, R.V. iii. 12, 8, and iii. 51, 9, as *vṛshṭi-dvârâ prerakatvam*, "the quality of impelling (or stimulating) *by means of* rain," and *apâm preraṇe*, "in the impelling (or sending) of rain."

In R.V. iii. 27, 11, the word *yanturam*, an epithet of Agni, is explained as either = *sarvasya niyantâram*, "the controuler of all things," or *kshipraṃ gantâram*, "quickly going."

*Ardhadeva*, in R.V. iv. 42, 8, is interpreted by Sâyaṇa as either "near the gods," or "half a god."

*Asaṣchat* is a participle of frequent occurrence in the R.V. One of the passages in which it is found, vi. 70, 2, is quoted in Nir. v. 2, where it is said to be equivalent to *asajyamâne*, "not attached together," or *vyudasyantyau*, "throwing apart, scattering." Sâyaṇa on this verse merely repeats Yâska. In i. 160, 2, where the word is again an epithet of heaven and earth, he explains it similarly, *asajyamâne paraspara-viyukte*, "not attached, separate from each other." In i. 112, 2, he takes it for an epithet of the worshippers, in the sense of *anyatrânâsaktâḥ*, "not attached to any one else." In vii. 67, 9, it is an epithet of the Aṣvins, and is in like manner interpreted by him *kutrâpy asajyamânau*, "not attached anywhere. In iii. 57, 6, he connects it with *pramati*, "the design" or "disposition" of Agni, derives it from *saṣch*, "to go," and explains it *asmad anyatra sangatim akurvâṇâ*, "not forming an union with any one but us." In. ii. 32, 3, it is an epithet of *dhenu*, "cow," and he there renders it *asaktâvayavâm*, "having her members unattached" (to what?). In ii. 25, 4, where he regards it as an epithet of "waters," (understood), he explains it, *asajyamânâḥ, aniruddhâḥ*, "unattached, unobstructed." In viii. 31, 4, where it is an epithet of *iḷâ*, "food," he derives it from *saṣch*, "to go," and renders it by *ăgamana-ṣîlam*,, "that whose character is not to go, or depart." In i. 13, 6, and i. 142, 6 (two verses which are partly identical in contents), the word *asaṣchataḥ* is an epithet of *dvârah*, "doors." In the former of the two texts (i. 13, 6), Sâyaṇa renders it *udghâṭanena praveshṭṛ-purusha-sanga-rahitâḥ*, "destitute of the contact or presence of persons entering in consequence of their being opened" (*i.e.* as Prof. Wilson explains "[hitherto] unentered"); whilst in the second passage (i. 142, 6) he renders *asajyamânâḥ paraspara-viprakṛshṭâḥ*,[1] "not attached or joined, distant or apart from each other." The renderings in the last two (parallel) passages seem to be mutually inconsistent, as the latter appears to mean that the doors, of which the two halves stood apart, were open, whilst the former, although we adopt Prof. Wilson's addition of "hitherto," imports that although they were about to be opened, they were still closed. In i. 13, 6, Rosen translates, "non frequentatæ" (which does not differ materially from Wilson's rendering); but in his note, subsequently composed, he says he should (in addition to other changes) prefer to interpret the word under consideration "non clausæ." I observe that in the quotation which he there adduces from Sâyaṇa's Commentary, his reading differs from that given by Müller, in adding a negative particle, as it runs thus, *udghâṭanena na purusha-sanga-rahitâḥ*, which would make the sense, "doors which from their being opened are *not* destitute of the contact or presence of persons entering." Westergaard, *s.v. saṣch*, follows Rosen's note in rendering *asaṣchataḥ* by "portæ non clausæ." Sâyaṇa, on i. 13, 6, derives the word from *sasj*, "to go," with *a* negative prefixed, but in the passages where he renders it by *asajyamâna*, or *anâsakta*, "not attached," he must, I suppose, be understood to ascribe to this root the sense of "being joined, or attached." Wilson, in his note on i. 142, 6, has noticed the variations in Sâyaṇa's rendering of the term *asaṣchataḥ*. In addition to this discrepancy between his translations of i. 13, 6 and i. 142, 6, I have to observe that Sâyaṇa's explanation of the word in viii. 31, 4, as meaning "that which does not depart," seems to be scarcely consistent

[1] I should add that Sâyaṇa here offers alternative renderings both of *asaṣchatah* —making it a masc. pl. with the sense, "devoid of persons entering,"—and of the verb *viṣrayantâm*, which he says may be explained not only "let them be opened," but "let them seek, or approach" (*sevantâm*).

with the signification "unobstructed," which he assigns in ii. 25, 4, which implies that the waters could depart elsewhere. At all events, the two meanings are quite different. I have no access to Sâyaṇa's explanations of the word where it occurs in the ninth and tenth books of the R.V.; but R.V. ix. 57, 1, is repeated in the Sâma-veda, ii. 1111, where I find from Prof. Benfey's Glossary that the Scholiast renders it *sanga-rahita*, "free from contact." Benfey himself, in his Glossary, translates it "free from pursuers, unhindered," or, when spoken of rain, "thick." In his translation of the passage of the S.V. however, he renders the word by "lovely;" and the cognate word *asaşchushî* in S.V. ii. 502, by "kindly-disposed." In his translation of R.V. i. 13, 6, in Orient und Occident, Benfey renders *asaşchataḥ*, "good" (from *a* privative and *saşchat*, "persecuting, enemy"); but in i. 112, 2, he gives "inexhaustible" (unversiegbar) as its equivalent. Prof. Roth (see his Lexicon, *s.v.*) proposes to render "unfailing." On the whole I think that the senses proposed by Sâyaṇa are either too various, too vague, or two forced, to be admitted as satisfactory, and have very much the appearance of being conjectural.

*Âhanas* is understood by Yâska (iv. 15, in his interpretation of R.V. ix. 75, 5, where it occurs in the plural as an epithet of *madâḥ*, "intoxicating draughts"), as = *âhananavantaḥ*, "smiting." In his explanation (Nir. v. 2) of R.V. x. 10, 8, where it is an epithet of Yamî, he adheres to the same etymology, and makes it signify "smiting as it were with uncivil words" (*âhamsîva bhâshamâṇâ iti asabhya-bhâshaṇâd âhanâ iva bhavati etasmâd âhanaḥ syât*). I have not access to Sâyaṇa's Commentary on these two verses, or on x. 125, 2; but on ii. 13, 1 (where he applies it to Soma) he takes it in a passive sense, "to be smitten, to be poured out" (*âhantavyo 'bhishotavyaḥ*), while on v. 42, 13, he gives it the active signification of *âhantâ sektâ*, "smiter, shedder." It seems unlikely that the term should have both these senses.

*Âtuje* in R.V. vii. 32, 9, is explained by Sâyaṇa as an epithet (in the dative) of Indra, with the meaning either "of destroyer of enemies, or giver of wealth." Müller makes it mean "to give." The last words of the verse, *na devâsaḥ kavatnave*, are rendered by Müller (Anc. Sansk. Lit. p. 544), "the gods are not to be trifled with." Wilson has, "the gods favour not the imperfect rite." In his note he shows a curious misapprehension of Sâyaṇa when he says: "The scholiast seems to render it, men do not become gods by such means, *devâ na bhavanti*." These last words merely mean, as I take them: "The gods are not for (*i.e.*, are not favourers of) a *kàvatnu*;" whether that adjective means, as Roth, *s.v.*, proposes, "a niggard," or, possibly,—as may be suggested, if we regard it as in opposition to the word *taraṇi* in the preceding clause,—"an inert or timid man." In illustration of the construction, compare iv. 33, 11, *na ṛte ṣrântasya sakhyâya devâḥ*, "the gods [are not disposed] for the friendship of the man who is tired of sacred rites" (though Sâyaṇa renders differently); and vii. 61, 5, *na vâṃ niṇyâny achite abhûvan*, "your secret things are not for the unthinking man." (Wilson does not translate Sâyaṇa accurately here).

In R.V. i. 84, 16, Sâyaṇa assigns to the word *kaḥ* the optional senses of "who?" or of "Prajâpati," and to *gâḥ* those of "horses," or "words of the Veda."

*Dhiyâvasu* is an .epithet of Sarasvatî in i. 3, 10 (=Vâj. S. 20, 84), and of Agni in iii. 3, 2, and iii. 28, 1. Yâska comments on the first of these passages in Nir. xi. 26, and there explains *dhiyâvasu* by the vague equivalent *karmavasu*, which may meàn, "rich in works," or "she who through works confers wealth." This last sense, though not in itself obvious, is the one extracted from the compound by Sâyaṇa, who render *skarma-prâpya-dhana-nimitta-bhûtâ*, "she who is the cause of the wealth which is to be acquired through works." He afterwards repeats the same explanation in the words, *dhiyâ karmaṇâ vasu yasyâḥ sakâṣâd bhavati sâ dhiyâvasuḥ*. On iii. 28, 1 he interprets similarly, and Mahîdhara on Vâj. S. 20, 84, not very differently. On R.V. iii. 3, 2, however, Sâyaṇa gives the word a totally different sense, *prajnayâ vyâptaḥ*, "pervaded by wisdom."

*Vidadvasu* is variously explained by Sâyaṇa in three different passages, i. 6, 6; v. 39, 1; viii. 55, 1. In the first, where he takes it for an epithet of the Maruts, he makes it signify *vedayadbhiḥ sva-mahima-prakhyâpakair vasubhir dhanair yuktam*, "possessed of riches which make known their greatness." Further on he gives the additional explanation, *audâryâtiṣayavattayâ jnâpayanti vasûni dhanâni yaṃ sa vidadvasuḥ*, "he whom his riches make known as exceedingly generous is *vidadvsau*." In v. 39, 1, the word is applied to Indra, and there the Scholiast gives it the sense of *labdha-dhana*, "he by whom wealth has been obtained."[1] In viii. 55, 1, where it is an epithet of the same god, it is declared by Sâyaṇa to mean *vedayadvasuṃ dhanâvedakam*, the god "who makes known riches." The term, however, was most probably intended by the authors of the hymns to have but one sense.

*Gabhasti*, in R.V. i. 54, 4, is interpreted by Sâyaṇa as either "taken with the hand," or "having rays."

*Hvârya*, in R.V. v. 9, 4, receives from Sâyaṇa a threefold interpretation, viz. either (1) "a wriggling serpent," or (2) "a horse performing the *âskandita* and other tortuous movements," or (3) "an unbroken colt." Compare Wilson's note.

*Kaṣâ* means a "whip," but in the Nighaṇṭus i. 11, it is also said to be one of the fifty-six synonymes of *vâch*, "speech." In R.V. i. 22, 3, and i. 157, 4, mention is made of the *kaṣâ madhumatî* or "honied whip" of the Aṣvins, and they are asked to moisten with it the sacrifice or the worshippers. In both these places Sâyaṇa gives an optional rendering of *kaṣâ*, as signifying either "whip," or "speech." Mahîdhara on Vâj. S. 7, 11, gives the word the sense of "speech" only. See Note 1 in p. 363 of my Article on the "Progress of the Vedic Religion," etc., in the last volume of this Journal.

*Krandasî* is interpreted by Sâyaṇa on R.V. ii. 12, 8, as either "heaven and earth making a sound," or "two armies, human and divine." On vi. 25, 4, he takes it for two disputants "crying and abusing" each other (*krandamânâv âkroṣantau*). I have not access to his commentary on x.

[1] Yâska quotes this verse (Nir. iv. 4) and explains *vidadvasu* by *vittadhana*, which may mean either "he by whom wealth is known," or "by whom wealth has been obtained."

121, 6, but I observe that Prof. Müller in his translation of the hymn (Anc. Sansk. Lit., p. 569) renders the term by "heaven and earth," which is also the only sense assigned to it by Mahîdhara on Vâj. S. 32, 7, where the verse is repeated.

*Nabhanya* is explained by Sâyaṇa in i. 149, 3, as = *nabhasi bhavo nabhasvân vâyuḥ*, "that which is produced, or exists, in the sky, the wind;" in i. 173, 1, as = *nabhasyam nabhasi bhavaṃ nabhovyâpinaṃ hiṃsakaṃ vâ râkshasâdikasya*, either "etherial, pervading the sky," or "destructive of Râkshasas," etc.; and in vii. 42, 1, as = *stotra*, "a hymn."

*Nṛchakshas*, which is not in the Nirukta, is generally translated by Sâyaṇa, "beholder of men" (R.V. iv. 3, 3; vii. 60, 2), or, "beholder of the conductors of rites" (*nṛnâm* being taken as = *karma-netṛîṇâm*). In i. 22, 7, however, though said to mean primarily, "he who sees men" (*nṛîṇṣ chashṭe*), it is (as an epithet of Savitri) explained by the words, "illuminator of men" (*manushyâṇâṃ prkaâṣa-kâriṇam*); and in i. 91, 2, by "he who shows to the conductors of sacrifices the desired fruit (of their rites)."

*Sûrachakshas* is found in Nir. xi. 16 (where R.V. i. 110, 4, is explained) as an epithet of the Ribhus. Yâska gives it the sense of "sun-speaking (?) or sun-wise," *sûra-khyânâ vâ sûra-prajnâ vâ*. Sâyaṇa does not adhere to more than one of Yâska's renderings, and proposes *sûrya-samâna-prakâṣâḥ sûrya-sadṛṣa-jnânâ vâ*, "having splendour like the sun," or "having knowledge like the sun." The word also occurs in R.V. i. 16, 1, where Sâyaṇa takes it for *sûrya-samâna-prakâṣa-yuktâ ṛtvijaḥ*, "having splendour like the sun, priests." The correctness of this last interpretation seems very doubtful; and I do not see why the word should not be, as Benfey makes it (Or. und Occ.), an epithet of *harayaḥ*, Indra's tawny horses. If so, the verse would run thus: "Let the tawny horses bring thee, the vigorous, to the soma-draught, Indra, thee, the sun-eyed steeds." The sense of "eye" or "sight" is assigned by Sâyaṇa in v. 66, 6, to *chakshas* in *îya-chakshasâ*, which he renders *vyâpta-darṣanau*; in *sahasra-chakshas*, an epithet of Varuṇa, in vii. 34, 10, which he interprets by *bahu-chakshus*, "many-eyed;" and, optionally, in the compound *ghora-chak-*

*shase* (vii. 104, 2), which he explains *ghora-darṣanâya parusha-bhâshiṇe vâ*. *Sûrachakshas* is rendered "sun-eyed" by Benfey in i. 116, 4, also; though in his note he doubts whether this means, "with eyes gleaming like the sun," or "with eyes which see all, like the sun." To the compound *uruchakshas*, Sâyaṇa gives the sense of "seer of many," in i. 25, 5, and vii. 51, 9; of "great seers," in viii. 90, 2; of "to be seen by many," in i. 25, 16; but of "possessing great brilliancy," in vii. 35, 8; vii. 63, 4.

*Châkshma*, in R.V. ii. 24, 9, is said by Sâyaṇa to signify *sarvasya drashṭâ sarva-saho vâ*, either "all-seeing," or "all-enduring."

*Jenya* is explained by Sâyaṇa on R.V. i. 74, 4, as meaning either "manifested," or "conquerors (of Râkshasas)."

*Pastyâ*, though generally rendered by Sâyaṇa "people," "men," house," "dwellers in a house" (i. 25, 10; i. 40, 7; i. 164, 30), has in one place (iv. 1, 11) the alternative sense of "river" assigned to it.

In R.V. i. 180, 7, the words *vi paṇir hitavân* are said by Sâyaṇa to mean either, "the vessel which receives the stipulated libation (?) has had the liquid put into it" (*paṇiḥ paṇâdhâro droṇa-kalaṣo vihitavân sthâpita-rasavân âsît*), or "let the trafficker, avaricious, unsacrificing, who, though possessed of wealth, does not sacrifice, be separated" (*paṇir vaṇik lubdhako 'yashṭâ hitavân niyata-dhano dhanâḍhyo 'py ayashṭâ vi yujyatâm*). The difference between these two explanations is evidently prodigious, and shows how greatly the Scholiast was at a loss. Compare Wilson's note *in loco*.

*Ûtayaḥ*, generally rendered "aids," is in i. 84, 20, explained by Sâyaṇa as = *gantâraḥ* "goers," or as standing (with the loss of the initial *dh*) for *dhûtayaḥ*, "shakers," meaning the Maruts. He also assigns to *râdhâṃsi* in the same verse the unusual sense of "spirits" (*bhûtâni*). He seems to have regarded these strange interpretations as necessitated by the following verb *dabhan*, which has commonly the sense of "injure," "destroy." But it may have here, as Roth proposes, *s.v.*, the signification of "fail."

*Dhṛta-vrata* is an epithet often applied to the gods, chiefly to Mitra, Varuṇa, and the Âdityas. It means, "one whose ordinance stands fast," "one by whom the order of nature is upheld," according to Roth, *s.v.*, and Müller, "Anc. Sansk. Lit." p. 534. Sâyaṇa on R.V. i. 15, 6, renders it by *svîkṛta-karmâṇau*, "those by whom works are accepted;" or, as Wilson translates, "propitious to pious acts." In i. 25, 8, also, Sâyaṇa explains the word *svîkṛta-karma-viṣeshaḥ*, "he by whom a particular work is accepted;"[1] whereas Müller (p. 536) makes it, "the upholder of order." In v. 1 of the same hymn the word *vrata* (with which *dhṛta-vrata* is compounded) is vaguely rendered by Sâyaṇa as=*karma*, "work;" and Wilson translates the phrase *vrataṃ praminîmasi* (which Sâyaṇa explains as= *karma pramâdena hiṃsitavantaḥ*), by "we disfigure thy worship by imperfections." Müller renders it, probably more accurately, "break thy laws." It is not clear which of the senses Sâyaṇa adopted; for in other passages, where there can be no doubt that the sense is what Müller makes it, Sâyaṇa uses the same terms of explanation. This is the case in ii. 38, 7, and v. 69, 4, where it is declared that no one can, or that the other gods cannot, hinder the ordinances of Savitri, or of Mitra and Varuṇa, in which passages it is far more likely that "decrees" or "designs," than "ceremonies," are contemplated. In ii. 28, 8, where it is said that the ordinances of Varuṇa rest unshaken on him as on a mountain, Sâyaṇa explains *vratâni* by *karmâṇi vidharaṇâni*, "works," "upholdings." And in ii. 38, 2, 9, he interprets the word of the "creative or impulsive act," *prasavâkhyaṃ karma*, of Savitri. So, too, in i. 101, 3, he gives it the signification of *niyama-rûpe karmaṇi*, *niyamanam* "controuling act," "controul;" in iii. 30, 4, of *karmaṇe*, *âjnâyai*, "command;" and in vii. 31, 11, of *rakshaṇâdîni karmâṇi*, "preservation and other works." But there are other passages in which he undoubtedly explains *vrata* by "rite," in accordance with the modern use of the word; as in i. 69, 4, where he takes it for *etâni paridṛṣyamânâni darṣa-pûrṇamâsâdîni karmâṇi*, "these rites which we see, the *darṣa*, *pûrṇamâsa*," etc.; and in i. 91, 3, where he takes it alternatively for *sarvâṇy agnishṭomâdîni karmâṇi*, "all the ceremonies, the

[1] On iv. 53, 4, he makes it=*dhṛtakarmâ*, "he by whom work is upheld."

*agnishṭoma*," etc., or *karmâṇi lokahitakâriṇi*, "acts promotive of the good of the world;" whilst in v. 63, 7, where Mitra and Varuṇa are said to uphold ordinances by their support, "through the wisdom of the divine Spirit," (*dharmaṇâ vratâ rakshethe asurasya mâyayâ*), he explains these words by *jagad-dhârakena vṛshṭy-âdi-lakshaṇena karmaṇâ vratâ yajnâdi-karmâṇi rakshethe pâlayathaḥ*, "ye support sacrifice and other rites by your world-sustaining action in the form of rain," etc. He interprets the word *vrata* in a similar manner in the following texts: i. 92, 12; i. 124, 2; ii. 28, 2; vii. 47, 3; vii. 76, 5. In most, at least, of these passages, however, there is little doubt the word *vrata* means "ordinances," or "laws." If there could be any question as to its having this meaning elsewhere, the point would be settled by R.V. x. 33, 9, *na devânâm ati vratam ṣatâtmâ chana jîvati*, "even the man of a hundred years does not live beyond the ordinance of (the term ordained by) the gods."[1] *Avrata* probably means quite as much "lawless," as "destitute of rites." (See Roth's Lexicon, *s.v.*) In x. 2, 4, where it is said that Agni rectifies whatever transgressions of the ordinances (*vratâni*) of the gods may be committed by the worshippers, the word probably alludes to sacred rites.

*Raṇva* in R.V. ii. 24, 11, means, Sâyaṇa tells us, *ramayitâ stotavyo vâ*, either "a giver of pleasure," or "one who is to be praised."

*Râti* in R.V. i. 60, 1, is a word about which Sâyaṇa is uncertain. He first explains it as "friend," a sense which he supports by the authority of Kapardin (whoever he may be), and then adds, "some say *râti* means "son," and in proof of this he quotes R.V. iii. 2. 4. But when we turn to that passage we find, strangely enough, that he renders the word by *abhilashitârthapradâtâram*, "giver of desired objects."

*Rudravarttani*, *hiraṇyavarttani* are epithets frequently applied to the gods, but diversely interpreted by Sâyaṇa. He explains the former in R.V. i. 3, 3, as meaning "leading in

[1] Compare R.V. viii. 28, 4, where a similar idea is expressed without the employment of the word *vrata*: *Yathâ vaṣanti devâs tathâ id asat tad eshâm nakir â minat*, etc., "As the gods wish, so it comes to pass; no one hinders that [will] of theirs," etc.

the front of the battle like heroes, who make their enemies weep." On viii. 22, 1, and 14, he renders it "those who in battle pursue a path characterized by weeping, or those whose path is praised." *Hiraṇyavarttani* in viii. 5, 11, he translates "they whose path is golden, or whose car is golden, or whose conduct is beneficent and pleasant" (*hita-ramaṇîyâcharaṇau.* On viii. 8, 1, he confines himself to the two latter senses. In vi. 61, 7, he makes it "having a golden chariot," and in viii. 26, 18, "having a golden path." Compare *kṛshṇa-varttani* and *ghṛtavarttani.*

*Stṛbhiḥ* is a word which Sâyaṇa translates by "stars" (*nakshatraiḥ*) in i. 68, 5; iv. 7, 3; vi. 49, 3, 12. Compare x. 68, 11. It is also found in ix. 68, 4, but I am not aware how he renders it there. Yâska explains the word in the same way, referring to one of these passages, iv. 7, 3, in illustration. In i. 87, 1, however, where it occurs in the following connection, *anjibhir vyânajre kechid usrâ iva stṛbhiḥ,* Sâyaṇa explains it by *svaṣarîrasyâchhâdakaiḥ,* "covering their bodies," a sense, which I suppose to be a purely conjectural one, based only on etymology. He separates it from its more immediate context and makes it an epithet of *anjibhiḥ,* rendering the clause thus: "The Maruts are seen distinct in the sky through the ornaments covering their bodies, like any rays of the sun shining in the sky." The position of *stṛbhiḥ* after *usrâḥ* is, however, rather adverse to this construction and rendering; and makes Roth's translation more probable, viz., "like many oxen with stars, *i.e.* white spots." See s. v. *usra.* Benfey translates differently, but retains the sense "stars," and thinks spots on the forehead may be meant. See Orient und Occident, ii. 250.

*Sahasramushka* is translated by Sâyaṇa on R.V. vi. 46, 3, (= Sâma-veda i. 286) as equivalent to *sahasraṣepha,* "mille membra genitalia habens;" and a story illustrative of Indra's lasciviousness is adduced from the Kaushîtakins to support this sense. In viii. 19, 32 the word is applied to Agni, and there Sâyaṇa renders it *bahutejaskam* "having many flames," *mushka* being considered as = *tejas,* from its stealing away, or removing darkness.

*Ṣundhyu* in R.V. i. 124, 4 is understood by Yâska (iv. 16) of the "sun," or of a "white water-fowl." Sâyaṇa repeats the same optional interpretation.

*Svarâj*, as an epithet of Indra, is differently explained by Sâyaṇa in R.V. 1, 61, 9; iii. 46, 1; vii. 82, 2; and viii. 12, 14. In iii. 46, 1, he makes it = *dhanâdhipati*, "lord of wealth," (*sva* here standing for "property"), and in the other places= *svenaiva tejasâ râjamâṇaḥ*, "shining by his own lustre," or *svayam eva anya-nirapekshayaiva râjamâṇaḥ*, "shining of himself, without reference to any one else," etc. In ii. 28, 1, where it is an epithet of Varuṇa, it is said by Sâyaṇa to mean "shining of himself," or "lord."

*Sakshaṇi* is differently explained by Sayaṇa in R.V. i. 111, 3, and in ii. 31, 4. In the former place it is said to mean "overcoming" (*asmân abhibhavantam*), whilst in the latter it is rendered, "to be served or reverenced" (*sachanîyaḥ sevyaḥ*). In viii. 22, 15, also, it is similarly interpreted *sachanîya-ṣîlau*. The word is also found in R.V. ix. 71, 4, and ix. 110, 1, but I have no access to the commentary on these two passages. The latter is, however, repeated in the Sâma-veda, i. 428, where Prof. Benfey renders the word "taming (enemies)." The sense of "overcoming" or "controuling" seems generally suitable in these passages. The word is, I presume, to be derived from the root *sah*, not from *sach*.

R.V. i. 140, 9. The word *tuvigrebhiḥ*, an epithet of Agni's attendants (*satvabhiḥ*) is explained by Sâyaṇa to mean either *prabhûtam ṣabdayadbhiḥ*, "much-sounding," or *prabhûta-gamanaiḥ*, "much-going." The apparently kindred word *tuvigraye*, R.V. ii. 21, 2 (an epithet, in the dative, of Indra) is said by him to mean either *pûrṇa-grîvâya*, "with full neck," or *bahubhiḥ stotavyâya*, "to be praised by many."

*Vṛtaṇchaya*, an epithet of Indra in R.V. ii. 21, 3, is declared by Sâyaṇa to mean either *abhîshṭasyâchetâ sanchetâ dâtâ*, "the bestower of what is desired," or (*vṛt ṣatruḥ, taṃ chayate hinasti iti vṛtanchayaḥ*, a "destroyer of enemies." *Radhrachoda*, in the following verse, is asserted to signify *samṛddhânâṃ prerakaḥ yadvâ hiṃsakânâṃ ṣatrûṇâṃ chodakaḥ*, either "a promoter of the affluent, or a driver of enemies."

*Varûtrî* appears to be explained by Sâyaṇa in i. 22, 10, as an epithet (*varaṇîya*, "to be desired"), of Dhishaṇâ, the goddess of speech. In vii. 38, 5, and vii. 40, 6, however, the word is treated as a proper name, denoting the goddess of speech, *Vâg-devî* or *Sarasvatî.* In Vâj. S. xi. 61, we have the word in the plural, *Varûtrîḥ*, where Mahîdhara says they are "goddesses personifying day and night" (*Varûtrayo devyo 'horâtrâbhimâninyaḥ* . . . "*ahorâtrâṇi vai varûtrayaḥ* | *ahorâtrair hi idaṃ sarvaṃ vṛtam*" *iti* (Ṣ. P. Br. 6, 5, 4, 6). In R.V. i. 22, 11, the epithet *achhinnapatra* is applied to the wives of the gods, and signifies, according to Sâyaṇa, "with wings uncut." For, he adds, "the wings of the wives of the gods, who have a winged form, are not cut by any one." Mahîdhara on Vâj. S. xi. 61, explains the term somewhat differently, as "those whose course or flight is not cut or hindered, constantly going," *achhinnam patram patanaṃ yâsâṃ tâḥ satatayâyinyaḥ.*

*Vihâyas* means, in modern Sanskrit, "sky," "bird." In the Nighaṇṭus 3, 3, it is given as one of the synonymes of *mahat*, "great." In Nir. iv. 15 (where Yâska quotes and interprets R.V. ix. 75, 5) it is said, as an epithet of *madâḥ*, "intoxicating draughts," to signify *vanchanavantaḥ*, "deceiving, deluding." The word occurs again as an epithet of Viṣvakarman in R.V. x. 72, 2 (=Vâj. S. 17, 26); and in Nir. x. 26, where that verse is explained, it is rendered by *vyâptâ*, "pervader." Mahîdhara interprets it as meaning either, "pervading like the ether," or "one who especially forsakes, a destroyer," *nabho-vad vyâpako yadvâ viṣeshena jahâti tyajati vihâyâḥ sanharttâ.* *Vihâyas* is also found as an epithet of Indra in R.V. iii. 36, 2, where Sâyaṇa, after stating that its constituent elements mean "the giver of the desired objects to suppliants," ends by assigning to it the simple sense of "great" (*vijahâty utsṛjaty arthân arthibhya iti vihâyâ mahân.* In iv. 11, 4, without entering into any explanation, he ascribes to it the same meaning. In his above cited comment on R.V. x. 72, 2 (Nir. x. 26), Yâska proposes no less than five different renderings for the participle *ishṭâni*, viz., *kântâni*, *krântâni*, *gatâni*, *matâni*, and *natâni.*

*Vishitashṭukâ*, an epithet of Rodasî ("the wife of the Maruts, or lightning," *Marutpatnî vidyud vâ*) in R.V. i. 167, 5, is said by Sâyaṇa to mean either "having a distinguished mass of hair," or "having a dishevelled mass of hair" (*viṣishṭa-keṣa-sanghâ viprakîrṇa-keṣa-sanghâ vâ*). Compare the different senses assigned to the word *pṛthushṭuka*, above.

*Mesha* occurs in the R.V. as a designation of Indra. On i. 51, 1 (=S.V. i. 376) Sâyaṇa renders it "striving with enemies, or ram, because Indra had come in that form to the rishi Medhâtithi when sacrificing, and drunk his soma," etc. On i. 52, 1 (=S.V. i. 377) the Scholiast only mentions the first of these two senses; but on viii. 86, 12, he returns to the second and gives it as the exclusive meaning. He here, however, says that Indra, in the form of a ram, carried Medhâtithi to heaven. In fact, there is a verse of the R.V. viii. 2, 40, which says, *itthâ dhîvantam adrivah Kâṇvam Medhyâtithim* | *mesho bhûto 'bhi yann ayaḥ* | "Thus, thunderer, having become a ram, and approaching the devout Medhyâtithi of the race of Kaṇva, thou didst carry him away, (or, thou didst depart)." Sâyaṇa gives to the verb *ayaḥ* here the causal sense of *agamayaḥ*. Compare the words of i. 51, 13, *menâ abhavo Vṛshaṇaṣvasya*, which either arose out of, or gave rise to, another story about Indra.

*Varîmabhiḥ*, in R.V. i. 55, 2, is rendered by Sâyaṇa either "coverings, or vastnesses," *saṃvaraṇair yadvâ urutvaiḥ*.

In regard to *ubhayâsaḥ*, in R.V. i. 60, 2, it is left doubtful by Sâyaṇa, whether it means both gods and men, or priests and those for whom they officiated.

*Varâha* is given in Nigh. i. 10, as one of the names for "cloud." In Nir. v. 4, two senses, "cloud" and "boar," are assigned to it, R.V. i. 61, 7 being quoted as a passage where it has the former meaning. Sâyaṇa, *in loco*, understands it either of "cloud" or "sacrifice." See Wilson's note.

The notes to the fourth volume of Prof. Wilson's translation of the Rig-veda (verified by reference to the original Commentary), and an examination of parts of the volume itself, supply the following additional instances of double renderings by Sâyaṇa, or of variations in interpretation between him and Mahîdhara, the commentator on the Vâjasaneyi Sanhitâ:—

R.V. vi. 62, 8. *Rakshoyuje* is explained by Sâyaṇa as "lord or instigator of Rakshases, or priest united with Rakshases;"

ibid. 10. *Nṛvatâ rathena*, as "chariot with a charioteer, or with horses;"

vi. 63, 8. *Dhenum isham*, as "gladdening food, or desirable cow."

vi. 71, 3. *Hiraṇyajihva*, "golden-tongued" (so rendered by Wilson), is explained by Sâyaṇa as "having a kind, pleasant voice," though in the next verse he translates *hiraṇyapâṇi*, "golden-handed."

In vi. 75, 11 (=Vâj. S. xxix. 48) the tooth of an arrow is said to be *mṛga*, which Sâyaṇa (following Yâska, ix. 19) understands either as meaning that it is made of "deer's horn," or that it "searches out the enemy." Mahîdhara adheres to the latter sense.

On vi. 75, 13 (=Vâj. S. xxix. 50), I quote Prof. Wilson's note, from which it will be seen that the interpreters are at variance: "*Prachetasaḥ* is applied by Yâska, ix. 20, and Mahîdhara, to *aśvân*, the intelligent horses; but Sâyaṇa is better advised, as there is no other nominative to the verbs *janghanti* and *jighnate*." I think, however, that from the position of *prachetasaḥ* in the verse it is difficult to conect it in the way Sâyaṇa does.

vii. 3, 7. *Pûrbhiḥ* is here rendered "cities," but "protectors" (*pâlakaiḥ*) in vi. 48, 8, where it occurs in a similar connection. It probably means "rampart," as in fact Sâyaṇa himself intimates on vii. 15, 14; *Pûḥ purî tad-rakshâ-sâdhana-bhûta-prăkâr-* (qu. *prâkâr-*) *âdir vâ*, "*Pur* is a city, or walls, etc., which are the means of its defence."

vii. 4, 7. *Parishadyam* is translated either as "fit" (*paryâptam*), or "to be taken away" (*pariharttavyam*); and *araṇa*, here rendered "freedom from debt," is in verse 8 explained as *aramamâṇ*, "not delighting."

vii. 5, 3. *Pûru*, here and in vi. 46, 8, explained as the "name of a king," is in vii. 8, 4, interpreted as the "name of an Asura;"[1] and in i. 63, 7, as an epithet of Sudâs, in the sense of, "satisfying with offerings." In iv. 21, 10, where the context is partly the same as in i. 63, 7, *pûru* is explained "man," "sacrificer." In i. 130, 7, after saying that *pûru* signifies "one who fills up, offers, what is desired," Sâyaṇa ends by telling us that the word is one of the names for "man."

ibid. 7. *Vâyur na pâthaḥ paripâsi* is explained as, "thou drinkest soma like Vâyu," or "thou drinkest up, driest, water like Vâyu."[2]

vii. 6, 4. The subject of the participle *madantîḥ* is said to be either "creatures" (*prajâḥ*), or "dawns" (*ushasaḥ*).

vii. 8, 4 (=Vâj. S. xii. 34). *Ṣṛṇve* is rendered by Sâyaṇa, "is renowned," whilst Mahîdhara makes it, "hears the invocation of the worshipper."

ibid. 6. *Dvibarhâḥ* is explained as "great in knowledge and works," or "great in two worlds."

vii. 16, 1 (=Vâj. S. xv. 32). *Arati* is explained by Sâyaṇa as goer" or "lord;" by Mahîdhara as "having competent understanding," or "of ceaseless activity."

ibid. 7 (=Vâj. S. xxxiii. 14.) *Yantâraḥ* is rendered by Sâyaṇa "givers," and by Mahîdhara, "controuling their senses." Sâyaṇa assigns to *sûrâyaḥ* in the same verse the sense of "impellers," or of "praisers."

vii. 18, 6. *Matsyâso nişitâḥ* is rendered either "like fish confined," or "Matsyas (people so called) harassed;" and *ṣrushṭi*, either "quick arrival," or "happiness," while in *v.* 10 it receives the former sense, and in vii. 40, 1 the latter.

ibid. 8. *Bheda* is explained either "unbeliever" (*nâstika*), or as the name of an enemy of Sudâs (which latter sense is also assigned in vii. 33, 3).

vii. 23, 4 (=Vâj. S. xxxiii. 18), *Âpaṣ chit pipyuḥ staryo na gâvaḥ*: Sâyana: "Let the waters increase like barren

[1] So, too, Mahîdhara on Vâj. S. xii. 34.

[2] Both explanations seem to be wrong. Compare the words *Vishṇurgopâḥ paramam pâti pâthah*, in iii. 55, 10, where Sâyaṇa himself renders the last three words "guards the highest place," though he adds an optional rendering of *pâthaḥ* as the "place of water, the atmosphere."

cows." Mahîdhara: "The waters swell the soma like the Vedic texts, with which libations are offered."

vii. 32, 18 (= S.V. i. 310), compared with viii. 19, 26. In the former passage, the words *na pâpatvâya râsîya*, which are common to both, are explained by *na dadyâm*: "I would not give, *i.e.* I would not give up, my worshipper to wretchedness." (Comp. Müller's transl. of this verse, in his Anc. Sansk. Lit. p. 545. In viii. 1, 22, *râsate* is explained by *dadâti*: "he gives.") In viii. 19, 26, however, the same words, *na râsîya*, though employed in a similar connection, are explained by *na âkroṣayeyam*: "I would not cause thee to be reviled." Prof. Wilson there translates as follows: "May I not be accused, Vasu, of calumniating thee, nor, gracious (Agni), of sinfulness against thee," etc.: instead of which Mr. Cowell proposes to render: "Let me not abuse thee by calumny or wickedness," which is no material improvement. There can be little doubt, I think, that Sâyaṇa, followed by his translators, is wrong, and that the verse should be taken in conjunction with the preceding (v. 25) and (omitting epithets) be explained as follows: "If, Agni, thou wert a mortal, and I an immortal, I should not give thee up to execration, or to wretchedness," etc.[1] We have Sâyaṇa's own authority on vii. 32, 18, as I have shown, for rendering *na râsîya*: "I would not give;" and although he does not explain *pâpatvâya* at all in either of these passages, he does distinctly assign to it the sense of "wretchedness" (*hînabhâvâya*) in a similar text, vii. 94, 3: "Do not, ye heroes, Indra and Agni, subject us to wretchedness (*pâpatvâya*), or to execration, or to reviling." Comp. Benfey's rendering of Sâma-veda, i. 310, and ii. 268.

vii. 41, 2 (=Vâj. S. xxxiv. 35.) *Tura* is rendered by Sâyaṇa "wealthy;" by Mahîdhara "sick," or as a designation of "Yama."

vii. 48, 3. *Uparatâti* is explained here as = *upalatâti*, "that which is carried on with stones, a battle." On i. 151, 5, it is explained as "that which has an extension of clouds."

[1] There are other instances in the hymns of the sense running on from one verse into another. See vv. 5 and 6 of this same hymn, viii. 19, and viii. 12, 32 f. in Prof. Wilson's translation.

vii. 64, 1. The words *ghṛtasya nirṇijaḥ* are interpreted either "forms of water" discharged by the clouds, or "forms of melted butter" offered to Mitra and Varuṇa.

vii. 66, 9. The verb *dhîmahi* is interpreted here, "we hold, or have;" on iii; 62, 10 (the celebrated *gâyatrî*), "we meditate" (*dhyâyâmaḥ*), or "let us hold in our mind as an object of contemplation" (*dheyatayâ manasâ dhârayema*), or "we hold" (*dhârayâmaḥ*). In vii. 15, 7, *nidhîmahî* is explained, "we have placed;" and in i. 17, 6, "we deposit as a treasure."

vii. 71, 4. *Viṣvapsnya* is explained as "pervading" (*vyâptarûpa*), or as a name of Vasishṭha.

vii. 77, 2. *Gavaṃ mâtâ* is said to mean the "former, either of voices, or of cows."

vii. 79, 3. *Angirastamâ*, an epithet of Ushas (the Dawn), is explained as either "the quickest of goers," or as a designation given to her, because night was produced along with the Bharadvâjas of the race of Angiras, and she (the Dawn) forms the end of the night!

vii. 82, 1. *Mahi ṣarma* is explained as either a "great house, or "great happiness."

ibid. 5. *Ṣubham îyate* is explained either, "obtains an ornament," or "sends water."

vii. 83, 2. *Svardṛṣ* is here explained "seeing heaven after quitting the body." In vii. 58, 2, it is interpreted, "seer of the sun, *i.e.* living creature," or "tree, from its seeing the sky."

vii. 90, 1 (=Vâj. S. xxxiii. 70.) *Vîrayâ* is taken by Sâyaṇa for a dative masc. "to the hero (Vâyu);" whilst Mahîdhara joins with it the preceding *pra* and makes *pravîrayâ* an epithet of the soma libations, with the sense, "having excellent heroes sprung from knowledge, priests."

ibid. 3 (=Vaj. S. xxvii. 24.) Sâyaṇa takes *nireke* for "in poverty," and Mahîdhara for "in a place crowded with people."

ibid. 5. *Vîravâham* is explained either to be "borne by worshippers, or by horses."

vii. 99, 3 (=Vaj. S.V. 16.) *Mayûkhaiḥ* is rendered by

Sâyaṇa "mountains,"[1] while Mahîdhara understands it of "various glorious lives (*sva-tejo-rûpair nânâ jîvaiḥ*), or his numerous incarnations in a Boar," etc.

vii. 104, 2. *Ghorachakshas* is explained as either "horrible in aspect," or "harshly speaking."

viii. 1, 2. *Ubhayâvinam* is explained as either "having both celestial and earthly riches," or "having both stationary and moving things to preserve," or "having persons both to praise and sacrifice to him."

ibid. 10. *Gâyatravepas* is explained here "having approved speed," whilst on i. 142, 12, it is interpreted as "having the form of the *gâyatra*."

Ibid. 31. *Yâdvaḥ* is explained as either "of the race of Yadu," or "renowned among men," and *paṣu* as either "having cattle," or "a perceiver of what is minute."

viii. 3, 5. *Samîke* is interpreted as either "at sacrifice," or in battle."

ibid. 9. *Yatibhyaḥ* is explained as either "from non-sacrificing men," or "for men practising rites."

ibid. 24. *Turîya* is explained either "fourth," or a "destroyer of enemies."

viii. 4, 8. *Dâna* is interpreted either a "breaker up," (*avakhaṇḍayitâ*) or a "giver."

viii. 5, 9. *Vi pathaḥ sitam* is explained either "shut up the paths that others may not enter," or the contrary, "open up, show the paths."

ibid. 13. *Brahma janânâm* is interpreted as either "the Brâhman-caste among men," or "the prayer, or the sacrificial food, of men."

ibid. 38. *Charmamnâḥ* is explained as either "practised in the wearing of cuirasses of leather," or "exercised in the use of horses and other instruments of motion." The word is interpreted by Mahîdhara on Vaj. S. xxx. 15, as "a person practised in the handling of leather (*charmâbhyâsa-karam.*")

viii. 6, 3. *Jâmi* is interpreted as either "useless," or "kinsman," *âyudham* as either "weapon," or "assailant," and

[1] Sâyaṇa adds, "For mountains belong to Vishṇu as his own, as the Veda says 'Vishṇu is lord of the mountains.'"

*kaṇvâḥ* as either "encomiasts," or "persons of the family of Kaṇva."

viii. 12, 1. *Mada* is explained as either the "exhilaration" of Indra, or "to be exhilarated," or "exhilarated."

viii. 13, 1. The words *kratum ukthyam* are explained either "the performer of the rite and the encomiast," or the "sacrifice called *ukthya*."

ibid. 3. *Bharâya* is explained either "to the battle," or "to the sacrifice," and it is added that the same words generally denote both these things.

viii. 15, 2. The word *ajrân* is taken as an epithet of the preceding term *girîn*, "mountains or clouds," and explained as "quickly moving." It is diversely interpreted in other passages. On viii. 27, 18, it is made to signify the "city of the enemy, although impregnable against the assaults of others," or "level ground;" on iv. 1, 17, "the undecaying, mountains," or "the moving, rays;" on iv. 19, 7, "travelling on the road;" on v. 54, 4, "clouds." I do not know how Sâyaṇa renders it in x. 44, 8, and x. 59, 3. Prof. Roth renders it "*ager*, field," and Prof. Goldstücker, "field, acre, plain," and also as an adjective, "quick." The sense of "plains" is fixed by the context of x. 59, 3, as, at least, one of the right ones: "Let us by our manly deeds overcome our enemy, as the sky (is over) the earth, and the mountains (over) the plains" (*girayo na ajrân*).

viii. 17, 5. *Kukshyoḥ* is interpreted either, in Indra's "two bellies; (as it is written 'fill both bellies, that of the slayer of Vṛttra, and that of Maghavat'") or "the right and left sides, or the upper and lower parts, of a single belly."

Ibid. 12. *Ṣâchigu* is explained as either "he who has strong cows," or "he who has manifest, famous, rays, or cows."

ibid. 13. *Ṣṛngavṛsho napât* is explained as either "the son of *Ṣringavrish*," or *ṣṛngavṛsh* is "the showerer of rays, the sun," and *napât* "he who causes not to fall, who establishes," and therefore the two words together mean "the establisher of the sun."

ibid. 15. *Pṛdâkusânu* is explained as either "having the

head erect like a serpent," or "to be propitiated like a serpent."

viii. 18, 21. *Trivarûtha* is explained as either "affording protection from three inconveniences—cold, heat, and rain," or "having three stories."

The following are some additional instances of the same description, chiefly from the earlier books of the Rig-veda.

i. 31, 2, and i. 112, 4. *Dvimâtâ*, an epithet of Agni, is explained by Sâyana as either "born from two pieces of wood," *i.e.* by friction, and so having two parents, or "maker of the two worlds." Compare *dvijanmâ* in i. 140, 2, and i. 149, 4, which, in the former place, he interprets either "born from two pieces of wood," or by "friction and the subsequent rite of consecration;" while in the second passage a third sense of "born from heaven and earth," is added. In i. 112, 4, the verb *vibhûshati* is rendered either "pervades," or "adorns." So, also, *paribhûshathaḥ* in iii. 12, 9, is declared to mean either "ye are adorned" (*alankṛtau bhavathaḥ*), or, "ye overcome" (*paribhavathaḥ*). See, above, the different senses assigned by Yâska to *paryabhûshat.*

i. 64, 10. *Vṛsha-khâdayaḥ*, an epithet of the Maruts, is explained as either, "having Indra for their weapon," or "having soma for their beverage." The word is rendered "adorned with ear-rings," by Bollensen (in Benfey's Orient und Occident, ii. 461, note), who refers for the meaning he assigns to *vṛsha* to Wilson's Dictionary, *s.v.*, *vṛshabha*, where one of the senses given is, "the orifice of the ear." *Khâdi* occurs frequently in the R.V. in the sense of an ornament worn by the Maruts, as in v. 53, 4; v. 54, 11, where it is rendered by Sâyana *kaṭaka*, and in vii. 56, 13, where he renders it *alankâra-viṣesha.* On i. 168, 3, he makes it mean "a guard to the hand," *hasta-trâṇaka*, and on i. 166, 9, either "eatables" or "ornaments." In the last passage he takes *prapatheshu* either for "resting-places," or "toes." Roth, *s.v.*, conjectures that the proper reading here must be *prapadeshu.*

i. 92, 10. *Ṣvaghnî* is here taken by Sâyaṇa for the feminine of *ṣvăhâ* (*lit.* dog-killer), and is rendered *vyâdha-strî*, a "hunter's wife." The word is, however, explained by Yâska

(Nir. v. 22, where he quotes R.V. x. 43, 5) as = *kitava*, "a gamester." This sense is adopted by Sâyaṇa himself on viii. 45, 38. On ii. 12, 4, dropping all reference to any feminine sense, he explains the word as "hunter" (*vyâdha*), viz., "one who kills wild animals with dogs" (*ṣvabhir mṛgân hanti*); and in the same way on iv. 20, 3, as *mṛgayu*, "a hunter." See Benfey's note on i. 92, 10, in his version of the passage in his Orient und Occident, ii. 257; and Bollensen's translation of the verse in the same vol., p. 464. If Yâska is right in explaining *ṣvaghnî* as a masculine noun, signifying "gamester," it can scarcely be also the feminine of *ṣvahâ*; or if it be the latter, it cannot well have a masculine sense also. I observe, also, that Sâyaṇa renders the word *vijaḥ* "birds" in i. 92, 10; and "one who causes distress" (*udvejaka*) in ii. 12, 5.

i. 128, 4. *Ishûyate* is said to mean either "to him who desires food," or "to him who desires coming."

i. 169, 5. The words *tve râyas toṣatamaḥ* are rendered either "thy riches are most gladdening," or "thy kinsmen, friends (the Maruts), are most destructive (to clouds which do not rain)."

i. 173, 6. *Opaṣa* is here explained as either a "horn," or "earth and atmosphere." On viii. 14, 5, the scholiast makes it either "a cloud lying near" (*megham upetya ṣayânam*), or "some particular manly power contained in himself" (*i.e.* in Indra, *âtmani samaveto vîrya-viṣeshaḥ*.

i. 190, 5. The words *chayase piyârum* are explained by Sâyaṇa as either, "thou visitest, with the view of favouring, him who drinks, offers, soma," or "thou destroyest the destructive man." The latter interpretation is supported by Nir. iv 25, to which Sâyaṇa refers; and is adopted by him in iii. 30, 8.

ii. 1, 4. *Asura* is explained here as either, "the expeller of foes" (*ṣatrûṇâṃ nirasitâ*), or "the giver of strength, the sun." This word is very variously interpreted by Sâyaṇa in different places. On i. 24, 14, he makes it = *anishṭa-kshepaṇa-ṣîla*, "the hurler away of what is undesired;" on i. 35, 7, *sarveshâṃ prâṇada*, "the giver of life to all;" on i. 54, 3, either, "the expeller of enemies," or "he who has breath, or force," or "the giver of breath, or water;" on i. 64, 2, and i. 174, 1, expellers of enemies;" on i. 108, 6, "thrower of oblations, priest;" on i. 110, 3, an unexplained designation of Tvashtri, perhaps in the later sense of "evil spirit;" on i. 131, 1, "expeller of unrighteous enemies;" on i. 151, 4, "strong;" on ii. 27, 10, *ṣatrûṇâṃ kshepaka*, "hurler away of enemies; on iv. 2, 5; iv. 53, 1; v. 12, 1; v. 15, 1; v. 27, 1; vii. 2, 3; vii. 6, 1; vii. 30, 3; vii. 36, 2, "strong; on v. 42, 1, "giver of breath;" ibid. *v*. 11, "strong," or "giver of breath;" on v. 51, 11, "expeller of enemies, or giver of breath, or force;" on v. 41, 3, "taker away of breath" (Rudra), or "giver of breath" (Sûrya or Vâyu); on iii. 3, 4 "giver of strength;" on iii. 29, 14, "the impelling" (*araṇi*-wood); on v. 63, 3, 7, "the expeller (or discharger) of water, Parjanya;" on v. 83, 6, the same sense; on vii. 56, 1, "wise" (*prajnâvân*); on viii. 20, 17, "a water-discharging cloud," or "rain water;" on viii. 25, 4, "powerful," or "as pervading all things, impellers;" on viii. 79, 6, "powerful, or possessor of life." In the Nighaṇṭus i. 10, *asura* is given as one of the synonymes of "cloud." In Nir. iii. 8, it is said to be = *asu-rata*, "devoted to breath," or to come from *sthâneshu* or *sthânebhyaḥ asta*, "thrown in, or from, places;" or *asu* is a synonyme of *prâṇa*, "life," a thing "thrown into the body. The Asuras are they who have it." And he adds, "it is well known that he (the creator) formed the *Suras* (gods) from *su*, "good," in which their essence consists, and that he formed the Asuras from *asu* (or *a* + *su*, "not good"), and that in this consists their essence." It is to be observed that the verse here explained by Yâska (R.V. x. 53, 4) is one of those later texts in which the word *asura* has the sense of evil spirit, as an enemy of the gods, a sense which it does not generally bear in the older hymns, in which it is a designation of the gods themselves. (In vii. 13, 1, however, Agni is called an "Asura-slayer," as is also Indra in vii. 22, 4).

ii. 11, 21. *Mâ ati dhak* is explained by Sâyaṇa either "do not give to others, passing us by," or "do not burn up our objects of desire."

vi. 2, 7. *Trayâyya* is explained by Sâyaṇa as either, "to be preserved,' or "one who has the three qualifications of science, austerity and works," or "one who has attained to the three births."[1]

viii. 24, 24. *Paripadâm* is explained by Sâyaṇa as either "persons who are sacrificing around," or "birds which are flying around."

*Ṣvâtra* is given in Nigh. ii. 10, among the synonymes of *dhana*, "wealth." In Nir. v. 3, it is said to mean "quick" (*ṣvâtram iti kshipra-nâma âṣu atanaṃ bhavati*); and the words of R.V. x. 88, 4, *sa patatrîtvaraṃ sthâ jagad yach chhvâtram Agnir akṛṇoj jâtavedâḥ* are explained: "Agni Jâtavedas made *quickly* whatever flies, goes, stands or moves." The term is also found in R.V. i. 31, 4, where the clause *ṣvâtreṇa yat pitror muchyase pari*, spoken of Agni, is rendered by Sâyaṇa: "When thou art released from thy parents (the two pieces of wood) by *rapid friction* (*ṣvâtreṇa*)," etc. In viii. 4, 9 (= S.V. i. 277), the word is found in the compound *ṣvâtrabhâj*, an epithet of *vayas* (there stated to mean "food"), and is declared to signify "associated with wealth." In viii. 52, 5, it occurs again in the phrase *ṣvâtram arkâ anûshata*, which the Scholiast interprets, "the worshippers praise *very quickly, very long.*" I am ignorant how he explains the word in x. 46, 7, where it occurs in the plural as an epithet of "fires;" but Mahîdhara on Vâj. S. xxxiii. 1 (where the verse is repeated), assigns to it the sense of *kshipra-phalaprada*, "quickly bestowing rewards." In Vâj. S. iv. 12, and vi. 34, *ṣvâtra* is found as an epithet of *âpaḥ*, "waters," and in the former of these verses (where "waters" are said to stand for milk) it is explained "quickly digested" (*kshipra-pariṇâmâḥ ṣîghraṃ jîrṇâḥ*), whilst in the second the sense of "quickly effecting the desired object," or "auspicious" (*kshipra-kârya-kâriṇyaḥ ṣivâ vâ*), is assigned. In Vâj. S. v. 31, *ṣvâtra* is used in a sacrificial formula as an epithet of a particular sort of little altar called *Maitravaruṇa-dhishṇya*, and is explained as signifying "friendly" (*mitraḥ*). *Ṣvâtrya* appears to be an epithet of Soma in R.V. x. 49, 10,

[1] In *v.* 11 of this hymn Sâyaṇa explains the pronoun *tâ*, "these," as meaning the "sins committed in another birth,"—a further instance of his ascribing more modern notions to the Vedic age.

as it is of *giraḥ*, "hymns," in x. 160, 2; but I am not aware how it is explained in those passages by the Commentator. On the whole, looking to the variety of senses ascribed to the word *ṣvâtra*, and to the artificial processes by which those senses are sometimes reached, I cannot but think that the Scholiasts were not always sure of its real signification.

I have, perhaps, already adduced a superabundance of instances in which Sâyaṇa, or Yâska, gives double, and, therefore, uncertain, interpretations of obscure words in the Rig-veda. But if any reader desires to pursue the subject further, he may examine for himself the following additional illustrations of the same fact which are indicated in the notes to the first three volumes of Prof. Wilson's translation of the Rig-veda, and have been verified by a reference to the Commentary of Sâyaṇa:—

R.V. i. 43, 4; i. 50, 4; i. 51, 4; i. 62, 4; i. 65, 3; i. 68, 1; i. 84, 16, 18; i. 89, 6; i. 95, 6; i. 97, 1; i. 100, 14; i. 102, 9; i. 105, 1, 8; i. 110, 6; i. 115, 1; i. 122, 2, 14; i. 123, 3; i. 124, 7; i. 125, 7; i. 127, 7; i. 129, 10; i. 130, 9; i. 132, 3; i. 141, 3; i. 143, 3; i. 145, 4; i. 146, 1; i. 149, 4; i. 150, 1 (comp. Nir. v. 11); i. 150, 3; i. 151, 2; i. 152, 1; i. 154, 4; i. 155, 2; i. 156, 4; i. 157, 2, 4; i. 164 (*passim*); i. 165, 5, 15; i. 169, 4, 6; i. 173, 2; i. 174, 7; i. 175, 4; i. 178, 2; i. 180, 7; i. 181, 3, 6; i. 182, 1, 2; i. 188, 5; i. 191, 8; ii. 2, 5; ii. 6, 2 (comp. viii. 50, 7); ii. 11, 3; ii. 12, 8; ii. 13, 11; ii. 18, 8; ii. 19, 4; ii. 20, 7; ii. 23, 17; ii. 24, 10; ii. 27, 8, 15; ii. 34, 2; ii. 38, 10; iii. 15, 1, 2; iii. 17, 1, 3; iii. 51, 3; iii. 60, 6; iii. 61, 2 (compared with i. 113, 12); iii. 61, 5; iv. 1, 5, 16; iv. 2, 1, 11; iv. 3, 7; iv. 9, 4; iv. 42, 1, 4, 8; iv. 44, 2; iv. 50, 6; iv. 53, 1; iv. 55, 1; iv. 56, 6; iv. 58, 1 and *passim*; v. 4, 6, 8; v. 7, 3; v. 8, 2; v. 9, 4; v. 33, 1; v. 36, 3; v. 50, 3; v. 69, 1; v. 73, 5; v. 74, 1, 8, 10; v. 75, 9; v. 76, 1; v. 79, 5; v. 86, 1; v. 87, 1; vi. 1, 4; vi. 4, 7; vi. 15, 3; vi. 17, 7; vi. 18, 14; vi. 26, 4;[1] vi. 26, 6; vi. 29, 2; vi. 34, 4;

[1] Sâyaṇa here refers, in illustration of one of his views, to another passage, x. 49, 4.

vi. 35, 5; vi. 44, 7; vi. 49, 7, 14; vi. 51, 6; vi. 56, 3; vi. 59, 6; vi. 61, 3.

In addition to these numerous instances, in which Sayaṇa proposes double interpretations, Prof. Wilson points out in his notes frequent differences of opinion between Sâyaṇa and Mahîdhara in regard to the rendering of passages which are common to the Rig-veda and the Vâjasaneyi Sanhitâ.

I will add some specimens of what appear to me to be mistranslations on the part of Sâyaṇa.

R.V. i. 22, 20 (=Vâj. S. vi. 5) he explains thus: "The wise ever behold with scriptural gaze (*ṣâstra-dṛshṭyâ*) that supreme station of Vishṇu, as the eye extended on every side in the sky, clear from the absence of any obstacle, beholds." He thus makes *chakshus*, "the eye," a nominative, and supplies *paṣyati*, "beholds." Mahîdhara, however, taking *chakshus* as an accusative, renders, as it appears to me, correctly, "like an eye extended in the clear sky," or (dropping the particle denoting resemblance) "that eye, the orb of the sun, which is extended in the sky;" and he quotes Vâj. S. vii. 42 (=R.V. i. 115, 1) and xxxvi. 24 (=R.V. vii. 66, 16) to show that the orb of the sun (represented here by Vishṇu) is called an "eye." Compare also R.V. vi. 51, 1; vii. 61, 1; vii. 63, 1; vii. 76, 1; x. 37, 1. "The wise" thus, according to Mahîdhara, "behold the highest station of Vishṇu fixed in the sky, like an eye." This construction is also adopted by Benfey in his version of the hymn.

i. 25, 11, is rendered by Wilson, following Sâyaṇa, "through him (*ataḥ* = *asmâd Varuṇât*), the sage (*chikitvân*) beholds," etc.; but better by Müller (Anc. Sansk. Lit. p. 536), "from thence perceiving (*chikitvân*)," etc., "he (Varuṇa) sees," etc. Similarly Benfey.

ibid. v. 13. The words *pari spaṣo nishedire* are explained by Sâyaṇa: "the gold-touching rays were diffused (*nishaṇṇâh*, placed) on every side." Müller renders better: "the spies sat down around him." So, too, Benfey. Compare A.V. iv. 16, 4, where there can be no doubt that the word *spaṣah* means "messengers" or "spies." See also the remarks which I have made above on this term.

i. 91, 3. The first words of this verse are rendered by Wilson, "thy acts are (like those) of the royal Varuṇa," in conformity with the second of the two interpretations proposed by Sâyaṇa. The first, which Wilson rejects, is as follows: "*Varuṇa* is soma bought for sacrifice and covered with a cloth (*vastreṇâvṛtaḥ*): all the ceremonies, the *agnishṭhoma*, etc., are connected with thee when purchased; hence thou art the instrument in all sacrifices."

vii. 32, 18 (on which, as well as on the passage to be next quoted, viii. 19, 25 f., I have already made some remarks), is rendered as follows by Professor Müller (Anc. Sansk. Lit. p. 545:) "If I were lord of as much as thou, I should support the sacred bard, thou scatterer of wealth, I should not abandon him to misery. 19. I should award wealth day by day to him who magnifies; I should award it to whosoever it be. We have no other friend but thee," etc. But Sâyaṇa understands the first clause of *v.* 19, not as a continuation of the words of the worshipper, as it appears to be, but as spoken by Indra: "Having heard these words of Indra," he says, "the rishi, delighted, exclaims, 'we have no other friend,'" etc. This appears to be wrong.

viii. 19, 25 f. is a passage closely resembling the preceding. It begins thus: *Yad Agne martyas tvaṃ syâm aham mitramaho amartyaḥ*, and should, I think, be translated as follows: "If, Agni, thou (wert) a mortal, (and) were I, o amicably-shining[1] god, an immortal, o invoked son of strength,—(26) I would not abandon thee to malediction, or to poverty; my worshipper should not be poor or distressed," etc. Verse 25 would thus form the protasis and verse 26 the apodosis. But Sâyana takes the 25th verse by itself and explains it thus: "If I, a mortal, were thou, *i.e.* if I should, by worshipping thee, acquire thy nature, then I should become an immortal, a god." My interpretation is borne out by a parallel passage (which is not, like the preceding, elliptical in construction), viii. 44, 23. *Yad Agne syâm ahaṃ tvaṃ tvaṃ vâ gha syâ aham | syus te satyâ ihâṣishaḥ*, which Sâyaṇa renders, "If I were thou,

[1] I adopt here Sâyaṇa's rendering of *mitramahas*, whether it be correct or not.

(wealthy), or thou wert I (a poor worshipper), then thy wishes would be fulfilled." Compare also viii. 14, 1, 2.

It is true R.V. i. 38, 4, 5, may be quoted on the other side. The original of this passage is as follows: 4. *Yad yûyam pṛṣnimâtaraḥ martâsaḥ syâtana* | *stotâ vo amṛtaḥ syât.* | 5. *Mâ vo mṛgo na yavase jaritâ bhûd ajoshyaḥ* | *pathâ yamasya gâd upa* | which Sâyaṇa renders: "Although you, sons of Priṣni, were mortals, yet your worshipper would be immortal, a god. (Prof. Wilson's version of this verse does not correctly represent Sâyaṇa). 5. Let not your panegyrist be an object of disregard (as a wild animal is not regardless of grass in a pasture), or go along the path of Yama." Rosen renders: "4. Licet vos, Prisnis filii! mortales fueritis, *tamen* laudator vester immortalis esse poterit. 5. Nunquam vester laudator, cervi instar in prato, sit negligendus, *neque* Yamæ viam calcet." Benfey translates: "4. If you, o children of Priṣni, were mortals, an immortal would then be your panegyrist. 5. Let not him who praises you be an object of indifference to you, like a wild animal at grass; let him not walk along the path of Yama." And he gives the following paraphrase of *v.* 4: "Ye are so great, that if ye were men, the gods would sing your praises." Professor Aufrecht would render: "Even if ye were mortals (and not gods, as you are in reality), it would require an immortal to praise you (worthily)." I cannot say that these interpretations appear to me particularly satisfactory. If we could suppose an aposiopesis at the end of *v.* 4, the sense might be: "If ye were mortals, and your worshipper an immortal, *i.e.* if you and I were to change places, I would not be so careless about my worshippers as you are about yours." Or can we suppose that the Rishi is expressing an aspiration that he could change places with the objects of his adoration? Or, possibly, the meaning might be: "If ye were mortal [*i.e.* if ye knew by experience the sufferings of mortality], your worshipper should be [ye would make him] immortal." This perhaps derives some confirmation from the deprecation of death in the next verse.

vii. 89, 1, is thus explained by Sâyaṇa: "Let me not go, o

king Varuṇa, to thy earthen house; but may I attain to thy resplendent golden house." The sense seems simply to be what Müller makes it: "Let me not yet, o Varuṇa, enter into the house of clay," *i.e.* the grave. Compare A.V. v. 30, 14, *mâ nu gâd mâ nu bhûmigṛho bhuvat,* "let him not go; let him not have the earth for his house."

x. 160, 4, is also, as it appears to me, incorrectly rendered by Sâyaṇa. His explanation, as translated by Prof. Goldstücker, in his Dictionary, *s.v. aratni,* is as follows: "Indra manifests himself (to the pious); (the sacrificer), who, though not wealthy, offers him the soma libation,—him, Indra, the wealthy, holds in his hand (lit. *fist, i.e.* he protects him), after having defeated his enemies," etc. I would propose the following as a correcter translation: "That man is observed by him (Indra) who, being rich, pours out to him no soma libation," etc. See my former paper "On the relations of the priests to the other classes of Indian Society," p. 293, note 2, where this translation is vindicated.

Some instances have already been given, in which Sâyaṇa imports the ideas of a later age into his interpretation of the hymns. I give a few more illustrations of this tendency, both as it regards mythological and speculative conceptions.

In i. 170, 2, it is said: "Why dost thou seek to kill us, Indra? the Maruts are thy brothers." On this the Commentator remarks: "The Maruts are Indra's brothers, from having been produced from the same womb of Aditi; and this production is celebrated in the Purâṇas." On this Professor Wilson annotates: "Here, probably, nothing more is meant than affinity of function." The Maruts are not Âdityas according to the Rig-veda, and even Indra himself is not generally so called in the hymns. See my Art. on "Vedic Cosmogony," etc., p. 39. In iii. 53, 5, the worshippers address Indra as "brother."

In vii. 72, 2, the Aṣvins are thus addressed: "For there are paternal friendships between us, a common bond,—acknowledge it." On this Sâyaṇa annotates: "Vivasvat and Varuṇa were both sprung from Kaṣyapa and Aditi. Vivasvat was the father of the Aṣvins (see my Art. on the Aṣvins, in "Contributions to a knowledge of Vedic Theogony," etc., No. ii. p. 2), and Varuṇa of Vasishṭha;" and then he quotes the Brihaddevatâ to prove the second of these relationships, which is also alluded to in R.V. x. 17, 2. The third is perhaps deducible from R.V. vii. 33, 10, ff.; see Sanskrit Texts, i. 75, ff., and Prof. Wilson's translation of the passage. It may be doubtful whether either of those other texts of the R.V. is so old as the one before us. Prof. Roth thinks the verses of R.V. vii. 33, in which Vasishṭha's birth is alluded to, are conceived very much in the taste of the epic mythology, and are attached to an older hymn. But even if both these Vedic legends about the birth of the Aṣvins and Vasishṭha, respectively, are as ancient as the verse I have quoted, vii. 72, 2, still the link by which Sâyaṇa connects them, and which is necessary to establish the relationship of the author of the hymn (supposing him to be Vasishṭha, or a descendant of Vasishṭha) with the Aṣvins, is certainly not Vedic, as we are nowhere told in the hymns that Vivasvat and Varuṇa were sons of Kaṣyapa and Aditi. If Vivasvat be identified with Sûrya, he would, indeed, be, according to some parts of the R.V., an Âditya, or son of Aditi, but not otherwise. See Art. on Vedic cosmogony, p. 75, f. In a later work, the Taittirîya Âraṇyaka i. 13, 3, he is named among the Âdityas. There is no difficulty in supposing that the passage before us does not contain any mythological allusion. In other places also reference is made to the former (vi. 18, 5) or ancestral (vi. 21, 8; i. 71, 10) friendship of the worshippers with the gods.

In i. 114, 6, Rudra is called the father of the Maruts. To explain this Sâyaṇa *in loco* tells a story that: "Indra, once on a time, overcame the Asuras, when Diti, their mother, desiring to have a son who should be able to avenge her vanquished sons by slaying the Thunderer, practised austerity and became pregnant by her husband. Indra, learning this news, entered into her womb in a very minute form, with a thunderbolt in his hand, divided her fœtus into seven parts, and again made each of those parts into seven. These fragments all issued from the womb and wept. At this conjuncture Paramesvara (Rudra), and Pârvatî (his wife), were passing by for amusement, and saw them. Pârvatî said to her husband: 'If you love me, make all these bits of flesh become severally sons.' He accordingly made them all of the same form and age, and decked with similar ornaments, and gave them to her, saying: 'Let them be thy sons.'" The Maruts ought thus to be $(7 \times 7 = 49)$ forty-nine in number. In R.V. viii. 28, 5, however, (if, indeed, the Maruts are there intended) they are only spoken of as seven. Sâyaṇa there gives a modified version of the story, to the effect that when Aditi (not Diti) desired to have a son equal to Indra, and her fœtus had, from some cause, been split into seven by Indra, the seven parts became seven troops (of Maruts).

It may be questioned whether, in styling Varuna, in conformity with modern ideas, "the deity presiding over the waters" (*jalâbhimânî devaḥ*), (as he does in R.V. i. 161, 14; viii. 58, 12), Sâyana does not derive some support from expressions in the hymns themselves. (See the passages quoted in pp. 86 f. of my "Contributions to a Knowledge of Vedic Theogony," etc.) In one of those texts, however, vii. 49, 3, the waters, in the midst of which Varuna is said to move, "beholding the truth and falsehood of men," seem to be rather aerial than oceanic, as the former, from their position above the earth, would appear to afford to the god (when anthropomorphically regarded) a more convenient post of observation than the latter. And in vii. 64, 2, the epithet, *sindhupatî*, "lords of the sea," (or "of rivers," *nadyâḥ pâlayitârau*, Sâyaṇa), is applied not only to Varuṇa but to Mitra also, who is not, that I am aware of, ever connected with the sea, even in later mythology. If we add to this, that these two gods are solicited to send *food and rain from the sky*, it may result that they are called *sindhupatî*, as supplying the aerial waters by which terrestrial streams are filled. But Sâyaṇa does not generally style Varuṇa the god of the sea, but in conformity with older conceptions, the deity who presides over the night. (See the paper above quoted, pp. 77 f.)

The epithet *Kauṣika* is applied in R.V. i. 10, 11, to Indra.

Sâyaṇa says it means son of Kuṣika, and repeats a story from the Anukramaṇikâ, or Index to the R.V., which relates that that person, wishing a son like Indra, practised chastity, in consequence of which Indra was born to him in the form of Gâthin. Roth, *s.v.* thinks the epithet may have originally meant "belonging, devoted to the Kuṣikas." The word is given in the Amara Kosha as denoting Indra, bdellium, owl, and snakecatcher.

I have mentioned above that Sâyaṇa understands R.V. i. 22, 16, 17, to refer to one of the incarnations of Vishṇu. On *v.* 16, he speaks of Vishṇu as *parameṣvara*, "the supreme deity." On i. 156, 4, he proposes either to take Vishṇu for the sacrifice, according to the idea of the Brâhmaṇas, or as the creator (*vedhas*) of the Maruts, whose function as preserver Varuṇa and the other gods recognize.

On i. 43, 1, Sâyaṇa derives the name Rudra from the root *rud*, "to weep," denoting the god who "makes everything to weep at the time of the end," and thus identifies him with the Mahâdeva of later mythology. (See Wilson's note *in loco*).

Sâyaṇa gives, optionally, a spiritual meaning to the words in i. 50, 10: "looking aloft to the upper light above the darkness, the Sun, a god among the gods, we have arrived at the highest luminary." He says the phrase "above the darkness" may mean "above the night," or "above sin;" and quotes a text which explains this passage and declares that "darkness is sin," etc.

On R.V. i. 71, 4, Prof. Wilson's note will further illustrate Sâyaṇa's practice of introducing later ideas into his explanations: "Mâtariṣvan is a common name of Vâyu, or wind; but it is here said to mean the principal vital air (*mukhya-prâṇa*) divided (*vibhṛta*) into the five airs so denominated, as in a dialogue between them, cited by the Scholiast, etc., etc."[1]

[1] Prof. Wilson has the following remarks in a note on R.V. v. 2, 1: "According to what is no doubt the most accurate interpretation of this verse, and of those which follow, they contain only a metaphorically obscure allusion to the lighting of the sacrificial fire: the mother is the two pieces of touchwood, which retain fire, the child, and will not spontaneously give it up to the father, the *yajamâna*, until

R.V. i. 115, 1 ("The sun, soul of whatever is moving or stationary, has filled heaven, air, and earth") is thus explained by Sâyaṇa: "The sun, existing within such an orb, being, from his pervasiveness, the supreme spirit (*paramâtmâ*), the mover of the universe, is the soul, the substance (*svarûpa-bhûtaḥ*) of whatever is moving or stationary. For he is the cause of all effects stationary or moving; and the effect is not distinct from the cause," etc. "Or, he is the life-soul (*jîvâtmâ*) of all creatures stationary or moving; for when the sun rises, all the world which was before nearly dead, is perceived to be again sentient." Though the latter explanation, no doubt, most nearly approaches the true one, still the first is also proposed by Sâyaṇa as admissible, at least, if not preferable.

Sâyaṇa translates *vedhasaḥ ṣaṣvataḥ* in i. 72, 1, by *nityasya vidhâtur Brahmaṇaḥ* "of the eternal creator Brahmâ." Though this sense of "eternal creator" is adopted by Benfey, in his version (Or. und Occ. i. p. 601), I should hesitate to admit that it can correctly represent the sense of the ancient bard.

The word *brahmâ* in R.V. i. 164, 35, is explained by Sâyaṇa as *Prajâpati*, though there does not appear to be any reason for supposing that it has that sense anywhere in the R.V., and though the other three clauses of the verse, which relate to sacrifice and objects connected therewith, the altar and the soma-juice, lead to the conclusion that "priest" is the proper rendering.

R.V. iii. 53, 9, is another passage in which Sâyaṇa's interpretation seems to have been influenced by post-vedic legends. We are told in the Râmâyaṇa (i. 60, 2 ff.; see Sanskrit Texts, i. 103), that Viṣvâmitra on a certain occasion created new constellations. Sâyaṇa appears to find a reference to this story in the words *mahân ṛshir devajâ devajûtaḥ*, "the great Rishi, god-born, god-impelled," which

forced by attrition: till then, also, people, the priests, do not behold it, but they see it when bursting into ignition: this, however, has not satisfied the commentators, and a curious and strange legend has been devised for the interpretation of the text, or has been, perhaps, applied to it by way of explanation, having been previously current: it is more probably, however, suggested by, than suggestive of, the verses," etc., etc.

refer to this personage, and which he explains: "The great Rishi, seer of objects beyond the reach of the senses, who had by austerity acquired intense power, generator of shining lights (*devajâ dyotamânânâṃ tejasâṃ janayitâ*), drawn by those lights" (*devajûtas tais tejobhir âkṛshṭaḥ*), etc. The real sense of the terms *devajâ devajûtaḥ* seems to be that which I have given above. *Jâḥ* is found in the Nighaṇṭus, ii. 2, as one of the synonymes of *apatya*, "offspring;" and *devajûta* is explained by Sâyaṇa in R.V. vii. 25, 5; viii. 31, 3, as "impelled by the gods" (*devaiḥ prerita*). [It is to be observed, however, that Yâska (x. 28) gives a double interpretation of this latter word, as meaning (in R.V. x. 178, 1) either *deva-gatam deva-prîtam vâ*, "gone to the gods," or "beloved by the gods."] Prof. Wilson partly follows, and partly deviates from, Sâyaṇa, in his translation of R.V. iii. 53, 9, which runs thus: "The great Rishi, the generator of the gods, the attracted by the deities," etc.; and observes, in a note: "*Devajâḥ* is explained by Sâyaṇa, the generator of radiances or energies . . . . . the compound is not *devajâ*, god-born, nor was Viṣvâmitra of divine parentage." In reference to this last remark see Wilson's note on R.V. i. 10, 11, and Sanskrit Texts, i. 82. The non-existence of any Puranic legend ascribing a divine origin to Viṣvâmitra ought not, however, to influence our translation of a Vedic text. And it is not undeserving of notice that, following Sâyaṇa, Prof. Wilson had but shortly before translated R.V. iii. 29, 15, thus: "The Kuṣikas, the first-born of Brahmâ," etc. etc. The Kuṣikas were the tribe to which Viṣvâmitra belonged. Sâyaṇa's words in explanation of this last text are these: *Brahmaṇah sarvasya jagataḥ srashṭuḥ prathamajâḥ prathamotpannaḥ*, "the Kuṣikas, the first-born of Brahmâ, the creator of the whole world." This translation is, however, the result of modern ideas, as I believe it is generally recognized (as already intimated) that there is no passage in the R.V. in which the personal creator (Brahman in the masculine) is mentioned, and in the present case the accent shows that the word is neuter, and therefore signifies "prayer." See the story about the birth of Vasishṭha in R.V. vii. 33, 10 ff. (Sanskrit Texts, i. 75 ff.), and compare the word *devaputra* applied to the Rishis in x. 62, 4, where, though the traditional accent makes the word a *Bahuvrîhi* compound, with the sense, "having gods for their sons," Prof. Roth, *s.v.*, thinks that, with a different accentuation, changing it into a *Tatpurusha*, the meaning may be conjectured to be, "sons of the gods." But if other Rishis were sons of the gods, why should not Viṣvâmitra also have been fabled to be so?

In R.V. iii. 62, 10, (the celebrated Gâyatrî), Savitri is interpreted "the supreme lord, the creator of the world, who impels by his all-pervading presence;" and *bhargas* is "the self-resplendent light, the glory of the supreme Brahma." Another explanation of Savitri as the sun is however given.

The word *tredhâ* in the last clause of R.V. vi. 69, 8, *tredhâ sahaṣram vi tad airayetham* ("ye then scattered a thousand into three parts"), is explained by Sâyaṇa as meaning "existing in the threefold form of world, veda, and speech;" and a Brâhmaṇa is quoted to support the interpretation. (See the entire passage in "Sanskrit Texts," iv. 72, note 42).

In vii. 59, 12. *Tryambaka* is explained as "the father of the three gods, Brahmâ, Vishṇu, and Rudra." This conception of a triad, consisting of these three gods, seems, however, to have been unknown in the Vedic age. Yâska mentions a triad, but it consists of Agni, Vâyu (or Indra), and Sûrya. (See "Sanskrit Texts," iv, 136 f.) I should observe that the passage of Sâyaṇa's Commentary from which this explanation is taken is put by the Editor, Prof. Müller, in brackets, as being derived from only one MS. See the extracts given from the other MSS. in p. 14 of the "Varietas Lectionis" prefixed to the 4th vol. of Müller's R.V. But even if the passage is not genuine, the style of interpretation found in it is that of the modern Indian commentators generally. Mahîdhara explains *tryambaka* as the "three-eyed Rudra." Prof. Wilson holds this text of the Veda to be spurious. The Ṣatapatha Brâhmaṇa, ii. 6, 2, 9, gives another sense of the word *tryambaka*: "He (Rudra) has a sister called Ambikâ, with whom he has this portion: and since he has this portion along with a female (*striyâ saha*), he is called Tryambaka," (*i.e.* Stryambaka). This passage of the Brâhmaṇa refers to Vâj. S. iii. 57, where it is said: "This is thy portion, Rudra, with thy sister Ambikâ."

In vii. 100, 4, it is said that "Vishṇu strode over this earth to give it for an abode to man (or Manu)." Sâyaṇa explains this last word, "to the host of gods who praised him," to whom he was about to give it, "after taking it from the Asuras." This explanation is, apparently, in conformity with more modern legends.

vii. 101, 1. The first clause of this verse, viz., "utter the three words of which light is the first," are explained by Sâyaṇa as meaning "the threefold praises in the form of rich, yajush, and sâman verses, preceded by the brilliant *praṇava*" (or sacred monosyllable Om). An alternative explanation is, however, given, according to which the three words or sounds are "the rapid, the slow, and the intermediate (thunderings), preceded by lightning."

viii. 12, 27. The first words of the verse, addressed to Indra, (which, translated literally, run thus: "when of thee Vishṇu, by the strength," and mean apparently, "when by thy strength Vishṇu strode," etc.), are rendered by Sâyaṇa, "when thy younger brother Vishṇu," etc. Prof. Wilson also observes that they might be translated "when Vishṇu by thy strength." The words "younger brother," *tavânujaḥ*, are not in the original. This idea of Vishṇu being the younger brother of Indra is, I believe, unknown to the Veda, and of modern origin.

In viii. 19, 5, we have the words, "the mortal who worships Agni with fuel, with an oblation, and with *veda*" (whatever that may mean), etc. etc. Sâyaṇa understands it of "reading the Veda," which can scarcely be the sense. See on the meaning of the verse Prof. Müller's "Anc. Sansk. Lit." p. 204 f., referred to by Prof. Wilson *in loco*.

Notwithstanding these instances (which might, no doubt, be considerably multiplied) of Sâyaṇa's tendency to allow the ideas of his own time to influence his exposition of the Veda, I think it must, in fairness, be admitted that, however incapable he may have been of fully comprehending and reproducing the real spirit and genius of the hymns, he introduces into his interpretation of them, on the whole, much less of positive modern mythology and speculation than might, in a writer of his age, have been expected. A similar remark may be made in reference to Yâska, that although in his general observations, Nir. vii. 4, ff., he regards all the deities as being, ultimately, members of the one Soul, he does not, in the sequel, allow this dogmatical view to interfere with his detailed explanations of their individual characteristics.

I extract from the notes to the fourth vol. of Prof. Wilson's translation of the R.V. a few admissions, in his own words, that he, too, occasionally failed to find in Sâyaṇa a perfectly satisfactory guide.

p. 6. "*Gâvaḥ* is rendered by Sâyaṇa *raṣmayaḥ*, "rays:" one of its meanings it is true, but rather incompatible here with the verb *vahanti, vehunt.*" [1]

p. 94. "The addition of the comment, *devânâm*, seems somewhat superfluous; human wives would have been more in keeping with the prayer." [2]

p. 102. ". . . . . the explanation is not very clear."

p. 103. verse 4. Prof. Wilson departs here, perhaps inadvertently, and I believe wrongly, from Sâyaṇa in rendering *savam*, "birth." The word is explained by Sâyaṇa as = *prasavam, anujnâm*, "permission," but it is rather "impulse." (See my "Contributions to Vedic Theogony," etc., pp. 118 ff.)[3]

p. 144. . . . "he (Sâyaṇa) seems rather puzzled."

p. 179. In his translation of a part of vii. 88, 6, Prof. Wilson deviates from Sâyaṇa's rendering, as he understands it: "*Mâ te enasvanto bhujema*, 'let us not, offending thee, enjoy'—it is not said what: the scholiast attaches the prohibitive to the verb, but gives a different turn to the sentence:

[1] *Atanavat* does not mean "not spreading or dispersing" as Prof. Wilson translates it in p. 28, note 3, but "going," *atana-vat* (not *a-tana-vat*).

[2] Prof. Wilson proposes, in p. 92, to take *ayâtuḥ* as the genitive of *ayâtṛ*, but I know of no such word as the latter with the sense of "one not sacrificing."

[3] In p. 114, Prof. Wilson proposes a translation of a word left unexplained by Sâyaṇa, *svapivâta*, which is founded on an analysis not sanctioned by the Pada-text, as the latter divides the compound *su* + *apivâta*, whilst Wilson would divide it *svapi* + *vâta*.

'being freed from sin through thy favour, let us enjoy enjoyments.'"[1]

p. 211. "The scholiast is rather puzzled how to interpret the duality here intimated."

p. 254. "The second part of the stanza is rendered intelligible by the scholiast only by taking great liberty with some of the terms; and after all the meaning is questionable," etc.

p. 285. *Śâchigo* is not very satisfactorily explained," etc.

p. 286. "The construction is loose, and the explanation is not very satisfactory."

To these admissions of Prof. Wilson, taken from the notes to vol. iv., I may add an observation from vol. i. p. 10, on Sâyaṇa's attempts to explain the word *ehimâyâsâḥ*: "It is more than probable that the origin and import of the term were forgotten when Sâyaṇa wrote." But if such was the case in this instance, why not also in many others, in which Sâyaṇa appears to have had no other guide than a fanciful etymology?

The following are some additional instances from the notes to the first, second and third volumes of Prof. Wilson's translation:—

vol. i. p. 211, note. "In this stanza, as usual in the more elaborate metres, we encounter strained collocations and elliptical and obscure illusions, imperfectly transformed into something intelligible by the additions of the scholiast," etc.

p. 215. "This . . . is rather obscure . . . Sâyaṇa does not make it more intelligible," etc.

p. 279. "The terms thus rendered, in conformity to the explanations of the scholiast would seem rather to be intended for proper names," etc. etc. . . . "The meanings may be supported by the etymology of the words, but the interpretation seems to be a needless refinement."

vol. ii. p. 5. "It would make better sense to render it," etc.

p. 36. "The scholiast is evidently puzzled by the phrase."

p. 82. "The scholiast repeats the *Pauranik* legend of the

[1] In a note to p. 193, Mr. Cowell corrects part of Prof. Wilson's translation of vii. 97, 6; but I do not see that the verse contains any word which can be rendered "friendship."

birth of Dîrghatamas from Mamatâ, : . . . . but there is nothing in the text to warrant the application: the persons are obviously allegorical," etc. etc. (Whether Prof. Wilson is right here or not I need not try to decide).

p. 94. "Some of these notions of the commentator are rather *Paurânik* than *Vaidik*."

p. 183. "The passage is not very clear, and Sâyaṇa's explanation does not remove the difficulty."

p. 293. "But this is more of a *Paurânik* than a *Vaidik* legend."

p. 300. "But this is *Paurânik*; apparently not *Vaidik*."

vol. iii. p. 44. "But this is a *Paurânik* notion, Vṛttra, according to the Purânas, being a Brâhman, and by killing him Indra was guilty of the heinous sin of *Brahmahatyâ*."

p. 155. "These explanations are rather, perhaps, derived from the *Paurânik* developments of the original legends, imperfectly handed down."

p. 173. "But this seems to be the notion of a later day."

p. 228. (R.V. v. 31, 7). Prof. Wilson does not follow Sâyaṇa in rendering *mâyâḥ*, "young women," but adheres to the usual sense "devices."

Prof. Wilson also in another place notices the gradual modification of the Vedic ideas by later Indian writers, vol. ii p. 87: "The Muṇḍaka Upanishad is also quoted for the attainment of heaven, *dyuloka-prâptiḥ*; the figurative expression of the text (R.V. i. 150, 3) having been converted into the assertion of a fact by the Upanishads; instancing the advance from simple metaphor to complex mythological notions."

In the translation of a part of R.V. vi. 59, 1, Prof. Wilson departs from Sâyaṇa. He renders the words *hatâso vâṃ pitaro devaṣatravaḥ* by "the Pitris, the enemies of the gods, have been slain by you, and you survive;" whilst in his note he says: "By Pitris, in this place, the scholiast says Asuras are intended, as derived from the root *pî* to inquire, *pîyatir hiṃsâ-karmâ*."

[The passage is a curious one. The proper translation seems to be: "Your fathers, to whom the gods were hostile, have been slain, whilst you, Indra and Agni, survive."

Professor Aufrecht suggests to me, that a former dynasty of gods is here alluded to as having been destroyed; and he refers, in illustration of this, to R.V. iv. 18, 12: "Who (o Indra) made thy mother a widow? Who sought to kill thee lying or moving? What god was present in the fray, when thou didst slay thy father, seizing him by the foot?"[1] In vii. 21, 7, mention is made of earlier gods: "Even the former gods admitted their powers to be inferior to thy divine prowess." And I apprehend that the two following verses, iv. 30, 3, 5, though otherwise rendered by Wilson (following Sâyaṇa), are to be understood of Indra fighting against the gods, and not with the gods, against the Asuras. 3. "Even all the gods assailed thee Indra, when thou didst prolong (?) day and night. 5. When thou didst fight alone against all the furious gods, thou didst slay the destructive." This interpretation is favoured by the tenor of verses 4, 6, 8–11 of the same hymn.[2] Earlier gods are also mentioned in x. 109, 4, though in conjunction with the seven rishis: "In regard to her the former gods said, the seven rishis who sat down to practise austerity," etc. An earlier age of the gods is mentioned in x. 72, 2, f.: "In the former age of the gods, the existent

[1] In explanation of this legend Sâyaṇa refers to the Taittiriya Sanhitâ, vi. 1, 3, 6. The following is the passage referred to, which I quote to show how little light it throws on the text of the R.V.:—*Yajno dakshiṇâm abhyadhâyat | tâm samabhavat | tad Indro 'châyat | so 'manyata "yo vâ ito janishyate sa idaṃ bhavishyati" iti | tâm prâviṣat | tasyâ Indra evâjâyata | so 'manyata "yo vai mad ito 'paro janishyate sa idaṃ bhavishyati" iti | tasyâ anumṛṣya yonim âchhinat | sâ sûtavasâ 'bhavat | tat sûtavaṣâyai janma | tâṃ haste nyaveshṭayata | tâṃ mrgeshu nyadadhât | sâ kṛshṇavishâṇâ 'bhavat | "Indrasya yonir asi mâ mâ himsîr" iti* | "Yajna (sacrifice) desired Dakshiṇâ (largess). He consorted with her. Indra was apprehensive of this. He reflected: 'whoever is born of her will be this.' He entered into her. Indra himself was born of her. He reflected. 'whoever is born of her besides me will be this.' Having considered, he cut open her womb. She produced a cow." etc. No mention is made of his killing his father.

[2] I should observe that the Brâhmaṇas constantly speak of the gods and Asuras as being both the offspring of Prajâpati; as contending together (Ṣ. P. Br. v. 1, 1, 1; vi. 6, 2, 11; vi. 6, 3, 2); and even as being originally equal or alike (Sanskrit Texts, iv. 52). And to prove that even malignant spirits may be called "gods," Prof. Roth, *s.v. deva*, quotes from the Taitt. Sanh. iii. 5, 4, 1, a verse to the effect: "May Agni preserve me from the gods (*devâḥ*), destroyers of sacrificers, stealers of sacrifices, who inhabit the earth;" and a second text from the A.V. iii. 15, 5: "Agni, do thou through the oblation repel the gods who are destroyers of happiness" (? *sûtaghnaḥ*).

sprang from the non-existent. In the first age of the gods the existent sprang from the non-existent." See "Contribu- to a knowledge of the Vedic Theogony," etc., Journ. R.A.S., for 1864, p. 72; and compare Nirukta xii. 41,[1] where a former age or generation (?) of gods, *pûrvaṃ devayugam*, is referred to. I may add that A.V. vi. 64, 1, speaks of "former gods," and A.V. i. 30, 2, of some of the gods being fathers and some sons (*ye vo devâḥ pitaro ye cha putrâḥ.*) R.V. viii. 48, 13, speaks of Soma in concert with the Fathers, having "stretched out heaven and earth;" and x. 68, 11, of the Fathers having "adorned the sky with stars." But in these two passages the forefathers of the worshippers, supposed to have been raised to the rank of deities, may be meant. In R.V. x. 97, 1 (=Vâj. S. 12, 75; Nir. 9, 28; Ṣ. P. Br. 7, 2, 4, 26) mention is made of certain plants which were produced three ages (*triyugam*) before the gods.]

I have alluded above to the fact that Prof. Goldstücker does not always coincide with the interpretations proposed by Sâyaṇa. I will cite from his Dictionary a few further instances of this disagreement.

On the sense of "one who does not praise the deity with

[1] The verse which is illustrated in this passage occurs both in R.V. i 164, 50, and in R.V. x. 90, 16, as well as Vâj. S. 31, 16. The concluding words are *yatra pûrve sâdhyâḥ santi devâḥ*, "where (in the sky) are the former Sâdhyas, gods." Yâska, as I mentioned above, tells us that the Nairuktas understood the Sâdhyas to be "the gods whose locality is the sky," *dyusthâno devagaṇah*, whilst, according to a legend (*âkhyâna*), the term denoted a former age of the gods." Prof. Wilson translates the word Sâdhyâḥ by, "who are to be propitiated," a sense not assigned by Sâyana, who proposes, first, that of *sâdhanâ yajnâdi-sâdhanavantaḥ karmadevâḥ*, "performers, performers of sacrifices, etc., work-gods." These words are rendered by Prof. Wilson in his note on i. 164, 50, "divinities presiding over or giving effect to religious acts." This does not, however, appear to be the real sense, as Mahîdhara on Vâj. S. 31, 17, tells us that "there are two kinds of gods, *karmadevâḥ*, "work-gods," and *âjânadevâḥ*, "gods by birth," the first being those who had attained to the condition of deities by their eminent works, and the second those who were produced at the beginning of the creation. The second class is superior to the first, and, according to the Brihadâraṇyaka, a hundred enjoyments of the latter (the work-gods), "are only equal to one single enjoyment of the former." See all this and more declared in the Bṛhadâraṇyaka Upanishad, pp. 817 ff. (p. 230 f. of translation), and Ṣatapatha Brâhmaṇa, p. 1087. The second sense proposed for *sâdhyâḥ* by Sâyaṇa on R.V. i. 164, 50, is that of the "deities presiding over metres," *chhando'bhimâninaḥ*, who, according to a Brâhmaṇa, by worshipping Agni were exalted to heaven, and became Âdityas and Angirases. Prof. Wilson remarks in his note: "It would seem that in Sâyaṇa's day the purport of the designation *Sâdhya* had become uncertain." Mahîdhara on Vâj. S. 31, 16, renders the term *virâḍ-upâdhi-sâdhakâḥ*, "producers of the condition of Virâj."

hymns," proposed for *amati*, he remarks (p. 343): "a doubtful meaning; it is proposed, besides the meaning 'poverty,' by Sâyaṇa on" (R.V. v. 36, 3).

On the word *amîvâ* he observes: "The same meaning (disease) applies satisfactorily to all other Vaidik passages where I have met with the word as a feminine; but Sâyaṇa has also the following interpretations, which seem artificial," etc.

On the alternative rendering of *amûra* by "combined with," etc., he remarks: "This meaning which is given by Sâyaṇa as an *optional one*, and the etymology on which it is founded by him, have little plausibility."

Under the word *ambi* he writes "(Ved.) water. Sâyaṇa holds that the word implies as well this meaning . . . as that of 'mother,' . . . so that it would express a double sense; but there seems to be no necessity to assign to it any other meaning than water."

Under *ayâ* he says: "Sâyaṇa here takes the instrum. *ayâ* as implying the *sense* of a genitive; . . . but it seems more probable that, as in other instances, some word, *e.g.* *âhutyâ*, etc., has to be supplied to it."

After giving under *ayâsya* the sense assigned by Sâyaṇa to that word, he observes, "but it seems that 'unable to be conquered,' might be more congenial with the context.

Under *araṇa* he remarks: "But Sâyaṇa has the improbable interpretation, 'unpleasant, painful;'" and again, "Sâyaṇa renders here *araṇa* in a very improbable manner, 'free from debt.'"

Under *aramati* he writes: "There seems no reason for adopting the other—rather artificial—meanings proposed by Sâyaṇa, and mentioned under ii. and iii."

Under *arari* iii. he says: "Both meanings appear to have been coined by Sâyaṇa for the sake of explaining the sense of *ararinda*."

If the principle that Sâyaṇa is open to free criticism of this description be admitted at all, the lengths to which dissent from his conclusions may be allowed to go must depend upon the discretion of the critic, and upon the philological principles which he adopts.

In rendering the particle *anâ*, "certainly," "indeed," Prof. Goldstücker *s.v.* departs from Sâyaṇa's explanation, at least in the only two places in which I have access to it, viz., R.V. iv. 30, 3, and viii. 47, 6, as on the former text he says it means *prâṇa-rûpeṇa balena*, "by strength in the shape of breath," and on the second that it signifies *prâṇa-yuktaḥ*, "possessed of breath." I am not aware how he renders it in x. 94, 3, 4.

Some apology is perhaps due to the Society for the long and minute examination into which I have entered of words and passages expounded by Yâska and Sâyaṇa. But it is evident that the only way in which a satisfactory estimate can be formed of the merits of any interpreter is by the presentation of such details. General assertions on such a subject, unless perceived to be founded on a sufficient induction of particulars carefully selected and thoroughly sifted, cannot be expected to command assent, especially if they run counter to opinions previously current.

It will be seen from the tenor of my observations that my object has not in general been to ascertain the true meaning of the words which I have discussed (though I have occasionally aimed at doing this), but to show either (1) that Yâska and Sâyaṇa are at variance with one another in regard to the sense of particular terms; or (2) that they have each given one or more alternative explanations of many words, and cannot therefore be supposed to have had in such cases any positive knowledge of the real signification; or (3), as regards Sâyaṇa, that he expounds numerous words differently in different places (without, as I presume, any justification of this variation in sense being in general discoverable in the context), and must, therefore, in some of those instances, at least, be held to have interpreted them wrongly.

From a consideration of these facts I am led to the conclusion that there is a large number of the most difficult words in the Rig-veda of the proper sense of which neither Yâska nor Sâyaṇa had any certain information, either from tradition or from etymology.[1]

[1] In regard to Indian tradition Prof. Benfey remarks as follows in note 450 to his translation of R.V. i. 51, 5, in his Orient und Occident: "If we compare

And this ignorance or uncertainty regarding the meaning of Vedic terms did not, as we have already seen, begin even with Yâska. It is clear from the preceding investigation that some important discrepancies in opinion prevailed among the older expositors, and the different schools of interpretation which flourished before his time. It has further been shewn that the Nighaṇṭus and the Nirukta are too limited in scope, as well, as in many instances, too general, or too uncertain, in their explanations, to serve as adequate helps for the elucidation of the hymns. The Nighaṇṭus, as we have found, do not expound nearly the whole of the obscure and obsolete words which they cite from the Veda, and the meanings which they do assign are often so vague as to leave us quite uncertain as to the specific signification of the terms. As we cannot tell for how long a period the hymns had ceased to be commonly understood, and particular words occurring in them had fallen into disuse before these vocabularies were compiled, it is possible that, in some cases, even the general meanings to which I have alluded may be incorrect, or, at least, may be different from those which the words had had in the earliest times. As regards the Nirukta, to say nothing of the fact formerly noticed, that it is but a very small portion of the hymns which it interprets at all, I think it is evident, from the instances I have given, that in the part which it does attempt to explain, the author depends very much upon etymological considerations for the senses he assigns; and this is made still more manifest by the fact of his frequently proposing two or more alternative or optional significations for the same word. Now it is possible that one or other of these explanations may be correct, or may be useful in suggesting the true sense; but the fact that Yâska offers us a choice of meanings seems to exclude the

the Indian interpretation, we recognize, as we have so often to do, how extremely little value we ought to attach to Indian explanations of words. On the other hand the correct explanation of things seems often to have been handed down, and such appears to be the case in the present instance"

On i. 61, 7, the same writer observes, note 614: "This is a strophe which is perhaps the best calculated to show how little use can be made of Indian tradition for the understanding of the Vedas, or rather how greatly it misunderstood them.'

supposition that he had any certain knowledge, from tradition or otherwise, that any of them were entitled to the preference. No one, I presume, will imagine for a moment that the writers of the hymns had, as a general rule, more than one meaning in their minds.

As regards Sâyaṇa, it seems doubtful if he had any other authorities than those which he cites, such as the Brâhmaṇas (among which he mentions the Aitareya, Kaushîtakî, Taittirîya, Ṣatapatha, Ṣâtyâyana, Shaḍvinṣa, Tâṇḍya, and possibly others), the Âraṇyakas, the Nirukta, the Bṛhaddevatâ, etc. In his remarks on R.V. iv. 24, 9, he also refers to "ancient teachers acquainted with tradition" (*sampradâya-vidaḥ pûrvâ-châryyâḥ*), whose verses he quotes; and as we have seen above, he adduces in one place the name of Kapardin as authority for one of his interpretations. As he so frequently quotes the works in question to support his views, there is every reason to suppose that, in all important cases, he made it a practice to prove his point by reference to an older text, when ever he found one extant which could serve his purpose; and if so, we may generally infer that when he cites no such evidence, he had none to produce.[1]

The specimens which I have brought together of Sâyaṇa's defects and mistakes have been collected in the course of a few weeks from a very small portion of his voluminous work. It is therefore perfectly just to conclude that, if his whole commentary were carefully examined, it would be found to be pervaded throughout by faults of the same description. But although I have no doubt whatever that such is, in reality, the case, I will not be so unreasonable as to deduce from

[1] In as far as Sâyaṇa was in the habit of confining his view to the single text before him (which I admit was not always the case) the following curious passage (Nirukta pariṣishta 1, 12) which gives a just view of the principles of Vedic interpretation, might seem to have been written with a prophetic reference to his case, and conveys a lesson not altogether inapplicable even to Christian divines, who have been too much in the habit of expounding *their* sacred texts without reference to the connection. "This reflective deduction of the sense of the verses is effected by the help both of oral tradition and reasoning. The verses are not to be interpreted singly, but according to the context. For one who is not a rishi or a tapasvin has no intuitive insight into their meaning. . . . . . When the rishis were departing, men said to the gods, 'Who shall be our rishi?' The gods gave them this reasoning for a rishi," etc., etc.

these premises the sweeping conclusion which might be expressed in the words *ex uno disce omnia*, but will merely draw the more moderate and much fairer inference that there is no unusual or difficult word or obscure text in the hymns in regard to which the authority of the Indian Scholiast should be received as final, unless it be supported by probability, by the context, or by parallel passages. It follows, as a necessary corollary, that no translation of the Rig-veda which is based exclusively on Sâyaṇa's commentary can possibly be satisfactory.

It would, however, be preposterous to deny that there is a large proportion of his interpretations from which most material help can be derived; that his Commentary altogether has been of the utmost service in facilitating and accelerating the comprehension of the Veda; that it has made many things clear at once which it might otherwise have taken long and laborious investigation to discover: and that it ought to be constantly consulted before any interpretation based on etymology, on the context, or on comparison of parallel passages, is proposed. No reasonable man will deny this. It would be simply absurd to neglect any aid derivable from the productions of extant Indian scholarship.

After all, however, there is probably little information of value derived from Sâyaṇa which we might not, with our knowledge of modern Sanskrit, with the other remains of Indian authorship, and our various philological appliances, have sooner or later found out for ourselves. It is not easy to conceive that many important problems presented by Vedic antiquity could have long remained, or can now long remain, insoluble by the resources and processes of modern scholarship,—a scholarship which has already decyphered the cuneiform writings of Persia and the rock inscriptions of India, and discovered the languages which lay hid under those mysterious characters.

But whatever may be our obligations to Sâyaṇa or Yâska, there is no reason why we should stand still at the point to which they have conducted us, if we have the means of advancing further. If a pupil possesses advantages denied to former generations, it is surely unreasonable to charge him with presumption if he seeks to go beyond his master. It is no disparagement to Sâyaṇa, if those European scholars who have begun by taking him for their guide should be able gradually to improve upon his lessons, and should end by rejecting a good deal that they have learned from him, as erroneous. This is the natural course of science in general, and there is no reason why Vedic philology should be an exception.

There can, as it appears to me, be no doubt that the understanding of the Veda has been already materially promoted by the labours of Professor Roth and the other philologists who belong to the same school. That in some cases their proposed interpretations are erroneous, is, if true, no argument against the judicious application of the correct and scientific principles on which they profess to proceed. The new school has existed but for a very short time; the labourers connected with it are few; and it is not to be wondered at, if, in a novel and untrodden field, some mistakes should have been committed. The merits of a method are not to be estimated by the results which have attended the first essays of its advocates. These earliest attempts may have partially failed from want of skill or experience. Complete success can only be expected to follow the efforts of several generations of scholars. The interpretation of the Old Testament is a parallel case to that of the Vedic hymns. In how many passages of the Psalms and Prophetical Books does the sense still remain obscure and disputed, notwithstanding all that has been done for their elucidation by the critical acumen of Hebraists during several centuries!

All this is admitted by Prof. Roth, who, far from claiming infallibility for his opinions, thus expresses himself in the Preface to his Lexicon (vol i. p. vi.):—

"This part of our Dictionary, as it is the earliest, will also be the first to grow old, for the combined labour of many able scholars, whose attention is now directed to the Veda, will rapidly promote our understanding of it, and determine many things with greater truth and precision than was possible for us on our first attempt. Centuries have toiled at the lexicographical interpretation of Homer, and yet his vocabulary is not entirely explained, though, in point of language, Homer presents incomparably fewer difficulties than the Vedic hymns. How could people expect to transfuse, without delay, into other languages, these monuments of a remote antiquity which is preserved to us in writing nowhere else but here, just as if they were a piece of modern book-making?"

Prof. Roth has already given sufficient proof of his readiness to correct any interpretations which further research has led him to regard as erroneous. Compare the meanings assigned to *anṛtadeva* and *antideva* with the close of the article *deva*; *arâyî, âpântamanyu, krivi, nûnam, paritakmyâ,* as explained in his Lexicon, with the senses previously given to the same words in his Illustrations of the Nirukta, p. 62, p. 95, p. 96, p. 6, p. 151.

# Art. X.—*An Attempt to Translate from the Chinese a Work known as the Confessional Service of the Great Compassionate Kwan Yin, possessing* 1000 *Hands and* 1000 *Eyes.* By the Rev. Samuel Beal, Royal Navy.

This work was presented to the Translator by the Priests of the Hai Chw'ang Temple of Honan.

*Imperial Preface to the Liturgical Services of the Great Compassionate Kwan Yin.* [*Written by Yung Loh, of the Ming Dynasty,* 1412 A.D.]

This Preface being written in the usual terse style of such compositions, and being without punctuation, is not translated *verbatim.*

It is reported that Kwan Tseu Tsai Bodhisattva, prompted by her great compassionate heart[1] has engaged herself by a great oath to enter into every one of the innumerable worlds, and bring deliverance to all creatures who inhabit them.

For this purpose she has enunciated the Divine sentences which follow, which, if properly recited, will render all creatures exempt from the causes of sorrow, and by removing them, render them capable of attaining Supreme Reason.

And if the virtuous man, who has already attained the happiness consequent on True Wisdom, still continue to recite these sentences, and by his correct line of conduct induce others who believe not to follow his example, and to accept the Truth and believe in it—how great his happiness!

So we, the Ruler of the Empire, because of our pity for those who ignorantly immerse themselves wholly in the affairs of the world, and are not acquainted with the virtue of these Sentences to obtain for them deliverance, do hereby bring before them a mode for attaining to the condition of Supreme Wisdom.

And we do so the rather, because Tathâgata when in the world, did principally enforce the practical duties of Fidelity

[1] I have followed the usual mode of considering Kwan Yin as a female.

and Obedience. From this it is plain that his religion is not a selfish system merely, but one which may do good to men and benefit the world.

As then by reciting these sentences we may attain to the Supreme condition which is termed "beholding Buddha"—so unless in practice we follow the duties of Fidelity and Obedience, naught but misery awaits us.

We therefore earnestly exhort all men, whichever course they are pursuing, carefully to study the directions of this work, and faithfully to follow them.

YUNG LOH, 9th Year, 6th Month.

*Liturgical Service of the Omnipotent and Omniscient Kwan Yin.*

PREFACE.

In preparing the altar of the great Merciful One the rules are these :—

The image of Ṣâkya Tathâgata Buddha must be reverently placed on an altar facing the south.

The image of the Omnipotent and Omniscient Kwan Yin Bodhisatwa should be reverently placed in the western quarter of the temple, facing east.

This figure of Kwan Yin may be either the one herein supposed (*i.e.*, exhibited in the accompanying Plate, and commonly known as Kwan Yin, with 1000 arms and 1000 eyes), or it may be one with forty arms, or six arms, or four arms—provided always it be made of the purest and best material, and with the greatest care.

At the dawn of day, before any act of worship be performed, the limits of the sanctuary [maṇḍala] must be well defined. The following is the mode—

First, take a knife, and mark out on the ground the prescribed limits of the sacred place, at the same time repeating the words.[1]

Then take pure water, and sprinkle it towards the four quarters, repeating the words.

Then take clean ashes, and scatter them on the ground, repeating the words.

[1] So, at least, I understand the expression in the original.

Then take a silken cord, consisting of threads of five colours, and bind it round the four sides of the sanctuary, repeating the words.

In all there must be twenty-one repetitions of the words.

The sacred limits having been thus determined, the next care must be to provide all necessary adjuncts of worship for the sanctuary, viz., flowing streamers, burning lamps, incense, flowers, offerings of food; all these must be carefully provided.

The incense, especially, must be prepared from sandal wood, not such as is commonly used, which may not be genuine, or, at least, not free from adulteration, but of the purest kind.

If the means be not found adequate to provide these necessary articles, there should be immediate consultation as to the best manner of laying out the funds in hand for the present necessity.

The western portion of the building should be covered with mats, or, if the ground be damp, kneeling stools may be provided.

The days appointed for worship and for reciting the sentences are the three seventh days of the month; the hours are six, viz., thrice in the morning and thrice in the evening. There must on no account be any abatement of the prescribed hours.

Before worship there must be due preparation, particularly the rules prescribed for the first of the seventh days (called "Fong-pien;" these rules are probably connected with the manumission of certain living creatures).

Before entering the sacred precincts due attention must be given to personal cleanliness; the garments worn must be new ones and clean, or, if not new, at any rate the best in the possession of the worshippers.

If during the service there be occasion to leave the temple, and visit any place of impurity, the clothes must be changed, and on returning from such a place the person must be washed, and on entering the place of worship the new clothes put on again. If there be no occasion throughout the whole day to visit such impure place, yet the person should be washed once.

One hour before and after service there should be no mixed conversation. On meeting one another there should be merely the customary mode of respectful salutation.

After the first service (*i.e.*, the service of the first canonical hour) the mind should be chiefly occupied in considering and weighing the nature of the ten vows of obligation entered on. The thoughts should be so occupied without intermission. Even whilst eating and drinking such thoughts should be persevered in, nor should the impressions received be allowed to be lost.

But if at time of prayer there be no devotional thoughts, but only a confused way of going through external duties, deceiving both oneself and others, and if after worship there be indifferent conversation, gossiping and babbling, hurrying to and fro, lounging about or sleeping, just as on ordinary days; if there be such criminal acts of careless self-indulgence, what benefit or assistance can we look for from our religious exercises?

The rules and directions for the service must also be properly studied and prepared; so that in going through it there may be outward decorum observed as well as inward devotion, whilst each portion of it is properly rendered.

Without such preparation, at the time of beginning the service, the mind and thoughts will be confused and hurried, and so the whole course of it will be unprofitable and nugatory.

Finally, let all disciples (*lit.* white-black) who have undertaken the precepts in earnest, and those who have not yet entered on a course of deep meditation (*i.e.*, laymen), strive after a firm faith, and excite in themselves an earnest intention; and so having purified the three faculties of thought, speech, and action, and engaging in this worship in a spirit of entire devotion, they shall obtain their prayers.

*End of Preface.*

*The Service of Kwan Yin.*

[*Direction.*]—The worshippers on entering the main court of the temple (*lit.* the Hall of Contemplation) shall reverently bow the head. On leaving it let them say—

[*Invocation.*]—Hail! Great Compassionate *Kwan Yin* Bodhisattva!

[*Direction.*]—Slowly and reverently reciting this invocation, let them enter the sanctuary, and having invested the altar three times, and arranged themselves in an upright position, let them reflect thus: "The body of the three precious objects of worship, and all the mass of sentient beings throughout the universe, differ in no essential respect from my own body and my own soul (heart). But all the Büddhas have arrived at complete wisdom, whilst all sentient creatures have been drawn away and deceived. For the sake, therefore, of these creatures, with a view to remove the obstacles and destroy the causes of delusion, I now enter upon this worship of the three precious objects." Having reflected thus, begin the following Hymn of Praise:—

[*Hymn*]—

Hail diffusive INCENSE CLOUD![1]
Bright mirror of the Divine excellencies!
Far spreading, boundless as the Heart of Wisdom.
Wherever lights one single ray (of that wisdom)
There is worship—there is praise—
To honor Him who reigns as king in the midst of all.

[*Invocation.*]—All Hail INCENSE-CLOUD-CANOPY, BODHISATTVA! MAHÂSATTVA. (To be repeated three times.)

[*Direction.*]—The Hymn of Praise being finished, then chant the following:—

[*Chant.*]—Profoundly Reverent,

In close communion[2] we adore the EVERLASTING BUDDHA, and the EVERLASTING LAW, and the EVERLASTING ASSEMBLY. (One bow after each ascription.) [Then continue], "This whole assembly, prostrate in adoration, holding flowers and incense, presents this bounden sacrifice.

[1] In all Buddhist Temples incense is continually burning before the various objects of worship.

[2] The phrase "in close communion" is an adaptation from the original, which is "one heart." This phrase "one heart" is explained in an appendix of the present work to signify that worshippers and the object of worship are both "one."

[*Direction.*]—Here the worshippers, holding flowers and incense in their hands, shall prostrate themselves and chant—

[*Chant.*]—Oh! may this Incense cloud and the perfume of these flowers spread through the worlds of space (*lit.* of the ten regions), and reach to every land of all the Buddhas. May each of these lands be infinitely enriched and adorned, filled with[1] the wisdom of the Bodhisattvas, and at length attain to the perfection of Tathâgata.

[*Direction.*]—Then let the worshippers light the incense and scatter the flowers, and with profound reflection, say—

I scatter these flowers and this incense
To signify the mysterious character and the excellence of the Doctrine we (profess),
Symbols of the harmony of Heaven and its holy joys (*lit.* precious perfume),
Emblems of angels' food and their sacred vestments.
How impossible is it to exhibit in words the infinite portions of the mysterious[2] universe!
Each single atom evolved from all the atoms,
Each single atom evolved from the aggregate of all,
Revolving thus unhindered they unite in one harmonious whole.
And thus diffused through space they appear before the three precious objects of worship,
And before the three precious objects of worship throughout the vast collective universe.
Thus as I with my body offer this sacrifice,
It is presented throughout each region of the universe,
Unhindered, unopposed by any external object;
And so through endless ages yet to come, discharging these sacred duties,
All sentient creatures united at length with the Divine essence,
(Thus united) shall attain the Heart of Wisdom,[3] and

[1] The expression "ku tsuh" is explained in the commentary on the twentieth section of the Kin-kong Sûtra.

[2] Miau fah, *i.e.* saddharma.

[3] I need not say that in the translation of such passages as the above I can only hope to attain to some obscure idea of the meaning of the original.

together enter on the State that admits of no Birth, the Wisdom of Buddha himself. Having concluded these offerings let all remain solemnly reverent.

[*Direction.*]—The officiating priest having finished this chant, bows once.

The body of worshippers, deeply meditating, having made their offerings, their incense still burning, and themselves still prostrate, ought to consider thus:—"The three precious objects of worship, although removed and distinct from us in respect of their essential purity, yet in respect of their very substance are one and the same with us, and therefore it is through their infinite love they continually regard and protect the whole body of sentient creatures. Can we only purify the three organs (body, speech, thought), they must of necessity come to us and remove sorrows and give joy. So let each one earnestly strive after this purity; then thrice invoked they will surely come and unite themselves with us." Let the worshippers now repeat the following chants.

[*Chant.*]—One in Spirit, respectfully we invoke thee. Hail! our own Teacher ṢÂKYA MUNI LOKAJIT.

[*Secret.*]—My nature being one with that of Tathâgata, if only the obstacles be removed, he will come and receive our offerings.

[The following invocations are similar to the above, following in order]; viz. to—

2. AMITÂBHA LOKAJIT of the world SUKHAVATÎ.
3. ṢÎLAPRABHA RÂJÂ LOKAJIT, of endless Kalpas past.
4. All the PAST BUDDHAS numerous as the sands of countless RIVERS GANGES.
5. CHING-FAH-MING.
6. All the Buddhas of the TEN REGIONS.
7. The 1000 BUDDHAS of the BHADRA KALPA.
8. All the DHÂRAṆÎs proceeding from the MERCIFUL HEART.
9. All the DHÂRAṆÎs spoken by KWAN YIN.
10. OMNIPOTENT, OMNISCIENT, GREATLY MERCIFUL, COMPASSIONATE KWAN SHAI YIN ÎṢVARA, BODHISATTVA, MAHÂSATTVA.
11. DHÂRAṆÎ RÂJA, BODHISATTVA, MAHÂSATTVA.
12. TAI-SI-CHI BODHISATTVA MAHÂSATTVA.

13. SÛRYAPRABHA BODHISATTVA, CHANDRAPRABHA BODHISATTVA MAHÂSATTVA.

14. RATNARÂJA BODHISATTVA.

15. LO-WANG BODHISATTVA, LO-SHANG BODHISATTVA MAHÂSATTVA.

16. AVATAṂSAKA BODHISATTVA, TAI CH'WANG YEN BODHISATTVA, PO-TS'ONG BODHISATTVA MAHÂSATTVA.

17. TI-TS'ONG BODHISATTVA VAJRA BODHISATTVA, HU-HUNG BODIHSATTVA MAHÂSATTVA.

18. MAITREYA B., BHADRIKA B., MANJUṢRÎ B., MAHÂSATTVAS.

19. All the BODHISATTVAS MAHÂSATTVAS of the THREE AGES of the TEN REGIONS.

20. MAHÂ KÂṢYAPA. teacher of countless great disciples.

21. The four illustrious Teachers of the Doctrine of TIEN TAI, great Doctors of the Law.

22. ṢÂNTI BRAHMÂ, GOPAKA DEVA, THE FOUR KINGS, THE EIGHT CLASSES OF DRAGONS, the large-eyed APSARASAS, Spirits of air, of rivers, of the sea, of fountains, of rivulets and pools, of plants and forests, of dwelling-places, water and fire, of wind, and sand, and mountains, of earth and rocks, Devas, dragons and demons who protect those who recite the Dhâraṇîs; and all related to these spirits.

[*Prayer.*]—Oh! would that our own Teacher, ṢÂKYA MUNI, and our merciful FATHER AMITÂBHA (and the rest), not passing beyond their own limits of perfect Rest and Love, would all descend to this sacred precinct and be present with us who now discharge these religious duties. Would that the Great, perfect, illimitable compassionate HEART,[1] influenced by these invocations, would now attend and receive our offerings. May the OMNIPOTENT AND OMNISCIENT KWAN YIN, bearing the sword of her own strong vow, now come amongst us reciting these Divine sentences, and remove from us the three obstacles (viz., of impure thought, speech, and action).

Would that the great CHE-TCHI BODHISATTVA and all the DHÂRAṆÎ RÂJAS, the GREAT BODHISATTVAS, the GREAT

[1] The word "Heart" probably corresponds to the Sanscrit *Âtmâ*.

Kâṣyapa, and all the Great Ṣrâvakas, all together manifesting (revolving) their compassionate natures, would now come and descend amongst us.

May Brahmâ, Ṣakra, and the Four Kings, and all the eight kinds of Heavenly Beings, according to our invocation, come now and protect this sacred place. May they defend us, as we recite these prayers, from the power of the evil demons, give us success, grant us strength ever to perform our vows.

[*Direction.*].—[All the above part of the Service, from the first invocation to Ṣâkya Muni, down to the last words in the Text, must be repeated only on the first day; on other days, after the sacrifice of incense and flowers, proceed as follows]—

[*Chant.*]—Hail![1] Saddharma Prabha Tathâgata of bygone ages ⊙.[2] And thou! our ever present Kwan-shai-yin-Bodhisattva, who hast perfected wondrous merit, and art possessed of Great Mercy, who in virtue of thine infinite power and wisdom art manifested throughout the universe for the defence and protection of all creatures, and who leadest all to the attainment of boundless wisdom, and teachest them the *rôle* of Divine Sentences ⊙. Thou who protectest us ever from the evil ways of birth, who grantest us to be born in the presence of Buddha, who dispellest all troubles, evil diseases and ignorance, who by thy power of spiritual perception art able to appear always to answer prayer, causing that which is desired to be brought about, who removest all doubts, who art able to cause speedy acquirement of the three degrees[3] of merit, and a rapid birth in the land of Buddha (or, in the position of Buddha); possessed of infinite spiritual power, beyond the capability of language to express, we therefore adore Thee and worship, with one heart and mind!

[*Direction.*]—The worshippers should be filled with holy joy and pious reverence, their hearts without confusion; they should render

[1] Namo ching-fah-ming-Ju-lai.

[2] The mark ⊙ in the original probably denotes a change of tone in the recitation of the chant.

[3] *Lit.* "the three vehicles."

due homage; bowing three times at the mention of ṢÂKYA BUDDHA, or the GREAT COMPASSIONATE DHÂRAṆÎS, or KWAN YIN BODHISATTVA, for these are worthy of chief honour and adoration. Say, therefore, these invocations:—

[*Invocation.*]—One in heart and mind, we worship Thee our own Teacher ṢÂKYA MUNI LOKAJIT!

[*Direction.*]—Repeat three times; bow three times; and with deep reflection say secretly, "The nature both of the object and subject in worship is empty (immaterial). Difficult is it to explain the blending of the one with the other. I regard this sacred altar as a Royal gem (a mirror?),—in the midst of it appears the shadow of Ṣâkya Tathâgata; my body also appears in the presence of Ṣâkya; prostrate thus upon my face and hands I worship him, that hereafter all the Buddhas and Bodhisattvas when invoked may duly appear."

[*Chant.*]—One in heart and mind we worship Thee AMITÂBHA of the Western world SUKHAVATÎ LOKAJIT.

[Here follow ascriptions of worship to all the Buddhas and Bodhisattvas named in the former part of this service.]

[*Direction.*]—After these acts of worship, all the worshippers should bow once, then let the officiating priest proceed.

The Scripture saith: Whatever Bhikshu or Bhikshuṇî, Upâsaka or Upâsikî, layman or laywoman, desires to recite the sentences of this service, in order to excite in the midst of all sentient creatures the operation of the COMPASSIONATE MERCIFUL HEART, ought first with us to go through the following vows:—

[*Direction.*]—Then all prostrate themselves and say,—

All hail! GREAT COMPASSIONATE KWAN SHAI YIN,
Oh! may I soon acquire perfect knowledge.

All hail! GREAT COMPASSIONATE KWAN SHAI YIN,
Oh! may I soon attain the eyes of Divine Wisdom!

All hail! etc.,
Oh! may I quickly deliver all sentient creatures!

All hail! etc.,
Oh! may I soon acquire a glorious emancipation!

All hail! etc.,
Oh! may I soon cross over to the other side, in the boat of Prajnâ!

All hail! etc.,
Oh! may I soon pass over the sea of sorrow!

All hail! etc.,
Oh! may I quickly obtain moral perfection (lit. the fixed way of the moral precepts).

All hail! etc.,
Oh! may I soon attain to Nirvâṇa (the hill of Nirvâṇa).

All hail! etc.,
Oh! may I quickly return to my original condition of passive inactivity (*wou wei*).

All hail! etc.,
Oh! may I soon be able to unite in one perfect whole the several parts of my nature! (Law, Nature, Body.)

Though I were cast upon the mountain of knives,
They should not hurt me!
Though thrown into the midst of the lake of fire,
It should not burn me!
Though hurled down to the lowest hell,
It should not hold me!
Though hungry ghosts surrounded me,
They should not touch me!
Though exposed to the power of Asuras,
Their malice should not reach me!
Though transformed amongst the lowest forms of life,
I should attain to heavenly wisdom!

[*Invocation.*]—Hail! KWAN YIN BODHISATTVA.

[*Direction.*]—To be repeated ten times, quickly. Let the worshippers here pray for deliverance from any particular calamity, such as fire, drowning, etc.

[*Invocation.*]—Hail! AMITÂBHA BUDDHA.

[*Direction.*]—Ten times quickly repeated. Then let the officiating priest continue thus,—

[*Lesson.*]—KWAN YIN, addressing Buddha, said,—World-honoured one! Whilst the recitation of these divine sentences is ineffectual to deliver creatures from the three evil ways of birth, I vow never to arrive at the condition of Buddha! So long as those who recite these divine sentences are not born in the various lands of all the Buddhas, I vow never to arrive at that condition myself! So long as those who recite these divine sentences are unable to attain every degree of spiritual perception, I vow never to arrive at the condition of Buddha! So long as those who recite these divine sentences do not receive full answer to their prayers, I vow to remain as I am! Then, in the midst of all the congregation—with closed palms, standing perfectly upright, exciting in all creatures the GREAT COMPASSIONATE HEART, her eyebrows raised, a smile on her lips—KWAN YIN forthwith began to deliver these comprehensive, effectual, complete, Great Compassionate Heart DHÂRAṆÎ, mysterious and divine sentences.

[*Direction.*]—Then let all the priests recite together—

Namo ho lo tan na to lo ye ye,
Namo ho li ye, Po lou ki ti lo che lo ye,
Bo ti sah to po ye, Mo ho ka lou ni ka ye,
Om!
Sah pa lah fah ye.

[These Dhâraṇîs being corrupt forms of Sanskrit or Pali words—chiefly names of popular objects of worship, interspersed with interjectional phrases, such as Om, svah, etc.,—I do not transcribe them further. The Sanskrit forms of the few written above appear to be Namo Ratnatrayâya, Namo Haraye, Avalokiteṣvarâya, Bodhisattvâya, Mahâsattvâya, Mahâkaruṇikâya, Om, etc., etc.]

[*Direction.*]—The worshippers having recited the DHÂRAṆÎ, must prostrate themselves on their faces and hands three times; then stand up four times in succession; then walk round the altar in procession eleven times; then stand up again three times in succession. In all twenty-one times.

This being finished, all standing upright, let the officiating priest continue thus,—

KWAN YIN BODHISATTVA having delivered these sentences, the great Earth trembled six times. The Heavens rained precious flowers, which fell down in commingled profusion. All the Buddhas of the ten quarters rejoiced. The powerful demons and the heretics shook with fear, and their hair stood on end. The members of the congregation immediately entered upon the paths, some on the path Sotâpanna, some on the path Sakadâgâmi, some on the path Anâgâmi, some on the path of a Rahat; others again obtained that condition which is known as the first platform (one earth), others the second, others the third, and so on, up to the tenth (daṣabhûmi), and numberless others attained to the Heart of Wisdom (*i.e.*, complete knowledge or Bodhi).

[*Direction.*]—One bow. The worshippers having finished the repetition of the sentences, ought to consider that all the connection of obstacles which prevent spiritual progress spring from sins committed in our condition as sentient creatures; that from the first till now, the sins of all created beings have been constantly going on, and that now the web of guilt has become intricate and complicated. Every age has intertwined its own peculiar crimes, which, descending from parent to child, have caused the obstacles to deliverance and the sorrows of our present condition. Without repentence there can be no remission. The law cannot be obeyed. Our sins, therefore, ought to be well considered and weighed that so they may be forgiven and destroyed.

Bowing low, say thus,—

We, and all men from the very first, by reason of the grievous sins we have committed in thought, word, and deed, have lived in ignorance of all the Buddhas, and of any way of escape from the consequences of our conduct. We have followed only the course of this evil world, nor have we known aught of supreme wisdom; and even now, though enlightened as to our duty, yet, with others, we still commit heavy sins, which still prevent us advancing in true knowledge. Therefore, in the presence of Kwan Yin, and the Buddhas of the Ten Regions, we would humble ourselves and repent us of our sins. Oh! that we may have strength to do so aright, and that they may cause all obstacles to be removed. [Here with a loud voice add]—

For the sake of all sentient creatures, in whatever capacity they be, would that all obstacles may be removed, we confess our sins and repent!

[*Direction.*]—A complete prostration. Then continue thus,—

We, and all men from the first, from too great love of outward things, and from inward affection to men, leading to sinful friendships, having no wish to benefit others, or to do good in the least degree, have only strengthened the power of the three sources of sin, and added sin to sin; and even though our actual crimes have not been so great, yet a wicked heart has ruled us within; day and night, without interval or hesitation, have we continually contrived to do wrong. There has been no desire after knowledge, no fear of misery, no alarm, no heart-chiding, we have gone on heedless of all consequences. Now, therefore, believing from the bottom of the heart in the certain results of sin, filled with fear and shame, and great heart-chiding, we would thus publicly repent us of our sins; we would cut off our connection with worldly objects, and aspire to the Heart of knowledge; we would separate ourselves from evil and pursue good; we would diligently recount all our past offences and earnestly pursue the path of virtue, ever remembering the blessedness of Heaven, and the power of all the Buddhas to deliver and rescue us and all men from evil. Hitherto we have only gone astray, but now we return. Oh! would that the Merciful Kwan Yin would receive our vows of amendment.

[*Direction.*]—An entire prostration. Then add,—

With all our heart do we (mentioning each one his name) repent of our sins. We all here prostrate ourselves before the sacred presence with all the countless beings of the infinite universe. [Here follow particular confessions of sin.] . . . . So were we helpless and lost till we found out Kwan Shai Yin, the Great Teacher of the Ten Regions, who has manifested to all the source of true wisdom, . . . . . so have we repented and returned. Would that the Great Compassionate Kwan

Yin Bodhisattva Mahâsattva, possessing 1000 hands and 1000 eyes, would overcome and destroy all obstacles in our way; . . . . . . would that our original power of acquiring knowledge might develop itself, . . . . so that quitting this body we might obtain perfect rest and repose. . . . . . Amitâbha Buddha! of the world Sukhavatî, receive our offerings!

Great Compassionate Kwan Yin, who art acquainted with all the sentences, fit to deliver every sort of creature, may all emerge from the wheel of transmigration and be saved.

[*Direction.*].—Having finished these vows connected with the confession and repentance of the worshippers, let adoration be once more paid to the three precious objects of worship.

All hail! Buddhas of the ten quarters!
All hail! Law of the ten quarters!
All hail! Assembly of the ten quarters!
Hail! Ṣâkya Muni Buddha!
Hail! Amitâbha Buddha!

[And so on as before.]

[*Direction.*]—Having walked round the altar in procession three times, once more returning before the image of Kwan Yin, proceed with these three forms of devout aspiration. (*Kwai-i.*)

Having myself returned to my duty to Buddha, I ought to pray for all men, that they may attain perfection of wisdom.

Having myself returned to my duty to the Law, I ought to pray that all men may be deeply versed in the wisdom of the Sacred Books, and acquire perfect knowledge.

Having myself returned to my duty to the Assembly, would that all men may agree in the great principles of Reason, and maintain Peace, and worship the Holy Assembly.

[*Direction.*]—(One bow.)

[*Invocation.*]—Namo! Kwan Shai Yin Bodhisattva.

[*Direction.*]—(Three times invest the altar, and then leave the sanctuary).

Kia King, 6th year, 7th month, 8th day.

May the merit of this book redound to the benefit of all men, so that I and all mankind may soon arrive at the condition of Buddha.

## Remarks.

As the Paradise of Amitâbha is the desire of the great body of Buddhist worshippers in China and Japan, so Kwan Yin is reverenced and worshipped as the "Saviour of men," able to remove the obstacles which prevent them from attaining that happy condition. Were the highest aspiration of the Buddhist, then, after annihilation, it would be difficult to account for the belief in the existence of such a beneficent and compassionate Being as their ideal of "Kwan Yin,"—a Being who has declared his purpose, under the most solemn oath,[1] to manifest himself to all creatures in the universe, for the purpose of delivering them from the consequences of sin, so long as any such creatures exist. But what is the deliverance promised? is it to lead to the annihilation of all such beings? No! but to their restoration to the "one condition"[2] of happiness, in which all were included before the delusion of sense and of the organs of sense led them astray.

The explanation of the difficulty arising from the apparently different tenets held by the philosophical and religious schools of Buddhist believers, is to be found in the fact of a most important development having taken place in their philosophical views. Up to the time of Âryâsangha (who was contemporary with Vasubandhu, the 21st Patriarch, and who died, according to Edkins, A.D. 117,—though I would suggest a later date,) the basis of every thing that exists was regarded as a "mere void,"—in other words, that nothing really existed; but the Yogâchârya system, which developed itself under his auspices, substituted for this void a *soul*, or âlaya, which was at once the basis and the receptacle, so to speak, of all existence. "This soul exists[3] from time immemorial and in every object, it reflects itself in everything like the moon in clear and tranquil water. It was the loss of its original purity that caused it to wander about in the various spheres of existence. The restoration of the soul to its purity can be attained by the same means as

[1] *Vide* the end of the Translation for the form of this oath.
[2] Called in Chinese the "One Heart," *yih sin*. [3] Schlagintweit, p. 39.

in the other systems (viz., by the practice of the Pâramitâs, etc.), but now its motive and the success become evident; ignorance is annihilated, and the illusion that anything ('except the soul') can be real is dissipated. . . . . . The dogma once established that an absolute pure nature exists, Buddhism soon proceeded, in the mystical school, further to endow it with the character of an all-embracing Deity." So that we have here something very definite, emerging from the uncertainty of previous systems. And it is to bring men back to this state of purity and happiness, that Kwan Yin, in different forms, is manifested to men, and by them worshipped and adored.

The method of proof on which this system rests, is well exhibited in the work called in Chinese, the Sing yan Sûtra (Ṣurangama Sûtra); in which, by a laboured process, but not altogether an illogical one, the existence of a Supreme Soul is demonstrated. And it is in this same work (Book vi.) that the character and office of the Bodhisattva Kwan Yin are properly explained. His character is one of pure mercy—his office to deliver men from all their troubles, and to bring them to happiness—and the peculiar mode of gaining his assistance is there declared to be by the recitation of a certain number of Dhâraṇîs, fully detailed in the same book (these Dhâraṇîs when restored to their Sanskrit originals, are found to be simple invocations of the deities and powers, known in the religions of India). The same method is also exhibited in the work here translated—a good portion of which consists of the invocations above-mentioned, which are repeated by the priests in a low monotonous voice, and are believed to have the power of commanding the presence and assistance of superior beings. There is, however, a thread of reasonable worship running through the whole service, which commends it to our careful consideration, and suggests frequent enquiries as to the model after which it was framed. We are unable to answer any such questions at the present time: perhaps some Sanskrit original may be discovered and translated for the benefit of future students, but at present we must rest contented with what we have—satisfied to know that Buddhism is not merely a cold philosophical system, or a system of morals only, or a system that binds men together as a community of religious mendicants; but beside all this, that it possesses a form of ceremonial worship, that includes in it a belief in future happiness and the existence of a Being of Supreme Power, and actuated by a principle of Supreme Love, manifested in His determination to deliver all creatures from their present evil condition.

The question now suggests itself, what do we know of the origin of the cultus herein described—Who is this Kwan Yin possessing the Power, Knowledge and Love, attributed to him in this ceremonial worship?

If written in full the Chinese title of this Bodhisattva would be Kwan Shai Yin, a title translated by Sir J. Davis, "She who hears the cries of men." By M. Rémusat it is rendered, "Vox contemplans sæculum;" whilst MM. Klaproth and Julien consider it as a mistaken version of the Sanskrit original, "Avalokiteṣvara."

Without doubt the original appellation of the Bodhisattva *was* Avalokiteṣvara; but I think the theory that "îṣvara" has been mistaken for "swara" is far-fetched.

It does not appear likely that the learned priests who superintended the translation of the originals into the Chinese, should have made such a mistake; on the contrary, we have proof that they did not, inasmuch as in the same chapter we frequently meet with both renderings "Kwan Tseu Tsai" and "Kwan Shai Yin" used indifferently; the first being the literal rendering of Avalokiteṣvara, and the other the popular equivalent.

With respect to the correct English translation of these titles, we know that the common rendering of Kwan Shai Yin, is "She who hears the cries of men," and hence the name, the "Goddess of Mercy," given to this Bodhisattva; but this appears rather to be a description of his character, than a true translation of the name itself. In the 6th Book of the Ṣurangama Sûtra, his character is fully described, as one who is always ready to assist and rescue men from trouble, hence he is always invoked in time of danger. Fah Hian, when nearly wrecked on the coast of Ceylon, tells us that he and his fellow religionists all called on the name of Avalokiteṣvara to save them from their peril. And so in many other cases that might be cited. The Temple of "Fei-loi Kwan Yin" in the city of Canton, was erected, or rather enlarged and beautified, after the first siege of that city by the English in 1842, because, as the printed account goes, "Kwan Yin appeared on that occasion over the city to protect and save it, in consequence of which the shot and shells of the Barbarians fell harmless among the people." It was a misfortune, however, for the votaries of this worship, that on the occasion of the last bombardment of that city, the fire of the assailants happened to be directed immediately against that quarter of the city where stood that very temple, and, as might be expected, it was soon reduced to comparative ruin, and when we entered it, after cessation of the fire, we found the incense still burning and a few of the last suppliants for mercy still hovering about the ruined courts. This all shews the aspect in which Kwan Yin *is* regarded, and Avalokiteṣvara *was* regarded, by modern and ancient worshippers.

Still I cannot think that the title the Bodhisattva bears can be literally Englished by "the Goddess of Mercy," or as M. Klaproth has it, "The Being who contemplates with love." I know it is hazardous to suggest any other version after M. Burnouf has sanctioned such a signification for the passive participle, "avalokita,"[1] but he appears to have lent his sanction to this rendering only on the ground that the Chinese and Thibetan equivalents required it. But if I am not mistaken the Chinese title, "Kwan Shai Yin," or "Kwan Tseu Tsai," may as well be rendered the "Manifested voice," or the "Manifested Self-Existent One," as by the active participle, "She who contemplates" or "the contemplating" the voices or cries of men. And if so, it seems only reasonable to suppose that in the original the passive participle was intended to have its real force: so that "Avalokiteṣvara," or,

[1] Introduction to Indian Buddhism, p. 226, note.

in Chinese, "Kwan Tseu Tsai," may very justly be rendered "the Manifested Deity."

This rendering is in absolute agreement with what is related concerning the peculiar attributes of this Bodhisattva, viz., that on being invoked by suppliants he manifests himself to deliver them. Hiouen Thsang relates how those who worshipped him, were rewarded by his coming out, as it were, from the image before which they said their prayers. And so, also, as to the origin of the worship, he tells us that on the top of Mount Potalaka (perhaps Pedura-Talla-Galla, in Ceylon) this divinity was accustomed to manifest himself under various forms, sometimes as Iṣvara, at others as one of the Paṣupatas, and so on, just as the occasion required. In fact, the secret of all the reverence paid to him is the belief that Avalokiteṣvara would reveal himself to the devotees who frequented his shrine, and bring them deliverance; hence it appears that the title, "the Manifested Deity," or "Îṣvara," is not an unlikely rendering of the original.

But it may be asked whence the title Kwan Shai Yin is derived, and how can such a translation as the one proposed, viz., the "Manifested Voice," be supported. In reply to this, it must be considered that the worship of Kwan Yin was probably introduced into China from the northern school of Buddhism, aud not from Ceylon. There is no such Divinity as Kwan Yin, or Avalokiteṣvara, known amongst the southern Buddhists. Yet most probably the cultus originated amongst them, if not in the island of Ceylon itself. But the worship of Avalokiteṣvara in those parts was simply the worship of Vishṇu, who we know is described as manifesting himself (as to Vijaya) in different forms to all those whom he regarded with favour, and we know also that Ceylon was always considered as being under the protection of Vishṇu; hence, I say, the possibility of this particular worship having been imported into Buddhism, from this popular belief in the South of India. But as the cultus spread further and wider, it necessarily came into contact with other legends and popular modes of religious worship, and so amongst the Ṣivite worshippers of the North, the idea of a "Manifested God" took the form of Ṣiva, and as the Buddhist philosophy developed itself, other forms and characteristics would be attributed to this popular and plastic Deity.

It is well known that a later development of Buddhism taught that each of the mortal, or Mânushi Buddhas, had a corresponding Dhyâni Buddha, just as Brahmá we may say, was developed from Brahmă. Now the Dhyâni Buddha, corresponding to Ṣâkya Muni, is Amitâbha Buddha, and hence the far extended worship paid to this particular Buddha; for as Ṣâkya Buddha is called the Saviour of our particular Sakwala, so Amitâbha is described as having even a paramount interest in our welfare, and not ours only, but in that of all the infinite Sakwalas composing his "platform" of existence (if we may so speak). Hence he is called the "God above all" by the Thibetans, and, if not so called, he is so regarded, by Chinese and Japanese Buddhists.

But in the North of India the theory of each Supreme Being having a female, or Ṣakti, representing the active power of that Being, had developed itself at an early date. Hence we find that the Ṣakti of Brahmâ was Vâch or Sarasvatî. But these names do but represent the power of speech, the connection being, evidently, between the faculty of speech and the hidden mind, of which speech is the exponent. Hence Buddhism (according to its facile character) was soon driven to adopt some similar theory, and as Amitâbha was regarded with supreme devotion, etc., his Ṣakti or active power was at first spoken of as Avalokiteṣvara, *i.e.* the *manifestation* of the Deity, and afterwards indifferently as Kwan Yin or the "Manifested Voice," corresponding to the female power called Vâch or Sarasvatî. Hence we find that Sarasvatî is adored in Thibet as the Ṣakti of Manjuṣrî,[1] simply because *he*, *i.e.* Manjuṣrî, is regarded as the chief divinity and protector of the country; and so also we may reasonably argue that as the belief in Amitâbha spread towards China, and afterwards to Japan, that the worship of Avalokiteṣvara under the title of Kwan Yin (or Vâch) accompanied it, and has ever after remained attached to it. We

[1] Schlagintweit, p. 65 n.

need not repeat that the two titles have the same meaning, and that as Sarasvatî was the Goddess of Speech, or as Vâch represented that power, so also that Kwan Yin is but the "Manifested Voice."

Hence again this Bodhisattva is nearly always represented in China under a female form, so much so, that to us she is familiarly known as the Goddess of Mercy, simply because when so represented she is the exponent of the character of Buddha, who is always regarded as being principally influenced by the attribute of *Love* in all he did for the benefit of men.

I have thus endeavoured to trace the origin of the title Kwan Yin, given in China and Japan to the Bodhisattva Avalokiteṣvara.

I may now say that Kwan Yin is there worshipped under many various shapes. It was my fortune some years ago to live for many months in the town of Hakodadi, in the North of Japan, and there on the different hills that surrounded the town, I found thirty-two images of this Being (called by the Japanese Kanōn), each possessing particular features—one, for instance, with two faces and four arms; another with three faces and six arms, etc.;—and I further discovered that these figures were well recognized models of different idols in the thirty-two chief temples of the country, in which the worship of Kanōn is particularly affected. So, also, in China, Kwan Yin is worshipped under very various shapes—at one time as "Kwan Yin of the Southern Seas," *i.e.*, no doubt, as inhabiting Potalaka (which is in Ceylon), and as such she is adored and invoked by sailors. Then she is worshipped by women as the Goddess of parturition, and so also she is represented, as in the present work, as being possessed of a thousand eyes and a thousand hands, indicating her supreme wisdom and power, to know all things and deliver all men. In the roll which accompanies the Chinese text, are representations of some forms under which Kwan Yin is known to the Chinese. Perhaps the most curious of all is the one in which he is described as the "Great Manes," no doubt referring to the Persian Manes, the founder of the Manichæan sect. We may gather from these representations the real mode of regarding this cultus: as being in fact adoration paid to every form of Wisdom and Beneficence, idealized under a particular figure and admitted, at an early period, as a proper personification of those attributes.

The work here translated does not profess to be a version of any Sanskrit original: it forms part of the Imperial collection of Sacred Books, and has a preface written by Yung loh the second of the Ming dynasty, A.D. 1412. It appears to have been re-printed at the Hai chwang Sze, near Canton (where I procured my own copy), in the 6th year of Kea King, *i.e.*, A.D. 1802.

I have been unable to revise the translation, and I am conscious of many faults being contained in it; but should it be considered of sufficient importance, the work of revision might be subsequently attended to, and perhaps the whole rendered more intelligible.

In the translation I have not hesitated to adopt words commonly understood to represent equivalent expressions in Chinese, as *e.g.*, in rendering the phrase "the thousand-handed and thousand-eyed Kwan Yin" by the expression Omniscient and Omnipotent, and also in other cases—in all of which I hope I have not been guided by anything but a wish correctly to render the original.

I have only to add that I have not in the translation written down all the Dhâraṇîs, as they are (unless restored to their originals) unmeaning sounds. They are repeated by the priests merely by rote, and with "no understanding." On examination, they are found to be invocations addressed to all the Buddhas, and to the popular idols of India; interspersed with frequent recitation of the words Om, Svah, Sri, &c.

*Dec.* 15, 1865.

ART. XI.—*The Hymns of the Gaupâyanas and the Legend of King Asamâti.* By Professor MAX MÜLLER, M.A., Hon. M. R. A. S.

HAVING lately received two new MSS. of Sâyaṇa's Commentary on the Rig-veda, I thought that a few lines on the character of these MSS., and on the proper use to be made of Sanskrit MSS. in general, might be of some interest both in England and in India. I owe these MSS. to the kindness and enlightened generosity of Dr. Bhao Daji, who is well known to the members of the Royal Asiatic Society, both as an intelligent collector of Indian antiquities, inscriptions, and manuscripts, and as a careful and successful inquirer into the history and chronology of India. I had explained to him and to other friends of mine in India the great difficulties I have to contend with in editing the two final Ashṭakas of the Rig-veda. Though I possess nine MSS. of Sâyaṇa's Commentary, yet, as I have stated in the prefaces to the four published volumes of the Rig-veda, these nine MSS. are only varieties of three original types, and as the later portions of Sâyaṇa's great exegetical work have evidently been much less read and studied in India than the former, the text is frequently in a very corrupt state, and in several passages past all hope of mending. This is the reason why I have waited so long before sending the last two Maṇḍalas of my edition of the Rig-veda to press, particularly as I had some hope of receiving an old and excellent MS. from the South of India. Whenever I heard of the existence of an old or otherwise promising MS. of Sâyaṇa, I always sent to my correspondent in India a number of test passages, in order to find out whether the MS. in question contained any independent readings. A collation of three or four passages in which all my MSS. shared exactly the same mistake, was generally sufficient to establish whether or not the new MS. represented an independent family, and a comparison of some other passages in which one of the three families had its peculiar faults or omissions, sufficed to show to which of the three the MS. belonged.

It is well known by this time that a mere collation of MSS. and an accumulation of various readings are of little use for critical purposes. MSS. are copied from one another, and if we have ten MSS. all copied from the same original, the various readings of these MSS. are clearly of no documentary value whatever. It is quite possible that here and there some of the more intelligent copyists may have been struck by the palpable errors of the original before them, and the corrections which they introduced may carry conviction to every reader. Yet, according to the principles of diplomatic criticism so well laid down by Lachmann, and at present adopted by all classical scholars of note, these corrections can claim no more authority than the conjectures of an individual, unless it can be proved, and this is very difficult, that the copyist had before him more than one MS. at the time. The object of diplomatic criticism is not to restore the most correct or the most plausible text, but that text, with all its mistakes and omissions, which a comparison of all the MSS. at our disposal places within our reach. Hence our first object in examining and collating MSS. must be to establish their respective worth and weight as witnesses. We ought to be most careful not to allow ourselves to be swayed either by the beautiful writing or by the age of any MS. Though the age of a MS. is always a matter of considerable importance, it happens not unfrequently that a modern copy possesses greater documentary value than an older copy, for the simple reason that it was copied straight from a MS. of greater age than any which we have access to. This is the case, for instance, with regard to the Ca. MS. of Sâyaṇa, which, although the oldest, is of far less value critically than the modern MS. A. Colebr. Let it once be established that out of ten MSS., B, C, D, are copied from A; that E, F, G, H, I, can all be traced back to a common source; and that J stands by itself:—then the office of an editor is simply to establish for each doubtful passage the reading of A, the reading that will account for the variations, if any, in E, F, G, H, I, and the reading of J. To give one of these readings in the printed text and the others in the notes, is all that can be required of him. After confronting in numerous places the evidence of three witnesses, it will, generally, be possible to arrive at an estimate of their respective value, and it is no doubt the greatest triumph of diplomatic criticism if it is possible, by conclusive evidence, to establish the paramount authority of one among three or more apparently independent traditions. In classical philology, where we have mostly to deal with MSS. which directly or indirectly must be traced back to the original MS. of an individual author, the establishment of one supreme authority is an object never to be lost sight of. In India, where the individual author is frequently merged in a school, and where oral teaching opens, even in modern times, so wide a door to disturbing influences, we must be prepared to arrive in the end at several independent authorities, generally localised in the principal seats of Brahmanic learning. Thus, although there may have been one original text of the Râmâyaṇa, it would clearly be in vain to attempt to restore that text by subjecting the two traditional texts to an eclectic criticism. All that an editor can do, is to give either the one or the other text according to the MSS. and to the commentaries, belonging to the one or the other school. The same applies to literary works which are ascribed to individual authors, as the play of Śakuntalâ, ascribed to Kâlidâsa. Here, too, the two traditional texts or 'recensions' must be kept apart, though, in this case, it is less difficult to decide which of the two is the original. With regard to the text of the Vedas, the Brahmans themselves recognised the existence of independent traditions or branches (śâkhâs); they chronicled the various readings of the hymns and even of the Brâhmaṇas, and this at so early a date, that we cannot ascribe these variations to the negligence of scribes, but only to the influence of oral tradition, kept up in different families and schools. What applies to the text of the Vedas, applies with equal, or even greater, force to their commentaries. Although the commentary of Sâyaṇa was composed as late as the fifteenth century of our era, and although I possess one MS., written not more than about a hundred years later, yet that MS. (Ca.) cannot claim the supreme authority, which for instance the codex Laurentianus A.

claims among the MSS. of Sophocles. The MS. of Colebrooke (A 2), although of a much more modern date, about 1761 A.D., represents in innumerable passages a less corrupt and less mangled text; at all events a text which could not possibly have passed through that phase which is exhibited in Ca. I have repeatedly, in the prefaces to my edition of the Rig-veda, explained the principles by which I have been guided in restoring the text of Sâyaṇa. Having to supply a text that should be practically useful, I have had to deviate from the strict principles of diplomatic criticism, so far as to place manifest blunders, even when they were supported by all the MSS., in the notes. I have chiefly done so when none of the readings of the MSS. would have yielded any sense whatever, or, when I was enabled, by consulting the originals from which Sâyaṇa quoted, to support my corrections by independent authority. I have on two or three occasions allowed an explanation, though it appeared in one or two MSS. only, and was clearly a marginal note of a later student, and not Sâyaṇa's own, to form part of the printed text, simply because I imagined it would be useful, and might be passed over if given only in the notes. Deviations like these from the strict rules followed by Lachmann, Haupt, and others, have always been noted in the *Varietas Lectionis*. I do not wish to defend them even in the edition of a work like Sâyaṇa's Commentary, and I have carefully avoided them in the later volumes.

In order to show the position which the two new MSS. of Sâyaṇa, lately received from Dr. Bhao Daji, hold in the well-established pedigree of Sâyaṇa's MSS., I have chosen a passage where Sâyaṇa gives a long extract from a Brâhmaṇa. These extracts are generally full of blunders, and unless they can be verified in the original from which they are taken, they are very troublesome to an editor. Their usefulness, however, for determining the relative position of our MSS. is all the greater, because the scribes, who had little difficulty in correcting blunders in the uniform and business-like style of Sâyaṇa, found it more difficult to deal with the antiquated words and grammatical forms of the Brâhmaṇas, and therefore contented themselves generally with copying letter by letter the original before them. It will be seen at one glance, by comparing the texts of the various MSS. in this passage, that of the two MSS. lent to me by Dr. Bhao Daji, the one which I mark B.D. belongs to the B. class, the other which I mark A.D. belongs to the A. class. The first MS. (B.D.) is written in a beautiful hand, with large and distinct letters, and contains both text and commentary. It has no date, at least not in that portion of it which I was able to examine. The other MS. (A.D.) is likewise written in a very distinct hand, but the letters are smaller and less carefully formed. In the centre of each page, space is left for inserting the text, but it is only in the sixth Ashṭaka, and in the seventh as far as fol. 51, that the text has been added. In the eighth Ashṭaka the commentary occupies the whole page, no space being left for the text. At the end of the eighth Ashṭaka a date is given, 1813, as it would seem, of Samvat, *i.e.* 1757 A.D. The name of the writer is not clear, but it may be meant for Sadâsîṁ, the son of Jagannâtha. Whoever the writer was, he lived, like the writer of Colebrooke's MS., at Benares, and this so far confirms my opinion that the A. class represents the Benares text, in the same manner as the B. class represents the scholastic tradition of Bombay and Poonah, and the C. class, at least in the earlier Ashṭakas, that of Calcutta. In order to explain the arrangement of the following extracts, I have only to add that the first class of MSS. comprises, besides the MSS. of Dr. Bhao Daji and Colebrooke, the two C. MSS., which, as I pointed out in the preface to the second volume of my edition (p. viii.), are in the later Ashṭakas derived from an A. source. Taylor's MS. too, which in the earlier Ashṭakas belonged to the B. class, and was therefore marked B. 4., belongs in the eighth Ashṭaka to the A. class. How this came to pass is easily explained by the fact that these MSS. were copied from different originals lent to Taylor, Mill, and Wilson by persons residing in different parts of India. The second, or C. class, is now represented by one MS. only, the oldest hitherto known in Europe, which I continue to quote as Ca. In the third, or B. class, B. 1. is the MS. of Stevenson; B. 2. the MS. of Burnouf, as copied by me in 1847; B. 3. is the new copy mentioned by me in the preface to the second volume, now in the hands of Dr. Goldstücker, and kindly collated by him for me; B.M. is a fragment of the last Ashṭaka which I received from Dr. Haug; B.D. is the MS. lent me by Dr. Bhao Daji. The last line gives the text as it may be re-established from an intercomparison of the three families of Sâyaṇa's MSS. I do not maintain that it represents exactly what Sâyaṇa wrote, still less that it gives the correct text of the Śâṭyâyanaka. It is simply impossible, with the MSS. at our disposal, to restore a text that might claim to be identical with Sâyaṇa's own writing. All that can be claimed for our text is that it represents Sâyaṇa's writing as far as it can *now* be restored with the help of our MSS. It gives what is obtainable with a strict observance of the rules of diplomatic criticism. It is not only possible, but extremely likely, that if to-morrow we obtained Sâyaṇa's own manuscript, whether from the ruins of Vidyânagara, where a complete collection of his works is said to have been buried, or from the MS. which Dr. Haug saw at Ahmadabad, and to which he assigns the date of Samvat 1526, A.D. 1470, we should find slight variations between Sâyaṇa's original and the nearest approach to it that is within our reach. It is still more likely that if a MS. of the Śâṭyâyanaka were recovered in India, there might be between it and our own restored text, considerable discrepancy. The students of Sâyaṇa's Commentary know that this is frequently the case when Sâyaṇa quotes from Brâhmaṇas and Sûtras, of which we possess both MSS. and printed texts; and he has his choice between supposing that Sâyaṇa quoted from memory and without caring about minute accuracy, or that he quoted from a śâkhâ different from that which is before us. It would be easy, no doubt, to improve the text of the Brâhmaṇa, as here printed, by conjecture. But those who know the mischief done by conjectural criticism in classical scholarship, will deprecate, most strongly, any countenance given to it by Sanskrit scholars. It may be truly said that the chief business of modern critics is to cleanse the text of the classics from the improvements introduced by the ingenious editors of the last three centuries, and we ought not to neglect this lesson in preparing our own *editiones principes*. Let an editor give what there is, and let the commentator and translator say what might be, or what ought to be.

| | | | | |
|---|---|---|---|---|
| A. D. | अत्रोक्ताख्येन | ग्राव्यायन ग्राव्यायनकं | असमातिं | राज्याप्रोष्ठं |
| A. | अत्रोक्ताख्येन | ग्राव्यायनकं | असमातिं | राज्याप्रोष्ठं |
| C. M. | अत्रोक्ताख्येन | . ग्राव्यायनकं | असमातिं | राज्याप्रोष्ठं |
| C. W. | अत्रोक्ताख्येन | ग्राव्यायनकं | असमातिं | राजाप्रोष्ठं |
| B. 4. | अत्रोक्ताख्येन | ग्राव्यायनकमममातिं | | राज्युत्प्रोष्ठं |
| | | | | |
| Ca. | अत्रोक्तास्तेन | ग्राप्यायनकं | असमातिराद्य | प्रौद्यं |
| | | | | |
| B. 1. | तत्रोक्ताख्याने | ग्राव्यायनकं । | असमितिं | राज्यात्षौष्ठ |
| B. 2. | तत्रोक्ताख्याने | ग्राव्यायनकं ॥ | असमितिं | राज्यात्षौष्ट |
| B. 3. | तत्रोक्ताख्याने | ग्राव्यायनकं | असमीति | राज्यात्प्रौष्ट |
| B. M. | तत्रोक्ताख्याने | ग्राव्यायनकं | असमीतिं | राज्यात्प्रौष्ठ |
| B. D. | तत्रोक्ताख्याने | ग्राव्यायनकं | असमीतिं | राज्यात्प्रौष्ठ |
| Text in M.M.'s edition. | अत्रोक्ता[1]ख्याने[2] | ग्राव्यायनकं । | असमातिं[3] | राथप्रौष्ठं |

| | | | | | |
|---|---|---|---|---|---|
| A. D. | गोपायना | अभ्यगामंस्ते | खांडवे | सत्रमासताद्य | हासमातौ |
| A. | गोपायना | अभ्यागमंस्ते | खांडवे | सत्रमासताद्य | हासमातो |
| C. M. | गोपायना | अभ्यगामंस्ते | खांडवे | सत्रमासताद्य | हासमातौ |
| C. W. | गोपायना | अभ्यगामंस्ते | खांडवे | सत्रमासताद्य | हासमातौ |
| B. 4. | गोपायना | अभ्यगासंस्ते | खांडवे | सत्रमासताद्य | हासमातौ |
| | | | | | |
| Ca. | गोपायनोयं | अभ्यगासंस्तेषां | खांडवे | सत्रमासताद्य | हासमातौ |
| | | | | | |
| B. 1. | गोपायना | अभ्यंगासंस्ते | खांडवे | सत्रमासतथा | हासमातौ |
| B. 2. | गोपायना | अभ्यंगासंस्ते | खांडवे | सत्रमास तथा | हासमातौ |
| B. 3. | गोपायना | अभ्यंगासंस्ते | खांडवे | सत्रमास | मातौ |
| B. M. | गौपयना | अभ्यंगासंस्ते | खांडवे | सत्रमास | मातौ |
| B. D. | गोपायना | अभ्यंगासंस्ते | खांडवे | सत्रमास | मातौ |
| Text in M.M.'s edition. | गौपायना[4] | अभ्यगमंस्ते[5] | खांडवे | सत्रमासताद्य[6] | हासमातौ |

A. D. राज्यप्रोष्टे किंलाताकुली दूषनुरसुमीयौ त ह स्मानग्नौ

A. राज्यप्रोष्टे किंलाताकुली दूषतुरसुमीयौ त ह स्मानग्नौ

C. M. राज्यप्रोष्टे किंलाताकुली दृषनुरसुमीयो त ह स्मानग्नौ

C. W. राज्यप्रो।ष्टे किंलाताकुली दूषनुरसुमीयौ त ह स्मानग्नौ

B. 4. राज्याप्रोष्टे किंलाताकुलीदूषतुरसमीयौत(म)हस्माहनग्नौ

Ca. राज्यप्रोष्टे किंलाताकुली दूषतुरसमीपौ न ह स्मानग्नौ

B. 1. राज्यात्षाष्टे कुली दूषनुरसुमीयौ तमह स्मानग्नौ

B. 2. राज्यात्षाष्टे कुली दूषनुरसुमीयौ तमह स्मानग्नौ

B. 3. राज्योत्प्रौष्टे किलांताकुली दूषनुरसुमीयौ नमह स्मानग्नौ

B. M. राज्योत्प्रोष्टे किलांताकुली दूषनुरसमीयौ तमह स्मानग्नौ

B. D. राज्यात्प्रोष्टे किलांताकुली दूषनुरसुमीयौ नमह स्मानग्नौ

Text in M.M.'s edition. राथप्रौ[7]ष्टे [8]किंलाताकुली ऊषतुर[9]सुरमायौ[10] तं [11]ह स्मानग्नौ

A. D. निधायोदनं यवतो ग्नौ मांस यथासुरा रा न्नं दग्धंत्वाकव:

A. निधायोदनं पवनो ग्नौ मांस यथासुरा रान्नं दग्धेत्वाकव:

C. M. नि ध्ययोदनं पवतो ग्नौ मांस पथासुरा रान्नं दग्धेचाकव:

C. W. नि ध्ययोदनं पवतो ग्नौ मांस पथासुरा रा न्नं दग्धेचाकव:

B. 4. निधायोदनं पचतो ग्नौ मांस मथासुरा अन्नं दग्ध्वेत्वाकव:

Ca. निधायोदनं पचतो ग्नौ मांसं यथासुरा त्रं दत्वा कवय:

B. 1. निधायौदनं पचतो ग्नौ मांसमधासुरा रान्नं दग्धेत्वाकव:

B. 2. निधायौदनं पचतो ग्नौ मांसमधासुरा रान्नं दग्धेत्वाकव:

B. 3. निधायौदनं पचतो ग्नौ मांसमधासुरा रान्नं दग्धेत्वाकव:

B. M. निधायौदन पचतो ग्नौ मांसमधासुरा रान्नं दग्धेत्वाकव:

B. D. निधायौदनं पचतो ग्नौ मांसमधासुरा रान्नं दग्धेत्वाकव:

Text in M.M.'s edition. ऽनिधायौदनं[12] पचतोऽग्नौ मांसमथा[13]सुरा अन्नंदग्ध्वेत्वाकव:

A. D. परावभूवुः तमसमाति रांयप्रोष्ठ गोपायनामाऊतयो

A. परावभूवुः तमसमातिं रायप्रोष्टं गोपायनमाऊतयो

C. M. पराबभूवुः तमसमातिं राद्य प्रौष्टं गोपायना मा ऊतयो

C. W. पराबभूवुः तमसमातिं राद्य प्रौष्टं गोपायना मा ऊतयो

B. 4. पराबभूवतुः तमसमातिं राज्यप्रौष्ठं गोपायनानामाऊतयो

Ca. पराबभूवुः तमसमातिं रायप्रौष्टं गापायनं मा ऊत तो

B. 1. परा समति रायत्प्रौष्टं गोपायनामाऊतयो

B. 2. परा समति रायत्प्रोष्टं गोपायनामाऊतयो

B. 3. परा समतिं रायत्प्रोष्टं गोपायनामां ऊतयो

B. M. परा समतिं रायत्प्रोष्ठं गोपायनामां ऊतयो

B. D. परा समतिं रायत्प्रौष्ठं गोपायनामां ऊतयो

Text in M.M.'s edition. परा[14]बभूवुः । तमसमातिं रायप्रौष्ठं गौपायनानामाऊतयो

A. D. भ्यनयन साच्च वोदिमौ किलाताकुली दूमां वै मा गौपा-

A. भ्यतपन सा च्च वीदिमौ किलाताकुलो दूमा वै मा गौपा-

C. M. भ्यतपन साच्च वीदिमौ किलाताकुली दूमा वै मा गौपा-

C. W. भ्यतपन साच्च वीदिमौ किलाताकुलो दूमा वै मा गौपा-

B. 4. भ्यतपन्स्तो ब्रवोदिंमौ किलताकुलो दूमा वै वे मा गोपा-

Ca. त्य तयन्सौ ब्रवीदिमौ कि रं ला राकुली दूमा वै गोपा-

B. 1. भ्यपतन्सो ब्रवीदिमो किलाताकुली दूमा वै मा गोपा-

B. 2. भ्यपतन्सो ब्रवीदिमो किलाताकुलो दूमा वै मा गोपा-

B. 3. भ्यपतन्सो ब्रवोदिमो किलाताकुलो दूमा वै मा गोपा-

B. M. भ्यपतन्सो ब्रवोदिमो किलाताकुली दूमा वै मा गोपा-

B. D. भ्यपतन्सो ब्रवीदिमो किलाताकुली दूमा वै मा गोपा-

Text in M.M.'s edition. ऽभ्यतपन्[15]सो ऽब्रवीदिमौ किलाताकुलो दूमा वै मा गौपा-[16]

| | |
|---|---|
| A. D. | यनानामाङ्कतयो भितपंतीति तावब्रूनां तस्य वा अवमेव |
| A. | यनानामाङ्कतयो भितपंतीति तावब्रूतां तस्य वा अवमेव |
| C. M. | यनानामाङ्कतयो भितपंतीति तावब्रूनां तस्य वा अवमेव |
| C. W. | यनानामाङ्कतयो भितपंतीति तावब्रूनां तस्य बा अवमेव |
| B. 4. | यनामाङ्कतयो नितपंतीति तावब्रूतां तस्य वा आवमेव |
| Ca. | यनानामाङ्कतयो भिनयंतीति तावब्रूतां तस्यं वा आवामच |
| B. 1. | यना अभिपतंतीति तावब्रूतां तस्य वा अवमेव |
| B. 2. | यना अभिपतंतीती तावब्रूतां तस्य वा अवमेव |
| B. 3. | यना अभिपतंतीति तावद्भूतां तस्य अवमेव |
| B. M. | यना अभिपतंतीति तावद्भूतां तस्य अवमेव |
| B. D. | यना अभिपतंतीति तावद्भूतां तस्य अवमेव |
| Text in M.M.'s edition. | यनानामाङ्कतयो[17] ऽभितपंतीति तावब्रूतां तस्य वा[18] आवमेव[19] |

| | |
|---|---|
| A. D. | भेजो स्था अवं प्रायश्चित्तिरापं तथा करिष्यावो यथा |
| A. | भेजो स्था अवं प्रायश्चित्तिरापं तथा करिष्यावो यथा |
| C. M. | भेजो स्था अवं प्रायश्चित्तिरापं तथा करिष्यावो यथा |
| C. W. | भेजो स्था अवं प्रायश्चित्तिरापं तथा करिष्यावो यथा |
| B. 4. | भिषजो स्थ आवं प्रायश्चित्तिरापं तथा करिष्यावो यथा |
| Ca. | भेषजौ स्न्यं अचं प्रापयश्चित्रिराचं तथा करिष्यावो यथा |
| B. 1. | भेषजौ स्थ अवं प्रायश्चितिरायं तथा करिष्यवो यथा |
| B. 2. | भेषजौ स्थ अवं प्रायश्चितिरायं तथा करिष्यवो यथा |
| B. 3. | भेषजौ स्थ अवं प्रायश्चित्तिरायं तथा करिष्यदो यथां |
| B. M. | भेषजौ स्थ अवं प्रायश्चितिरायं तथा करिष्यदो यथा |
| B. D. | भेषजौ स्थ अवं प्रायश्चित्तिरायं तथा करिष्यदो यथा |
| Text in M.M.'s ediuon. | भिषजौ[20] स्व आवं प्रायश्चित्तिरावं तथा करिष्यावो यथा |

A. D. न्वैता नाभितपंतीति तौ परेत्य सुवधोगौंपायनस्य स्वपत:
A. न्वैता नाभितपंतीति तौ परेत्य सुवंधोगौंपायनस्य स्वपत:
C. M. न्वैता नाभितपंनीति तौ परेत्य सुवंध्येगौंपायनस्य स्वपत:
C. W. न्वैता नाभितपंनीति तौ परेत्य सुवंध्येगौंपायनस्य स्वपत:
B. 4. न्वेता नाभितपंतीति तौ परेत्य सुबंधोगोंपायनस्य स्वपत:

Ca. त्यैता नाभिनयंतीति त्यै परेत्य सु ंधोगोंपायनस्य स्वपत:

B. 1. न्वेता ॥ तीति तौ परेत्य सुबंधुगोंपायनस्य स्वपत:
B. 2. न्वेत ॥ तीति तौ परेत्य सुबंधुगोंपायनस्य स्वपत:
B. 3. वेत तीति तौ परेत्य सुबंधुगोंपायनस्य स्वपत:
B. M. न्वेत तीति तौ परेत्य सुबंधुगोंपायनस्य स्वपत:
B. D. न्वेत तीति तौ परेत्य सुबंधुगोंपायनस्य स्वपत:
Text in M.M.'s edition. न्वेता[21] नाभितपंतीति तौ परेत्य सुबंधोगौं[22]पायनस्य स्वपत:

A. D. प्रत्तस्यासुमाऊत्यात: परिधि न्यधत्तानमित्यादि ॥
A. प्रमत्तस्यासुमाऊत्यात: परिधिं न्यधत्तानमित्यादि ॥
C. M. प्रमत्तस्यासुमाऊत्यात: परिधिं न्यधत्तानमित्यादि ॥
C. W. प्रमत्तस्यासुमाऊत्यात: परिधिं न्यधत्तानमित्यादि ॥
B. 4. प्रमत्तस्यासुमाऊत्यांत: परिधिं न्यधत्तानमित्यादि ॥

Ca. प्रमत्तस्यासुमाह्न्यात: परिधिं निधत्तानमित्यादि ॥

B. 1. प्रमतस्यासुमाऊत्यांत: परिधि न्यधतामित्यादि ॥
B. 2. प्रमतस्यासुमाऊत्यांत: परिधि न्यधतामित्यादि ॥
B. 3. प्रमतस्यासुमाऊत्यांत: परिधि न्यधातामित्यादि ॥
B. M. प्रमतस्यासुमाऊत्यांत: परिधि न्यधतामित्यादि ॥
B. D. प्रमतस्यासुमाऊत्यांत: परिधि न्यधतामित्यादि ॥
Text in M.M.'s edition. प्रमत्तस्यासुमाऊत्यांत: परिधि न्यधत्ता[23]मित्यादि ॥

[1] The B. MSS. differ from the A. and Ca. MSS. by putting तत्र instead of अत्र. The repetition of ग्रात्यायन is a slip of the writer of A.D.

[2] All B. MSS. have आख्याने right, while the A. MSS. have the mistake आख्येन, which reappears in the still more corrupt Ca. उक्तास्तेन.

[3] All the B. MSS. blunder in the third vowel of असमातिं; the A. MSS. are right; Ca. blunders in leaving out the *anusvâra*.

The patronymic name of Asamâti, which I suppose to be राथप्रौष्ठं, is corrupt in all MSS. The A. MSS. agree in राज्याप्रोष्ठं except B. 4, which has been corrected, and C. W., which has the slight variation of राजाप्रोष्ठं; while the B. MSS. support throughout at all events the *vṛiddhi* vowel of the third syllable, which also appears in the faulty reading of Ca. B. 1 and 2 are more closely united, and so are B. 3, B.M., and B.D.; the former giving राज्यात्षौष्ठ or °ष्ट, the latter राज्यात्प्रौष्ठ. See R.V. x, 60, 5. On Asamâti, see Lassen, Indische Alterthumskunde (first edition), vol. i. p. xiii. note 31; Colebrooke, Misc. Essays, i. p. 25.

[4] B.M. stands alone in furnishing the right reading गौपयना, the correction probably of an individual copyist, unsupported even by the nearest MS. B.D. The short vowel in the second syllable is equally peculiar to B.M.

[5] The right reading अभ्यगमंस्ते is nearly preserved in A. Other MSS. belonging to this class, C. M. and A.D. slide into अभ्यगामंस्ते. B. 4 seems to give अभ्यगासंस्ते, and this is the reading of Ca. The B. MSS. add to it a new mistake अभ्यंगासंस्ते.

[6] The A. class and Ca. have throughout the right reading आसत, followed by अद्य, which I think is meant for अथ. B. 1 and 2 have taken तथा as one word, and left आस without the त, thus rendering it unintelligible. B. 3, B.M. and B.D. have the same lacuna.

[7] The patronymic has again puzzled the scribes. The A. and Ca. MSS. now agree in राज्यप्रोष्ठे or राज्यप्रोष्टे. B. 4 brings in the long आ in राज्याप्रोष्ठे, which seems to come from B. unless it is accidental. B. 1 and 2 have राज्यात्षाष्ठे and °ष्टे, to which they inclined before; while B, 3, B.M., and B.D. approach to their former blunder राज्यात्प्रौष्ठ.

[8] The *anusvâra* in किं is the characteristic mark of the A. class. B 1 and 2 are held together by their common lacuna; B. 3, B.M. and B.D. by the *anusvâra* on the second syllable.

[9] The spelling of दूषतुः or दुषनुः seems to point to ऊषतुः The verb वस्, to dwell, may be construed with a locative, in the sense of "to dwell with."

[10] असुमीयौ is probably intended for असुरमायौ. The readings of the different MSS. might seem to suggest समीपौ or असमीपौ, but I

prefer असुरमायौ because this word is used in the Tâṇḍya-brâhmaṇa, xiii. 12. There we find two Mâyâ's, evidently treated as females, but acting a similar part to that assigned to the two priests in our legends. I subjoin the text and Sâyaṇa's Commentary (MS. Wilson, 396, p. 161 *a*): गौपायनानां वै सत्रमासीनानां किरातकुल्यावसुरमाये अंतःपरिध्यसून्प्राकिरतां तेऽग्ने त्वं नो अंतम इत्यग्निमुपासीदंस्तेनासूनस्पृण्वंस्तद्वाव ते तर्ह्यकामयंत कामसनि साम गौर्द्रः काममेवैतेनावरुंध इति ॥ Com. गौपायनानां गौ(गो?)पगोत्राणां सत्रमासीनानां सत्रासनं कुर्वतामृषीणामसून्प्राणान्किरातकुल्यौ। किराता म्लेच्छाः। तत्तु(*sic*)ल्यरूपे असुरमाये असुरसंबंधिन्यौ माये अंतः परिधि आहवनीयस्य परिधीनां मध्यदेशे प्राकिरतां। प्रकर्षेण व्याक्षिपतां। कॄ विक्षेप इति धातुः। ततस्ते गौपायना अग्ने त्वं नो अंतम इति तृचेनाग्निमुपासीदन्। उपागच्छन्। अस्तुवन्नित्यर्थः। तेनोपसदनेनाग्नेः प्रसादात्पुनरात्मीयानसूनस्पृण्वन्। अबलयन्। मायापरिक्षिप्तान्पुनरादाय प्रबलानकुर्वन्नित्यर्थः। ते गौपायनास्तस्मिन्समय एतदेव तर्ह्यकामयंत तस्माद्गौर्द्रः। कामसनि कामप्रदं। गतमन्यत् ॥ Here then किरातकुल्यौ would have to be taken in the sense of "of the race of, or similar to Kirâtas," it would be a feminine, corresponding to असुरमाये, and the singular in the feminine would therefore be किरातकुली, masc. किरातकुलः In our passage, on the contrary, किलाताकुली must be a masculine in the nom. dual, and would therefore lead us to suppose that किरात and अकुलि were the names of the two sorcerers. They occur again as male demons in the Śatapatha Brâhmaṇa I. 1, 4, 14, and in the Bṛihaddevatâ. Sâyaṇa in his commentary on the Śatapatha Brâhmaṇa explains किराताकुली by किरातश्चाकुलिश्च द्वावसुरपुरोहितौ बभूवतुः। In another passage, the Tâṇḍya (xiii. 7) uses the fem. termination of the dual, (ध्वस्ने for ध्वस्नौ) for the masc. Here, however, the commentator calls it लिंगव्यत्ययः.

[11] The A. MSS. agree on त ह, *i.e.* तं ह, for the म of B. 4 is from the margin. The B. MSS. on the contrary all point to तमह.

[12] निधायोदनं marks the A. and Ca. MSS.; निधायौदनं the B. MSS.

[13] The A. MSS. agree in मांस यथा, instead of मांसमथा which is intended by the B. MSS. B. 4 has the B. reading, and alone of all MSS. supplies the reading अन्नं. Ca. mixes up the two readings.

[14] In the lacuna after परा and in समति we have marked features of the entire B. class. B. 4 has its own peculiar mistake, पराबभूवतुः which could only refer to the two Asuras, while it is meant for the Ikshvâkus, *i.e.* Asamâti and the Rathaproshṭhas.

[15] The A. class is again marked by retaining the correct अभ्यतपन् though not always clearly written, whereas the B. MSS. have clearly अभ्यपतन्.

[16] The B. MSS. again agree in the mistake गोपायना.

[17] The B. class is sharply marked by the lacuna of आहुतयो and again by अभिपतंति instead of अभितपंति, and the short vowel in करिष्यवो.

[18] The omission of वा shows the close relationship of B. 3, B.M. & B.D.

[19] The original reading was probably आवमेव; cf. Śatapatha-brâhmaṇa, I. 1, 4, 15, आवमिति ह्रस्वोच्चारणं.

[20] The mistake भेजो in A. D., A., C. M., and C.W. indicates a closer relationship between these three MSS.

[21] The lacuna after त्वेता in the B. MSS. is important; likewise the coincidences between B. 1 and B. 2 on one side, and between B 3, B.M. and B.D. on the other.

[22] सुबंधुर्गों° is a mistake that distinguishes the B. MSS. from the A. and Ca.MSS. सवंध्ये in C.M. is a mere *lapsus calami*, repeated in C.W. So is गौपा° in A.D. and B. 4, and again प्रत्तस्य. Is आहुत्य intended for आहृत्य?

[23] The A. MSS. agree in न्यधत्तानमि° instead of न्यधत्तां. Ca. stands alone with निधत्तानमि°, while the B. MSS. just miss the right reading by the omission of one त. B. 3 has न्यधाता°, where the long â is a blunder of the copyist.

Having thus established the fact which I wished to establish, viz., that at present, in spite of repeated researches set on foot by my friends in India, no MSS. of Sâyaṇa's have been discovered that could claim to be anterior to the branching off of the three great families, A.B.C., I only intended in conclusion once more and in this public manner to convey my thanks to Dr. Bhao Daji for his great kindness, and to express a hope that other countrymen of his might follow his example, and take an active and enlightened interest in researches concerning the ancient literature, religion, and history of their noble country. But as I have once touched on the hymns of the Gaupâyanas, and on the legend of king Asamâti, quoted by Sâyaṇa in explanation of the four hymns of the Rig-veda (x. 57–60), I gladly add a few extracts from my manuscript notes on these hymns themselves, hymns which are in many respects of peculiar interest to the student of the Veda. In offering a double translation of these hymns, one according to Sâyaṇa, the other according to my own view, I need not enter fully into the principles which I think ought to be followed in the interpretation of the hymns of the Rig-veda. I have frequently stated my opinions on this subject in the prefaces to my edition of the Rig-veda, in the specimens that I have given in my History of Sanskrit Literature, and in my Essay on the Funeral Ceremonies of the Brahmans, and I may have to defend these opinions again when I come to publish my translation of the Rig-veda. The following is a specimen of what I intend to give in that translation, though, as the hymns of the Gaupâyanas occur in the last Maṇḍala, I have here to take account of M. Langlois' translation only, and have not to examine, as in the earlier books, the valuable explanations proposed by other scholars, such as Rosen, Nève, Benfey, Wilson, Kuhn, Regnier, Aufrecht, Muir, and others. Whenever it is possible to ascertain from his Dictionary the opinion of my learned friend, Professor Roth, with regard to the meaning of certain words in certain passages, I have to take careful account of his interpretations, and I hope to be able to avail myself in like manner of Professor Goldstücker's Lexicon and of the Vedic Glossary and translations promised by Professor Aufrecht. All I need say at present is that I am convinced as strongly as ever that all interpretation of the Vedic hymns must begin with an examination of the traditional explanations collected by Sâyaṇa. No one can doubt that the commentary of Sâyaṇa is the result of a long line of scholastic tradition, gathered up by Sâyaṇa, but the first fibres of which can easily be traced back to Kâtyâyana, Śaunaka, Yâska, and the authorities quoted in the Brâhmaṇas. We may be certain that Sâyaṇa does not invent traditions; he hardly ventures to choose between them, but gives them as he finds them, unconcerned about their palpable contradictions. Thus, in our case, the traditions of the Brahmans, with regard to the four hymns in question, are by no means uniform, though they all agree in giving to the four hymns (x. 57–60) an historical character. How the orthodox Brahmans can reconcile these allusions to historical personages and events with the pre-Adamite or pre-Mânavite character which they claim for the Veda, it is difficult to understand. In other cases they have tried to give to proper names occurring in the hymns or Brâhmaṇas an allegorical character, but, as far as I know, they seem to have made no such attempt with the names of king Asamâti and his priest Subandhu. But, however that may be, the important point to us is this, that as far as we can trace back the exegetical tradition of the Brahmanic schools, we find that these four hymns are grouped together, and are supposed to allude to certain historical events. As the simplest account of these events is given in the Sarvânukrama of Kâtyâyana, it will be best to begin with this.

According to Kâtyâyana, then, these four hymns were seen, *i.e.* composed, by the Gaupâyanas, the same Ṛishis to whom four other lines are ascribed by Kâtyâyana in Rig-veda, v. 24. In that passage Kâtyâyana calls them Gaupâyanas or Laupâyanas,[1] and gives their names as Bandhu, Subandhu, Śrutabandhu, and Viprabandhu. What Kâtyâyana tells us in explanation of the events that called forth the four hymns of the tenth Maṇḍala, is simply this: "King Asamâti, of the race of Ikshvâku, left the Gaupâyanas, Bandhu, etc., who had been his chief priests, and selected two wizards whom he considered better, or the very best that he could get. Then the others were angry and used incantations against the king. Thereupon the two wizards attacked[2] the vital spirits of Subandhu. Then his three brothers recited[3] the Gâyatrî-hymn (x. 57) to obtain a blessing.[4] Afterwards they recited the next Anushṭubh-hymn (x. 58), in order to cause the soul (of Subandhu) to return. In the next hymn (x. 59) they recited four verses to drive away Nirṛiti,[5] and in the fourth they likewise praised Soma. In the two next following verses they praised the divine Asunîti (fem.) in order to remove Mṛityu or death; in the seventh verse they invoked certain deities by name, and in the remaining verses Dyâvâpṛithivî (heaven and earth); likewise Indra in the first line of the tenth verse. Then follows the Anushṭubh-hymn (x. 60) in which they praised Asamâti in four verses, and in the fifth, Indra. In the sixth verse their mother, the sister of Agastya, praised the king. With the others they invoked

[1] The name of Laupâyana receives no further explanation. It may be mentioned, however, that Lopâmudrâ is the name of the wife of Agastya (R. V. i, 179), and that Agastya is quoted in these hymns as the ancestor, it would seem, of the race.

[2] आचिक्षिपतुः आच्छादयतां.  [3] जप्त्वा, छांदसत्वादनिट्त्वं.

[4] Sâyaṇa has अविनाशप्राप्तिहेतुभूतं.

[5] Nirṛiti, according to Sâyaṇa, removes the vital spirits from the body.

the life of Subandhu, and with the last they touched him after he had recovered consciousness."

Sâyaṇa follows in general the tradition of Kâtyâyana, but he likewise takes some particular points from other sources, from the Śâṭyâyanaka and the Bṛihaddevatâ. The Śâṭyâyanaka is one of the Brâhmaṇas very frequently quoted by Sâyaṇa, but unfortunately not yet recovered in manuscript. The text, as restored above from a comparison of the principal MSS., is not always clear, but as far as it is possible to make it out, the tradition, as there given, seems to have been as follows: "The Gaupâyanas had come to Asamâti Râthapraushṭha. They had performed a Sattra sacrifice in Khâṇḍava. Then two demoniacal wizards, Kilâta and Akuli, dwelt with Asamâti Râthapraushṭha. The two Asuras cooked their porridge without putting it into the fire, and then the meat on the fire.[1] The Ikshvâkus having burnt their food, failed. The oblations of the Gaupâyanas burnt Asamâti Râthapraushṭha. He said to those two, Kilâta and Akuli, 'These oblations of the Gaupâyanas burn me.' The two said, 'Of that we two indeed are the healers, we two are the penance. We shall so arrange that these do not burn.' Then the two, going off, and offering the soul of Subandhu Gaupâyana, who was asleep and unconscious, placed it inside the sacrificial ring.'" Another extract from the Śâṭyâyanaka follows at the seventh verse of the last hymn: "Then they praised Agni with the Dvipada-hymn.[2] Agni being praised, approached, and having approached, he said, 'With what desire did you come?' They said, 'Let us obtain again the spirit of Subandhu.' He said, 'That spirit is inside the sacrificial ring, take it.'"

Here then we see that some sacrificial minutiæ have been added, of which the Sarvânukrama takes no notice. Though the language of the Brâhmaṇa is by no means clear, yet it would seem that its author knew nothing of any incantations

[1] This translation is very doubtful, and the text decidedly incorrect. असुरा might be taken as a nominative dual, but the use of the particle अथ is not in accordance with the ordinary style of the Brâhmaṇas. We must wait for the help of other MSS.

[2] This refers to the hymn R.V. v. 24.

being used by the Gaupâyanas against King Asamâti, unless the same idea is expressed by the words, "the oblations of the Gaupâyanas burn me." The Ikshvâkus, *i.e.* the people of Asamâti, according to the Śâṭyâyanaka, simply made a mistake at the sacrifice and burnt their food in the fire. It is not even said that this failure was caused by the Gaupâyanas, as priests of Asamâti. But after it has happened, Asamâti complains to the two wizards that the oblations of the Gaupâyanas burn or hurt him. Thereupon the wizards seem to have sacrificed Subandhu, or to have placed his spirit inside the sacrificial ring, whatever that may mean. The Gaupâyanas, in order to save the life of their brother, invoked Agni, who gave it back to them from within the sacrificial enclosure.

A third, and again somewhat different, account is given in the Bṛihaddevatâ[1] :—

सूक्तमाख्यानसंयुक्तं वक्तु[2]कामस्य मे शृणु ॥
संमोहाच्च विसंज्ञस्य[3] शत्रुणा[4]भिहतस्य च[5] ।
जीवावृत्तिः[6] सुबंधोर्वा[7] यद्दिवा[8] मनसः स्तवः[9] ॥ १ ॥
राजासमातिरैक्ष्वाको[10] रथप्रोष्ठः[11] पुरोहितान्[12] ।
व्युदस्य बंधुप्रभृतीन् द्वैपंदा[13] ये[14]ऽग्निमंडले ॥ २ ॥
द्वौ किराता[15]कुली[16] नाम ततो मायाविनौ द्विजौ ।
असमातिः[17] पुरोऽधत्त[18] वरिष्ठौ[19] तौ हि मन्यते[20] ॥ ३ ॥

[1] The text is printed from a MS. kindly presented to me by Dr. Bhao Daji, and which I mark B. The various readings (H.) are taken from a MS. belonging to a small but valuable collection presented to the Bodleian Library by Dr. Fitzedward Hall, and which, by an unfortunate mistake, was in the printed catalogue mixed up with other collections. MS. *b.* was sent to me by my friend Dr. Buhler. Another MS., belonging to Dr. Fitzedward Hall, is an incorrect copy of H.; and another, just received from Bombay, is unfortunately only a second copy of the same original from which *b.* was taken.

[2] पक्ष H. [3] ज्ञवृ H. [4] शत्रूणांद् H.

[5] तु H.; the first and second lines wanting in *b.* [6] धूर्त्तिं H.; वृति *b.*

[7] र्था H. [8] यद H. [9] सस्त H. *b.* [10] नि H. [11] ष्ठाः H.

[12] के रथप्रोष्ठात्पु° B.; न्यु° *b.*

[13] ती द्वे H.; तिनद्वै *b.* [14] दान्ये H. B. [15] तै B. *b.*

[16] लि H. The Anukramaṇî-bhâshya says, किराताकुलि इति बृहद्देवतोक्तनामानौ । The Nîtimanjarî gives किराताकुली नाम ।

[17] ति H. *b.* [18] वंतौ H.; धत *b.* [19] सि H.

[20] तौ ह्यमन्यत is a conjecture confirmed by the Nîtimanjarî.

तौ कपोतौ द्विजौ[1] भूत्[2]वा गत्वा गौ[3]पायनानभि[4] ।
मायाब[5]लाच्च योगाच्च सुबंधुमभिपेत[6]तुः ॥ ४ ॥
स दुःखादभिघाताच्च मुमोह च पपात[7] च ।
तौ ततो ऽस्या[9]सुमालुच्[10]य राजानम[11]भिजग्मतुः ॥ ५ ॥
ततः सुबंधौ पतिते गतासौ[12] भ्रातरस्त्रयः ।
जेपुः[13] स्वस्त्ययनं सर्वे[14] मेति गौ[15]पायनाः सह ॥ ६ ॥
मनस्वावर्तयंतो ऽस्य[16] सूक्तं य[17]दिति ते जगुः[18] ।
जेपुश्च भै[19]षजार्था[20]य प्र तारीति परं तत[21]ः ॥ ७ ॥
सूक्तस्याद्यस्तृचस्तत्र[22] निर्ऋतेरपनोदनः[23] ।
त्र[24]यः पादा मो ष्विति तु[25] सौम्या नैर्ऋत उत्तमः ॥ ८ ॥
ऋक् सौम्यनैर्ऋ[26]ती चैषासुनीतेः[27] स्तुतिः[28] परे ।
द्वृचे त्[29]वानुमतं पादसंत्यं य[30]ास्कस्तु मन्यते ॥ ९ ॥
भूर्द्यौः सोमश्[31]च पूषा च खं पथ्या[32] स्वस्तिरेव च ।
सुबंधोरेव शांत्यर्थं पुनर्न ऋचि[33] संस्तुताः[34] ॥ १० ॥
तृ[35]चः शमिति[36] रोदस्योरिंद्रोऽर्धर्चः समि[37]त्यृचि ।
रपसो[38] नाशनार्थ[39] ते तु[40]ष्टुवुश्[41]चैव रोदसी ॥ ११ ॥

[1] जो H. [2] त्वां युक्तानो H. [3] कौपा° B. [4] निह H.
[5] त्वयात्व H. [6] येव H.
[7] पयात *b.* [8] तो *b.* [9] तौ तो स्या° B. [10] लुच्च्य B.; लोच्य *b.*
[11] स्य समालुप्य राजनभ H. [12] deest H. [13] ययुः H. [14] पूर्वे B. s.m.
[15] गो H. [16] मन आचर्तनंसस्य H. [17] यदि त्ते भ्ययुः B.
[18] भ्ययः H.; भ्ययुः *b.* [19] भेष *b.* [20] जार्थ यं *b.*
[21] The whole line wanting in H
[22] यस्त्रितच : प्रेति H. [23] नाः H. [24] यच्च H.
[25] दो मो ष्वित्यस्याः H. [26] म्या नि H.
[27] नीतिः B. *b.* The first अ of *asunîti* ought to be pronounced. MSS. H. *b.* write चैषा असुनी°.
[28] तेरतः H. [29] ताद H. [30] दं मव्यया H.
[31] द्यौमश्च H.; द्यौः सोमस्तु B. *b.* [32] स्वययश्याः H. [33] च H.
[34] तु स्तुताः B.; तु स्मृताः B. *b.* [35] त्रि H. B.
[36] समति H.; समिति B. [37] त्यु H. [38] शो H. [39] यार्थं H.
[40] चै तुष्टु B.; वै तुष्टुवुस्त्वथ *b.* [41] ष्टुवित्स्विद्र H.

रप इत्य[1]भिधानं[2] तु गदितं पापकृच्छ्रयोः ।
ऋग्भिरेति [3]चैतसृभिस्तं[4]त ऐक्ष्वाकमस्तुवन्[5] ॥ १२ ॥
इंद्र चचेत्यृ[6]चा चास्य स्तुत्वाशंसिषुराशिषः ।[7]
अगस्त्य[8]स्येति माता च तेषां तुष्टा[9]व तं नृपं ॥ १३ ॥
स्तु[10]तः स[11] राजा सव्रीड[12]स्तस्थौ गौ[13]पायनानभि[14] ।
सूक्तेनाप्यस्तुव[15]न्नग्निं द्वैप[16]देन यथाचिषु ॥ १४ ॥
अग्निरप्य[17]ब्रवीदेनानयमंतः परिध्य[18]सुः ।
सुबंधोरस्य चेत्क्ष्वा[19]कोमया[20] गुप्तो हितार्थिना[21] ॥ १५ ॥
सुबंधवे प्रदायासुं[22] जीवे[23]त्युक्त्वा च[24] पावकः ।
स्तुतो[25] गौपायनैः प्रीतो जगाम त्रिदिवं प्रति[26] ॥ १६ ॥
अयं मातेति हृष्टास्ते[27] सुबंधोरसुमाह्वयन् ।
शरीरमभिनिर्दिश्य[28] सुबंधोः[29] पतितं भुवि ॥ १७ ॥
सूक्तशेषं जगुश्चास्य चेतसो धारणाय ते ।
लब्धासुं[30] चायमित्यस्यां[31] पृथक् पाणिभिरस्पृशन् ॥ १८ ॥

"Hear of me the hymn together with the story which I wish to tell! It is the revival of Subandhu who from trouble had lost his consciousness, and had been struck down by his enemy; or it contains the praise of the soul. King Asamâti Rathaproshṭha, of the race of Ikshvâku, having sent away the Purohitas, Bandhu and the rest, who composed the Dvipada verses in the Atri-maṇḍala (R.V. v. 24), the same Asamâti afterwards elected two Brahman wizards, Kirâta and Akuli by name, for he believed them to be the best. These

[1] त्या H. [2] सं H. [3] श्वादैश्च H. [4] सृभित H.; स्तृभिस्त b.
[5] एक्ष्वाकुसरभूवत् H.; ऐक्ष्वाकुमस्तुवन् b. [6] चेचेत्यृ B.; तृ b.
[7] This line wanting in H. [8] स्त्ये b. [9] ष्टा b. [10] सु H. [11] तश्च b.
[12] सुप्रीतः Sây. संहृष्टः Nîtim.; deest in H. [13] गो H. B. [14] भी b.
[15] सूक्तेनैषां स्तु° B. b.; सूक्तेन ते ऽस्तु° Sây. [16] ग्नि द्वै b. [17] अथाग्निर H.
[18] पराव्यसुः B.; चैनामयं मत्तः परैत्वसून् H.; द्वेवानयमतः पराव्यसुः b.
[19] चै B. b. [20] को मपा H. [21] तैषिणा H. [22] ष्पु H.
[23] वंत्य H. [24] तु H. [25] तौ b. [26] पुनः H. [27] शेषेण H.
[28] ष्टं H. [29] धो H. [30] लब्धामुं H.; लब्ध्वासुं b. [31] त्यृगभ्यां H.

two Brahmans, having become doves,[1] and having gone towards the Gaupâyanas, flew upon Subandhu by the strength of their spells and their magic. He, from pain and violence, staggered and fell. Then these two, after plucking out his soul, went to the king. Then after Subandhu had fallen and given up his spirit, all the three brothers, the Gaupâyanas, recited together a blessing, beginning with the word *Mâ* (x. 57); and in order to cause his spirit to return they sang the hymn beginning with *Yad* (x. 58). And after that, in order to effect a cure, they recited the hymn beginning with *Pra târi* (x. 59). The first three verses in that hymn are meant to drive away Nirṛiti; the three quarters beginning with *Mo shu* (x. 59, 4) are addressed to Soma, the last quarter to Nirṛiti, and the whole verse is therefore addressed to Soma and Nirṛiti. In the next two verses Asamâti is praised, but Yâska holds the last quarter of the sixth verse to be addressed to Anumati. The earth, heaven, Soma, Pûshan, the air, Pathyâ, and Svasti, these are praised together in the verse beginning with *Punar naḥ*, in order to give comfort to Subandhu. The three verses (8–10) beginning with *Śam* are addressed to the two Rodasî, but in the verse beginning with *Śam* (10) half the verse is addressed to Indra. And they praised the Rodasî in order to destroy *rapas*, and the word *rapas* is used for sin and evil. Then with the four verses beginning with *Â* (x. 60, 1–4) they praised the Aikshvâka (Asamâti), and having praised him, they invoked blessings upon him by the verse *Indra kshatrâ* (x. 60, 5). Their mother also praised that king with the verse beginning with *Agastyasya* (x. 60, 6). Then, after thus being praised, the king felt ashamed, and went to the Gaupâyanas, and they praised also Agni with the Dvipada-hymn, as it is found among the Atris, *i.e.* in the Atri-maṇḍala (R.V. v. 24). And Agni said to them: 'This spirit of Subandhu has been kept inside the sacrificial ring by me, being a well-wisher also of this Ikshvâku (Asamâti).' And

[1] This change into doves is not mentioned elsewhere, and in a passage of the commentary on the Sarvânukrama we read अथ मायावहितपुरोहितौ काश्यपौ तौ भूत्वेति बृहद्दे॰ ॥

having given the spirit to Subandhu, and having said, Live!, Agni, praised by the Gaupâyanas, and pleased, went towards heaven. Then these were delighted and called the spirit of Subandhu with the verse *Ayam mâtâ* (x. 60, 7), pointing to the body of Subandhu that was lying on the ground. And they sang the rest of the hymn in order to confirm his mind, and they touched him separately, after he had recovered his spirit, with the verses beginning with *Ayam* (x. 60, 12)."

What is chiefly important in this version of the legend is the transformation of the two wizards into doves, always supposing that the text is correct. It should be observed also that the Bṛihaddevatâ knows of the spirit of Subandhu having been preserved inside the sacrificial ring, and of Agni restoring it, after he had been praised with the four verses given in the Atri-maṇḍala. If this be so, if the four verses of the hymn (R.V. v. 24) were recited by the three brothers, before the resuscitation of the fourth brother, Subandhu, it would be difficult to reconcile with this the statement of Kâtyâyana, who says that the four brothers saw or composed the four verses of that hymn.

We now come to the Nîtimanjarî which derives two of its moral maxims from our four hymns. The first is that one ought not to trust in kings; the second that there is no friend like a brother.

I give the extracts of this little work as they stand in my MS. in order to show how the work has been put together. If one knows the sources from which the author has taken his information, it is easy to supply the omissions and to correct palpable mistakes. Thus he begins with the Anukramaṇî; then from ततो to the next इति he quotes from Sâyaṇa. Then follows a passage from the Bṛihaddevatâ, all full of mistakes, but easily corrected by a reference to the originals:—

प्रभोर्विश्वसनं न कुर्यादित्यर्थ आह ॥ प्रभुप्रसादे विश्वासं न कुर्यात्स्वप्नसंनिभे। अग्र्यांस्तत्याज बंध्वादीनसमातिः पुरोहितान् ॥ तथानुक्रमणी अथ हैक्ष्वाको राजासमातिर्गौपायनान्बंध्वादीन्पुरोहितांस्त्यक्त्वान्यौ मायाविनौ श्रेष्ठतमौ मत्वा पुरोदधे इति। ततो बंध्वादयः क्रुद्धाः संतः इमं राजानमभिचारितवंत इति । द्वौ किराताकुली नाम ततो मायाविनौ

असमातिः पुरोहितौ वसिष्ठौ तौ ह्यमन्यत। तौ च कपोतौ द्विजौ भूत्वा तान् गोपायनानभि मायाबलाच्च योगाच्च सुबंधुमभिपेततुः। तदर्थेयमृक्। मा प्र गाम पथो वयं॥ बंध्वादयस्त्यक्ताः संतो विश्वान्देवांस्तुष्टुवुः। हे इंद्र वयं गौपायनाः पथः समीचीनान्मा प्र गाम मा गच्छाम। तथा सोमवतो यज्ञान्मा प्र गाम। नो ऽस्माकमंतर्मार्गे अरातयो मा तस्थुः। मा तिष्ठंतु।

भ्राता महान्सुहृदित्यर्थ आह॥ भ्रातासमः सुहृन्नास्ति भ्रातरः समजीवयन्। सुबंधुं शंतनुर्भ्राता नृपं कृत्वा वनं ययौ॥ बृहद्देवता।

ततः सुबंधौ पतिते भ्रातरि भ्रातरस्त्रयः।
ययौ स्वस्त्ययनं सर्वे मेति गौपायनाः सह॥
त्रिभिः सूक्तैर्यथान्यायं तुष्टुवुः सर्वदेवताः।[1]
अगस्त्यस्य स्वसा माता तेषां तुष्टाव तं नृपं॥
स्तुतो ऽसमातिः संहृष्टस्तस्थौ गौपायनानभि।
सूनाप्यस्तुवन्नग्निं द्वैपदेन यदग्निषु॥
सुबंधवे प्रदायासु जीवं त्यक्त्वा नु पावकः।
स्तुतो गौपायनोः प्रीतो जगाम त्रिदिवं पुनः॥

ततो जीवितं भ्रातारं हस्तेन स्पृशन् हस्तं तुष्टाव अयं मेत्यनया ऋचा। अयं मे हस्तो भगवान्॰ अयं मे मम हस्तः भगवान् यतो जीवंतं सुबंधुं स्पृशंति। तथा चायं मे हस्तः भगवत्तरः अतिशयेन भाग्यवान् तथा चायं विश्वभेषजः सर्वभेषजः। कथंभूतो हस्तः। शिवाभिमर्शनः मंगलस्पर्शः।

These extracts from the Nîtimanjarî, printed here with all the mistakes of the MS., contain nothing that is not mentioned by earlier authorities, and need not therefore be translated.

If now we turn to Sâyaṇa's Commentary, we shall see that he explains the four hymns in accordance with the legend they are supposed to illustrate:—

### Hymn 57

The Gaupâyanas, coming from Khâṇḍava to Asamâti in order to receive the spirit of Subandhu, say:—

1. "O Indra, may we not go away from the right way! (may we go to the house of Asamâti!) May we not go away

[1] This line is not in the Bṛihaddevatâ.

from the sacrifice of the Soma-sacrificer, viz., of Asamâti! May the enemies not stand in our way!"

2. "May we obtain that thread, (the fire) always offered, the accomplisher of the sacrifice, spread out by the priests!"

3. "We (Bandhu and the rest) invoke the soul (of Subandhu) quickly, with Soma offered in the sacrificial cups of our ancestors, and with the hymns of our fathers."

4. "O Subandhu, may thy soul come hither, for work, for strength, for life! and for seeing the sun a long time!"

5. "May the assembly of our fathers,[1] and the assembly of the gods give us life and our senses! May we obtain both, (life and our senses)."

6. "O Soma, may we (Bandhu and the rest) keeping our mind on thy service and on thy members, obtain with our offspring, both (life and our senses)."

## Hymn 58.

1. "O dead man, thy soul which went far away to Yama the son of Vivasvat, we turn it back, here to dwell and to live."

2. "O Subandhu, thy soul which went far away to heaven and earth, we turn it back, here to dwell and to live."

3. "O Subandhu, thy soul which went far away to the four-cornered earth, we turn it back, here to dwell and to live."

4. "O Subandhu, thy soul which went far away to the four great regions, we turn it back, here to dwell and to live."

5. "O Subandhu, thy soul which went far away to the watery sea, we turn it back, here to dwell and to live."

6. "O Subandhu, thy soul which went far away to the onward moving splendours, we turn it back, here to dwell and to live."

7. "O Subandhu, thy soul which went far away into the water and the shrubs, we turn it back, here to dwell and to live."

[1] Sâyaṇa must have read जनः instead of मनः

8. "O Subandhu, thy soul which went far away into the sun and into the dawn, we turn it back, here to dwell and to live."

9. "O Subandhu, thy soul which went far away to the great mountains, we turn it back, here to dwell and to live."

10. "O Subandhu, thy soul which went far away into the whole world, we turn it back, here to dwell and to live."

11. "O Subandhu, thy soul which went far away to distant distances, we turn it back, here to dwell and to live."

12. "O Subandhu, thy soul which went far away into the past and into the future, we turn it back, here to dwell and to live."

### Hymn 59.

1. "May the life (of Subandhu) be increased so as to be longer and newer; as two men standing on a chariot (are increased or advanced) by an active (charioteer). Thus he (Subandhu) having fallen (from life), increases his object (his life). May Nirṛiti leave further away and well!"

2. "While the song is sung, we make also for our wealth (*i.e.* our health) treasured food; we make oblations well, and in many ways. May she who is praised (Nirṛiti) taste all our offerings; may Nirṛiti leave further away and well!"

3. "May we well overcome our enemies with power, as the sun overcomes the earth, as the thunderbolt overcomes the clouds. She who is praised (Nirṛiti) knows all our praises; may Nirṛiti leave further away and well!"

4. "O Soma, do not well surrender us to death; may we see the sun that is now rising. May old age, sent by days, be well to us! May Nirṛiti leave further away and well!"

5. "O life-leading goddess, place soul into us again! Lengthen well our life, that we may live! Place us in the sight of the sun! Swell thou the body with (sacrificial) butter!"

6. "O life-leading goddess, give to us (to Subandhu) again the eye, again here to us breath, and pleasure! May we long see the rising sun! O Anumati, pity us, hail!"

7. "May the Earth again give us life, again the bright

heaven, again the sky! May Soma give again our body, may Pûshan give speech, and what is bliss!"

8. "May the great Heaven and Earth, the mother of the sacrifice, give a blessing to Subandhu. Whatever evil there is, may they both carry it off! O heaven, o earth! if there is patience! O Subandhu, may no evil whatever hurt thee really!"

9. "From Heaven medicines descend, double and threefold; (*i.e.* the two Aśvins, and the three goddesses, Iḷâ, Sarasvatî, and Bhâratî); a single medicine walks on earth. Whatever evil there is, may they both carry it off! O heaven, o patient earth! O Subandhu, may no evil whatever hurt thee really!"

10. "O Indra, drive the cart-drawing ox, who draws near the cart of Uśînarâṇî (a herb with which they rub the sick). Whatever evil there is, may they both carry it off! O heaven, o patient earth! O Subandhu, may no evil whatever hurt thee really!"

## Hymn 60.

1. "We (Bandhu and the rest) bringing praise, have come to a man (viz. king Asamâtî)[1] of bright aspect, praised by the great."

2. "To Asamâti, the smasher (of enemies), the brilliant, (like unto) a conquering chariot, born of the race of Bhajeratha,[2] the lord of the brave."

3. "He who by fight overcomes men, like oxen, whether he has a dagger, or whether he has no dagger."

4. "The king of this country, Ikshvâku, thrives in his work, rich, and killing his enemies. His five tribes are as if in heaven."

5. "O Indra, keep the powers with Asamâti Rathaproshṭha, as thou keepest the sun in heaven to be seen."

6. The mother of Bandhu and the rest, the sister of Agastya, says: "O King Asamâti, for the sake of Agastya's

[1] Or, we have come to a country belonging to the life-leading goddess, to Asunîti; not to Asamâti, as might be expected.

[2] Or, conquering an enemy called Bhajeratha.

nephews, harness the two red horses. Conquer all the miserly merchants!"

7. Bandhu and the other brothers say: "This is the mother, this the father, this life-giver has come. O Subandhu (who art now in a cover of life), this (thy body) is thy means of moving.[1] Come here, come out (of thy cover of life)!"

8. "As they tie a yoke with a rope that it may hold, so has Agni held thy soul (in the cover), for life, not for death, ay, for safety."

9. "As this great earth has held these trees, so has Agni held thy soul, for life, not for death, ay, for safety."

10. "I have brought the soul of Subandhu from Yama, the son of Vivasvat, for life, not for death, ay, for safety."

11. "The wind blows down, the sun shines down, the cow gives milk down; may thy sin go down!"

12. The brothers touching the reviving Subandhu with their hands say: "This my hand is blessed; this my hand is more blessed; this my hand holds all healing herbs; this has a happy touch."

The translation of these four hymns is a fair specimen of what a translation of the Rig-veda would be, if we followed strictly and unhesitatingly the explanation given by Sâyaṇa. Many verses would give a perfectly satisfactory sense, nor is there any necessity for going beyond Sâyaṇa's interpretation, whenever that interpretation satisfies both the rules of grammar and the requirements of common sense. Three-fourths of the Veda may thus be translated by anybody who can understand Sâyaṇa's commentary. But there occur from time to time lines and verses where Sâyaṇa's interpretation offends clearly both against grammar and against sense. Here the fault must either rest with Sâyaṇa or with the text of the Veda. The poets of the Veda, who strictly observe a grammar of their own, and who in by far the greater part of their hymns utter thoughts that are both intelligible and coherent, cannot be supposed suddenly to have forgotten themselves,

[1] Or, o Subandhu, this is thy mother, this the father, this thy son, come here; all have come, full of grief.

and to have set grammar and sense at defiance. In such cases we must see whether their words do not lend themselves to a different interpretation from that given by Sâyaṇa. Sometimes the misapprehensions of Sâyaṇa are palpable. Thus in hymn 57, 5, it is clear that Sâyaṇa mistakes *manaḥ* for *janaḥ*. Regardless of the accent, he takes *pitaraḥ* for a nominative, and he does further violence to grammar by making *pitaraḥ* an apposition to *janaḥ*. Instead of translating, as he does, "May the assembly of our fathers and the assembly of the gods give us life," it is clear that we ought to translate, even though adopting the rest of Sâyaṇa's Commentary, "O fathers, may the assembly of the gods give back our soul." The following words are likewise wrongly rendered by Sâyaṇa. He takes *jîvam* for life, and *vrâtam* for the collection of the five senses. *Jîva*, no doubt, means life, and *vrâta* mean a collection. But, first of all, we should then expect the two words to be joined by *cha*; or, if that might be passed, the difficulty would still remain that *vrâta* never means the collection of the five senses, but simply collection, mass, multitude. This can be proved by many passages, such as R.V. i. 163, 8; iii. 26, 6; v. 53, 11; vi. 75, 9; x. 34, 8, and 12. It is true the phrase *jîvaṁ vrâtaṁ sachemahi*, does not occur again, but as there are many passages in which *jîva* is used as an adjective, in the sense of living, and as *jîvaloka* is used in the sense of the world of the living, everything seems to favour the natural explanation of the last line, "Let us join the living multitudes." Then the question arises, can *sach* be used with the accusative? It generally governs the instrumental, as R.V. i. 116, 17; 136, 6; 152, 1; 183, 2; 185, 9; ii. 8, 6; v. 50, 2; x. 7, 1; 64, 11; 106, 10. But there are numerous passages where it governs the accusative, such as i. 136, 3; 180, 1; ii. 41, 6; iii. 39, 3; 52, 15; vii. 88, 5; viii. 5, 2; 102, 22. We may therefore translate our passage: "May we join the living multitudes," while with the instrumental, we should have had to translate, "May we be together with living multitudes!" Thus we read R.V. i. 136, 6, *jyok jîvantaḥ prajayâ sachemahi*, "May we long live and be together with offspring, *i.e.* possess offspring."

The question whether *daivyaḥ janaḥ* means really the assembly of gods, or whether it should be translated by Agni, fire, the heavenly man, has been raised on a former occasion, and I still adhere, though, with regard to some passages, rather doubtfully, to the opinion which I then expressed.[1] I should therefore translate: "O fathers, may the heavenly man, Agni, give us back our soul, may we join the living multitude."

The next verse again is not well explained by Sâyaṇa. The words *vrate tava manas tanûshu bibhrataḥ* cannot well mean, "keeping our mind on thy service and on thy members." *Tanu* is not used in the sense of members, nor does *bhṛi*, "to bear," with *manas*, "mind," mean to keep one's mind on something, or to attend. Here again, a little reflection shows that we ought to translate, "May we in thy service, keeping the soul in our bodies, *i.e.* keeping alive, join the living multitude." The ellipsis is somewhat unusual, yet as the two verses follow each other, *jîvam vrâtaṁ* may well be supplied after the second *sachemahi*. Although *saṁ sachâvahai* occurs (vi. 55, 1) in the sense of "let us join," this meaning would hardly be applicable in our passage.

But while in passages like these, a little reflection and a consideration of similar passages will generally remove all difficulties, it happens not unfrequently that the work of interpretation becomes really a work of deciphering. Nothing will avail but to look at every passage in which we may examine each single word that occurs in the verse to be deciphered; and even after that has been done, the labour is frequently in vain, and we are driven to admit either that the text is corrupt, or that we possess no longer the means of discovering behind the strange words and phrases of the Veda the thoughts which the early poets intended to express. Here lies the real work which a translator of the Veda has to perform; and although different Sanskrit scholars in England, France, and Germany have explained many words and pas-

[1] Zeitschrift der Deutschen Morgenländischen Gesellschaft, vol. ix. p. xxii. 1855. The heavenly host would be *divyo janaḥ* (R.V. vi. 22, 9).

sages, and removed many difficulties that Sâyaṇa was unable to remove, yet a really satisfactory translation of the whole of the Ṛig-veda will for many years be simply impossible.

In accordance with the principles of translation which I have explained more fully on former occasions, I shall now endeavour to translate the four hymns which, before, were translated according to the tradition of the Brahmans. And here I have to confess, first of all, that I cannot bring myself to believe in the historical reality of the legend which, according to Sâyaṇa, forms the background of our hymns. This may seem gratuitous scepticism, and at this distance of time, and with the utter absence of historical documents, it is so safe that it seems hardly fair, to throw the burden of proof on those who believe in the legend. I do not mean to say that it is impossible that there ever was a king Asamâti; that he had four priests, brothers of the family of the Gaupâyanas; that he dismissed them and appointed two others in their place; that the Gaupâyanas injured him; that the new priests carried off one of the brothers and nearly killed him, possibly in order to sacrifice him; that the Gaupâyanas then made their peace with the king, and that their brother was finally restored to them. All this may have happened. Nor could any scholar in Europe avail himself of the argument that might be used in the theological schools in India, viz. that no historical events can be referred to in the Veda, because the Veda is believed to have been composed before all time. But what may be urged is this, that the legend itself varies, and varies on essential points; that large portions of the legend owe their origin to a misunderstanding of some antiquated expressions occurring in the Veda and the old Brâhmaṇas; and lastly, that if the hymns had been composed for the occasion, the allusion to the events would naturally be more marked and palpable.

Several variations in the legend have been pointed out before, but a more important one remains to be noticed. Who were the two priests appointed in the place of the four Gaupâyanas? Kâtyâyana calls them simply *mâyâvin*, which we may translate 'possessed of power,' but more particularly 'possessed of supernatural or magical power.' Sâyaṇa speaks of them as Ṛishis, or sacred and inspired poets. The Śâṭyâyanaka is more explicit, and, if our text is correct, it speaks of them as *asuramâyau*, 'possessed of demoniacal powers,' and calls them asuras or evil spirits. The Bṛihaddevatâ calls them *mâyâvinau dvijau*, Brahmans endowed with magic powers, and gives their names as Kirâta and Akuli.[1] Here we have already several conflicting statements, enough to stagger an orthodox Brahman. But a more important point remains to be noticed. In the Tâṇḍya-brâhmaṇa, the story of the Gaupâyanas occurs in a much more simple and primitive form, and here the two demoniacal Brahmans are no Brahmans at all, but females, whatever else they may be. Nothing is said there of King Asamâti or of the one brother Subandhu, but the legend simply states: "Two demoniacal Mâyâs, of the race of the Kirâtas,[2] scattered about, inside the sacrificial enclosure, the spirits of the Gaupâyanas who were performing a Sattra sacrifice. These worshipped Agni with the hymn,[3] 'Agni, be thou nearest to us.' By it they took again[4] their spirits." If this is the foundation of the later stories of the Gaupâyanas, we can see clearly what has happened. The two Mâyâs, or female spirits, of the race of the Kirâtas, Kirâta-kulyau, were changed into two men of the name of Kirâta and Akuli. The name of Subandhu occurring in the hymn was taken to be the name of one of the Gaupâyanas, and the name of Asamâti, likewise occurring in the hymn as a name of Indra, was supposed to be the name of a king who,

[1] Whether it is Akuli or Âkuli cannot be settled from the passages hitherto known. It may be right to mention that in the S'atapatha-brâhmaṇa the MSS. really give किराताकुली, which is explained by the commentary as किरातस्चाकुलिश्च द्वावसुरपुरोहितौ बभूवतु:

[2] It may be right to mention that the MSS. of the Tâṇḍya-brâhmaṇa really give किरातकुल्यौ, not किराताकुल्यौ, as printed by Boehtlingk in his Dictionary, *s.v.* किलात. The text and commentary of this passage are given on p. 13.

[3] R.V. v. 24. Sâyaṇa, in his commentary on the Tâṇḍya-brâhmaṇa, calls this hymn *tṛicha*, consisting of three verses, which would have been appropriate, according to the account of the Bṛihaddevatâ, while in the Rig-veda there are four lines, forming two verses.

[4] अस्पृण्वन् is explained by अबलयन्, both meaning "to cherish."

somehow or other, was connected with the Gaupâyanas. The remaining details would be supplied at demand, and the legend would gradually grow into that form in which we now find it in the Śaṭyâyanaka, in the Sarvânukrama, and in the Bṛihaddevatâ. The reasons imagined for the anger of the Gaupâyanas are truly Brahmanic. It was the professional hatred of one set of priests against another, and the reason for their dismissal savours equally of modern Brahmanism, viz., some little mistake that had occurred in the cooking of the sacrificial viands.

But although we can thus explain in a natural manner the growth of the legend of the Gaupâyanas, by simply supplementing the story of the Tâṇḍya with little indications taken from the hymns themselves, I do not lay much stress on this. Whether there ever was a king Asamâti or not, whether he exchanged one set of priests for another or not, what is all that to us? The only real thing we have to deal with are the hymns of the Veda, and one single intelligible thought contained in them, and giving us an insight into the mind of those ancient poets, is worth all the genealogies of shadowy kings and spirits. That there are some valuable thoughts in the hymns which are ascribed to the Gaupâyanas, must have become clear even from Sâyaṇa's translation. It will become still clearer if we forget altogether what we have heard about Asamâti and the Gaupâyanas, and translate the hymns as we find them, and as possibly even Śaunaka understood them, when he said that they either contained an account of the revival of Subandhu, or praises of the soul.

## Hymn 47.

1. "Let us not swerve from the (right) path, nor from the Soma-sacrifice, o Indra. May our enemies not stand in our way!"

2. "May we obtain the fire which is (to be) offered, which is the accomplisher of the sacrifice, the thread[1] that reaches unto the gods."

[1] The sacrifice was considered as a thread or a connecting link between God and men. See M. M., Die Todtenbestattung bei den Brahmanen, Zeitschrift der D. M. Gesellschaft, vol. ix. p. xxii.

3. "We now call hither the soul, with libations as offered by our blessed ancestors, and with the songs of our fathers."

4. "May thy soul come back for work, strength, and life; and that it may long behold[1] the sun!"

5. "May the heavenly man, Agni, (the fire), give us back our soul, o fathers.[2] May we join the living host!"

6. "May we join it with our offspring, in thy service, o Soma, keeping the soul in our bodies."

## Hymn 58.

1. "Thy soul which went far away to Yama Vaivasvata,[3] we turn it back, here to dwell and to live."

2. "Thy soul which went far away to heaven and to the earth, we turn it back, here to dwell and to live."

3. "Thy soul which went far away to the four-cornered earth, we turn it back, here to dwell and to live."

4. "Thy soul which went far away to the four quarters, we turn it back, here to dwell and to live."

5. "Thy soul which went far away to the watery ocean, we turn it back, here to dwell and to live."

6. "Thy soul which went far away to the onward rays,[4] we turn it back, here to dwell and to live."

7. "Thy soul which went far away to the water and the shrubs, we turn it back, here to dwell and to live."

8. "Thy soul which went far away to the sun and the dawn, we turn it back, here to dwell and to live."

9. "Thy soul which went far away to the great mountains, we turn it back, here to dwell and to live."

[1] If *jîváse* and *dṛiṣé* are called infinitives, why not *krátve* and *dákshâya*? The name of infinitive might well be given up and replaced by a more appropriate term.

[2] It is more natural to join *naḥ* with *manaḥ* and translate, our soul. In that case the subject of the hymn would change, and what follows would certainly harmonise with this view.

[3] On Yama Vaivasvata, the king of the departed, see Ueber die Todtenbestattung, in the Zeitschrift der D. M. Gesellschaft, ix. p. xiv.

[4] *Marîchî* does not occur again in the R.V. (exc. *márîchînam*, x. 177, 1), but there is no reason to doubt that it had in the Veda the same meaning as in the later literature, viz., ray, splendour. *Pravat*, which, by Professor Roth, is given as a substantive only, must be taken as an adjective, not only in this, but in several other passages, such as vii. 32, 27. It means 'moving onward,' possibly 'eastern,' like *prâch*.

10. "Thy soul which went far away to the whole world, we turn it back, here to dwell and to live."

11. "Thy soul which went far away into the distant distances, we turn it back, here to dwell and to live."

12. Thy soul which went far away to the past and the future, we turn it back, here to dwell and to live."

## Hymn 59.

1. "Life has advanced forward afresh, like the two skilful drivers of the chariot; yea, moving on, man rises to the goal. May Nirriti (the goddess of destruction) indeed go far away!"[1]

2. "On our hearth are riches, our food is garnered,—let us

[1] There is clearly not much sense or coherence in this verse as translated according to the commentary of Sâyaṇa. Sâyaṇa is guided by the traditional notion that this hymn refers to certain details in the story of the death and resurrection of Subandhu, but even thus his explanation can hardly be called natural and happy. The train of thought which he discovers in the words of the poet is this: May the life of Subandhu be increased or advanced, as persons advance who stand in a chariot. Having lost his life Subandhu regains it; may the goddess of mischief fly away! This seems easy enough at first sight, but difficulties soon appear on further consideration. The first half verse means certainly, May life be lengthened, or, life is lengthened; and it will be best to take this in a general sense, without thinking much of Subandhu. Then follows a simile. Now that simile does not speak of one person, but of two, *sthâ'târâ iva. Sthâ'tṛi*, with the accent on the first (not to be confounded with *sthâtri*) means a driver, not one who stands, but one who makes stand, one who controls horses. Thus Indra is frequently called *sthâtar harînâm*, not he who stands on the horses, but he who makes them stand, who holds, checks, and drives them (viii. 24, 17; 33, 12; 46, 1). He is also called *sthâ'tâ rathasya* (iii. 45, 2), or *sthâtri* by itself. R.V. i. 33, 5; vi. 41, 3, *harivaḥ sthâtaḥ ugra*. The Maruts are called simply *sthâtâraḥ*, riders or rulers (R.V. v. 87, 6), and *jagataḥ sthâtaḥ* is used R.V. vi. 49, 6, and seems to mean 'ruler of the earth.'

The real difficulty, however, lies in the dual. Why two riders instead of one? We can hardly say in the Veda *metri causâ*, nor can I think of any explanation except by ascribing to the simile a more special reference to the two most famous drivers in the Veda, the two Asvins, the *vrishṇaḥ sthâtârâ* (R.V. i. 181, 3), the *rathîtamau* (R.V. i. 182, 2, etc.). As in their original conception, the two Asvins represent the succession of day and night, light and darkness, morning and evening, and other correlative powers, the simile becomes even more telling, if taken in that special sense. But, it may be said, why not take the explanation of Sâyaṇa? Why not take *kratumat* in the sense of driver, and then translate, "like two who stand on a chariot are moved on by the charioteer." For the simple reason, that the adjective *kratumat* is never used in the Veda as a substantive, least of all in the special sense of *sârathi* or charioteer. I confess I can make nothing of the instrumental *kratumatâ*, but I have only to change it into *kratumantâ* and it becomes the recognised epithet of the Asvins, the clever, the wise, cf. R.V. i. 183, 2, *suvrít ráthaḥ vartate yán abhí kshâ'm yát tishṭhathaḥ krátumantâ ánu prikshé*. To read *sthâtrâ iva kratumatâ rathasya* would sanction a hiatus, which might be accepted if supported by the authority of MSS., but which I hesitate to adopt in a conjectural reading,

The meaning of the next sentence is even more difficult. *Chyávâna*, though it might mean fallen, does not occur in the Veda in the sense of departed, dead.

make good and manifold feasts! The bard may enjoy all that is ours. May Nirṛiti indeed go far away!"[1]

3. "Let us with our forces overcome the enemies altogether, as the sky the earth, as the mountains the fields. The bard knows all that is ours. May Nirṛiti indeed go far away!"

4. "O Soma, do not altogether deliver us unto death; may we see the sun rising! May old age, sent by the days, be kind to us! May Nirṛiti indeed go far away!"

5. "Thou guide of life, preserve our soul in us, lengthen our age well, that we may live. Grant us to see the sun, and fill thy body with the offered ghee."[2]

6. "Thou guide of life, bestow again upon us sight, again breath, here to enjoy. May we long see the rising sun! O (increasing) Moon,[3] be gracious to us with mercy!"

7. "May the Earth again give us life, again the Heaven, again the Sky! May Soma give our body again, and Pûshan the path[4] which is bliss."

In R.V. x. 61, 2, *chyavânaḥ* means moving on, arriving; and the same sense is, by Professor Roth, assigned to other forms of *chyu*.

The expression *uttavîti artham* is without a parallel in the Rig-veda.

Langlois translates. Que cette existence nouvelle soit prolongée, et menée (par le maître de la vie) comme un char l'est par un habile écuyer. Ainsi celui qui était tombé se rélève. Que Nirriti s'eloigne.

[1] This is again a difficult verse, and, as it stands, simply unintelligible. I read *râyo* instead of *râye* in order to get at anything like sense. The two *nu*'s show that the first half-verse contains two sentences. The second of these is clear, literally, our food is possessed of repositories, *i.e.* our garners are full of food. The first also must have a nominative, and this we get by reading *râyo* instead of *râye*. *Sâman* is a locative, which I derive from *sâman*, in the sense of hearth or house. This meaning is conjectural; but there are several passages in the Veda where *sâman* cannot well mean song or poem. Whether it be derived from *san*, to acquire, so as to mean acquisition, property, or from *so*, to finish, so as to mean establishment, *sâman* seems to have some meaning like hearth or home in passages such as R.V. viii. 89, 7; ix. 111, 2; 145, 3. However, I only propose this interpretation until a better one can be found, for I cannot bring myself to translate, "When there is a song sung, there are riches."

[2] There is nothing to show that Asunîti is a female deity. Yâska (x. 39) takes Asunîti as a masculine, Sâyaṇa as a feminine. It may be a name for Yama, as Prof. Roth supposes; but it may also be a simple invocation, one of the many names of the deity. The metre requires a syllable in the third half verse, which may easily be supplied by reading *saṁ-dṛiśike.*

[3] Anumati means compliance, grace, and Sâyaṇa takes Anumati as a female deity, a personification of grace. Anumati, however, is likewise a name of one of the phases of the moon, which go by the names of Anumati, Râkâ, Sinîvâlî, and Kuhû. In a prayer for life the moon would naturally come in for an invocation.

[4] The explanation of *pathyâ* by speech is evidently old, for Sâyaṇa supports it by a passage from the Brâhmaṇa. It must be confessed, too, that speech would be more appropriate in this passage; yet *pathyâ* in the Rig-veda means path or

8. "Ye mighty Heaven and Earth, mothers of right, may there be happiness to our dear friend.[1] Whatever evil there is, may they both carry it off! Heaven and gentle Earth! may no evil whatever hurt thee!"

9. "Medicines come down from heaven, double and three-fold. A solitary medicine moves about on earth. May they both carry off whatever evil there is! Heaven and gentle Earth! may no evil whatever hurt thee!"[2]

10. "Indra, stir up the cart-ox that brought here the chariot of the dawn. May they both carry off whatever evil there is! Heaven and gentle Earth, may no evil whatever hurt thee!"[3]

## Hymn 60.

1. "Bringing praise we came to the man of radiant aspect,[4] who is praised by the great,—"

2. "To the matchless, the roaring, the radiant; to the crushing chariot, the good lord of Bhajeratha,—"[5]

3. "He who overcomes men in battle like oxen, whether he has his weapon or whether he is weaponless,—"[6]

walk, and only by a well-established metaphor could this have been used to express speech.

[1] Subandhu may be a proper name, but even then it would mean good friend, and nothing is lost therefore by keeping to the natural meaning.

[2] I take this and some of the later verses as formulas used by wise men or women in effecting medical cures. Such formulas are often very meaningless, and, at all events, we must not look in them for any deep wisdom. The suffixes *ke* and *kâ*, used for forming repetitive adverbs, are curious. In later Sanskrit we have only *ṣas*, the Greek κις or χα.

[3] Another verse used for incantations or witchcraft. As the poet speaks of the ox that brought (*i.e.* that is in the habit of bringing) the chariot of Uṣînarâṇî, we should naturally think of the chariot of the dawn. Sâyaṇa, however, takes *uṣînarâṇî* in the sense of a medicinal herb, and it may have been so understood by the medical charlatans of India.

[4] Most of the epithets here used of the man to whom praise is offered refer to Indra, who, in the fifth verse, is invoked by name. *Asamâti*, it is true, does not occur again as applied to Indra, and hence the commentators might easily have been led to take it as a proper name. But in *asamâtyojas*, of incomparable strength, *asamâti* clearly is the same as *asamâna*, incomparable. Hence I surrender king Asamâti and all that the Brahmans tell us about him. I believe he took his origin from this verse, and the same verse must be his grave. Professor Roth, if I understand him right, takes the same view. He takes *nitoṣana* in the sense of dripping, evidently connecting it with *ratha*. But the verb *tuṣ* expresses sound, and the sense of roaring is appropriate to all its derivatives.

[5] Bhajeratha must be taken as the name of a people or a country, like Ikshvâku in the next verse. It may be a dialectic form of Bhagîratha.

*Niyayinam ratham* is a simile introduced without a comparative particle. The adjectives which precede refer to Indra, not to *ratha*.

[6] I tried to explain *pavîravân* and *apavîravân* in the Beiträge zur Verglei-

4. "He in whose service Ikshvâku[1] grows, rich, and strong to kill, as the five tribes in heaven."

5. "O Indra, preserve the power among the matchless Rathaproshṭhas, as the sun to be seen in heaven."[2]

6. "Thou harnessest thy two bright horses for the descendants of Agastya. Thou steppest down upon the enemies, upon all, o king, who are ungenerous."[3]

7. "This is the mother, this is the father, this thy life came back. This is thy escape, o good friend; come here, come forth!"[4]

chenden Sprachforschung, vol. iii. p. 444 seq. Though the Pada text does not give *pavira-vân*, yet I think it right to give up my explanation of *pavî-ravân*, because I now see that it is possible to give a grammatical explanation of *pavîra*. Professor Roth derives *pavîra* from *pavi*, but this is impossible in Sanskrit. *Pavi*, with the Taddhita *ra* would give *pavira*, like *sushira* from *sushi* (Pâṇ. v. 2, 107), but never *pavîra*. There is, however, the possibility, of which I had not thought before, of classing *pavîra* with such words as *śarîra*, formed by the Uṇâdi *îran* from *śri*, with *guṇa* of the radical vowel (Uṇâdi-Sûtras, ed. Aufrecht, iv. 30). As this seems unobjectionable, I now take *pavîra-vân* as a possessive adjective in the sense of 'possessed of a thunderbolt or a weapon.' We thus get a proper climax which was wanting in former translations. As to *pavîrava*, it may now be explained as formed by the possessive Taddhita *va* (Pâṇ. v. 2, 109), like *keśava* from *keśa*.

[1] This is the first mention of Ikshvâku, and the only one in the Rig-veda. I take it not as the name of a king, but as the name of a people, probably the people who inhabited Bhâjeratha, the country washed by the northern Gangâ or the Bhâgîrathî.

[2] I think it best to take Rathaproshṭha as the name of a tribe. The word does not occur again in the Rig-veda. Professor Roth seems to take it in the sense of chariot, or seat of a chariot, but in that case the prayer for preservation of power would not be appropriate, for *kshatra* always refers to powers wielded by gods or men. We have seen two rare proper names in the preceding verses, and we need not be surprised at a third, though none of them occurs again in the Rig-veda. In the Mahâbhârata the Proshthas occur as a people.

[3] Another difficult verse, chiefly on account of the word *nadbhyaḥ*, which does not occur again, Professor Roth derives it from *nah*, in the sense of rope, and he compares *akshânah* (R.V. x. 53, 7), fastened to the axle, the name of a horse. I confess I do not see how, with such a word in the dative or ablative, any sense can be elicited from our verse. If one might indulge in conjectures, I should read *naptṛibhyaḥ*, for *Agastya* occurs both with three and four syllables. But why should so simple a word have been changed into *nadbhyaḥ?* The Pada gives *nat-bhyaḥ*, and this Sâyaṇa derives evidently from the verb *nand*, which has given rise to several derivatives in the sense of son, or relative, or descendant. It might be possible, etymologically, to derive *nah* from *nah* or *nabh* (from which *nâbhi*, relationship), and to take it in the sense of relatives, literally, ties. But *nadbhyaḥ* may also be an old dat. plur. of *napât*. The Pada-form of *napât*, if we may judge from the fem. *naptî*, *neptis*, would have been *napt*. This, before *bhyaḥ*, would have been regularly changed into *nap*, This, with *bhyaḥ*, would have become *nabbhyaḥ*. Now in order to avoid the want of euphony, we see that *ab-hyaḥ* is changed to *ad-bhyaḥ*. Why not *nab-bhyaḥ* into *nad-bhyaḥ?*

The Rishis Bandhu, Subandhu, S'rutabandhu, and Devabandhu, are called the sister-sons of Agastya in the Mantrârshâdhyâya. See Ind. Stud. iii. 459.

[4] The last verses are evidently formulas used for restoring health or life. Like most of such formulas they are not always very coherent or very wise. Their

8. "As they tie the yoke with a guard, that it may hold, thus I have held thy soul for life, not for death, ay for safety."[1]

9. "As this great earth has held these forest trees, thus I have held thy soul for life, not for death, ay for safety."

10. "I have brought back the soul of our dear friend from Yama Vaivasvata, for life, not for death, ay for safety."

11. "Down blows the wind, down shines the sun, down milks the cow, down be thy sin!"

12. "This hand of mine is blessed; this hand of mine is more blessed; this hand of mine is all-healing, this has a lucky touch."

If now we ask ourselves for what purpose these four hymns could have been composed, it must be confessed, first of all, that, with the exception of the second hymn, the rest are not very closely strung together, and it is by no means certain that they are not rather a collection of verses than consecutive poems. Taking, however, the hymns as they stand, we may observe a difference between the first, second, and fourth on one side, and the third on the other. The former are addressed to some friend, spoken of in the second person, whose life is in danger, while, in the third, the poet, speaking in the first person plural, seems to fear for his own safety, at least in the seven verses in the beginning. In the concluding verses the friend is addressed again in the second person, and recommended to the protection of the gods. The situation thus brought before us by these hymns seems to be a battle-field or a siege, in which the enemies have wounded one person who lies like dead among his friends, and whom his friends try to recall to life. Their endeavours of awakening the

efficacy would seem to depend on a certain amount of mysterious obscurity. Observe the apparently irregular gender in *ayam mâtâ*, also in *ayam jîvâtuḥ*, for *jîvâtuḥ* is usually feminine. It may be, however, that the speaker, who evidently is the enchanter or mesmeriser, points to himself, saying, as if with the Greek ὅδε, "This is the mother, this is the father, this is thy life, *i.e.* I who bring thee back to life." Professor Roth translates *prasarpaṇa* by unterkommen. Does he mean livelihood? The *nir ihi*, come forth! seems to show that *prasarpaṇa* means the escaping of the soul from the place where it is supposed to be held captive.

[1] *Varatrâ* means a guard, *i.e.* a guard chain. *Dâdhâra* I take to be the first person, considering the construction of verse 10.

wounded from a swoon, or their attempts—whether successful or not, we know not—of calling one really killed in battle back to life, are accompanied with sacrificial oblations, with laying on of hands, and with the recitation of certain charms. If we were at liberty to re-arrange the hymns, I should propose to end the third hymn with verse 7. The three remaining verses would then form an invocation by themselves. Then, again, verses 1–6 of the fourth hymn would form a perfect address to Indra, while the concluding verses by themselves look like a collection of medical charms, such as are very common among poor and ignorant people. The last verse clearly shows that the healing powers of the hands, or what we now call mesmeric strokes, were known long before Mesmer's time. This is interesting; but far more interesting even in these hymns, which are by no means fair specimens of the best religious poetry of the Brahmans, is the constant dwelling on the divine powers which govern the life of man. Whether they are addressed as Indra and Soma, or as Heaven and Earth, or as Guide of Life and Good Lord, it is the gods who reward their worshippers with health and wealth, who give life and death, who destroy evil or sin. The hymns with which the fathers praised the gods, possibly the cups in which they offered their libations, are kept with religious care, nay, the fathers themselves, departed this life, but enjoying immortality, are invoked to bestow blessings on their descendants. The sacrifice is kept up in each family, and this sacrificial succession is looked upon like an unbroken chain uniting each generation, like a new link, with the generation that preceded, and at last with the gods themselves, who were worshipped by the ancient prophets. Let us also observe, particularly in the second hymn, the clear conception of a soul as separate from the body; of a soul, after death, going to Yama Vaivasvata, the ruler of the departed, or hovering about heaven or earth, the sun, the dawn, the water or the plants, ready to be called back to a new life. If we reflect on these germinal thoughts and on the vast proportions they were intended to assume in the later history of the Aryan world down to our own time, we shall have to admit that, even if we lose the legend of king Asamâti and the squabbles of his rival priests, there is still enough left, even in these meagre hymns, that will repay the student for the patient deciphering of the sacred records left to us by the fathers of our own, the Aryan, race.

॥ अथ माधवीयवेदभाष्यं ॥

मा प्र गामेति षडृचं पंचदशं सूक्तं गायत्रं वैश्वदेवं । ऐक्ष्वाको ऽसमातिर्नाम राजा । तस्य बंधुः सुबंधुः श्रुतबंधुर्विप्रबंधुश्चेति चत्वारः पुरोहिता आसन् । ते च गौपायनाः । स च राजा तांस्त्यक्त्वान्यौ मायाविनावृषी पुरोहितत्वेनावृणीत । ततो बंध्वादयः क्रुद्धाः संत इमं राजानमभिचरितवंतः । एतज्ज्ञात्वा मायाविनौ पुरोहितावेषामन्यतमं सुबंधुं प्राणैर्वियोजितवंतौ । मृतस्यास्य भ्रातरो बंधुः श्रुतबंधुर्विप्रबंधुरित्येते ऽविनाशप्राप्तिहेतुभूतमिदं दृष्ट्वा जपंति स्म । अतस्ते ऽस्य सूक्तस्यर्षयः । प्रतिपाद्यत्वादावर्तमानं मनो देवता । तथा चानुक्रांतं । अथ हैक्ष्वाको राजासमातिर्गौपायनान्बंध्वादीन्पुरोहितांस्त्यक्त्वान्यौ मायाविनौ श्रेष्ठतमौ मत्वा पुरोदधे । तमितरे क्रुद्धा अभिचेरुः । अथ तौ मायाविनौ सुबंधोः प्राणानाचिक्षिपतुरथ हास्य भ्रातरस्त्रयो मा प्र गामेति षट्कं गायत्रं स्वस्त्ययनं जप्त्वेति ॥ अग्निसमीपाद्देशांतरगमनसमय इदं सूक्तं जप्यं । सूत्रितं च प्रव्रजेदनपेक्षमाणो मा प्र गामेति सूक्तं जपन्निति ॥ महापितृयज्ञे ऽप्येतदृत्विग्भिर्जप्यं । सूत्रितं च । मा प्र गामाग्ने त्वं न इति जपंतः । आ० २. १८. । इति ॥ निविदः स्थानातिपत्ताविदं सूक्तं शस्त्वा सूक्तांतरे निवित्प्रक्षेप्तव्या । सूत्रितं च । स्थानं चेन्निविदो ऽतिहरेन्मा प्र गामेति पुरस्तात्सूक्तं शस्त्वा । आ० ६. ६. । इति ॥

मा । प्र । गाम । पथः । वयं । मा । यज्ञात् । इंद्र । सोमिनः । मा ।
अंतरिति । स्थुः । नः । अरातयः ॥ १ ॥

अत्रोक्ताख्याने शाट्यायनकं । असमातिं राथप्रौष्ठं° न्यधत्तामित्यादि । तं सुबंधोरसुमादातुं खांडवादसमातिं प्रतिगच्छंतो गौपायना वदंति । हे इंद्र वयं गौपायनाः पथः समीचीनान्मार्गान्मा प्र गाम । मा परागच्छाम । असमातिगृहमेव गच्छाम । मा च सोमिनो ऽसमातेर्यज्ञात्प्रगाम । मा स्थुर्मा तिष्ठंतु नो ऽस्माकमंतर्मार्गमध्ये ऽरातयः शत्रवः । यद्वा सोमिनः सोमवतो यागान्मा प्रगाम ॥

यः । यज्ञस्य । प्रऽसाधनः । तंतुः । देवेषु । आऽततः । तं । आऽहुतं ।
नशीमहि ॥ २ ॥

यो ऽयमग्न्याख्यस्तंतुराहवनीयादिरूपेण विस्तृतो यज्ञस्य प्रसाधनः प्रकर्षेण साधयिता देवैः स्तोतृभिर्ऋत्विग्भिर्विस्तारितो वर्तते वेद्यां तमाहुतं सर्वतो ह्रयमानं नशीमहि । प्राप्नुयाम । नशतिर्व्याप्तिकर्मा ॥

पिंडपितृयज्ञे मनो न्वा हुवामह इति तृचेन पिंडाभिमानिनः पितर उपस्थेयाः । सूत्रितं च । मनो न्वा हुवामह इति चतसृभिरथैनान्प्रवाहयेत् । आ° २. ७. । इति ॥

मनः । नु । आ । हुवामहे । नाराशंसेन । सोमेन । पितृणां । च ।
मन्मऽभिः ॥ ३ ॥

वयं बंधुश्रुतबंध्वादयो मनः सुबंधोः संबंधि मायाविभिरपहृतं नु क्षिप्रमा हुवामहे । केन साधनेनेति तदुच्यते । नाराशंसेन नराशंसचमसगतेन सोमेन । नरैः शस्यंत इति नरा-

ग्रंसाः पितरः । तेषां चमसानां कंपनमेव होमः । तथाविधेन सोमेन पितृणामंगिरसां मन्मभिर्मननीयैः स्तोत्रैश्च ॥

आ । ते । एतु । मनः । पुनरिति । क्रत्वे । दक्षाय । जीवसे । ज्योक् । च । सूर्यं । दृशे ॥ ४ ॥

हे सुबंधो ते मनः पुनरैतु । अभिचरतः सकाशात्पुनरागच्छतु । किमर्थमित्युच्यते । क्रत्वे कर्मणे लौकिकवैदिकविषयाय दक्षाय बलाय च । यद्वा क्रत्वे ऽपानाय दक्षाय प्राणाय । प्राणो वै दक्षो ऽपानः क्रतुरिति हि श्रुतिः । जीवसे जीवनाय च । ज्योक् च चिरकालं सूर्यं दृशे सूर्यं द्रष्टुं । अत्यंतंचिरजीवनायेत्यर्थः ॥

पुनः । नः । पितरः । मनः । ददातु । दैव्यः । जनः । जीवं । व्रातं । सचेमहि ॥ ५ ॥

नो ऽस्माकं पितरः पितृभूता अंगिरसो जनः । तेषां संघ इत्यर्थः । स च जीवं व्रातं प्राणादींद्रियसंघातं पुनर्ददातु । तथा दैव्यो जनः । जनशब्दः संघवचनः । देवानां संघो ऽपि जीवं व्रातं च ददातु । वयं च तदुभयं सचेमहि । प्राप्नुयाम ॥

वयं । सोम । व्रते । तव । मनः । तनूषु । बिभ्रतः । प्रजाऽवंतः । सचेमहि ॥ ६ ॥

हे सोम देव वयं बंध्वादयस्तव व्रते त्वदीये कर्मणि । व्रतमिति कर्मनाम । तव तनूषु त्वदीयेष्वंगेषु च मनो बिभ्रतस्तात्पर्ययुक्तां बुद्धिं धारयंतः प्रजावंतः प्रजाभिः पुत्रपौत्रादिभिर्युक्ताः सचेमहि । संगच्छेमहि । जीवं व्रातं चेति शेषः ॥

॥ इत्यष्टमस्य प्रथम एकोनविंशो वर्गः ॥

यत्ते यममिति द्वादशर्चं षोडशं सूक्तमानुष्टुभं । बंध्वादय

ऋषयः सुबंधुदेहान्निर्गतस्येंद्रियवर्गसहितस्य मनसः पुनस्त-स्मिन्प्रवेशनार्थमिदं सूक्तं दृष्ट्वाजपन्। अतस्ते ऽस्यर्षयः। प्रति-पाद्यत्वादावर्तमानं मन एव देवता। तथा चानुक्रांतं। यत्त इति द्वादशर्चमानुष्टुभं मनआवर्तनं जेपुरिति। गतो वि-नियोगः॥

यत्। ते। यमं। वैवस्वतं। मनः। जगाम। दूरकं॥
तत्। ते। आ। वर्तयामसि। इह। क्षयाय। जीवसे॥१॥

पुरुषस्य म्रियमाणस्य मनो नाम महद्भूतं बहुधा विशीर्णं भवति। तस्य पुनःसंभरणमत्रोच्यते। हे म्रियमाण पुरुष यत्ते तव मनो वैवस्वतं विवस्वतः पुत्रं यमं दूरकमत्यंतं दूरं यथा भवति तथा जगाम ते तव तन्मन आ वर्तयामसि। आवर्तयामः। किमर्थं। इह क्षयाय। इह लोके निवासाय। जीवसे चिरका-लजीवनायेत्यर्थः॥

यत्। ते। दिवं। यत्। पृथिवीं। मनः। जगाम। दूरकं॥
तत्। ते। आ। वर्तयामसि। इह। क्षयाय। जीवसे॥२॥

हे सुबंधो यन्मनो दिवं जगाम यच्च पृथिवीं दूरकं। दूर-कमिति क्रियाविशेषणं। तदिह निवासाय जीवनाय चाव-र्तयामः॥

यत्। ते। भूमिं। चतुःऽभृष्टिं। मनः। जगाम। दूरकं॥
तत्। ते। आ। वर्तयामसि। इह। क्षयाय। जीवसे॥३॥

हे सुबंधो यन्मनो भूमिं चतुर्भृष्टिं। चतुर्दिक्षु भ्रंशो यस्याः सा। तां जगाम तदावर्तयामः॥

यत्। ते। चतस्रः। प्रऽदिशः। मनः। जगाम। दूरकं॥
तत्। ते। आ। वर्तयामसि। इह। क्षयाय। जीवसे॥४॥

हे सुबंधो यत्ते मनः प्रदिशः प्रकृष्टा महादिशस्तत्रो जगाम तदावर्तयामः ॥

यत् । ते । समुद्रं । अर्णवं । मनः । जगाम । दूरकं ॥
तत् । ते । आ । वर्तयामसि । इह । क्षयाय । जीवसे ॥ ५ ॥

हे सुबंधो यत्ते मनोऽर्णवं । अर्णांस्युदकानि । तद्वंतं समुद्रं मेघं वा जगाम तदावर्तयामः ॥

यत् । ते । मरीचीः । प्रऽवतः । मनः । जगाम । दूरकं ॥
तत् । ते । आ । वर्तयामसि । इह । क्षयाय । जीवसे ॥ ६ ॥

हे सुबंधो यत्ते मनः प्रवतः प्रगच्छंतीर्मरीचीर्दीप्तीर्जगाम तदिति गतं ॥

॥ इत्यष्टमस्य प्रथमे विंशो वर्गः ॥

यत् । ते । अपः । यत् । ओषधीः । मनः । जगाम । दूरकं ॥
तत् । ते । आ । वर्तयामसि । इह । क्षयाय । जीवसे ॥ ७ ॥

हे सुबंधो यत्ते मनोऽप उदकं यदोषधीर्वनस्पतीनिति तदिति गतं ॥

यत् । ते । सूर्यं । यत् । उषसं । मनः । जगाम । दूरकं ॥
तत् । ते । आ । वर्तयामसि । इह । क्षयाय । जीवसे ॥ ८ ॥

हे सुबंधो यत्ते मनः सूर्यं सूर्यमिव यदुषसं तदिति गतं ॥

यत् । ते । पर्वतान् । बृहतः । मनः । जगाम । दूरकं ॥
तत् । ते । आ । वर्तयामसि । इह । क्षयाय । जीवसे ॥ ९ ॥

हे सुबंधो यत्ते मनो बृहतः पर्वतान् तदिति गतं ॥

यत् । ते । विश्वं । इदं । जगत् । मनः । जगाम । दूरकं ॥
तत् । ते । आ । वर्तयामसि । इह । क्षयाय । जीवसे ॥ १० ॥

हे सुबंधो यत्ते मनो विश्वमिति तदिति गतं॥ चतस्र ऋचा निगदसिद्धाः ॥

यत्। ते। पराः। पराऽवतः। मनः। जगाम। दूरकं॥
तत्। ते। आ। वर्तयामसि। इह। क्षयाय। जीवसे ॥ ११ ॥

हे सुबंधो यत्ते मनः पराः परावतोऽत्यंतं दूरदेशाज्जगाम तदिति गतं ॥

यत्। ते। भूतं। च। भव्यं। च। मनः। जगाम। दूरकं ॥
तत्। ते। आ। वर्तयामसि। इह। क्षयाय। जीवसे ॥ १२ ॥

हे सुबंधो यत्ते मनो भूतं च भव्यं चेत्यनेन भूतभव्यात्मकव्यतिरेकेण कस्यचिदभावाद्वर्तमानस्य पृथगेवाभिधानात् कृत्स्नं प्रपंचमुक्तं भवति । तत्र सर्वत्र गतं मनो जीवनाय निवासाय चावर्तयामः ॥

॥ इत्यष्टमस्य प्रथम एकविंशो वर्गः ॥

प्र तारीति दशर्चं सप्तदशं सूक्तं बंध्वादीनां त्रयाणां गौपायनानामार्षं। आदितः सप्त त्रिष्टुभः। अष्टमी पंचाष्टका पंक्तिः। नवमी षडष्टका महापंक्तिः। दशमी पंक्त्युत्तरा। आद्यौ दशकावष्टकास्त्रय इत्युक्तलक्षणसद्भावात्। एकाक्षराधिक्याद्भूरिग्विशेषणेयं वेदितव्या। सूक्तस्यादितस्ततस्तो देहात्प्राणान्निर्गमयित्र्या निर्ऋतेर्निवृत्त्यर्थं बंध्वादयोऽजपन्। मो षु णः सोमेति चतुर्थ्यामेव मृत्युनिवृत्त्यर्थं सोममस्तुवन् अतस्तत्रणां निर्ऋतिर्देवता चतुर्थ्याः सोमस्य। असुनीते मन इति द्वाभ्यामसुनीतिनाम्नीं देवीमस्तुवन् अतस्तयोः सा देवता। पुनर्नो असुमित्यस्याः पृथिव्याद्या लिंगोक्ता देवताः। ततस्तिसृभिः शिष्टाभिः पंक्तिमहापंक्तिपंक्त्युत्तराभिर्द्यावापृथिव्याविति द्या-

वाप्टथिव्यौ देवते। समिंद्रेत्यर्धर्चस्येंद्रो देवता। तथा चानुक्रांतं॥ प्र तारीति दशर्चं चतस्रो निर्ऋत्यपनोदनार्थं जपुस्रतुर्थ्यां सोमं चास्तुवन्मृत्योरपगमायोत्तराभ्यां दैवीमसुनीतिं सप्तम्यां लिंगोक्तदेवताः शिष्टाभिः पंक्तिमहापंक्तिपंक्त्युत्तराभिर्द्यावाप्टथिव्यौ समिंद्रेतींद्रं चार्धर्चेनेति। गतो विनियोगः॥

प्र। तारि। आयुः। प्रऽतरं। नवीयः। स्थातारा ऽइव। क्रतुंऽमता। रथस्य॥
अर्ध। च्यवानः। उत्। तवीति। अर्थं। पराऽतरं। सु। निःऽऋतिः।
जिहीतां॥१॥

सुबंधोरायुरायुष्यं प्र तारि। प्रवर्धतां। प्रपूर्वस्तिरतिर्वर्धनार्थः। कथं प्रवर्धतामित्युच्यते। प्रतरं प्रवृद्धतरं नवीयो नवतरं। यौवनोपेतमित्यर्थः। निर्ऋत्यनुग्रहादेवमायुर्वर्धतां। तत्र दृष्टांतः। क्रतुमता कर्मवता सारथिना रथस्य स्थातारेव रथे स्थिताविव वर्धेते तद्वत्। अधाथ च्यवानो जीवितात्प्रच्यवमानोऽर्थं स्वाभिलषितमायुर्लक्षणमुत्तवीति। वर्धयति। सुबंधुप्राणापहर्त्री निर्ऋतिः पापदेवता परातरमत्यंतं दूरतरं परिजिहीतां। परित्यजतु। गच्छतु॥

सामन्। नु। राये। निधिऽमत्। नु। अन्नं। करामहे। सु। पुरुध।
श्रवांसि॥
ता। नः। विश्वानि। जरिता। ममत्तु। पराऽतरं। सु। निःऽऋतिः।
जिहीतां॥२॥

सामन्नु साम्नि गीयमाने सति। नु चार्थे। राये जीवायूरूपधनार्थं निधिमन्निधानवदन्नं हविस्स करामहे। कुर्मः। अत्र न्विति चार्थे। निर्ऋत्यै स्तुतिं हविस्रोभयं कुर्म इत्यर्थः। तदेवाह। सु सुष्ठु पुरुध पुरुधा बहुप्रकारं श्रवांस्यन्नानि हवींषि करामहे।

ता तानि हवींषि नोऽस्माकं संबंधीनि विश्वानि सर्वाणि जरिता जीर्णा स्तुता वा । जरा स्तुतिः । नि० १०.८.। ममस्तु । स्वदतां । आस्वाद्य च निर्ऋतिः परातरमत्यंतं दूरदेशं जिहीतां । गच्छतां ॥

अभि । सु । अर्यः । पौंस्यैः । भवेम । द्यौः । न । भूमिं । गिरयः । न ।
अज्रान् ॥
ता । नः । विश्वानि । जरिता । चिकेत । पराऽतरं । सु । निःऽऋतिः ।
जिहीतां ॥ ३ ॥

वयमर्योऽरीञ्छत्रून्पौंस्यैः पुंस्त्वैर्बलैः सु सुष्ठ्वभिभवेम । द्यौर्न भूमिं । सूर्यो यथा स्वरश्मिभिर्भूमिमभिभवति तद्वत् । गिरयो नाज्रान् । गिरिर्वज्रः । ते यथाज्रानजनशीलान्मेघानभिभवंति तद्वत् । ता तानि यानि नोऽस्माभिः कृतानि स्तोत्राणि तानि विश्वानि सर्वाणि जरिता स्तुता सती निर्ऋतिश्चिकेत । जानाति । शिष्टमुक्तं ॥

मो इति । सु । नः । सोम । मृत्यवे । परा । दाः । पश्येम । नु । सूर्यं ।
उत्ऽचरंतं ॥
द्युऽभिः । हितः । जरिमा । सु । नः । अस्तु । पराऽतरं । सु । निःऽऋतिः ।
जिहीतां ॥ ४ ॥

हे सोम नोऽस्मान् सु सुष्ठु मृत्यवे मो परा दाः । मैव परादानं कुरु । मृत्य्वधीनान्नोऽस्मान्मा कार्षीः । किंतु न्विदानीमुच्चरंतमूर्ध्वं गच्छंतमुदयंतं सूर्यं पश्येम । चिरकालं जीवेमेत्यर्थः । जीवाभावे सूर्यादर्शनादित्यभिप्रायः । किंच द्युभिः । अहर्नामैतत् । अहोभिर्दिवसैर्हितः प्रेरितो जरिमा जराभावो नोऽस्माकं सु सुखकरोऽस्तु । शिष्टमुक्तं ॥

असुऽनीते । मनः । अस्मासु । धारय । जीवातवे । सु । प्र । तिर । नः । आयुः ॥
ररन्धि । नः । सूर्यस्य । संऽदृशि । घृतेन । त्वं । तन्वं । वर्धयस्व ॥ ५ ॥

हे असुनीते मनुष्याणामसूनां नेत्रि देवि अस्मासु मनः पुनर्धारय । किंच जीवातवे जीवितुं सु प्र तिर सुष्ठु वर्धय नोऽस्माकमायुः । किंच रारंधि स्थापय नोऽस्मान् सूर्यस्य संदृशि चिरसंदर्शने । त्वं च घृतेनास्माभिर्दत्तेन तन्वं शरीरं वर्धयस्व । वर्धय ॥

॥ इत्यष्टमस्य प्रथमे द्वाविंशो वर्गः ॥

असुऽनीते । पुनः । अस्मासु । चक्षुः । पुनरिति । प्राणं । इह । नः । धेहि । भोगं ॥
ज्योक् । पश्येम । सूर्यं । उत्ऽचरंतं । अनुऽमते । मृळय । नः । स्वस्ति ॥ ६ ॥

हे असुनीते प्राणदायिनि देवि अस्मासु । अस्मदीये सुबंधावित्यर्थः । पुनश्चक्षुः प्रकाशकं नयनं । ईक्षणसामर्थ्यमित्यर्थः । किंच पुनः प्राणमस्मासु धेहि । स्थापय । वयं च ज्योक् चिरमुच्चरंतमुद्गच्छंतं सूर्यं पश्येम । हे अनुमते देवि स्वस्त्य विनाशं यथा स्यात्तथा नोऽस्मान्मृळय । सुखय ॥

पुनः । नः । असुं । पृथिवी । ददातु । पुनः । द्यौः । देवी । पुनः । अंतरिक्षं ॥
पुनः । नः । सोमः । तन्वं । ददातु । पुनरिति । पूषा । पथ्यां । या । स्वस्तिः ॥ ७ ॥

पृथिवी देवी नोऽस्मभ्यमसुं प्राणं ददातु पुनः । द्यौर्देवतासुं ददातु । तथांतरिक्षमंतरिक्षदेवतासुं ददातु । तथा सोमो नस्तन्वं शरीरं पुनर्ददातु । तथा पूषा पोषाभिमानिनी

देवता पथ्यां । पंथा अंतरिक्षं । नि० ११.४५. । तत्र भवां वाचं । वागात्मकः शब्दो ह्याकाशादुत्पद्यते । तां पुनर्ददातु । किंच या स्वस्तिर्या लोके वेदे च स्वस्तिरुच्यते तामपि पूषा प्रयच्छतु । यद्वा पूषा पोषं प्रयच्छतु । या स्वस्तिर्वाग्नाम्नी देव्यस्ति सा पथ्यां वाचं प्रयच्छतु । वाग्वै पथ्या स्वस्तिरिति ब्राह्मणं ॥

शं । रोदसी इति । सुऽबंधवे । यह्वी इति । ऋतस्य । मातरा ॥
भरतां । अप । यत् । रपः । द्यौः । पृथिवि । क्षमा । रपः । मो इति ।
सु । ते । किं । चन । आममत् ॥ ८ ॥

इदमादिभिस्तिसृभिर्द्यावापृथिव्योः स्तुतिः । रोदसी द्यावापृथिव्यौ सुबंधवे शं सुखं प्रयच्छतां । कीदृश्यौ ते । यह्वी महत्यौ । ऋतस्य यज्ञस्योदकस्य वा मातरा निर्मात्र्यौ । यद्रपः पापं कृच्छ्रमस्ति तदप भरतां । अपहरतां । अपनयतां । हे द्यौः हे पृथिवि हे द्यावापृथिव्यौ क्षमा क्षमायां सत्यां । यद्वा क्षमा पृथगप्युच्यते । क्षमाप्यपहरतु । एवमुक्त्वा सुबंधुं बंध्वादयो ब्रुवते । हे सुबंधो ते त्वां मो षु मैव सु सुष्ठु किंचन परं रपः कृच्छ्रमाममत् । हिनस्तु ॥

अव । द्वके इति । अव । त्रिका । दिवः । चरंति । भेषजा ॥
क्षमा । चरिष्णु । एककं । भरतां । अप । यत् । रपः । द्यौः । पृथिवि ।
क्षमा । रपः । मो इति । सु । ते । किं । चन । आममत् ॥ ९ ॥

दिवो द्युलोकाद्भेषजा भेषजानि द्वके द्विकं त्रिका त्रिकं चाव चरंति । अत्राश्विनौ द्विकमवचरतः । इळा सरस्वती भारती त्रिकमवचरंति ॥ क्षमा क्षमायां चरिष्णु चरत्येककमेकं भेषजमित्यभिप्रायमाह । तानि सर्वाणि सुबंधोः प्राणं रक्षंत्विति शेषः ॥

सं । इंद्र । ईरय । गां । अनड्वाहं । यः । आ । अवहत् । उशीनराण्याः । अनः ॥
भरतां । अप । यत् । रपः । द्यौः । पृथिवि । क्षमा । रपः । मो इति । सु । ते । किं । चन । आममत् ॥ १० ॥

हे इंद्र समीरय प्रेरय । किं । गां गंतारमनड्वाहमनोवहनसमर्थं । यो ऽनड्वानावहदावहत्यस्मान्प्रति किं । अनः शकटं । कस्य । उशीनराण्या एतन्नामिकाया ओषधेः । ययार्तमनुलिंपंति सोशीनराणी । भरतामित्यादि गतं ॥

॥ इत्यष्टमस्य प्रथमे त्रयोविंशो वर्गः ॥

आ जनमिति द्वादशर्चमष्टादशं सूक्तं । गौपायना बंध्वादय ऋषयः । षष्ठ्यास्त्वगस्त्यस्य स्वसैषां मातर्षिका । आदितः पंच गायत्र्यः । अष्टमीनवम्यौ पंक्ती शिष्टा अनुष्टुभः । आदितस्तिसृणामसमातिनाम्नो राज्ञः स्तूयमानत्वात् स एव देवता । पंचम्या इंद्रः । षष्ठ्या अप्यसमातिः । ततः पंचानां सुबंधोर्जीविताह्वानरूपोऽर्थो देवता । अयं मे हस्त इत्यस्या लब्धसंज्ञस्य सुबंधोः स्पर्शनहेतुभूतो देवता । तथा चानुक्रांतं । आ जनमिति द्वादशर्चमानुष्टुभं चतसृभिरसमातिमस्तुवन्पंचम्येंद्रं षष्ठ्यागस्त्यस्य स्वसा मातैषां राजानमस्तौत्पराभिः सुबंधोर्जीवमाह्वयंस्तमंत्यया लब्धसंज्ञमस्पृशन् पंचम्याद्या गायत्र्यो ऽष्टम्याद्ये पंक्ती इति ॥

आ । जनं । त्वेषऽसंदृशं । माहीनानां । उपऽस्तुतं । अगन्म । बिभ्रतः । नमः ॥ १ ॥

इदमादिभिस्तिसृभी राजानं स्तुवंति । वयं बंध्वादयो जनं जनपदमसुनीतिस्वभूतमागन्म । अभिगताः ॥ गमेर्लुङि मंत्र

घसेति च्लेर्लुक्। म्वोश्चेति मकारस्य नकारः॥ कीदृशं जनं। त्वेषसंदृशं। दीप्तदर्शनं। माहीनानां महतामुपस्तुतमुपगतस्तुतिं॥ तादौ चेति गतेः प्रकृतिस्वरः॥ कीदृशा वयं। नमो नमस्कारं बिभ्रतो धारयंतः। कुर्वंत इत्यर्थः। यद्वा जनमसमातिमित्यर्थः। शिष्टं समानं। नमो बिभ्रत इति राजकृते नमस्कारं धारयंत इत्यर्थः॥

असमातिं। निऽतोशनं। त्वेषं। निऽययिनं। रथं। भजेऽरथस्य
सत्ऽपतिं॥ २॥

असमातिं राजानं नितोशनं शत्रूणां हंतारं। नितोशतिर्वधकर्मा। त्वेषं दीप्तं। निययिनं रथमित्युपमाप्रधानो निर्देशः। रथवत्सर्वाभिमतप्राप्तिसाधनं भजेरथस्यैतन्नामकस्य राज्ञो वंशे जातं। यद्वैतन्नामा कश्चिदस्य शत्रुः। तस्य निययिनं॥ हलदंतादिति सप्तम्या अलुक्॥ सत्पतिं सतां पालकं॥

यः। जनान्। महिषान्ऽइव। अतिऽतस्थौ। पवीरवान्। उत। अप-
वीरवान्। युधा॥ ३॥

योऽसमातिर्जनान् स्वविरोधिभूतानतितस्थौ अतिक्रम्य तिष्ठति। पराभावयतीत्यर्थः। क इव। महिषान् सिंह इव। कीदृशः सन्। पवीरवान्। पवीरः पविः। खड्गवान्। उतापि चापवीरवान्। अपगतखड्गः सन्। शस्त्रसाहाय्यमपि कदाचिन्नापेक्षत इत्यर्थः। उतापि च किं कुर्वन्। युधा योधनेन युध्वेत्यर्थः॥

यस्य। इक्ष्वाकुः। उप। व्रते। रेवान्। मराय्ी। एधते। दिविऽइव।
पंच। कृष्टयः॥ ४॥

यस्य जनपदस्येक्ष्वाकू राजा व्रते कर्मणि रक्षणरूप उपैधते

प्रवर्धते । कीदृशः सन् । रेवान् रयिवान् मरायी शत्रूणां मारकश्च सन् । विशेषणद्वयेन जनानां दानादिरूपेण धनलाभः परराजोपद्रवापत्तिश्चोक्ता भवति । एवं सति तद्विषयस्याः पंच कृष्टयो निषादपंचमाश्चत्वारो वर्णा दिवीव द्युलोके यथा संकल्पसिद्धाः संतः सुखिनो भवंति तद्वत्सुखिनो भवंतीति शेषः ॥

इंद्रं । क्षत्रा । असमातिषु । रथऽप्रोष्ठेषु । धारय । दिविऽइव । सूर्यं । दृशे ॥ ५ ॥

अनयेंद्रमाह्वयतेऽसमात्यर्थं । हे इंद्र क्षत्रा क्षत्राणि बलानि रथप्रोष्ठेष्वसमातिषु । एकस्मिन्बहुवचनं पूजार्थं । रथप्रोष्ठेऽसमातौ धारय । दिवीव सूर्यं दिवि यथा सूर्यं दृशे सर्वेषां संदर्शनाय स्थापितवानसि तद्वदत्र बलं धारय ।

अगस्त्यस्य । नत्ऽभ्यः । सप्ती इति । युनक्षि । रोहिता ॥

पणीन् । नि । अक्रमीः । अभि । विश्वान् । राजन् । अराधसः ॥ ६ ॥

अनयागस्त्यस्य स्वसा बंध्वादीनां माता राजानं स्तौति । हे राजन् असमाते त्वमगस्त्यस्यर्षेर्नद्भ्यो नंदयितृभ्यो बंध्वादिभ्यो निमित्तभूतेभ्यस्तेषां धनप्राप्तये सप्ती सर्पणस्वभावावश्वौ रोहिता रोहितवर्णौ युनक्षि । योजय रथे । तथा कृत्वा विश्वान् सर्वानराधसोऽदातॄन् अयजमानान्पणीन् वणिजो लुब्धकान् नि निकृष्टं नितरां वाभ्यक्रमीः । अभिभव ॥

॥ इत्यष्टमस्य प्रथमे चतुर्विंशो वर्गः ॥

अयं । माता । अयं । पिता । अयं । जीवातुः । आ । अगमत् ॥

इदं । तव । प्रऽसर्पणं । सुबंधो इति सुऽबंधो । आ । इहि । निः । इहि ॥ ७ ॥

अत्र शेषे शाट्यायनकं । अथाग्निं द्वैपदेन सूक्तेनास्तुवन् अग्निः स्तुत आजगाम । आगत्य चाह किंकामा मागच्छतेति ।

सुबंधोरेवासुं पुनर्वनुयामेत्यब्रुवन् । एषांतःपरिधीत्यब्रवीत्त-मादद्धमिति । तन्निराह । अयं मातायं पितेति । शौनकश्च ।

स्तुतः स राजा सुप्रीतस्तस्थौ गौपायनानभि ।
सूक्तेन तेऽस्तुवन्नग्निं द्वैपदेन यथाच्चिषु ॥
अथाग्निरब्रवीदेनानयमंतःपरिध्यसुः ।
सुबंधोरस्य चेत्त्वाकोर्मया गुप्तो हितार्थिना ॥
सुबंधवे प्रदायासुं जीवेत्युक्त्वा च पावकः ।
स्तुतो गौपायनैः प्रीतो जगाम त्रिदिवं प्रति ॥
अयं मातेति हृष्टास्ते सुबंधोरसुमाह्वयन् ।
शरीरमभिनिर्दिश्य सुबंधोः पतितं भुवि ॥
सूक्तशेषं जगुश्चास्य चेतसो धारणाय त इति ॥

अयमग्निर्माता । अयमेव पिता । अयं जीवातुर्जीवयिता-गमत् । आजगाम । अतो हे सुबंधो जीवपरिधौ वर्तमानेदं तव शरीरं तव प्रसर्पणं प्रकर्षेण सर्पणसाधनं । अत इदं प्रत्येहि । आगच्छ । निरिहि । निर्गच्छ परिधेः सकाशात् । अन्य एवं व्याचचत् । हे निर्गतप्राण सुबंधो अयं । विभक्तिव्यत्ययः । इयं मातायं पितायं जीवातुर्जीवनफलभूतः पुत्रश्चागमदिति संब-ध्यते । सर्वे त्वामागता दुःखिताः संतः । शिष्टं समानं ॥

यथा । युगं । वरत्रया । नह्यंति । धरुणाय । कं ॥
एव । दाधार । ते । मनः । जीवातवे । न । मृत्यवे । अथो इति ।
अरिष्टऽतातये ॥ ८ ॥

यथा युगं वरत्रया पाशेन नह्यंति बध्नंति धरुणाय रथा-दिधारणाय । कमिति पादपूरणः । एवैवं ते मनो दाधार परिधावग्निः । किमर्थं । जीवातवे । जीवनाय । न मृत्यवे मरणाय न । अथो अपि चारिष्टतातये । अविनाशाय । स्वार्थिकस्तातिः ॥

यथा । इयं । पृथिवी । मही । दाधार । इमान् । वनस्पतीन् ॥
एव । दाधार । ते । मनः । जीवातवे । न । मृत्यवे । अथो इति ।
अरिष्टऽतातये ॥ ९ ॥

यथेयं पृथिवी महीमान्वनस्पतीन्वृक्षादीन्दाधार । शिष्टमुक्तं ॥

यमात् । अहं । वैवस्वतात् । सुऽबंधोः । मनः । आ । अभरं ॥
जीवातवे । न । मृत्यवे । अथो इति । अरिष्टऽतातये ॥ १० ॥

इयं निगदसिद्धा ॥

न्यक् । वातः । अव । वाति । न्यक् । तपति । सूर्यः ॥
नीचीनं । अघ्न्या । दुहे । न्यक् । भवतु । ते । रपः ॥ ११ ॥

वातो वायुर्द्युलोकान्न्यक् निचीनमव वाति । गच्छति । सूर्यश्च न्यक् तपति । अघ्न्याहननीया गौर्निचीनं दुहे । दुग्धे । एवं ते रपो पापं न्यक् निचीनं भवतु ॥

अयं । मे । हस्तः । भगऽवान् । अयं । मे । भगवत्ऽतरः ॥
अयं । मे । विश्वऽभेषजः । अयं । शिवऽअभिमर्शनः ॥ १२ ॥

अनया बंध्वादयो लब्धजीवं सुबंधुं पाणिभिरस्पृशन् । अयं मे हस्तो भगवान् यस्मात्सजीवं सुबंधुं स्पृशति तस्मात् । तथायं मे हस्तो भगवत्तरः । अतिशयेन भगवान् । तथायं मे हस्तो विश्वभेषजो जीवचिकित्सासाधनसर्वौषधवान् तत्स्थानीयो वा । अयं शिवाभिमर्शनो मंगलस्पर्शनः । यतो जीवंतं स्पृशत्यत इत्यर्थ ॥

॥ इत्यष्टमस्य प्रथमे पंचविंशो वर्गः ॥
॥ दशमे मंडले चतुर्थोऽनुवाकः ॥

## Art. XII.—*Specimen Chapters of an Assyrian Grammar.* By the Rev. E. Hincks, D.D., Hon. M.R.A.S.

A great number of years have now elapsed since I began to collect materials for an Assyrian grammar; an object, of which I have never since lost sight. Of late, I have been preparing my materials for publication; but a preliminary question has suggested itself:—"If I were to publish a grammar, who would read it?" The persons for whose instruction I should naturally write would be either persons who were acquainted with other Semitic languages, and who were desirous of comparing the grammars of these with that of the oldest and the best developed language of the family; or else persons, who desired to study this language for its own sake, and who sought the aid of a grammar, in the absence of an oral instructor, to teach them the first principles of this "Sanskrit of the Semitic tongues," which they might afterwards improve upon by their own studies.

I believe that persons of both these classes would derive benefit from such a grammar as I should publish, if they would only make use of it. I fear, however, that no person of either of the classes has so much faith in me, and in my knowledge of Assyrian grammar, as to make use of it. My only readers would probably be my critics;—those, who have attained *some* knowledge of the Assyrian language—considerable knowledge, I may say, so far as respects *the meaning of words,*—but whose published translations show that, as respects *grammar,* their views are extremely different from mine; and, of course, if my views be correct, extremely erroneous. My only readers would thus be, with perhaps one or two exceptions, *hostile* critics, who must condemn what I have written, because, by laying down rules which they have disregarded and violated in their translations, it indirectly condemns those translations.

In the case of one eminent Assyrian writer on the continent, the certainty that I should meet with hostile criticism is more obvious than it is in the case of others. Dr. Oppert has published an Assyrian grammar, of which I have already stated that, besides minor errors, it was pervaded by three erroneous general principles, "so as scarcely to leave a page free from what I consider pernicious error." One of these three principles, Dr. Oppert, in a late article in the *Journal Asiatique,* intimates that he has abandoned, or is disposed to abandon. To the other two he clings pertinaciously. Now, as I cannot retract the unfavourable opinion above expressed, and as, according to my views of Assyrian grammar, I cannot think the translations from Sargon, which MM. Oppert and Ménant have published, to be even approximately correct, I could not possibly expect any criticism from those gentlemen but of the most adverse description.

Under these circumstances, I have thought it advisable to deviate materially from my original plan. Instead of publishing an entire grammar, I will, in the first instance, publish specimen-chapters only; treating of the declensions of substantives and adjectives, and of the permansive forms of verbs;—a subject on which Dr. Oppert, in the *Journal Asiatique* for last year (Tome vi. p. 297), has mis-stated both my views and the facts to which he appeals. Instead, too, of stating what I believe to be the grammatical rules of the Assyrian language, dogmatically, as would be the natural course of the writer of a grammar, I will deduce them from those leading positions on which all are agreed, by inductive proofs, in the order which appears to me the best for this purpose; different as this order is from what I should adopt if I were exempt from the necessity of writing otherwise than dogmatically. My examples must be numerous, because they are not merely illustrative, but justificatory. It will readily be understood that where I bring forward a number of proofs in support of any assertion, it is one which is not generally accepted, and is likely to be controverted; but except in the one case of the permansive forms of the verb, which I have already mentioned, I do not mean to point out directly what I believe to be the errors of others. It will answer my end, and will be pleasanter to myself, if I merely seek to establish the correctness of my own views. This being done, the incorrectness of any views that are inconsistent with them will follow as a matter of course.

A few words should be said here on the principles on which I have conducted my investigations. I have sought the rules of Assyrian grammar by induction from passages, the meaning of which I considered to be perfectly known, occurring in writings of a good age; the induction being guided by a general knowledge of Semitic grammar. I have taken no account of passages, however well their meaning may be known, which are found in texts of a late age, probably written by persons who had a very imperfect knowledge of Assyrian, and of whom it was not the native tongue. Neither have I assumed the identity of Assyrian and Hebrew rules of grammatical construction in cases where there is no inductive evidence of it.

As to the transcriptions of Assyrian words and texts which I give, I think that it is unnecessary to say much. Were I to publish a grammar, it should contain a list of all the characters representing syllables consisting of a single vowel, or a vowel preceded or followed by a consonant, and of all those whose values were syllables consisting of a vowel both preceded and followed by a consonant, and which occurred in any text quoted in the grammar. To each character its transcription should be attached. I represent, as every one else does, ב, ג, ד, ז, כ, ל, מ, נ, פ, ר, and ת, by *b*, *g*, *d*, *z*, *k*, *l*, *m*, *n*, *p*, *r*, and *t*. I also represent ח by *ḥ*, ט by *ṭ*, ס by *ṣ* (which was anciently sounded either *st*, or *sk*; the former being, like ש, represented by the Arabic س, the latter by ش, and by the Greek ξ, which occupied the same position in the alphabet, and had the same figure as the Phœnician ס), צ by *ẓ*, ק by *q*, and ש by *s*. The remaining five letters, א, ה, ו, י, ע, are indiscriminately transcribed as ʿ with the following exceptions: 𒅀 is transcribed by *ya*; [illegible] by *ʿu* or *yu*; 𒀀 after another 𒀀 by *ʿa* or *yâ*; 𒅇, when a copulative, by *va*; and 𒄴 by *h* or *ih*. I use the vowel *e* alone to represent 𒂊,

è standing for . The grave accent over a vowel is not intended to mark a distinction of sound, but to show that a homophone of the character usually representing the syllable without the accent is used in place of that character. I use four vowels in transcriptions, *a*, *i*, *u*, and *e*, which I believe the Assyrians pronounced as long *i*, or *î*. I think that no Assyrian scholar will find any difficulty in restoring the text of my transcriptions; but if he do, he can consult the original text, to which I refer him. To explain my references, I will observe that B. means Botta's plates; L., the first series of British Museum plates, edited by Mr. Layard; I. and II., the two volumes of the second series of British Museum plates, edited by Sir H. Rawlinson. The number which precedes this is the number of the plate in each series, and the number at the end is the line in the plate; with a distinctive mark before it, *if necessary*, the meaning of which will be seen when the plate is referred to. In some of the plates of the second series, I use *r*, *c*, and *l* for right, centre, and left. In these references, and in the transcriptions, I have followed as closely as I could Mr. Norris.

I believe that the main point in which I differ from Mr. Norris in my transcriptions is that I do not attempt to distinguish in most cases between the several breathings and semivowels. I do not think that we can distinguish them by inspection of the Assyrian characters. We can only do so by knowledge derived from some other source. I find, for instance,  occurring in four words; between *ma* and *du*, between *na* and *du*, between *ṭa* and *bu*, and between *da* and *nu*. I transcribe it in the four instances by ʿ*a*. I happen to know from the Hebrew that in the first word the ʿ*a* represents אָ, in the second הָ, in the third וָ, and in the fourth יָ; the four words signifying *much* or *great* from מאד, *glorious* from נהד, *good* from טוב, and *a judge* from דין. In another word which had no Hebrew equivalent, I should not know how to render the characters so as to make a distinction; and I therefore do not make it in the cases where I am able to do so. Some persons would in all these instances represent the by accenting the preceding vowel. In most cases, however, I think that this would be an error. Where it is plain to me that two characters represent together but one syllable, I cut off one of the vowels by an apostrophe; but I do not consider it a matter of course to do so, nor do I use an accent in all cases where I do so.

When two syllables are joined together without a point, it will be understood that they are, in the original, not represented phonetically, but by monograms, ideograms, or Accadian roots, as they have been variously called. In such cases I generally give the cuneiform characters in brackets, with *i.e.* after them, before I give the words that I read. When, however, the signification of the monogram is well known and universally admitted, I omit the cuneiform characters.

[Chapter V.] *On Verbs, and first on their permansive parts.*

1. Generally speaking, a verb admits of seven principal conjugations, of which the first six correspond to the first six of the recognized Hebrew conjugations; the seventh being the causative of the third. I denote them by the seven first Roman numerals. Other conjugations are occasionally met with, but are less frequent. It will, of course, be understood that no one verb is used in all the conjugations.

2. Each of these seven admits of a secondary or augmented conjugation, which I denote by the proper Roman numeral followed by t. The augmented conjugation regularly inserts *t* or *te* after the first radical letter, or in the conjugations V.–VII. after the preformative *s*. In some cases the insertion of this letter or syllable is the only difference between the augmented conjugation and its principal one; but in other cases, other changes are introduced which will be mentioned in the sequel.

3. The inserted *t* is sometimes changed into *d* or *ṭ*, through the influence of the letter with which it comes in contact; and sometimes through its influence that letter undergoes a change. Another irregularity, which is apt to be more puzzling, is that in most verbs defective in the second radical

(concave verbs) the dental precedes the first radical in place of following it. Thus, we have from בוא, in the aorist of I. t, *it.bu.ni*, instead of *ib.tu.ni*, "they came on" (90 L. 63).

4. Generally speaking, again, the verbal forms belonging to each conjugation may be divided into two great classes, which I call permansive and mutative. The former denotes continuance in the state which the verb signifies in that conjugation; the latter denotes change into that state. Each portion of the forms belonging to the conjugation has tenses and verbal nouns. The permansive tenses are analogous to the so-called Hebrew preterite, having no preformatives, but having terminations added, (except in the third person singular masculine, which has none, as in Hebrew), by which the number, person, and gender are distinguished. The mutative tenses, on the contrary, are analogous to the so-called Hebrew future, having one or other of the preformatives אֵיתָן always prefixed to the root, whether or no there be any distinctive addition at the end.

5. The distinction here made between permansive and mutative forms is in my judgment a fundamental one, on the proper development of which all accurate knowledge of the Assyrian language must depend. Now, Dr. Oppert, has in a recent number of the *Journal Asiatique* (Tome vi. p. 297), ridiculed the existence of any such forms as what I call permansive, characterising them as being a mere fancy of mine. The first thing then that I have to do is to establish the existence of such forms by a number of clear examples.

6. I will begin with comparing two sentences from adjoining columns of Taylor's Cylinder, in which the same root occurs,—a perfect root having three letters incapable of change,—namely, כתם. It signifies in Arabic *celavit* (Frey. iv. 10), and this *may* be the meaning in the single passage in the Hebrew Bible where it occurs (see Ges. 723). At any rate this seems clearly the meaning in the two Assyrian passages which I will cite. In the former of these, 40 I. 68, Sennacherib, after mentioning the destruction of certain towns concluding with *'ak.mu*, "I burned," proceeds thus. I omit a simile which is evidently parenthetical. *Qu.ṭur n'a.ak.mu.ti.*

*su.nu* . . . . . *pa.an* [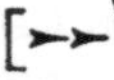 *i.e.*] *same.'e rap.su.ti 'u.sak.tim,* "the smoke of their being burned (like a ponderous cloud) the face of the wide heavens I made to conceal." The verb is here in the 1. s. of the aorist of (the causative) Conjugation V., having two objects expressed, that which is made to produce, and that which is made to undergo, the change. The preceding verb *'akmu* is the 1. s. of the aorist of I. of the verb כמה. Let us now proceed to 41 I. 45. I omit another comparison to a cloud, which is parenthetic. [ *i.e.*] *epir sepi.su.nu* . . . . *p'a.an same.'e rap.su.ti ka.t'i.im,* "the dust of their feet (like, etc.) the face of the wide heavens is concealing." In my judgment, nothing can bc clearer than that *katim* is the 3. m. s. of the principal permansive tense. Dr. Oppert says that I "substitute participles for the 3. s. m." By a participle I presume he means what I call the *nomen mutantis.* No doubt the latter would be *katim,* or, as I should write it for distinction, *kâtim*; but this would stand before what it governs; it should then be translated "the concealer of (the face of the wide heavens)," and it would require a verb to complete a sentence. It might as well be said that the second word in Genesis was a participle, or any other 3. m. s. of the preterite in the Bible. In this portion of Taylor's Cylinder we have no less than six long lines and a half in which there is nothing that he acknowledges to be a verb. In l. 43, Sennacherib begins to describe an attack upon him by an immense multitude of his enemies, whom he compares to locusts. All are doing the same things in constant succession, and accordingly, in speaking of what they do, he uses only permansive tenses. In l. 44 we have *te.bu.'u.ni,* "they are coming on," the 3. m. p. of the permansive of I.t. of the verb בוא. It has exactly the same relation to *it.bu.ni,* "they came on," cited in § 3, as *ka.t'i.im* in l. 47 has to *iktum,* "it concealed." Passing over a permansive verb in l. 48, the discussion of which would lead to a digression, we have in l. 49, after the description of the position taken by his enemies, *ẓab.tu.va,* "they are occupying, and," followed by a mutative verb. Surely it cannot be maintained with any show of reason that ẓab.tu, followed as it is by the copulative enclitic which connects verbs, and verbs only, and this by an acknowledged verb, is anything else than a verb, and yet it has no preformative. The verb צבת is a very common one in the mutative tenses of both I. and V.

7. Before going further, I will give paradigms of the declension of the three principal tenses of the imaginary verb פגל;—the *permansive present*, the *aorist*, and the *mutative present*, or *present* simply. The latter is written indifferently with *g* or *gg*; the duplication of the second radical being euphonic, and not characteristic of the third conjugation. What really characterizes this conjugation is the use of *u* as the vowel of the preformative. It is *invariably* so used in Conjugations III., V., and VII., and their augmented conjugations; and *never* so in any other conjugation, unless the first radical of the verb be ו. Each of these three principal tenses admits a secondary tense formed by the addition of *u* to forms which end in the third radical, and of *ni* to those which end in an added vowel. The most important of these secondary tenses is that derived from the present, which is clearly a *future*.

8. Paradigms of the three principal tenses of Conjugation I.:—

| | Permansive Present. | Aorist. | Present. |
|---|---|---|---|
| 1. *s.* | paglaku, or paglak | ʿapgul | ʿapaggil, or ʿapagil |
| 2. *m.s.* | pagilta | tapgul | tapaggil |
| 2. *f.s.* | pagilti | tapguli | tapaggili |
| 3. *m.s.* | pagil | ipgul | ipaggil |
| 3. *f.s.* | paglat | tapgul | tapaggil |
| 1. *p.* | pagilnu | napgul | napaggil |
| 2. *m.p.* | pagiltunu | tapgulu | tapaggilu |
| 2. *f.p.* | pagiltina | tapgula | tapaggila |
| 3. *m.p.* | paglu | ipgulu | ipaggilu |
| 3. *f.p.* | pagla | ipgula | ipaggila |

The forms of the second person plural may require correction; but I believe that all the others may be depended upon. I use *i* as the vowel after the second radical in the permansive and ordinary present, and *u* in the aorist. These are the most common vowels, but many verbs have different ones. Perhaps the third person feminine singular sometimes ends in *a*, that is *'a*, like the Hebrew הָ. An apparent example is in 18 I. 62, where the nominative is singular, *sa*, referring to *'u.ba.nu 'a.ẓi.tu*, "a projecting summit;" and we have *su.qa.lu.la* in the printed text, and *lat* as a variant. The latter is, however, the reading of far the most copies, *if not of all*. In 33 I. 2·48, we have *su.qa.lu.la*; but there the nominative is plural, *'u.ba.n'a.at sad.e*, "the summits of the mountain." In 24 I. 51, we have also *su.qa.lu.la*, but here the nominative is masculine singular; and the final *a* is, as very often happens, a representative of *va*, the copulative enclitic, and not an inflexion of the verb.

9. What are called the personal pronouns of the first and second persons are really, as I have stated long since, permansive presents of a verb signifying "to be here," *adsum*; and *'ana*, "ad," "to," or "for," is to be referred to the same root, אוֹן. The *true* personal pronouns are the afformatives of the permansive present, *'aku*, *nu*, and *ta*, with its derivatives. It is *these* which the comparative grammarian should compare with the Indo-European pronouns. By the way, I never said, as Dr. Oppert represents me to have said, that the second person of the permansive present ended in *ka* and *ki*, as in Ethiopic. What I said was, that the fact of the first persons ending alike in Assyrian and Ethiopic ought not to be relied on as proof of a special connection between those two languages, because the Ethiopians had *k* in the second person, as well as in the first, while the Assyrians had not.

10. I will now give some other examples of permansive presents: In the descriptions of permanent features of a country, which are so frequently found in the historical inscriptions, the permansive tense is constantly used. Thus *e.g.* in 11 I. 43, etc., we read of "high mountains, which, like the edge of a sword, *sam.ṭu*, are piercing; which, for the passing of chariots, *la.'a na.ṭu.'u*, are not fitted." The exact force of the roots שמט and נטע or נטא may be questioned, but the general sense is clear. The king tells us that he left his chariots behind, and crossed the mountains without them;

and *here* he uses the aorist. In 22 I. 105, we have *kir.hu.su kima ʿu.bʾa.an sad.e sa.kin*, "Its top (or head) like the summit of a mountain was lying," or simply "was." The verb שכן in its mutative parts signifies, actively, "to place," or "make;" in the permansive parts "to lie," or "be." This is something like what happens in several Greek verbs, as ἵστημι, and in Latin, where *facio*, as well as *fio*, is etymologically connected with *fuo*.

11. The permansive present is also habitually used in the passive conjugations; for the state denoted by these forms is generally a permanent one. So in Greek we have τετυμμένοι εἰσί, and in Latin, to a greater extent, *pulsatus sum*, etc., as well as *pulsati sunt*. Thus, we have 42 I. 11, *ra.ki.bu.sʾi.in di.ku*, "their riders were killed," and soon after, *si.na mus.su.ra*, "they (*f.*) were abandoned." In 38 L. 8, we have *ẓʾu.uḥ.ḥu.rat su.bat.ṣa*, "its site (was made, *i.e.* as often in Hebrew) was judged to be small." Examples might be quoted almost without end.

12. I will now pass to the first person. Dr. Oppert objects to an example which I gave formerly. In 19 I. 101, we read, as it is printed, *ina li.me ù.ma, ina Ninua uẓ.ba.ku*, which I have translated "In the eponymy of a certain person, in Nineveh I am stopping." I ought, however, to have translated it, "In the same eponymy." The character in two copies that I have collated is not that for *ù*, the copulative conjunction, but that which occurs so commonly on the tablets, signifying "the same." There can, I think, be no doubt that this is the correct reading in all the inscriptions; and that the copyists have substituted a common character for one which was not familiar to them. In 18 I. 69, we have *Ina li.me an.ni.ma*, "in the eponymy of this person," that is, "of myself." This is one of the many substitutes for the pronoun "my," which we meet with in the Assyrian inscriptions. This is sometimes contracted into *an.ma*, as in 40 L. 50. The  seems to be used to indicate that a peculiar mode of expression is used; or perhaps it may signify "and so forth." Speaking of these substitutes for the possessive pronouns, I consider it due to Dr. Oppert to acknowledge the great merit of his late dis-

covery of the signification of *raman,* which had been so long a puzzle to Assyrian students. I adopt his explanation as perfectly correct, and I have met with five or six passages, besides those cited by himself, which it explains in the most satisfactory manner. *O si sic omnia!*

13. The explanation of *uẓ.ba.ku* given above, "I am stopping," clashes with Dr. Oppert's view in two respects. It is a permansive present, a tense which he does not acknowledge; and it is that of the verb וצב, a defective in "פו, of which he has affirmed in his grammar that the Assyrians had none. It appears then absolutely necessary for the maintenance of hiṣ system that he should do away with this passage; and I will quote from p. 297, what he says on the subject: "D'abord, on ne lit jamais *usbaku,* mais toujours *uśbakuni* dans les inscriptions de Sardanapale III., dans la phrase; 'Pendant qu'ils me retinrent à Ninive, etc.' *Uśbakuni* est la 3[me] pers. du pluriel de סבך à l'iphteal avec le suffixe. Sans suffixe, ce serait *yuśśabaku* יִסַּבְכוּ, ou même *yuśabaku* יִסַבְכוּ (G.A. § 128), et contracté avec le suffixe (ibid. § 197) יִסַבְכוּנִי. Voilà à quoi se réduit la 1[re] personne en *ku.* Et ce *seul* example, si même il était avéré, ne pourrait avoir une grande portée, quand on le compare aux milliers de formes des aoristes fournies par les textes."

14. I have given the whole of this passage from M. Oppert's text; and I must say, that I think I have never read a passage of the same length, in which there are so many mis-statements as to matters of fact. The word *uẓbaku* does occur in the passage cited; and when he denied that it did so, Dr. Oppert must have trusted to a treacherous memory. There is no *ni* after it in the printed text; there is no various reading noted in 19 I. 101; and, morover, I collated, some years ago, very carefully, all the copies of the inscriptions brought over by Mr. Layard, which substantially coincide with that which is printed, and I am thus in possession of some important various readings which are not printed; and I can say most positively that there is *not a single copy* which contains *any other* reading than *uẓbaku,* which Dr. Oppert says "on ne lit JAMAIS!" Elsewhere, *e.g.* in l. 94 of the same plate, *ni* is added; but there the sentence begins with *ki,* "when;"

and I translate "when in Ṣur I was stopping." This is the secondary permansive tense noted at the end of § 7. Where there is no *ki* at the beginning of the sentence, there is no *ni* at the end of *uẓbaku.* In the second place, the existence of the verb סבך is, so far as I am aware, a pure fiction. I never recollect to have met it, and I believe no one else has met it. It has been imagined purely for the purpose of neutralizing a text, the existence of which is inconsistent with two grammatical dreams. But in the third place, even if the existence of this verb bê granted, it could not produce by any legitimate process such a grammatical monstrosity as *yuṣbakuni.* Dr. Oppert cannot produce any similar form. *Iṣbakuni* would be legitimate; and so would *iṣabkuni*, or with *ṣt* or *ṣṣ* in the place of *ṣ*; *yuṣabkuni* might pass also for Conj. III.; but the substitution of *yu* for *i* before *ṣb*—such a form as *yupgaluni*—is unparalleled. *Yu* and *i* are not interchangeable, as he says in his grammar, the former is used in Conj. III., the latter in Conj. I.; but these two conjugations, the Pihel and Qal of the Hebrews, he has blended together in hopeless confusion.

15. But, perhaps, the most extraordinary sentence in the passage I have quoted is the last. The first question at issue is, whether the Assyrians had, like the Hebrews, at least one tense in each conjugation, in which there were no preformatives. It is in regard to this tense that we are at issue; that they had also a tense or tenses in each conjugation, which had preformatives, we are agreed. Now if I can establish even a single instance, in which a verb has no preformative, my case is proved. The fact is, however, that there are hundreds of instances of permansive verbs in inscriptions of every age, from Tiglath Pileser to Darius. Dr. Oppert says that *sarraku*, even if it should not be read *sarratus,*—a supposition which the variant form in *ak* (of which presently) proves to be untenable,—may mean "I am a king," and yet not be a verb. Here I differ from him. I say, in common I believe with all grammarians, that a word which includes in itself a pronominal subject, a copula and a predicate, is essentially a verb. It might as well be denied that *malakta* in 2 Sam. iii. 21, was a verb, because *malkê*, "kings of," is a noun. In 17

I. 32, etc., there are, after the completion of a sentence, no less than eleven words ending in *aku*. I take them to be permansive presents in the 1. s., ten of them belonging to triliteral verbs in the first, third or fourth conjugations, and the eleventh to a quadriliteral. It is not the slightest objection to this view that substantives or adjectives are in use, containing the former part of the alleged verb. So it is in all the Semitic languages. There is a *nomen permanentis*, and a *permansive present*, the beginnings of which generally agree, though their endings are generally as different as the cases of *rex* and the persons of *rego*. In the proper names *Nabu-na.ʿid*, "Nebo is glorious," and *Na.ʿid-Mar.duk*, "Marduk is glorious," as well as in *na.h.da.ku* in l. 32, we have the permansive present; in E.I.H. I. 3, on the contrary, *ru.ba.ʿa na.ʿa.dam*, "the glorious prince," gives us the *nomen permanentis*, here an adjective.

16. In the Babylonian inscriptions the *u* at the end of the 1 s. is dropped. Thus in E.I.H. I. 39, we have *p'i.it.lu.ḥ'a.ak be.l'u.ut.ṣ'u.un*, "I am habitually worshipping their lordships." The *u*, it will be observed, is also dropped in this affix, as it sometimes is in the affix *su*, when added to a word ending with a vowel. This is the 1. s. of the permansive present in the first augmented conjugation of פלח. Before this, in l. 10, the king had used the permansive past (badly spelled), *b'i.it.l'u.ḥu b'i.e.l'u.ut.ṣ'u.un*, "he has been habitually worshipping their lordships." •In the Nakshi-Rustam inscription, l. 9, we have *s'a.al.ṭ'a.ak*, "I am ruling," as the translation of *patiyakhshiya*, or rather of the latter part of this Persian word; for the preposition at the beginning is expressed in the Babylonian text by a separate preposition. I was curious to see what Dr. Oppert would make of this, and I turned to his transcription of it into Hebrew characters in the Z. D. M. G. XI. 136. I was no little surprised to find that he makes two words out of these four characters, namely, שְׁלֵט אֶעְבַּשׁ. The latter of these two words he has substituted for the termination *ak*, which he did not understand! This led me to look further into his transcriptions. In l. 24 there is a passage, the true reading and signification of the first word of

which was suggested to me by Mr. Talbot.  is *ẓub* as well as *lib*. The reading is *ẓub.bu.'u sa 'ana.ku ẓi.ba.'a.ka*. I take the *ka* to represent *ak*, which would look very awkward after *ba.'a*; while if the  were omitted it would be natural to read *ẓibak*; the word is really *ẓiba'ak*. I translate, "they are always made to will what I am willing." Here, again, Dr. Oppert transcribes the four characters by צְבָא יְעָרֵשׁ instead of צְבָאָךְ, introducing a second imaginary word in place of a termination which he does not understand.

17. These are not the only instances of permansive verbs in the Nakshi-Rustam inscription. In l. 26, we have *kul.lu*, "has been holding," a deponent verb like *dominatus erat;* and in the following line we may restore the damaged word of Conj. IV. *na.su.'u*, "are carrying," from נשא. This word occurs again l. 18 ("The Ionians who maginat on their heads) are carrying;" as does the preceding word in l. 11 ("my laws) they are holding;" , which must be here read *ha*, being added to the singular, to form the feminine plural. An eighth permansive form occurs in l. 21, where in speaking of the depraved state of the people before Darius became king, the obscure word *ṣummuḥu* is used. To these eight instances of permansive words I think myself entitled to add two others in which *'anaku* is used as a verb, there being no other in the sentence. Now, I can only count thirty-one mutative verbs in this inscription; so that the permansive verbs are in the inscription about a fourth of all the verbs. In the inscriptions generally they are perhaps a fifth or sixth of the whole; but this is a very different proportion from "one to thousands."

18. I will now give some examples of permansive forms of two verbs, the meanings of which have been strangely misconceived, ישא, "to have," and בשא, "to be." Both are used in the mutative, as well as in the permansive tenses; and in the former verb, there is a great liability to confusion, the aorist being in both the first and third persons singular *i.si*, as in E.I.H. 10, 15, where we have the derivative form *'a.ya 'i.si na.ki.ri*, "let me not have enemies." The 3 s. of the permansive form would, I presume, be written precisely alike; and *i.su.'u* and *i.sa.'a* would be the 3 p. m. and f. in both the

aorist and the permansive tense. We have, however, in 9 I. 58, a form which is clearly permansive, *ma.ḥi.ra* (in another copy *sa.ni.na*) *'as taḥazi la i.sa.'a.ku*, "a confronter (or rival) in the close combat I have not." In l. 44 of the same plate we have *ma.ḥi.ru la i.su.'u*, "a confronter has not had;" and in 42 L. 40, the name given by Sennacherib to his palace is *sa sa.ni.na la i.su.'u*, "which has not had a rival."

19. The verb "to be" occurs frequently in a variety of mutative forms; as in 3 m. s. Conj. I. *sa.nin ul ib.si*, "rival (or adversary) there was not," 18 I. 43; *mal.ku gab.r'a.a.'a ul ib.si*, "king prevailing against me there was not," 145 B. 1; for which we have in 171 B. 7, *gab.r'a.a.su ul ib.su.'u*, "one prevailing against him (whom) there was not." Here the *u* at the end of the verb is not the formative of the preterperfect, but a relative enclitic; and it may be so in some of the instances of the permansive past which I have given. It is to be observed that the *u* and *ni* of all the secondary tenses are annexed immediately to the primary tense; whereas, if an objective affix follow, the enclitic is placed after it. Thus, in 89 L. 40, we have, after *sa*, *i.qa.bu.su.ni*, "which (the people of Ḥatti) call." Here *i.qa.bu* is the 3 p. m. of the present of קבה; *su* the affix "it," which, in combination with the preceding *sa*, must be translated "which," as in Hebrew; and *ni* the relative enclitic is after the affix. Were the perfect to be expressed, we should have *i.qa.bu.ni*.

20. Other forms of this verb are *i.b'a.as.su.'u*, 3 m. p. present "do not exist," E.I.H. 2, 20; I have also met *i.b'a.as.si* in the singular; and on Bellino's cylinder l. 31 we have the infinitive *'a.di la ba.s'i.e 'u.sa.lik.su.nu.ti*, "till there was none (left) I made them depart." In 38 I. 18, this is repeated with two various readings, *i* for *e*, and *su* for *su.nu.ti*. The singular *su* is very often used, when there is no definite antecedent, in the sense of "people," as in 47 B. 88, etc. In 65 I. 2, 13, we have *'u s'a.al.m'i.is* (for *'usalmisu*) to express the *ma.da 'u.s'a.al. mi* of E.I.H. 6, 43, "the people I caused to see." Once more we have the 1 s. of the aorist of בשא in Conj. V. in 42 L. 44, *'a.gam.mu 'u.sab.si* "a lake I made" (*lit.* "I caused to be.")

21. The permansive form of this verb is most commonly

found in the parenthetic formula *ma.la* (or *mal*) *ba.su.ʿu*, "as many as there are." I must here observe that while I have always, in common with Sir H. Rawlinson, assigned to *mala* an affirmative signification, instead of a negative one, as Dr. Oppert assigned to it in his grammar, I never attributed to *basuʿu* the signification of number, as I am represented to have done in Dr. Oppert's late paper. He now admits that *mala basuʿu* means "all," though he does not yet see his mistake in supposing *ba.su.ʿu* to mean "bad" or "contemptible." That this word and its Accadian equivalent  *nal.la*, as I read it with some small doubt, means simply "to be," I feel perfectly sure. But, as this is rather a matter for a lexicographer than a grammarian, I will not discuss it here.

22. It remains for me to give the forms of the permansive tense in the different conjugations; of pagil Conj. I. enough has been said; I have also given examples of pitgul Conj. I. t. Another occurs in 37 I. 66, where Sennacherib speaks of people, "who to the kings my fathers," *la kit.nu.su*, "were not submissive," from כנש. The conjugation generally indicates repeated action, and the tense that this repeated action was continued for a length of time.

23. The permansive of Conj. II. is of the form napgul; and of II. t. I presume it would be naptegul. I have, however, met with no instance of the latter, and only one of the former. It occurs in 40 L. 3, *sa.qis n'a.an.zu.zu*, "they were fixed on high." The root is נזז. The *n* of the root is here preserved, but it is often assimilated to the *z* when it comes in contact with it; and we have thus apparently, though not really, a root of which all the letters are ז. In the present text, which is to me in great measure obscure, the verb quoted lies between two other permansive ones, *pit.hu.lu* Conj. I. t. and *n'u.uṣ.ṣu.ru* Conj. III., which, again, is followed by *n'u.um.mu.ru* in the same conjugation.

24. The permansive form of Conj. III. is but rare: the form is paggal. Examples are *qar.ra.da.ku*, "I am very strong," 17 I. 32; and *ʿal.la.ka bir.k'a.a.ʿa*, "my knees are moving briskly," 16 II. c. 30. This is the 3 f. p. from הלך. In the following line we have another permansive verb, *la.ʿa*

*ni.ḥa se.p'a.a.' a*, "my feet have not any rest." This is from נוח in a conjugation peculiar to concave verbs, which is in the mutative parts analogous to Conj. III. of perfect verbs, but in the permansive parts has generally a passive or neuter signification. Another example will be found in § 11. Examples of Conj. IV., of which the form is puggul, have been already given in §§ 11 and 17. The verbs in the last section are כלה and סמח.

25. I have not met with the permansive form of Conj. III. t. or IV. t., nor of V. or V. t. The former of these I should from analogy expect to be sapgal; and the latter, perhaps, satpegal. Conj. VI. makes supgul; so, at least, I infer from the defective and otherwise irregular verbs in this tense which alone I have hitherto found. From הלך we have certainly *su.lu.ku*, "they were made to go," 49 I. 4, 30; and I suspect *su.qu.ru*, in an obscure passage, 39 L. 44, to be another 3 m. p. from יקר. On the other hand we have *su.qa.lu.la* and *su.qu.lu.la* from קלל in 18 I. 62, as if the form had an additional syllable. The fact, however, of the additional vowel being in different copies *a* and *u*, suggests that it is irregularly introduced; perhaps in order to distinguish to the eye a derivative of this root from one of גלל or כלל, which were both in use; or perhaps, because the liquid *l* admitted a vowel before it (see § 24 of Chap. II.) I would therefore read *suqlula*.

26. There are two verbs in a permansive tense beginning with , of which the conjugation has been doubted. In the one this character is followed by *qul*, in the other by *kun*. There can be no doubt that the verbs are שקל and שכן; but the initial character admits two readings. It may be *sit*, and the verbs would then be in Conj. I. t.; or it may be *muṣ*, which, as a variety of examples prove, may be interchanged with *mus* before ק or כ. Thus, *mus.ki* and *mu.uṣ.ki* are both used for the name of the country, *Musuk*, Heb. מֶשֶׁךְ. Thinking that the significations of the verbs in question were not such as suited the Conj. I. t., it occurred to me that *m* was here substituted for *s* as a preformative, on account of the first radical being *s*, the conjugation being VI. As, however, I have found no such tense beginning with *mu*, or *mus*, and as '*u.s'a.as.kin* is met with in Conj. V., with the preformative

*s* before a first radical *s*, I am now inclined to think that the sixth conjugation has never *m* for its preformative, and that we should read *sit.ku.nat su.bat.ṣuǹ* in 41 B. 39, "their dwelling is lying;" and in the Equinox tablet, K. 15, *sit.qu.lu*, (the day and night) "are balancing one another."

27. Of the permansive form of Conj. VI. t. I have as yet met only one example. It is in some respects a very valuable one, as it clearly establishes the existence of a permansive past, terminating in *u*. The nominative is singular, and there is no relative particle on which it could depend. It occurs in 51 I. 1, 32, where we have *la su.te.su.ru mu.ẓe.ʿe mi.ʿe.sa*, "the exit of its waters had not been made straight." The verb is ישׁר, and the form is probably *sutpegul*; but from the weakness of the first radical, this is not certain. I have not met with the permansive form of either VII. or VII. t.

## [Chapter II.]—*Nouns.*

1. In the present chapter I propose to consider the declension of Assyrian substantives and adjectives. In the following chapter I will treat of their syntax, endeavouring to show under what circumstances each of the forms, the connexion of which is explained in the present chapter, is found to be used. In a future chapter I will treat of the connexion between the primitive forms of nouns and their significations; nouns which have the same primitive form bearing, in a very great degree, the same relation in their meanings to their verbal roots.

2. I think it best to reserve the full consideration of the forms of nouns, as connected with their significations, till I have treated of the verbal forms of roots; but as I shall have to speak of these forms occasionally in connexion with declensional differences, I feel it necessary to define the terms of which I shall have to make use.

3. A perfect Assyrian root consists of three consonants, which are called its radical letters; and every Assyrian word derived from such a root consists of three consonants at least, and two vowels at least. Words which differ from one another only in their radical letters are said to be of the same

form. Thus *marẓi* and *namri* are of the same form; as are *puluḥti* and *tukulti; musaskin* and *musalbir; gabsa'ati* and *rapsa'ati*, etc.

4. If we assume a root of three letters, we can always exhibit a derivative of this root of the same form as any derivative of any other root that we may meet with. It has been the custom with Hebrew and Arabic grammarians to assume פעל as a standard root. It was chosen on account of its signifying "to do" or "to make," which seemed the most natural type of a verbal root; but it is objectionable on account of the weakness and uncertainty of sound of the second radical. I substitute for this a ג, which gives an imaginary root, but one which is very convenient. The words in the preceding section would become, by substituting the three letters of this root for the three in each of them, *pagli, pugulti, musapgil, pagla'ati;* and I take these as the names of the forms to which these words respectively belong.

5. All the forms given in the preceding section are forms of nouns; but there is a difference between them. One of the four, *musapgil*, is a *primary form*, or *theme;* the three others are *derived forms*, or *cases*. Observe that, besides the principal theme, which is singular, there are plural and dual themes, and sometimes feminine themes, singular and plural. In the present chapter I will show how the cases are derived from the theme, and to a certain extent how the theme may be recovered from one of its cases. The same derived form may, however, be derived from different primary forms. For example, *pagli* is a case, the theme of which may be *pagal, pagil*, or *pagul*. Had we only the words *marẓi* and *namri* before us, we should have no means of judging to which of three possible themes we should trace each of them. Other derivatives of the themes in question are required before we can say that the former theme is *maruẓ*, the latter *namir*.

6. The themes last given differ from *musapgil*, in that they contain no consonant but the three letters of the root. I call such themes as consist of the three radical letters, with two short vowels intervening, *simple themes*. Those which contain *any* addition, reckoning as such a quiescent letter, א, י, or ו,

which may be considered as lengthening a vowel, I call augmented themes.

7. The following are the different kinds of augmentation which an Assyrian root may have, and it may have two or more of them at the same time. First, it may have a prefixed addition consisting of one or more servile letters with a vowel or vowels, as in *musapgil;* 2nd, it may have a medial addition of a servile letter, as in *pitgul,* or in *pâgil,* where the the first syllable would be in Arabic فَا, in Hebrew פוֹ or פֹּ; 3rd, it may have the middle radical doubled, as in *paggal;* 4th, it may have the final radical doubled, as in *paglal;* or 5th, it may have one or more servile letters added at the end as in *puglân* or *paglût.* I do not consider the *at* or *it* at the end of feminine nouns as constituting an augmented theme, but as a declensional modification of a theme. The form *pugulti* in § 4 I consider to be a feminine case of *pugul,* or a case of *puglat,* the feminine theme of *pugul.*

8. There are many feminine themes of this description. Some of them are substantives denoting females, or what are considered to be such, where the true themes denote the corresponding males. Thus *ṣa.p'i.in* is "a sweeper away," applied to a king, 40 B. 25; *ṣa.pi.n'a.at* is the same, applied to a chariot, which is conventionally feminine, 41 I. 82; *mu.rap.pis,* 33 L. 9, and *mu.rap.pi.sat,* 38 L. 5, mean "enlarger," and are applied to the king and to the sceptre respectively. Adjectives, which always agree with their substantives in gender, form feminine themes of this description: they are, however, rarely used in the theme, either masculine or feminine. A few nouns are used in the masculine and feminine forms without distinction, as *puluḥ* and *pulḥat,* "fear;" and there are several which are only found in the feminine form, as *ḥirat,* "a wife;" *'irẓit,* "a land," or "the earth;" *'isat,* "fire;" *'amat* or *tamat,* "a sea."

9. Besides these, there are many feminine themes, which have a collective signification, and may very often be translated as plurals. In 42 B. 70, we have *'u.kin lib.n'a.aṣ.ṣu,* "I made fast its bricks;" *aṣ.ṣu* stands for *at.su* by a euphonic change which will be explained in § 56 of this chapter. The word

is *libnat*, the feminine theme of *libin*, which would signify "a single brick." It is not a plural, as might perhaps be thought. The plural would be, according to analogy, assuming *libin* to be a feminine, *lib.na.ʿa.ti.su*. Besides, it is declined as a feminine singular; and similar nouns are accompanied by adjectives in the feminine singular. It is, as I have stated, a collective singular, used for a plural. There are above a score of such collectives, from perfect and imperfect roots, in frequent use in the texts.

10. *All* nouns terminating in *at* or *it* servile are feminine; other nouns *may be* so. Examples of such are *ḥal*uz, "a castle" (I put the second vowel of the theme in roman, because I am not sure what it is; see § 5). In 52 I. N^o. 3, 2.16, we have *ḥa.al.ẓi ra.bi.tim*, "of the great castle;" and the plural occurs with feminine adjectives (➤➤ being used for the first syllable) 146 B. 6, 7. In 17 II. 32 *l.* we have *li.sa.an li.mut.tu*, "a sore tongue," the adjective being feminine. Other examples of feminine nouns, not so by syllabic addition (or, as Hebrew grammarians express it, by *motion*), are *ʿum*, "a mother;" *ʿistar*, "a goddess;" (I believe, a loan word, originally signifying "a star;") *ʿumman*, "an army;" *ʿuzun*, "an ear; *qat* or *qaʿat*, "a hand" (we have *qa.aṣ.ṣu*, "his hand," 49 B. 32 and 8 II. 45 *r*; the plural in the principal case is *qa.ta.tu* 8 II. 40 *r*, which proves that the *t* is radical), and all augmented forms ending in *ût*, as *sarrût*, "a kingdom" or "reign."

11. Nouns have three numbers, the singular, the dual, and the plural. The dual is not often used, and only, I believe, in the theme (§ 5); the cases of the dual do not seem to be distinguished from those of the plural. The dual is of course most frequently used for nouns which express objects that are in their nature double; but I think that I have met with duals of other nouns.

12. Nouns in the singular number have three cases in addition to the theme. I call these the first or principal case, the second case, and the third case. They are used so differently from the nominative, genitive, and accusative cases of European languages, that I think, on mature considera-

tion, the use of these terms decidedly objectionable, as likely to mislead. Their use will be explained in the following chapter. Here it will suffice to say that the first case ends in *u* or *um*: it appears from the grammatical tablets that the Assyrians considered this to be the leading form of the noun. The second case ends in *i*, *e*, or *im*; and the third in *a* or *am*. The third case is only used in the singular number.

13. Before I speak of the formation of these cases from the theme, I must go back to the classes of roots. I stated in § 3 that a perfect Assyrian root consisted of three radical consonants. It does not follow, however, that every root which consists of three consonants is perfect. Not to speak of roots having for the first radical a נ, which is often assimilated to the following consonant, and which sometimes disappears altogether; nor of surd roots, as they are called, of which the second and third radicals are the same, and which have some peculiarity consequent upon this; there are certain weak letters, the existence of which in a root renders it imperfect.

14. I consider א, ה, ו, י, and ע to be weak letters; I do not include ח in the list; preferring to regard those roots in which a weak letter is found where cognate languages have ח, as substituting an ה or ע for it. This is the case in a few roots, of which the most common are רחק, פתח, and לקח. I consider the corresponding Assyrian roots to be רעק, פתע, and לקע; as I consider the Assyrian root corresponding to the Hebrew צער to be צחר. In this root the second radical never exhibits any symptom of weakness.

15. All these letters are capable of causing the assimilation of the preceding and following vowels, which sometimes causes the contraction of two syllables into one; for when a weak letter has the same vowel before and after it, the two may coalesce, though they do not necessarily do so. An example may be given in the third person singular of the present of a verb with a weak letter for its first radical, suppose הלך. Instead of *iʿallak*, which would be the regular form, the Assyrians first substituted *i* for *a*, assimilating the vowels, and then contracted *iʿil* into simple *il*. Thus they wrote *illak*, a dissyllable, where a regular verb would have three syllables.

16. So, when the second radical was weak, they wrote *ruʿuq* for *raʿuq*, like *maruz*, and perhaps pronounced 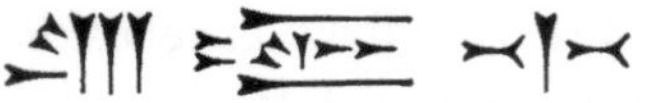 *ru.uq.ti* as a dissyllable, when the corresponding form of a perfect root would have three syllables. It must be observed, however, that when the two vowels of the form were characteristically different, an assimilation could not take place; for example, in the form pâgil, the *nomen mutantis*, no assimilation is permitted. We have 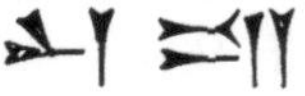 *qâʿis*, 17 I. 9, and  *qâʿi.sat*, 66 II. 9, "an ensnarer (of the living)," applied to a god and a goddess. See Gesenius under קוש, 2. Examples of assimilation when the third radical is weak will be given presently.

17. Besides these irregularities, which are common to the five weak letters, three of them, א, ו, and י, are liable to be dropped altogether. In the case of one of these being the middle radical, this may always be considered a case of contraction, and it may be so sometimes when the first or third radical disappears; but the dropping of a letter of which I speak here, and of which I will shortly give examples, is not the result of contraction. Where a perfect root would have a complete syllable, though a short one, a root beginning or ending with one of the letters in question will sometimes drop it, apparently on the principle that a short unaccented vowel, having no substantial consonant to support it, is a nullity. Such Hebrew forms as וַיָּגֶל, צֵאת, and חֵטְא will show what I mean. In the first and second, weak letters, called by Hebrew grammarians ה and י, are altogether omitted; of these letters, the latter is in Assyrian certainly ו, and the former is possibly י. In the second and third examples an א is written, but regarded as a nullity.

18. I now come to consider the different modes of declining themes. The most natural mode is simply to add to the theme the three terminations, which I will here call *u*, *i*, and *a*, reserving till the next chapter an explanation of the modifications of these terminations indicated in § 12. This natural declension is always used when the theme terminates in a strong consonant preceded by a long vowel, such as that of

the form pagâl, the infinitive, or *nomen mutationis*, or that of the augmented forms in *ân* or *ût*, whatever may precede the last syllable. It is also used when the last consonant of a monosyllabic theme is strong, provided that the theme be not derived from a surd root. Examples are *mut*, "a husband," whence *muti*; *ab*, "a father," whence *abu*, *abi*. Lastly, it is used when, the last consonant being as before, the last vowel, though short, is so completely separated from the preceding vowel, that a contraction is impossible. This happens in many forms where a double letter intervenes, as tapgal, pitgul, musapgil, etc.

19. There are three cases indicated in the preceding section in which the noun is not declined in the natural manner there indicated. 1st, The last consonant may be a weak one; 2nd, the theme may be a monosyllable derived from a surd root; and 3rd, the theme may terminate in a strong consonant, preceded by a short vowel; and this may be separated from the preceding vowel by so thin a partition that a contraction becomes possible, and generally takes place; the last vowel being dropped. I will treat of these three cases in their order.

20. If the theme terminates in a weak letter, the preceding vowel is assimilated to that of the case. Thus from *'aẓ'i*, "going out" (root יצא), we have  *'a.ẓu.'u*, 67 I. 2. 37. So we have from the theme which signifies "a crown"—it is uncertain what it is— *'a.gu'u*,  *'a.ge.'e*, and  *'a.ga.'a* in the three cases. In 30 II. 19 *r.* we have *'a.gu.'u e.lu.'u*, "the high crown," where both adjective and substantive end in weak consonants. Examples of the other cases will be found in 9 I. 5 and 21. So again from the theme for "mouth," we have 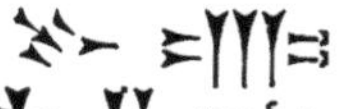 *pu.'u* in 39 II. 1 *l*, 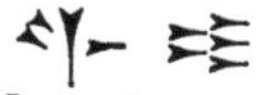 *pi.'i* 39 II. 5 *l*, and 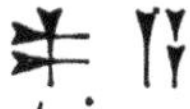 *pa.'a* 1 L. 14. Here also the actual theme is uncertain; nor is the root itself less so. Perhaps it is פאי. If so, two weak letters would come together, and a contraction would take place, as it certainly does in  *e.pi.si 'a.ḫi*, "another work," 16 I. 20.

I cannot think, however, that a contraction takes place as a matter of course, and that we should read *'agû, elû, pû,* etc., when a second vowel is expressed.

21. In monosyllabic themes derived from surd roots, or from which surd roots are derived (for I suspect that many of these themes are adopted from foreign languages, and that the verbal form, if in use, is derived from the substantive or adjective), the final consonant is repeated before the case-ending. Thus from *sar,* "a king," we have *sar.ru;* from *lib,* "a heart," *lib.bu;* from *'um,* "a womb" or "mother," *'um.mu.* A few dissyllables also double their last letter, as *'agam,* "a lake," whence *'a.gam.mu,* 41 L. 44. Perhaps this should be considered as derived from a quadriliteral root. The word is singular, for it is referred to by  *sa.*

22. The omission of the last vowel before the case-ending is very common. It always takes place in the forms pagal (but not pagâl, the infinitive), pigil, and pugul, and in augmented forms like muptagil, in which the second radical stands alone between the last two vowels. It takes place for the most part in the forms pagil and pagul, as in *n'a.am.ri,* from *namir, mar.ẓi* from *maruẓ,* and many others; but there are exceptions. In 7 I. F. 24 we have *bit.ṣu la.bi.ru,* "his old house;" older inscriptions have *la.be.ru,* 20 I. 3; and it is only in the inscriptions of Nebuchadnezzer that I find  *l'a.ab.ri,* 65 I. 2. 39. We must, however, distinguish the form pâgil, the *nomen mutantis,* and pagûl, *nomen mutati,* from pagil and pagul, which like pagal belong to the *nomen permanentis.* Both forms may belong to the same root, and to the eye may be the same. Thus  may be "ruler," *'mâ.lik,* which would make *mâ.li.ku,* and in the feminine *mâ.li.kat,* 66 II. *a.* 4; or "king," *ma.lik,* which would make *mal.ku,* 145 B. 1. So *dal.ḥu,* 74 B. 13 (whence *da.li.'ḥ.tu*), means "troubled, being in disturbance;" but *dâliḥ, dâ.li.ḥat,* means "the putter in disturbance, the disturber," 66 II. *a.* 4.

23. The three forms piggal, piggul, and puggal require special notice. The two former are derived from the third

conjugation, and the last from the fourth. It will appear very strange to an Hebraist, but it is certainly the case, that the duplication of the second radical is very apt to disappear, and the initial vowel to be the sole characteristic of the conjugation; the forms thus become pigal, pigul, and pugal, and the first two of these generally, though not always, drop the second vowel in their declension. Thus for *gissar*, the intensive form of *gasar*, we have *gisar;* and in the second case  *gis.ri*, 17 I. 1, a little more forcible than *g'a.as.ri*, which we have in the parallel text, 32 I. 1. The meaning is "bold, daring;" and we have the feminine *gi.sar.tu*, 66 II, *a*. 1. The word which is constantly used for "enemies" in the Behistun inscriptions is similarly contracted. It is *nikrutu;* in the singular it would be *nikru*, from *nikar*. So 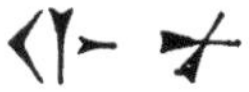 *lim.nu* in 48 B. 31 is from *liman*, for *limman*, "annoying" or "injurious." But this word gives occasion for another remark. The word *limnu* may come from a theme *limun*, as well from *liman;* from the *nomen mutati* as well as from the *nomen permanentis*. We have, in fact, in 17 II. 32. 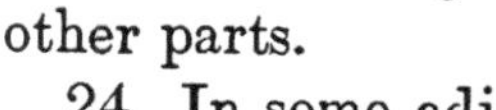 *pu.'u lim.nu*, "an injured mouth;" followed by *li.s'a.an li.mut.tu* (for *limuntu*), "an injured tongue;" the text evidently speaks of wounds. The two adjectives are distinct in the feminine singular, which would be with active signification *li.mat.tu*, but are confounded in all other parts.

24. In some adjectives, however, of these forms the final vowel of the theme is not dropped. I have met *i.sa.ru* from *isar* for *issar*. The reason of this I take to be that the initial vowel is here virtually formed by contraction. The root is ישר; and the *i* of the root and the *i* of the form combine together, so as to form an obstacle to further contraction. The retention of the vowel in *suturu* may be explained on the same principle, the root being ותר and the form supgulu, so that two *u's* combine in the first syllable. It is less easy to account for *pumalu;* perhaps the *a* is long by nature, or perhaps the liquid third radical may have rendered it desirable that a vowel should precede it. I am the more inclined to

think this, because I find *ba.ṭa.lum* in 38 II. 74 *r.*; but in 50 I. 4, 28, I find *b'a.aṭ.lu.ti.* The theme is *baṭil,* as the feminine form *ba.ṭ'i.il.tu* in 172 B. 5 proves conclusively; the *a* before the *l* must therefore be euphonic.

25. The feminine theme may be said to be formed from the principal case of the masculine by changing *u* into *at* or *it.* I am not able to give any rule by which it can be absolutely determined which vowel should be used; and in most adjectives it cannot be known, the theme not being in use, and its vowel being dropped in the cases. On the whole, however, I find *at* to be more frequently used than *it;* and I believe it is exclusively used when the theme is a *nomen mutantis* of any of the conjugations, or a monosyllable derived from a surd root.

26. The feminine cases are generally formed by adding *tu, ti,* and *ta* to the theme, properly so called; sometimes, however, by adding *u, i,* and *a* to the feminine theme. The latter mode is the only one possible, if the theme be a monosyllable derived from a surd root. Thus from *sar,* "a king," we have *sarrat,* "a queen," in the theme, and *sarratu* in the principal case. From *ḥirat,* "a wife," on the contrary, we may have *ḥirtu,* though *ḥiratu* is also in use. So also from *napsat,* "a life," theme *napis,* we have sometimes *napsatu,* but more frequently *napistu.* Adjectives almost always form their feminine cases by adding *tu,* etc. to the proper theme, at least if the root be a perfect one, though they sometimes admit the other form also. Thus we have *saplitu,* "low," as well as *sapiltu; maḥritu,* "old," as well as *maḥirtu.* From *dan,* however, we could only have *dannatu*; and, on the contrary, from *eli* only *elitu.*

27. The addition of the feminine case-endings to the theme sometimes causes a change in its last letter. For instance, *n* is changed into *t,* as in the instances already given in § 23; the masculine case 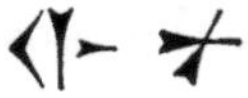 *lim.nu* corresponding to the feminine  *li.mut.tu,* for *limuntu.* So we have  *li.bit.tu,* for *libintu,* 49 B. 52. The feminine theme is *libnat.* It is probable that

*d* and *ṭ* when final were also assimilated to *t* when they preceded it in the feminine cases; but the Assyrians did not in writing distinguish these letters from *t* when terminating a syllable.

28. The letters *s*, *z*, *ṣ* and *ẓ*, were sometimes, but not necessarily, changed to *l* before the *t* of the feminine cases. I believe, however, that none of the three last-mentioned letters is ever found preceding the *t*. It is changed either into *s* or into *l*. Thus in 17 II. 27 *l.* we have *ma.r'u.us.tu*, evidently the feminine of *mar.ẓu*. In 16 I. 76 we have *ma.r'u.us.ta;* and in a parallel text, 27 I. 92, we have *ma.ru.ul.ta*. In the upper part of 27 I. 10 we have *ris.ti* for *riẓti;* and, again, in 12 I. 90 we have *ri.ḥ'i.il.ti*, evidently for *riḥiẓti*. As to *s* itself we have *lu.b'u.us.ti*, "clothing," 38 II. 48 *m.*, but much oftener  *lu.bul.ti*. A comparison of the text last quoted with 67 II. 62 must, I think, satisfy every one that these are the same word. I at one time read the initial character *ṭib*, and translated it, "what was dyed with;" and I perceive that Dr. Oppert and M. Ménant have done the same; but here we have *lubulti matisunu*, "clothing of their people," just as in 38 II. 48, 49 *m.* we had *lubusti ilutisunu*, "clothing of their godships." It follows that *birmi*, which usually follows *lubulti*, does not signify a dye-stuff but a material; no doubt "wool," ϝερϝιον; compare *vellus* for *velves* (as *mollis* for *molvis*). The other word, which is commonly joined with *birmi*, 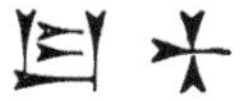, *ku.kum*, or *kum?* for I suspect that the first character is a nonphonetic determinative of names of plants, I take to mean "flax" or "cotton."

29. The Assyrians formed their plurals in several ways, of which I will treat in succession. Some plurals are formed by the addition of *n* for the theme, and  *nu* and  *ne* for the case ending, to the third case of the singular. These are sometimes written in full phonetic characters; but very often the theme, or the principal case of the singular, is accompanied by the character . This combination must be understood to denote the proper plural form, which the reader is presumed to know;—and this constitutes one of the chief

difficulties in reading Assyrian. Sometimes, however, as a guide to him  is added, which I read *ne;* because, while *ne* and *ni* were expressed alike, *te* and *ti* were distinguished; and it is  *te* which is used similarly to  when the plural theme terminates in *t*.

30. Examples are  *dup.p'a.a.ne,* "clay tablets," K. 116; where K. 131 has  and K. 136  only. All these tablets contain the same text. So we have  *ḥal.ẓa.ne,* "castles." 32 I. 50 and  *ḥal.zu* with plural sign (to be read *ḥalẓan* or *ḥalẓane*) 146 B. 6, 7, 8. Observe that the 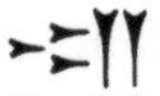 prefixed to this word is a nonphonetic determinative. In 28 I. 1, 12, we have *ḥar.s'a.a.nu,* "woods;" and in 145 B. 2, *ḥar.sa.ne,* in the second case. In 39 II. 11 *l., pa.ʿa.nu.* from *pa.ʿa* (§ 20) is "mouths," as the Accadian equivalent proves; but in 17 II. 31, *pa.ʿan* is used for "a face;" it takes, however, a plural adjective. In 33 L. 6, *e.mu.q'a.an,* "powers," and in 30 II. 14 *r., ri.s'a.an,* "heads," are written in full. The singulars *emuq* and *ris* are in common use.

31. The plural in *an* only appears in a limited number of substantives, some of which admit also different plurals. It is, I believe, never used in the case of an adjective or of a substantive which is feminine by termination. Several plurals in *an* are, however, feminine, as well as the singulars from which they are formed, as appears from the adjectives which accompany them. Such are *emuqan, risan,* and *ḥalẓan,* cited in § 30. It would, therefore, be incorrect to say that *an* was the termination of the masculine plural. I believe that originally, in the language from which all of the Semitic family have diverged, the addition of *am* or *av* to the singular theme rendered it plural; and that *at* was added as a feminine termination to both singular and plural. Thus the theme alone was of *either* gender, as was the plural in *am* or *av;* but *at* in the singular and *avat* in the plural were distinctively feminine. From the original *am,* which was retained in Phenician, came the Hebrew *im,* and the Assyrian and Himyaritic *an;* from

the *av* came the Egyptian *u*. The Aramaic and Arabic forms, in which both vowel and consonant are different from what they were originally, are probably of later origin than the others.

32. Another form of the plural ends in *t* in the theme, and in *tu* and *ti* in the cases. Originally, I conceive, as I stated in the last section, this termination was *avat* or *awat*, and was peculiar to feminines by termination. This was in time changed to *aʿat*, sometimes contracted to *ât*; but in the cases there is generally, though not always, an  between what belongs to the theme properly so called and the preceding; and this should, I conceive, be sounded as a distinct syllable. In Arabic, as well as in Masoretic Hebrew, the termination اَت or וֹת is pronounced as one syllable, but the quiescent letter which is always inserted indicates contraction; and the Hebrew *ḥolem* manifestly stands for *awa*.

33. This plural in *at* is almost always used for feminine adjectives, and for substantives feminine by termination. It is also used for many substantives which are feminine otherwise than by termination. Thus we have *ʿum.ma.n'a.at*, "armies," 146 B. 4, and *ʿum.ma.na.te*, 151 B. 12, from *ʿumman*. In 37 II. 11; the plural of "mouths" is stated to be  *pa.ʿa.tum* or *pa.ʿa.nu*; *pu.ʿu* in the singular and *pa.ʿan* have masculine adjectives, 17 II. 32 and 31 *l*. I presume, however, that *pa.ʿa.tu* would take a feminine one. Irregularities of this kind are found in all languages.

34. Examples of this plural when the singular is feminine by termination are *ẓi.ra.ʿa.te* "high, supreme," 33 L. 6; *e.la.tum*, "high," 30 II. 14 *r.*; *dan.na.ʿa.ti*, "strong," 146 B. 6; *mar.ẓa.ʿa.ti*, "difficult of access," 146 B. 7; all which adjectives are in concord with the plurals in *an* mentioned in § 31; *ḥi.ra.ti ra.ba.ʿa.ti*, "great wives," 153 B. 12, from *ḥirat*. This is a theme feminine by termination; but it must not be supposed that *ḥir* would mean "a husband." The latter I take to be *ḥa.ʿar*, whence  *ḥ'a.a.ʿa.ru*, 36 II. 40 *l.*; *ḥi.ra.tum* and *ḥ'i.ir.tum* in line 43 *l.*

are equivalent forms (see § 26), or perhaps dialectic variations, of the principal case of *ḥirat*, "a wife," which is in the same relation to the former theme as *din* or *dinat*, "a law" or "judgment," to *daʻan*, "a lawgiver" or "judge."

35. Besides the two plurals of which I have hitherto spoken, which I take to have been the original forms common to all the Semitic languages, there are other forms which the Assyrians appear to have developed after their separation from those who used the other languages of the family. One of these is the masculine plural in *ut* in the theme, and *utu* and *uti* in the cases. It differs from the feminine plural last mentioned in having *u* in place of *a* at the end of the theme, and  *ʻu* for  *ʻa*. The *ʻu* is, however, oftener omitted than expressed, contrary to what takes place in the case of *ʻa*.

36. This plural is used by all adjectives and by the *nomina mutantis* of all the conjugations. All these admit feminines by termination; and it may be laid down as a general rule that a masculine plural in *ut* can be changed into a feminine plural in *at*; or if not into that, into *et* (see § 37); but many feminine plurals in *at* do not admit masculine plurals in *ut*. For example, *sarraʻate* is good Assyrian for "queens," but for "kings" they would say *sarrane*; *sarruti* would come from *sarrut*, "a kingdom" or "reign." Examples of these plurals need not be given here. They will appear in the following chapter, and are everywhere to be met with.

37. Some feminine ṣubstantives and adjectives form their plurals in *etu, ete*, in place of *atu, ate*; or, perhaps, I should say, as well as in *atu, ate*. In 33 I. 10 we have *ʻa.na ru.q'e.e.ti*, "to distant places (he fled);" in 153 B. 12 we have *is.re.ti nam.ra.ʻa.ti*; the latter word is certainly an adjective in the feminine plural, "shining," or the like. Whatever, then, may be the meaning of *isreti*, it is clearly used as a substantive feminine and plural. Nebuchadnezzar speaks E. I. H. 3. 13 of having made and purified (?) the *isreʻet* of Babylon, and l. 65 those of Borsippa. The spelling is not exactly the same in any two of the three passages, but there can be no reasonable doubt that the word is the same. These examples establish the existence of the feminine plural in *et*; and I confess

that I cannot affirm with confidence anything more than that it exists.

38. I may, however, mention a conjecture which has occurred to me. Can *et* be a feminine plural of adjectives used in place of *ât* when they are not accompanied by substantives, but are used as substantives, with "persons, places, or things," understood after them? This explains the *ruqeti* of 33 I. 10, and the *muqalleti* of E. I. H. 10, 16, "may I not sinfully incline (*'ar.si*, from רשע) to the blasphemous persons!" the feminine plural being used to express contempt. In a similar context in 68 I. 2. 30, *ḥi.ṭe.ti*, "sinful persons," is substituted. It explains also the  of N.R. 8, where the adjective *an.ne.ti* cannot be attached to the substantive which follows it; but we must translate, "these (are) the countries;" and so in similar contexts. But how, it may be asked, can *isreti* be explained on this supposition? May it not be the feminine plural of ישר *isar*, meaning "the straight places, the avenues?" "lightsome avenues" well suits the context in 153 B. 12; and Nebuchadnezzar may have said, "avenues of Babylon (and Borsippa) I caused to be made, and I cleansed, or kept clean." In a future chapter I will give reasons for assigning to זנן the primary sense of "cleansing." It does not appear to me that the spelling of *isret* is inconsistent with its derivation from *isar*. So far as I have observed  *is* is preferentially used when a word begins with a radical letter, and  when it begins with a servile *i*. In the Assyrian text, and in one of the Babylonian ones, the word begins with ; in the other Babylonian one the first syllable is expressed by  *e.is*, which, however, may have only meant that the initial *i* was very long, and which, on the authority of the other two passages, we may safely pronounce to be bad spelling. I do not recollect any place in which *et* occurs as a formative of the feminine plural, which is inconsistent with the theory which I have here proposed. Nevertheless, I am far from having the same confidence in it as I have in my other statements. I can only say that if the difference between *et* and *ât* be not

what I have suggested, I am quite unable to explain what that difference is.

39. A very common form of the Assyrian plural remains to be spoken of, namely, that in which no syllable is added to form it, but the plural cases are either the same as the singular, or modifications of the singular forms. The distinction between the two numbers is indeed sometimes made by a change of case, as will be shown in the following chapter; but even this is often not to be perceived, and the context becomes our only guide. I will first give examples in which the singular and plural are identical.

40. As this identity of the singular and plural is what most persons would consider very improbable, it is necessary to give some very clear instances of it. I do not rely on such a passage as *'i.lu.ti.su.nu*, "of their godships," already quoted in § 28. In fact, *'iluti* is here singular; derived nouns in *ut* not admitting a plural. In 15 I. 106, 113, it occurs joined to an adjective in the feminine singular. Neither do I rely on *lib.bi.k'u.un*, "your hearts," 9 I. 19, though I have myself no doubt that *libbi* is here plural, because words which are certainly singular occur elsewhere, accompanied by plural affixes. I will, however, bring forward clear instances of plurals, the same as the singular, accompanied by plural adjectives.

41. In 152 B. 2, 1, we have  *ṣuk.ki nak.lu.ti*, which I would translate "well-built houses;" but whatever be the exact translation, it is clear that *ṣukki* is here used as a plural, and equally clear that it is the second case of the singular. Again, we have in 41 B. 57, *mal.ki la.bi.ru.ti*, "ancient kings," another example that cannot be contested. And so in 41 I. 74, *s'u.u.ri ma.ru.ti*, "fatted oxen;" in 144 B. 10, 11, *yu.me ma.'h.du.ti*, "many days."

42. In other cases forms identical with the singular are substituted for the theme with a plural sign. Thus in 38 B. 67, we have  for "gates;" in another copy of the same inscription, 50 B. 74, *ba.bi* is substituted. This noun

admits also a plural in *at*. We have in 39 L. 22, *ba.ba.ʿa.ti*. Variations of this sort occur in almost all languages; and there does not appear to me to be any difference in the use of these plurals, so that one could be called definite and the other indefinite.

43. A similar example occurs as to , *ba.tul*, with the determinative of males prefixed, and the plural sign added, 21 I. 43; in 22 I. 109, *ba.tu.li*, with the same determinative, but without the plural sign, is substituted. To both of these words is added *ba.tu.la.ti* with the determinative of females  prefixed. The meaning is obviously "pure boys" and "pure girls." Other instances occur in which two nouns are coupled together, one of which is evidently plural from its form, while the two are evidently in the same number. Even if the passage 21 I. 43 did not exist, we might infer that *ba.tu.li* in 22 I. 109 was plural, from its being coupled with *ba.tu.la.ti*, which is manifestly so.

44. The same principle applied to the formula "oxen" and "sheep" gives us two more plurals of this sort. In 67 II. 41 we have , the monogram for an ox, followed by , the plural sign, and 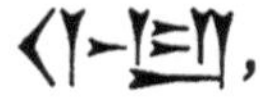, *ù*, the copulative conjunction; then comes *ẓ'e.e.ne*, "sheep," which the context proves to be a plural. In 41 I. 82 we have, in place of this, *rag.ge ù ẓe.ne*, and in E.I.H. 2. 28 *r'a.ag.ga ù ẓ'e.e.nim*. The construction, it will be observed, in the last two passages, is different. Surely, it is a fair inference that *raggi* is plural as well as *ẓ'e.e.ni*. I am rather disposed to draw a further inference, namely, that *ʿalap*, which corresponds to , was only used in the singular number, and that *raggu* was used as its plural. On this question, however, I do not think that I have evidence which warrants a *positive* opinion.

45. The above examples, to which might be added many others, must, I think, satisfy every one that the Assyrians had a plural of the same form with the singular; though there was some slight difference in the use of the cases. I now proceed to consider plurals which are modifications of the singular, not identical with it. The principle of these

modifications is that in dissyllables, the last of which is not lengthened by a quiescent letter, the singular inclines to have the accent on the former syllable, and the plural on the latter. Monosyllabic themes admit no such modification; nor those in which, the middle radical being weak and the two vowels the same, they coalesce in the declension into one, as צאן, *ẓiᶜin*, whence *ẓenu*. Nor again is this distinction possible where the last vowel of the theme is necessarily long, as in *batul*, § 43.

46. As a general rule, however, such a noun as *pigil* would add its case-ending, in the singular to *pigil* with the accent on the first syllable, and would thus form *piglu*, etc., with the second vowel suppressed; while the plural would retain the second vowel; and would perhaps admit also another change consequent on this. For example *nakru* is used for "an enemy," but *nakiri* for "of the enemies," the theme being *nakir*.

47. I have spoken of this distinction being rendered more marked by another change consequent on this. The Assyrians were accustomed to double the consonant of an accented syllable. This is the reason why the second radical is commonly doubled in the present of the first conjugation, as in *i.qab.bi*, "he says," and numerous other instances, which must not be supposed to be Pihel forms. In conformity with this usage the last consonant of the noun is often doubled in the plural. Thus, in 43 I. 43, we have *sal.gu na.ḥal.lim*, "the snows of the valleys;" while in the parallel text, 40 I. 77, we have *na.'ḥ.li*, "of the valley."

48. Where the first radical was a very weak one, that admitted of being altogether dropped, it was, I think, dropped in plurals of this kind. Instances of this are neceesarily rare; and I am not sure that there are sufficient to establish the usage. I remark, however, that in the same nouns that could drop the initial syllable in the plural, that syllable is dropped in the singular when the noun is in what Hebrew grammarians call the state of construction. It may have appeared strange that I have spoken of the noun, when without a case-ending, as the theme and not as the construct form. I have done this

advisedly. It will be seen in the following chapter that the second case is repeatedly used,—almost, if not quite, as often as the theme,—where the Hebrews would use the construct form; and it will be seen also that the theme is repeatedly used where the Hebrews would use the absolute form. If I were, therefore, to give the name of construct form to the theme, I should be using a term that would certainly mislead. I think, however, that the theme was in some instances pronounced differently when it did and when it did not indicate a state of construction; that the theme pigil, for instance, was pronounced pigíl when in construction, and pígil when not so; and I think that, consequent upon this difference, when the first radical was so weak that the first syllable might be dropped, it was dropped when the noun was in construction.

49. Taking, then, *ʿagal* or *ʿagil* as a type of such a noun as I have described, I think we should have for the theme when absolute *ʿágal* or *ʿágil*; for the theme in construction, *gal* or *gil*; for the first case of the singular, *ʿaglu*; and for the first case of the plural, *galu* or *gilu*. Such is the conclusion at which I have arrived by induction; but I give it doubtingly; the examples being few, and what others would probably explain differently from what I do. I think there are three nouns following this type which occur with and without the initial syllable, namely, those which signify "a son," "a servant," and "a bull." From the first we have *ʿa.b'i.il.su*, "his son," E. I. H. 1. 33; *ʿab.lam*, "son," 51 I. No. 1, 2. 16, in one of the copies, the other having the usual monogram for "son." Without the initial syllable we have, I think, *ba.lu.sa*, "her sons," in 66 II. 5. It must be owned, however, that this passage is obscure; and others would interpret it otherwise. On Hebrew and Greek transcriptions but little reliance can be placed, so far as the vowels are concerned; but I am disposed to take "Baladan" as authority for the theme being *ʿabal* as well as *ʿabil*.

50. As respects the second noun, we have in 95 B. 6, *ʿar.du* for "servant," before *kan.su*, "obedient," where 145 B. 24 has the monogram 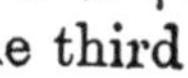; also in 10 II. 15 *l.* we have *ʿar.da*, "a servant," in the third case. On the other hand, in 1 L. 1,

we have, I think (but I admit that there is no positive proof, and others take it differently), *rid* for "servant of (Assur)." As for the third word, *r'i.i.mu* is given in Porter's transcript of portions of the E. I. H. inscription as the equivalent of , 3. 59. This group certainly signifies "bulls." On the other hand, *'ar.mi* is a singular noun in the second case, denoting some male animal; and it appears to me probable that it is the singular of the other word. A fourth example may perhaps be the plural *ni.si* from *anis*, see § 57. This is a case in which the few examples bearing on the question appear to throw light on one another. Without, therefore, maintaining that the positions advanced in the last three sections are established, I think that they are highly probable; and I state them here in order that they may be tested by further examples, should such occur.

51. It remains for me to speak of the dual number of nouns; but here again I confess that I can only speak doubtingly. It appears to me that a dual theme in *a*, formed precisely as the third case of the singular, must be admitted to exist. I have only met with it, however, in a few nouns; *qa.ta*, "hands," (where the *t* is radical, for we have the plurals *qa.ta.tu*, *qa.ta.te* in 6 II. 40, 41), *se.pa*, "feet," *bir.ka*, "knees," and perhaps *ma.ta* or *ma.da*, "peoples." I once thought that a distinction might be established between the second case of the dual and that of the plural; but I rather think now that such is not the case.

*Appendix on the possessive pronominal affixes.*

52. It has been necessary in several places to assume a knowledge on the part of the reader of the possessive pronominal affixes attached to nouns. A complete knowledge of these affixes is essential to a grammatical knowledge of the inflexions of nouns; and I believe that no complete and correct list of them has yet been published. I will therefore endeavour to supply the deficiency in the following sections.

53. The affixes attached to the case endings are always

expressed by the addition of one or two characters to those which express the noun. They are the following:

1. s. *'a*; instead of which we find more commonly after the second case *ya*, "my."

2. s.m. *ka*, and f. *ki*, "thy."

3. s.m. or *su*, "his," f. or *sa*, "her."

1. p. *ni*, "our."

2. p.m. *ku.nu*; f. *ki.na*, "your."

3. p.m. *su.nu* or *s'u.un*; f. *si.na* or *s'i.in*, "their."

is used for the affix of the 3. p. of both genders; it is interchanged with *s'u.un*, cf. 164 B. 23 and 165 B. 17; and with *s'i.in*, cf. 38 B. 69 and 46 B. 76.

54. The affix of the 3 s.m. after an unaccented *u* is often shortened to *s*; this happens most commonly after the feminine first case *tu*; and the *tus* is then expressed by .

On the other hand, after an accented *u*, an additional character is generally introduced after the first case, as it would be written without the affix. This character is or before *'a*, the affix of the first person singular (which, however, is not to be read as an additional syllable) and before those of the second and third persons *uk* and *us* respectively. Before the affix of the first person plural I should from analogy expect *un*, but I have as yet met with no example of it.

55. Although this reduplication, which may be compared with that of § 48, may be used after the *u* of the first case whenever it is not preceded by a *t*, formative of the feminine; there are some words, after which it occurs, which should be particularly noticed. Such are the prepositions, *kirbu*, "within," *ẓiru*, "upon," and *panu*, "before," which are used before pronominal affixes in place of the *kirib*, *ẓir*, and *pan*, which are used before nouns. Examples are *ẓi.r'u.u.'a*, "upon me," 41 I. 45; *pan.uk.ki*, "before thee (f.)," 66 II. 2. 7, 8; in a similar inscription addressed to Nebo, 85 L. 15, *pan.uk.ka*;

*k'i.ir.b'u.us.sa*, "within it," E. I. H. 10, 12; *ẓi.r'u.us.su.un*, "upon them," 39 I. 78. Such also is the noun of non-existence *yanu*, whence *ya.n'u.u.ʿa*, "I am not," 42 II. 14 *r.*; and in the two preceding lines, *ya.n'uk.ka*, "thou art not," *ya.n'u.us.su*, "he is not." I may also notice *ki.bi.t'u.uk.ka*, "it is thy will" or "in pursuance of thy will," E. I. H. 10, 1; *ki.bi.tus.su*, "in pursuance of his will," 16 B. 141. The *t* of this word is radical. I think it is invariably used of the divine will, which was not to be resisted.

56. The affixes annexed to the theme are the same as those annexed to the case endings, except for the first person singular; and for the third person in all its forms, when the theme ends in a dental or sibilant. In the last case, *ṣ* is substituted for *s* in the affix; the preceding consonant being sometimes retained, sometimes omitted, but most frequently changed into another *ṣ*. That is to say, the affixes of the third person given above can never follow , , , , , , , , or ; or any character, the value of which terminates with any of these; but after these letters  is substituted for ,  for , and  for 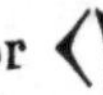. Examples are *ḥi.r'i.it.ṣu*, "its ditch," E.I.H. 6. 60, or *ḥi.ri.ṣu*, 65, I. 2. 7, or *ḥi.r'i.is.ṣu*. E.I.H. 6. 30. All these are used in parallel texts, and are evidently equivalent. The last of the three forms is, however, the commonest. Other examples are *ru.pu.uṣ.ṣu*, "its breadth," from *rupus*, 7 I.F. 23; *e.pi.ṣu.un*, "their work," from *epis*, 132 B. 18. It is needless to multiply them, as they are everywhere to be met with. To the rule here laid down there are no exceptions; and the student, if he thinks that he sees it violated, may be quite sure that he is mistaken as to his reading of the text.

57. The affix of the first person attached to a theme which ends in a consonant is generally *i*; sometimes *a* is substituted, but only, I believe, in Babylonian inscriptions. Examples are *ʿa.ba*, "my father," E. I. H. 7, 48; *b'i.e.la*, "my lord," 66 I. 18. This affix, whether *i* or *a*, is not represented by a separate character, but by a change of the last

character of the theme, which, with this affix, is the same as the second or third case. Examples are very numerous; but they appear to have been overlooked, or set down as mistakes, by others. I will give a very few out of a long list. In 151 B. 16, Sargon says, *'ak.ẓu.ra 'us.ma.ni*, "I prepared my camp." Five lines after, speaking of his enemy, he says, *ik.ẓu.ra 'us.m'a.an.su*, "he prepared his camp." These translations may be only approximate; but there can be no doubt as to the "I," "my," "he," and "his." Again, *b'i.in.ti 'ad.din.su*, 145 B. 18, is, "my daughter I gave to him;" *'u.s'a.az.bil ra.ma.ni*, 49 I. 4, 11, is, "I caused myself to carry." Both these texts are correct as they stand; and the *emendations* that have been proposed would render them the contrary. We have also *qa.ti* for "my hand," 10 I. 98; *mu.ti*, "my husband, 10 II. 4 *l*, *'as.sa.ti*, "my wife," do. 10 *l*. This last is for *an.sa.ti*, the feminine theme of *anis*, "a man," from which I derive the plural *ni.si* mentioned in § 50. All these nouns occur with other affixes, *qa.aṣ.ṣu*, "his hand," 49 B. 32, *m'u.uṣ.ṣu*, "her husband, 10 II. 2 *l*.; and *'as.sa.ti.su*, "to his wife," do. 9 *l*.

58. The use of *ṣu* for "her" in this ancient text must not be passed over. We have also *'at.ta* for "thou (woman);" do. 10 *l*. This fragment of the ancient laws of Assyria is probably the oldest text in the language that we possess. The tablet, indeed, is not older than the seventh century B.C.; but it is a transcript of one of the highest antiquity. Now, it is very remarkable that, in the Hebrew Pentateuch, the masculine pronoun of the third person singular is often used for the feminine; that is to say, if we go by the written letters and neglect the Qeri and vowel points. The distinction between the pronouns of the second person, masculine, and feminine is also in several places only made in the vowel points. I think it is a fair inference from this, that in the earliest stage of the language "thou" and "thy," masculine and feminine, had but one representative; and that "his" and "her" were expressed alike, as they were in Latin, and as they still are in the languages derived from it.

# INDEX.

STEPHEN AUSTIN, PRINTER, HERTFORD.

# ROYAL ASIATIC SOCIETY.

## PROCEEDINGS

OF

## THE FORTY-THIRD ANNIVERSARY MEETING OF THE SOCIETY,

*Held on the 4th June*, 1866,

SIR EDWARD COLEBROOKE, BART., M.P.,

PRESIDENT, IN THE CHAIR.

---

THE following Report of the Council was read by the Secretary :—

The Council of the Royal Asiatic Society have much satisfaction in being able to state that the effective condition of the Society is more promising than it has been for some years past, and that its immediate prospects are sufficiently encouraging to ensure a marked extension of the scope and usefulness of its operations. For not only has there been a steady preponderance of accessions to the ranks of its members over the corresponding losses through death or retirement; but, apart from this source of increased prosperity, other additions to its resources are forthcoming.

The losses by death during the past session amount to eight resident and seven non-resident members, and to four resident and four non-resident members by retirement. The provisions of Art. XLth of the Society's regulations respecting defaulters have been put in force against three members. The elections during the same period have been, of resident members, fourteen, and of non-resident members, fifteen.*

* *Elections.—Resident :* Major E. Bell; E. B. Cowell, Esq.; Dadabhai Naoroji, Esq.; Sir F. H. Goldsmid, Bart., M.P.; Col. C. S. Guthrie; E. Isaac, Esq.; Capt. W. R. M. Holroyd; Major-Gen. W. Lang; E. Maltby, Esq.; E. H.

Foremost among the distinguished members whose loss the Council record with regret, stands the name of His late Majesty *Leopold I., King of the Belgians*, who was one of the earliest members of the Society, and for upwards of thirty-five years one of its Vice-Patrons. The warm interest taken by His Majesty, during the many years of his residence in England previous to his accession to the Belgian throne, in the various literary and scientific institutions of this country, and the enlightened liberality with which he promoted their object, suffered no abatement from his attendance to the cares of royalty or the infirmities of advancing age. His appreciation of oriental studies was evinced by his continuing to be to the very last the most liberal subscriber to the Oriental Translation Fund.

Among the other names of members recently deceased, the Society laments that of *Mr. Alexander Kinloch Forbes*, of the Bombay Civil Service. Mr. Forbes was a ripe student of oriental literature, and always took a keen interest in the proceedings of the Society. His service in India commenced on the 15th of November, 1843, when he first arrived in Bombay, having been appointed a member of the Civil Service there on the 30th of December in the year previous. He passed quickly in Hindustani and Marathi, and after being successively assistant to the collectors of Ahmednagar and Khandesh, and Assistant-Judge and Session Judge at Ahmedabad and Surat, he was, on the 26th of

Palmer, Esq.; V. Pleignier, Esq.; T. C. Plowden, Esq.; J. R. Robinson, Esq. G. Smith, Esq. *Non-Resident:* Dr. A. Bastian; J. Burgess, Esq.; C. R. Cama, Esq.; the Hon. G. Campbell; R. C. Childers, Esq.; H. H. the Rao of Kutch; J. d'Alwis, Esq.; Dr. J. R. Dickson; L. H. Griffin, Esq.; Kursondas Mahdewdas, Esq.; W. G. Palgrave, Esq.; Babu Siva Prasâd; R. Temple, Esq.; Dr. A. Vámbéry; W. Young, Esq.

*Retirements.—Resident:* Rev. T. F. Crosse; H. W. Hammond, Esq.; Major J. G. Stephens; General Sir W. F. Williams. *Non-Resident:* Prof. M. Amari; Dr. F. Dini; Count C. Marcolini; N. J. Samsâmu 'd Dowlah, Bahâdur. *Struck off:* C. Bruce, Esq.; G. R. Haywood, Esq.; Dr. R. G. Latham.

*Deaths.—Resident:* H. M. Leopold I., King of the Belgians; N. Bland, Esq.; J. R. Butlin, Esq.; J. Constantine, Esq.; Capt. P. Maughan; Rev. J. Reynolds; A. Spottiswoode, Esq.; T. Thornton, Esq. *Non-Resident:* Dr. H. Barth Rajah V. L. P. N. of Conjeveram; G. W. Earl, Esq.; A. K. Forbes, Esq.; Col. de Havilland; Juggonnathji Sunkersett, Esq.; Capt. A. Troyer.

March, 1851, appointed Commissioner at Surat to introduce the Act to enable improvements to be made in towns. Mr. Forbes discharged the delicate duty of making this law first applicable in Western India with much tact and judgment, and received the thanks of Government for his services. In August, 1852, he was appointed Political Agent in the Mahî Kântâ, and went to Europe on furlough in 1854, when he published his Râs Mâlâ, or Hindu Annals of Gujarât, a work which Sir H. Lawrence pronounced to be superior to that of Tod. Mr. Forbes returned to Bombay in November, 1856, and was appointed Agent for the Governor at Surat. One of his most important duties there was the trial for treason and murder of a large number of persons concerned in the Muhammadan outbreak of May, 1857. He had also to conduct a confidential investigation, which he managed so well as again to merit the thanks of Government. In October, 1859, he received charge of the Political Agency in Kâtiâwâr, and ably directed affairs during the serious insurrection of the Bâghars, who, having been driven by the force under Col. Scobie out of Okhâmaṇḍal, took up a strong position in the fort of Abhpûra, which was stormed by Major Honner on the 18th December, 1859. In March, 1861, Mr. Forbes was appointed Acting Secretary to Government in the Political and Persian Departments, Puisne Judge of the Sadr Dîwânî in the December following, and Judge of the High Court of Judicature in August, 1862. He was also at the time of his death Vice-Chancellor of the University of Bombay.

In *Mr. Nathaniel Bland* the Society has lost a most zealous member and valuable contributor to the Journal. Mr. Bland was a descendant of Francis Crumpe, Esq., of Randalls Park, Surrey, who married Dorothea, daughter of Mr. Bland, of Derriquin Castle, in the county of Kerry. The issue of this marriage, Mr. Nathaniel Crumpe, took the name of Bland, and inherited property in Ireland, which, as well as Randalls Park, descended to Mr. Nathaniel Bland, the subject of this notice. The Blands were an ancient Yorkshire family, who settled in Ireland about the middle of the 17th century. Mr. N. Bland went to Christ Church, Oxford, as a gentleman commoner in 1823, and took his degree of B.A. on the 16th of June, 1825. He subsequently devoted himself to the study of oriental languages, and became one of the first Persian scholars of the day. His first contribution to the Journal of the Society was an account of the Âtesh Kedah, a biographical book on the Persian poets, by Hajjî Lutf Ali Beg, of Ispahân, which was read on June 24th, 1843, and forms Article xxxiii. of vol. vii. This article shews a great amount of reading, and is very useful for reference, though it is, perhaps, to be regretted that a complete list of the names of the 842 poets whose works are noticed in the Âtesh Kedah, was not appended. Mr. Bland's next paper was a Letter to R. Clarke, Esq., the Hon. Secretary of the Society, on the Oriental MSS. in the Library of Eton College, and was read on the 16th of March, 1844. It will be found at p. 104 of vol. viii. of the Society's Journal. This paper was followed by one "On the earliest Persian Biography of Poets, by Muhammad 'Aufî, and on some other works of the class called Tazkirat ul Shu'arâ," read on the 17th November, 1846, and occurring at p. 111 of vol. ix. of the Journal. If some late writers of eminence in this country had known these papers, it is probable they would have been more guarded in their assertions as to the sterility of Persian literature. On the 18th of June, 1847, an interesting paper by Mr. Bland, "On the Persian Game of Chess," was read and subsequently printed as Article I. of the 13th vol. of the Journal. Mr. Bland's last contribution to the Journal was read on the 5th of March, 1853. The subject is "The Muhammadan Science of Tâbîr, or Interpretation of Dreams." It forms Article IX. of vol. xvi. Besides these papers, Mr. Bland published in 1844, the Makhzan ul Asrâr, "The Treasury of Secrets," being the first of the five Poems, or Khamsah, of Shaikh

Nizâmî of Ganjah, which he edited from ancient MSS. for the Society for the Publication of Oriental Texts. He had intended that the text should be accompanied by various readings and a selected commentary, but these never appeared. Mr. Bland died on the 10th of August, 1865, and thus some other works on which he was engaged have not been completed. Among these were editions of the Sihar i Ḥalâl, "Lawful Magic," and the Shama' va parwânah, "The Taper and Moth," by Maulavî Ahlî of Shîrâz.

*The Rev. James Reynolds* was the son of Cornwall Reynolds, Esq., of Clapton. This gentleman had sailed as a naval surgeon with Admiral Lord Nelson, who honoured him by standing godfather to his son, an elder brother of the subject of this notice. James Reynolds was educated at a private school, and he afterwards entered as a sizar at St. Catharine's Hall, Cambridge, where he obtained a fair knowledge of the Arabic language. He took his Bachelor's degree in 1826, was ordained deacon in 1827 by Dr. Howley, and priest in the following year by Bishop Blomfield. The late Lord Munster appointed Mr. Reynolds his private chaplain, and in the year 1837 obtained for him the Perpetual Curacy of St. Mary's Hospital Chapelry, which he held up to the time of his death. Mr. Reynolds became Secretary to the Oriental Translation Fund early in 1837, and retained the office until the close of its operations. He died at Great Ilford, in Essex, on the 19th of April last, in the 62nd year of his age, after a long decline of bodily powers. He was the author of the following works:—A History of the Temple of Jerusalem, translated from the Arabic of the Imâm Jalâlu 'd dîn al Siûtî, with notes and dissertations, 1837. A Memoir of the late Sir Gore Ouseley, Bart., prefixed to that gentleman's posthumous work, "Biographical Notices of Persian Poets, with critical and explanatory remarks," 1845. The Kitâb i Yamînî; "Historical Memoir of the Sultan Mahmud of Ghazna," translated from the Persian version of Al 'Utbî, 1859.

In the death of *Dr. Heinrich Barth* the kindred sciences of ethnology, geography, and glossology, have lost one of their most distinguished and devoted investigators. He was born at Hamburgh on the 16th of February, 1821, and gave promise at a very early period of that extraordinary aptitude for the acquisition of languages which was subsequently so useful to him in his perilous travels. At the University of Berlin he applied himself chiefly to the study of classical philology and antiquities, and the lectures of Carl Ritter inspired in him the desire of visiting those countries in which the great dramas of classical antiquity had been enacted. With this view he set out, at the beginning of 1845, on a three years' journey round the coasts of the Mediterranean; but he had only been able to bring out the first volume of his travels when he accepted an offer of joining the scientific expedition which the English Government had decided on sending to the Sudan, in the summer of 1849. That he, the first European, reached Ágades, the principal place of the oasis of Aïr, in the autumn of the following year, and from thence traced his course of geographical conquest by way of Kátsena and Kanó to Kúkawa, making this the basis for his further extensive excursions to Adamaua, Musgu, Baghirmi, and other territories in the vicinity of Lake Tsad;—that he arrived at Timbuktu on the 7th of September, 1853, and after a seven months' perilous sojourn in that city of the desert, returned to Kúkawa, and thence to Tripoli, the point from which he had started five years and a half before,—and that he accomplished all this without ever using or needing the services of an interpreter: these are facts which have placed the name of Dr. Barth amongst those of the most daring and successful explorers of all times and all countries. The five volumes in which the account of his travels is contained will long remain the chief, and in many respects the only, source of information on the geography, history, commerce, politics, and ethnology of Central Africa north of the equator. Of no less importance are his researches on the languages spoken in Central Africa, the third volume of which has just been published. But the favourite subject of his youthful studies became again uppermost in his mind, when, after years of toil, anxiety, and constant exertion, he might have allowed himself an uninterrupted repose: and he revisited in successive years various countries adjacent to the Mediterranean, viz., Spain, Italy, the Maritime Alps, European Turkey, and Asia Minor, with a view to supplementing his researches on the geography, history, and commerce of that cradle of the ancient civilization of Europe. He succeeded Carl Ritter in the chair of Geography in the University of Berlin, and in the Presidency of the Berlin Geographical Society; but his great merits as an African explorer will only be duly appreciated when European commerce shall be extended to those central regions of the vast continent, with so large a portion of which he has been the first to make us acquainted. Dr. Barth died at Berlin on the 25th November last, in the 45th year of his age.

It will be matter of much gratification to the Society to find in the list of gentlemen, who have been enrolled among its members during the past session, the name of H. H. the Rao of Kutch, to whose father the Society is indebted for a munificent donation of coins transmitted to it, some years since, through General Jacob. In congratulating the Society on this accession, the Council trust that other native princes may likewise testify their enlightened patriotism by coming forward to join the ranks of an association, one of whose principal objects is India, under all its religious, historical, literary, and physical aspects.

The *Library* of the Society has continued to receive a great variety of additions since the last annual meeting, consisting partly of works presented by their authors or publishers, or by other friends and patrons of the Society, partly of Transactions of learned Societies in England, on the Continent, in

Asia and America. Among these donations, the Council would especially advert to a number of valuable Dictionaries and other oriental publications, the gift of the Secretary of State for India.

From its honorary member Îsvarachandra Vidyâsâgara, of Calcutta, the Society has received a series of Sanskrit and Bengali Works. To E. W. Lane, Esq., the Society is indebted for a copy of vols. I. and II. of his great Lexicon of of the Arabic language. E. Maltby, Esq., has established his claims to the acknowledgments of the Society by the presentation of a series of large photographic views of Tanjore and Trivady, and of the photograph, 20 feet in length, of an inscription around the basement of the Vimâna, or Great Pagoda, at Tanjore. The inscription is said to date from the beginning of the 14th century A.D., and to be in the old Tamil language, but to have baffled all attempts at a complete decipherment. The Council therefore take this opportunity of inviting the attention of Dravidian scholars to the subject. The Rev. Dr. Hoole presented a copy of the late Dr. Graul's edition and translation of the Kural of Tiruvalluvar, and accompanied this gift with a memoir, which was read before the Society early in the present session, on the age and poetry of that most celebrated of ancient Tamil moralists, paying at the same time a graceful tribute to the memory of the accomplished translator of this work. H. H. the Raja of Burdwan sent, for presentation to the Society, the first volumes of the Sanskrit Text, and of the Bengali Translation of the Mahâbhârata, now publishing under his auspices.

The Council, while duly appreciating the talent and scholarship bestowed by learned Hindus and Mohammedans on the cultivation of their ancient literature, and the patronage still accorded to it as of old by the native princes, cannot refrain, on this occasion, from recording their full concurrence in the regret, frequently reiterated by M. Mohl in his annual reports, that, on the one hand, the editors and publishers of works which issue from the native presses of India, do not sufficiently consider the desire of European scholars to possess these books; and on the other, that such desire is not sufficiently brought home to them by those who have the power and opportunities of doing so. Were it not for these reasons it might be matter of surprise to the Society that the Council should have to mention only two donations under this head, notwithstanding the praiseworthy activity displayed by the native presses of Benares, Calcutta, Bombay, and Madras in the production and reproduction of the standard literature of ancient and modern India, and the increased facilities for literary intercourse between England and her eastern dependencies.

The only *Branch Societies* which have forwarded continuations of their Transactions are those of *Shanghai* and *Bombay*. The former of these, since its reconstruction, has shown great activity in its literary operations. Frequent meetings have been held, at which papers have been read and new discoveries communicated; the number of its members has been constantly on the increase, and its Journal embodies a vast amount of valuable information on a wide range of subjects, embracing the geography, geology, ethnology, history, religion, antiquities, philology, and literature of China and Japan. To an elaborate article, in its last number, entitled "The Medicine and Medical Practice of the Chinese," by the late Dr. Henderson, the Council would especially invite attention. The fluctuations incident on the temporary character of resident membership in the East have but too obvious a tendency to affect the progress or decline of literary associations, such as the North China Branch; but in this case the Council consider they are warranted in expressing a confident hope that, with the increasing prosperity of the Shanghai settlement, there will always be a sufficient number of working members on the spot able and willing to continue and extend the useful operations of their Society.

The new part, just issued, of the Journal of the *Bombay Branch Society*, appears to be calculated to make amends by the value and interest of its contents for the long period that has been allowed to elapse since the publication of the preceding part. The historical data concerning the Sah, Gupta, Valabhi, and other ancient dynasties, as gleaned by the Hon. Mr. Justice Newton from coins, and by Dr. Bhao Daji from inscriptions, though modestly put forth by the latter as speculative rather than as authorative, the Council consider to be of great importance in tending to bring the vexed question of the chronology of those obscure reigns very much nearer its solution; and they trust that the Bombay Branch Society may long continue to sustain its well-established reputation for supplying the best original materials for the study of the antiquities of Western India.

The Council have now the gratifying duty to state that two new Societies have been formed during the past year, which, though not standing in the relation of branches to the Royal Asiatic Society, are intimately connected with it by similarity of scope as well as by local association. These are the Palestine Exploration Fund and the Sanskrit Text Society.

At a meeting, held at Willis's Rooms on the 22nd June of last Year, His Grace the Archbishop of York in the chair, the *Palestine Exploration Fund* was constituted as "a Society for the accurate and systematic investigation of the archæology, the topography, the geology, and physical geography, the manners and customs of the Holy Land, for Biblical Illustration." The association is under the patronage of Her Majesty the Queen, and counts amongst its supporters the most eminent men in church, state, literature, and science. To carry out its objects, it is proposed to send out "an expedition, composed of thoroughly competent persons in each branch of research, with perfect command of funds and time, and with all possible appliances and facilities, who should produce a report on Palestine which might be accepted by all parties as a trustworthy and thoroughly satisfactory document." How much has already been accomplished has been briefly stated in the occasional papers issued by the Committee; and it is hoped that, by the combined and well-organized investigations of many men, far more complete results may be arrived at than could be expected from the isolated researches of individual travellers, however eminent their qualifications. An application made to the Council by the Committee of the Fund some weeks since to have the use of the ground-floor of the Society's house for the transaction of their current business, has been granted on the understanding that the arrangement do not interfere with the general meetings of the Society.

The *Sanskrit Text Society* has been instituted for the diffusion of Sanskrit literature, and it is thus calculated essentially to forward one of the objects for which the Royal Asiatic Society was established. The position held by the above-mentioned institution with regard to the "Bibliotheca Indica," which, though not exclusively confined to Sanskrit, but including also several Arabic and Persian works, amounts now to about 300 fasciculi, is clearly defined in the preface to its first part as follows :—"So far from intending to interfere with the activity of that distinguished body, the Sanskrit Text Society feels satisfied that it will increase its strength by performing that part of the common work which is favoured by better opportunities in Europe than exist for it in India, and which might else have been long delayed or left undone. For, in view of the difficulties which have hitherto prevented European scholars from joining the Asiatic Society of Bengal in its labours, and convinced, too, that the vast treasures of Sanskrit literature as yet concealed in the public and private libraries of Europe and India can only be brought to light if European assistance, material as well as intellectual, is added to that which India affords, the Sanskrit Text Society trusts that its objects will be welcomed by all true friends of India, and receive their support, wherever literary, philological, or political considerations create a desire for a knowledge and a diffusion of the works of the Hindu mind." The series of its publications is inaugurated by the celebrated compendium of the Mîmânsâ philosophy, the Jaiminîya-nyâya-mâlâ-vistara, by Mâdhavâcharya, the great commentator on the Vedas, which is edited by Professor Goldstücker, and is likely to be succeeded by the Yogasûtra, with Vyâsa's commentary; the Sânkhya-sûtra, with Aniruddha's commentary; the Vâyu-purâṇa, the Vishṇupurâṇa, Bharata's Nâṭyaṣâstra, and other works of equal interest and importance. The labours of the Society are yet in their earliest stage, and their success will depend upon the support which may be further accorded to it in Europe, and by the wealthier and more influential portion of the Hindus. But with the patronage already received in this country, and the encouragement that has been promised it from other quarters, it bids fair gradually to attain to the higher ulterior objects with which it has been founded.

In connection with this subject, the Council wish to bring to the notice of the Society the good services rendered to *Sanskrit Bibliography* by the Curators of the Bodleian Library, in the publication of Dr. Aufrecht's descriptive catalogue of the non-Vedic Sanskrit MSS., belonging to that celebrated institution. This catalogue is indeed everything that can be desired, and takes its stand worthily by the side of Weber's description of the Sanskrit MSS. of Berlin. Printed catalogues exist also of the Paris, Copenhagen, St. Petersburg, and Tübingen collections, and, through them, Sanskritists have been enabled to find and consult the MSS. they might be in search of with far greater facility than they could have done without such aid. It may in truth be said that, with such a descriptive and classified catalogue as those by Aufrecht and Weber, the vast and important collection of

Sanskrit MSS. now in the possession of the India Office, though it has alone supplied more materials for research and for the publication of original texts than all the other European libraries together, would probably have been still more assiduously and more successfully consulted. The Council, therefore, in the interest of Oriental Literature, trust that their learned associate, the present Librarian to the India Office, who, by his wide range of Sanskrit reading, his intimate acquaintance with the contents of some of the richest collections of Sanskrit MSS. in India, and the publication of his Bibliography of the Indian philosophical systems, and of other valuable contributions to Hindu Literature, is pre-eminently qualified for such a work, may not shrink from accomplishing the laborious task bequeathed to him by his predecessors. And if Dr. Hall could be induced to publish also a catalogue of his own Sanskrit MSS., which are understood to be the richest private collection anywhere out of India, he would confer an additional obligation on all Sanskrit scholars.

It will be in the recollection of the Society that, in the year 1828, Professor H. H. Wilson edited, at Calcutta, a descriptive catalogue of the Oriental MSS., collected by the late Col. Colin Mackenzie. Amongst them many were in Sanskrit, some of great interest and rarity, which have since been deposited in the India Office Library. Another collection, chiefly formed by the late Dr. John Leyden, and purchased by the Court of Directors at his death, was transferred in 1844, on the application of the Madras Literary Society, to the custody of that body; and soon after a still larger body of MSS. was incorporated, by Mr. C. P. Brown, with those already deposited in the library of that society, to which many additions were made by that gentleman up to the time of his return to England, in the year 1855. The Sanskrit MSS. in these two collections alone amount to about 2600 volumes. Last, not least, the existence of a most remarkable Sanskrit Library, belonging to the late Raja of

Tanjore, is mentioned by Professor Goldstücker in the preface to Part I. of the Sanskrit Text Society's publications.

An estimate of the richness of these various collections may be formed from a glance at the printed catalogues, in which works are, not unfrequently, enumerated that would seem either to have wholly disappeared, or at least, to have become very scarce, north of the Dekhan. Moreover, it has been observed that Sanskrit MSS., written in the Dekhan, are as a rule very correct, and that at the same time they often differ so materially from the more generally received texts as to be calculated to supply essential assistance in supplementing and correcting them. The Council consider it right to draw attention to the great importance attaching to this class of Sanskrit MSS., inasmuch as there has been much reluctance on the part of Sanskrit scholars to avail themselves of the aid derivable from the study of these resources, so far as they are accessible in England. It is true, the variety of rather complicated Dravidian alphabets in which they are written, and the minuteness of the writing itself, as it is traced on the palm leaves, are by no means inviting to the eye. But these drawbacks, serious as they may appear, cannot be held to stand in any just proportion to the value of the results to be gained, and may, it is hoped, by patience and perseverance be gradually overcome. It would appear that even in India, where no excuses of this nature could be pleaded, the three before-mentioned collections have not been turned to any substantive use; and the Council would therefore strongly advocate any scheme that might be set on foot to rescue those MSS. from the early destruction with which they are threatened by the ravages of the climate and of the white ants, by transferring them to London, where with the new impetus that has been given to Sanskrit studies, they might be duly appreciated and turned to good account.

The Council have been led to make the foregoing remarks by a similar collection which has been now for thirty years in possession of the Royal Asiatic Society, and they deem the present a fitting moment for bringing this collection more prominently than has hitherto been done to the consideration of its members. The *palm-leaf MSS.* of which it consists, upwards of 180 in number were collected by the late *Mr. C. M. Whish*, of the Madras C.S., author of several valuable articles on Hindu Astronomy, and were presented to this society on his death by his brother, Mr. J. C. Whish. They are all in Sanskrit, and nearly all in the Grantham character. Now that catalogues of the MS. treasures of the most celebrated Oriental libraries, including even the famous Armenian collection of Etchmiadzin, have been printed, or are printing, it may fairly be expected that the Royal Asiatic Society should not remain behind in this respect; and its members may, perhaps, be glad to learn that a descriptive catalogue of the Whish collection, as well as of the other Sanskrit MSS. in the Society's possession, is in course of preparation.

In proceeding to a brief survey of the share which the *sister societies* have taken in the furtherance of the common objects of enquiry, the Council have the gratification of stating that the Journal of the *Asiatic Society of Bengal*, for the past year, fully maintains its character for antiquarian and scientific research. The volume contains the concluding instalment of the results of the archæological pilgrimage on which General Cunningham had set out for the purpose of tracing the sites of the ancient cities of Buddhistic renown in Behar and Oudh,—results deduced from the most ingenious geographical and historical combinations. Among the various other papers of interest there are two contributions by Mr. E. Thomas, on ancient Indian Weights, in which many important collateral questions, archæological as well as historical, are treated; a Note on the Pronunciation of the Tibetan language, by the Rev. H. A. Jæschke; a Notice of the coins of the nine

Nâgas, by Gen. Cunningham; a Paper by Rajendralal Mittra on the Sena Rajas of Bengal; and two by Dr. F. Mason on Religion, Mythology, and Astronomy among the Karens. The plan of dividing that Journal into two parts, one for philology and archæology, and the second for science, appears on its very first trial to have failed, and is not likely to approve itself to those members of the Society whose claims on the Journal for their antiquarian, philological, and literary contributions it is calculated to trench upon.

In the Sanskrit series of the "Bibliotheca Indica" the following works have been completed:—the Bṛhatsanhitâ of Varâhamihira, Kapila's Sânkhyasûtras, Dhananjaya's Daṣarûpa with Dhanika's commentary, and Gotama's Nyâyadarṣana with the commentary of Vâtsyâyana; and the Yoga Aphorisms of Patanjali with the gloss of Bhoja and an English translation, are in the press. In the Persian series the Ikbâlnâmah i Jahângîrî has been completed, and the Bâdshâhnâmah and the Âlamgîrnâmah have been commenced, which, with the Târîkh i Daulatshâhî, will terminate for the present the publication of the principal historians of Delhi. A revised text of the Âyîn i Akbarî is also in contemplation.

While the Asiatic Society of Bengal must deeply regret the departure for Europe of General Cunningham and Mr. Cowell, the latter of whom, by his learning, industry, and conscientious care, has done such good service on the editorial staff of the "Bibliotheca Indica," it will be matter of congratulation to the Royal Asiatic Society if their ministrations be henceforth as zealously bestowed on the younger, as they have been for so many years on the elder sister society.

It may not perhaps be generally known that the foundation of the Asiatic Society of Bengal followed by six years that of the *Batavian* "*Society of Arts & Sciences*," which was established in the year 1778 as a branch of the Royal Society of Amsterdam. The earlier volumes of its Transactions contain much miscellaneous matter not exclusively relating to the

Dutch possessions in the East. But its operations have for the last twenty years been strictly confined to inquiries concerning the Indian archipelago. Reserving its transactions for more extensive papers, the Society began in the year 1853 the publication of a Journal, 14 volumes of which, in addition to 2 volumes of Proceedings, have been presented to this Society up to the present time. In consequence of the new impetus which these researches were receiving in the Colonies, a *Royal Institute* was originated at *Amsterdam* in the year 1851, for the investigation of the languages, literature, geography, and ethnology of the Dutch East Indies. Its Journal has just reached its 13th volume, and an equal number of valuable monographs, chiefly geographical, have been issued. By the exertions of these two societies, a great mass of new information has been brought to light, as may be expected, concerning those islands over which the Dutch rule or influence extends. However, since the appearance, in the earlier volumes of Logan's "Journal of the Indian Archipelago," of some papers translated from the Transactions of the Batavian Society, which were read with much interest at the time, no further cognizance of their operations would seem to have been taken in this country, though a variety of contributions to their publications are closely associated with the objects to which the investigations of this Society are principally directed. The Council would call especial attention to the excellent papers published by the two Societies on Indian palæography, architecture, chronology, and the interpretation of Kawi and Sanskrit inscriptions, all of which bear on the early introduction of Hindu civilization into Java, Sumatra, and the other islands of the Archipelago, and will be studied with the greater advantage by all those interested in Hindu archæology, inasmuch as they supply indispensable materials for correcting or supplementing the accounts given by Leyden, Marsden, Anderson, Raffles, Crawfurd, and other earlier writers on the subject.

The *German Oriental Society*, with no national colonies to restrict the scope of its activity, is wont to consider the whole of Asia as its legitimate territory: and the pages of its journal give evidence of the wide range over which the various contributions to it extend. Notwithstanding, much preponderance is allowed to papers on Semitic languages and literature, and it is natural that it should be so in a country in which Semitic studies have for centuries been cultivated with such success. The following papers in the volume for the past year deserve especial notice: the first part of the late Dr. Osiander's decipherment of the Himyaritic Inscriptions published by order of the Trustees of the British Museum, (the second part will bring a survey of the linguistical and archæological results deducible from an examination of all the known Himyaritic Monuments); the continuation of Geiger's researches on the Samaritans; and a new analysis of Phœnician Inscriptions by Dr. O. Blau and Professor E. Meier. On Iranian palæography and history there is a further instalment of Dr. Mordtmann's interpretation of Pehlevi coin legends.

The last four numbers of the "Memoirs" published by the Society contain the Sanskrit text of Âṣvalâyana's Gṛhyasûtras, with a German translation and notes by Professor Stenzler; the Sanskrit text of Ṣântanava's Phiṭsûtras, with commentaries, a German translation and notes, by Dr. Kielhorn; and a dissertation on the Parsee origin of the Jewish Angelology and Demonology, by Dr. Kohut. Of other publications printed at the expense of the Society, the Kâmil of el-Mubarrad, an Arabic grammatico-lexiological work, edited by Dr. W. Wright, of the British Museum, is the latest and at the same time the most important.

Though the Journal and Memoirs of the Society are the chief, yet they are by no means the only repertory of Oriental research in Germany. Besides four or five periodicals devoted to especial subjects of enquiry connected with the East, there are the Transactions of the five Academies of Vienna, Munich, Berlin, Leipsic, and Göttingen, each of these counting among its members several Oriental scholars of renown, whose contributions in many cases extend far beyond the limits of ordinary essays. The publications of the three first-named Academies are regularly supplied to the Library of the Royal Asiatic Society, and are available to its members.

The Oriental Section of the *Imperial Academy of St. Petersburg* has continued its labours during the past year with unabated energy. The great Sanskrit Dictionary by Bœhtlingk and Roth has been carried on to the letter M, and at the same time the third volume of Bœhtlingk's "Sententious Poetry of the Hindus" has appeared. Turanian philology has received a most important contribution by the publication of Dr. W. Radloff's researches on the Tatar dialects of Southern Siberia. Lastly, the Academy has earned the thanks of linguists by its efforts to rescue from oblivion the languages of the Caucasus, before the small and scattered communities by whom they are spoken perish from the face of the earth. Dr. Schiefner, who has been entrusted with the difficult task of constructing grammars and vocabularies from texts written down from the mouths of the natives, has already acquitted himself successfully in the case of five of these tongues, and is at present engaged upon the language of the Kasikumüks, from materials collected on the spot by the indefatigable Baron Uslar.

The *Journal Asiatique* for the past session has been rich in articles of great merit. M. Barbier de Meynard has finished his translation of, and annotations on, the book of routes and provinces of Ibn Khordadbah, the Arabic text of which he had given in the previous volume. M. Oppert has brought his analysis of the great Khorsabad inscription to a conclusion, and M. Ménant has greatly enhanced the value of this paper by the addition of a glossary. The Royal Asiatic Society has the more reason to welcome every new contribution to a better understanding of the Assyrian Monuments; as the pages of its own journal have given the first impulse to a scientific and methodical treatment of the linguistical and palæographical questions affecting the successful decipherment of those ancient documents. Professor Nève has furnished a new translation, with introduction and exegetical commentary, of the Âtmabodha, a popular text-book of the Vedânta philosophy, by Ṣankara Âchârya. Lastly, M. E. Prudhomme has translated from the Russian M. K. Patkanean's researches on the history of the Sassanides from Armenian sources. In the series of Oriental authors published by the Société Asiatique in the original text and with a French translation, the fourth volume of Masûdî's "Golden Meadows" has appeared, which brings the History of the early Ḳhalifs down to the death of Ali. It is much to be hoped that M. Mohl, whatever other arrangements he may propose, may be prevailed upon to continue his annual surveys of the progress of Oriental literature, which have for so many years constituted a most instructive and valuable addition to the essays contained in the Journal Asiatique.

While the centralization of Oriental studies in Paris enables the Société Asiatique to carry on its operations in all their ramifications, and to bring out the monthly or bi-monthly parts of its Journal, with unvarying regularity, it cannot be denied that, in the case of the *American Oriental Society*, the unavoidable absence of centralization has made the labours of that body and the appearance of its Journal more or less contingent on external circumstances. Though the semestrial meetings of the Society have never suffered any interruption through late political events, only one volume of its Journal has been published since the year 1862. The Society has, indeed, ever since its commencement in a measure been dependent for contributions on a small staff of eminent scholars at home, but still more so perhaps on its correspondents in all parts of the world, and more especially on the Missionaries of the American Board. Some of the most important articles in the last three volumes of the Journal treat of Hindu astronomy: and two of these, contained in the part that was presented to this Society at the last meeting, deserve especial notice as touching upon questions which were subjects of discussion in the Journal of this Society last year. In the one, the Rev. E. Burgess, the translator of the Sûrya Siddhânta, endeavours to assign, "from the evidences and materials for judging now available," the origination of the lunar zodiac, as represented in the Nakshatras and Manâzil, to the Hindus or their immediate ancestry: whereas in the other, Professor Whitney, whose authority on all questions of this sort stands unchallenged, states it as his opinion, that "every attempt hitherto made to prove any one of the three systems [Hindu, Arabic, Chinese] derived from either of the others is demonstrably a failure," and inclines to think that "some fourth people is most likely to have been the originator of the primitive lunar zodiac." It is probable that the researches into the primitive astronomy of the Chaldeans, on which the Director of the Royal Asiatic Society is now engaged, will throw important light on this most interesting subject.

In reference to the *activity of this Society* during the past session, the Council offer the following statement:—

Besides two of the papers adverted to in the last Annual Report,—viz., "Contributions to a knowledge of Vedic Theogony and Mythology," Part II., by Mr. Muir, and "Translation of the Amitâbha Sûtra from the Chinese," by the Rev. S. Beal,—the first part of Vol. II. of the Society's Journal, which has just been distributed to the Members, contains a translation, also by Mr. Muir, of such "Miscellaneous Hymns" from the Rig and Atharva Vedas as possess a more general interest from the light which they throw on the social condition of the times in which they were composed.

The Rev. J. Long, of Calcutta, has contributed a series of questions and desiderata designed to draw attention to, and elicit information on, subjects relating to native social life in

Bengal and other parts of India. It is hoped that this guide to statistical and sociological enquiries may, in the hands of educated natives and with the co-operation of Europeans interested in the subject, be the instrument of bringing to light a variety of new data and facts which, when properly sifted and arranged, will be laid before the Society.

During his stay in London, in May of last year, Dr. H. N. van der Tuuk examined the Malay MSS., about 90 in number, belonging to the Royal Asiatic Society. His "Catalogue Raisonné," incorporated in the last number of the Journal, is far more accurate than the list of these MSS. that was given by Dulaurier in the "Journal Asiatique" for the year 1840. It may interest the Society to know that the Dutch Colonial Office is having a translation of this Catalogue made, to form the basis of a more extensive work on the literature of the Malays, by the same scholar.

From a critical examination of about a thousand silver coins which had originally formed part of a large hoard discovered in the Protected State of Kooch Bahâr three years ago, and now belonging to Colonel C. S. Guthrie, Mr. Thomas has derived the leading materials for a paper "On the Initial Coinage of Bengal." The coins in question range over a period of 107 years down towards the end of the 14th century, A.D., and record ten mint cities and the reigns of ten kings: and their historical bearings, in connection with the slender data furnished by Persian and Arabic writers of that period, have been brought out by Mr. Thomas with great ingenuity.

Mr. Norris, who has for many years been engaged in collecting materials for an Assyrian Dictionary, has, in the concluding paper, supplied the commencement of his work, as a specimen of the plan and arrangement he has adopted. Of the difficulties with which his task is attended on all sides, only those few scholars can form an adequate idea who have themselves had the courage to grapple with them. Mr. Norris is now engaged in carrying his Dictionary through the press in a larger form than that of the Society's Journal, as being better adapted for a work of such extent.

A further very important aid to the prosecution of Cuneiform studies has been recently afforded by the publication of the 2nd volume of the "Cuneiform Inscriptions of Western Asia," a work on which Sir Henry Rawlinson, assisted by Mr. Norris, has been long engaged, under the auspices and at the expense of the Trustees of the British Museum. This volume contains 70 plates, devoted for the most part to explanatory bilingual lists which, although too often fragmentary and half-obliterated, are still of great value in solving those difficulties of Turanian expression that have hitherto proved the chief impediment to the interpretation of the Assyrian texts. The Society will be glad also to learn that the Trustees of the British Museum have made a further application to Her Majesty's Government for funds to enable them to continue the publication of Cuneiform texts; and that, if this application be granted, Sir Henry Rawlinson will at once proceed to lithograph the large collection of Nineveh Clay Tablets referring to legal transactions on the one hand, and to astronomical and astrological formulæ on the other, of which repeated mention has been made in the pages of the Society's Journal.

The forthcoming number of the Journal is in a forward state, and will be out at the beginning of the autumn. On account of the accumulation of important materials, it will be speedily followed by an extra number, which is to contain among other papers an Assyrian grammar by the Rev. Dr. Hincks, and one or two of the Memoirs, adverted to in the last Annual Report, by Sir Henry Rawlinson. It must be as gratifying to the other members of the Society as it is to the Council, to see the usefulness of their association so much on the increase through the excellence and importance of the contributions to its Journal. Though its labours are carried on noiselessly and without parade, the Society continues to fulfil its literary and scientific mission in accordance with the high standard of Oriental scholarship and research it has ever sought to maintain.

It will be in the recollection of the Members that, when the stock and copyright of the translation of the History of *Tabari* was presented by the Oriental Translation Fund to the

Royal Asiatic Society, it was proposed to continue this publication. Arrangements have since been made with Dr. Zotenberg, in Paris, for undertaking this task, and the printing has been commenced. The work is to consist of four volumes 8vo., including a revised reprint of the portion translated by M. Dubeux, and an ample index of names: and it will be completed, if possible, by the end of the year 1868. It will be offered to the Members of the Royal Asiatic Society, as well as to those of the Société Asiatique and the German Oriental Society, who may send in their names to the Secretary, at the net price of five shillings per volume. To non-subscribers a higher price will be charged.

With a view to the better control of the *Library* and to obviate any irregularities in the return of books, the Council have resolved to frame a rule making it the Secretary's duty to call in every book borrowed from the library, once a year, in the month of March. With regard to MSS. lent to Oriental scholars abroad, the Council have determined to reserve to themselves every case for their especial consideration.

## AUDITORS' REPORT.

Your auditors have examined the accounts for the past year and compared them with the vouchers; they find them correct, and remark with satisfaction that the income has been not only equal to the expenditure, but that nearly £100 has been added to the balance in the Bankers' hands.

They have formed a careful estimate of the probable receipts and expenses for the ensuing year, and find that owing to a considerable increase to be expected in the expenditure in printing the Journal, no such saving can be anticipated this year, but that the current income of the Society is quite equal to meet the expected expenditure.

NEIL B. E. BAILLIE, *Auditor for the Council.*

J. FERGUSSON, H. LEWIS, } *Auditors for the Society.*

*London, May,* 1866.

Sir Edward Colebrooke, the President, in moving the adoption of the report, observed that his first duty was the very gratifying one of having to congratulate the Society on the improvement of its finances. Our annual meetings had so often given occasion for comment on our financial difficulties, that it was the more cheering now to have to notice these signs of returning public confidence and support. They afforded evidence, he believed, that the exertions of the Society were appreciated by those branches of the public service to whom we usually looked for aid, and he need not add that with increased resources we should be enabled to extend the sphere of the Society's activity, and add to our library, which had been much neglected during these years of difficulties.

It would perhaps be imprudent to count too much on these indications of prosperity. It was not to be expected that this Society, still less the parent Society in Calcutta, would again occupy the leading position which belonged to it when the study of Indian literature was young, and when the exertions of those who had been interested in the antiquities of Asia, or in scientific enquiries connected with the East, were concentrated in a few learned associations.

The question was put to him lately, by one of the most eminent of our oriental scholars, how it was that the public service in India produced so few eminent scholars compared with its state formerly. If we were to inquire into the cause of this falling off in the zeal for the study of Indian antiquities in India itself, we should perhaps find less ground for surprise at the small number who now devote themselves to such researches, than for wonder at the extraordinary activity of the pioneers of research, who, amid the pressure of public avocations, achieved so much formerly. A remarkable impulse was given to these studies during the freshness of their novelty, when the mine was unwrought, its resources unknown, and the student was cheered by the applause of European scholars, who looked with eagerness to the result of his labours. Such motives cannot be expected to operate with the same force now, and it was undoubtedly to this falling off in the number of earnest scholars connected with the Indian service that we should attribute the abatement in the support we have for some years received from these public bodies, whose sympathies with the objects of the Society were in no small degree attributable to the pride they felt at the learning and reputation of some of their number, and which threw so much lustre on the whole body.

He made these remarks because the Society must place its principal reliance for support on those who were bound to India by ties of public duty. Everything which can elucidate its past history and literature, and the connection between ancient traditions and modern modes of thought, should command the attention of those whose lot is cast with the inhabitants, whether for Government or commerce. He could not too strongly appeal to those whose duties or interest carried them to the East to promote these researches and give their support to Societies, one of the first objects of whose foundation was to advance our knowledge of these interesting questions.

But if we have to report some falling off in the number of active students among members of the Indian service, on the other hand, he saw no ground to apprehend any decline in the Eastern research in the great centres of literary activity, and especially on the Continent of Europe. Of this we have evidence before us in the notice which the report of the Council contains of the labours of kindred societies, both in the East and West. The seats and centres of learning have multiplied. Professorships have been liberally endowed, and scholars are increasing. In the preface to Professor Max Müller's Sanscrit Grammar, recently published, he had noted the interesting fact that in the University of Leipsic alone, as many as twenty-five pupils attend the classes of Professor Brockhaus, in order to acquire the elements of Sanscrit, previous to the study of comparative philology. In this country where motives of utility act more powerfully, were it not for the public examinations for the Indian Service, it was to be feared that the number would be very limited. It was interesting, however, to observe that, in the last report of the Civil

Service Commissioners, out of forty successful competitors for the Indian Service, twenty-five obtained marks for their knowledge of Sanscrit, and among the unsuccessful competitors no less than forty-nine showed some proficiency in the language. Amid these evidences of increasing activity in the centres of literary research, it was satisfactory to observe that one of the affiliated societies in China was showing signs of new life. With the opportunities afforded of access to the interior of the country, and with increased cultivation of its language, we might hope for larger information as to the antiquities and social state of a nation differing in manners so widely from our own.

Among the contributors to the Journal of the Society he thought we should look with especial interest on the exertions of our indefatigable members, Mr. Muir and Mr. Thomas, in their several departments of Vedic study and numismatic antiquities. It was, he thought, by following up separate and detached questions bearing on the mythology and writings of the Vedic period, that we should arrive at clear views of the whole of that remarkable literature, and of its relative position to Buddhism and the religious opinions of modern times. Though much has been done to impart a method to our knowledge, and determine the position which different branches of the literature held to the rest, he confessed that he entertained slender hope of deciding, with any approach to precision, on the epoch to which the more ancient writings belonged. The record of ancient astronomical observation certainly left too wide a margin for errors to afford more than an approximation, and we had no other scientific data to which we could refer. It would be too much, perhaps, to expect that anything would be added to our knowledge of the more remote period through the medium of ancient inscriptions and coins; but they had assisted in determining periods of considerable antiquity in Indian history, and indirectly threw light on what was more ancient, and they must soon be regarded as important landmarks, by the aid of which the outline of Indian history may be ultimately mapped out.

On one department he could have wished that the Council

had a more definite report to offer. It was gratifying to know that the language and antiquities of ancient Assyria are studied with unabated interest, and that we have before us in the last number of our Journal, the commencement of an Assyrian Dictionary, by Mr. Norris, and we have further promise of a contribution to an Assyrian Grammar, by Dr. Hincks. These were hopeful signs of agreement among the learned as to the value of the several signs and symbols which compose the ancient inscriptions. They should serve, he thought, to dispel any lingering feelings of scepticism, if any such are still entertained; but they would be of higher value if they encouraged others to enter upon a field of discovery so well begun. The Society would receive with satisfaction the announcement that our learned Director was still actively engaged on the labours which the world regards with such interest. They might at the same time regret that the hope that was held out last year, of some contributions to our knowledge of the astronomy and astrological lore of the ancient Chaldæans remained still unfulfilled. Considering the difficulties which belonged to the attempt to trace the evidence of scientific knowledge, and determine its character and value through the medium of a language only imperfectly known, we ought not to feel impatient at any delay which may serve to mature his views on this interesting question; but if the subject matter of his studies were not ripe for publication, it would be gratifying to hear from him some account of their progress, and we might be indulged with a Barmecide's feast while waiting for the more solid entertainment that was promised to us.

Sir Edward Colebrooke concluded by congratulating the Society on the advance which the great objects of its researches were now making, and on the honourable position which the Society continued to hold in furthering them. If we did not now look for proofs that literature and science were cultivated in the East at periods of extravagant antiquity, and shining with a lustre that rivalled the early civilization of Europe,—on the other hand, we year by year acquired clearer views of the state of the ancient world, its races, manners, the changes its religion and opinions have undergone, and, above all, as to the structure of its languages, and their affinities with those of modern Europe. In this last subject of enquiry the study has long ceased to be peculiarly Asiatic, and has assumed the position of a science in which every step adds to our knowledge, and paves the way for future discoveries.

The motion having been duly seconded and carried,

Sir Henry Rawlinson explained that having found himself much impeded in his researches into the astronomy and astrology of the Assyrians by the very copious use which was made of the primitive Babylonian language in all documents relating to these sciences, he had judged it advisable to undertake, in the first instance, a thorough examination of this ancient and most difficult tongue; and he had already made so much progress in the enquiry that he thought himself justified in stating the general results to the Society, in so far, at any rate, as regarded the ethnographical question. He doubted whether it would be ever possible to institute a direct comparison between the primitive Babylonian and any living language of the present day: all the contiguous links in the chain seemed to have been lost; but he was inclined to regard the group of tongues to which it belonged, and which he proposed to call Erythræan, because they were spoken by the nations around the Erythræan sea, as intermediate between the African languages on one side and the Proto-Turanian or Finno-Ugrian on the other. This language seemed to have been introduced into Babylonia from the uplands of Central Arabia; and he suggested that the terms of Akkad and Sumir, by which the primitive colonists were designated, represented the Nejd and Shomar of the present day. At any rate, Akkad meant "a highlander" in the old language, just as Nejd meant "highlands" in Arabic; and with regard to the etymology of the latter term, the initial *n*, although now supposed to be a radical letter, might very well be a secondary development, as in *nur*, "light," from *ur*; *nis*, "man," from *ish*, etc. etc. He had been first led to speculate on this Arabian origin of the Akkad race of Babylonia, from recognizing what seemed to be an identity between the Ante-Semitic names of the old Himyarite gods, and the Akkadian equivalents given in the bilingual tablets for the titles of the deities of Assyria. Thus he believed the *Almaqah* of the Himyarites to be "the moon," which was always the head of any system of astral and planetary worship; and this was evidently the same name as the *Lamga* of the bilingual tablets, corresponding with the Assyrian *Sin*. (The native name of the moon in Babylonia before the Akkad immigration was *Nannar*, and it would appear that this god was transferred as *Asshur* to the head of the Assyrian Pantheon, and irrespective of the position of *Sin* in that mythology). The *Gudibir*, again, of the Akkadian lists, which answered to the Assyrian Merodach, was represented apparently by the *Júdfúr* of the old Arabian idolators. He had further traced a very considerable number of Akkadian nouns and roots to that portion of the Arabic vocabulary which was unrepresented in any other Semitic dialect, and which he believed accordingly had been inherited by the Semitic Arabs from their African predecessors. The Mosaical genealogies which associated Nimrod with Cush and Misraim were also in favour of this Ethnic relationship: and the Greek traditions of Memnon and Cepheus, fluctuating between a Susian and an Egyptian nationality, pointed to the same connection. He observed further that Berosus had expressly named an Arabian dynasty as having preceded the great Chaldæan line of Babylonia; and he thought that the Mahomedan tradition of the Himyaric Toba' having led an expedition from Yemen to Semarcand, was in the same way to be explained by a real immigration of colonists from Arabia, who had penetrated through Babylonia into Central Persia, where they had ultimately coalesced with the resident Scythic population, prior to the spread of the Arians to the westward. Sir Henry added that much time and labour would still have to be expended on the Proto-Babylonian language before the many curious notices regarding the ancient religion and traditions of the Akkadian race contained in the Nineveh tablets could be adequately understood; but he had already made so much progress in this direction, that he could look with confidence to the result; and he thus hoped before the next anniversary to have laid before the Society a detailed memoir on the subject.

The following resolution was moved by the Right Honourable the EARL of POWIS, seconded by Sir JOHN BOWRING, and unanimously adopted :—

"That the thanks of the meeting be tendered to the President, Director, Vice-Presidents, and other officers of the Society for the efficient manner in which they have forwarded the interests of the Society during the past year."

The PRESIDENT then read to the meeting the names of the twelve candidates whom the Council had decided on recommending to the Society for election as Honorary Members,—viz.: Professor T. Aufrecht, Dr. S. Birch, the Rev. J. Edkins, Don P. de Gayangos, M. N. de Khanikoff, E. W. Lane, Esq., Professor C. Lottner, the Duc de Luynes, Professor J. Oppert, Ahmed Vefik Effendi, Professor A. Weber, and Professor W. D. Whitney. They were accordingly proposed from the chair, and on a show of hands being taken they were declared elected as Honorary Members of the Society.

The Right Honourable Lord STRANGFORD moved, and Sir F. HALLIDAY seconded, a vote of thanks to the President for his able and courteous conduct in the chair. The vote was carried unanimously; and E. B. Cowell, Esq., and the Rev. W. Arthur having been requested to act as scrutineers, the ballot was had recourse to for the election of one Vice-President and six new members of Council in the room of those whose term of office has expired. The result of the ballot was declared as follows: *Vice-President:* Oswald de Beauvoir Priaulx, Esq. *Council:* N. B. E. Baillie, Esq.; J. W. Bosanquet, Esq.; General J. Briggs; E. B. Cowell, Esq.; General A. Cunningham; J. Dickinson, Esq.; M. E. G. Duff, Esq., M.P.; E. B. Eastwick, Esq.; Professor T. Goldstücker; Sir F. Halliday, K.C.B.; the Right Hon. Holt Mackenzie; J. C. Marshman, Esq.; Sir C. Nicholson, Bart; E. C. Ravenshaw, Esq.; and A. Russell, Esq., M.P.

The Chairman then declared the meeting adjourned till July 2nd.

# ABSTRACT OF RECEIPTS AND EXPENDITURE FOR THE YEAR ENDING DECEMBER, 1865.

**1865. RECEIPTS.**

| | | £ s. d. | £ s. d. |
|---|---|---|---|
| 139 Resident Members, at 3 guineas ... ... | | 437 17 0 | |
| 66 Non-Resident Members, at 1 guinea ... ... | | 69 6 0 | |
| 6 Original Members, at 2 guineas ... ... | | 12 12 0 | |
| Arrears paid up ... ... ... ... ... ... | | 29 8 0 | |
| Compositions:—C. W. Gainer, Esq. | 31 10 0 | | |
| M. P. Edgeworth, Esq. | 21 0 0 | | |
| | | 52 10 0 | |
| | | | 601 13 0 |
| Donation of India Council ... ... ... ... | | | 210 0 0 |
| Dividends on Consols, £1200 ... ... ... ... | | 35 5 0 | |
| Sale of Publications ... ... ... ... ... | | 16 2 0 | |
| | | | 51 7 0 |
| Donation of Oriental Translation Fund ... ... | | 20 0 0 | |
| Ditto towards Printing Expenses:— | | | |
| By Sir H. Rawlinson ... ... | 25 1 6 | | |
| ,, Mr. J. Muir ... ... ... | 3 0 0 | | |
| | | 28 1 6 | |
| | | | 48 1 6 |
| Total Receipts ... ... | | | 911 1 6 |
| Balance at Bankers', 1st January, 1865 ... ... | | 139 2 4 | |
| Ditto in Treasurer's hands, ditto ... ... ... | | 0 0 2 | |
| | | | 139 2 6 |
| | | | £1050 4 0 |

**EXPENDITURE.**

| | £ s. d. | £ s. d. |
|---|---|---|
| House Rent for the Year ... ... ... ... | 280 0 0 | |
| Assessed Taxes do. ... ... ... ... | 19 17 2 | |
| Parochial Rates do. ... ... ... ... | 40 12 6 | |
| Water Rate do. ... ... ... ... | 5 19 0 | |
| Fire Insurance do. ... ... ... ... | 5 12 6 | |
| | | 352 1 |
| House Expenses, 21*l.* 6*s.* 5*d.*; Housekeeper's Wages. 36*l.* ... ... ... ... ... ... ... | 57 6 5 | |
| Coals 12*l.*; Gas 5*l.*, as per agreement ... ... | 17 0 0 | |
| | | 74 6 5 |
| Secretary, 200*l.*; House Porter, 54*l.* 12*s.* ... ... | | 254 12 0 |
| Out Postage ... ... ... ... ... ... ... | 8 10 0 | |
| Sundries, and In-Postage (including 7*s.* paid by Bankers) ... ... ... ... ... ... | 20 2 4 | |
| Stationery ... ... ... ... ... ... | 4 12 6 | |
| Messrs. Trübner & Co., for publishing Journal ... | 76 18 3 | |
| Mr. Watts, for Warehouse room ... ... ... | 16 0 0 | |
| | | 126 3 1 |
| Liabilities of 1864 paid up:—Stationer ... ... | | 7 15 7 |
| Total Expenditure ... ... | | 814 18 3 |
| Balance at Bankers', 31st December, 1865 ... ... | 234 9 10 | |
| Ditto in Treasurer's hands, ditto ... ... ... | 0 15 11 | |
| | | 235 5 9 |
| | | £1050 4 0 |

*29th May*, 1866.

NEIL B. E. BAILLIE,
JAS. FERGUSSON,
HENRY LEWIS.

Amount of Society's Fund,
Three per cent. Consols ... ... £1,200.

# LIST OF THE MEMBERS

OF THE

# ROYAL ASIATIC SOCIETY

OF

## GREAT BRITAIN AND IRELAND:

5, NEW BURLINGTON STREET, LONDON.

CORRECTED TO JULY, M.DCCC.LXVI.

LONDON:
TRÜBNER AND CO., 60, PATERNOSTER ROW, E.C.
1866.

# ROYAL ASIATIC SOCIETY.

# Members :

## RESIDENT AND NON-RESIDENT.

---

N.B.—The marks prefixed to the names signify—

§ Original Members.

* Non-resident Members.

† Members who have compounded for their Subscriptions.

†† Members who, having compounded, have again renewed their Subscriptions, or given donations.

‖ Members whose Subscriptions are in abeyance during absence.

His Royal Highness the Prince of Wales.

Alexander, Colonel Sir James Edward, K.C.L.S., F.R.G.S., *United Service Club*, S.W.; *Westerton, Bridge of Allan*, N.B.

*†Ali Mahomed Khan, *Consul for the Ottoman Porte, Bombay.*

*Alison, Charles, Esq., *H.B.M. Minister to the Court of Persia.*

*Alves, Colonel N., *St. Helier, Jersey.*

Ameuney, Professor A., *King's College*, W.C.

Anstruther, Major-General, 1, *Chapel-street, Grosvenor-place*, S.W.

Anderson, H. Lacon, Esq., *India Office*, S.W.

*†Ardaseer Cursetjee, Esq., *Bombay.*

*†Ardaseer Hormanjee, Esq., *Bombay.*

†Arrowsmith, J., Esq., 35, *Hereford-sq., South Kensington*, W.

Arthur, the Rev. W., M.A., *Wesleyan Mission House*, E.C.

Ashpitel, Arthur, Esq., 2, *Poet's Corner, Westminster*, S.W.

†Astell, J. H., Esq., *Union Club*, W.C.

†Babington, B. G., Esq., M.D., F.R.S., 31, *George-street, Hanover-square*, W.

Baillie, N. B. E., Esq., 93, *Gloucester-terrace, Hyde-park*, W.

Baker, Major-General W. G., R.E., *India Office*, S.W.

†Balfour, F. C., Esq., 2, *Brunswick Place, Cheltenham.*

§Ball, Samuel, Esq., *Sion Hill, Wolverley, Kidderminster.*

Baskerville, Henry, Esq.

*Bastian, Dr. A., *Bremen, Germany.*

Batten, J. H., Esq., *Bengal C.S., Bloomfield, Torquay.*

†Baxter, H. J., Esq., *Oakfield Lodge, E. Cowes, I. Wight.*

*Bayley, E. C., Esq., *Bengal C.S.*

*Beal, Rev. S., *Tower House, Southsea.*
Beamont, Rev. W. J., *Trinity College, Cambridge,*
*Beaufort, W. Morris, Esq., *Bengal C.S.*
Bell, Major Evans, 37, *Holland-villas-road, Kensington,* W.
†Benson, Robert, Esq.
‖Bettington, Albemarle, Esq., *Bombay C.S.*
*†Bhau Daji, Dr., *Bombay.*
Bicknell, Herman, Esq., 7, *Royal Crescent, Ramsgate.*
*Blunt, J. E., Esq., *H. M. Consul, Adrianople.*
Bosanquet, J. W., Esq., 73, *Lombard-street,* E.C.
†Bowring, Sir John, LL.D., *Athenæum,* S.W.
*Brandreth, J. E. L., Esq., *Bengal C.S., Calcutta.*
*Brice, Charles Alexander, Esq., *India.*
††Briggs, General John, F.R.S., *Oriental Club,* W.; *Bridge Lodge, Hurstpierpoint, Sussex.*
§Broughton, the Right Hon. Lord, F.R.S., 42, *Berkeley-sq.,* W.
Brown, Charles P., Esq., 8, *Queen's-road, Bayswater,* W.
*Burgess, James, Esq., *Bombay.*
*Burnell, Arthur, Esq., *Calicut, India.*
*†Burns, David Laing, Esq., *Allahabad.*
*†Burton, Captain R. F., *H. M. Consul, Santos, Brazil.*
Burzorjee, Dr., *Northwick Lodge, St. John's Wood,* N.W.
†Cabbell, Benj. Bond, Esq., F.R.S., 1, *Brick-court, Temple,* E.C.
*†Caldwell, Colonel Hugh, *late of the Bengal Army.*
Calthorpe, the Right Hon. Lord, 33, *Grosvenor-square,* W.
*Calvert, Edmund, Esq., *H. M. Consul, Monastir.*
*Cama, K. Rustomji, Esq., *Bombay.*
*Cameron, Captain C. D., *H. M. Consul, Massowah, Abyssinia.*
*Campbell, the Hon. George, *Bengal C. S., Calcutta.*
Campbell, R. H. S., Esq., 5, *Argyll-place, Regent-street,* W.
Capon, Major-General David, C.B., *Anglesea House, Shirley, Southampton.*
*Carmichael, David F., Esq., *Madras C. S.*
*Carr, Captain M. W., *Madras.*
†Cautley, Colonel Sir Proby T., K.C.B., F.R.S, 31, *Sackville-street,* W.; *India Office,* S.W.
†Chase, Lieut.-Colonel Morgan, 31, *Nottingham-place,* W.
*Chetty, G. Latchmee Narrasoe, Esq., *Madras.*
Chenery, Thomas, Esq., 7, *Eaton-pl. South, Belgrave-sq.* S.W.
*Childers, Robert C., Esq., *Ceylon C. S.*
*Churchill, H. A., Esq., C.B., *H. M. Consul-General, Algiers.*

†Clark, Gordon W., Esq., 72, *Gt. Tower-street*, E.C.
Clerk, the Right Hon. Sir George R., K.C.B., K.S.I., *Athenæum*, S.W.
Cole, C. J. D., Esq., *The Avenue, Sydenham*, S.W.
*Cole, Lieut. R. A., *Madras Staff Corps, Mysore.*
††Colebrooke, Sir Thomas Edward, Bart., M.P., 37, *South-street, Park-lane*, W.
*Coomaraswamy, M., Modeliar, *Colombo, Ceylon.*
Cowell, Edward B., Esq., 1, *England-lane, Haverstock-hill*, N.W.
†Crawford, R. W., Esq., 71, *Old Broad-street*, E.C.
*†Cruttenden, Captain C. J., *Indian Army;* 8, *Talbot-terrace, Westbourne-park*, W.
Cunningham, General A., *Bengal Army;* 18, *Clarendon-road, Kensington*, W.
Curzon, A., Esq., 181, *Euston-road*, N.W.
Dadabhai Naorojee, Esq., 32, *Gt. St. Helen's*, E.C.
*†Dadabhai Pestonjee, Esq., *Bombay.*
*D'Alwis, James, Esq., *Colombo, Ceylon.*
*Dalyell, Sir Robert A. O., *H. M. Consul, Jassy.*
*Dashwood, H. W., Esq., *Bengal C.S.*; *Tonning, Reading.*
Davies, the Rev. John, *Walsoken Rectory, near Wisbeach.*
†Davis, Sir John Francis, Bart., K.C.B., *Athenæum*, S.W.; *Hollywood, near Bristol.*
De Grey and Ripon, the Right Hon. the Earl, 1, *Carlton-gardens*, S.W.
De Salis, William, Esq., *Hillingdon-place, Uxbridge.*
Dent, William, Esq., 2, *Moorgate-street*, E.C.
Dent, Thomas, Esq., 12, *Hyde-park-gardens*, W.
Deutsch, E., Esq., *British Museum*, W.C.
Dickinson, John, Esq., 13, *York-street, Portman-square*, W.
†Dickinson, Sebastian S., Esq., *Brown's Lodge, Stroud.*
*Dickson, C. H., Esq., *H.B.M. Consul, Sukoum Kalé.*
*Dickson, J. R., Esq., M.D., *H. M. Legation, Persia.*
*Dickson, W., Esq., *Teheran.*
*Dowleans, A. M., Esq., *India.*
Dowson, Prof. John, *Staff College, Sandhurst, Wokingham, Berks.*
†Drane, Thomas, Esq., *Marychurch, Torquay.*
†Drysdale, William Castellan, Esq., 26, *Austin Friars*, E.C.
Duff, Mountstuart Elphinstone Grant, Esq., M.P., 4, *Queen's-gate-gardens, South Kensington*, W.
Dymes, Danl. D., Esq., 9, *Mincing-lane*, E.C.

††EASTWICK, Captain Wm. J., 12, *Leinster-terrace, Hyde-park*, W.; *India Office*, S.W.

†EASTWICK, E. B., Esq., F.R.S., *Athenæum*, S.W.; 38, *Thurloe-square*, S.W.

†EDGEWORTH, M. P., Esq., *Mastrim House, Anerley*, S.; *Athenæum*, S.W.

*EGERTON, Ph. H., Esq., B.C.S., *Dharmsala, Kangra, Punjab.*

ELLIOTT, Sir Walter, K.S.I., *Wolfelee, Hawick; Travellers' Club*, S.W.

ENGEL, Carl, Esq., 54, *Addison-road, Kensington*, W.

*ERSKINE, C. J., Esq., *Bombay C. S.*

†EVEREST, Col. Sir Geo., C.B., F.R.S., 10, *Westbourne-st.*, W.

FERGUSSON, James, Esq., 20, *Langham-place*, W.

‖FORBES, Charles, Esq., *Bombay C. S.*

†FORBES, Professor Duncan, LL.D., 58, *Burton-crescent*, W.C.

†FORBES, James Steward, Esq., 3, *Fitzroy-square*, W.

FORSTER, W. E., Esq., M.P., *Reform Club*, S.W.

FOX, Sir Charles, 8, *New-street, Spring-gardens*, S.W.

FRASER, Charles, Esq., 15, *Lancaster-gate, Bayswater-road*, W.

FREELAND, H. W., Esq., *Athenæum*, S.W.

*FRERE, W. E., Esq., *Bombay C. S.*

FRITH, J. G., Esq., 13, *Wimpole-street*, W.

FROST, the Rev. George, M.A., 28, *Kensington-square*, W.

*FRYER, George, Esq., *Madras Army.*

FULLER, the Rev. J. M., M.A., 2, *Ebury-street*, S.W.

†GAINER, W. C., Esq., M.A., 11, *Grove-street, Oxford.*

GALLENGA, Mrs., *The Falls, Llandogo, Coleford, Monmouthshire.*

GARDEN, Robert, Esq., 63, *Montagu-square*, W.

‖GARSTIN, Lieut.-Col. Robert, *late of the Madras Army.*

GILLETT, William Stedman, Esq., *Harefield, Southampton.*

GLADSTONE, William, Esq., *Fitzroy-park, Highgate*, N.

*GLASFORD, Captain C. L. R., *Nagpore.*

*GOLDENBLUM, Dr. A. J., *Odessa.*

GOLDSMID, Sir Francis H., Bart., M.P., *St. John's Lodge, Regent's-park*, N.W.

*GOLDSMID, Colonel F. J., *Madras.*

GOLDSTÜCKER, Prof. T., 14, *St. George's-sq., Primrose-hill*, N.W.

*GORDON, the Hon. Arthur, *Governor of Trinidad.*

GRAHAM, C. Cyril, Esq., 9, *Cleveland-row, St. James's*, S.W.; *Delroe House, Watford.*

*†GREGORY, John, Esq., *late Governor of the Bahamas.*

‖GREY, the Right Honourable Sir Charles E.

*GRIFFIN, Lepel H., Esq., *Bengal C. S., Lahore.*
*GRIFFITH, R. T. H., Esq., M.A., *Benares.*
*GRINDLAY, Captain Robert Melville.
†GUEST, Edwin, Esq., F.R.S., LL.D., *Master of Caius College, Cambridge.*
GUTHRIE, Colonel C. Seton, *late Bengal Engineers.*
HAIGH, Rev. B. B., D.D., *Bramham College, Tadcaster.*
HALL, Fitzedward, Esq., D.C.L., 18, *Provost-rd., Haverstock-hill*, N.W.
†HALL, Richard, Esq., 92, *Eaton-place*, S.W.
HALLIDAY, Sir Frederick, K.C.B., 28, *Cleveland-square, Bayswater*, W.
*HAMILTON, Colonel G. W., *Commissioner, Mooltan.*
HAMMOND, W. P., Esq., 74, *Camden-road-villas*, N.W.
†HAUGHTON, Richard, Esq., 137, *High-street, Ramsgate.*
*HAY, Sir J. H. D., K.C.B., *H.M. Minister, Morocco.*
HAY, the Right Hon. Lord W., M.P., *Boodle's Club*, S.W.
HEATH, the Rev. D. I., *Esher, Surrey*, S.
†HEMING, Dempster, Esq.
HENDERSON, James, Esq., *Oriental Club*, W.
HENTY, Walter, Esq., *Northlands, Chichester; Windham Club*, S.W.
†HEYWOOD, James, Esq., F.R.S., *Athenæum*, S.W.
†HOBHOUSE, H. W., Esq., *Brookes's Club, St. James's-street*, S.W.
†HODGSON, Brian Houghton, Esq., *The Rangers, Dursley.*
†HODGSON, David, Esq., *South-hill, Liverpool.*
HOGG, Sir James Weir, Bart., 4, *Carlton-gardens*, S.W.; *India Office*, S.W.
†HOLROYD, Thomas, Esq., *Oriental Club*, W.
HOLROYD, Captain W. R. M., *Bengal Staff Corps.*
HOOLE, the Rev. Elijah, D.D., *Sec. Wesleyan Miss. Soc.*, E.C.
*HUGHES, T. F., Esq., *Oriental Secretary, H.B.M. Embassy, Constantinople.*
HUGHES, Captain Sir F., *Ely House, Wexford.*
††HUNTER, Robert, Esq., F.R.S., *Southwood-lane, Highgate*, N.; *Oriental Club*, W.
HUTT, Benjamin, Esq., *E. India U. S. Club*, S.W.
ISAAC, Ezra, Esq., 12, *Talbot-terrace, Westbourne-park-road*, W.
JACOB, Maj.-Gen. G. Le Grand, C.B., *Bonchurch, Isle of Wight.*
*†JEEJEEBHOY, Sir Jamsetji, Bart., *Bombay.*
*JONES, C. T., Esq., *H.M. Consul, Shanghai.*
KAYE, J. W., Esq., *India Office*, S.W.
*†KEMBALL, Col. Sir A. B., C.B., K.S.I., *Baghdad.*
†KENNEDY, R. H., Esq., 22, *The Mall, Clifton.*

†KERR, Mrs. Alexander.
‖KNIGHTON, W., Esq., *Assistant Commissioner, Lucknow.*
*KNOX, Thomas George, Esq., *British Consul, Siam.*
*†KURSONDAS MAHDEWDAS, Esq., *Bombay.*
*†KUTCH, H. H., the Rao of, *Bhooj, India.*
LAIDLAY, J. W., Esq., *Seacliff House, North Berwick, N.B.*
LANG, Major-General W., *Craigend Castle, Milngavie, Glasgow.*
†LAW, J. S., Esq., *Oriental Club*, W.
†LAWFORD, Henry S., Esq., M.A., 28, *Austin Friars*, E.C.
*LAWRENCE, His Excellency Sir J. L. M., Bart,, G.C.B., *Calcutta.*
*LEITNER, Gottlieb W., Esq., *Lahore, India.*
LE MESSURIER, A. S., Esq., 26, *Connaught-sq.*, W.; *Oriental Club*, W.
*LE MESURIER, Hy. P., Esq., *Chief Engineer, Jubbalpore Railway.*
LEWIS, Lt.-Col. John, 27, *Dorchester-place, Blandford-sq.*, N.W.
LEWIS, Henry, Esq., R.N., *Oriental Club*, W.
†LINWOOD, the Rev. Wm., *Birchfield, Handsworth, Birmingham.*
§LOCH, John, Esq., 15, *Great Stanhope-street*, W.
LOEWE, Dr. L., M.S.A. Paris, 48, *Buckingham-place, Brighton.*
†LOW, Lieut.-Genl. Sir John, K.C.B., *Clatto, Fifeshire.*
LUDLOW, Major-General J., 9, *Pelham-crescent, Hastings.*
†MACDOUALL, Prof. C., M.A., *Queen's College, Belfast.*
*MACFARLANE, Charles, Esq., *Mooltan, India.*
MACKENZIE, the Right Hon. Holt, 28, *Wimpole-street*, W.
MACKENZIE, J. T., Esq., 9, *Old Broad-street*, E.C.
§MACKILLOP, James, Esq., 11, *King's Arms Yard*, E.C.
MACKINLAY, D., Esq., 42, *Clarges-street, Piccadilly*, W.
MACKINTOSH, Alexander Brodie, Esq., *Oriental Club*, W.
†MACKINTOSH, Eneas, Esq., 17, *Montagu-square*, W.
MACKINTOSH, Lieut.-Gen. A. F., 7, *Tilney-street*, W.
MACLEOD, Sir J. MacPh., K.S.I., 1, *Stanhope-st., Hyde-park*, W.
§*†M'NEILL, Sir J., G.C.B., F.R.S., *Granton-house, Edinburgh.*
MACPHERSON, Wm., Esq., 6, *Stanhope-street, Hyde-park*, W.
†MADDOCK, Sir T. Herbert, *Union Club, Trafalgar-square*, W.C.
MALCOLM, Major-General G. A., 67, *Sloane-street*, S.W.
*MALLOUF, Nassif, Esq., *H.M. Consulate, Smyrna.*
MALTBY, E., Esq., *late of the Madras C. S.*; 12, *Cleveland-square*, W.
*†MANOCKJEE CURSETJEE, Esq., *Bombay.*
MANNING, Mrs., 44, *Phillimore-gardens, Kensington*, W.
†MARDON, Thomas Todd, Esq., 30, *Wimpole-street*, W.
MARSHMAN, John Clark, Esq., 7, *Palace-gardens, Kensington*, W.
MARTIN, Sir J. Ranald, F.R.S., 37, *Upper Brook-street*, W.

*Mason, the Rev. Francis, D.D., *Tounghoo, Burmah.*
†Matheson, Sir James, Bart., M.P., 13, *Cleveland-row*, S.W.
Matheson, Farquhar, Esq., *Oriental Club*, W.
Mayer, J., Esq., F.S.A., 68, *Lord-street, Liverpool.*
Melvill, Philip, Esq., *Ethy House, Lostwithiel.*
Melvill, Major-General Sir P. M., *Bombay Army.*
†Mexborough. the Right Hon. the Earl of, *Travellers' Club*, W.C.
*Miles, Captain Joseph, *India.*
*Miles, Lieut. S. B., *Bombay Army, Poonah.*
*Milligan, Joseph, Esq., F.G.S., F.L.S., *Tasmania.*
Mills, Rev. John, 40, *Lonsdale-square, Islington*, N.
Moffatt, G., Esq., M.P., 103, *Eaton-square*, S.W.
Montefiore, Sir Moses, Bart., 7, *Grosvenor-gate, Park-lane*, W.
†Moor, Rev. A. P., M.A., F.R.G.S., *Subwarden, St. Augustine's College, Canterbury.*
*Moore, Niven, Esq., C.B., *late H.M. Consul General, Beyrut.*
*Mouatt, Fred. John, Esq., M.D., *Bengal Medical Service.*
Muir, John, Esq., D.C.L., LL.D., 16, *Regent-terrace, Edinburgh; Athenæum*, S.W.
*†Munmohundass Davidass, Esq., *Bombay.*
*†Murray, the Honourable C. A., *H.M. Envoy, Copenhagen.*
*Murray, E. C. Granville, Esq., *H.M. Consul General, Odessa.*
*†Nelson, James Henry, Esq., *Madura, India.*
*Neale, Colonel E. St. John, *Secretary of Legation, Japan.*
Nicholson, Sir Charles, Bart., D.C.L., LL.D., 26, *Devonshire-place*, W.
*Niemann, G. K., Esq., *Rotterdam.*
Norris, Edwin, Esq., 6, *Michael's Grove, Brompton*, S.W.
*Norris, Captain Henry MacFarlane, *Madras Army.*
Ogilvy, Thomas, Esq., 62, *Princes Gate*, W.
*Oliphant, Lawrence, Esq., *Athenæum*, S.W.
*Osborne, Capt. Willoughby, C.B., *Tudor House, Richmond*, S.W.
*Palgrave, W. G., Esq., *Baghdad.*
Palmer, Edward H., Esq., *St. John's College, Cambridge.*
‖Palmer, George, Esq., *Bengal C. S.*
‖Parbury, George, Esq.
†Parker, John F., Esq.
*Pelly, Lieut.-Col. Lewis, *Bombay Army.*
Perry, Sir T. Erskine, *India Office*, S.W.
Pilkington, James, Esq., M.P., *Reform Club*, S.W.
*Pisani, Count Alexander, *Constantinople.*
††Platt, William, Esq., *Conservative Club, St. James's*, S.W.

Pleignier, V., Esq., *College-green, Castle Town, Isle of Man.*
Plowden, Trevor C., Esq., late B.C.S., *Oriental Club*, W.
Pollock, General Sir George, G.C.B., K.S.I., *Clapham-common*, S.
Powis, the Right Hon. the Earl of, 45, *Berkeley-square*, W.
Priaulx, Osmond de Beauvoir, Esq., 8, *Cavendish-square*, W.
Prideaux, F. W., Esq., 13, *Avenue-road, St. John's Wood*, N.W.; *India Office*, S.W.
Prinsep, H. Thoby, Esq., *Little Holland-house, Kensington*, W.; *India Office*, S.W.
*Puckle, Major James, *Mysore.*
Purushottam, C., Modeliar, 5, *Old Quebec-street, Oxford-street*, W.
Pusey, S. E. B., Esq., *Pusey House, Faringdon.*
Ravenshaw, Edward Cockburn, Esq., 36, *Eaton-sq.*, S.W.
††Rawlinson, Major-Gen. Sir H. C., K.C.B., F.R.S., D.C.L., M.P., 1, *Hill-street, Berkeley-square*, W.
Redhouse, J. W., Esq., 16, *Kilburn Priory*, N.W.
†Renouard, the Rev. George Cecil, B.D., *Swanscombe, Kent.*
Reynolds, Major P. A.
||Ricketts, Mordaunt, Esq.
*Roberts, A. A., Esq., C.B., C.S.I., B.C.S., *Jud. Comm., Punjab.*
Robinson, J. R., Esq., F.R.G.S., F.S.A.Scot., etc., *South-terrace, Dewsbury.*
Rolland, S. E., Esq., *Junior United Service Club*, W.
Rollo, the Right Hon. Lord, *Duncrub Castle, Perthshire.*
Russell, A. J. E., Esq., M.P., 2, *Audley-square*, W.
Ryan, the Right Hon. Sir Edward, 5, *Addison-road, Kensington*, W.
St. Maur, the Right Hon. Earl, *Admiralty*, S.W.
Salomons, D., Esq., M.P., 26, *Cumberland-st., Hyde-park*, W.
Sassoon, Albert D., Esq.
Sassoon, Reuben D., Esq.
Scarth, the Rev. John, *Conservative Club, St. James's*, W.; *Milton-on-Thames.*
*Schlagintweit, Baron Hermann de, *Jägersburg, Forchheim, Bavaria.*
*Schlagintweit, Dr. Emil, *Würzburg, Bavaria.*
*Scott, Matthew Henry, Esq., *Eastfield, Westbury-on-Trym.*
Selwyn, the Rev. W., D.D., *Cambridge.*
*†Seraj-ul-Mulk Bahadur, *Hyderabad.*
Sheil, Major-General Sir Justin, K.C.B., 13, *Eaton-place*, S.W.
*Showers, Major C. L., *India.*
*Siva Prasâd, Babu, *Inspector of Schools, Benares.*
†Sigmond, George Gabriel, Esq., M.D.

*Skene, J. H., Esq., *H.B.M. Consul, Aleppo.*
*Sleswig-Holstein, H.S.H. Prince Frederick of, *India.*
†Smith, George, Esq., LL.D., F.A.S., M.R.S.L., *Trevu, Camborne, Cornwall.*
Smith, George, Esq., 41, *Crowndale-road, Camden Town*, N.W.
Smith, John B., Esq., M.P., 105, *Westbourne-terrace*, W.
Smith, Mrs. Newman, 34, *Gt. Cumberland-place, Hyde-park*, W.
†Smith, Thomas Charles, Esq., 25, *Oxford-square*, W.
Smollett, Patrick Boyle, Esq., M.P., *Cameron House, Alexandria, Dumbartonshire; Conservative Club*, S.W.
Spooner, the Rev. E., D.D., LL.D., *Kirk-Harle, Newcastle-upon-Tyne.*
††Spottiswoode, Wm., Esq., F.R.S., 50, *Grosvenor-place*, S.W.
†Stanley, the Right Hon. Lord, M.P., 36, *St. James's-square*, S.W.
*Stanley, the Hon. H. E. J., 40, *Dover-street, Piccadilly*, W.
Strachey, William, Esq., *Oriental Club*, W.
Strangford, the Right Hon. Viscount, 58, *Cumberland-street, Hyde-park*, W.
*Strickland, Edward, Esq., *Barbadoes.*
*Stubbs, Capt. F. W., R.A., *Bengal.*
†Talbot, W. H. Fox, Esq., F.R.S., *Lacock Abbey, Chippenham.*
*Taylor, J. G., Esq., *H.M. Consul, Diyarbekr.*
*Taylor, Major R. L., C.B., *Bombay Army.*
§Teignmouth, the Right Hon. Lord, F.R.S., *Langton Hall, North Allerton.*
*Temple, Richard, Esq., C.S.I., *Bengal C. S., Nagpore.*
Tennant, Sir J. Emerson, LL.D., K.C.S., 66, *Warwick-square, Belgravia*, S.W.
†Thomas, Edward, Esq., 4, *Madeley-villas, Kensington*, W.; *Athenæum*, S.W.
Thomas, Henry H., Esq., 77, *Pulteney-street, Bath.*
†Thompson, Lieut.-Col. T. P., F.R.S., *Eliot-vale, Blackheath*, S.E.
*†Tien, Rev. Antonio, 109, *Queen's-road, Dalston*, N.E.
§Toone, Francis Hastings, Esq., 31, *Portland-place*, W.
||Trevelyan, Col. H. W., C.B., *Bombay Army.*
*Tronson, Major R. N., *Moultan.*
†Urquhart, David, Esq., 76, *Jermyn-street*, S.W.
*Vámbéry, Dr. A., *Pesth, Hungary.*
*Van Drival, M. l'Abbé, *Arras.*
Vaux, W. S. W., Esq., *British Museum*, W.C.
Vawdrey, W. D., Esq., 65, *Gt. Russell-street*, W.C.

†VERNEY, Major Sir Harry, Bt., M.P., 32, *South-street, Park-lane*, W.
†VYVYAN, Sir Rd. Rawlinson, Bart., F.R.S., *Athenæum*, S.W.
†VYVYAN, R. H. S., Esq., F.R.G.S., *Conservative Club*, S.W.
WATSON, Dr. J. Forbes, M.D., *Fife House, Whitehall*, S.W.
WAUGH, Major-General Sir A. S., C.B., *Athenæum*, S.W.
*WELLS, Charles, Esq., 28, *Sussex-street, Pimlico*, S.W.
WESTWOOD, John, Esq., 8 and 9, *Queen-street-place*, E.C.
†WHITE, General Martin, *Combe Down, Bath.*
†WHITE, James, Esq., M.P., 2, *Queen's-gate, Hyde-park*, W.
WHITE, John, Esq., *Oriental Club*, W.
||WILBRAHAM, Major Richard, *Gibraltar.*
†WILKINSON, Robert, Esq., 22, *Cumberland-terrace, Regent's Park*, N.W.
WILKINSON, Lieut.-Col. Sir Thomas, K.S.I., 23, *Hanover-sq.*, W.
†WILLIAMS, Monier, Esq., A.M., Boden Prof. of Sanskrit, *Oxford.*
WILLOUGHBY, J. P., Esq., *India Office*, S W.; 18, *Westbourne-terrace*, W.
†WILLCOCK, Major G., K.L.S., *Bath.*
†WILSON, the Rev. John, D.D., *Bombay.*
*WRIGHT, the Ven. Archdeacon H. P., *Southsea.*
†YATES, W. Holt, Esq., M.D., 5, *Sumner-terace, Onslow-sq.*, S.W.
*YOUNG, W., Esq., *Bengal C.S.*
*ZOHRAB, James, Esq., *H.M.V. Consul, Mostar, Turkey.*

## Honorary Members.

HIS MAJESTY KING JOHN OF SAXONY.
HIS HIGHNESS NAWÂB IKBÂL UD DAULAH BAHÂDUR.
HIS MAJESTY THE KING OF SIAM.

Professor T. Aufrecht, *Edinburgh.*
The Rev. Prof. K. M. Banerjea, *Calcutta.*
Paṇḍita Bâpû Deva Ṣâstri, *Benares.*
Dr. Bhâu Dâjî, *Bombay.*
S. Birch, Esq., LL.D., *British Museum, London.*
The Rev. Robert Caldwell, LL.D., *Tinnevelly.*
The Rev. J. Edkins, *Shanghai, China.*
Professor Gustavus Flügel, *Dresden.*
Don P. de Gayangos, *Madrid.*
The Rev. R. Spence Hardy, *Headingley, Leeds.*
The Rev. Edward Hincks, D.D., *Killyleigh, Down, Ireland.*
Paṇḍita Îṣvarachandra Vidyâsâgara, *Calcutta.*
M. N. de Khanikoff, *Paris.*
Kûkel Kelu Nâyaru, District Munsif, *Malabar.*
E. W. Lane, Esq., *Worthing.*
Professor C. Lottner, *Dublin.*
The Duc de Luynes, *Paris.*
Bâbû Râjendralâl Mittra, *Calcutta.*
Professor Max Müller, *Oxford.*
Professor J. Oppert, *Paris.*
Syed Ahmad Khân, *Ghazipur.*
Ahmed Vefik Effendi, *Constantinople.*
Professor A. Weber, *Berlin.*
Professor N. L. Westergaard, *Copenhagen.*
Professor W. D. Whitney, *Newhaven, Conn., U.S.*

## Foreign Members.

[By the Regulations of the Society, as amended in 1850, no further additions can be made to the lists of the Corresponding or Foreign Members; the Elections being restricted to Resident, Non-resident, and Honorary Members.]

Professor Jacob Berggren, *Stockholm.*
Professor Francis Bopp, *Berlin.*
Baron de Cetto, *Bavarian Minister.*
Professor F. B. Charmoy, *Toulon.*
M. Alexandre de Chodzko, *Paris.*
Professor Bernhard Dorn, *St. Petersburg.*
Professor Garcin de Tassy, *Paris.*
William B. Hodgson, Esq., *New York.*
Professor Stanislas Julien, *Membre de l'Institut, Paris.*
Mirza Alexander Kasem Beg, *St. Petersburg.*
Professor Christian Lassen, *Bonn.*
Senhor Joaquim José da Costa de Macedo, *Lisbon.*
Dr. Julius Mohl, *Membre de l' Institut, Paris.*
Professor Charles Frederic Neumann, *Berlin.*
Monsieur Reinaud, *Paris.*
Professor Gustavus Seyffarth, *United States.*
The Hon. Martin van Buren, *United States.*

## Corresponding Members.

[See Note, p. 15.]

Sir Rutherford Alcock, K.C.B., *H.B.M. Envoy Extr. & Min. Plen. at Pekin.*

M. le Chevalier E. G. Arbanère, *Paris.*

General G. Balfour, C.B., *Madras Army.*

Sir F. W. A. Bruce, *H.B.M. Min. Plen. at Washington.*

Archibald Campbell, Esq., M.D., *late of Darjeeling.*

Dr. E. Carmoly, *Brussels.*

Dr. J. F. J. Cassel, *Paderborn.*

The Chevalier Clot-Bey, M.D., *Cairo.*

Monsieur N. D'Avezac, *Paris.*

James Finn, Esq., *H.B.M. Consul, Erzeroum.*

Professor J. Goldenthal, *Vienna.*

Maharaja Kali Krishna Bahadur, *Calcutta.*

Francis C. McGregor, Esq.

Colonel James Mackenzie, *Bengal Army.*

W. H. Medhurst, Esq., *H.B.M. Consul, Tang-chow.*

Signor G. Michelotti, *Turin.*

Dr. A. D. Mordtmann, *Constantinople.*

Professor F. Nève, *University of Louvain.*

M. Cæsar Maria Noy, *Venice.*

The Rev. P. Parker, M.D., *Canton.*

Sir Harry P. Parkes, K.C.B., *H.B.M. Min. Plen. in Japan.*

The Chevalier Etienne Pisani, *Constantinople.*

Christian A. Rassam, *H.B.M. Vice-Consul, Mosul.*

Raja Radhakant Deb, K.S.I., *Calcutta.*

M. Augustus Sakakini, *Egypt.*

The Rev. W. M. Thomson, *Beyrut.*

J. W. Walker, Esq.

Richard Wood, Esq., *H.B.M. Consul-General, Tunis.*

STEPHEN AUSTIN, PRINTER, HERTFORD.

Lightning Source UK Ltd.
Milton Keynes UK
UKHW020026160219
337399UK00010B/604/P

9 781331 102649